For Reference

Not to be taken from this room

EARLY CHILDHOOD EDUCATION

EARLY CHILDHOOD EDUCATION

An International Encyclopedia

Volume 4
The Countries

Edited by
Rebecca S. New and Moncrieff Cochran

Westport, Connecticut
London

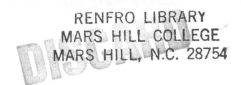
Library of Congress Cataloging-in-Publication Data

Early childhood education [four volumes] : an international encyclopedia / edited by Rebecca S. New and Moncrieff Cochran.

     p. cm.

   Includes bibliographical references and index.

   ISBN 0-313-33100-6 (set : alk. paper)—ISBN 0-313-33101-4 (vol 1 : alk. paper)—
   ISBN 0-313-33102-2 (vol 2 : alk. paper)—ISBN 0-313-33103-0 (vol 3 : alk. paper)—
   ISBN 0-313-34143-5 (vol 4 : alk. paper)

   1. Early childhood education—Encyclopedias.   I. New, Rebecca Staples.   II. Cochran, Moncrieff.

  LB1139.23.E272   2007

  372.2103—dc22   2006035011

British Library Cataloguing in Publication Data is available.

Library of Congress Catalog Card Number: 2006035011
ISBN: 0-313-33100-6 (set)
     0-313-33101-4 (vol. 1)
     0-313-33102-2 (vol. 2)
     0-313-33103-0 (vol. 3)
     0-313-34143-5 (vol. 4)

First published in 2007

Praeger Publishers, 88 Post Road West, Westport, CT 06881
An imprint of Greenwood Publishing Group, Inc.
www.praeger.com

Printed in the United States of America

The paper used in this book complies with the Permanent Paper Standard issued by the National Information Standards Organization (Z39.48-1984).

10 9 8 7 6 5 4 3 2 1

Contents

Alphabetical List of Entries   vii

Guide to Related Topics   xi

Preface   xix

Acknowledgments   xxiii

Introduction   xxv

The Handbook, *Volume 1, A–D*   1

The Handbook, *Volume 2, E–N*   307

The Handbook, *Volume 3, O–Z*   567

The Countries, *Volume 4*   861
    Introduction to Volume 4   861
    Australia   867
    Brazil   914
    China   971
    The Czech Republic   1017
    France   1063
    Italy   1110
    Japan   1155
    South Africa   1194
    Sweden   1240
    United Kingdom   1281

Bibliography   1319

Index   1323

Editorial Advisory Board and International Coordinators   1365

List of Editors and Contributors   1367

Introduction to Volume 4

As acknowledged in the overall Introduction to this handbook, the field of early childhood education has a long history of being influenced by people and ideas across cultural and national boundaries. The provocative ideas of Freidrich Froebel and, later, of Maria Montessori helped establish features of the field that continue to be salient today—a belief in the importance of the early years, sustained interest in the nature and role of a prepared environment, and culturally and philosophically distinct points of view about the nature of the child and the concept of a developmentally appropriate early education. These and other influences with international origins were often the result of privately funded travel by American women who cared deeply about improving conditions for young children—especially those living in deep poverty. Their contributions have been described in the entries in Volumes 1, 2, and 3 of this set. Volume 4 highlights a more recent contribution to the field—that of cross-national perspectives on what is increasingly understood as early childhood education in a new global era.

As the World Turns

The second half of the twentieth century was a period of worldwide transformation in the social and economic structure and dynamics of families with young children, and in the relationships between the private sphere of family life and the public spaces in local communities. Within industrialized societies, the most visible manifestation of this shift has been the movement of mothers into the labor market to engage in paid work. In societies still in the process of industrialization, the change can be seen most strongly in the movement of whole family units from the countryside into the cities, accompanied by a shift from extended to nuclear family structure, or in migratory labor systems where one parent (once typically the father, now increasingly the mother) travels to the city or even abroad for work for extended periods, leaving the other parent or a relative back in the village with full responsibility for the home and family.

Accompanying these changes in the private sphere of the family, and heavily influenced by them, is growing public interest in systems of early education and care worldwide. Although that interest is not new per se, its manifestation and level of intensity within policy circles has reached unprecedented heights since the 1960s. Visible first in the eastern European countries following World War II (within socialist political systems at that time), *public systems* of early education and care spread into the Scandinavian countries during the 1960s, and into France and Italy soon thereafter. Developments in the still industrializing nations of Asia, Africa, and South America during this same time period were also notable. For instance, in China interest in early childhood education is increasing, and the majority of children aged 3–5 now attend early childhood education programs. South Africa has gone through dramatic changes in early education policy since apartheid was abolished in 1994, shifting from separate services for black, white, and colored children to an emphasis on the rights of all children, with early childhood development as a key area in the process of reconstruction and development. Beginning in the 1980s, South Africa's early care and education policies expanded significantly and program coverage has also grown, despite economic challenges. The World Bank has recognized the importance of early child development and early education as strategies to develop human resources and reduce poverty, expending an estimated $1.5 billion in the areas during the 1990s.

This interest has been matched by a burgeoning body of scholarship on culture and child development—some of which is acknowledged in topics discussed in Volumes 1, 2, and 3—as well as international and comparative social policy analyses of early childhood education. The literature describing and analyzing early childhood education policies, programs, and concepts in multiple societies and cultures, while not copious, has been significant both in quality and in regularity. The International Study Group for Early Child Care, established in 1969, made the first major contribution, producing extensive monographs addressing child care in nine countries: Hungary, Sweden, the United States, Switzerland, Great Britain, France, Israel, Poland, and India. No attempt was made by this group, however, to compare policies, or the forces shaping policies, across cultures. The work of Sheila Kamerman and Alfred Kahn has been foundational to the cross-national study of early care and education, beginning in 1979 with an introductory examination of family policy in fourteen countries and followed in 1981 with an extensive comparative analysis of child care policies and programs in six countries, all Western and highly industrialized. The next decade (1991) saw publication of yet another Kamerman and Kahn analysis, this time focused on policy innovations in Europe in response to increased demands for child care and parental leave for infants and toddlers. In 1995, the late Sally Lubeck* described cross-national comparative work as not only necessary to our understanding of what is possible under diverse economic and cultural conditions, but also as *essential* to gaining insights into the political positioning of children, their mothers, and the period of early childhood.

---

* Sally Lubeck was keenly interested in this handbook, particularly its emphasis on cross-national contributions, and had agreed to serve as a member of the Editorial Advisory Board. Her premature death of pancreatic cancer was a major loss to those who knew her as a friend and a colleague as well as to the field of early care and education.

By the late 1980s and early 1990s, interest in countries beyond Europe began to be more heavily reflected in the literature. In 1989, a volume edited by Olmstead and Weikart presented fourteen national profiles of child care and early education, six of which were Asian or African. Little cross-cultural comparison was attempted by these authors in that initial publication, but a second volume edited by the same scholars five years later provided comparative data on service usage, the nature of organized facilities, and children's daily routines in eleven of the fourteen countries. In 1992, a pair of Americans (Lamb and Sternberg) and a pair of Swedes (Hwang and Broberg) edited a collection of twelve analytical case studies drawn from five of the six inhabited continents, that placed nonparental child care in social and cultural context and made "cautious and informed comparisons." The following year one of the editors of the current work (Cochran) edited a 29-country International Handbook of Child Care Policies and Programs (also published by Greenwood Publishing Group), including six continents and 80 percent of the world's population. This work included an extensive analysis of the major themes cross-cutting early care and education in these countries, and creation of an analytic framework that has since been further refined by the author (1997) and used as the basis for the development of U.S. policy proposals (2006).

A quantum leap in our understanding of the interface between early childhood education and care and community development was provided in 1992 by Robert Myers' remarkable book *The Twelve Who Survive*, which drew a rich set of examples from African, Asian, and South American countries to identify three general early childhood education-focused development strategies—imposed development, self-actualized development, and partnership—and argued persuasively in favor of the partnership approach. This relationship between early childhood education and community development also caught the attention of global entities dedicated to economic investments. World Bank interest in early childhood education came to the fore in the 1990s, highlighted by a Bank-sponsored conference in 1996 titled *Early Child Development: Investing in the Future*. The proceedings from that conference, published in 1997, emphasized policies and programs in "developing" countries and included papers on the fit between cultures and policies, elements of program quality, parent education and child development, home-based programs for early childhood education, and the financing of early childhood education systems.

Most recently the Organisation for Economic Co-operation and Development (OECD) conducted an extensive review of early childhood education policies and programs in many of its member countries in response to recognition that improving the quality of, and access to, early childhood education and care has become a major policy priority in those countries One of the editors (New) participated in this review. An integrative report, published in 2001 and titled *Starting Strong, Early Childhood Education and Care*, documents the various strategies that these countries have applied to policy development in this field, noting that these policies and subsequent program development strategies are deeply embedded in particular country contexts, values, and beliefs. The report also documents common challenges and issues shared across diverse national contexts and proposes eight key policy elements for decision makers wishing to "promote equitable access to quality early childhood education and care." Within the context of what some have referred to as a global era of early childhood education, the U.S. National Research Council commissioned a special Board of Comparative and International Studies to review and write a report on the varying degrees to which cross-national or international studies on education have influenced educational practices in the United States. The title of this report— *Understanding Others, Educating Ourselves*—might well be the subtitle for this fourth volume.

In the preface to the set, we describe the primary purpose of this four-volume work as providing a comprehensive resource on early childhood education for teachers and caregivers, parents, teacher educators, policy planners, and researchers. Given the increasingly global nature of the field of early childhood education and the growing body of knowledge about the cultural variability of interpretations of and provisions for young children's learning and development, this fourth volume is devoted to profiles of early childhood education systems in a diverse set of countries in Asia, Africa, South America, and Oceania as well as eastern and western Europe. Unlike the *International Handbook* published by Greenwood Press in the early 1990s, this volume contains no integrative cross-national analysis of thematic similarities and contrasts. That rich opportunity is left to the reader, and a wealth of information is available to anyone with such interests. For example:

- All twenty-one of the major early childhood education topics included in this volume are addressed by experts from at least two of the ten participating countries, and ten of the topics have five or more national contributors. These subjects are also addressed by American authors in Volumes 1, 2, and 3. This feature allows the American reader not only to learn what an American expert has to offer about curriculum through an American lens and in U.S. settings, but also to compare and contrast this American viewpoint with those of specialists from ten other countries (those countries being Australia, Brazil, China, the Czech Republic, France, Italy, Japan, South Africa, Sweden, and the United Kingdom). Many of the great thinkers from abroad whose ideas and approaches to early education have influenced practices in the United States—not only Montessori and Froebel, but also others, such as Piaget and Malaguzzi—receive attention from American authors in the first three volumes and then are discussed from different perspectives in Volume 4 by writers seeing them from within other cultural frames, in some cases the home cultures of those thinkers themselves. Contributors to Volume 4 also acknowledge the influence of other, lesser-known Western European philosophers and postmodern scholars such as Bakhtin, Foucault, and Bourdieu, whose ideas are entering the U.S. discourse thanks to scholars committed to reconceptualizing the field of early childhood education (see the **Reconceptionalists** entry). And, of course, there are still others who have influenced early childhood education in other nations who remain unknown to American early childhood educators. Thus the writings in Volume 4 permit the American reader to peer beyond the natural ethnocentrism of American authors on subjects like pedagogy, play, curriculum, quality, family involvement, inclusion, and teacher preparation by examining these topics through the eyes of experts in cultures as diverse as Sweden, Japan, South Africa, and Brazil.
- Because the four volumes, taken together, include in-depth information about early childhood education in eleven different countries, the contents should be as relevant to audiences abroad as they are to Americans. Both similarities and differences

across cultures provide insights not only to audiences in the countries included in this set, but also to those in other nations as well. For instance, Volume 4 contains five contributions on the topic of play, from Sweden, China, Italy, Brazil, and Japan. In those entries, it is fascinating to find both a common emphasis on play as a way of learning, especially about social norms, rules, and ways of being, and reflections of characteristics specific to each individual culture (e.g., the idea of solidarity in Sweden, the Chinese emphasis on modesty, the Brazilian concept of public spaces). Careful study of articulations of the same topic from different cultural perspectives will enrich the reader's understanding both of concepts in early care and education that transcend individual cultures and the ways that particular cultural beliefs and traditions shape early development through early childhood education. In like fashion, the different disciplinary interpretations of children and early childhood begin to become apparent when contrasting the discussion of play as written by a developmental psychologist in the United States. and as written by scholars of diverse disciplines in other nations. Although these disciplinary distinctions could easily be found in the United States—and in fact, they are apparent in the various entries on "Play"—it is also the case that the field of child development and the discipline of developmental psychology is much more salient in American discussions of early childhood education than in any other country in the world. This set provides the reader with new insights into the various ways in which the social sciences—psychology, philosophy, and sociology—have contributed to contemporary understandings in the field of early childhood education.

• The country profiles and accompanying topical entries in Volume 4 provide a "snapshot" of ten national early education and care systems at a single point in time, the year 2005. But as the brief literature review presented earlier documents, earlier snapshots are available as well. For example, the *International Handbook of Child Care Policies and Programs*, also published by Greenwood Publishing Group, contains in-depth case studies covering nine of the ten nations included here, developed in 1991. Using this reference, and others listed in the Bibliography, together with entries in this set, it is possible to examine patterns of change over time, both in individual societies and across societies. This kind of temporal analysis will reveal early childhood education as a dynamic process, adapting to broader societal changes while at the same time sustaining cultural continuities and exploring creative ways of engaging and supporting children and their families.

References: Berfenstam R., and I. William-Olsson (1973). Early child care in Sweden. *Early Child Development and Care* 2(2), 97–249; Committee on a Framework and Long-Term Research Agenda for International Comparataive Education Studies (2003). *Understanding others, educating ourselves*, C. Chabbott and E. J. Elliott, eds. Washington, DC: The National Academies Press; Cochran, M., ed. (1993). *The international handbook of child care policies and programs.* Westport, CT: Greenwood Press, Cochran, M. (1997). Fitting early child care services to societal needs and characteristics. In Mary E. Young, ed., *Early child development: Investing in our children's future.* Amsterdam: Elsevier; David, M. and I. Lezine (1974). Early child care in France. *Early Child Development and Care* 4(1), 1–148; Hermann, A., and S. Komlos (1972). Early child care in Hungary. *Early Child Development and Care* 1(4), 337–459; Kagan, Sharon Lynn, and V. Steward (2005). A new world view: Education in a global era. *Phi Delta Kappan* 87(3), 184–187; Kamerman, S. (2000). Early childhood education and care: An overview of developments in the OECD countries. *International Journal of Education Research* 33, 7–29, Kamerman, S., and A. Kahn, eds. (1978). *Family policy: Government and families in 14 countries.* New York: Columbia

University Press; Kamerman, S., and A. Kahn eds. (1991). *Child care, parental leave, and the under 3s: Policy innovation in Europe.* New York: Auburn House; Kamerman, S., and A. Kahn (1981). *Child care, family benefits, and working parents: A study in comparative policy.* New York: Columbia University Press; Kellmer-Pringle, M., and S. Naidoo (1974). Early child care in Britain. *Early Child Development and Care* 3(4), 299–473; Khalakdina, Margaret (1979). Early child care in India. *Early Child Development and Care* 5(3/4), 149–360; Lamb, M., K. Sternberg, K.-P. Hwang, and A. Broberg, eds. (1992). *Child care in context: cross-cultural perspectives.* Hillsdale, NJ: Lawrence Erlbaum; Lubeck, Sally (2001). Early childhood education and care in cross-national perspective. *Phi Delta Kappan* 83(3), 213–215; LeVine, A. Robert, and Merry I. White (1986). *Human conditions: The cultural basis for educational developments.* New York: Routledge and Kegan Paul; Luscher K., V. Ritter, and P. Gross (1973). Early child care in Switzerland. *Early Child Development and Care* 3(2), 89–210; Myers, R. (1992). *The twelve who survive: Strengthening programmes of early childhood development in the third world.* London: Routledge; New, R. (2003). Culture, child development, and early childhood education: Rethinking the relationship. In R. Lerner, F. Jacobs, and D. Wertlieb, eds., *Promoting positive child, adolescent, and family development: A handbook of program and policy innovations.* Thousand Oaks, CA: Sage Publications; New, R. (2005). Learning about early childhood education from and with Western European nations. *Phi Delta Kappan* 87(3), 201–204; OECD (2001). Starting strong, early childhood education and care. Paris: The Organization for Economic Cooperation and Development; OECD (2006). *Starting strong II.* Paris: The organization for Economic Cooperation and Development; Olmstead, P., and D. Weikart, eds. (1989). How nations serve young children: Profiles of child care and education in 14 countries. Ypsilanti, MI: High/Scope Press; Rapaport, et al., (1976). Early child care in Israel. *Early Child Development and Care* 4(2/3), 149–345; Robinson, H., N. Robinson, M. Wolins, U. Bronfenbrenner, and J. Richmond (1973). Early child care in the United States of America. *Early Child Development and Care* 2(4), 359–582; Young, M., ed. (1997). *Early child development: Investing in our children's future.* Amsterdam: Elsevier; Ziemska, Maria (1978) Early child care in Poland. *Early Child Development and Care* 5(1/2), 1–148.

Moncrieff Cochran and Rebecca S. New

Australia

Early Childhood Education and Care in Australia

Introduction

Australia is a nation characterized by distance, diversity, and change. As a democracy, with a federal system of government, power and responsibility are shared between the Commonwealth (the Australian government) and the six-state and two-territory governments. The Australian government is based on the Westminster system. Under the Constitution, citizens elect members of the House of Representatives and the Senate (the house of review of legislation). The states and territories vary in size, population, and their specific systems of democratic government. The state and territory parliaments regulate a further tier of local government by around 750 democratically elected Municipal and Shire Councils.

The Australian government has prime responsibility for collection and distribution of Income Tax and the Goods and Services Tax (GST) and sets policy in many areas, including social security, education, and health. While the states and territories also collect a range of taxes, the bulk of their funds are distributed from the Australian government.

A multicultural society of just over 20 million people, Australia occupies a continent with a land area only slightly smaller than the coterminous states of the United States. Most of the population is concentrated on the southeast and east coast, and to a lesser extent in the southwest of the continent, with the majority of Australians living in the capital cities of the states and territories.

The distances between population centers in rural and regional Australia can be vast and the population density varies greatly. Half of the total land area is home to only 0.3 percent of the population. In contrast, the most densely populated 1 percent of the land area is home to 84 percent of the population, making Australia arguably one of the most urbanized nations on the planet.

Indigenous Australians have lived on the continent for over 50,000 years, or 2,000 generations. Seminomadic hunters and gatherers, they moved in small family groups in both the inland and the coastal regions, inhabiting areas of extreme diversity in climate and terrain from the central desert to the wet tropical north. At the time of European settlement in 1788 their population has been estimated at between 300,000 and one million, with 600 tribes each with its distinct territory, language, and culture. Identification with land, cultural diversity, and mobility strongly characterize Indigenous Australians. Today, there are still 170 Indigenous languages that are spoken by 21 percent of those over 5 years of age. The 410,000 Indigenous Australians recorded in the 2001 census are approximately 2.2 percent of the population.

Migration has added further richness to the diversity of Australia. Since European settlement, the increasingly multicultural character of Australian society has been the result of successive waves of **immigration**, predominantly from the United Kingdom and Europe, although increasingly from Asia and the Middle East. At the last census, around 4 million residents had been born overseas, in one of 200 countries, and a similar number had a parent who had been born outside of Australia. Apart from the Indigenous languages, 111 languages other than English are spoken in this country. In recent years migration has been the major contributor to the average annual increase of 1 percent in Australia's population.

Like most countries in Europe, Australia has experienced considerable change in the age mix of its population. Only 20 percent of the general population is aged under 15 and 6.4 percent under 5. This contrasts with the figures for the Indigenous population, of 38.9 percent and 13.1 percent, respectively. The proportion of the population aged over 65 has been increasing and now represents 12.8 percent of the population. Again, this is in marked contrast to the Indigenous population where only 2.9 percent of the population is over 65 years, reflecting marked differences in health and life expectancy.

The total fertility rate (TFR) of Australia has declined steadily over the last hundred years. The current rate of 1.81 babies per woman is well below the replacement level (2.1), although recently there has been evidence that the TFR continues to rise. The age at which mothers give birth to their first child is rising, with a median age in 2002 of 30.2 years. The infant mortality rate of 5.2 deaths per 100 live births, in 2000, is lower than the UK (5.6) and the USA (7.1) but higher than in Sweden (3.4) and Japan (3.2). Indigenous babies have a mortality rate that is three times that of the general population (15.5 deaths per 1000 live births). In total, at the Census in 2001, Australia had 1.3 million children under 5 years of age, 2.2 million aged from 5 to 12 and 1.4 million aged 13–17.

With regard to family types, most children were born to married couples (69%) and most lived in two-parent families (80%). But only 38.6 percent of all families comprised couples with dependent children. Single-parent families with dependent children have increased from 6.5 percent in 1976 to 10.7 percent in 2001.

One of the most marked social trends has been the rapid increase in the participation of Australian women in the workforce. Approximately 70 percent of women are in some form of paid employment and they account for around 43 percent of the total workforce. Nearly half of those women with a child under 4 years of age worked, although only 15 percent were employed full time while their children were this age. Those with a partner are more likely to work than those who are sole parents. Mothers' workforce participation increases as their children grow older. Of all those with children aged less than 15, two-thirds participate in the workforce.

Early Childhood Education

Australia has a universal system of school education, provided by a mix of government and nongovernment (church and other religious bodies and independent providers). Almost three-quarters are government schools, while 17 percent are under the auspices of the Catholic Church and 10 percent are independent.

The Department of Education, Science and Training (DEST) has responsibility for administering policies and programs for schools and providing financial assistance to state and territory governments and other school education providers. DEST also has a significant responsibility for Indigenous education, including through the provision of preschool education for Indigenous students. The Australian government has taken a leading role in the development of national benchmarks for literacy and numeracy, as part of its commitment to the improvement of attainments in these areas. Early literacy has been a particular focus, nationally.

Responsibility for children's services and education policy involves all levels of government. The national government, however, has a prime responsibility for Child Care Support and for supporting the national quality assurance schemes, via the National Childcare Accreditation Council (NCAC). The Department of Family and Community Services (FaCSIA) has the major responsibility for children's services, excluding schools. Its Child Care Program sets policy and funding for long day-care services, including family day care; multifunctional services and multifunctional Aboriginal services; some occasional care centers; and outside-school-hours care services. Subsidies are also provided to central playgroup associations in each state and territory to foster and support playgroups.

Major developments like the National Agenda for Early Childhood and the Head Start for Australia, along with the emergence of advocacy groups such as the National Investment for the Early Years (NIFTeY) and research networks including the Australian Research Alliance for Children and Youth (ARACY), highlight the priority that Australia places on its young children. Major initiatives such as the Australian government's Stronger Families and Communities Strategy designed to build community capacity to support young children, and complementary state and territory developments, further underscore the continued prominence of early childhood in Australia.

To cater for the education and care of its young children, and to support women's workforce participation, Australia has developed and sustained an extensive and diverse system of children's services including long day-care centers, family day-care schemes and outside-school-hours care services. These services are primarily provided to meet the needs of working parents, but are also used by nonworking parents and those families requiring respite care. Preschools and early learning centers provide educational experiences for children on a sessional basis, prior to school entry.

Service Provision

Early childhood education and care in Australia is a priority policy focus for all levels of government. Of most policy interest are issues related to improving the affordability and access to child care and the enhancement of the educational and developmental benefits for children of participation in early childhood services. While the focus remains on supporting mothers' workforce participation, increasingly the role of children's services in prevention and early intervention is being highlighted.

Provision of such services is through a mix of public, nongovernment not-for-profit, private for-profit, and private not-for-profit organizations. The private sector provides over 70 percent of center-based child care. Most other early childhood services are provided by state and territory governments, local government, and the nonprofit sector.

Issues of supply, access, affordability, on the one hand, and quality and staffing of children's services, on the other, are of current concern. In terms of supply, around 1.5 million Australian children in the age range from birth to eleven years used care (around half of this age-group). The Australian government expended $1646 million in 2001–2002 on the provision of child care, with the bulk of this paid as the Child Care Benefit (CCB) to parents, on the basis of the family's income and use of approved child-care services.

The states and territories also provide funding to children's services and are responsible for their regulation and licensing. Their primary responsibility, however, is for the provision of school education, including preschools, and some occasional care centers. Some also contribute financially to outside-school-hours care, long day-care centers, playgroups, and other children's services. The states and territories vary as to where responsibility for early childhood education and care resides. In some it is split between departments of education and community services. In others it is in a single department, typically education.

Local government is involved in the provision of a wide range of services for young children and their families. In addition to providing a wide array of community facilities it may also subsidize or provide long day care, out-of-school hours, and occasional care services, as well as immunization services and parenting courses. The larger councils typically employ an early childhood coordinator.

Access to Services

Australians enjoy a relatively high standard of living, and while there is poverty, it tends not to be concentrated in inner city locations. There are, however, higher than average levels of unemployment, poverty, and disadvantage in rural and remote areas. Distance makes provision of social, health, and educational services a challenge in rural and remote Australia. Provision of early childhood services in these locations is not easy.

Quality

Quality in early childhood centers is directly addressed through the national accreditation program managed by the National Child Care Accreditation Council and through state and territory regulatory and licensing systems. Staffing of children's services remains a major issue, and if Australia is to maintain the high quality of its children's services the supply of well-qualified early childhood educators will need to be increased.

Further Readings: Australian Government (2004). Stronger families and communities strategy. Available online at http://www.facs.gov.au/internet/facsinternet.nsf/aboutfacs/programs/sfsc-sfcs.htm; Commonwealth Taskforce on Child Development, Health, and Wellbeing (2003). *Towards the development of national agenda for early childhood.* Canberra: Commonwealth of Australia; deVaus, D. (2004). *Diversity and change in Australian families: Statistical profiles.* Melbourne: Australian Institute of Family Studies, Commonwealth of Australia; Martin, J. (2004). "'More than just play dough'—A preliminary assessment of the contribution of child care to the Australian economy." In *Australian Social Policy* (2004). Canberra: Department of Family and Community Services, pp. 3–19; New South Wales Commission for Children and Young People and Commission for Children and Young People (Qld) (2004). *A head start for Australia: An early years framework.* Sydney and Brisbane: New South Wales Commission for Children and Young People and Commission for Children and Young People (Qld); Press, F., and A. Hayes (2000). *OECD Thematic review of early childhood education and care: Australian background report.* Canberra: Commonwealth of Australia.

Alan Hayes

The Sociology of Childhood

The sociology of childhood has been used increasingly as a theoretical perspective in early childhood education since the late 1980s. In Australia, those who draw on the sociology of childhood have tended to use it in similar ways to European counterparts, being guided by six major tenets identified by Prout and James that form the basis of the sociology of childhood. These include the notion that childhood is a "social construction", that childhood is a "variable of social analysis" and is closely connected to other variables such as class and gender, and that children's relationships and cultures are "worthy of study in their own right." Further, children are considered as active (rather than passive) agents in their daily lives and to be competent and knowledgeable about their own lives. Although the sociology of childhood is comparatively young, there has been little analysis of the key tenets of the position. Morss is an exception and raises some fundamental issues for consideration, which include refining the notion of the "socially constructed child," a term that is used widely in much that is written about the sociology of childhood.

The key tenets of the sociology of childhood have been used in various ways throughout the world in research projects that feature children. One way in which this has occurred is through the focus on children's rights. The United Nations (1989) *Convention on the Rights of the Child* (CRC) has had significant impact internationally on child protection and human rights, notably the debate about child labor, and also on flow-on effects such as the contested area of the protective regulation of children. This manifests itself in continuing tension about the dubious line between adult regulation of children's lives and children's protective rights, especially as the former can restrict the latter and that legislatively in many countries, adults have different rights from children.

With regard to children's protective rights, the sociology of childhood has been used to investigate a range of circumstances such as the ethical responsibilities of involving children in research as participants, the preferences of children in foster care, and decisions about with whom children will live when their parents divorce or separate. Another way that the sociology of childhood has been used in empirical research is to investigate children's perspectives about their education environments in both before-school settings and the early years of schooling. For the purposes of this encyclopedic entry, examples are drawn from research in Australia that includes involving children as research participants and the understanding that children are competent and knowledgeable about their own lives.

In their attempt to develop a model whereby children can have "input [in]to the process of identifying children's needs in care" Mason and Urquhart confront the complex issue of attempting to balance relationships of power between researchers and children. Their motivation was that research about substitute care for children (such as foster care) continually told stories about children "feeling that their needs were discounted and that they were treated as objects." Mason and Urquhart contend that decisions about the placement of children are based on generalizations about ideological and budgetary considerations that are supported by understandings of the universality (rather than individuality) of children's needs. Although they claim that children are being listened to, they point out that this does not necessarily mean that they are "being heard and responded to in terms of the needs they articulate."

One way around this impasse, the complexities of achieving children's participation in decision making, and ensuring systemic responses that meet their needs is to involve children "actively in the design and development of the processes and structures intended to hear their contributions." (New South Wales Child Protection Council, cited in Mason and Urquhart). In their attempts to develop a collaborative approach that is based on social justice and achieves a balance between what they call Adultist and Children's Movements, Mason and Urquhart's first step was to consult children about how and why children should contribute, and to ask what children needed in the way of support and assistance to be able to contribute. Methodologically, a number of ways for children to participate were offered (focus group discussions, individual or group drawings, writing individual or group narratives), as were feedback sessions where member checking was to be undertaken. The ultimate aim is to develop an approach that integrates children's perspectives with those of carers and decision makers that is informed by social theories, all the while recognizing that children have individual responses and should not be confined to one research category.

The case for developing social capital through responsive and integrated child and family services has been made by Farrell, Tayler, and Tennet. An integral part of this approach has been to seek not only adult, but young children's views about service provision, mainly because of the scarcity of children's voices in such research. Informed by the sociology of childhood, data were gathered from 138 children aged 4–8 attending two public elementary schools in a rural/remote locality and two public elementary schools in an urban setting in the state of Queensland. A practitioner-researcher engaged children in informal conversations in their classrooms to ask about six dimensions of social capital (participation in community activities, neighborhood connections, family and friend connections, feelings of trust and safety, proactivity in a social context, and tolerance of diversity). Teachers also asked children informally about why they came to school or preschool, what they liked and disliked about coming, and advice they would give to children new to the setting to ensure that they were happy.

According to the children's responses, the social capital of children in the urban community was higher than those in the rural/remote locality. High numbers of children in all age-groups reported feeling safe in the community in which they lived, and responses to the questions asked informally by teachers showed variations in the different age-groups, confirming that purposes, attitudes, and reasons for coming to school change with age. Unsurprisingly, children were troubled by acts of physical and verbal aggression by other children, but were not asked about how they thought such acts should be handled. The children provided advice about effective transitions between early childhood settings and made suggestions about what newcomers need to know that could be incorporated by practitioners, administrators, and policy makers to help children transition successfully to new educational environments.

The impetus for a study by Dockett and Perry was that much of the research about children starting school positions children as research objects by assessing, testing, and observing them. They wanted to know from children's experiences what starting school is like and ways to improve the experience for others. Based on the premise that children have expert knowledge about their own lives and that adults have different understandings of children's lives and their experiences, these researchers gathered children's drawings, photographs that children elected to take, and engaged in conversations with children to gain insight into their perspectives about starting school. Children from four schools in two states of Australia were involved in the project that asked the children to share their expertise with those who were soon to begin school. The four schools reflect a cross section of socioeconomic, rural, urban, isolated, and religious characteristics, and some of the photographs taken by the children are included in the article. This study recognizes the knowledge children have about their own lives in regard to starting school, and aims to use their expertise to improve transition programs and experiences associated with beginning school. It is further evidence of the value of involving children as research participants and seeking their perspectives about matters that are significant to them and that pertain directly to them and their successful movement into school environments.

As well as using the expertise of children to improve transitions to school, the sociology of childhood has been employed to show the competence of young children in everyday language interactions in constructing their own social orders in a preschool classroom (Danby). To illuminate understandings of the sociology of childhood, Danby contrasts viewing young children as competent language users with typical child development perspectives such as Jean **Piaget** and Lev **Vygotsky**, where children are considered to be in the process of developing language skills and achieve competence as adults. A detailed analysis of several excerpts from a transcript of three boys aged 3–4 who are playing in the block area, reveals the intricacy and intensity of the interactions and emotions and how relationships can change quickly. Although the teacher was engaged at one stage, she retreated after a short time, advising the boys to sort the situation out for themselves. The verbal and nonverbal language competence of the boys was unmistakable, causing Danby to make some suggestions for practitioners to reflect on how they understand children.

From the analysis provided, the point that these three boys are highly competent and knowledgeable about their own lives and experiences is undeniable. However, practitioners would do well to consider some of the other tenets of the sociology of childhood alongside such evidence. For example, while much of the sociology of childhood is given over to research and discussion about adult regulation of children's lives and children's protective rights, it is also necessary to consider the rights and responsibilities of children as they 'play' in early childhood educational environments, and how they are to learn about and respect such rights and responsibilities.

In Australia, while research informed by the sociology of childhood is in its infancy, it has much to offer to children and adults, especially adults working in early childhood settings who must do more than merely observe children's play.

Further Readings: Danby, S. (2002). The communicative competence of young children. *Australian Journal of Early Childhood 27*(3), 25–30; Dockett, S., and B. Perry (2005). You need to know how to play safe: Children's experiences of starting school. *Contemporary Issues in Early Childhood 6*(1), 4–18; Farrell, A., C. Tayler, and L. Tennet (2004). Building social capital in early childhood education and care: An Australian study. *British Educational Research Journal 30*(5), 623–632; Mason, J., and R. Urquhart (2001). Developing a model for participation by children in research on decision making. *Children Australia 26*(4), 16–21; Morss, J. R. (2002). The several social constructions of James, Jenks, and Prout: A contribution to the sociological theorization of childhood. *The International Journal of Children's Rights* 10, 39–54; Prout, A., and A. James, (1997). A new paradigm for the sociology of childhood? Provenance, promise and problems. In A. James and A. Prout, eds., *Constructing and reconstructing childhood: Contemporary issues in the sociological study of childhood.* 2nd ed. London: Falmer, pp. 7–33; United Nations (1989) *Convention on the Rights of the Child.* Adopted by the General Assembly of the United Nations on November 20, 1989.

Susan Grieshaber

Multicultural Education and Cultural Diversity

The initial phase of multicultural education in Australia was primarily conceived as a project to improve the educational and social opportunities of cultural and linguistic "minorities." Although being of a cultural and linguistic "minority" does not automatically predestine a child to educational failure or lack of social mobility, it is undoubtedly the case that the educational prospects of particular cultural and linguistic groups are adversely affected under particular circumstances. A view of multicultural education as something that exclusively addresses "minorities," either as groups inequitably excluded from social access or as a positive presence, however, has its own limitations and difficulties.

From this early experience in Australia, it was realized that new visions of multicultural education were needed, visions that have the potential to transform pedagogy for all students, and to reconstitute mainstream social and educational practices in the interests of all.

Differences in Educational Success Rates

We know that some groups of students are more successful in school than other groups. We acknowledge that not all opportunities are evenly distributed and we refer to this as a question of "disadvantage." This is usually conceptualized as a checklist of educationally disadvantaged groups:
- Aboriginal and Torres Strait Islander students.
- Students from non-English speaking backgrounds.
- Students in poverty, or from low socioeconomic status families and localities.
- Girls, and sometimes also on some measures, boys.
- Students with disabilities.
- Students in rural and/or isolated communities.

In the Australian context, however, it has become evident that these groups are in fact habitually, perennially disadvantaged, giving lie to any claim that opportunities are equal. The problem in each case is the distance between these worlds of community experience and the world of institutionalized education and valued knowledge.

However, despite its undeniable truth, the checklist represents a view that is too simplistic, since:
- Some students in these groups do succeed, background is not all-determining. Indeed, sometimes it is a student's "disadvantaged" background that is the basis for their particular resilience, their peculiar success.
- There are more disadvantaged citizens than those found in the groups in the list; and many more individuals who fail as a result of particular conjunctions of community or lifeworld experience.
- The groups are not separate; they are overlapping, simultaneous, multilayered. In fact, virtually every individual represents a peculiar conjunction, a unique mix of group or community experiences.
- The groups are defined via relationships—of comparative power, privilege, and access to resources. Each group is created through a series of historical and ongoing intergroup relationships. These relationships (e.g., racism, sexism, comparative socioeconomic privilege) often play themselves out through schools and classrooms.
- The group categories oversimplify critical success and failure-determining differences within groups and between individuals.
- They create labels for categories, implying a deficit on the part of the student, when in fact they may be an opportunity upon which we might build a worthwhile learning experience.

The Notion of "Lifeworld"

Recognizing the notion of the "lifeworld," one's everyday life or community experience, is important since it represents an opportunity to encapsulate the full spectrum of differences across all the students in the classroom. Note that when we are talking about cultural differences as a critical determiner of outcomes, we are talking about the broad dynamics of power and privilege, of history and location, and of the accident of birth and life experience

Ethnic and Linguistic Diversity in the Classroom

When we consider ethnic and linguistic diversity in classrooms, the two big-group categories Indigenous and Non-English Speaking are too simple and over-generalized to account for relative advantage or disadvantage of students in our schools. A fine-grained understanding of every student's cultural and linguistic background and lifeworlds would include the following information about the students:

- Country/place of birth; country/place of birth of parents
- Indigenous ancestry, or recency of **immigration**; if recent, parents' visa category (e.g., refugee, business)
- Ethnic or Indigenous identity
- Religion
- Perceptions of "race"
- First language spoken; language(s) spoken at home
- English language proficiency of student and parents
- Variant of English spoken (e.g., Aboriginal English, working-class Australian English, "wog" English)
- Literacy level of parents in first or other languages

In addition, gender, socioeconomic status, and other variables such as disability, may be integral and inseparable aspects of culture, ethnicity, and language. Consistent with recent developments in multicultural policy in Australia, in which the category "non-English speaking background" (NESB) has been contested and calls made to abandon it, the above pointers focus on the following:

- The cultural and linguistic profile of every student; and
- A much broader range of variables than those identified by the category "NESB" which, for curriculum and school planning purposes, are (a) more closely related to categories of the Australian Bureau of Statistics (ABS) data and (b) represent a more finely grained predictor of educational outcomes.

Working with Cultural Differences in Education: Alternative Models

In dealing with cultural differences, there are four archetypical forms of modern education approaches: exclusion, assimilation, superficial multiculturalism, and a more inclusive approach we have called pluralism.

Exclusion. Education as exclusion means not being able to gain access for success in the education system. It also includes those who experience failure once in the system. There can be a variety of reasons for exclusion, and these all reflect the kind of distance that exists between the student's lifeworld and institutionalized education. Distancing features include, for example, the education you can afford; what you know you can realistically wish for from education; what you expect; and what you can slip into more or less comfortably. In the modern era, where education is compulsory and the promise of equity through education universal, exclusion can also exist as a powerful form of inclusion. As a consequence of this exclusion, you will do certain kinds of work, become a certain kind of citizen, have a certain kind of relationship to the icons of belonging—and the results of your education will have in part "explained" this for you.

Assimilation. Education as assimilation means gaining access to institutionalized education and succeeding by adhering to the protocols and practices inherent to it. Assimilation requires leaving behind your old self and lifeworld as past experience, and then gaining experience and expertise in those lifeworlds closest to the culture of education.

Superficial multiculturalism. Education as a superficial multiculturalism means that, at a surface level, the system recognizes the variability of lifeworlds—a kind of "spaghetti and polka" multiculturalism. However, in reality, it requires adopting the image of those lifeworlds closest to the culture of institutionalized learning and "mainstream" power. Different lifeworlds might be made an object of study or celebrated as folkloric color, but only insofar as the fundamental framework of seeing, valuing, and knowing remains singular and undisturbed.

Cultural pluralism. Education as pluralism recognizes that you don't have to be the same to have similar opportunities. Pluralism involves a subtle but profound shift from a more superficial multiculturalism. Pluralism means that the mainstream—be that the culture of the dominant groups or such institutional structures as education—is transformed. Instead of representing a single cultural destination, the mainstream is a site of openness, negotiation, experimentation, and the in-terrelation of alternative frameworks and mindsets. Learning is not a matter of "development" in which you leave your old selves and lifeworlds behind. Rather, learning is a matter of repertoire—starting with the recognition of lifeworld experiences and using them as a basis for extending what you can do. The pluralist process of transformation, then, is not a matter of vertical progress but one of expanding horizons. These new horizons have an impact on the lifeworld: learners still engage in and with their lifeworlds in new ways, but not necessarily to leave those lifeworlds behind.

Genuine equity cannot be achieved in any but the pluralist alternative. In fact, the first three forms of inclusion are simultaneously rationalizations of exclusion; the first explicitly so and the other two by way of practice. In all three, the pattern of those who are more likely to miss out on opportunities reflects the relative distances of lifeworlds to the culture of power and the culture of institutionalized education. The crossover is more possible for some than for others. Only pluralism is even-handed, because negotiating cultural differences is the main objective.

The Dichotomy of Pluralism

Pluralism is both an ambitious program and a minimalist, unambitious program. It is ambitious in the sense that it is based on the argument that the mainstream needs to be transformed. It is unambitious in that it does no more than take the limited equity argument at its word. To the question of what are the conditions of mere equity—not equality—the only answer can be an educational system that does not habitually favour and reward some lifeworld experiences over others. This is to do no more than to take at its word the apologetic rhetoric of a society which does not pretend to have an equality of outcomes, just "opportunity" for all. Pluralism is the only way the system can possibly do even that; the only way it can possibly be genuinely fair in its distribution of opportunity, as between one group and another, one kind of lifeworld experience and another.

Making curriculum culturally inclusive. Cultural differences are interwoven through the patterns of relative advantage and disadvantage that characterize schooling, as well as society. One of the fundamental purposes of education is to provide learning, and as a consequence, social opportunities for all. Equity, however, can only be achieved through a curriculum that engages every student in such a way that their opportunities are optimized. Education for pluralism requires a culturally inclusive curriculum that recognizes the differences among students and provides every student with learning experiences that optimize their opportunities. The key features of an inclusive curriculum are (a) recognition of students' differences, (b) classroom and curriculum flexibility and curriculum customization such that every student is provided learning experiences that engage their particular capacities, needs, and interests, (c) measurable outcomes which optimize each student's learning and social possibilities. Inclusive curriculum requires a complementary mix of strategies focused on opportunity and strategies focused on diversity.

Opportunity. It is important to design educational strategies that provide access to the dominant or "mainstream" culture, its ways of thinking, communicating, and being. Dominant educational values are expressed and measured at the key points of assessment and credentialing. Key access strategies might include English as a Second Language instruction and explicit teaching to the rules of the assessment and credentialing system. In this task, education has a crucial intervention role to play in the politics of *redistribution* of social resources.

The balance between *strategies for opportunity* (or access) and *strategies for diversity* is critical. Strategies to improve access that neglect diversity tend to drift toward discredited and ineffectual educational strategies akin to "assimilation." The underlying message of a curriculum which overemphasizes access is that the ideal knowledge and skills are those expressed by the dominant culture, and other cultures are, in one way or another, inferior. It also leads to old-fashioned, didactic forms of "transmission" pedagogy, which fail for their lack of relevance, and for their failure to mesh with students' interests and aspirations.

Diversity. Diversity recognizes curriculum strategies honoring differences amongst students by including those differences as the subject matter of the curriculum, by valuing different learning styles, and by allowing for different learning outcomes depending on student background and aspirations. Such strategies should aim to build constructively upon student experience, interest, and motivation. In this task, education has a crucial interventionary role to play in the politics of social and cultural *recognition*, the politics of belonging.

Strategies for diversity that neglect access may appear "relevant" or "appropriate" yet fail to challenge students or fail to take them into realms of opportunity outside of their existing or community experience. They may, in fact, silently help the already advantaged and hurt the disadvantaged. This is the danger of a superficial multiculturalism. Multicultural education is not about the unreflective preservation of differences, since keeping things just the way they are preserves the relationships of inequality. It is about transformations whereby learners change themselves in and through learning, while nevertheless remaining true to their selves, their lifeworld experiences, and their communities. This is a matter of cultural transformation through self-determination and self-redefinition. A pluralistic version of multiculturalism extends the dominant culture and even transforms what is considered mainstream. It helps redefine the "mainstream" as multicultural, as a place that is diverse in its very nature and in which all people can benefit from that diversity.

Further Readings: Cope, Bill and Mary Kalantzis (1997). *Productive diversity: A new Australian approach to work and management.* Sydney: Pluto Press; Cope, Bill and Mary Kalantzis (1997). White noise: The attack on political correctness and the struggle for the western canon. *Interchange: A Quarterly Review of Education* The Netherlands: Kluwer Academic Publishers, *28*(), 283–329; Cope, Bill and Mary Kalantzis, eds. (2000). *Multiliteracies: Literacy learning and the design of social futures.* Melbourne: Macmillan and London: Routledge; Kalantzis, Mary and Bill Cope (1999). Multicultural education: Transforming the mainstream. In Stephen May, ed., *Critical multiculturalism: Rethinking multicultural and anti-racist education.* London: Falmer Press, pp. 245–276; Kalantzis, Mary (2000). Multicultural citizenship. In W. Hudson, ed., *Rethinking Australian citizenship*. Melbourne: Cambridge University Press.

Mary Kalantzis and Bill Cope

Families and Children in Australia

Many factors, including improved contraception, the legalization of abortion, and the widely publicized detrimental effects of institutionalization, have resulted in nearly all Australian children growing up in a family even if it is not their biological family. In fact, in Australia (2003), very few children grow up in institutions (200) or in correctional centers (500). However, currently children of refugees are held in detention centers with their families while their claims are being processed.

Although most Australian children grow up in families, children's experiences of childhood differ as a function of the structure of their family, their parents' socioeconomic circumstances, and the cultural background into which they are born.

Changes in the Structure of Australian Families

Women's participation in the workforce. Over the past few decades there have been several major changes in conceptualizing what constitutes an Australian family. There has been a decline of the "traditional" family type of mother as homemaker, father as breadwinner, and children. The most obvious area of change has been the increased participation of women with dependent children in the paid workforce. Currently the most common pattern in families with children under 15 years of age is both parents are in paid employment. Eight percent of children in Australia, however, are in families where both parents are unemployed.

The increase of one-parent families. The other major change in family structure has been a large increase in one-parent families (an increase of 53% between 1986 and 2001). One-parent families now make up 23 percent of all families with dependent children. More than one in five children under 15 years of age is now living with one parent, generally their mother (20.3% of families with dependent children are headed by a single-parent mother and 2.7% are headed by a single parent father).

Cohabitation before marriage. In addition, about three-quarters of couples in Australia now live together before they marry, in contrast to patterns of the mid-1980s. De facto relationships are now recognized by law, and as a result many couples are choosing not to marry. This trend not to marry may partly explain why close to a third of the children in Australia are now born outside a formal marriage.

Socioeconomic circumstances of families. In affluent families, the expectation of health and access to good health care, combined with a low birth-rate and a greater use of prenatal testing, has led to an assumption that if they chose to have children, parents will have one or two *perfect* children. The emphasis has moved beyond desiring the basic survival of children, to the desire that children must fulfill "their potential." To achieve this goal, a growing number of families invest resources in private education and extra tuition fees for their children. Such expectations for children have led to less emphasis on children's useful contributions to the family in terms of responsibility and work at home. At the other end of the spectrum, for children from economically disadvantaged families, there seems to be an increasing sense of social alienation as they struggle to find the money to participate in such basic activities as school excursions, much less afford the fees for child care and preschool.

Cultural Diversity in Australian Families

Australia is a country characterized by the migration of a diverse range of people. Recent statistics show that the first Australians, or Indigenous Australians, currently comprise 2.2 percent of Australia's population of just over 20 million people. The British colonized Australia in the eighteenth century and this is reflected in the population today. The three most common ancestries reported in the 2001 census were Australian (people born in Australia of various ancestries including Indigenous people), English, and Irish. Immediately following the Second World War, people from Europe (largest groups were from Italy, Germany, Poland, and the Netherlands) imigrated to Australia. More recently, people of Lebanese, Vietnamese, Indian, Chinese, and many other ancestries (approximately 160 in total) have joined the Australian population. In the 2001 census, over half of the children under the age of 15 reported having Australian ancestry, with most having been born in Australia and having at least one Australian-born parent. Within some ancestry groups, notably Vietnamese, Lebanese, and Chinese, many families speak a language other than English at home. The diversity of languages and cultures in Australia adds to its social wealth as well as challenging the English language and Anglo-Saxon cultural dominance of many services for children and families in Australia.

Indigenous Families

In the 2001 census, 410,000 people considered themselves to be of Aboriginal or Torres Strait origin. While most live in major cities or in regional centers, proportionally more Indigenous than non-Indigenous people live in remote areas of Australia. As a group, Aboriginal and Torres Strait Islander people suffer multiple disadvantages: poor health, a higher rate of infant mortality, a reduced life expectancy compared to non-Indigenous Australians, lower rates of employment, lower rates of educational achievement, higher rates of incarceration, a high incidence of domestic violence and child abuse and neglect, and limited infrastructure and services in remote areas.

While forecasts for the general Australian population over the next few decades predict that there will be a larger proportion of older people than children in the population, the reverse is true for the Indigenous population, where it is predicted that there will be more children than older people. This has implications for services for Indigenous and Torres Strait Islanders, particularly in health and education, as there are a large number of dependents and relatively few adults to provide for them. In addition, Indigenous parents are often poor, young, and relatively uneducated—characteristics that point to the need for parenting support. High levels of unemployment, domestic violence, and abuse also create an unpredictable and sometimes dangerous backdrop for Indigenous children.

This need for support is counteracted, to some extent, by the strong sense of family and community in Indigenous culture. This characteristic leads to a lesser sense of isolation than might be experienced by non-Indigenous families in the same circumstances. However, since life expectancy is twenty years shorter for Indigenous Australians than for the non-Indigenous Australians, grandparents are not as available to provide support to families and children.

Managing Work and Family

Women in the paid workforce. Over the past twenty years, Australian women have become increasingly involved in the paid workforce. As a result, families have needed to actively manage their work and family responsibilities. Despite the increased dependence on the wages of both parents, the patterns of women's involvement in the labor force is consistent with mothers rather than fathers assuming most family responsibilities at home. As their children grow older, more mothers join the paid labor force and mothers are more likely to shift from part-time to full-time work. In contrast, patterns of fathers' participation in the workforce are unaffected by the ages of their children and as a result, most fathers work full-time jobs.

Managing work and family in Australia has been made more difficult for dual wage earners and single-earner families because of a shift away from standard working hours to longer hours and to "flexible" yet "unsocial" working hours involving early mornings, evenings, and weekends. There is considerable concern over the impact of these changes on parents and their relationships with their children and each other. In addition, there has been a trend toward more casual work, with one in three positions now offered on a casual basis. This has led to greater financial insecurity that has a detrimental effect on family well-being.

Child care is difficult for parents to organize as there is a shortage of places and trained staff in formal child care, such as long day-care centers and family day-care schemes. This is especially the case for children under 2 years, and as a consequence, child-care hours are generally structured around a standard working day. As a result, parents are forced to create a patchwork of formal and informal care arrangements, resulting in a third to a half of Australian children in their first three years attending two or more care settings a week.

Support from within the extended family is a crucial resource for families. Without support in the form of information, financial and practical help such as grandparents' assistance in the care of young children, families become isolated and their children suffer. It is unusual in Australia for members of the extended family to live in the household of "nuclear" families, although this is more likely in Aboriginal and Torres Strait Islander households, reflecting a wider kinship system.

The role of grandparents in the lives of children has been of increasing interest to researchers and policy makers. Non-Indigenous grandparents are living longer and having a longer period of shared lives with their grandchildren. When grandchildren are of preschool age and their parents are in the workforce, many grandparents act as regular part-time caregivers and are increasingly awarded custodial care of their grandchildren when parents are unable to care for them. In this way, they often take on shared parenting roles in the care of their grandchildren.

Children's Services and Families

In their engagement with families and children, children's services in Australia need to cater to the diversity of family structures and cultural and language backgrounds. While services attempt to include culturally sensitive practices, from the viewpoint of culturally and linguistically diverse families, children's services are often seen as institutions that teach the values of mainstream Australian culture. Some migrant groups enroll their children in centers for this very reason, to learn about Australian society. Other groups, including Indigenous families, prefer not to send their children to children's services because of the perceived difference in child rearing approach and values (as well as other reasons such as cost and lack of transport and services). Indigenous children have a very low rate of participation in prior to school services in Australia.

Australian policy. In Australian government policy, child-care services are seen as primarily serving the needs of employed parents. In some cases, child care or preschool is used to give families in need or with histories of abuse respite care for their children. There is a legislative requirement through the national accreditation system for children's services to work in partnership with parents. Australian centers are working on finding ways to effectively develop this partnership; however, one constraint limiting family involvement is the long hours of employment, limiting parents' availability for participation. Another constraint is that the majority of child care in Australia is now privately owned and more likely to have a "service" than "partnership" orientation toward families.

Increasingly in Australia, children's services are seen as one of many community services, government and nongovernment, that help support families with young children. In North Queensland, for example, community hubs have been established around many children's services to provide "one-stop shopping" for family support services. This is also the model used around Australia in many children's services for Indigenous children and families.

In line with this trend, children's services in Australia are providing formal support for families as well as care and education for children under school age. This has been done in a number of ways such as encouraging parents to form social networks, and providing parent education sessions on topics as diverse as nutrition and approaches to discipline. Additionally, informal support regarding children's services has always been provided for parents. The involvement of children's services in interagency collaboration with other services for children and families has only just begun to happen in Australia and this holds great promise for an integrated approach to assisting families in raising their children during the early years.

Further Readings: Australian Bureau of Statistics (2003). *Australian social trends 2003*. Catalogue No. 4102.0. Canberra: Australian Government Publishing Service; Bowes, J. M. (2004). *Children, families and communities: Contexts and consequences*. Melbourne: Oxford University Press; De Gioia, K., J. Hayden, and F. Hadley (2003). *Enhancing participation by Aboriginal families in early childhood services: A case study*. Bankstown: Center for Social Justice and Social Change, University of Western Sydney; Hughes, P., and G. MacNaughton (2002). Preparing early childhood professionals to work with parents: The challenges of diversity and dissensus. *Australian Journal of Early Childhood* 28 (2), 14–20; Secretariat for National Aboriginal and Islander Child Care and Center for Community Child Health (2004). *Early childhood case studies*. Northcote, Victoria: Secretariat for National Aboriginal and Islander Child Care.

Jennifer Bowes

Pedagogies in Early Childhood Education

Pedagogy is not a readily used term to describe teaching and learning practices in the Australian preschool (before formal schooling) context. Instead, early childhood educators refer to their program or curriculum approach, teaching techniques, and personal philosophy; and it is this combination that makes up their pedagogy. Pedagogies in early childhood education vary from setting to setting due to the individual's personal teaching and learning style, their underpinning educational philosophy and epistemological beliefs, state curriculum policies and requirements, religious and philosophical orientation of the actual early childhood setting, and the type of community that the preschool is situated within. Here we review *traditional* and *emerging pedagogies* within Australian settings for early childhood education, and focus on the pedagogies found in preschool programs (programs for under 6-year-olds) that are located in schools, kindergartens, and child-care centers.

One of the main reasons that the term pedagogy has traditionally *not* been used in preschool education is that it has been viewed by early childhood practitioners as (primary) school terminology denoting formal teaching and learning, one that implies a direct transmission of knowledge approach. Pedagogy in preschool education is largely determined instead by the teachers' own personal philosophy, usually built from theories acquired in their initial teacher training or gained through teaching experience. In the case of the state of Victoria, where there is no recommended, prescribed nor mandated curriculum framework operating for teachers of under 6-year-olds, one significant educational implication this brings is the issue of teachers' curricula freedom, where the teachers are able to determine and devise their own curriculum framework, content, and pedagogy. More often than not, this results in a teacher-devised curricular framework and pedagogy that ultimately rests upon dominant discourses, dominant theories, and practices familiar and accepted by the teacher. The dominant early childhood teaching and learning practices in Australia will now be explored.

Child-Centered Pedagogies

Foundational to many preschool programs are *child-centered pedagogies*, practices that are informed by child development theories and developmentally appropriate practice (DAP). Child-centered pedagogies view the child in individual terms or as a person who is not yet developed or underdeveloped, and this child is then observed, assessed, and planned for within a child development frame. The child is the focus of the educator's study and is planned for individually through the lens of the main developmental domains; social and emotional development, cognitive, fine, and gross motor development. Acting as a catalyst, the child's "interest" is used to drive the curricula content decisions while being embedded within a developmental frame, one that singles out and matches the interest to the child's developmental "need." In many cases this type of learning entails minimal adult interaction except for the educator setting up the learning environment, monitoring, "scaffolding," and sanctioning the type of play and learning the child engages in.

Other child-centered pedagogies that feature within Australian early childhood programs have their own distinctive traditions and practices, including **Montessori** and **Steiner** education, and programs' using Gardner's multiple intelligences theory as the basis for their educational direction. Depending on the program, they can be either highly teacher-directed or highly child-initiated with the common feature being their child-centeredness that features *planning for the individual child* based on the child's needs, interests, and strengths. This is in stark contrast to the school context, where the curriculum content shapes the pedagogy and the educator's main role is to teach specific knowledge sets and skills. However, having said this, this distinction is now becoming less defined as recent examples show that there are more intersections between school and preschool pedagogies, with some primary schools adopting **Reggio Emilia**-inspired pedagogy and some preschool educators taking on board principles from *Productive Pedagogies,* an inquiry-based pedagogy with its origins deriving from the Queensland school system.

Although *play-based pedagogies* can share some common elements with that of child-centered pedagogies, such as basing practices upon child developmental theories, they are not necessarily the same in pedagogical terms. This is due to the main feature of play-based pedagogies, the belief that children learn through play. This can be witnessed in the form of uninterrupted play, free play, structured play, with the teaching techniques ranging from highly adult interventionist to minimal or no adult intervention. Play-based pedagogies are the foundation of most early childhood programs and are interpreted and practiced in many ways.

Sociocultural and Inquiry-Driven Pedagogies

New pedagogies are changing the educational landscape within preschool education. Viewing children as capable, competent persons and co-constructors of their learning are the common features of these new teaching practices and are inspired by inquiry-driven, critical, and postmodern pedagogies. This shifts the frame from seeing the child in individualist terms, or as a child who is underdeveloped with developmental needs, to that of seeing them as capable people traveling on their lifelong learning journey. One such pedagogy, inspired by sociocultural theories, has resulted in a growing number of research projects and publications that describe early childhood practices from this frame. Fleer and Richardson provide an example by documenting how early childhood practitioners have moved across educational paradigms, in this case from a constructivist-developmental framework to a sociocultural pedagogical approach. Drawing from the sociocultural theories of Lev Vygotsky, Malaguzzi, Rogoff, and others, Fleer and Richardson highlight some of the tensions and resistance that can occur when pedagogy shifts and new conceptual tools replace the familiar. In this particular study, new key pedagogical principles and practices are revealed and a transformation of theoretical understandings takes place. This type of work is shifting the pedagogical frame in the Australian early childhood context.

Even though sociocultural theories and practices are making inroads, at the forefront of pedagogical change within Australian early childhood settings is the phenomenon of the Reggio Emilia approach. Stemming from the small region of Reggio Emilia, Italy, innovative early childhood programs founded by Loris Malaguzzi relatively recently appeared on Australian shores and the approach barely requires an introduction to worldwide early childhood educators. The effect of this educational approach and its wide-ranging pedagogical influence is paramount as an increasing amount of early childhood programs are based on some sort of connection to this orientation. Early childhood educators are being hired based on their knowledge of "Reggio," and their ability to "do Reggio" are keenly sought after pedagogical skills. The discrimination of the transference of this pedagogy to the Australian context varies, with some programs taking the "best aspects" of Reggio Emilia and others taking on board and duplicating as many Reggio Emilia principles and practices that they can. The pedagogical impact of the Reggio Emilia approach is overwhelmingly positive, with educators incorporating inquiry-driven teaching and learning practices including child-initiated projects, and carrying out comprehensive documentation practices. Even though the early childhood programs and approaches of Reggio Emilia have broadened early childhood teaching practice within Australia, some skepticism should be maintained to ensure that the process of pedagogical reconceptualization is an ongoing process; a process that includes curricular renewal to best fit the educational context, and a process aware of the many curricular theories and pedagogies that are available. Reconceptualizing early childhood pedagogy guided by postmodern and critical theories is one example of how to distill the familiar, as practice guided by this frame of reference reveals educational inequities so that they can be challenged and ultimately overcome.

Postmodern and Critical Pedagogies

Currently gaining momentum in early childhood education are pedagogies that aim to transform culture and change the status quo, derived and informed by postmodernism, poststructuralism, feminism, postcolonialism, and critical theories (MacNaughton, 2003). These postmodern pedagogies have entered preschool educational discourse and practice, but still have a long way to go, educationally speaking, and much more to offer early childhood education. These critical pedagogies are driven by principles of social transformation and democratic education and provide educators a language of critique and possibility. Critical pedagogies unravel salient and critical issues within educational contexts and provide educators with the ability to examine "hidden" aspects of their curriculum. In their text, MacNaughton and Williams categorize early childhood teaching techniques into two main areas, *general teaching techniques* that are common pedagogical techniques and *specialist teaching techniques* that originate from diverse theoretical perspectives. The general teaching techniques category is comprised of commonly found early childhood teaching approaches such as demonstrating, describing, encouraging, facilitating, modeling, questioning, and so on, whereas specialist teaching techniques that are quite new to early childhood education are co-constructing, community building, deconstructing, empowering, and philosophizing, and so forth. Of pedagogical interest here are the specialist teaching techniques that generate new and different ways to view pedagogy and ultimately educate young children. By drawing from new and diverse philosophical and epistemological theories, the challenge that the Australian early childhood community has set itself is to promote and sustain new pedagogies, in order to continue to shift the pedagogical frame to accommodate the changing nature of society and education. It is for this reason that early childhood pedagogies are thought of in multiple terms, highlighting the theoretical choices, discourse alternatives, and practice possibilities that are available to educators.

Critical perspectives are most useful for early childhood education as they view the preschool site as an environment that can be inequitable and unjust for some, particularly disadvantaged groups who often consist of lower socioeconomic groups, Indigenous Australians, recent immigrants, or other people of disadvantage. Arguably one of the least known critical pedagogies is that of Indigenous Australians. As Fasoli and Ford found out, there is little research literature on Indigenous Australian pedagogies in early childhood contexts. These writers consequently maintain that it is vital to employ Aboriginal educators where possible when educating Aboriginal children, and non-Aboriginal educators should become aware of the complex relationship structure and the importance placed on relationships within Australian Indigenous perspectives, rather than just apply an Anglo-Australian version of "culturally appropriate activities." They argue that, ". . . in understanding Indigenous practices, was not so much to modify programs to include Indigenous content but rather to focus on relationships as critical when dealing with Indigenous children in an early childhood setting." As some of the most disadvantaged people within Australia, Indigenous Australian pedagogies require close and careful consideration to rethink and change educational bias and prejudiced practices.

The emergence of new technologies is also changing the way that early childhood education is practiced. O'Rourke and Harrison have reported that the inclusion of new technologies, particularly the computer, can be a catalyst for reconceptualizing the early childhood program and pedagogy. Preschool educators in their study claim that by introducing the computer to their early childhood program it has broadened the preschool's horizons and has had positive program implications.

Not all pedagogies could be mentioned here and even though pedagogies have been discussed as separate entities it is common for early childhood practitioners to be eclectic in their approach and combine varying pedagogies to make up their own teaching and learning repertoire. By discussing various pedagogies it is anticipated that early childhood educators will appreciate the limitless bounds of theoretical inspiration from which their pedagogies can draw, and the educational impact on our young children that these pedagogies can ultimately have.

Further Readings: Fasoli, L., and M. Ford (2001). Indigenous early childhood educators' narratives: Relationships, not activities. *Australian Journal of Early Childhood 26*(3), 18–22; Fleer, M., and C. Richardson (2004). Moving from a constructivist-developmental framework for planning to a sociocultural approach: Foregrounding the tension between individual and community. *Journal of Australian Research in Early Childhood Education* 11(2), 70–87; MacNaughton, G. (2003). *Shaping early childhood: Learners, curriculum and contexts.* Maidenhead, England: Open University Press; MacNaughton, G., and G. Williams (2004). *Techniques for teaching young children: Choices in theory and practice.* 2nd ed. Frenchs Forest, New South Wales: Pearson; O'Rourke, M., and C. Harrison (2004). The introduction of new technologies: New possibilities for early childhood pedagogy. *Australian Journal of Early Childhood 29*(2), 11–18.

Anna Kilderry

Creativity and Imagination

Creativity is a concept that has a wide range of meaning and understandings, particularly in the education sector. In Australia, the Victorian Schools Innovation Commission (VSIC) initiated a creativity pilot program with four schools during 2004. The intention of the pilot was to raise teachers' awareness about creativity, to test ideas as to how best to promote children's creativity, and to identify how to embed creative learning across the curriculum. This work has been continued and expanded through the Australian Centre for Effective Partnerships, who have brokered a range of innovative partnerships between schools and creative practitioners.

Conceptualizing Creativity

An advisory group on creativity was established by VSIC consisting of representatives from a wide range of creative sectors and industries. The group set
out to describe creativity in such a way that it would be useful for teachers and
the education sector in general and developed the following guiding concept in
2004:

> When we are creative we see the world in new ways, we ask new questions, we
> imagine new possibilities and we seek to act in such a way that makes a difference.

They maintained that creativity entails the following:
- use of imaginative, intuitive, and logical thinking
- a fashioning process where ideas are shaped, refined, and managed
- pursuing purposes to produce tangible outcomes from goals
- disciplined application of knowledge and skills to make new connections
- originality or production of new ideas, perspectives, or products
- expression influenced by values
- the value of what is produced is open to the judgments of others
- collaboration, evaluation, review, and feedback

In this conception of creativity, imagination is intrinsic to the creative process
and operates as children develop their capacity for creative thinking and action.
Imagination is concerned with the generation of ideas through exploration, representation, and conjecture. Imaginative thinking and creativity are significant as
children construct knowledge and learn to communicate ideas.

The Role of Creativity in Learning: Rationale for a National Focus

Creativity is increasingly being seen as a key component to the individual's well-
being, sense of fulfillment, cultural identity, and economic success. In response to
such international imperatives, the VSIC Advisory Group identified the following
four points as rationale for increasing the focus on creativity in schools:

1. *Creativity enables individuals to structure rewarding and fulfilling lives.* The
   world that our children face will be complex, ambiguous, and uncertain. They
   need to be equipped with curiosity and confidence in order to exercise choice
   and respond positively to opportunities, challenges, and responsibilities. Children
   need creativity to manage risk and cope with change and adversity. A creative
   life generates excitement and personal delight. Creativity also emerges from the
   struggle to negotiate conflicts between ourselves and our surrounding world.
2. *Creativity stimulates learning.* When provided with the opportunity to be creative, children are more likely to make full use of the information and experiences
   available to them and extend beyond habitual or expected responses. When children are encouraged to think independently and creatively, they become more
   interested in discovering things for themselves, more open to new ideas, and keen
   to work with others to explore ideas. As a result, self-motivation, pace of learning, levels of achievement and self-esteem increase. By developing the capacity of
   teachers to use their own creativity in their teaching practices, we increase the

opportunity for students to develop their ideas in safe, creative, learning environments. This capacity to transfer, transform, create, and innovate is an important dimension of twenty-first century literacy practices.

3. *Creativity as a driving force of economic growth.* Today's global economy increasingly relies on knowledge, creativity, and innovation. Knowledge, imagination, and individual creativity are the wellspring of innovation as nations attract, retain, and develop creative people. This ability to innovate is increasingly acknowledged as *the* critical corporate asset of the twenty-first century and a major source of individual, corporate, and national competitive advantage. By supplanting land, labor, and capital, nations use creativity to stay "ahead of the pack." Creativity, innovation, inventiveness, entrepreneurship, and enterprise are valued social capital.

4. *Creativity in response to social, cultural, and environmental issues.* Flexible, creative approaches are required if society is to respond positively to the challenges and responsibilities associated with rapid change, uncertainty, and adversity. Schools and communities that equip students to be creative will generate individuals capable of fueling a vibrant and innovative cultural, social, and economic life. Individuals can transform society if they learn to act together and generate new ideas. The state of social cohesion, environmental sustainability, economic prosperity, and effective governance will depend on the abilities of people to unlock their creative potential. Current social, cultural, and environmental attitudes and beliefs can be reconsidered when people respond to new interactions and fresh connections, and collaborate.

The implications for education are therefore significant. Teachers face a major challenge as they go beyond simplistic understandings of creativity as self expression. Creativity must be understood in the classroom beyond children's responses to open-ended tasks. This will require teachers to reconsider creativity as a rich and disciplined inquiry vital for the effective communication of ideas.

A Framework for Creativity: Where to Look in Assessment

Teachers in the creativity pilots adopted and continue to use the following conceptual framework developed by the IDES network in conjunction with Learning and Teaching Scotland:

The Person—characteristics, abilities, and skills we encourage and give space for. These include the following:
- predispositions
- preferences
- cognitive and metacognitive abilities
- knowledge and specific skills

The Process—the relevant strategies and approaches we adopt and employ in successful creative exploits. These include the following:
- flexibility and openness
- facilitation of specific knowledge
- skills
- acceptance of alternatives
- stimulus and ownership

The Product—the outcomes of the creative endeavor. These include the following:
- tangible products
- personal satisfaction
- social worth

The Place—the environment and resources that are provided and developed. These include the following:
- ethos and culture
- physical space
- organization
- equipment

Creative Curriculum and Pedagogy

What is significant about these frameworks is the notion of interrelationships. We can only understand teaching for creativity if we consider it as part of a complex range of interdependent factors. There are implications for assessment and a need for a new assessment paradigm.

Rather than judging students by what they produce, the *relationships* between learners, teachers, and their environment should be assessed and analyzed in order to plan for future action and intervention. If we consider how students take risks, participate in critical reflection, remain open and flexible, use general and detailed knowledge, and make decisions, we can assess how students have engaged in the creative processes as they occur. In order to better understand how students are learning, we need to consider whether students are informed about the structure of the learning, have opportunities to negotiate criteria, and are supported in their work.

We need to consider the environment and relationships in the classroom in the same way. When we evaluate the particular atmosphere, the approaches employed, and the facilities, we can make better decisions about the creative learning environment. By looking at the partnerships and relationships that form in the classroom, we can see how relationships affect creative processes. We should acknowledge how students help each other to focus on the learning, how relationships encourage risk-taking, and how students support each other's expressions of ideas. We cannot assess a student unless we assess the pedagogy of the teacher and the learning environment being offered at the same time. The following cases illustrate this complexity in action.

A Case Study: The Potential of Animation in the Classroom

Rachael is an early childhood teacher who passionately believes in the importance of creativity in children's lives. She participated in a two-year research project with twelve other teachers exploring the use of information and communications technologies (ICT) with young children. It became apparent to her that although ICT had the potential to stimulate children's creativity, the software programs that were available were not facilitating the process. By chance she came upon a professional opportunity that enabled her to learn about how to create animations and she realized its potential to act as a powerful narrative device by which children could create contexts for telling stories using new media.

A visit to an animation studio clarified for Rachael that animation was essentially about well-constructed narrative. She began an exploration of animation with her class and provided children with the opportunity to observe and critically reflect on animations they had encountered. She also allotted time for children to develop a foundational understanding of how the various technologies worked. The children played, experimented, and were given small teaching clinics on both the technical and narrative aspects of animation. The children also spent time talking about their ideas to each other and thinking about how the animation process could facilitate telling their story effectively. Rachael supported and guided them to find effective ways to communicate their ideas.

Prompted by their discussions, the children created a storyboard of their ideas together with a script. Both the storyboard and the script indicated features of the technology, such as camera angles, the placement of sound effects, and the use of voice-overs. Once Rachael taught the children the basic principles of visual design and camera work, they quickly increased control over equipment and the medium. The project created a need for learning new vocabulary (e.g., wide-shot, mid-shot, close-up, etc.), which was incorporated into the curriculum. The class also investigated how to combine a sequence of shots based on film-making principles. This newly gained expertise and knowledge provided children with the power to critique their own and others' work.

Rachael's classroom moved beyond other classrooms where the technical or foundational aspects of animation predominated. When only the foundational aspects are emphasized, the results are animations that are technically clever but not necessarily communicating a message of interest or worth in the eyes of the audience (neglect of some aspects of the human dimension).

The teamwork required during the creative process inevitably facilitated the development of such skills as communication, negotiation, decision making, time management, and general organization. Creativity is therefore not something that occurs in isolation from other learning. The children in Rachael's class exhibited many of the characteristics of creative people: curiosity, passion, drive, and confidence. They used their imagination to pursue purposeful goals and demonstrated tolerance for ambiguity and uncertainty as they persisted with their tasks and identified ways forward when confronted with problems.

Importantly, Rachael created an environment where children could work in a sustained way when needed. For example, when one group of students were clearly working well and in the final stages of producing their animation, she allowed them to spend the better part of two days to complete it rather than be constrained by the timetable. Children as young as seven and eight years were able to sustain their concentration and perseverance.

Rachael encouraged learners in her class to believe in their own ideas and articulate back and forth between logic and imagination. Her own beliefs in children's creative and learning capacity meant that her expectations of what they were capable of doing were high. Consequently she created a learning environment where there was clear evidence of children feeling challenged by their goals and tasks, freely moving around and taking the initiative to find relevant

892 EARLY CHILDHOOD EDUCATION

information, interacting with others, gaining support and encouragement from their teachers, and willingly put forward new ideas and alternative views. This is consistent with the research on creative learning environments and demonstrates how important both environment and pedagogy were in enabling children in Rachael's class to develop their creative capacity.

Links to Literacy

One of the reasons the animations produced by Rachael's students communicated powerfully with their audiences was because she went beyond the technical to emphasize a need to communicate something of worth. Creativity and multiliteracies are intrinsically linked if literacy is understood to involve the following dimensions: the human, the foundational, the critical, and the creative.

The *human* dimension of literacy is a reminder that literacy is not simply a technical endeavor. Literacy is shaped and influenced by individuals as they make sense of life experiences and communicate new knowledge. An individual's knowledge develops through experience, and the way an individual interprets experience changes. This growing knowledge includes not only discipline knowledge (e.g., Arts, Science), but also knowledge gained from other people, situations, and contexts. The communication of emotions is particularly evident in multiliterate practice when music is used to create a mood or feeling associated with a message.

The *foundational* dimension of literacy refers to the particular skills and knowledge that generally need to be directly taught, then practiced in order for students to become proficient. In schools, a huge emphasis has been placed on the development of skills associated with reading and writing and to a lesser degree, listening and speaking. The foundational skills associated with visual, aural, spatial, and gestural modes of communication do not receive that same emphasis and are more often addressed through specialized or elective subjects.

The *critical* dimension of literacy has serious implications for educators' pedagogy and the following series of questions arises:
- How do we examine the educational intentions of the tasks we set students? For example, are we aiming to simply engage students with technology or are we providing opportunities for genuine critical engagement?
- To what extent are students encouraged to use higher order thinking, develop deep understandings, and reflect on the content of their work?
- How well do we encourage students to identify the relevance of their work at a local and global level?
- To what extent are students able to reflect on the appropriateness of the mode of communication they have used to exhibit their knowledge and ideas?
- Is the learning environment designed physically, socially, and culturally to be a place where students regularly give and receive feedback?
- How much time is provided for students to revisit and reshape their initial ideas after discussion and feedback?

The quality of questions, scaffolding, and support that teachers provide to guide students' thinking contribute to how well the critical dimension of literacy is developed.

The *creative* dimension indicates where learners manipulate and reconstruct situations to make their experiences more meaningful. This involves the expression, testing, and elaboration of ideas as they take place. Other dimensions of literacy are adapted, adopted, and innovated for the individual's own purposes. Understanding how well other dimensions of literacy have been assimilated provides opportunities to assess creative literacy.

Future Directions

Creativity has long been valued in the early childhood sector, particularly by preschool teachers who are adept at creating curriculum that enables children to explore and develop their ideas. Creative approaches, in addition to being effective, also match calls for reform of teaching pedagogy. Students become engaged in novel ways and build a strong base of skills, techniques, knowledge, and understanding.

When teachers create an environment that fosters honesty of interaction, they also create an atmosphere for challenge. Teachers still have a strong role to play, as the early stages of the creative process often involve teachers articulating the challenge and engaging in direct teaching or modeling. Later, children draw on new and existing skills, knowledge, and understandings to develop their ideas and thinking. A curriculum that fosters creativity in the classroom encourages empathy and consideration of multiple perspectives, with a high premium also placed on communication and interpersonal skills.

Creative learning contexts need to foster a wide sense of student responsibility for learning. Students can identify what to do, organize their time, identify priorities, determine how best to approach tasks, and balance their commitments. Communication of ideas in multiple modes creates a demand for multiliteracies in learning and teaching. In examining creativity, a shift from evaluating isolated student achievement to using a new assessment paradigm that evaluates *relationships* is called for. This refers to *relationships* between teachers' pedagogy, the physical and cultural environment they create for students, and the learning or outcomes demonstrated by students. Considering the interplay of such relationships in assessment will enrich our understanding of how best to develop young children's creative capacity and improve our teaching practice.

Further Readings: Cotton, R. (Spring 2003). *Assessing creativity: Where to look.* IDES Network. Available online at http://ides.org.uk/idespublications/index.asp; Craft, A. (2001). *An analysis of research and literature on creativity in education.* Report prepared for the Qualifications and Curriculum authority. Available online at http://www. ncaction.org.uk/creativity/creativity_report.pdf; Department for Culture, Media, and Sport (2001). *Culture and creativity: The next ten years.* Green paper. Available online at http://www.culture.gov.uk/PDF/creative_next10.pdf; Learning and Teaching Scotland and the IDES Network. (2004). *Creativity counts: A report on the findings from schools.* Dundee, Scotland. Available online at http://www.ides.org.uk/files/creativitycountslts2004.pdf; Loveless, A. (2002). *Literature review in creativity, new technologies and learning.* NESTA: Futurelab series. Report 4. Available online at http://www.nestafuturelab.org/research/reviews/cr01.htm; The New London Group (2000). A pedagogy of multiliteracies: Designing social futures. In B. Cope and M. Kalantzis, eds., *Multiliteracies: Literacy learning for social futures.* London:

Routledge; VSIC Advisory Group. (2004). *Creativity rationale and guiding concept.* Melbourne: Victorian Schools Innovation Commission.

Maureen O'Rourke

Curriculum in Early Childhood

Overview

In Australia curriculum is developed and implemented at the level of states and territories. Attempts in the past two decades to develop a national curriculum for schools have been unsuccessful, and as a result, each state and territory government is solely responsible for the development and implementation of its' own regulatory frameworks for the curriculum. Each state and territory has agreed on a set of Key Learning Areas. Although the names for these may vary, the discipline areas remain common and refer to English, mathematics, science, the arts, technology, society and environment, health and physical education, and languages other than English. In this section I will refer specifically to the school curriculum for early childhood (kindergarten to year 3) since child care in Australia is regulated by a national accreditation scheme. The child-care sector does not usually adopt curriculum designed by education authorities although in some states child-care directors are required to be trained teachers. Most Kindergarten and preschool programs are offered free to children who are 3–5 years of age, although these programs are not compulsory and school (i.e., year 1) starting ages also vary, as they too are determined by individual states and territories.

Curriculum

The curriculum emphasis in each Australian state and territory differs, with a shift in recent years toward "essential learnings." Essential learnings are a response to recognition of the need for a new curriculum paradigm, able to embrace multiliteracies, changing technological conditions and futures. Curriculum frameworks in the Northern Territory, Tasmania, South Australia, New South Wales, and Queensland reflect this shift in thinking toward essential learnings or the "new basics." Queensland's New Basics Framework also promotes multifaceted and authentic or "rich" tasks for assessment as an alternative to large scale testing (The State of Queensland Department of Education and the Arts, 2001). Baker, Trotter, and Holt (2003) note considerable diversity in the categorization of these essential learnings. While some frameworks regard essential learnings as curriculum itself, others describe them as a component part of curriculum.

Stages of Schooling

Within the frameworks there is a reliance on developmental continua to demarcate early, middle, and upper schooling into phases/bands or stages. Although these stages of schooling in fact attract slightly different names in each state and territory, the underlying principle of these levels is hierarchical and increasingly focuses on specialized rather than integrated knowledge. It is usually the case that children of the same chronological age are grouped together in the same classroom. Multiage groupings often exist in small schools for reasons of administration rather than pedagogy while some larger schools have taken a multiage or family grouping approach for philosophical or pedagogical reasons.

There is policy provision for early entry to school for children of high ability and this is usually measured by an intelligence test that is administered, at the cost of families, by an independent psychologist. Equity is clearly an issue in the access to dominant cultural discourses and funds of knowledge that are tested. The actual provision of early entry to school has been very limited and many families have encountered considerable resistance from education authorities to early entry or differentiated curriculum in the early years. The social and emotional development of children is often cited as the major reason for not accelerating students of high ability (Senate Committee, 2001).

Outcomes and Standards Frameworks

In a climate of accountability and economic rationalism it is now the case that outcomes frameworks are used in all Australian schools. Each of these frameworks identifies a set of predetermined learning outcomes for all students although these also vary across jurisdictions in the type and scope of learning outcomes used. The outcomes are essentially curriculum organizers that emphasize observable student achievement using terms such as "compare," "describe," or "investigate." They are not intended as assessment criteria (Baker, Trotter, and Holt, 2003). However, as Luke (1999) notes, "the multiple outcomes approach is 'technocratic'" (p. 7) based on positivist principles and is potentially intellectually reductionist. It also deskills teachers and teacher professional learning communities. MacNaughton (2003) also notes that outcomes-based education and standardized testing disempower educators and perpetuate a conforming position in relation to curriculum in early childhood education.

National Benchmarking

National testing in literacy and numeracy is conducted with all students in year 3 (approximately 8-year-old children) and testing is again conducted nationally in tests during the school years 5 and 7. These tests are based on achievement targets identified by education authorities. These tests are decontextualized, standardized, and offer students a single opportunity to demonstrate their knowledge and understandings in a high-stakes curriculum area. Our concern with such approaches is informed by critical theory and a multiliteracies framework (Cope and Kalatzis, 2000) that recognize that many students undertaking such tests will be unable to demonstrate what they know and can do due to the Eurocentric cultural knowledge that is inherently valued and normalized within them.

Financing of Early Years Provision

The Australian Council of Deans of Education have identified that "prior to school education is probably the sector most in need of help in Australia . . . (it) remains seriously under funded" (2004, p. 47). The inadequate funding of prior to school settings, insufficient remuneration of early years teachers, and increasing child/staff ratios have a negative impact on the types of programs offered in early childhood. In this climate it is difficult to imagine how the profession can adequately provide learning environments where children "are to develop into well rounded, competent, productive and socially responsible citizens" (p. 47).

Recent Research

The popular appeal of recent developments in brain research has contributed to a renewed emphasis on the significance of the environment in the early years. In particular, there is concern regarding the so-called "windows of opportunity" in early childhood being fully exploited in order to generate competent and productive adults. Curriculum in the early years emphasizes early education as a significant foundation for future development particularly in social, emotional, and physical well-being and the development of literacy and numeracy to be an economically "legitimate" citizen. The notions of "opportunity and investment" are closely linked to the now renowned RAND Corporation's statement that $1 spent in early childhood nets a $7 return in the long term (RAND, 2005). Hopes expressed by politicians that Australia would be regarded internationally as a "clever country" have been fertile ground for conservatism that unapologetically declares Australia can no longer afford to carry the "warm bodies" draining our education, welfare, and justice systems (Smart Population Foundation, 2005).

Curriculum Approaches

Despite the mandatory nature of early childhood curriculum in Australia there are numerous philosophical approaches to programming at the "grassroots" level. Arthur, Beecher, Death, Dockett, and Farmer (2005) identify no less than sixteen approaches evident in Australian early childhood programs. Among these are models of early childhood education informed by developmentally appropriate practice, **behaviorism**, sociocultural theory, postmodern, poststructural, and critical theories. MacNaughton (2003) makes a crucial distinction among these approaches, identifying social justice and equity as crucial indicators for evaluating whether curriculum approaches perpetuate conforming, reforming, or transforming educational practices. MacNaughton's model is a useful one for exploring the ways in which dominant cultural discourses shape the perspectives of race, ethnicity, class, culture, childhoods, and families that inform mandated curriculum frameworks and day-to-day, classroom-based curriculum decisions.

What Lies Ahead?

Redefining curriculum in Australia has begun in earnest (The State of Queensland, 2001; Luke, 1999; MacNaughton, 2003) and will continue to evolve, provided that a purposeful dialogue regarding identity, diversity, language, and a problematizing of what constitutes essential learnings in the knowledge era persists. The major threats to this dialogue are political conservatism, cconomic rationalism, and the deprofessionalizing of educators through the development of a technocratic approach to curriculum in the early years of education.

Further Readings: Arthur, L., B. Beecher, E. Death, S. Dockett, S. Farmer (2005). *Programming and planning in early childhood settings.* Melbourne: Thomson; Australian Council of Deans of Education (2004). *New teaching, new learning: A vision for Australian education.* Canberra: Australian Council of Deans of Education; Baker, R., H. Trotter, and J. Holt (2003). *Curriculum provisions in the Australian states and territories: Research report for the ministerial council on education, employment, training and youth affairs.* Canberra: Curriculum Corporation; Luke, A. (1999). *Education 2010 and new times: Why equity and social justice still matter, but differently.* Online conference October 20, 1999. Available online at http://education.qld.gov.au/corporate/newbasics/html/; MacNaughton, G. (2003). *Shaping early childhood.* Berkshire: Open University Press; RAND Corporation (2005). *The economics of investing in universal preschool education in California.* Santa Monica: RAND Corporation; Senate Employment, Workplace Relations, Small Business and Education Committee (2001). *The education of gifted children.* Canberra: Commonwealth of Australia; Smart Population Foundation (2005). *Why smart population?* Available online at http://www.smartpopulation.com; State of Queensland Department of Education and the Arts (2001). *The new basics project.* Available online at http://education.qld.gov.au/corporate/newbasics/index.html.

Libby Lee

Multiliteracies

Now, more than ever, the lives of young children are saturated with multimedia, in the form of DVDs, CD-ROMs, computer games, digital music, e-mail, text messaging, and digital photography, to name just a few. This has required new thinking about the new forms of literacy. One of the ways that this rethinking has occurred has been encapsulated in the pedagogy of multiliteracies, which has expanded our view of reading, writing, speaking, and listening to include the various multimedia symbol forms. In this way computers are "symbol machines" that allow young children to negotiate a complex interplay of multiple sign systems (e.g., video clips, music, sound effects, icons, virtually rendered paint strokes, text in print-based documents), multiple modalities (e.g., linguistic, auditory, visual, artistic), and recursive communicative and cognitive processes (e.g., real time and virtual conversations, cutting/pasting text, manipulating graphics, importing photographs).

The term multiliteracies in fact covers what has also been regarded as electronic literacies, technoliteracies, digital literacies, visual literacies, and print-based literacies. To explore multiliteracies we require an understanding of semiotic theory to know how symbols, in the form of letters and words, drawings, icons of various types, photographs, colors, and animation movement can communicate meanings. Semiotics offer a wide lens to describe the ways in which meanings are made and goals accomplished using "semiotic resources" such as oral language, visual symbols, and music. As the figure shows below, emergent and early literacy is not simply a question of print-based versus electronic or digital literacies, but a consideration of the multimodal context of multiliteracies that makes it unique and relevant to contemporary early childhood education.

Multiliteracies incorporate print-based literacies

While being multiliterate is extremely relevant to the early childhood context, a review of the research into new technologies and early childhood by Lankshear and Knobel found a preponderance of the use of multimodal resources to promote decoding and encoding alphabetic texts. The authors claim there has been an underrealization of the potential of new technologies to orient children toward literacy futures that will be very different from those of the past. These authors also affirmed that the interrelated fields of new technologies and literacy in early childhood were radically underresearched when compared to other age-groups. Interestingly the authors contend that much new learning was occurring in out-of-school settings rather than in classroom settings. This review of research alerted Australian researchers to the need for involving teachers as researchers in exploring the possibilities of new learning and multiliteracies.

In other research into the integration of technology and literacy pedagogy Durrant and Green found that in various Australian states there has been an overly technical skills approach to integrating technology literacy pedagogy. This "skills orientation" was outside of an authentic context of situated social practice and at odds with social constructivist theories that underpin much of early childhood pedagogy. Durrant and Green's research into digital literacies provided a conceptual framework known as the "3D" view of new literacy learning to bring together three dimensions—"operational," "cultural," and "critical"—that need to be addressed simultaneously to enable a holistic, cultural, and critical view of pedagogy.

Building on the work of these two research teams an Australian early childhood research project titled *Children of the New Millennium* involved twenty teacher-researchers exploring 4- to 8-year-old children's knowledge and understanding of multiliteracies. In the first instance, the teachers and researchers undertook a "technotour" of children's homes that revealed a high level of use of new technologies by children that was far greater than teachers had anticipated. In most cases the children had access to and could use information and communication technologies (ICT) far in advance of the equipment that existed in many of the schools and preschools. Children were able to go online to websites that were often linked to their favorite television shows, use search engines to find information, and often played interactive games online and with game software. New ways of building on the skills and interests from home emerged when teachers engaged some children as coaches or mentors in the classroom and capitalized on children's funds of knowledge by using similar software in school as at home. This was particularly so for children with special learning needs. The pedagogies of the teachers using new technologies were inquiry-based, and autonomous investigations and problem posing and solving were promoted. The multimedia software supported the creation of animations, movies, slideshows, and explorations of digital-still photography and video.

Situated practice—making learning meaningful and based on real-life experiences by focusing on children's interests and understandings—was highlighted in the learning stories compiled by the teacher-researchers. The teachers commented on the need for authentic, real life, purposeful engagements in early childhood settings because children at home were able to quickly locate an enormous amount of resources and material through the use of the information-rich Internet. Teachers wrote that the visual aspect of the Internet was a valuable tool to further enhance young children's understanding of their world.

A framework for mapping the depth and complexity of young children's learning with multiliteracies was developed by the teacher-researchers. The four interrelated dimensions provided a lens for teachers to analyze what children know about multiliteracies and helped reveal the next steps in planning for learning.

Functional user	**Meaning maker**
◆ Locating, code breaking, using signs and icons ◆ Selecting and operating equipment ◆ Moving between mediums: cameras, videos, computers	◆ Understanding multimodal meanings ◆ Purpose of text and text form ◆ Connecting to prior knowledge 
Critical analyzer	**Transformer**
◆ Discourse analysis ◆ Equity ◆ Power and position ◆ Appropriate software / hardware	◆ Using skills and knowledge in new ways ◆ Designing texts ◆ Producing new texts

The multiliteracies map (Hill, 2005)

The teacher-researchers found that children thrived on generating new multimodal texts and this led to the need to understand principles of multimodal meanings. For example, the use of graphics and story-making software encouraged communication and other emergent literacy behaviors as well as enhanced interpersonal interactions among learners. The electronic books in various software programs supported the development of children's readings and rereadings and this was particularly evident with children with special needs. The use of electronic multimedia options opened up an interactive world that can support children's literacy development in a digital world and provide them with stories that may be beyond their reading level.

Projects such as *Children of the New Millennium* have shown that children as young as 3 and 4 years of age can represent meaning with digital photographs about their learning, can play with these photographs; importing them into slide shows, changing the layout, the colors, and the shape. They can make books with photographs and their own artwork using myriad of colors and backgrounds, and this can have audio voice and sound effects and animation added to it. The project has also revealed that the traditional content of reading and writing needs to be broadened to include the use of multiple-sign systems that represent meaning. Children in early childhood have always used construction, drawing or illustrations, movement, and sound to represent meaning. The newer multimodal technologies merely add to children's choice of medium to represent ideas and to comprehend the meanings in a range of texts.

Indeed, as an example of how quickly the concept of multiliteracies has taken hold over the past three years, most Australian state departments of education have embraced the concept of multiliteracies. Education of Queensland and the South Australian Department of Education promote literacy learning in the context of the pedagogy of multiliteracies and encourage teachers to create contexts for learning that are multimodal and incorporate the use of new technologies where appropriate.

Very quickly, over the past five years it has become evident that digital literacies and print-based literacy are not oppositional concepts. Both are required for effective functioning in the twenty-first century. In fact traditional print-based reading and writing was found to be vitally important for success in digital contexts. Writing was significantly important as a memory tool, for planning, designing, and recording ideas and information. Reading was critically important for predicting, scanning, interpreting, analyzing, and selecting from the abundance of information. Interestingly, in *Children of the New Millennium*, the children switched effortlessly between genres, scanning material for information, following procedures, searching by scrolling through menus, and interpreting icons and written instructions on tool bars. In other words, although reading, writing, listening, and speaking are paramount, today's students must be able to do more, as they decipher, code-break, achieve meaning, and express ideas through a range of media incorporating design, layout, color, graphics, and animation.

In fact, learning to critique the digital media, and consider whether the information is appropriate or accurate, is far more important than ever before considering the amount of time children are engaged with the screen. For many children preschool and school is the only place where they can learn to question the values and intentions of the many software programs and numerous websites. Teachers have commented about the need for practical examples of strategies they can use to support children to develop a critical orientation to multiliteracies.

It is clear that more research is needed into the long-term effects of prolonged use of screen-based learning. Children as young as 2 and 3 years of age are choosing to play with computers for long periods of time at home; in some learning stories teachers wrote of children whose main leisure activity at home was playing with the computer for extensive periods without adult supervision. Add to this long periods of screen-based learning at school, and the length of time interacting with the screen is significant. Long-term use may affect children's health, social and communicative abilities, and thought processes.

Further research into multiliteracies in early childhood education is important because technological change is increasingly defining the nature of literacy. Reading and writing will become even more important in the future due to the increasing need for acquiring and communicating information rapidly in a world of global competition and information economies. We live in a time where speed of information is central to success and reading and writing proficiency will be even more critical to our children's futures.

There has been a plethora of research regarding the impact of television on children. However, the Internet, as a source of information, education, and entertainment, is set to have a far greater impact on the lives and learning of young children than television. It is essential for us to consider the following questions: How will interactive game-based entertainment affect children's play and learning? How will new technologies transform children's dispositions or "habitus", or ways of thinking? As children play, think, and learn, this learning becomes internalized as structures, schemas, or ways of thinking that can be used in other contexts. How will the increasing engagement with multimodal literacies change the ways children think and learn? New technologies have already transformed the lives of young children in their home and informal learning contexts—such questions will be vital if we are to have an education system that is meaningful and relevant to the lives of young children in the twenty-first century. Becoming multiliterate is viewed as being an essential part of successful learning for these new times.

Further Readings: Durrant, C., and B. Green (2000). Literacy and the new technologies in school education: Meeting the l(IT)eracy challenge? *Australian Journal of Language and Literacy* 23(2), 89–108; Hill, S. (2005). *Mapping multiliteracies: Children of the new millennium.* Report of the research project 2002–2004. Adelaide: University of South Australia; Hill, S., and N. Yelland. *Children of the New Millennium: Using information and communication technologies (ICT) for playing and learning in the information age.* Australian Research Council Large Grant LP0215770 2002–2003; Kress, G., and T. Van Leeuwen (2001). *Multimodal discourse: The modes and media of contemporary communication.* London: Hodder Headline Group; Lankshear, C., and M. Knobel (2003). New technologies in early childhood literacy research: A review of research. *Journal of Early Childhood Literacy* 3(1), 59–82; New London Group (1996). A pedagogy of multiliteracies. *Harvard Educational Review* 60(1), 66–92.

Susan Hill

Numeracy: An Australian View

In the context of Australian education mathematics is generally regarded as the knowledge and skills base for the discipline, and the term *numeracy* relates to the application of this knowledge and skills in authentic or real-world contexts. As such the importance of developing a numerate populace who can function effectively with the practical mathematical demands of everyday life in the twenty-first century has been recognized in the Australian context. In fact, there is recognition that the process of becoming numerate is ongoing and the years from birth to eight years of age represent an age of unparalleled growth when the foundations of skills and concepts are established. It also represents a time of opportunity to develop positive attitudes towards mathematics and the ways in which it can contribute to everyday life in a variety of ways. It has become evident that children use mathematical ideas and processes in the years before they attend school in a number of informal ways. They develop understandings about money when shopping and about time as they embark on journeys in the family car, or on trains. Such informal learning contexts are enriched when parents or caregivers support the learning via reading stories, highlighting real world applications involving numeracy concepts and making links between numeracy and play activities. However, much of this support will be intuitive and we need to be clear about the importance of the early childhood years for later development and the ways in which we as parents and educators can support the foundations of numeracy in a variety of contexts.

It has now become apparent that new demands in the high-performance workplace mean that a traditional view of mathematics which focused on memorization, rote learning, and knowing facts devoid of context and application has been replaced with one in which mathematics has some purpose and application, and where becoming numerate is conceptualized in a broad way. Such a vision considers mathematics and becoming numerate in the context of societal and individual expectations. This vision has been accompanied with a shift in pedagogy which emphasizes the use of both whole class and small group teaching, active exploration, inquiry and problem solving, engagement with mathematical ideas via collaborations and creative explorations, mathematical representations incorporating a variety of media which include the use of information and communication technologies (ICT), and the communication of findings with peers and authentic audiences.

Environments that Promote Numeracy Learning

The importance of a solid foundation in literacy and numeracy was epitomized in Australia in the Adelaide Declaration on National Goals for Schooling in the twenty-first century, which stated the following:

> Students should have attained the skills of numeracy and English literacy; such that, every student should be numerate, be able to read, write and spell and communicate at an appropriate level.

Such a vision has implications for the organization of teaching and learning opportunities in mathematics that will enable children to become numerate or mathematically literate in Australia. The *Numeracy for All Report* recognized that "No single approach to teaching numeracy will be effective for all learners," but declared that it was a major policy objective that students should attain strong foundations in literacy and numeracy in the early childhood years, so that key enabling skills for achieving success in schooling could be achieved. In 1999 Perry noted the importance of early learners being confident about their ability to solve problems mathematically and being challenged and engaged to create opportunities to use and extend their existing skills. He also stated that since children actively construct their own knowledge they should be able to learn in a variety of contexts and ways that are characterized by play, talking about their discoveries and strategies, and working with others in collaborative ways. He stressed the importance of teachers and parents working in partnerships to support student learning since this was a major factor that influenced effective learning in the early years.

Because of the high priority placed by the government on attaining numeracy for all students in Australian schools the various states created mathematics programs that were designed to create contexts in which children could develop skills which they could utilize in real-world contexts, and thus provide contexts for becoming numerate in new and dynamic ways. These have included the following:
• Count me in (New South Wales)
• The early years numeracy project (Victoria)
• First steps to numeracy (Western Australia)
Additionally, benchmarks for mathematical achievement were developed to ensure that it was possible to measure if such programs were successful in reaching their objectives. The programs initiated in each of the states not only focused on student attainment but also recognized that teachers needed professional development and additional support in their classrooms if outcomes in numeracy were to be achieved. The early years numeracy interview, which is part of the project in Victoria, is, for example, conducted on a one-to-one basis and provides teachers with rich data about the knowledge and abilities of young children with regard to their mathematical ability. Evaluations of the program have indicated that teachers feel more confident about their skills in mathematics as a result of their participation in the project, and that they were able to teach more effectively to improve outcomes for the children in their class.

In a recent study, Yelland and her colleagues have illustrated the ways in which young children may become numerate in the information age. They suggest a new view of numeracy that allows for the application of mathematical skills in a diverse range of contexts. Thus, to become numerate young children should have the opportunity to participate in both problem solving and problem posing in authentic contexts. This involves a model of learning that is active and related to engagement, with ideas that have meaning for the child so that they can build new understandings. This has meant moving beyond a basic use of mathematical skills for problem solving. It incorporates a model (see figure) that involves inquiry, communication, and the generation of new knowledge as well as the application of knowledge in a variety of authentic contexts. Further, it is asserted that there is a fundamental link between the ability to become numerate and the skills and knowledge base that children require to function effectively.

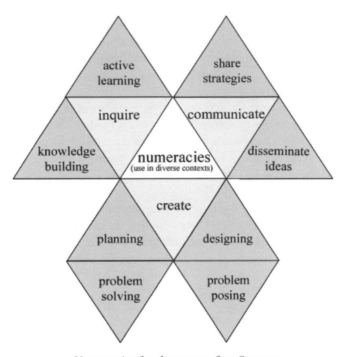

Numeracies for the twenty-first Century

These are based in tasks that children engage with in schools and it is suggested that these range on a continuum from unidimensional to multidimensional, which directly relate to the skills base and application that children need to draw upon to demonstrate a capacity to become numerate. Unidimensional tasks were simple sequences of activity that usually had a single outcome, and were often used as an introduction to concepts and processes. The pace of activity was largely related to the ability of the whole group yet the tasks were completed individually by each child in the class. An example would be when a teacher is teaching the concept of "doubling" to 5-year-olds and asks them to represent numbers by drawing squares and writing the addition equation (e.g., $5 + 5 = 10$) underneath their drawing.

Multidimensional tasks, in contrast, were generally build on these basic tasks in a significant way and consisted of integrated investigations in which skills and concepts were used in innovative ways to solve authentic problems which often could not be categorized into traditional subject areas of the curriculum. An essential element in completing such investigations was the opportunity to communicate ideas and discuss concepts and issues that were an inherent part of authentic problem posing and solving during multidimensional tasks or investigations. For example, the children might plan and create a garden in their center or school. They mapped the garden beds that had already been planted, and decided what new plants and areas could further enhance these gardens based on various ideas from the collaborative group. The children then measured, mapped, and drew the gardens so that they could purchase and plant the new vegetation. The types of gardens included: "A Grasses Garden," the "Entrance Garden," a "Pea Garden," and a "Bird Garden." The children then organized a "working bee" of volunteer parents and community members to assist them in the building process.

Conclusions

In Australia, the importance of becoming numerate has been given a high priority by both Commonwealth and state governments who have become increasingly concerned with being able to measure outcomes in simple ways to demonstrate that their policies have been effective in raising standards in our schools. However, it is apparent that such conceptualizations of numeracy are intrinsically linked to traditional views of mathematics that focus on skill and knowledge acquisition which can be easily assessed in pencil and paper tests. It has also been suggested that new conceptualizations of numeracy are needed for the twenty-first century which provide contexts in which young children are able to inquire and generate their own investigations and create new knowledge which can be shared and communicated to others using new technologies. In this way mathematics and numeracy teaching and learning contexts are utilizing new pedagogies that promote such types of learning, and innovative programs in each of the states have been implemented to ensure that young children have the opportunity to learn and use such skills and knowledge and build on them in the later years of schooling.

Further Readings: Australian Council for Educational Research (1990). *Being numerate: What counts?* Victoria, Australia: ACER; Clarke, D. M., P. Sullivan, J. Cheeseman, and B. A. Clarke (2000). The early numeracy research project: Developing a framework for describing early numeracy learning. In J. Bana & A. Chapman, eds., *Mathematics education beyond 2000* (Proceeding of the 23rd annual conference of the Mathematics Education Research Group of Australasia). Fremantle, Western Australia: MERGA, pp. 180–187; Department of Education Training and Youth Affairs (1999). *The Adelaide declaration on national goals for schooling in the twenty-first century.* Available online at http://www.deet.gov.au/schools/adelaide/text.htm; Department of Education Training and Youth Affairs (2000). *Numeracy, A priority for all: Challenges for Australian schools.* Canberra, ACT: DETYA; Department of Further Education and Employment (1998). *The implementation of the national numeracy strategy: The final report of the numeracy task force.* Available online at http://www.dfee.gov.uk/numeracy/index.htm; Hunting, R. P. (1999). Rational-number learning in the early years: What is possible? In J. V. Copley, ed., *Mathematics in the early years.* Reston, VA: NCTM, pp. 80–87; Kilderry, A., N.J. Yelland, V. Lazarides, and S. Dragicevic (2003). ICT and numeracy in the knowledge era: Creating contexts for new understandings. *Childhood Education* 79(5), 293–298; Perry, R. (1999). Early childhood numeracy. Australian Association of Mathematics Teachers. Available online at http://www.aamt.edu.au/projects/numeracy_papers/perry.pdf; Yelland, N.J. (2005). Curriculum practice and pedagogies with ICT in the information age. In N.J. Yelland, ed., *Critical issues in early childhood.* Buckingham, UK: Oxford University Press, pp. 224–242.

Nicola Yelland

Gender and Equity in Australia

Gender equity is a broad and politically charged term, holding different meanings for different groups of teachers, parents, administrators, and policy makers. In Australia, the concept of equity recognizes that the historical inequities of children from different social groups (gender, race, sexuality, and class) exist and that groups of children do not enter early childhood services from a level playing field. A number of social factors, including gender, are often associated with reduced access and participation in schooling. Gender equity also recognizes that different gender relationships of power and privilege exist within educational settings and society. Gender equity does not imply equality of treatment to girls and boys, as there are many factors that may disadvantage children in achieving equitable outcomes. Therefore, curriculum, teaching strategies, and policies created from a gender equity perspective favor those children who have been discriminated against or marginalized. Until recently, most policy and research on gender and education focused on girls and girls' issues. Currently, there has been a growing shift toward examining boys' education, debating how boys can, do, and should fit into gender equity programs.

Theoretical Perspectives

In Australia, the field of early childhood education has taken the ideas and concepts of gender equity seriously, and for over a decade has been using alternative theoretical perspectives to explore how gender is constructed. The gender research conducted in early childhood settings, by Davies, Yelland, MacNaughton, and Taylor and Richardson, challenges traditional understandings of gender, uncovering the subtle processes by which children actively construct themselves as girls and boys. This research sheds light on the need for early childhood teachers to understand the part that children play in the construction of gender. What makes the gender research conducted in Australia unique is how these scholars are drawing from postmodern perspectives to conceptualize gender in early childhood settings. For example, Davies, Yelland, and Mac Naughton all use feminist poststructuralist understandings of subjectivity, discourse, agency, resistance, and power-knowledge regimes to analyze gender relations and social interactions of young children. Richardson and Taylor expand on these ideas by using queer theory to comprehend gender further.

Findings from these studies about gender depart from the Western cultural assumption that gender is biologically or socially determined. Instead, gender is seen as a social, cultural, historical, and political construct, recognizing the active part that children take in the social construction and reconstruction of their gender identities. For example, Davies' groundbreaking work (originally done in 1989) was the first Australian study in early childhood to use feminist poststructuralism as a means for critiquing mainstream understandings of gender. Her work shows the possibilities of feminist poststructuralism for understanding children's gender differently by exploring how children construct their gender identities. She shows how children position themselves conceptually, physically, and emotionally as male or female in the classroom. Feminist poststructuralism is used to analyze how children maintain and resist the male–female binary. According to Davies, gender equity will not be achieved until children are given access to new gender discourses, which open up new and multiple ways of being gendered.

Theory in Practice

MacNaughton's (2000) action research project with twelve early childhood teachers shows how feminist poststructuralist ideas about gender might be practical in early childhood for exploring how young children learn and live their gendered identities. This work shows the possibilities for teachers to transform the traditions of early childhood curriculum by seeing and understanding gender from a feminist poststructuralist perspective. This requires early childhood teachers to conduct different kinds of observations in order to uncover the gender dynamics between children. Rather than looking simply at individual children's behavior, which only reinforces gender differences, teachers should look for patterns in how girls and boys relate to each other, attempting to find out what kinds of power relations exist between children and groups of children. Recognizing the power relations and gender dynamics that exist in the classroom enables teachers to challenge inequitable gender relations. Working towards gender equity is not only done by recognizing children's talk and actions in the classroom and reviewing the curriculum resources, materials, and goals, but it also includes challenging these inequities in practice. Change in children's gendered behaviors will most likely occur through teachers' efforts at inventing new gender discourses for children to access and explore.

Yelland's (1998) edited book, *Gender in Early Childhood* presents gender research done by various early childhood researchers in Australia. The studies presented in this book all draw upon contemporary understandings of gender. A variety of perspectives that influence gender are considered, including the family, community, and society as contexts for how gender is enacted in the everyday lives of young children. Several studies also explore the role of the school and its relation to the construction of gender and gender expectations.

New gender research conducted by Taylor and Richardson is building on these feminist poststructuralist understandings of gender by using queer theory to problematize gender further. These researchers look at how gender norms are being contested and defended by young children in the early childhood classroom. By critically analyzing heterosexuality and its position in the social construction of gender, the heterocentrism of developmentally appropriate practices becomes evident. This study shows how children's space in the early childhood curriculum is gendered and how children's gendered identities are spatialized. By viewing children's play at the home corner from a queer perspective, Taylor and Richardson show how new opportunities can be created in the curriculum for young children to challenge and transcend gender norms. This research also highlights the fluidity of gender and the various ways that children position themselves strategically in the classroom as different kinds of girls and boys. This work challenges the field of early childhood education to continue exploring gender in radical ways, in hopes of transcending gender inequities.

The scholarship of these researchers recognizes the importance of the structures and processes of the social world and the impact these have on children and their capacity to take an active part in the construction of gender.

Impacts on Curricula and Policies

These contemporary understandings of gender have begun to influence early childhood curriculum and policies for gender equity in Australia. For instance, most current Australian state-based early childhood curricula identify the preschool years as significant to young children's identity formation and make the identity of the young child as a future learner and citizen a key responsibility of early childhood teachers. Gender is seen as an important facet of young children's identity, and these curriculum frameworks are recognizing how the active role that children take constructing and reconstructing their gender identity can limit their learning and produce unjust classroom relationships. As a concept of social justice, gender equity recognizes that gender issues do impact on children, the classroom, and society.

Although gender equity policies do not flourish in the early childhood sector, when compared to primary and secondary education, Early Childhood Australia does have a Policy on Gender Equity. This policy states the following: "All children have an equal right to life opportunities that promote well being and support their development in all areas. Comprehensive knowledge about both societal and structural inequity based on gender should be understood and responded to in a manner that does not further promote gender discrimination." It is evident that the research discussed earlier has influenced this policy in that gender is conceptualized throughout the document as a social, cultural, historical, and political construction. Not only does the policy recognize the importance of gender for girls and boys, believing it to be an all-pervasive and ever-present factor for all children, but it also sees sexuality as a significant aspect of identity. This policy highlights the vital role that early childhood settings play in the development of a range of femininities and masculinities through children's relationships with peers, teachers, the classroom culture, and curriculum. This policy also implies that the role of the teacher is vital in promoting gender equity as it positions the teacher as an interventionist, ensuring that gender bias is identified and challenged in the classroom.

The state of current gender understandings is a direct result of the impact of 1970's feminism on government and society in Australia. This movement has made huge gains in transforming the lives of women. Although these improvements are often under threat, they have been significant toward influencing early childhood gender research, curriculum, and policies in Australia.

Further Readings: Davies, B. (2003). *Frogs and snails and feminist tales: Preschool children and gender.* 2nd ed. Sydney: Allen & Unwin; Early Childhood Australia (2005). ECA Policy: Gender Equity. Available online at http://www.earlychildhoodaustralia.org.au/abtus_pol_genderequity.htm; Mac Naughton, G. (2000). *Rethinking gender in early childhood education.* London: Paul Chapman Publishing; Taylor, A., and C. Richardson (2005). Queering home corner. *Contemporary Issues in Early Childhood* 6(2), 163–173; Yelland, N., ed. (1998). *Gender in early childhood.* London: Routledge.

Mindy Blaise

Learning and Assessment

Camp Kilda (CK) is regarded as being a quality early childhood center, and has many features you would typically expect to see in settings across Australia. The children are busily engaged in hands-on activity, playing indoors and outdoors, in the sandpit, under the shade of a big mango tree. The learning environment is planned to offer a variety of activities, including dramatic play, climbing equipment, balls, painting, drawing, clay, books, blocks, writing materials, scissors, manipulative materials. The children are free to access all the materials, and they play either individually or in small groups. The teachers encourage and stimulate the children's learning, through interactions and thoughtful planning. Learning and assessment at CK is embedded within the cultural and social contexts of the children and their community. Children's learning is made visible through a rich variety of strategies, including recorded observations, work samples, photographs, and other artifacts. Parents are actively encouraged to build on these "stories" of their children. Planning is based around the teachers' analysis of the information they gather daily as they interact with the children and their families.

Introduction

Like most Australian early childhood educators, the CK teachers subscribe to the theories that young children learn best through play. Play-based programs are widely supported in initial teacher training and the literature, although they vary widely in application and in assumptions made about the type and place of play in learning. It is the kind of pedagogy in place that is an important factor. The teacher's role in supporting learning generates varied child learning outcomes.

There is no national core curriculum for the early years in Australia but increasingly government initiatives at a federal level are calling for the introduction of a national standardized curriculum. Education is organized on a state-by-state basis and, as in many areas of Australian life, the states vigorously resist most moves for federal intervention. This results in a flexibility and range of differences across the programming and services available to young children and their families. For instance, across Australia, the starting age for formal schooling varies. Broadly, approaches to learning and assessment are distinctive to three stages in the early years: infants and toddlers (generally birth to 2 years), preschool (3–5), and early primary school (6–8). There is general agreement that identifying and building on children's interests and maintaining informal approaches is of primary importance, and various models for curriculum are embraced, including child-centered, Developmentally Appropriate Practice (DAP), antibias, emergent, and inquiry-based learning.

All early childhood workers who are involved in the planning of young children's programs are professionally qualified with at least two years of tertiary training, and preschool and early primary teachers hold university degrees. Compartmentalizing curricula that separates learning into distinct domains and lessons for mastery is viewed as problematic in regard to young children's development and learning. In their initial training, early childhood educators are urged to plan for learning that is holistic, play-based, active, hands-on, in a planned and supportive environment, with a strong developmental framework, and taking into account the cultural and social contexts.

In recognition of the complexities of learning, assessment is through congruently multiple and holistic methods. Teachers build a rich picture of each child, combining strategies such as using the traditional tools of child study (for example, observations, anecdotal records, checklists) with newer documentation technologies such as photos, portfolios, and recorded conversations. These rich data provide them with opportunities for reflection and analysis, which, in turn, informs their planning for further learning.

Learning and assessment in the early years are coming under increasing social and political scrutiny. Brain research is currently enjoying a high profile, with its advocacy for early intervention. The rapidly expanding child-care sector is having both social and economic impact. Corporate and managerial models of organization are being overlaid onto education. The rhetoric makes for an interesting mix with calls for the recognition of the necessity for lifelong learning and creativity, ironically juxtaposed with calls for getting "back to basics," standardized testing, and a lamenting of a so-called "drop in standards" of literacy and numeracy. Along with calls for accountability, performance indicators, benchmarks, outcomes and standards, economic rationalizations question how the education dollar is spent, what is the product, who is the client, and what evidence is available to demonstrate positive outcomes. The high level of professionalism in early childhood educators has contributed to their ability to resist the increasing pressure for a more academic approach to learning and assessment, but they are being called on to find new ways to convince others of the worth of their educational approach.

In this situation, the discursive construction of play both enables and constrains. While the idea of facilitating children's learning through exploration and discovery is enduringly attractive, for some educators, this has been interpreted as a *laissez faire* hands-off *role* for the teacher, which is a misreading of the principles for active learning and child-centered practice. Teachers will variously describe their work as guiding, facilitating, supporting, directing, scaffolding, being reluctant to use the word *teach* when describing the ways they work with children. Their understanding of child-centeredness does not permit them to take the position of teacher; rather, they strive to *teach without teaching*. There is a variety of nomenclature for staff in early childhood settings, for example, directors, group leaders, carers, assistants, teachers. In this entry all staff who work with young children in supporting their learning are referred to as teachers.

Palimpsest

A second reading of the CK center can build a palimpsest, locating traces of any number of influences, a mix of some of the enduring traditional approaches, as well as the more recent thinking about learning and assessment.

Infants and toddlers—long day care. For the youngest children at CK, the interface between education and care for this age-group shapes approaches to learning and assessment. In the rapidly expanding child-care sector, standards vary widely, but at CK the infants and toddlers are seen as actively learning about their world through interactions and explorations. Proactive adults with a sound knowledge of young children and high expectations of their capacity make a positive difference to their learning. They support the babies in their sensory, perceptual, and motor development. The teachers bring an awareness of the expected patterns of growth and development, balanced with knowledge of each individual child, and their social and cultural contexts.

Planning for this age-group is not a matter of teacher-initiated "activities." Rather, routine times, such as nappy (diaper) changing, are considered as learning opportunities, through one-to-one language experiences, music, and interactions. The teachers listen and respond to the children, develop communication skills through modeling and immersion, play games with them, and tend to their physical and emotional needs in a relationship of mutual respect and trust. The children are supported in the reaching of developmental milestones. Their cognitive development, creativity, and divergent thinking are all appreciated and encouraged. Planning is individually based, and directly relevant to the individual's needs.

While there is no mandated curriculum, as such, for this age-group, the childcare sector is accountable to a national accreditation system. This applies to all long day-care centers, and CK's continuing funding is tied to satisfactorily meeting the principles (e.g., *Staff interact with children to stimulate their curiosity and thinking*). Like all such standardizing devices, meeting all these principles sets only minimal standards for quality.

Along with this checklist as a tool for assessment of their program, teachers at Camp Kilda employ authentic forms of assessment daily, in order to inform their planning and improve the teaching and learning. They see the child as rich and competent, and they gather information and evidence of the children's needs, interests, strengths, abilities, and achievements. They monitor children's growth and development and learning through the use of traditional tools of child study, including observations, anecdotal records, and checklists. They use photography and other newer technologies for documentation. This "story-building" is shared with the children themselves, and their parents and families. The teachers use this pedagogical documentation as a reflective tool for themselves and their colleagues, to trace children's thinking and communication.

Preschool—3- to 5-year-olds. The teachers at CK work at helping children to become decision makers, critical thinkers, problem solvers, theorists. The processes of doing and talking to clarify thinking, are seen as integral to children's learning and development. Children's curiosity and the questions they ask provide a key to learning about children's understandings and learning processes. Basic understandings are constructed by children through self-directed problem solving.

In the process of co-constructing meaning, teachers act as co-players, co-learners, co-artists. Art as a language is considered an important means through which the children can make their learning visible. The children are invited to draw, paint, and construct daily. They are given instruction in skills and techniques when required, they visit the art gallery in their local community, a dance specialist works with each group weekly, and artists are frequently invited to visit the center. The children's artwork has also been hung in the local gallery, and these close connections with the community help to make learning purposeful.

Each state has developed its own curriculum guidelines for this age-group, but they share many commonalities. Learning programs for children of this age are child-centered and holistic, with an emphasis on developing thinking and communicating skills. In response to political pressure, literacy and numeracy are emphasized, along with recognition of the importance of learning social skills and understandings. Learning through play is in the foreground. There are those who critique "play-based" learning, and compare this unfavorably with "knowledge-based" learning. Others insist that the two are not oppositional.

Assessment is not considered as being the sole purpose, or even the main goal of teaching and learning but, rather, is relative, cultural, and dynamic. Teachers employ multiple strategies for assessing the diversity of children's abilities and strengths, taking into account the cultural, social, and family contexts for learning. As with the younger children, strategies for assessment can include observations, anecdotal records, running records, some checklists and diagnostic tests, photographs, portfolios, work samples, recorded conversations, and other artifacts. At CK, this pedagogical documentation is shared daily and openly with parents.

Early Primary—5–8 Years. In the January that they have turned five, the children from CK leave and go on to a primary school. Although the starting age differs from state to state, you can expect a general "look" to these learning environments. Most children wear school uniforms; the daily timetable separates "learning" from "play"; classrooms usually accommodate each child with a desk and chair.

Teachers in the early primary years all have a university degree, and they are accountable to a state-mandated curriculum, which is organized hierarchically around the traditional key learning areas: Literacy, Mathematics, Science, Studies of Society, Health, Arts, and so on. While the syllabus documents are mandated, they are outcomes based, and teachers have a certain degree of autonomy to implement the curriculum according to what they consider is the best way to meet the outcomes. Many early childhood educators working in the early years of primary schooling bring with them an appreciation of the role of play in children's learning, and build this into their programming.

There is an increasing interest in interdisciplinary approaches to learning at this level, and the rhetoric, at least, recognizes the place of active and purposeful learning. As in the preschool settings, there is much variation and flexibility in how learning and assessment is enacted across settings. But a quality early primary classroom would see the children engaged in purposeful and active learning, across the disciplines. Integrating devices vary, but might be through a thematic approach, or through projects or "rich tasks." In general, it would be safe to say that teacher-initiated activity is predominant.

National standardized testing has been introduced for the third, fifth, and seventh years of primary schooling, with a strong political interest in levels of literacy and numeracy. Results are compared across states, and influence policy-makers. This places downward pressure on the earlier primary years, where formal assessment is required. Commonly, this takes the form of mapping individual children against indicators of outcomes, organized on a developmental continuum. Parents receive a written report, and are also invited to an interview with their child's teacher. Some teachers in the early primary years, committed to the principles of child-centered learning, also use the broader range of assessment strategies, such as observations, portfolios, and other forms of pedagogical documentation.

Conclusion

Early childhood teachers in Australia are increasingly called on to resist the downward pressure for a more academic approach to teaching and learning, and they strive to advocate for young children through making their learning visible. When you walk into the CK center, you see and hear busy, happy children, who are viewed as rich and competent beings in the now. Their teachers are actively engaged with them in the co-construction of meaning, encouraging their curiosity and enthusiasm for learning. They do this through their interactions, and through planning a dynamic learning environment, in thoughtful response to their daily assessments of the children's strengths, abilities, and needs.

Further Readings: Kolbe, U. (2001). *Rapunzel's supermarket: All about young children and their art.* Paddington, New South Wales: Peppinot Press; Luke, A., and S. Grieshaber (2004). New adventures in the politics of literacy: An introduction. *Journal of Early Childhood Literacy* 4(1), 5–9; MacNaughton, G., and G. Williams (2004). *Techniques for teaching young children: Choices in theory and practice.* 2nd ed. Frenchs Forest, New South Wales: Pearson Education Australia; McArdle, F. (2001). A method of ironic research. In P. Singh and E. McWilliam, eds., *Designing educational research: Theories, methods and practices.* Flaxton, Queensland: Post Pressed; Yelland, N., ed. (2000). *Promoting meaningful learning: Innovations in educating early childhood professionals.* Washington, DC: National Association for the Education of Young Children.

Felicity McArdle

Brazil

Early Childhood Education in Brazil

Introduction

In Brazil, early childhood education is conceived as attendance in *crèches* (day-care centers for infants and toddlers) and preschool for children of up to 6 years of age, prior to eight years of compulsory elementary education.

Brazilian early childhood education (ECE) initiatives date back to the last quarter of the nineteenth century, but only in the second half of the twentieth century did day-care centers and preschools undergo a significant expansion in the country. In the beginning of the twentieth century the few existing day-care centers were characterized as a charitable initiative, and it wasn't until the 1940s that child care became the norm, although even then services were very limited and with strong health orientation. In 1942, the Consolidation of the Labor Laws defined the care of lactating children of working mothers as the duty of the companies. Within the school system preprimary education arose as an addition to state establishment of compulsory primary education and also emerged in private institutions.

In the mid-1970s and the 1980s, the federal government instituted initiatives within two sectors, the Brazilian Legion of Assistance (LBA) and the Ministry of Education (MEC), aimed at expanding admission, especially to children of low-income families. The MEC supported the states and municipalities both technically and financially in the expansion of preprimary education provision, on a part-time basis, giving priority to the age-group closest to 7 years (the beginning of compulsory school education). The LBA used a strategy of contracts with community and philanthropic institutions and with local municipalities to cater to children between 0 and 6 years of age, on a full-time or part-time basis, providing a subsidy per child that only partially covered admission costs. The expansion that occurred in this period was due in great part to the utilization of local community and nonqualified human resources, resulting in low quality services, in which the primary goal was to compensate for the effects of poverty. UNESCO and UNICEF played influential policy roles. This two-pronged insertion of ECE institutions into both education and social welfare constituted a remarkable aspect of the history of Brazilian ECE, resulting in clashes between the sectors not as yet overcome.

In the mid-1980s the social movements in defense of rights, including the right to education in day-care centers and preschools, had an important effect, highlighted in this case by the women's movements. The decade ended with the proclamation of the new Brazilian Constitution (1988). Admission in day-care centers and preschools of children from zero to six is recognized in the constitution as an educational responsibility of the state (Art.208) as is the social right of the urban and rural workers to free attendance of their dependent children of up to 6 years of age in day-care centers and preschools (Art.7, XXV). However, this last article has not been implemented yet, perhaps due to recent reductions in labor rights.

The early 1990s were marked by several Education Ministry initiatives. Experts and educational administrators discussed national policy proposals that would meet the constitutional purposes, especially regarding the recognition of day-care centers as part of education. MEC documents laid out the conception of ECE as the first phase of basic education, extending from birth to six years, in which the functions of educating and caring for the children must be carried out in an integrated manner. The terms day-care center and preschool were redefined, in order to differentiate two age brackets (day care, for children up to 3 years of age, and preschool for those between four and six), with both having to present adequate quality standards. During this period, the Legislature discussed the proposed Law of Guidelines and Bases of National Education (LDB), which was finally approved in 1996. However, the implementation of these legal advances has encountered obstacles resulting from the absence of adequate financing mechanisms.

Despite great difficulties, ECE expanded in the decade of the 90s. According to the Brazilian Institute of Geography and Statistics (IBGE, 2003), 11.7 percent of children from 0 to 3 years of age and 68.4 percent of those between 4 and 6 attended ECE programs. Almost 70 percent of these places are provided by the local municipalities.

Organization and Coordination of Services

Early childhood education is part of a complex educational structure in which the Union, the twenty-six states, the Federal District, and the 5,560 municipalities each have their own responsibilities at specific levels of education. It is up to the municipalities to provide ECE and, together with the states, the compulsory elementary education. The states are also responsible for providing the high school education. The Union, in addition to maintaining a network of institutions of higher education, is responsible for the coordination of national policy, articulating the different levels and systems and exerting a normative, redistributive, and supplemental function in relation to the other jurisdictions.

The institutions that provide ECE shall have their functional operation authorized and supervised by the educational system of the respective municipality, or by the state jurisdiction when the municipality opts to belong to the state system. Although the law emphasizes that the functions of caring and educating should be inseparable in ECE, stressing a child's overall development, many institutions still limit themselves to caring for the child and custodial care routines, while others emphasize preparation for elementary school.

Following international trends, in 2006 the National Congress approved a law that included 6-year-old children in elementary education nationwide, thereby extending the period of compulsory schooling from 8 to 9 years. As a result, ECE will cover the 0–5 age range.

Brazilian ECE policy guidelines are grounded in the Law of 1996 and the National Educational Plan of 2001. The Law defines ECE as the first phase of basic education, whose objective is the integral development of the child of up to 6 years of age through provision of day-care centers and preschools. The Law establishes that the evaluation of this educational phase be focused on development and cannot have the goal of assessing and measuring the learning of the child as a means of promotion to elementary school.

The 1996 Law also assigned the responsibility for providing ECE to the Municipalities and specified a period of three years for the day-care centers and the preschools to integrate themselves to the educational systems.

The National Council on Education (CNE) and the State and Municipal Councils on Education issued complementary laws. The regulatory challenge is considerable, especially because prior to the 1996 Law ECE did not have the status of a phase of education, and its history in the educational system did not include day-care centers. Difficulties also arise from the fact that ECE is assigned to the Municipalities, the majority of which suffer from precarious technical, political, and financial conditions.

The National Educational Plan establishes goals and objectives for ECE that include aspects like the national coverage of day-care centers and preschools, the definition of quality standards, and the implementation of actions for the initial and ongoing teacher preparation and training. The goal for 2011 is to have 50 percent of the children from zero to three and 80 percent of the children between four and five enrolled in ECE institutions. Those of 6 years of age should all be in primary school.

Financing

One of the main obstacles to the implementation of the expansion and the improvement in quality objectives foreseen in ECE is found in the pattern of financing Brazilian education. The Constitution determines the distribution of public revenue (taxes and social contributions) received in the three levels of the government for the financing of education. Since 1998, however, 60 percent of these state and municipal resources have been placed in a special fund, FUNDEF, in each state to finance compulsory elementary school. Thus ECE is forced to compete with other educational expenses for municipal resources not assigned to this fund. The situation is especially grave in those municipalities where local revenues are very low. Although the Union has responsibility for supplementing the resources of the municipal educational systems, its investments in the provision of higher education and the priority given to compulsory primary education result in an insignificant investment in ECE. The largest investment of federal resources in day-care centers and preschools comes from the Ministry of Social

Development (MDS). But since 2000 the MDS has been orienting state and municipal social assistance to apply these resources in other areas (for example, toy centers, home day care, social-educational family support initiatives), since the educational sector was assigned responsibility for the day-care centers. Thus the present financing situation is unfavorable. A new educational financing proposal, FUNDEB, which will also include early childhood education and high school in the fund that at present only deals with elementary education, is being discussed in the National Congress. For this purpose, the resources shall be increased to 80 percent of the state and municipal resources destined to education. The initial proposal for this new fund, sent to National Congress by the Executive Powers in June 2005, excludes financing for the enrollment of children from zero to three. The reason given for this was the higher cost of serving this age bracket, but it also became clear that many do not yet recognize and accept the day-care center as a legitimate institution within the educational sector. However, due to the actions of the social movements in defense of the right to early childhood education amongst parliament members, the enrollment of children from zero to three was included in the proposal of the fund approved by the Chamber of Deputies in January 2006. The proposal still must be approved in the Federal Senate. The resources of the fund shall be distributed proportionately according to the number of children and pupils registered in the different educational levels and modalities, utilizing factors of differentiation that take into account the cost differences between levels. The law regulating this distribution is still being discussed. The actual situation of the financing of ECE in the country will depend to a great extent on what factor of differentiation will be defined in the law for the registration of children 0–3 years of age (day-care centers) and 4 to 6 (preschool).

Teacher Preparation

For preservice teacher preparation the 1996 Law defined optimal qualification of a university degree, but accepted the minimum educational qualification of secondary level at a teacher training school (licensure). Data for 2004 show that about 6 percent of the preschool teachers and 17 percent of day-care-center workers did not even have the minimum preparation demanded. A national program for the preparation of these professionals—ProInfantil "Program of Initial In-Service Training of Teachers in Early Childhood Education"—started in 2005. Another problem involves the curricula of the teacher preparation courses, which do not always deal adequately with the specificities of ECE. Regarding in-service training, there is no national regulation, this being up to the educational systems and to the school institutions to provide it to its teachers.

Curriculum

The 1996 Law stipulates that all Brazilian day-care centers and preschools, both public and private, design their programs in accordance with the National Curricular Guidelines for Early Childhood Education instituted in 1999 by the National Council of Education. The municipalities generally have a common pedagogical plan for all the schools in their network. In 1998, the Ministry of Education released the National Curricular Reference for Early Childhood Education to pro-vide guidance in the preparation of the curricula. Unlike the National Guidelines, the National Reference is not mandatory. In actual practice local programs reflect the influences of different theoretical approaches, models, and experiences.

The Family

The idea of early care and education as complementary to the roles of both the family and the community performed by the ECE institutions is affirmed in the laws referenced earlier. Because the preschool educational phase is not compulsory, enrollment of the child is a family option. Demand is not always met, because there are insufficient spaces for all those who seek them. There are no data available to estimate the unmet demand.

The importance of the participation of the families in the definition and imple-mentation of pedagogical proposals is stressed in the national and local guidelines and references. However, the way in which this partnership is actually carried out in local programs varies greatly, and in most cases is rather limited.

In cases where abuse and maltreatment of children by members of the family is suspected, the program is to direct the problem to the local Protective Council. According to the 1990 Statute of the Child and Adolescent this is the organiza-tion entrusted by the society to care for the welfare and rights of the child and adolescent. It is up to this Council to refer the family to programs of promotion, orientation, or treatment, or to take the case to judicial authorities.

Access and Supply

One of the challenges for ECE policy in Brazil involves the inequalities in gaining access to admission in day-care centers and preschools due to the socioeconomic level of the family. 2003 National IBGE data show that in families with a per capita monthly income of less than 1/2 the minimum salary the rate of admission is only 8 percent of children from 0 to 3 years of age and 61 percent for those from 4–6. In families with a higher income, above two minimum salaries, these percentages are 20 percent and 82 percent respectively. Many low-income families that do not manage to enroll their children in an ECE program resort to dangerous alternatives, such as leaving them at home in the care of older siblings or even at home on their own. In rural Brazil children sometimes accompany their mothers into the plantations and help with the work there.

The National Education Plan proposes that, given the limitations of financial and technical resources, public ECE provision should give priority to the children of lower income families, locating programs in the areas of greatest need. The deficiencies in the sectorial policies, especially in the areas of education, social assistance, and health, need to be overcome in order for the rights of 0- to 6-year-old children, already recognized in the legal documents, to be guaranteed in fact.

Further Readings: Conselho Nacional de Educação. Câmara de Educação Básica (1999). *Diretrizes Curriculares Nacionais para a Educação Infantil (National curricular guidelines for early childhood education)*. Parecer CEB 01/1999, aprovado em 19 de janeiro de 1999; *Lei de Diretrizes e Bases da Educação Nacional (Law of guidelines and bases of the national education)* LDB (1996). Lei n. 9394, de 20 de dezembro de 1996; MEC, COEDI (1994). *Política nacional de educação infantil (National policy of early childhood education)*. Brasília: MEC/SEF/DPEF/COEDI; Ministério da Educação (1995). *Critérios para um atendimento em creches que respeite os direitos fundamentais das crianças (Criteria for attendance in day-care centers that respect children's fundamental rights)*. Brasília: MEC/SEF/DPEF/COEDI; Ministério da Educação (1999). *Referencial curricular para a Educação Infantil (National curricular reference for early childhood education)*. Brasília, MEC/SEF/DPEF/COEDI. 3 vols; Ministério da Educação. Secretaria de Educação Infantil e Fundamental (2003a). *Política Nacional de Educação Infantil: pelos direitos das crianças de 0 a 6 anos à Educação. Documento preliminar (National policy of early childhood education: For the rights of children from 0 to 6 years to education)*. Preliminary paper. Brasília, MEC; Ministério da Educação. Secretaria de Educação Infantil e Fundamental (2003b). *Padrões de Infra-estrutura para as Instituições de Educação Infantil e Parâmetros de Qualidade para a Educação Infantil (Standards of infrastructure for ECE institutions and parameters of quality for ECE)*. Preliminary paper. Brasília, MEC; *Plano Nacional de Educação (National Education Plan)*. 2001. Lei n. 10172, de 9 de janeiro de 2001. Available online at www.mec.gov.br.

Angela Rabelo Barreto and Sonia Larrubia Valverde

The Ecology of Childhood

The decades of the 1960s and 1970s brought significant changes in values and customs in family relations as well as in the broader social structure. The intensification of urbanization, the expansion of working women followed by the increasing presence of mothers with young children in the labor market, the decrease in number of siblings and of urban spaces for collective games, and the greater concern with childhood rights, all led to a redefinition of the boundary between public and private, indicating a new place of childhood, characterized by a change in the locus of child socialization from single to multiple places.

In Brazil, this change was set off in the context of the political transition that was leading toward the redemocratization of the country, and must be comprehended within the confluence of several factors. These included the legal accomplishments in the fields of children's, women's, and family rights, changes in family structure, the contributions in the diverse areas of knowledge that challenged the idea of a fragile and incomplete child, and the impact of this new vision of childhood as a subject with legitimacy for early childhood education (ECE) public policies.

The Broad Range of Achieved Rights

Despite a long regime of dictatorship installed with the military coup of 1964, the 1970s were marked by a true revolution in the field of social and individual rights. The accomplishments are reflected in the Federal Constitution of 1988, with the recognition of the universal right to education for children from zero to six years of age, and the right of working men and women to day-care centers and preschools for their children. These changes offer a new vision of the child, of childhood, of early childhood education, of women, of the professional, and of gender relations and family responsibility. The right to education from birth presupposes a social responsibility for the child and the creation of alternatives in childhood socialization that complement the role of the family. The child begins to be seen as occupying a place in the present as a protagonist of his own life, a citizen in development. Women become the target of important policies promoting gender equality and the elimination of all the forms of discrimination. The integration of the social and educational dimensions, resulting from the fact of the right to the day-care center and preschool stated in the chapters of the Law on Education and Work, legitimizes the idea of responsibility shared between the family and the state, establishing an intersection between private matters and those of a public order regarding the education/socialization of the young child. The expansion of rights shall also benefit the professionals through the requirement that there be specific training for early childhood teachers and caregivers.

Transformations in the Brazilian Family

The place of childhood in the contemporary context is related to the transformation in the composition of the Brazilian family. The progressive increase in participation by women with young children in the labor market coincides with a reduction in the percentage of extended families, a reduction in the birthrate and an increase in the number of single-parent families. Studies of trends in the work patterns of Brazilian women reveal a 54 percent increase in workforce participation between the 1980s and the 1990s. In 2002 women increased their participation in the labor market more than men (2.5% vs. 1.6%). The birthrate dropped from 6.3 births per woman of child bears in age in 1960 to 2.3 in 2003. Persons per household went from 5.1 percent in 1970 to 3.6 percent in 2003, while the proportion of women household heads grew from 15 percent in 1980 to 29 percent in 2003, revealing a growth of almost 30 percent over the last ten years.

These changes reflect broader international patterns, but they have not been accompanied by mechanisms of support for families with young children. Although the provision of places in day-care centers and preschools has been increasing in the past years, the rates of coverage are still unsatisfactory. In 2003, 37.7 percent of the children from 0 to 6 years of age attended an ECE setting, reflecting a direct association among parents' level of education, (especially of the mother), family income, and admission to day-care centers or preschools. The probability of children attending a day-care center or preschool increases according to the educational level of the parents, and it is the poorest families that have the least access to these services, even though legislation places a priority on the children in those families.

The transformations in the family are also qualitative: they point to a crisis in the traditional family form consisting of two parents and their related children, which, although still predominant, start to cede space to more heterogeneous forms. Separations and remarriages create new relations and roles; the proportion of married couples decreases while the quantity of singles and separated parents increases, constituting a segment that is predominantly made up of women.

From Private to Public Spaces

The more intense and effective participation of the woman in economic, political, and social life and the significant expansion of the role of mother creates pressure for a revision of the traditional female contributions in the domestic space as well as a redefinition of the masculine role, and calls for the construction of relations of a more equal nature regarding the reproduction and care of the children. The decline in the children's sources of socialization within the interior of the domestic space has led to the creation of other spaces and relations outside of the family sphere. While in the past children were gathered most frequently within the home and the family, at present we see a broad circulation of children in formal or nonformal public spaces, showing the multiple contexts of extra-family socialization, especially in the urban centers.

Within the academic sphere the production of knowledge on the present development of public ECE policies from the perspective of the ecology of childhood is still scarce and has little impact on the planning of the policies and the attitude of professionals and users in general. Very little research addresses this new place of childhood at the intersections of family responsibility, out-of-home paid work, and child care. There is little research on the nature of the socialization processes in these nonfamily contexts. There are also very few studies that deal with ECE institutions as a new experience of child socialization, an issue that gains space in some research groups, but still finds very little relevance amongst the ECE professionals, or within the curricula of the teacher training courses.

Changes in the Focus of ECE Research

Up until the 1970s, research showed a great concern for the development of the child. The studies on day-care centers in general reflected an interest in the effects of maternal deprivation on the development of children attending these institutions, and research on preschool was directed to the development of strategies to avoid a future school failure, from the point of view of cultural deprivation.

Researches on day-care centers took a qualitative leap in the 1980s, by shifting the focus of the developing child to the institutional contexts, situating the day-care center as the legitimate field for data collection. Strongly inspired by foreign literature, these research projects brought new elements previously not contemplated in the area: maternity, the status of woman, the role of the professional, the pedagogical dimension, the family and institution relationship, and the role of the state.

Upon shifting the attention away from the day-care center as a place primarily of "family absence" and of the adult as the only provider of affection, new perspectives were established in the field of developmental psychology, demonstrating that young children are capable of establishing affective bonds with adults other than the mother, and revealing the importance of the day -care center as a context of socialization where the children establish a wide range of relationships with their peers.

By the 1990s investigation of childhood was also observed in other fields, like the history of childhood, revealing the childhoods constituted in different contexts and present within diverse social practices, educational projects, and public policies. In anthropology the work on childhood in the indigenous societies stands out, presenting the manner in which these peoples experiment and express themselves in their social life, and demonstrating how little interest in indigenous children was shown in most of the research and writing carried out previously. However, this important area of research does not intersect at all with early childhood care and education studies.

The Sociology of Childhood

The recently established sociology of childhood, that arose in Europe and in the United States as a field of investigation within the social sciences in the 1990s, has been a source of inspiration for various centers of research in childhood education. The conception of childhood as a social category is guiding the creation of new methodologies that place the child as the protagonist of its own life, seeking to study the children by means of their voices, their practices, and their possibilities of creating and recreating the social reality in which they are placed.

The place of childhood as subject legitimizes the ECE contexts as settings of socialization and spaces where the children can live their childhoods in the present, and not as a promise for the future, occupying different places, experimenting in diverse interactions with their peers and participating in cultural production in their interaction with others. It also legitimizes the ECE institutions as settings where fathers, mothers, and others responsible for children may share in the care and the education of the young child and participate in the construction of the institutional culture. This new sense of place has direct implications for ECE policies and practices. It presupposes an integrated, unified, universal approach, strong public investment, directed at the 0–6 age-group and attuned to the needs and interests of the children and their families.

The Gap between Rhetoric and Reality

However this conception, although implicit in the Brazilian Constitution, is still an ideal that has not been debated or become concrete in the form of social practices. This gap reflects the changes in the national and international political and economic scenario that have served as the theater for our legislation. Between the proclamation of the Constitution (1988) and its regulation (1996) a new world economic order has imposed itself, marked by the restriction of the role of the state in social policies, including the reduction of public investment in education, threatening many accomplishments in the rights arena, especially for women and for childhood. The law that regulates the inclusion of day-care centers and preschools in the educational sector was elaborated within the context of these neoliberal reforms, when the policies for basic education were redefined and the resources channeled primarily to elementary education. At the present time the constitutional Article that guarantees the right to day-care centers and preschools for the children of working men and women has not been carried forward into regulations; the social movements that motivated this conquest are demobilized. The topic finds little resonance in the educational sector, the main source of public policies for ECE, which has no tradition of dealing with a nonscholarly conception of ECE.

The Influences of International Agencies and Organizations

In addition, the international treaties and the action plans of international conferences have played a role in the definition of the educational policies and are incorporated into national plans, demanding adjustments that are not always suited to the guidelines already established in national legislation.

The 1990 Declaration of Jomtien (Education for All), that adopted as its first goal "Expand and improve the early childhood care and education, in an integrated fashion, especially for the most vulnerable and less favored children" recommends a realignment of the early childhood care and education policies in the developing countries. Haddad observes the coexistence of two sets of priorities in response to fulfilling this goal, which differ according to age-group. One refers to the expansion of preschool classes for the age that precedes compulsory schooling, with a view to universalize admission to ages of 4–5, as a form of guaranteeing full access to formal schooling. The second refers to programs for families and communities directed at children under 3 years of age, reflecting the orientations of international organizations led by the World Bank. In this latter case these organizations use different terminologies to refer to the early childhood programs in developing countries (*Early Childhood Care and Development* (UNESCO), *Early Childhood Development* (World Bank), and *Early Childhood Care for Survival, Growth and Development* (UNICEF)), and give different meanings to the terms childhood and early childhood education. In the name of combating poverty and of a holistic view of childhood development, supported by research on the development of the brain, these terms have subtly altered the concept of childhood as a social category and of early childhood education as the legitimate space for the child to live its childhood, undermining the concept of social responsibility and accentuating the gap between developed and developing countries. In contrast to what is proposed for developed countries, the literature of international organizations regarding developing countries advocates that programs should be less costly and run by mothers or community leaders; parents and close caregivers (such as older siblings) should be an equal target population; settings should be community or home-based; and private sector involvement should be encouraged. These premises de-emphasize the accomplishments that have led to recognizing a specific ECE culture, which were hardly achieved and require a correspondingly specific pedagogy. Whether we will be able to resist these regressive outside influences is a question both for the present and the future.

Further Readings: Campos, Maria M. and Lenira Haddad (1992). Educação infantil: crescendo e aparecendo. (Early Childhood Education: Growing and appearing). *Cadernos de Pesquisa* São Paulo, 80, 11–20, Feb.; Educação E Sociedade. Revista de Ciência da Educação. Sociologia da infância: pesquisas com crianças (Sociology of childhood: Research with children). Campinas, 26(91), 337–712, May–Aug; de Faria, Ana Lúcia G., Demartini, Leila de Brito S., and Prado, Patrícia D. (orgs.) (2002). *Por uma cultura da infância (For a culture of childhood)*. Campinas: Autores Associados; Haddad, Lenira (2002). *An integrated approach to early childhood education and care*. UNESCO Early Childhood and Family Policy Series Number 3. Paris, France: UNESCO; Kuhlmann, Jr., Moysés (1998). *Infância e Educação Infantil: uma abordagem história (Childhood and early childhood education: A historic approach)*. Porto Alegre: Mediação; Nascimento, Maria Letícia B.P. (2003). *Creche e Família na constituição do "eu": um estudo sobre as imagens e as representações de crianças no terceiro ano de vida na cidade de São Paulo (Crèche and family in the constitution of the self: A study on children in their third year of life in the city of São Paulo)*. Doctorate thesis in Education. São Paulo: FEUSP.

Lenira Haddad and Maria Letícia Nascimento

Culture, Race, and Ethnicity

Culture, race, and ethnicity themes have only recently entered the political and academic debate in Brazilian Early Childhood Education (ECE) and they are just beginning to be addressed. These themes deal specifically with the ethnic-racial inequalities that blacks (45%) and indigenous (0.4%) populations experience compared to whites (54%). Historic processes of construction and combat of these inequalities are not the same for black and indigenous peoples.

Blacks

After having practiced slavery for over three centuries (until 1888), Brazil was the last country to abolish the enslavement of African blacks. During slavery, the domination of African blacks extended beyond slaves, it also affected free blacks. The educational legislation of that time prohibited slaves, free blacks, and people suffering from contagious diseases from obtaining an education.

The abolition of slavery was gradual and was regulated by a series of laws: in 1871 freedom was conferred to children born of slave mothers (Law of the Free Womb—*Ventre Livre*). As a result of this law, the first text on day-care centers (crèches, 1879) was published in Brazil. These documents revealed that day-care centers (crèches) were conceived as the institutions designed to shelter the newly freed children of mothers who were forced to continue as slaves.

After the complete abolition of slavery, the processes summarized below marked the social, economic, and political relations between whites and blacks:

• Unlike the United States, Brazil did not adopt a legislation of racial segregation; therefore the legal definition of slavery as belonging to a specific ethnicity or race did not occur.

• Brazil did not develop a specific policy to integrate the newly freed blacks into the broader society, which strengthened the bases of racial inequalities.

• In accordance with the state policy of "whitening" the population in accordance with the eugenic racial policies developed in Europe in the nineteenth century,

Brazil encouraged European **immigration** during the late nineteenth century and beginning of the twentieth century.

- The country adopted a system of racial classification based on appearances resulting from the simultaneous consideration of physical traits (skin color, facial features, hair), social-economic condition, and region of residence. This is one of the reasons that explains the use of the word blacks and not Afro-Brazilians.

- The existence of a large mixed population (38% identify themselves as "brown," *pardos*) that is diversely distributed throughout the national territory. The poorest regions—in the Northeast—are those that have the largest percentage of *Negros* (black/*preto* and brown/*pardo*) due to the "whitening" policy discussed earlier.

- The commingling of standards of simultaneous vertical racial relations, producing intense social inequality, and horizontal ones in which no open hostility or racial hatred is observed, permitted interracial marriages and friendly commingling in certain social spaces under specific circumstances.

This last peculiarity of the racial relations in Brazil, associated with the process of racial classification based on appearance, created a belief in the myth of Brazilian racial democracy. This myth presupposes not only friendly and cordial relations, but also equality of opportunities for whites and blacks. Since the 1950s the myth of racial democracy has been challenged by white and black researchers and by activists of the Black movement. In the late 1970s, researchers highlighted the racial inequality regarding access to material and symbolic goods, urging people to interpret this inequality as expressions of racism, and to propose policies that permit supplanting it. In 1996, the Brazilian government recognized for the first time that the country is structurally racist, having assumed its historic debt with black and the indigenous people.

Three Schools of Thought in Brazil

Three perspectives characterize Brazilian social thought regarding racial relations. The first one postulates the existence of racial democracy. The second one recognizes a deep inequality between the white and black segments of the population, but interprets the racial relations in the postabolitionist period as remnants of the ancient regime, incompatible with the new social order that is shaping itself into a competitive society of classes. Despite the fact that this perspective recognizes the existence of racial inequalities, it is optimistic, hoping that the racial inequality will eventually disappear with the development of industrialization. This perspective greatly influenced the Brazilian educational thought. While recognizing the massive concentration of black students in the poorer layers of the population, Brazilian educational thought tends to identify the educational difficulties experienced by blacks exclusively with the inequalities caused by poverty, and fails to consider the specific impacts of racial membership.

Without denying that the destiny of the black population is associated with the political and economic history of the Brazilian society, the third perspective views these inequalities as also due to the unequal opportunities for social mobility after the abolishment of slavery, and the contemporary racism (structural and symbolic) faced by the black and indigenous populations.

Race Inequalities in Early Childhood Education

The concern with race inequalities in ECE is very recent in Brazil. Neither researchers nor activists of the black and indigenous movements have dedicated any attention to the theme. Their concern has been oriented more to the educational situation starting with primary school education. In this context, the written work is limited and there is no consensual political agenda to orient the action.

This inattention is worrying, since blacks and residents in the Northeast between 0 and 6 years of age comprise the greatest percentage of the poor and very poor people of Brazil, with the highest rates of mortality and infant malnutrition and the least access to basic sanitation. Quality indicators indicate that the ECE of the Northeastern region is also of the poorest quality in the nation.

Supply and access. In 2003, 11.7 percent of Brazilian children 0–3 years of age and 68.4 percent 4–6 years of age attended some kind of ECE. Despite an incredible growth rate between 1970 and 1990, studies from the 1990s showed that ECE grew the least in that decade, and presented totally unsatisfactory quality indicators. From a budgetary perspective, ECE is the educational level in which the per-pupil investment is the lowest in the country. The ethnic-racial inequalities in ECE appear on several different levels: in the access and in the quality of the service offered, in the retention of children 7 years of age and older, in the institutional segregation and in the discriminatory processes observed in the institutional practices.

In Brazil, children of higher income levels and white children have the greatest access to ECE. However, due to the expansion of ECE during the 1980s as a strategy to combat poverty, day-care centers, preschools, and improvised literacy classes of low quality were opened for the poor, in poor population regions (slums, urban outskirts). As a result, it is possible to find in some strata of income and age a greater percentage of black children attending day-care centers and preschool. The same expansion policy of ECE for regions considered "politically dangerous" (the "pockets of poverty" of the Northeast) during the last decade of the military dictatorship (1978–1985) caused a specific pattern for the rates of coverage: the Northeastern region presents the best rates of ECE coverage both for white as well as for nonwhite children 4–6 years of age. However, better rates of coverage may be associated with the worst ECE quality indicators. Therefore, the Northeastern region simultaneously presents the greatest coverage and the greatest rate of teachers without qualification, who receive the worst salaries and who work in child-care settings presenting the worst material conditions, including poor basic sanitation.

ECE expansion and racial segregation. This same model of ECE expansion adopted in states with a high percentage of blacks has resulted in the most homogenous clientele at all the levels of public education. Public day-care centers and preschools receive almost exclusively poor children. While this may seem positive, it can also be negative, since social and racial segregation occurs and there is little ethnic-racial or economic diversity.

Financing. Due to this process of antidemocratic expansion and the low financial investment of the state, the ECE has been failing children. This distortion of the system (that has been diminishing recently) especially affects poor, black children of the Northeast. Until 1987 no data were collected on how disadvantaged children functioned in ECE. It was commonly believed that black children started primary school education at a later age than white children, when in fact, substantial quantities (in 1995 an estimated one million children) were retained in preschool. This finding is in accord with research results and the claims of black leadership, which describe the Brazilian school system as having "hostile ambience" for black children or at the very least being indifferent to the racism that occurs both in the school institution and in the broader society. To quote Pinto (1993) "This hostile ambience has been detected in the curriculum, in the didactic material of the most diverse disciplines, in the relations amongst the pupils and in the relations between teachers and pupils." At least since the 1970s studies of school texts, children's literature, and other pedagogical materials (toys) have demonstrated the racial discrimination found within ECE. This discrimination manifests itself in the less representation of black and indigenous characters that can serve as positive role models, omitting and even denying the contributions of black and indigenous people to the cultural formation of Brazil.

Research conducted in the schools has uncovered the discriminatory practices that reflect the ways in which black children are seen in a negative light in terms of their intellectual possibilities. Among white children, the exclusion of black peers and the use of pejorative nicknames for them is not unusual, and most of the time this behavior is ignored by the teachers. In addition, there is little help from the government or from private institutions for improving teacher preparation regarding human rights. Some initiatives have been taken; for example the inclusion of the theme of "multiculturalism" in the national curriculum. However, a recent law that requires the inclusion of the history of Africa and of the contributions of the Afro-Brazilian culture to the Brazilian society does not include ECE, being aimed only at primary and secondary school levels.

Indigenous Peoples

In Brazil, it is estimated that between 350,000 and 500,000 Indigenous people reside on indigenous lands. There are 219 different indigenous nations speaking 180 different languages. At the last census (2000), 739,000 people declared themselves Indigenous. The process of Portuguese colonization adopted in Brazil, as well as the later indigenous policies, exterminated indigenous peoples and their descendants, and banished innumerable languages from human culture. In the process of Portuguese and later Brazilian colonization, the schools played a fundamental role as the institution "domesticating" the "savages." The situation only changed after the dictatorship (in the 1980s), when the Constitution of 1988 was approved and recognized Brazil, for the first time, as a multiethnic and multilinguistic nation.

928 EARLY CHILDHOOD EDUCATION

Supply and access for indigenous peoples. Among other rights, the Constitution of 1988 assured the indigenous peoples' access to a specific intercultural and bilingual school education. The National Council of Education recognized and established norms for the creation and operation of "indigenous schools." In accord with the legal requirement, in 1999 the Ministry of Education carried out for the first time the "Indigenous School Census," which collected the basic information available on education in indigenous territories.

ECE makes up 20.6 percent of the total school registrations in the Indigenous School Census (1999). Ninety-eight percent of these children are in public settings, 56 percent are between 4 and 6 years old, and 72 percent come from Indigenous cultures. Over one-third of school registrations in ECE consist of children of 7 years and above.

ECE and indigenous nations. Not all the indigenous nations favor the creation of ECE settings for their children. These nations fear the diffusion of values that are incompatible with their culture, the loss of their mother tongues, and practices that remind them of the "domesticating" education their ancestors suffered. Despite the fact that the theme of indigenous education is increasingly a subject of academic study, ECE has not been highlighted in these efforts. This is an important and unjustifiable gap in the efforts of researchers. In April of 2005, a national debate was held on ECE and indigenous peoples for the first time. One of the issues under discussion was how compatible the ECE model known and disseminated by the western world is for peoples whose primary socialization does not occur in the context of the normative model of the nuclear family found in the West.

Further Readings: Cavalleiro, Eliane. (2000). *Do silêncio do lar ao silêncio escolar (From home silence to school silence).* São Paulo, Contexto; Pinto, Regina P. (1993). Multiculturalidade e educação de negros (Multiculturality and negros education). *Cadernos Cedes*, (32), pp. 35–48; Rosemberg, Fúlvia (2003). Multilateral organizations and early child care policies for developing countries. *Gender & Society*, 7(2), 250–266; Rosemberg, Fúlvia (2005). Childhood and social inequality in Brazil. In H. Penn, ed., *Childhoods: Young children's lives in poor countries.* London: Routledge, pp. 142–170.

Fúlvia Rosemberg

Poverty

Brazil is not a poor country, but rather a country with many poor people. This is the thesis on Brazilian poverty that is most accepted at present, based on the fact that Brazil ranks amongst the world's highest rates of social inequality, a situation that has not undergone great alterations despite the progress achieved in the country's economic development and modernization throughout the twentieth century.

According to official statistics, the proportion of the poor in the country decreased from 39 percent to 33 percent between 1977 and 1998, but the absolute number grew from 40 million to 50 million people. This total has only started to diminish only recently.

Data reproduced from a table elaborated by Almeida (2000) provide an idea of what the differences in mean income in Brazil are compared to other countries. Of a total of sixteen countries, six were selected for this illustration. The difference between the average income of the countries and the income of the poorest 20 percent supplies a measure of its internal inequality. One country may be richer than another (for example, Brazil compared to India), but present a substantially larger indicator of inequality.

Comparison between the average annual *per capita* income of the total population with the poorest 20% in six countries (1993, in US$)

Country	A (Average *per capita* income of the total population)	B (Average *per capita* income of the poorest 20%)	Relation A/B
United States	24,240	5,814	4.2
Chile	8,400	1,386	6.1
Brazil	5,370	564	9.5
Indonesia	3,150	1,370	2.3
India	1,220	537	2.3
Guinea-Bissau	840	88	9.5

Source: PNUD—1996 (*apud* Almeida, 2000, p. 36).

The classification of the countries according to the Human Development Index, reported periodically by the United Nations Program for Development, situates Brazil in the group of countries of Average Human Development. In 2005, the country was classified in the 63rd position, having shown a tendency toward improvement on this indicator over the past few years.

Brazil has no legal definition of a poverty line. The most commonly used classification of the population brackets considered poor and extremely poor is based on a monthly *per capita* family income calculated in minimum salaries (MS). In 2005 the monthly MS was 300 *Reais* or US$125. The poor are considered those people with a *per capita* income of less than 1/2 MS (approximately $2 per day) and extremely poor those with less than 1/4 MS. This poverty line corresponds to the income necessary to provide their needs with feeding, dwelling, clothes, and transportation, amongst others; the line of extreme poverty refers exclusively to feeding needs. According to this definition, in 1998 there were 50 million poor people (32.7%) in Brazil, 21 million of whom (13.9% of the total population) were extremely poor.

Monteiro (2003) calculates the proportion of the Brazilian population considered poor by regions, using the criteria of the *Projeto Fome Zero* (Zero Hunger Project), a program launched in 2002 by the *Partido dos Trabalhadores* (Workers Party). These criteria combine the family income and cost of living of the different regions, considering the domestic production of the agricultural families and not taking into account the expenditures with rental and acquisition of their own homes.

Percentage of poor population in Brazil by regions
(1999)

| Region | Área | | |
	Urban	Rural	Total
Northern	35.4	38.1[a]	36.2
Northeastern	42.9	59.7	48.8
Southeastern	14.9	34.3	17.0
Southern	15.7	28.4	18.3
Central-Western	20.0	34.0	22.3
Brazil	23.1	46.1	27.8

[a] Includes only the state of Tocantins, excluding the rest of the
rural Amazon. *Source*: Monteiro, 2003, p. 10.

Table shows that the greatest contrast is observed between the rural and urban
zones and amongst the large geographical regions of the country. The Northeast
is a region that presents the greatest proportions of poor people, far above the
others, both in the urban as well as in the rural zone.

The condition of poverty in Brazil aligns itself with the color/ethnic origin of the
population. According to *IBGE* (Brazilian Institute of Geography and Statistics),
of almost half of the 180 million Brazilians who classify themselves as *Negroes*,
41 percent are brown and 6 percent black. Although the rates of illiteracy among
these two groups have been dropping, in 2003 they still represented more than
double that registered for whites. The *Negro* population is proportionately larger
in the Northeastern and Central-Western regions, where the average income of
the blacks and browns is only slightly more than half that of the whites. There is
no comparative data for the Indigenous population, which totaled almost half a
million people according to the last Census.

Childhood Poverty

Several studies have already shown that poverty in Brazil affects the young
child population most intensely, especially children between 0 and 6 years of age,
the age bracket that corresponds to early childhood education. Various factors
contribute to this: (1) the family life cycle, since the families with young children
bear heavier expenses and count on a smaller quantity of people in the workforce
than the others; (2) the fact that the poorest families, with less school education
and who live in the less developed regions, have a higher average number of
children than the others; (3) and less access to the basic public services both in
the less developed regions as well as in the poorest neighborhoods of the large
cities.

Kappel (2005) developed a careful characterization of the young child population in the 0–6 age-group, based on IBGE data. In 2001, there were, approximately
22 million children between 0 and 6 years of age in the country. A decrease in
the birthrates from 2.7 to 2.4 in the country between 1992 and 2001 was combined with an increase of newborn life expectancy to keep the total young child

population relatively stable over the past ten years. The regional differences in the birth rates also decreased during that period. These differences continued to be strongly associated with the level of the mothers' schooling: those women with less than four years of education have an average rate of fertility of 3.2 children, while those with more than eight years of study have an average of 1.6 children.

In 2001, of the total of 50 million Brazilian families, 16 million (32%) had children from 0 to 6 years of age. Of these, 38 percent presented *per capita* monthly family incomes below 1/2 an MS, that is, they were considered poor. The proportion of families in the lowest income bracket is significantly higher in the Northeastern region, as shown in the table.

Families with children from 0 to 6 years of age, per classes of *per capita* monthly family income in minimum salaries, according to the regions-Brazil, 2001

| | | Families with at least 1 child from 0 to 6 years of age | | | | | |
| | | Classes of per capita monthly family income in MS (%) | | | | | |
Brazil and Great Regions	Total[a]	Up to 1/2 MS	More than 1/2 up to 1	More than 1 to 2	More than 2 to 3	More than 3 to 5	More than 5 MS
Brazil[b]	16,143,638	38.1	25.1	16.6	5.3	3.4	2.9
Northern[b]	1,017,114	42.5	26.0	13.7	3.7	2.7	1.9
Northeast	4,889,150	60.1	18.2	7.2	2.0	1.4	1.2
Southeast	6,592,766	26.2	27.8	21.3	7.1	4.7	4.0
Southern	2,413,616	26.6	28.8	23.9	7.3	4.2	3.4
Central-Western	1,203,979	32.0	30.2	16.7	6.2	4.0	3.9

Source: Kappel, 2005, Table 2, p. 187, based on data from PNAD 2001, IBGE.
[a] Including those without income and without declaration of income.
[b] Excluding the rural population of the Northern region.

An important aspect to consider is the number of families headed by women: in 2001, 27.3 percent of the total families were in this situation. The infant mortality rates decreased significantly between 1992 and 2001, but they still reveal a significant regional inequality.

Monteiro (2003) shows how the rates of infant undernourishment in children between 0 and 5 years follows the same tendency of increasing poverty in the rural zone of the Northeastern region (25.2% compared to 16.6% in the urban). In addition, there is a significant difference in the rates of the urban zones in the Northern (16.6%) and Northeastern regions (13%) compared to the Central-Southern region (4.6%).

This author identifies the lack of access to public health services, education, and sanitation, among others, as an important factor associated to the incidence of childhood undernourishment, in addition to the family income. In this sense, the rural population is more affected than the urban. A longitudinal study during the period 1989–1996 showed that the decline observed in the rates of childhood undernourishment in Brazil are more due to the increase in the coverage of basic services of health, schooling of mothers, and the supply of water than to the small increase in family income recorded over these years. These data demonstrate that progress in the living conditions of the population is not obtained simply through higher economic growth rates, but requires the mediation of greater investments in basic public services.

However, the younger children are precisely those that benefit least from public expenditures in the social area. Based on estimates of the proportion of expenditures on social programs that reach the different age and income brackets of the population, Camargo (2004) demonstrated that social policies in Brazil present a pro-elderly, antichildren, and antipoor people pattern. Of a total of 200 billion *Reais* that the country spends annually on social programs (health, education, social welfare, social assistance, and work), more than 60 percent are targeted to retirement funds and pensions. In addition to these expenditures there are those spent on social assistance, half of which (5 billion *Reais*), go to the elderly.

Comparing social expenditures on the aged with those invested in the 0–14 age-group, this author calculates 12 percent of the GNP for elders (6% of the population) compared with 3.6 percent of the GNP for children (29.6% of the population—a total of 50 million in 2000). This bias is even more evident when children between 0 and 6 years of age are highlighted. Although Brazil practically universalized access to obligatory elementary education for children between 7 and 14 years of age during the decade of the 1990s, in 2003 only 11.7 percent of the children from 0 to 3 years old and 68.4 percent of those from 4 to 6 years old actually attended ECE institutions (see Country Profile).

School attendance rates are higher for the higher income segments and the white population. In 2001, the chance of a higher family income child (more than three minimum salaries family income *per capita*) being enrolled in ECE, compared to those of a lower income child, were 3.5 times greater for the 0–3 age bracket and 1.6 times greater for the 4–6 age bracket.

Attendance rates were higher for children classified as white. In the 0–3 age bracket 11.4 percent of the white children were enrolled in ECE, compared to 9.6 percent of the black and brown children. In the 4–6 age bracket the difference was 67.9 percent for white versus 63.3 percent for the black and brown children.

These data show quite clearly that the social policies of the country are not able to significantly alter existing patterns of social and racial inequality, and that the young children are at a relative disadvantage in relation to other segments of the population, not only regarding access to income but also in terms of access to the social programs.

Social Policies and Poverty

Without ever having implemented a universal social welfare system, as occurred in several European countries in the post World War II period, Brazil is currently accumulating the contradictions of a society that was industrialized and urbanized with the impasses of a nonhegemonic country in a globalized world. The neoliberal policies of weakening the capacity of the state to intervene are combining with the postindustrial society, high unemployment, and social exclusion to become firmly established as structural characteristics.

Over the past years, several programs to supplement family income were adopted and directed to the poorer families. The *Bolsa Escola* (School Scholarship) program was one of the first, and required in return from the families that their children between 7 and 14 years of age attend schools. The shape of these programs evolved over the past five years together with significant expansion. With the commencement of the *Fome Zero* (Zero Hunger) program, the main social proposal of the 2002 government, the diverse types of income supplementation programs were unified into what is now called *Bolsa Família* (Family Scholarship), coordinated by the Ministry of Social Development and Combat to Hunger.

One of the consequences of this unification under the auspice of social assistance is a weakening of the emphasis on the children's school attendance as an obligation of the families receiving assistance. In addition, at the intersection with the crèche programs, the previous stimulus to education has been switched to a stimulus for mothers to stay at home and take care of their young children, contradicting the purpose of the *Bolsa Escola* program.

Bolsa Família is an income transfer program aimed at families in poverty situations that expects a contribution by the families, in the form of participation in health activities, enrolling their children in schools, and participating in nutrition education programs. In 2005, a total of 6,562,155 families were being catered to, receiving an average of 66 *Reais* ($28) a month. The goal defined for 2007 is to reach 11.4 million families.

Neither research nor evaluations are yet available on how these programs are affecting the living conditions of the children from 0 to 6 years of age. But it should be considered that the education policies aimed at young children in Brazil must overcome inequalities in access to day-care centers and preschools, Otherwise these efforts to combat poverty will not have a long-term effect on the future of the poorest children.

In any case, it seems that income supplementation programs, whether or not associated to education and other social policies, have come to stay. They have political support, have gained support among international organizations and, more importantly, correspond to pressing and dramatic social necessities. However, in a society that commingles these programs with patronage-oriented political practices and confuses social policy with benevolence and rights with favors, it is difficult to disseminate a conception of social policy and income supplementation based purely on rights of citizenship, which also creates obligations for those benefited and which does not cause discrimination in social life. Social inequalities cannot be understood exclusively in terms of the right to receive certain goods and services. It is also necessary to consider the rights of integration that would permit individuals to be active citizens, with full rights to live in society.

Further Readings: Almeida, Evaristo (2000). *Programas de garantia de renda mínima*: inserção social ou utopia? *(Minimal income guarantee programs: Social insertion or utopia?)*. São Paulo: EDUC/Fapesp; Barros, Ricardo Paes de, Ricardo Henriques, and Rosane Mendonça (2000). *Desigualdade e pobreza no Brasil: retrato de uma estabilidade inaceitável (Inequality and poverty in Brazil: The portrait of an unacceptable stability)*. *Revista Brasileira de Ciências Sociais* 15(42), Feb., 123–142; Camargo, José Márcio (2004). *Política social no Brasil: prioridades erradas, incentivos perversos (Social policy in Brazil: Wrong priorities, perverse incentives)*. *São Paulo em Perspectiva*

18(2), 68–77; Campos, Maria Malta (2003). *Educação e políticas de combate à pobreza* (Education and policies to combat poverty). *Revista Brasileira de Educação* (24), Sept./Oct./Nov./Dec., 183–191; Fitoussi, Jean-Paul, Pierre Rosanvallon (1997). *La nueva era de las desigualdades* (The new era of inequalities). Buenos Aires: Manantial; Kappel, Dolores Bombardelli (2005). *As crianças de 0 a 6 anos no contexto sócio-demográfico nacional* (Children from 0 to 6 in the national socio-demographic context). In Sonia Kramer, (org.), *Profissionais de educação infantil: gestão e formação* (*Early childhood education professionals: Management and training*). São Paulo: Ática, pp. 178–201; Monteiro, Carlos Augusto (2003). *A dimensão da pobreza, da desnutrição e da fome no Brasil* (The dimension of poverty, undernourishment and hunger in Brazil). *Estudos Avançados* 17(48), May/Aug., 7–20.

Web Site: www.fomezero.gov.br.

Maria Malta Campos

Violence

In Brazil, as in many other Western capitalist societies, the largely urban phenomenon of violence assumed endemic proportions beginning in the 1980s, and challenged the efficacy of socially controlled institutions.

Although *violence* (and its consequences) attacks all social segments, its diverse *forms of manifestation* produce a hierarchic complexity that affects social groups differentially, depending on their particular vulnerabilities. Exposure to violent events occurs differently for blacks and whites, young and old, men and women, poor and rich, residents of central or peripheral regions of large urban centers. To these characteristics are added those related to age, given that the risk of victimization occurs especially in the economically nonproductive groups. The main victims of homicides in Brazil, for example, comprise a predominantly young, male population residing in regions where the processes of social exclusion are accentuated.

Structural Violence

Violence in its *structural* manifestation is defined in terms of life conditions produced as a result of economic decisions. In its cruelest form this type of violence takes as its victims those families that live in poverty or misery, and especially affects the children. In Brazil its result can be seen through the historical and social conditions that produced the institutionalization of poor children in shelters, child-juvenile labor as a form of supplementation of the household budget and the phenomenon of the boys and girls that live in the streets. In the case of early childhood education (ECE), this violence was reproduced in the sphere of the national public policies aimed at expansion of child-care places which, supported in the name of low-cost investment, generated only small coverage with public financing and established a range of different types of admission (public, private, philanthropic, home-based). This process makes access difficult on behalf of children coming from poor families, who receive less attention (see Country Profile), and creates institutions that provide the children with services of varying quality.

Other forms of violence, labeled *social*, *intra-family*, and *institutional*, also have the greatest impacts on children and adolescents, violating their rights and shaping both the conditions for and their opportunities for development.

Intra-family Violence

In relation to intra-family or domestic violence, its physical form is the most visible, being both the most common type in the country and also including cases so severe that they require the attention of the Health System. It is manifest as physical and sexual abuse, where intentional use of force may even lead to a risk of death. From 1997 to 2003, the National Secretariat of Human Rights received 8,600 reports of sexual and commercial exploitation of children. A National Program has been developed as a form of combating mainly the sexual exploitation linked to tourism. Girls are especially the victims of sexual violence. In relation to physical violence, according to IBGE data 20 percent of Brazilian children are victims and in 80 percent of the cases parents are the aggressors. Studies by the Center for the Study of Victims of Violence show that child abuse is a grave public health problem, having become the main cause of death of children under age 5.

As part of a national culture centered on the adult and permissive with punitive forms of childhood discipline, physical violence is combined with *negligence and psychological violence*, in which a process of humiliation and submission of the child occurs provoked by adults or by other children. This culture results in a lack of knowledge of the real situation of victimized children, because it produces a "plot of silence" which leads to the helplessness of the children and a continuation of the fear and negligence.

Psychological Violence: Bullying in Schools

Within the sphere of the school, psychological violence has been discussed mainly through studies on *bullying*, characterized as a combination of aggressive, intentional, and repetitive behavior perpetrated by one or more pupils against others, causing pain, anguish, and suffering. Generally prejudice and nontolerance to differences are at the base of this behavior.

These are also the factors that appear associated to *school violence* in a broader context expressed in terms both of how the institution understands the problem and of its educational practices as (re)producers of social violence. Studies in the area, which have intensified in the last decade and become more centered on the educational settings serving children from 7 to 14 years of age, raise issues regarding institutional violence specific to the school and also to its articulation with extramural violence.

If the issue of school violence in the elementary and high school has received more attention recently in research and in Brazilian educational policies, this has in general not been the case in early childhood education. There are some research projects that study the day-care centers and preschools as protected spaces for the child regarding domestic violence. The concept is that daily attendance provides the child with other adults who can accept some responsibility for their physical integrity, acting more rapidly when threatening situations occur in the realm of

936 EARLY CHILDHOOD EDUCATION

the family. At the same time there are a few recent research projects that seek to understand how violence is manifest within the day-care centers and preschools themselves, mainly concerned with the fact that these children occupy an even more fragile position than older children in relation to the education settings they attend. This violence is manifested in two ways: (1) through processes of discrimination by race and gender resulting from differentiated treatment by the teachers, especially affecting girls and Negroes, and (2) through some care/educational routines that treat children as objects of intervention rather than as subjects with rights.

The History of Violence Against Young Children in Brazil

These processes of child victimization can be traced to a long history of Brazilian society's relationship with childhood. Violence against young children has existed since the colonization of Brazil, via the physical and mental indoctrination of indigenous children by the Jesuits. Cases of pederasty and racial prejudices appear in the historical records of a society—Brazil—that founded itself on a patriarchal model. From a judicial point of view, it was only when childhood was consolidated as a social category that the first laws emerged aimed specifically at children. As in European countries and the United States, this process occurred early in the twentieth century. In 1923, the first Brazilian Tribunal for Minors (*Tribunal de Menores*) was established and in 1927 the first Minor Legal Code was promulgated. This landmark consolidation of the doctrine called *irregular situation* was based on a discourse and a practice that preached the necessity of "moral protection" of those children in conditions judged as potential for marginality, particularly children of the poor. Thus the origin of this legislation for childhood reflects and legitimates a repressive relationship with the child, characterized by the concern for social control. In this way it consolidates a culture of penalization of childhood, of marginality and blaming the poor, and of violation of basic rights. The judicial ordinance of the *doctrine of irregular situation* persisted until 1990, when the Statute of the Child and of the Adolescent (ECA) was promulgated.

Violence and Children's Rights

The ECA resulted from the social mobilization that occurred in the process of democratization of the 1980s, and is guided by principles contained in international documents and regulating article 227 of the Federal Constitution. This legal framework proposes a new view of the child, inserting childhood into the arena of human rights. Developed with the support of UNICEF and considered one of the most advanced models for other countries of the world, this legislation introduces the *doctrine of integral protection*, which postulates rights to all children and adolescents, recognizing their particular stages of development. It furthermore establishes a systematic guarantee of basic rights (education, health, protection from work, culture and leisure) and of special protection (to victimized children and adolescents victimized and from the perpetrators of crimes). Two types of public councils are proposed to monitor children's rights: one responsible for the elaboration of the public policies for childhood (Council of Rights) and consisting of members of the government and civil society; another responsible for admitting or of directing children to the appropriate agencies in cases of violation of basic rights or of victimization (Ward Council), composed of five members elected or appointed by the community. In each municipality there shall be a Rights Council and at least one Ward Council.

Every citizen is co-responsible for the child and has the obligation of reporting rights violations to the Ward Councils. The professionals that deal directly with the children, like those in early childhood education, are particularly relevant to the legislation since, in addition to being promoters of the rights within the ECE settings and in direct relation to the children, they are also obliged to report evidence of abuse and exploitation occurring in the family. However, the fragility of the institutions responsible for following up the cases reported to the Ward Councils generates a situation of helplessness in the responsible professionals, who express fear of reprisals on the part of the abusers since there is no protection after the report and its delivery to the Ward Council.

Although, in the 1990s the development of ECA passed through an intense process, including the participation of the media and of children's rights defense organizations, priority was given to certain themes, such as child labor and adolescents perpetrating infractions. In the ECE field, a document published by MEC entitled "Criteria for a provision that respects children's fundamental rights" (*Critérios para um atendimento que respeite os direitos fundamentais das crianças*) deserves special mention. This document presents principles based on the conception of children's rights both for actions within early childhood settings as well as for the elaboration of policies of early childhood education. The development of this document, which was interrupted in the decade of the 1990s by changes in national policy, is now beginning anew.

Despite the legal advances, there still is a great deal of resistance in relation to the construction of a culture that respects the rights of the child. The existence of a system of guaranteeing rights does not lead directly to a transformation of the life conditions of the Brazilian children. On the contrary, it exposes the historical and cultural complexities and demands the reorganization of activities and practices in the different social spaces, including the educational institutions that are confronting old and new conceptions of the child.

Efforts within Early Care and Education

In the case of early childhood education, there is a lot yet to be done. National policy has not addressed the issue of children's rights and of violence against early childhood with the necessary force and urgency. In the ECE professional preparation courses and in the curricular proposals these themes are not considered.

Localized efforts and advances are documented in different regions of the country. Concrete experiences that have already proved to be more successful are those that seek to organize the institutions by means of Childhood Protection Networks, articulating the day-care centers and preschools with other areas and public and private services. This model expands the possibilities of acting preventively in the process of victimization of the children and at the same time of qualifying, via dialog with partners, the professionals that work in the day-care centers and preschools. In this qualification, however, one of the main challenges created by ECA needs to be overcome: the need to substitute the conception of the child as an object of attention with one that considers the view of the child as a *subject of rights* and a participant in its own development, on a daily basis and in the execution of pedagogical projects and activities.

Nonviolence and a Peace Culture

Other initiatives that deserve to be highlighted are those that, in contrast to the concept of violence, seek to distinguish constructive reflections based on the concept of nonviolence. It is in the bosom of civil society that the majority of the proposals in favor of a peace culture are born. NGOs, foundations, and movements directed to guarantee the basic rights of children stimulate research and publications that seek to influence public policies, exploring methodologies among the children that allow all to comprehend and expand the knowledge of the child's integral development. The construction of this peace culture, if it is to be effective, requires a multidisciplinary approach and the participation of children and adolescents, family members, educators, and other members of the community. The early childhood education settings, due to the central importance of their activities and their proximity to the family, occupy important and privileged spaces for these activities. Educating for solidarity, building ways of dealing with conflicts not mediated by violence, and breaking down prejudices and intolerance are currently our great challenges for the education of our children in more humanized relations.

Further Readings: Azevedo, M. A., and V. N. A. Guerra (2001). *Hitting mania: Domestic corporal punishment of children and adolescents in Brazil.* São Paulo: Iglu, p. 303; Campos, M. M., and F. Rosemberg (1995). *Critério para um atendimento que respeite os direitos fundamentais das crianças.* Brasília: MEC/SEF/COEDI; COPIPAZ. Comitê Primeira Infância na Cultura de Paz (2004). *A Primeira Infância na Construção de uma cultura de paz (Early Childhood Committee in the construction of a culture of peace)*, www.copipaz.org.br; *Estatuto da Criança e do Adolescente* (1990). Lei Federal 8.069/90; Fante, C. (2005). *Fenômeno Bullying: como prevenir a violência nas escolas e educar para a paz.* 2nd ed. Campinas: Verus.; Ferrari, Dalka C.A. (org.) (2004). *O Fim da Omissão: A implantação de Pólos de Prevenção à Violência Doméstica.* São Paulo: Fundação Abrinq; Mendez, E.G., and A. C. G. Costa (1994). *Das necessidades aos direitos.* São Paulo: Malheiros.

Ana Paula Soares da Silva and Adriana Friedmann

Child Care and Early Childhood Education for 0- to 3-Year-Olds

History

The social movements for the democratization of Brazil, which increased during the military regime (1964–1985), greatly influenced the Brazilian Constitution of 1988. This also brought about great advances in the field of individual and collective rights. As a result, the Constitution recognizes the child and the adolescent as subjects with rights, thus revolutionizing the protective doctrine of previous legislations. It guarantees the universal right to health and education, as well as assistance to those in need. It also affirms that all workers' children have the right to admission in day-care centers and preschools, extends the period of maternity leave from 90 to 120 days, and creates a paternity leave. It also institutes, as a responsibility of the state, the provision of day-care centers and preschools for children from 0 to 6 years of age. Specific laws regulate these constitutional precepts, including the Statute of the Child and of the Adolescent (1990), the law that establishes the Single Health System (1990), the Organic Law of Social Assistance (1993), and the Law of Guidelines and Bases of National Education (1996). It also promoted the decentralization of services of the Union to states and municipalities and the establishment of councils in the various areas: education, health, social assistance, and rights of the child and of the adolescent. Representatives of the government and civil society participate on these councils in establishing the guidelines for public policies and in the follow-up of the services provided.

Health Care Initiatives

In the field of health, a single system has been established that includes the union, the states and the municipalities, as well as private institutions financed by the public sector. Over the last several decades, different actions were introduced to reduce infant mortality and to prevent childhood diseases. Mass vaccinations in childhood were introduced, along with attention to prenatal care. This message about the importance of prenatal care was accompanied by campaigns targeting breastfeeding. Seeking to reach the entire population, the strategy of family visits by community health agents was expanded, providing information regarding basic care, health and hygiene, and child development follow-up. Volunteers of a nongovernmental organization, the "Pastoral da Criança," linked to the Catholic Church, carry out similar work.

These initiatives have resulted in a significant reduction in the infant mortality rate over the last twenty years. In 2003, the rate was estimated at 27.5 per thousand, representing a drop of 60.2 percent from 1980. Even so, Brazil's infant mortality rate is still the third highest in South America (UNICEF, 2005). Infant mortality becomes more serious as the income level and the mother's educational level decrease. Children who are born into low-income families have twice as great a chance of not surviving the first year of their lives than those with higher incomes. Additionally, children with mothers who have only completed three years of schooling have almost double the risk of dying before their first birthday than children of mothers with eight or more years of schooling. The incidence of abdominal Caesarian delivery and pregnancy in adolescence is also higher in these groups.

ECD Programs

Assistance to the most needy families and children is the responsibility of the Ministry of Social Development (MDS) and of the Secretariats and Municipal Organs of Social Assistance. MDS designs the assistance policies, and it supports home-shelters (temporary dwellings), services for those with disabilities, and financial help programs for the most needy, especially the "*bolsa-família*" family aid program. "Bolsa-família" is the main aid program for poor families; "bolsa" means a kind of scholarship for the families. See Poverty entry. The program that supports the maintenance of day-care centers and preschools (public and private nonprofit) that cater to children of low-income families is especially noteworthy. This program consists of a per capita monthly sum provided by the federal government per child attended. Since this per capita value is insufficient, these resources have to be supplemented by other segments of the government and other sources. In 2003, 1,650,608 children aged 0–6 benefited from this program. There are no precise figures regarding how many of these children are in the 0–3 age-group, but we know that the percentage is far lower than for children in the 4- to 6-year-old group (UNESCO, 2003). Because day-care centers were recognized as educational institutions in the Constitution of 1988, negotiations are under way for these resources to be managed by the Education Ministry.

In Brazil, actions in the areas of education, health and assistance for children 0–3 years of age and their families still suffer from past traditions. Instead of a cohesive system of services, emergency measures dominate, which are both overlapping and disjointed. The Councils invoke the importance of articulation of concrete activities in the different areas. However, this articulation is lacking within the various spheres of the government. The Committee of Early Childhood, which functioned between 2000 and 2003 in the precinct of the federal government, took some initiatives in this direction, but this was not a high priority for the organizations involved.

Day-Care Centers and Preschools

The inclusion in the Constitution of 1988 of day-care centers and preschools as a "right to education" reflects a fundamental milestone in Brazil, especially as relates to the day-care centers. This clause in the Constitution provides recognition, on behalf of society, of the right of the child to education in the earliest years of life. Among the factors that contributed to the accomplishment of this recognition were the scientific advancements related to the development of the child, the social movements in support of the child and children's rights, the women's movements, movements by administrators and researchers in different areas, and the general social consciousness about the meaning of childhood.

In consonance with this new vision, the Educational Law of 1996 redefines the terms day-care centers and preschool. Whereas earlier day-care centers were meant mainly for children aged 0–6 from low social-economic families, now they are defined as institutions for children aged 0–3, and the preschools are for those aged 4–6. The municipalities are responsible for providing this public provision.

Teacher Preparation

Other important milestones are the requirement that (1) teachers be licensed at a higher level or have completed a course on a secondary level, in the "*Normal*" modality for work in day-care centers as a professional, and (2) that all day-care centers have their operations authorized and supervised by the educational system, as defined by the LDB. Just as in preschools, day-care centers now must develop their pedagogical plans in accordance with the *National Curricular*

Guidelines for Early Childhood Education of 1999 (DCNEI). Specifically for younger children aged 0–3, the document emphasizes articulation with social policies, integration between development and the individual child, social and cultural life, forms of expression (especially oral and corporal) games and play, and the intense and constructive commingling between families and teaching teams. The RCNEI, published by the Ministry of Education in 1998, also supplies specific guidelines for the construction of practices in the day-care centers (see Curriculum entry, below).

The official documents explicitly define conceptions that are consistent with contemporary views of human and child development. The documents explain that children have rights, and that they are complete beings, total and indivisible. However, these official requirements are not generally complied with across the country. Many educational systems are still in the process of restructuring themselves to take on the supervision of the day-care centers, and many of these (as crèches) are not regulated. In general they are characterized by practices limited to health care and feeding.

Financing Early Childhood Education

The current pattern of financing the educational sector does not guarantee resources for early childhood education (ECE). As with many social policy initiatives, money is limited and ECE funding competes with other educational programs. The federal resources are limited, and the majority of them are committed to the previously mentioned program of day-care-center maintenance, administered by the MDS (see Country Profile). This financing system contributes to the fact that the day-care centers are identified more with care than with education. As a result, the effective integration of the day-care centers in the educational area is still in process. A new educational financing proposal (FUNDEB) that will also include early childhood education is being discussed in the National Congress (see the Early Childhood Education in Brazil entry, above). Apart from the technical and financial difficulties in the educational sector, low standards of quality exist in many of the institutions, which make it difficult for them to meet the requirements of the educational system.

Research

Recent findings regarding children's day-care-center status (IBGE, 2003) show that 62 percent of registered day-care centers are public (60.5% municipal) and 38 percent private, including nonprofit ones. Regarding coverage, of the 13.8 million children from 0 to 3 years of age in the country, only 11.7 percent attend day-care centers, far from the 30 percent goal stipulated in the National Education Plan to be accomplished by 2006. This percentage decreases as the family's income level falls. The rate of access of the children from 0–3 coming from families with an income under 1/2 MS is about four times less than that found for families with an income bracket between three and five minimum salaries *per capita*.

If we consider this low level of enrollment in day-care centers in the context of a labor market participation rate, which is 51.9 percent for women with children under 2 (only slightly less than the rate of 54 percent in the total population

(IBGE, 2002)) we easily conclude there is a lack of correspondence between child-care provision and the parent's working policies. To remain in the workplace, mothers with young children have sought other child-care solutions, such as family arrangements, home day care, or unregulated day-care centers.

Data from 2004 show that 17 percent of day-care-center professionals lack the minimum preparation. Since the data refers only to the registered institutions, the overall percentage must be higher. The physical condition of the centers and the variety and quantity of materials available in them are also inadequate, according to the ECE Census held in 2000.

There is a great diversity of practices observed in the Brazilian day-care centers: those that emphasize care and those that promote early schooling, those that value the participation of the families and those that do not consider relations with the family as part of their work. At the same time, there are institutions that serve as fine examples of conceptual and practical advancement, including some linked to the public universities, unions, associations, or private entities, in addition to several successful experiences in the public sector.

Although there is not yet a national instrument to evaluate the environments provided specifically in the day-care centers, some municipal networks have developed their own instruments and conduct an annual system of evaluation of the quality of the day-care centers.

In scientific research the field of psychology continues to carry out the greatest number of projects on children younger than 3 years of age in day-care centers. Through the 1970s the role of the affective link between children and significant adults, especially between mothers and their children, and their effects on child development dominated inquiry. Since the 1990s there has been growth in the number of studies and topics, including themes related to adaptation, communication, the meaning of gestures, and the nature of language in interactive situations or in the production of meaning. These studies are showing that children are capable of multiple relations from a very tender age. Studies have also investigated the interaction of the infant and toddler with its immediate surroundings and the relations between the environment and the frequency of babies' interaction.

There is still little research on the development of babies in the collective space of the day-care centers. Recent contributions in psychology, the social sciences, and pedagogy have expanded the understanding of basic childhood processes, including other perspectives, of the children's production of meaning, of their insertion process in the collective spaces, and of the different social roles that they play, as determined by their life contexts (Rocha, 1990; Strenzel, 2001; Rossetti-Ferreira, Amorim, Silva and Carvalho, 2004).

Conclusion

To summarize, the number of child-care places for children under the age of 3 in Brazil is low, the policies and their financing are still fragile, the conceptions of custodial assistance and the resistance to accepting day-care centers as a right continue in many sectors. The educational sector has no consolidated history of provision to this age-group, and the neoliberal policies and the programs proposed by international organizations do not proceed in the same direction as that achieved through previous successes. There is conflict among the needs of the population, the political and scientific advances, and the decisions of the governmental jurisdictions. Despite these fragilities, the system of care and education for children aged 0–3 is progressing. This can be seen in the policy of the right to services and is present in policy debates and in research. Since this system can easily fall prey to ideologies, maintenance of it requires constant vigilance, care, and commitment.

Further Readings: Rocha, Eloísa A. C. (1999). *A Pesquisa em Educação Infantil no Brasil: Trajetória recente e perspectivas de consolidação de uma pedagogia da educação infantil. (Research in ECE in Brazil: Recent trajectory and perspectives of an ECE pedagogy).* Florianópolis: UFSC—Centro de ciências da Educação Infantil, Núcleo de Publicações; Rossetti Ferreira, M.C., K.S. Amorim, A.P.S. Silva, and A.M.A. Carvalho (orgs.) (2004). *Rede de significações e o estudo do desenvolvimento humano (Network of meanings and the study of human development).* Porto Alegre: ArtMed; Strenzel, Giandréa R. (2000). *A Educação Infantil na Produção dos Programas de Pós-Graduação em Educação no Brasil: Indicações Pedagógicas para a Educação da Criança de 0 a 3 anos (ECE in the production of post graduation programs in education in Brazil: Pedagogical indications for the education of the child from 0 to 3).* Florianópolis: Dissertação (Mestrado em Educação) UFSC; UNESCO (2003). *Early childhood services in Brazil: Some considerations on services for creches and pre-school and co-ordination of public policies for early childhood.* Brasília: UNESCO Brazil; UNICEF (2005). *Situação Mundial da Infância* (Worldwide childhood situation). Brazil.

Telma Vitória and Angela Rabelo Barreto

Teacher Preparation in Brazil

Brazilian early childhood education has progressed over the course of the past century, ultimately gaining its own legal status. Historically, the development of this field has been affected by a lack of relevant governmental policies, as well as polarization due to the custodial care/instruction/compensatory education divisions within the field of early childhood education. Since the first services for children 0–6 years of age were established in the nineteenth century, two types of institutions have been configured to care for young children: day-care centers, which focus on physical health and care; and nursery schools, kindergartens, and preprimary education classes, which were linked with formal education and incorporated into the official system of education. The training paths for early childhood professionals reflect this dualism.

In the day-care centers, professionals have several designations: including caregivers, monitors, and child development assistants. The people hired to work with young children are, in large part, unspecialized lay workers or have a low educational level, not exceeding the eighth grade of elementary education. Although Brazilian day-care centers have been in existence for nearly a century, prior to the 1990s the few basic training initiatives provided to day-care educators were connected with hygienist and *"puericultura"* programs (child welfare term used in medicine), and were frequently private programs. In addition to receiving poor preparation for their work, these professionals lacked any kind of career or salary plan.

For the teachers in preschools and kindergartens, the training process has historically been merged with that of teacher preparation for the early grades of elementary education (previously primary education). Originally, nursery school and kindergarten teachers were not grouped with teachers trained in "*escola normal*" (basic teacher certification on a secondary level), the training course for teaching in primary education. The selection criteria for these preschool teachers were based on abstract concepts like having the "vocation" for working with children, and defined by the absence of jobs in primary education, resulting in a transitory nature and turnover in the profession. To perform professionally was seen as requiring specific training in certain techniques and pedagogical materials (Froebelian, Montessorian, and Decrolyan) and, in the case of nursery schools, introduction to basic concepts of hygiene.

The National Education Law of 1971: Two Paths of Teacher Training

The Law of Guidelines and Bases of National Education (LDB) of 1971 specified two paths of teacher training for preschool: one through high school graduation (secondary education) and the other at the university level.

Secondary Level Preparation. At the secondary level, teacher training specific to preschool takes place in the last year of a four-year teacher preparation course. The curriculum for preschool teacher preparation at this level, as specified by the *Educational National Council Report of 1972*, contains the following four focus subject areas:

• Foundations of Preschool Educati0on, addressing historical, legal, philosophical, and sociological aspects;
• Development of preschoolers, including biological and psychological aspects;
• Didactics of Preschool Education;
• Practice of Preschool Education, including a supervised practicum training period.

A set of additional activities proposed in the law complement the curriculum of this single year of preparation: physical education, with an emphasis on recreation and games; artistic education; and health programs, especially regarding preschool nutrition and hygiene and moral and civic preparation. For those teachers already graduated from a teacher training course for the early grades of primary school it is possible to study for one year in a specific preschool preparation course lasting 720 hours. Although the legislation defines early childhood as extending from 0 to 6 years of age, the contents of the teacher preparation curriculum emphasize work with 5- to 6-year-olds.

Preparation in Higher Education. At the higher education level, the course of pedagogical studies gives peripheral attention to preparing teachers for early childhood education, addressing this education in one or two required subjects or in optional subjects but not allowing sufficient space to consider issues of educational practice. Historically, pedagogy has characterized itself as a course for early childhood education and the first grades of elementary education and administration. The list of topics addressed emphasizes general knowledge of fundamentals, reserving limited space in the curriculum for more specific focus on teaching practice, which in turn is directed at elementary school teaching.

The National Education Law of 1996: Advances and Gaps

The National Law of 1996 affirmed the concept of special preparation for and professionalization of early childhood education (ECE) teachers, in accordance with the acknowledgment of the rights of children 0 to 6 years old to education issued by the Federal Constitution 1988 and reaffirmed by the Statute of the Child and the Adolescent of 1990. The 1996 Law was preceded by publications of the Ministry of Education (MEC), resulting from a series of studies carried out by specialists and professionals in several educational sectors, that proposed a national ECE policy. The major contribution to the thinking regarding teachers' preparation was a publication dedicated especially to the topic: For a Policy of the Preparation of the Early Childhood Education Professional (*Por uma Política de Formação do Profissional de Educação Infantil*).

In accordance with this Law, the preparation of teachers/initial training for basic education should occur on a higher education level, in a full licensure course, offered in universities and institutes of higher education. The Law accepts as minimum preparation for ECE teachers the course on a medium level, in the "*Normal*" modality (teacher certification on a secondary level). It also specifies programs of continuing education and in-service training, with both in-the-classroom and distance learning approaches.

Secondary Level Preparation. A Federal Resolution of 1999 institutes National Curricular Guidelines for Teacher Preparation in Early Childhood Education and of the first years of Elementary Education, which define the secondary level preparation as the *Normal* modality. This modality of training is aimed at students who have completed their eight years of elementary education. It is to be offered in institutions with their own pedagogical-administrative organization. The duration of the *normal* course shall be at least 3,200 hours, distributed over four school years. The curricular contents of this preparation are quite vague.

Preparation in Higher Education. At this level two possible pathways are foreseen in the National Law of 1996: a *Normal Superior* course of study and the Pedagogy course of study offered in universities, university centers, and institutes of higher education. A proposal for structuring the *Normal Superior* Course is presented in a document issued by the National Council of Education in 2000. There the curricular components for the preparation of both ECE teachers and those teaching in the early years of elementary education are described together. The following areas of didactic content are highlighted: Portuguese Language, Mathematics, Natural Sciences, History, Geography, Art, and Physical Education. The focus on the traditional school subjects leaves little room for topics specific to early childhood education, especially relative to the 0–3 age-group.

The Pedagogy course of study is addressed by the National Council of Education in the 2005 Resolution Project that institutes the National Curricular Guidelines for Graduation Courses in Pedagogy. Specific training is proposed for licensure in Pedagogy for teaching in Early Childhood Education, involving a course of 2,800 hours of academic work, of which at least 300 hours are to be on-site practicum training. This document, still under discussion, reignites an old controversy in the area of education, between those in favor of a course of study in Pedagogy that is a general preparation for teachers and educational experts in education, as is now the case, and one with more specific contents directed to each of the educational modalities, including early childhood education.

Uncertainties continue in the field of education regarding the intended profile of the early childhood education professional and the nature of the teacher preparation courses for this area, but advances at the level of legislation are indisputable. However, the legal accomplishments are neither being translated into governmental policies nor into real programs on the ground despite the profusion of documents, often containing progressive ideas. Financing programs provide a good example: they have not been favorable to the institution of a national ECE policy, and this has prevented progress in the preparation of professionals for the area.

Initiatives seeking the specific preparation of teachers for early childhood education are timid. In 2004 the Ministry of Education reported that Brazil currently contains 300,000 teachers in early childhood education. Of these, 12.4 percent do not even possess the minimum secondary school preparation demanded by law. Entry into the profession occurs without the least preparation, especially for working in day-care centers. To meet this demand, in 2004 the federal government signaled the possibility of promoting initial in-service and continuing training for teachers, through the following projects: ProInfantil "Program of Initial In-Service Training of Teachers in Early Childhood Education" and "National Network of Continuing Education of Teachers in Basic Education," which are in their initial implementation phase.

In several Brazilian states, in-service teacher training initiatives, combining face-to-face and distance learning strategies and technologies, have been developed by means of partnerships between nongovernmental foundations, public and private universities, and the state and municipal governments. These are both secondary and higher level courses, targeting teachers working in day-care centers and preschools, respectively. There are also initiatives by several training centers at the higher education level promoting specific ECE training, in most cases via extension courses.

Related to the search for equity in the ECE teacher preparation processes is the need to institute career and salary plans, ratifying the rhetoric in the National Law of 1996 and other later documents. Very little data is available regarding career patterns and salaries. A document published by the Education Ministry in 2002 indicates the presence of inequities within the municipal network between the salaries of elementary and ECE teachers. There are municipalities in which the salary differences between elementary and ECE teachers involve additional amounts linked to hours of planning and other extracurricular activities. At the level of designation for the director/coordinator, no attention is paid to the legal criterion that establishes a minimum of two years teaching experience as a prerequisite for that position.

Inequities are evident especially in the real world of the day-care centers. Throughout the national territory a fairly irregular professionalization process continues to exist, from the issue of entering the profession to the inadequacies of working conditions, a lack of space and time for studies and for the preparation of long-term educational action plans. Differences in professional profile, denomination, salaries, career plans, and workdays are common.

The great challenge at the moment is to move beyond mere words in the documents, from their intentions to propositions, starting with the fundamental issue of teacher preparation specific to the early childhood education and care, contemplating the specificity of the age bracket of 0–6 years old as a formal part of a national training policy. From this basic need are derived several other issues as yet hardly explored, like work with the family, care and education of the youngest children (0–3 years of age), multiculturalism, and inclusion. Only by addressing these issues will it be possible to achieve the professionalization so needed in early childhood education.

Further Readings: Barbosa, Raquel L.L. (org.) (2004). *Trajetórias e Perspectivas da Formação de Educadores (Trajectories and perspecitves of the educators training)*. São Paulo. Editora UNESP, Kishimoto, Tizuko M. (1999). *Política de Formação Profissional para a Educação Infantil: Pedagogia e Normal Superior (Policy of professional training for ECE: Pedagogy and Superior Certification)*. *Educação e Sociedade* XX(68), 61–78, Dec.; Ministério da Educação. (1994). *Por uma Política de Formação do Profissional de Educação Infantil. (For a policy of preparation of the ECE professional)*. Brasília/DF: MEC/DPE/COEDI; Movimento de Interfóruns de Educação Infantil do Brasil (org.) (Movement of interforums of ECE of Brazil). (2002). *Educação Infantil: construindo o presente (ECE: Building the present)*. Campo Grande/MS: Editora UFMS.

Marieta Lúcia Nicolau Machado and Mônica Appezzato Pinazza

Curriculum for Early Childhood Education in Brazil

One of the several challenges set for the different agents entrusted with formulating early childhood education (ECE) policies in Brazil today, is the issue of the curriculum. It is one of the structural components of national policy that interacts with a number of policy-relevant issues, including the specific preparation of the ECE professionals, the regulations that specify the qualifications and authorizations for operation of ECE programs, the financial resources invested in ECE resources, and the integration of the work carried out by the day-care centers and preschools within a comprehensive policy for childhood, shouldered jointly by the public agencies and by society in general.

In Brazil early childhood education curriculum has been an area of debate and confrontation involving different views of child, family, and the function of the day-care center and preschool. The idea of a curriculum for early childhood education has not always been accepted as it has been most closely associated with compulsory education for children over 6 years of age. Expressions like "pedagogical project" or "pedagogical proposal" are more often used, especially when dealing with the education of children less than 3 years old.

Until recently, the systematizations of pedagogical experiences with children in day-care centers and preschools in terms of guidelines or general orientations were rare and diffuse. Only in the last decade have official orientations and national references been established to guide the specification of educational programs for these institutions. This has resulted from the inclusion of Early Childhood Education in the sphere of Basic Education defined by the National Educational Law of 1996. This Law defines the goal of ECE as "the integral development of the child up to six years of age, in his/her physical, psychological, intellectual and social aspects, complementing the actions of the family and of the community." The importance of structuring and organizing quality educational activities to promote the integral development of the children is articulated with the recognition of the great importance of the professional who works with children 0 to 6 years old in the educational institution. The Law now requires that such professionals attain a medium or upper level of qualification that prepares them for the appropriate social and educational responsibilities (see Teacher Preparation, above). Finally, the Law foresees as one of the requirements of the Federation, in collaboration with the states, D.C., and municipalities, the establishment of competencies, guidelines, and minimum contents, in order to guarantee a common basic curricular formation.

The National Curricular Guidelines for Early Childhood Education (DCNEI)

The common norms for ECE practices are defined in the *National Curricular Guidelines for Early Childhood Education* (DCNEI) instituted in 1999 by the National Council of Education (CNE). These norms specify the principles, foundations, and procedures of ECE. They orient the ECE institutions of the Brazilian educational system in the organization, articulation, development, and evaluation of their pedagogical plan. The *Guidelines* specify the following eight elements for the pedagogical plans:

1. respect for the following guiding fundamentals: *ethical principles* of autonomy, responsibility, solidarity, and respect for the common good; *political principles* of the rights and duties of citizenship, of the exercise of critical thinking, and of respect for democratic order; and *aesthetic principles* of the sensitivity, creativity, playfulness, and diversity of artistic and cultural manifestations;
2. explicit recognition of the importance of the children's personal identity, their families, teachers, and other professionals, and the identity of each educational unit in the context of their organizations;
3. promotion of educational and caring practices which integrate the physical, emotional, affective, cognitive/linguistics, and social aspects of the child's development in educational and care practices, the child being conceived as a total being, complete and indivisible;
4. guarantee of the interaction between the diverse areas of knowledge and aspects of citizen life, like basic contents for the constitution of knowledge and values, via activities that are at times more structured and at other times less restrictive;
5. organization of evaluation strategies through the follow-up and documentation of the phases reached in the care and education of children from 0 to 6 years of age, without the objective of promotion, even for access to elementary education;
6. be conceived, developed, supervised, and evaluated by teachers with at least the Teacher Certification Course.
7. be democratically coordinated in their execution,
8. guarantee conditions for the implementation of the educational strategies, with specific reference to physical space, timetable, and calendar, jointly with the internal regulations of each ECE institution.

National Curricular References for ECE (RCNEI)

A document titled *National Curricular References for ECE* (RCNEI) was developed by the Ministry of Education in 1998. Although it differs from the DCNEI in that it is not compulsory, this document guides the development of ECE institutions' curricula and lays out a number of goals to guarantee the integral development of child recognizing his/her rights to childhood as part of his/her rights as a citizen. In addition to some theoretical foundations, the document orients the ECE professionals in important aspects of their practice, including organization of time, use of space and materials, selection and design of subject-matter into blocks, in addition to being concerned with "curricular components" like objectives, contents, didactic guidelines, and general orientation for the teacher. The curriculum contents are organized around two axes: *Personal and social formation,* addressing the processes of children's construction of identity and autonomy and *Knowledge of the world,* the latter divided into six subgroupings: music, movement, visual arts, oral and written language, nature, society, and mathematics.

Related Research

In 1995, the Office of General Coordination of Early Childhood Education in the Ministry of Education carried out a study to identify the pedagogical-curricular guidelines in use in the various units of the Federation. This study pointed out the fragility and the inconsistencies in the majority of the existing guidelines. It also highlighted the multiplicity and heterogeneousness of the proposals and practices in ECE, a characteristic peculiar to Brazilian society. Any national guidelines should take into account multicultural differences at the setting level as they are intersected by severe historical, social, and economic stratification. These guidelines should also guarantee that differences by gender, age-group, ethnicity, culture, and the children with special educational needs are respected. Also such a guideline should guarantee the rights inherent to all the Brazilian children from 0 to 6 years of age, in such a way as to assist with overcoming inequalities. In this sense, the great challenges set at that time were: how to contribute to the educational settings in the reformulation and/or development of its pedagogical plans without supplying ready-made models, how to guarantee respect for diversity and, at the same time, a qualitative unity to the pedagogical plans of the ECE institutions, and how to provide theoretical substance to teachers and to their institutions (Brazil, 1996).

In a way, the DCNEI tried to absorb the recommendations of this study, resulting in specification of general goals without laying down the means by which goals shall be attained. However, it has had very little impact on the teachers and ECE programs, because it was not properly publicized, debated, or followed up with an investment in training and/or supervision that supported its practical implementation and the changing processes that result from them.

The RCNEI was written in another context, intended to be a didactic guide to the ECE professionals. It was well distributed to the ECE institutions throughout the country. Nevertheless, it has been the object of controversies among academics and experts of the field since its elaboration. Criticisms vary in their concerns. These include the priorities assigned to various contents, the incorporation of teaching models oriented to specific disciplines, and specially the fact that it did not dare to advance beyond the mere issues of the teaching-learning process to include a broad perspective that encompasses a wider and more contextualized perspective of childhood and early childhood education.

Implementation

The Law delegates to the ECE institutions the task of developing their own pedagogical plans, within the general parameters and norms of the educational system. This means that effectively all the Brazilian day-care centers and preschools, public and private, should follow the DCNEI guidelines, which are general in nature. Although the ECE settings may complement them, the basic curriculum and the pedagogical practices are defined by the scope of the ECE institutions, both public and private. At the moment there is no way of evaluating the extent to which the guidelines are being implemented by Brazilian ECE institutions. Although the institutions have total freedom to develop their own pedagogical proposals, in the case of ECE networks, public or private, their technical teams generally define a common pedagogical project, or general lines to be followed.

In practice, the ECE settings and their professionals feel some disorientation. The public settings and those under contract with governmental agencies are especially impacted, due to their lack of knowledge regarding how to develop a pedagogical plan. In that context, the RCNEI has been largely accepted and implemented by professionals in the field, despite the fact that it has been the object of intense controversy in the academic milieu. This general willingness to accept the guidelines by many Municipal Secretariats of Education can be understood as a confluence of many factors: the long tradition of custodial assistance; the absence of early childhood traditions and adequate pedagogical models due to the impact of compensatory educational programs that have accompanied the great expansion of low-cost services that took place in the 1970s; the absence of a policy of specific preparation for ECE professionals; and the dominance of elementary education as the main source of inspiration for preschool education in the country.

Current Tensions

The controversies surrounding the existence or absence of a national curriculum to guide the practices in day-care centers and preschools have made a qualitative improvement when compared to the impasses of the past. These controversies reflect disagreements regarding the functions of ECE in the contemporary world that have yet to be resolved in most other countries. ECE, increasingly considered the first phase in basic education, is viewed by policy-makers on a continuum that ranges from the goal of strengthening children's capacities to assimilate information useful to their future education and life to the idea of creating a socialization context where the child can fully experience childhood without being submitted to the ritualized practices present in school, home, and health routines. At one end of the continuum the focus of attention is on the teaching-learning relation, keeping in mind the acquisition of basic knowledge and the development of competences and abilities necessary to the child's social integration and future success. From this perspective, the ECE institutions are responsible for promoting the conditions and opportunities of learning, knowledge being linked to a didactic project oriented in the realm of experience or areas of knowledge from a view of disciplines adjusted to the age-groups in question. At the other end, the emphasis falls on the specific activities of ECE, which shares with the family the task of caring for and educating the child and does not associate itself with the same norms and parameters traditionally assigned to compulsory education. This distinction defines the objectives and functions of ECE in a qualitatively different way from those of the school institutions. While the school has as its subject the *pupil* and as its fundamental object *teaching* in the different areas, via *classes*, day-care centers and preschool have as their object *educational relations* locked in a collective living space that has as its subject the child from 0 to 6 years of age (Rocha, 2001). Knowledge, from this perspective, is linked not to didactics, but to the general processes that constitute the development of the child as a human being in different social contexts including its culture, and his or her intellectual, creative, aesthetic, expressive, and emotional capacities. The combination of relations that the child establishes with the natural and social environment, between peers and with the different adults, constitutes the object of the pedagogy of ECE, whose focus is the child, with its unique peculiarities.

When the present federal government policy establishes the goal of nine years of elementary education, including the 6-year-old child in the system of compulsory education, new issues in the national debate on the curriculum are introduced. Firstly, it calls attention to the need to strengthen the interface between ECE and elementary education through integrated planning that respects the temporality of the child of 6 years of age and the separate concepts of education at these two educational levels. From the standpoint of promoting a conceptual connection between the two levels of education to make possible an educational approach that respects the specificities of childhood, the initiative is praiseworthy and desired. However, the risks of pushing the pedagogical standards of formal education down into the preschool years are great if we consider that ECE is still a fragile area constructing its own culture. The challenge is to transcend the adult-centered culture, and work, above all, on the sensitivity of the professional to comprehend the situations through the child's eyes.

Further Readings: ARTMED (2004). Que currículo para a educação infantil? (Which curriculum for early childhood education?). Porto Alegre: *Pátio Educação Infantil* II(5), Aug./Nov.; Bennett, J. (2004). *Curriculum issues in national policy making.* Paris: OECD/Malta, EECERA; Bujes, M. I. (2003). *Infância e Maquinaria.* Rio de Janeiro: DP&A; Cerisara, Ana, B. (2000). O Referencial Curricular Nacional para a Educação Infantil no contexto das reformas (The national curricular reference for ECE in the context of the reforms). *Educação e Sociedade*, Campinas, 23(80), Sept., 326–345; Craidy, Carmem, and Kaercher, Gládis. E. (orgs.) (2001). *Educação Infantil: pra que te quero?* (ECE: What for?) Porto Alegre, Artmed; Haddad, Lenira. (1998). *O Referencial Curricular Nacional para a Educação Infantil no contexto das políticas para a infância*: uma apreciação crítica *(The National Curricular Reference for ECE in the childhood policies context: A critical appreciation)*. Presented at the 21st Annual Meeting of ANPED, Caxambú, September 1998; Kramer, Sônia. (1997). Propostas pedagógicas ou curriculares de educação infantil: subsídios para uma leitura crítica (Pedagogical or curricular proposals for ECE: subsidies for a critical reading). *Educação e Sociedade*, Campinas, 18(60), Dec., 15–35; MEC/COEDI (1996). *Propostas Pedagógicas e Currículo em Educação Infantil (Pedagogical proposals and curriculum in ECE)*. Brasília: MEC/SEF/DPEF/COEDI; Rocha, A.C. (2001). A pedagogia e a educação infantil (Pedagogy and ECE). *Revista Brasileira de Educação* (16), Jan/Feb/Mar/April, 27–34.

Lenira Haddad and Zilma Ramos de Oliveira

Creativity and Imagination

The concepts of "imagination" and "creativity" are discussed here in terms of their relevance to shaping the child as a human, a historical, and a cultural subject. This relevance has strong implications for pedagogy. Imagination and creativity are discussed as they are significant and situated within the official Brazilian principles and goals. The application of these principles and goals is then considered within the daily reality of early childhood education programs.

Defining the Concepts

Imagination and creativity are defined as the abilities to visualize new ways of thinking and acting. These possibilities are conceived of through visual, auditory, plastic, tactile, spatial, and verbal images. Creative individuals integrate emotion, perception, intuition, and cognition as they examine the significance of humans in relation to the world. Because imagination and creativity are human dimensions, they develop within a cultural context and are shaped in the exercise of life itself. Imagination and creativity are present in the work of every individual, but are most evident in the activity of the scientist, the artist, and the child. As conscious beings, humans are compelled to understand life and to create. Creativity is the essence of humanity; an incessant process of developing, restructuring, and deepening life experiences. We see this process in the development of great artists and in the growth of children.

Creativity in Childhood

Creativity manifests itself in the unbound, diffuse, and spontaneous activities of children. Through play, children make associations and create symbols to better understand their world. For the child, creating is living. Children are in a state of continual physical, psychological, emotional, and cognitive transformation. These changes sharpen their attentive and experimental spirit. In childhood, life itself is an adventure, and children see a world to be conquered.

Children establish a sensory and aesthetic relationship with reality through a process of perceiving, imagining, and creating. Their relationship to the real world is profoundly rooted in culture and in the sensitive forms of reality. As children engage in the world, they grow, make meaning, and find affirmation. In this way, children meet the world and the world meets the children's needs.

Children adjust themselves to the social world of their elders, whose external interests are carried out through the rules of society. Children also come to understand the physical world. According to Jean **Piaget**, children need to adapt to these social and physical realities and find an emotional and intellectual balance. Children will naturally adapt an activity to their own perception of reality, without reinforcement or sanctions. Through children's play, what is real is transformed because of the need to make meaning. Assimilation and accommodation of external models help children understand and think about their world.

The young child lives in a world of infinite possibilities and is far more curious and adventurous than an older child. Despite limitations in dealing with complex logical relations, young children possess a symbolically intuitive, imaginative, and creative thinking ability that allows them to establish powerful analogies. If this initial ability to make connections is fomented, it may become part of their cognitive processes and cognitive structures. As children develop, they are more apt to think in inventive, perspicacious, and flexible ways. It is significant to recognize that the origins and the foundations of creative thought are established in these early moments of affirmation.

Imagination in early childhood. In early childhood, imagination is constituted as the first form of thought. According to Lev **Vygotsky**, imagination is a new psychological process for the child; it represents a specifically human form of conscious activity. It arises first in the guise of play, which is imagination in action.

Imagination arises from the child's action and encounter with the material and perceptible world. Through fantasy and multiple forms of experimentation, the world becomes more apparent and the child's imagination is engaged. The child establishes a relationship with the surrounding culture through imaginative thinking. By imagining, she/he is affected by what is perceived of the culture and simultaneously defines the culture based on what is perceived. Thus, the child begins to make meaning of experience by imagining. Through imagination, the child is the protagonist of his/her own story. Creation can then be seen as individual acts, immersed in the collective context of interpersonal and cultural relationships.

Children's imaginations are an inexhaustible source of ideas and projects. Using the languages of play, painting, drawing, sculpture, music, literature, and others, the child gains new creative skills and expressive possibilities. Children's imaginations expand and connect to their cultural-historical knowledge. This understanding is necessary as they begin to construct their personal and cultural identities.

Importance in Current Contexts

Imagination and creativity are human dimensions that have always been present in the field of early childhood education (ECE) in Brazil. But how and where they are relevant have not been clearly defined. Creativity and imagination are terms that appear in official documents and in the discourse of educators during different historical moments. They are associated with young children's curiosity as exhibited in their playful and expressive behavior. By putting faith in humanity's creative and imaginative power, these terms reflect a democratic and humanistic concept of education.

A look at pedagogy: why now? At the present time, a deeper discussion of these concepts has been developing. This current conversation points to the fact that imagination and creativity are crucial to the process of the constitution of the child as a historical and cultural human subject. Therefore, they are also crucial to the pedagogy of childhood. The pedagogy that emphasizes imagination and creativity, considers children as the author of their childhood. Creation gives the child the possibility to express his/her voice in multiple languages. This pedagogy considers the child's expression, action, and imagination as axes of educational practice.

A new vision in Brazilian pedagogy. We currently seek to solidify childhood education as a right of all Brazilian children and their families, and to improve the quality of the pedagogical projects provided for them, as stated in the different legal documents referring to ECE (Constitution of 1988, LDB of 1996, DCNEI 1999). As we work toward this goal, one aim is to recover what is known about imagination and creativity. We are faced with a pedagogical tradition that is either driven by concerns of social assistance or focuses narrowly on the child's schooling at a very early age. The challenge is to counteract these traditions with a pedagogy that places a high regard on play and aesthetics. This pedagogy values the expressive languages appropriate to the needs of the child, and the child's appropriation of cultural knowledge in a way that is meaningful and emancipating, as he/she develops. Imagination and creativity play a leading role both for children and for educators.

Imagination and creativity are terms that now inspire the construction of a pedagogy that respects the rights of both children and educators. A new kind of work in education, in which childhood may be fully experienced, should develop at day-care centers and preschools. This requires the development of high quality programs for teacher preparation, which will help educators to better understand and work more in-depth with all the human dimensions of young children.

National Positions on Imagination and Creativity in Early Childhood Education

The work with imagination and creativity in ECE acquires an even broader social dimension when we take into account the deep economic and social inequalities that have left their mark in Brazil. According to Paulo Freire and Maxine Greene, when imagination and creativity are put to use in the service of democratic social projects, they can lead to great transformations.

Rights to creativity and imagination. Over the last few decades, official documents have incorporated imagination and creativity as essential aspects in early childhood education. In *Critérios para um Atendimento em Creches que Respeite* *os Direitos Fundamentais das Crianças* (MEC 1995) *(Criteria for Daycare Centers Child Caring that Respects Children's Fundamental Rights)*, children are assured of their "right to develop their curiosity, imagination, and capacity of expression in the service of the construction of their cultural, racial and religious identity." This right is linked to "the right to a welcoming, safe and stimulating environment which includes contact with nature; individual attention, with the guarantee of essential attention to cleanliness, health and healthy food, to protection, affection and friendship, with special attention given to the child during the period of adaptation; the right to play as the foremost form of expression, developed in different languages and cultural manifestations."

In these statements creativity and imagination are understood as broad and integrating concepts. By establishing creativity and imagination as rights, the mechanisms necessary for implementing this pedagogy in educational practice is being valued.

National Curricular Guidelines

The 1999 National Curricular Guidelines for Early Childhood Education (DCNEI) include the following among their guiding principles:
- aesthetic principles of sensitivity, creativity, playfulness, and the diversity of cultural and artistic manifestations
- ethical principles of autonomy, solidarity, and respect for the common good
- political principles regarding the rights and duties of citizenship, the exercise of critical reasoning, and respect for the democratic order

The DCNEI understands and demonstrates that these principles are interdependent.

Imagination and creativity have been the subject of different publications, translations, seminars, and training courses for childhood educators over the last decade in Brazil, demonstrating their importance for childhood education and for teachers' education. These publications highlight for teachers how work with play and expressive languages links to the genesis of knowledge construction, the appropriation of culture, and the constitution of the child as a human subject. They indicate that educators need and deserve aesthetic experiences in the arts and sciences. In teaching and learning, aesthetic experiences expand the teacher's creative ability with the children, if they are included in the daily reality of the school or day-care center.

Current Challenges in Creative Curriculum

An analysis of the current practices in Brazil's ECE programs reveals an enormous distance between official statements and declarations and actual reality. The national documents value imagination and creativity, but Brazilian programs frequently standardize activities, which are centered on the teacher.

Problems leading to standardized teaching. Teacher training has not prepared teachers to understand the dynamics involved in the processes of knowledge construction, appropriation of culture, and child development. Teachers face difficult working realities, due to overpopulated classes and unsatisfactory physical and material conditions. As a consequence, teachers' work is devoted mainly to containing and controlling the children. These circumstances greatly hinder the possibilities for creative, imaginative thought and action.

Building a more independent pedagogy in the face of insufficient materials, precarious working conditions, and inadequate training is a difficult challenge for teachers. But in order to use imagination and creativity in the interests of cultural empowerment and creation, this pedagogy is necessary. We see the lack of specific training for teachers in the artistic languages, so essential to early childhood, as another major problem for educators.

A cultural paradox. Brazil is a country whose ethnic diversity is unparalleled, a country rich with artistic and cultural manifestations. In a country where Carnival, one of its most important national cultural manifestations, is also one of the most well-known cultural celebrations in the world, why isn't creativity and individuality more valued in school? We can see that a major paradox exists in Brazil, where the national cultural reality is separated from the artificial culture of its schools.

Moving Forward

We can see a strong and increasing movement, present in both public and private educational institutions, toward the implementation of programs that value imagination and creativity. These programs are making it possible to integrate imagination and creativity into their curriculum. Programs are organizing educational spaces, materials, and proposals so that children are invited to act, interact, think, and express themselves in creative, imaginative ways. Projects are introduced that consider diverse artistic expressions. With a view toward appropriating knowledge and producing children's cultural manifestations, many different cultural institutions such as art and science museums, libraries, and theaters, are being integrated into educational projects.

Experiences such as these are structured by means of relationships. These relationships have constructed a balance of power. They are founded on rules of mutual respect that favor the shared involvement of adults and children in the development of a curriculum in action, where imagination and creativity play a leading role. Play and expression are valued in all their dimensions. Through activities such as make-believe playing, building, painting, and clay modeling, and experiences with music, dance, puppets, storytelling, computer activities, and nature, children form relationships with their world. All these activities are incentives to experiment, invent, and imagine. These experiences expand the child's repertory of existential, human, artistic, and cultural experiences. It is then possible for the child to build an identity that is investigative, strong, sensitive, participative, and solidly established in relation to the world.

The expansion of a program that values imagination and creativity can be seen as one of the current challenges that Brazil must face in early childhood education.

Further Readings: Almy, M., and C. Geneshi (1979). *Ways of Studying Children.* New York: Teachers College Press; Dias, M.C.M. and M. Nicolau (2003). *Oficinas de Sonho e Realidade na Formação do Educador da Infância (Workshops of dreams and reality in childhood teacher education).* São Paulo: Papirus; Friere, P. (1992). *Pedagogia da esperança: um reencontro com a pedagogia do oprimido (Pedagogy of hope: A reencounter with the pedagogy of the oppressed).* Rio de Janeiro: Paz e Terra; Green, M. (1995). *Releasing the imagination, the arts and social change.* S. Francisco: Jossey-Bass Publishers; Moreira, A.A.A. (1985). *O Espaço do Desenho e a Educação do Educador (The space of art and the educator's education).* São Paulo: Loyola; Ostrower, F. (1984). *Criatividade e Processos de Criação (Creativity and creation processes).* Petrópolis: Vozes.

Marina Célia Moraes Dias

Play

Play as a Societal Value

In the general context of society there is a strong play culture in Brazil. Children play in their homes, their backyards, in condominiums, parks, and on the tranquil streets of towns in the interior. There are cultural events in museums that exhibit memories, paintings, and sculptures that value playing. There has also been a considerable advance in the inclusion of play on a theoretical plane, in research, in public policies and a strong indication of innovations in pedagogical practices. Play projects aimed at the child population conducted through public policies have utilized circuses, itinerant buses that transport toys and stimulate games in streets and common areas, workshops producing toys, courses and activities integrating music, dance, theater, and the visual arts with play, all as forms of manifestations of childhood culture throughout the country. In hospitals, with the admission of the children comes respect for their right to play, with the recent approval of a legal measure making this compulsory for children living under hospital care. Nongovernmental organizations, working with private companies and with toy manufacturers interested in providing social programs for children (especially low-income children), have stimulated the creation of toy-playing centers around the country and have promoted social events in which playing is the object of attention. The creation of specialized publications, early childhood education (ECE) magazines, and the publicizing of the right to play have stimulated research and practices on play. The expansion of higher level courses to train early childhood education teachers and the multiplication of *brinquedotecas*/toy-playing centers since the 1980s, in addition to the creation of toy museums in the 1990s, are other factors that stimulate the importance of play. Specific to Brazilian educational culture at present is the recovery of regional traditional childhood cultures of play, and the introduction of toy-playing centers in universities, children's schools, hospitals, and population centers.

Play in the Context of Early Childhood Education Settings

Despite the focus on play by the society as a whole, in the majority of the ECE institutions the idea of play as a free activity, with imaginary elements, initiated and maintained by the child, perhaps with rules, varying in time and space, related to a process and to learning, is often is obscured by other conceptions of play; play as a reward, as rest from structured activities, as a way of filling time, as a recreational activity, under adult supervision and not of great importance.

The inclusion of ECE as the first phase of basic education in the public educational system (see earlier entries) led to a spate of documents aimed at improving the quality of childhood education, where respect for the child's rights, especially of playing, are defended. The concern with the quality of childhood education, resulting in efforts to improve teacher training for day-care centers and preschools, has generated a conception of education that integrates playing as the mediator in the child's development.

In Brazil, the introduction of Froebelian kindergartens at the end of the nineteenth century brought the first concerns about games as pedagogical instruments predominating over skill and job-related activities. Teachers that worked in kindergartens during the first decades of the twentieth century, like Alice Meirelles Reis and Helena Antipoff, demonstrated pedagogical practices with free and directed play, drawing upon other references such as John **Dewey**, Maria **Montessori**, Agazzi, and Decroly. However, fragmented activities like copying letters and numbers, drawings and graphic exercises prevail in the majority of the pedagogical practices in the twentieth century.

Academic Interest in Play

The increase in scientific research on play in the 1970s resulted from factors like the creation of the national system of postgraduate education and research, the expansion and insertion of early childhood education into the public system of education, the increase in teacher training courses at this level of education, the expansion of discussions on play in the pedagogical approaches to childhood, the circulation of studies and research on play in congresses, websites, specialized journals, teacher training courses, and the emphasis on the right to play by public policies. In the 1970s, when postgraduate training was structured into the nation's higher education system, the first postgraduate discipline on play was introduced within the Institute of Psychology at the University of São Paulo (USP). In the following decades, research associations began to release the findings of studies carried out on play. For instance, in a survey of researches on play carried out by Bomtempo, in the area of psychology, conducted in the period between 1970 and 1995, play-related topics were found with the following frequencies: role-playing (44.5%), preferred play (16.7%), turbulent play (13.9%), free and gender play (11.3%).

Reflecting the pattern in the foreign literature, Brazil has also observed the increase of studies on "role play" in the areas of education and psychology, highlighting its influence on cognition, creativity, and language, with a greater emphasis on the action of playing itself and less on objects that give support to play. In a study that reviewed research on early childhood education by Brazilian social and human services researchers presented at annual congresses between 1990 and 1996, Rocha identified thirty-eight works on games, and classified them as follows: pretending (29%); psychological, historical, or anthropological representation (26%); space (24%); teacher training (18%); and language (13%), along with others with smaller percentages (interaction, children with special needs, preference for toys, gender, social class, objectives of childhood education, and theoretical approaches).

From the point of view of learning and the development of the child, the theories that stand out in these studies are those formulated by Lev **Vygotsky**, A.R. **Luria**, Leontiev, Wallon, and also Jean **Piaget**, Jerome **Bruner,** and Friedrich **Froebel**. The recognition of the mediator role of the child's play in its relation to the world stimulates studies that show play as a pivot of pedagogical practice in ECE. Increasingly studies utilize the conceptions of Brougère in a sociological perspective and feminist theories to understand toys and play in an analytic perspective that considers ethnic, religious, and gender differences, and which denounces the prejudices existing in the child's daily routine.

As a result of this research, public and private universities and different organizations have created projects involving the construction of toys, stimulating social activities that seek to recover the local culture of play and have released their experiences on websites. The practice instituted in 1984, by the Laboratory of Toys and Pedagogical Materials of Faculty of Education of USP, of including toy-playing centers as an area for research, training, and community services, has been highlighted as meritorious in the national evaluation of teacher training courses on a superior level.

Play and Children with Special Needs

In the area of children with special educational needs, play-related initiatives are under way in organizations like the Association of Parents and Friends of Exceptional Children (APAE) and in other centers addressing multiple disabilities throughout the country. The public and private universities in several states are conducting studies on play and the acquisition of language, anchored in interaction processes, related to physical space and materials. Worth highlighting, among others, are programs in São Paulo with virtual Braille containing digital games that provide free instruction in the Braille language to sighted people. Educational toys for all the modalities of needs are introduced in specialized courses, as occur in Marília, in the state of São Paulo. Institutions like the Fundação Laramara, the Instituto Padre Chico, the Fundação Dorina Nowill, and the Centro de Reabilitação de Cegueira Dr. Newton Kara José (Blind Rehabilitation Center), have stimulated the use of games for the blind. Groups installed in Rio de Janeiro and public and private institutions of São Paulo transmit digital games, and educational toys for the deaf have been developed in Rio Grande do Sul.

Play and Pedagogy

The relationship between play and the pedagogical proposals for ECE has stimulated criticism of approaches that are primarily cognitive in nature. Studies in several fields, including Education, Psychology, Arts and Linguistics, have stimulated the integration of play with speech, graphics, gestures, and mathematical languages in the activities experienced by children. In this process the educators, influenced by the constructivist or social-constructivist perspective, are supported by Bachelard, who sees daydreaming as the act of playing with thought; by Bruner, for whom it is playing with words that provides narrative thinking; and by Bakthin and Benjamin, who point out the pleasure of meaning whether in the sketch of a child's drawing or in the words created as expressions of the childhood culture.

The discussion of curricular approaches like Reggio Emília, High/Scope, Freinet, the Pedagogy of Projects, among others, has expanded the presence of the toy and play in the discussions and the processes of professional training, but with little evidence of permanent impacts on the quality of play in pedagogical practice.

The gap between investigation and innovation and pedagogical practice can be attributed to the resistance of the schooling and institutional culture, which does not focus on the specific child, and to the educational policies that do not maintain successful programs and that preserve the structural problems related to adult–child ratio, financial resources, time, space, materials, and training of the teachers.

The physical space of the ECE institutions, although recognized within the theoretical plan as the environment of learning that leads to the playful exploration of material in the physical world and that must guarantee the right to play as part of the pedagogical plan, does not always retain these meanings in practice. Materials like sand, water, soil, leaves, flowers, paints, plasticines, foodstuffs, scrap materials, cardboard boxes, and toys are beginning to be understood by teachers, timidly, as important resources to relate play to learning. But there is difficulty with their organization, and in many cases the tendency is to use play with the goal of transmitting knowledge. In the institutions that place priority on the practice of taking care of the child, where there are no organized activities with and for the children, there are few materials in a world of few interactions. In others, time for fragmented activities dominates, with little time for playing. In the majority of institutions there is not coherence between conceptions and practices.

Structural Problems

The lack of resources invested in early childhood education, which results in inadequate adult–child relationships, the absence of objects and toys, and the organizing of space more for collective control than for promoting exploration in dyads, triads, etc., impedes the permanent inclusion of play practices in day-care centers and preschools. Another difficulty is the frequent acquisition of miniature toys, which are inadequate both for collective use, due to their fragility for use by small children, and because they restrict the play to individual practices.

In the experience of many municipalities, the effort to expanding the play space in ECE institutions results in the practice of using toys in one room named a toy-playing center, but within a conception that shows little comprehension of the more general role of playing in an educational setting. These rooms usually are maintained as toy demonstration windows or are used only for directed activities. Even if they are used for childhood play the toy-playing centers are often utilized on a shift schedule, due to the great quantity of children, and so are available only on a weekly or biweekly basis for each age-group.

The inclusion of play in the pedagogical practices requires the adoption of constructivist or social-constructivist conceptions that are not present in the majority of Brazilian academic and institutional cultures and that depend on the professional training and the solution of structural problems of organization and functioning in the ECE institutions. From the perspective of teacher training, the systematic observation of and listening to the children in play situations has increasingly been pointed out as essential for understanding how play is associated to childhood learning, development, and culture, and thus how play can be included appropriately within educational practices.

Further Readings: Atas do Seminário Internacional da OMEP (2000). *Infância— Educação Infantil. Reflexões para o início do século.* Rio de Janeiro: Ravil Editora; Kishimoto, T.M. (1993). *Jogos Infantis. O jogo, a criança e a educação.* Petrópolis: Vozes; Kishimoto, T.M. (2003). Toys and the public policy for child education in Brazil. In Anders Nelson, , Lars-Erik Berg, and Krister Svensson, eds., *Toys as communication. Toy research in the late twentieth century.* Part 2. Stockolm: SITREC, pp. 149–159; Rocha, Eloisa Acires Candal (1999). *A pesquisa em educação infantil no Brasil. Trajetória recente e perspectiva de consolidação de uma Pedagogia da Educação Infantil.* UFSC Santa Catarina-Centro de Ciências da Educação. Núcleo de Publicações—NUP; Salgado, Pereira e Jobim e Souza (2002). *Children's games and cartoons: A dialogue with young superheroes.* London: ITRA Congress. Available online at www.gips.psi-puc-rio.br/txingles/texto4.htm.

Tizuko Morchida Kishimoto

Inclusive Education in Brazil

History

At the end of the World War II, concern about human rights triggered a renewed focus on human values, which resulted in the Universal Declaration of Human Rights. Created in 1948, this Declaration affirmed, among other things, the right of all people to education. However, the Declaration did not give visibility to the disabled, who were segregated and denied access to an education that considered their specific needs. In 1975, the UN General Assembly approved the Declaration of Rights of Disabled People, for the first time fully expressing the needs of disabled people and formally recognizing their citizen rights and duties. In that decade, the National Movement in Defense of Disabled People's Rights gained force in Brazil. One of the Movement's main objectives was to replace the existing segregated educational system with an integrated one in which disabled people could commingle in regular schools. This concept of integration was ruled by the idea of normalcy, and its goal was to "modify the person with special educational needs, that this person could be as similar as possible to the other citizens, so this person could be included and integrated into a commingling within society." To this end, special classes were created in schools (partial integration), with the purpose of preparing the child for total integration in regular classes, which would only occur once he or she was capable of following the curriculum.

In 1990, upon agreeing with the Worldwide Declaration of Education for All, signed at the UNESCO World Conference, Brazil formally announced its decision to create an inclusive educational system. In 1994, upon signing the Declaration of Salamanca, Brazil reaffirmed this commitment, giving visibility to Special Education. Since then, the Brazilian educational system has been in a process of deep transformation, resulting in changes in the legislation and in the development of national guidelines for education. All these changes have been oriented around the idea of inclusive education.

The idea of *inclusion* is an advance beyond the unilateral "the child must change" perspective, toward a bidirectional process, involving actions both on the part of those people with special educational needs and on the part of society: "instead of presupposing that the pupil must adjust to the standards of 'normalcy' to learn, it appoints the school the challenge of adjusting itself to respond to the diversity of its pupils." Instead of only focusing on the limitations, difficulties, and/or disabilities of children, inclusion considers the human dimension. The concept of inclusion goes beyond merely bringing the child to school. On the contrary, it implies a posture of involving, comprehending, learning, and building new possibilities.

The concept of special education has also undergone deep changes. Instead of focusing only on the development of competences and abilities of the person with special educational needs the concept has shifted to a concern with how special education can contribute to the construction of an inclusive society for everyone.

National Guidelines for Special Education in Basic Education

The National Guidelines for Special Education in Basic Education issued in 2001 by the National Council of Education define special education as follows:

> An educational process defined in a pedagogical proposal, ensuring a set of special educational resources and services, organized institutionally to support, complement, supplement and, in some cases, substitute the regular educational services, in order to guarantee school education and promote the development of the potential of the pupils that present special educational needs, at all levels, phases and modalities of education.

The conception of *special* refers to the criterion of meaningful difference in relation to what is normally provided to the pupils in a regular school, where the special educational needs are defined as those that "require from the school a series of resources and support of a more specialized character, that provide the pupil means of access to the curriculum." These needs may result from high abilities or difficulties to learn, and are not associated with the condition of the disability.

Understanding special education in this context provides an opportunity for any child to have his or her specific needs recognized, whether they are transitory or not, and it creates the demand for solutions that are also specific to and adequate for each situation. This conception demands flexibility and the capacity for reflection on practice, which is only possible when there is involvement and good working conditions for the teachers.

These guidelines determine that the schools should enroll all the special need pupils and organize themselves to provide them quality provision in regular classes. They indicate the importance of considering the unique bio-psychosocial situations and characteristics of those being educated, in order to ensure their requisites with respect and human dignity, and the development of their identity and citizenship. The guidelines recommend that educational intervention for pupils requiring special support be provided as soon as possible, which shall make it more effective in the long run. In this sense, admission to early childhood education (ECE) is understood as preventive and desirable for children with special needs. They also recommend reflection, the exchange of experiences amongst the protagonists of the educational action and a search of partnerships with institutes of higher education and research, seeking to develop a theoretical elaboration on inclusive education.

Education and Care for Seriously Handicapped Children

For children that are seriously handicapped and who could not benefit from the common curriculum, a functional curriculum shall be considered. This curriculum emphasizes the development of social competences. The education of children with special needs may require few curricular adaptations (small adjustments in the planning or organization of the classroom) or significant ones. The document further anticipates the need for pedagogical support services in the day-care centers and preschools, which would help identify a child with special needs. Additionally, such identification may promote more curricular flexibility and adaptation with alternative pedagogical practices. This service may be provided in an itinerant fashion, developed by a teacher specialized in special education and ECE, or through resource classrooms, where the specialized teacher would carry out complementary and/or supplementary curricular activities with small groups, as an alternative to the school routine.

Also foreseen to consolidate the process of inclusion is the creation of *early intervention services* from birth to three years of age, in specialized institutions, whose admission shall be complementary to (and not a substitute for) the day-care center or preschool. It is understood that these admissions are essential to promote the development of potentialities present in this early childhood period, and that they shall be integrated with the health and social action areas.

Admission to ECE may also be made in *special schools* in those cases in which it is necessary to provide "intense and continuous help and support, and when the need for curricular adaptations is so significant that the common school cannot provide them." Some studies challenge this idea and point out, specifically in

ECE, that it is possible to create conditions for the admission of all the children in the regular day-care centers and preschools, in a manner that brings benefits to all the children (Sekkel, 2003). *Hospital class* and *family home care* are special admission possibilities, on a temporary basis, in situations where health treatment hinders attendance at a regular school.

Nevertheless the Guidelines as well as the National Education Plan have been treating special education as a chapter aside of the national education. The absence of a specific treatment of special education in early childhood education causes it to remain as a topic for specialists only and impedes educators from engaging in the discussion, generating a feeling of helplessness and paralysis of action.

Support for Implementation

In 2003 the Secretariat of Special Education of the Ministry of Education (MEC/SEESP) published the collection *Saberes e Práticas da Inclusão— Educação Infantil (Knowledge and Practices of Inclusion Early Childhood Education)*, composed of nine volumes that discuss specific themes in the education of children from birth to six years of age with special needs. The topics covered in this collection are the following:

• An introduction covering the concepts of inclusive education for the programs and goals of ECE
• Profound Learning Difficulties or Limitations in the Development Process
• Profound Learning Difficulties—Autism
• Profound Learning Difficulties—Multiple Disabilities
• Difficulties of Communication and Signaling—Physical Disability
• Difficulties of Communication and Signaling—Deaf and Blind/Multiple Sensorial Disabilities
• Difficulties of Communication and Signaling—Deafness
• Difficulties of Communication and Signaling—Visual Disability
• High abilities / Gifted / Superior Abilities

These volumes, available on the site of the Ministry of Education (www.mec. gov.br), have helped nationwide to fill a fundamental gap between implementation of inclusive education, the supply of important technical support for inclusive practices, and initial and continued in-service preparation of ECE teachers.

Research

The data provided by the Secretariat of Special Education shows that the number of special needs pupils enrolled grew from 201,142 in 1996 to 500,575 in 2003. According to the School Census of 2003 inclusive admissions in Brazil grew from 24.7 percent in 2002 to 28.7 percent in 2003 while enrollment in the special classes diminished from 75.3 percent to 71.3 percent. However, the data available is very general, not allowing for deeper analyses or identification of the challenges faced by the families or schools involved.

The National Education Plan itself recognizes the lack of knowledge regarding the real circumstances facing special needs students in the educational process. Complete statistics on the number of people with special needs and the quality of the education provided to them simply isn't available. Until the 1990s there were no official data at all on Brazil's disabled population. The Population Census of 1991 included, for the first time, questions regarding the disabled population, but the methodology utilized was faulty and compromised interpretation of the data. The Population Census of 2000, relying on the technical assistance of the *National Coordination for the Integration of Disabled People* (CORDE) utilized an expanded concept of disability, compatible with the International Classification of Functioning, Disability, and Health, provided by the World Health Organization and recommended as the theoretical benchmark by the United Nations. In this census 14.5 percent of the Brazilian population identified themselves as having some kind of disability, which amounts to 24.5 million people. Of this total 48.1 percent are visually disabled, 22.9 percent motor disabled, 16.7 percent hearing disabled, 8.3 percent are mentally deficient, and 4.1 percent have physical disabilities. In 2004, CORDE published a report, based on data obtained in twenty-one Brazilian cities that highlighted the close relationship between social inequalities and these incapacities, and emphasized the need for social policies that positively identify the population with disabilities.

The amount of ECE research in this arena is not impressive, and in general shows the feelings of abandonment and isolation suffered by teachers and other ECE professionals who work with special needs children. It also allows us to foresee the great advance that inclusion represents for the construction of a humane society. The pioneering experiences developed at the Creche/pre-escola Oeste (Western Daycare center) of the University of São Paulo show the impact that the inclusive ECE proposal has had on the lasting transformation of attitudes in the children, parents, teachers, and employees, caused by the collective confrontation of the attitudinal barriers that result from the influence of the stereotypes and prejudices regarding disabled people. The construction of an inclusive ambience, sensitive to the individual and group issues, articulating channels of participation at all levels, proved to be fundamental for the collective construction of an inclusive educational project.

Further Readings: Carvalho, R. E. (1997). *A nova LDB e a Educação Especial.* Rio de Janeiro: WVA; Emílio, S. A. (2004). *O cotidiano escolar pelo avesso: sobre laços, amarras e nós no processo de inclusão.* Thesis (Doctorate in Psychology). Institute of Psychology, University of São Paulo, São Paulo; Ministério da Educação e do Desporto (2000). *Projeto escola viva: garantindo o acesso e permanência de todos os alunos na escola – alunos com necessidades educacionais especiais (Project alive school: Guaranteeing access and permanence of all the pupils in the school—pupils with special educational needs).* Brasília: MEC/SEESP. Available online at www.mec.gov.br; Ministério da Educação (2001). *Diretrizes Nacionais para a Educação Especial na Educação Básica.* Brasília: MEC, SEESP. Available online at http://portal.mec.gov.br/seesp; Palhares, M., and S. Marins (2002). *Escola inclusiva.* São Carlos: Ufscar; *Saberes e práticas da inclusão (Educação Infantil)* (2003). 2nd ed. rev. Brasília: MEC, SEESP. Available online at www.portal.mec.gov.br/seesp; Sekkel, M.C. (2003). *A construção de um ambiente inclusivo na educação infantil: relato e reflexão sobre uma experiência (The construction of an inclusive environment in early childhood education: Report and reflection on an experience).* Thesis (Doctorate in Psychology). Institute of Psychology, University of São Paulo, São Paulo.

Marie Claire Sekkel

Gender and Equity: A Brazilian Perspective

The Concept of Gender

In Brazilian dictionaries, the term gender is defined as a way of classification and a means of real or imaginary expression of the characteristics of human beings, with emphasis on the stereotypes attributed to each sex. Beginning in the 1980s the concept of gender began being incorporated by sociology with reference to social organization in the relation between the sexes. The elaboration of this concept also received and still receives considerable attention in areas of knowledge such as linguistics, psychoanalysis, psychology, history, and anthropology, with anthropologists credited with demonstrating the cultural variability of the behaviors considered masculine and feminine. These findings have demonstrated that the masculine and the feminine are understood as shaped fundamentally by the culture as well as by biology. In the 1990s in Brazil, the studies of the American historian Joan Scott had a significant influence on the studies of gender and on critical reflections on education. Her work provided a greater understanding of sexual differences and the multiple meanings that this knowledge acquires in various socialization contexts, including the institutions responsible for education.

However, for a long time the focus of gender issues was limited to the conditions faced by women, which made the political consolidation of the concept of gender difficult, rejecting a dynamic and dialectic vision of the social relations between men and women. Even today both in the political and the academic realms, attention to gender is sometimes limited to a focus on women. At the same time, among those that defend the relational dimension of gender there is the risk of restricting the analysis to a single standard of masculine and feminine, immutable and polar. At present the adoption of a gender perspective, whether in academic studies or in the policy arena, requires the recognition that men and women are not equal, the relations that they establish are asymmetrical, there is no single model of masculinity or femininity, and the relations of power touch on relations between women themselves as well as between women and men. Thus gender must be associated with the dynamics of social transformation, and with meanings that go beyond the bodies and the sexes and that which supports the notions, ideas, and values in the different areas of social organization. These meanings are found in the culturally constructed and visible symbols of masculinity and femininity, heterosexuality and homosexuality, in the development of normative concepts within the scientific, political, and judicial fields, in the formulation of public policies that are implemented in social institutions like day-care centers and preschools, and in subjective and collective identities.

Gender and Early Education

The incorporation of the concept of gender in education starts with recognition of its fundamentally social character, and the way that it has been constructed historically around inequalities based on physical and biological differences. This orientation sometimes challenges the supposedly fixed and polar character of categories such as feminine and masculine. In the case of the early childhood education (ECE), the issue of gender was powerfully present during the 1980s in the construction of policy directed at early childhood care and education, and influenced propositions for the preparation of professionals and the academic undertakings of that period. By the end of the 1990s the gender perspective associated with development of ECE policies had shifted more to the interior of the institutional spaces, with concerns more directed to childhood socialization, development, and learning.

Gender and Early Childhood Education Policies

The insertion of the perspective of gender in ECE is the result of changes that permeated the entire process of redemocratization of Brazilian society over the last four decades, the legal manifestation of which, apart from direct elections for the presidency of the Republic, has been development of the Federal Constitution of 1988. The latter brought to an end a period characterized by the violation of human rights under the protection of a dictatorial government, and guaranteed the recognition of the demands of various social movements, including the women's movement; marked above all by reflections initiated in 1975 with the first Women's Worldwide Conference organized by the UN in Mexico. The women's movement engaged itself in the Constitutional Campaign, with the objective of assuring rights and guarantees for women's equality within the constitutional text. At that time, the National Council of Women's Rights (CNDM), created in 1985, and the State Council on the Conditions of Women (CECF), in São Paulo, played an important role in the introduction of the theme of sexuality and gender in ECE.

Faced with the intense process of urbanization of the 1970s and 1980s and the necessity of intensifying their involvement in the labor market and facilitating redistribution of domestic and family responsibilities between the sexes, women managed to introduce ECE as a right by using an argument that brought together the issues of paid work, gender equality, child care, and education. In this sense, the recognition by the Constitution of maternity as a social function and of the duty of the state to guarantee extra-familial care and assistance through day-care centers and preschools for 0- to 6-year-old children represented a significant advance in social policy and in the promotion of gender equity in Brazil. Thus Brazilian feminism views the day-care-center proposal through a double lens: both as a woman's right to day-care center and to preschool for her children and as an achievement of the child's right, whether poor or rich, to an educational and pedagogical setting and to extra-familial care as an effective means of articulating family with occupational and social responsibilities. The right of every child to early childhood education, through day-care centers and preschools, also meant the expansion of citizenship and became a turning point in the history of the social construction of this subject of rights: the young child.

Neoliberal Reforms

Beginning in the mid-1990s, these legal advances were restrained by the neoliberal reforms that followed, with less state participation and the restriction of the social and work policies. Some advances were maintained, as in the case of equity between the sexes with respect to admission into early care and education programs. In 2001, 531,102 girls and 562,245 boys attended day-care centers and 2,372,038 girls and 2,446,765 boys preschools. However, Article 7 of the Constitution, which called for free admission to day-care centers and preschools for the children or dependents of rural and urban workers as a social right, has not been enforced. The educational policy, which was not based on a tradition of viewing ECE from the perspective of sharing child care with the family, also applied the logic of the liberal reform that allowed for no increase in costs. There was no effort to direct resources to the improvement of teacher salaries or to the broad provision of day-care centers, as foreseen in the Constitution. The proposed creation of a day-care-center salary (*salario-crèche*) was defeated in the voting process of the National Law of Guidelines and Bases of National Education (LDB), which was approved in 1996.

This defeat was aggravated by new educational financing rules, and especially the law that created the FUNDEF, a measure of the federal government that modified the Constitution by giving priority to elementary education as the primary investment in national education (to detriment of ECE and the education of youth and adults) (see Country Profile). This political context results today in a situation where less than 40 percent of Brazilian children are enrolled in day-care centers and preschools, still far from the ideal, and in the priority given to part-time admission of children aged 0–6, instead of to full-time admissions. The expansion of ECE as the first phase of basic education, without the social component that articulates family responsibility and duty to the state and a guarantee of the extra familial care and assistance (a part of feminist demand for day-care centers and preschools that shaped the Constitution), is considered one of the greatest obstacles to implementing a policy that truly integrates care and education from the perspective of the rights of the child and of the families.

The Preparation and Practices of the Early Childhood Education Professional

Gender is also reflected in professional preparation, and in the practices and curriculum directed to ECE. The conception that women are, by nature, capable of caring for and educating young children served as an excuse for reinforcing ECE as the *locus* of voluntary or poorly remunerated female work, reflecting the low public investments and the absence of sound policies of initial and in-service training. With the 1996 Educational Law, the qualification of the ECE professional was also regulated, foreseeing the secondary level as *Normal* modality (the minimum preparation for this educational level), collaboration for the improvement of the preparation of day-care-center educators, until then mainly lay people without any appropriate preparation. (see the Teacher Preparation entry). But there continues to be a strong need for greater attention to the specific competencies that characterize the professional and to the shortage of men among the ECE professionals. In Brazil, the practices developed in these two institutions are aggravated by disagreement and imprecision regarding the responsibility of the family, in the private sphere, and the responsibility of the day-care centers and preschools, in the public sphere, for the care and education of the young child.

Inside the Early Childhood Education Settings

From the point of view of the gender relations in the interior of the ECE settings, there is criticism regarding the stereotyped socialization of boys and girls in early childhood that is commonly occurring within the institutionalized spaces of early childhood education and care. There is great difficulty, for example, in perceiving gender-related education as part of the work to be developed by day-care centers and preschools. Professionals, in general, do not know how to deal with situations that contradict traditional behaviors for girls and boys (for example, a boy liking to play with dolls or pots and pans). It is observed that children use as objects for gender representation what the adults—responsible for their education— provide and reflect. From this perspective, the emphasis is on the transmission of values of equality and respect amongst people of different sexes, as described in the National Curricular Referential (RCNEI) of ECE (1998), which highlights the construction of the identity of gender and of sexuality itself as more than the mere biological configuration of human beings. This vision understands the education of the children as extending beyond the reproduction of stereotyped patterns. The proposals for a nonsexist education also highlight the role of educators, both men and women, in deconstructing the meanings of gender in childhood relations, an aspect of the most recent policies aimed at the professional preparation of ECE.

Attention in Academic Circles

The intersection between relations of gender and ECE gained greater visibility in the Brazilian educational research with the systematization of efforts to establish, in the sphere of the state and of public policies, measures against the discrimination of women and in support of the education of young children as a right that articulated work, equality of gender, and early childhood education and care. In the last decade, this focus has lost ground to themes that are more focused on the relations established in the interior of the ECE settings: in the development of child sexuality, in the children's learning processes, in the production of the identities of boys and girls, in the games amongst young children, and in the relations between adults and children. These studies draw attention to the necessity for deepening the question of gender in the ECE period, for considering that the identities of gender are directly related to this phase of childhood development. The 0–6 age bracket is an important period for the construction of identities. ECE, from this perspective, must adopt a view of gender that recognizes the transforming opportunities in the crystallizing conception of masculine and feminine.

Studies on the character of gender of masculine behavior in day-care centers and preschools are rare. Some authors point out that entry into this field of work demands the mobilization of knowledge linked to the production and reproduction of life, and therefore relate in our society to the female condition, even when performed by men. Moreover, one must consider that the masculine presence, as a reference for the construction of the identity of gender in ECE, involves professionals, children, and families, as well as the redefinition of the function of the ECE institutions in order to overcome the rigid models of separation between family and school.

Further Readings: Carvalho, M., and C. Vianna (1994). Educadoras e mães de alunos: um (des)encontro (Educators and pupil's mothers: A (dis)encounter). In Bruschini, Cristina e SORJ, Bila (orgs.) *Novos olhares: mulheres e relações de gênero no Brasil (New looks: Women and gender relation in Brazil)*. São Paulo: Marco Zero/FCC, pp. 133–158; Cerisara, A. B. (1996). *A construção da identidade das professoras de Educação Infantil: entre o feminino e o profissional (The construction of the identity of the ECE teachers: Between the feminine and the professional)*. Doctorate Thesis. São Paulo: USP; Cruz, E. F. (1998). "Quem leva o nenê e a bolsa?" o masculino na creche ("Who carries the baby and the bag?" the masculine in the daycare center). In Margareth Arilha, Sandra Unbehaum Ridenti, and Benedito Medrado (orgs.) *Homens e masculinidades: outras palavras (Men and masculinities: Other words)*. São Paulo: ECOS/Ed.34, pp. 235–258; Haddad, L. (2004). Creches e pré-escolas no sistema de ensino: desafios para uma política pró-integração (Daycare centers and preschools in the teaching system: Challenges for a pro-integration policy). In PEC-Formação Universitária Municípios, *Educação Infantil (Early childhood education)*. São Paulo: Secretaria de Estado da Educação, pp. 169–177; Pro-Posições (Sept./Dec. 2003). *Dossiê: Educação infantil e gênero (ECE and gender)*. Campinas: Unicamp; Rosemberg, F. (Mar. 2002). Organizações multilaterais, Estado e políticas de educação infantil (Multi-lateral organizations, the state and ECE policies). *Cadernos de Pesquisa*, São Paulo (115), 25–64; Saparoli, E. (1997). *Educador Infantil? uma ocupação de gênero feminino (Childhood Educator? A female gender occupation)*. Dissertação (Mestrado). São Paulo: PUC-SP.

Cláudia Vianna and Sandra Unbehaum

China

Early Childhood Education in China

Introduction

Located in Eastern Asia, People's Republic of China is the most populous country in the world, with a population of 1.3 billion. There are fifty-six ethnic groups in the nation, with the Han making up about 92 percent of the population and other ethnic groups including the Zhuang, Uygur, Hui, Yi, Tibetan, Miao, Manchu, Mongol, Buyi, and Korean. Both ethnic languages and the official language of mandarin are used in ethnic areas. In the last few decades, the nation has made great progress in economic development, especially since 1978 when the country began to adopt an open door policy and market-oriented economic development. As a result of this economic growth, living standards have improved dramatically in the past ten years for much of the population, However, in 2002, 5 percent of the population was still below the national poverty line and the developmental gap between the urban and rural areas was great. Currently, the number of children aged 0–6 is about 99.3 million, 8.14 percent of the total population. Among the child population, more than 50 percent are less than 3 years of age. More than 60% percentof these children live in rural areas.

After the Communist Party took over mainland China, gender equity was on the government's working agenda. Mothers were encouraged by the government to join the workforce, leading to the care of the children as a social issue. The Ministry of Education issued the first program regulation titled Kindergarten Provisional Operation Regulation (Initial) in 1952. It specified that "the purpose of the early childhood program is to ensure that children have a healthy physical and mental development upon entering the elementary school; meanwhile the program is to relieve the burden of child care from mothers, so mothers are able to have the time to participate in political, productive and educational activities." The double purposes of the early childhood program have not been changed in the past five decades, while the fostering of the development of children has been expanded to include the development of physical, intellectual, social and emotional, and aesthetic.

A good beginning will provide an important foundation for children's lifetime development and this idea has been well accepted by the policymakers in the government since 1990s. To provide optimal conditions for children's learning and development, important policies have been made and implemented. In the two versions of the same government document titled Chinese Children Development Guideline (1990s and 2001–2010), the purpose of early childhood development is related to the nation's economic and social progress, and is tied to the improvement of the quality of human resources in the nation. Although many specific goals have been established for the improvement of children's survival conditions in rural areas in this document, the goal for providing equal education and universal access to all children is not mentioned. In recent years, the idea of equal education has been discussed primarily in the sector of compulsory education, and not yet in early childhood education.

Key Historic Figures

Xingzhi Dao (1891–1946) established the first early childhood program for farmers and factory workers in Nanjing and Shanghai in the 1920s. After Dao studied with John **Dewey** in the United States in 1910s, he returned to China to make great efforts for poor families and their children. He proposed that children's education should start before the age of 6 and that education should encourage children to employ both hands and minds; to learn by doing. He was also an advocate for the education of creativity.

Xuemen Zhang (1891–1973) was a well-known child educator in North China and Taiwan. He worked with children as an ordinary teacher for many years. In his behavioral curriculum, he proposed that curriculum is experience and life is education for children.

Heqin Chen (1892–1982) was a well-known child psychologist and child educator. He studied psychology and pedagogy at Columbia University in the United States with Kilpatrick early in the twentieth century. After returning to China, he worked in Nanjing Normal University as a professor of child psychology and education. Chen was the founder of the first experimental child education center *Gulou Kindergarten* in Nanjing, and also established the first public early childhood education teacher training school in the early 1940s in Jiangxi province. He was the first researcher to study children's psychological development in China. The curriculum research he conducted in Nanjing provided a solid foundation for the establishment of the first Kindergarten Curriculum Standard in China. He proposed the theory of "Life Education", which emphasized: (1) the goal of the education as to foster a good Chinese citizen; (2) use of the nature and the social life as the resource of the curriculum; (3) the principle for teaching young children as "to learn by doing, to teach by doing and to make progress by doing."

A Brief Sociology of Childhood in China

Chinese children's position in society has been changing in the last few decades. Historically, children did not have many rights in a Chinese family. They were treated not as independent persons, but instead as the personal property of adults. Young children, particularly girls, could be killed at birth, abandoned, sold, or sent as a gift to relatives. Even as adults they usually did not have rights equal to the older adults in the family until they had a family of their own. This situation has been changing since early 1950s, following the Communist Party takeover of the country. However, in many rural areas today, girls may still not be treated equally with boys in terms of rights and position in the family.

The popular metaphor "children are flowers of the country, the future of the country" has been used to describe Chinese children. The idea that children should have special protection and care is not only written in the constitution but broadly accepted in Chinese society. During the past few decades, the conditions for the survival and development of Chinese children have been improving steadily. For example, the mortality for children under the age of 5 has decreased from 225 per 1,000 births in 1960 to 36 per 1,000 births in 2001; the infant mortality has decreased to 30 per 1,000 births. In 1991, the People's Congress passed the Young Citizen Protection Law, which specifies the purpose, principles, and responsibilities for the protection of children. In the same year, China signed The Convention on the Rights of the Child. In order to achieve the child protection goals an important government document was issued in 1992, titled "Chinese Children Development Guideline in the 1990s." The document made children a top priority. Ten specific goals for child survival, protection, development, and education were established. In 2001, the State Council Women and Children Commission declared that almost all the goals proposed in that guideline have been reached. A new Chinese Children Development Guideline for 2001–2010 has just been released, which proposes specific goals and implementation strategies in four areas: health, education, legal protection, and the environment.

However, changing people's perspective on children's rights in family life has been relatively slow, particularly in rural areas. Family planning policy may have made a positive change for children's position in the family. Because of the pressure of population growth on the nation, the government initially encouraged and then (starting in 1979) enforced the policy of one child per family. As a result, over 90 percent of families in urban areas today have only one child. Needless to say, the only child in the family has been able to receive more care and have a better education. Parents invest more money and time in their only child's health and education. In the family, the only child experiences the situation called "4-2-1 Syndrome," four grandparents and two parents give their love and attention to the single child. One result has been overprotection and not enough discipline for the child in some families. It is also possible that the change in children's position within the family may be reflected more in the distribution of attention and resources to the child, and not so much in respect for the child's rights. For example, parents and grandparents usually have very high expectations for the child's academic achievements. Many children in the urban areas are now expected to take extracurricular classes at an early age, such as English, computer, music, and visual arts. These children and their parents are often busy during the weekends, running from one training class to the other. In many cases, children's own interests and choices are not considered and respected.

The Purposes of Early Childhood Education Policies

The Ministry of Education, the Ministry of Health, and the National Women's Federation play important roles in formulating the national policies for the development and education of young children. The purposes of the policies are to (1) protect young children and mothers by improving their living conditions and the quality of service; (2) set up the national program and curriculum standard and to improve the quality of early childhood education; (3) coordinate the administration and management for early childhood education programs between different social sectors at the national, provincial, and local government levels; (4) improve teacher training and professional development system; (5) provide better support and child-care service to families and parents; and (6) provide support for the development of the early childhood education program in undeveloped areas.

Extent of Provision

Up to 3 years of age, the majority of Chinese children are usually cared for at home by grandparents, other relatives, or a hired nanny. In some cases, if family resources allow, the mother may quit her job for a few years to take care of the child. Before the mid-1990s, many workplaces provided child-care services for their workers. Many mothers returned to work after sixty days of maternal leave (the current policy allows for at least ninety days of paid maternal leave) and left their child in the on-site program. However, in recent years the number of employer-based services has been decreasing, because many state owned businesses have been sold to private individuals, resulting in closure of some of the child-care services. In urban areas, at the age of $1^1/_2$, some children go to kindergartens that provide toddler programs, while others go to private home day care. A high percentage of children stay home until age 3. In some urban areas these children may go to early childhood education centers or stations for some parent–child educational activities. The percentage of children who enroll in regular education programs for children before three in urban areas is usually less than 20 percent. The early childhood education service for children aged 0–3 is not available in rural areas.

At the age of 3, the majority of the children in urban areas attend kindergartens for three years of early childhood education. Most of these programs provide full-day services and some also provide a boarding program. In urban areas the percentage of the children enrolled in early childhood programs is over 90 percent, while in rural areas it is only 39 percent. In 2002 there were 11.2 million kindergartens in China, serving 20.36 million children.

Program Types

The most popular type of kindergarten program is called *You Er Yuan*. This is usually a full-day program for children aged 3–6, or in some areas age 5 only and age 6 only. The school day lasts from 7:30 AM to 5:00 PM Children either have one meal and two snacks or three meals and two snacks in the center each day. Parents are responsible for paying the cost of the food. In recent years, the service of boarding kindergarten (overnight accommodations) has been welcomed by some busy working parents in urban areas. Half-day programs are rare. The children in this kindergarten program are usually grouped by age, although mixed age grouping does exist. Teachers who work in kindergartens are required to have at least three years of professional training.

An independent early childhood education institute for children below the age of 3 is another type of program called *Tuo Er Suo*. This is an infant nursery that usually provides full-day service. The operation of these nurseries is the same as that of kindergartens and may be partially funded by the government, workplaces, or individuals. In recent years, this type of program has been integrated into kindergarten programs in some urban areas. Teacher qualification in these programs is usually not as good as that of kindergartens.

A third type of program that has emerged recently is called *Zao Jiao Zhong Xin*. This is an early childhood education center. These centers also provide services for children below the age of 3. Financially supported by local governments or other resources, these centers usually provide free or hourly rate education programs such as teacher-directed activities for infants and toddlers, or parent–child activities. Some of these centers are independently built and others are affiliated with regular kindergartens. In either case, the teachers in regular kindergartens play an important role in providing the service. These centers may have some branches called early childhood education stations, which are located in local communities. An informal child-care service for children before the age of 3 is the private home care, which is provided by individual families. This kind of service usually has a flexible schedule and the payment can be negotiated.

Supply and Access

A great gap still exists between urban and rural areas in terms of children's survival and development. Millions of young children continue to need help in obtaining nutritional foods and basic care. Because of the rapid urbanization in the recent years, many farmers have moved into urban areas to find jobs. Some of these workers bring their children with them, but most leave their children in the care of their grandparents or other relatives. In either case, the care and the education for these children have been a great problem. Migrant children may not be able to go to local child-care programs because their parents cannot afford such services. These children may be brought to their parents' worksite and often cause a safety problem. Children who are left behind with relatives may have more emotional and discipline problems in addition to the lack of parental protection. The number of the children affected by HIV/AIDS has also been increasing in some areas in the recent years. In some urban areas the government has been adopting special policies to help these children and their parents.

Financing

Before the mid-1990s, a high percentage of early childhood education programs in China were partially publicly funded, and some were partially supported by workplaces. In either case, parents shared about 40 percent of the cost. However, in the last ten years, the number of public or work site funded kindergartens has been decreasing. In many areas, some of these kindergartens have been sold to private organizations or individuals to become private education programs. In some of these private kindergartens the cost to parents has increased, while the quality of the education has not risen. The number of private early childhood education programs has been increasing steadily in the past ten years and the monitoring of the quality for these programs has been a challenge for local governments.

Further Readings: In Chinese: Chinese Preschool Education Research Association (1999). *The collection of important government documents of the People's Republic of China on early education.* Beijing: Beijing Normal University Press; Ministry of Education (2003). *Early childhood education programs. Yearbook of China Education.* Beijing: People's Education Press; National Women Federation (2001). *Chinese children development guideline, 2001–2010,* issued by the State Council; Preschool Education Research Association, ed. (2003). *The century Chinese preschool education: 1903–2003.* Beijing: Educational Science Press.

Web Site: China at a Glance. Available online at http://www.worldbank.org.cn/.

Xin Zhou

Family and Early Childhood Education in China

China is a country that devotes much attention to the functioning and responsibility of the family. Rearing children is a very important issue for Chinese families. The concepts of "carrying on the ancestral line" and "having offspring as a provider for old age" are characteristics intrinsically linked to Chinese culture and are still valued by most Chinese families today. Chinese families, including parents and grandparents, both in rural and urban areas, would spend all they have and do all they could for their children. Families try the best they can to provide support for their children's care and education.

The Historical Context

Although the earliest history regarding the cooperation between the family and early childhood education programs may trace back to 1904 when the Qing Dynasty issued the first regulations related to early childhood education programs, the progress in parents' involvement in children's educational programs has been slow. Historically, it has been the teacher's duty to communicate with parents about their child's progress in early childhood programs, also known as kindergartens. Teachers held conferences or conducted home visits. However, the program usually treated parents as the receiver of the service or of parent education. Parents believed that once their child was sent to a program, the task of educating children was mainly the teacher's responsibility.

This situation has been changing in the recent years, and there are several reasons for this change. First, the national government and organizations issued a series of documents regarding the issue of parent involvement, including the following:

1) Kindergarten Operation Regulations, issued by the Ministry of Education in 1989. This document devoted a separate chapter to outlining the requirements for the cooperation between the family and the program.
2) China Child Development Outline in the 1990s, issued by the Chinese National Women's Federation, set a goal for family education. This goal stated that at the beginning of the twenty-first century, 90 percent of the parents who have children under the age of 14 should be able to obtain basic knowledge about child development and care.
3) The national curriculum standard titled "Kindergarten Education Guidelines" issued by the Ministry of Education in 2001 proposed for the first time that respect, equality, and cooperation should be the principle for working with parents.
4) In the document of Innovation in the Primary Education in 2003, the national government established a law and policies for family education. In this innovation, the parent's important role in family education was pinpointed through the cooperation of the family and the school. The government promised to help to bring coordination between the school and the family into play.
5) Regulations issued by some provincial and local governments have also promoted the change. These regulations propose that parents have the right, as well as the duty, to become involved in their child's kindergarten education. Parents have the right to know the education program the kindergarten provides, including the policies, the management of the center, the curriculum goals and the implementation of the curriculum.

A second contributing factor has been the program evaluation of kindergartens that began in the early 1990s, which has emphasized cooperation between the family and the program as an important quality indicator and supported the idea that kindergartens should take a more active role in involving parents. Still another important reason for the change is that many parents with only one child have little experience in child rearing, and may feel the need to seek professional help. The kindergarten is a natural place for parents to communicate with trained professionals, or with each other, to obtain information on child care and/or education. Chinese parents' education has improved in the recent years, particularly in urban areas. Educated urban parents are taking a more active role in their children's education.

The Current Status of Family and Program Cooperation

Cooperation between the family and the kindergarten includes the following different strategies:

1) At the beginning of each semester, the kindergarten and parent may work together to discuss a plan for the semester. In general, this may start with the parents' proposals for the kinds of activities they wish the kindergarten could organize. The parents' proposals may generate discussion between the kindergarten and the

parents. Finally a detailed schedule is created for the semester, detailing the time, activities, and support the parents need to provide.

2) The regular information exchange between the teacher and the family includes the following:
   • Parents' conference, which is held once or twice a semester;
   • Family–kindergarten contact notebook, which is used once a week by either the teacher or the parent to leave messages for each other;
   • A family–kindergarten contact board, where parents may find a message from the teacher or leave a message, where children and their parents' photographs may show parent's involvement in the program, etc;
   • Some kindergartens in urban areas may also develop websites where they can develop a special section for parents or family education. The section could include more information on issues in which parents may have an interest;
   • Home visiting or telephone contacts are also used;
   • Short conversations take place when parents send or pick up their children in the kindergarten.

3) Parents are often involved in the educational process by collecting and contributing materials for children's learning; for instance, making tools or toys, demonstrating their professional skills to children, participating in field trips.

4) Some educational programs or trainings on special topics may be provided for parents.

5) Kindergartens may have special strategies for cooperation with parents who have children with special needs. For example, for children who have autism or are handicapped with cerebral palsy, it would be helpful if the kindergarten would keep in regular contact with their parents. Regular communication would facilitate discussion and educational strategies for the child. Additionally, for children who are from religious families or have special diets, the program would cooperate with their parents and have special arrangements for foods and activities that are adapted to their cultures and special customs.

There are various organizations involved in the issue of cooperation between the family and the program, including the following:

1) The Parent Committee, which is organized at the program level. This committee is responsible for the monitoring of the program as well as the organization of parents' involvement in activities.

2) The Community Education Coordinating Committee, which is organized at the community level in some urban areas, consisting of parents and community workers. This committee works to provide help in connecting families to programs. For example, the committee can help parents identify children who need special assistance and make arrangements with appropriate programs or supporting organizations.

3) The National Family Education Association and Early Childhood Education Research Association. Both of these national organizations have a branch on family and program cooperation (including the affiliating association at the provincial level). The organizations consist mainly of teachers, education researchers, administrators, women workers, and others. The work of these associations is to probe into the problems of family and kindergarten education.

Problems and Challenges

As regards the position of the family and the kindergarten in their cooperation, both parties firmly believe that the kindergarten should take a leadership role in the cooperation and that it has a responsibility to direct and help parents with their special training and skills. Kindergartens usually do take an active role in the cooperation between the parent and the program and this situation may easily lead to the neglect of parents' equal partnership and equal rights. In some areas, parents may be given no right to choose programs for their children, to know important relevant facts about the programs, or to negotiate with kindergartens on issues concerning their children. For instance, in some kindergartens, whether the parents like it or not, they are required to participate in certain extracurricular activities. Therefore, the challenge in facilitating cooperation between the family and kindergarten is not only in finding the strategies to encourage parents to be actively involved in their children's education, but also in developing ways to protect parents' rights in this potentially unequal relationship.

Further Readings: In Chinese: Beijing Educational Committee (2000). Education guidelines for early childhood education in Beijing; Beijing Government Documents (1996–2000). Family education programs for young children in Beijing; Ministry of Education (2003). Early childhood education programs. Yearbook of China Education. Beijing: People's Education Press; Preschool Education Research Association, ed. (2003). *The century Chinese preschool education: 1903–2003.* Beijing: Educational Science Press.

Web Site: (in Chinese): Chinese Education Research Network: http://www.chinaeducationresearchnetwork.

Lan Gao

Early Childhood Program Quality

Quality in early childhood education may be defined at two levels, the system level and the program level. Current discussion of quality in early childhood education in the Chinese context mainly focuses on quality at the program level, although professionals in the field do believe that the quality at the system level has significant impact on the quality at the program level. In the last five decades, the central government has made important contributions to the quality in early childhood education programs by setting up a quality framework, making program regulations and curriculum guidelines, and improving the training and the status of staff. The provincial and local government is responsible for the monitoring of program quality. The evaluation of the program in most locations mainly focuses on kindergarten, the program for the children aged 3–6, and in some locations on the program for children aged $1^1/_2 - 6$.

National Regulations for Program Quality in Early Childhood Education

The central government has played an important role in the regulating of the quality of early childhood education programs over the last five decades. The national regulations have evolved through several versions over time.

Starting in the 1950s, the Ministry of Education has issued several versions of program quality regulations. The earliest effort in establishing the regulation for the quality in early childhood education programs was issued by the Ministry of Education in 1952. Titled *Kindergarten Provisional Guidelines,* this document was produced with the help of former Soviet Union early childhood education experts. The regulation was composed of eight chapters and forty-three items: The purpose of the program and educational goals; years of provision; leadership and administrations; care and educational principles and curriculum content, enrollment, group size, adult–child ratio and staffing; financing, physical environment and facilities, etc.

The second version of this regulation came out in 1979, titled *Urban Kindergarten Provisional Regulation.* Comparing to the first version, this regulation gave less attention to overall organizational issues such as finance, leadership, and administration, since these issues had been well settled in the program by that time. However, the discussion of curriculum was expanded from one chapter to three chapters. Play appeared for the first time in the regulation and was treated as children's fundamental activity and an important means in the education of children. The encouragement of children's autonomy and creativity in play was emphasized.

The third version of this regulation, issued in 1989 and titled *Kindergarten Operation Regulations (Initial Version),* clearly specified for the first time the purpose of the regulation as to raise the quality of center-based child care and education. Three years of teacher training or similar qualifications were required for working in early childhood education programs. The qualifications for other staff were also proposed. More specific regulations were made regarding finance, expenditure, and parent's payment management. A separate chapter was devoted to program–family cooperation. This version of Kindergarten Operation Regulations was finalized in 1996 with minor modifications: the respect and protection of children from abuse, discrimination, physical punishment, and other behavior that is harmful to children was emphasized.

National Curriculum Guideline

The first National Curriculum Guideline came out in 1981, with three main components: (1) Educational goals and children's developmental characteristics; (2) curriculum areas and objectives; (3) teaching strategies and important issues The eight learning areas were: life skills and habits, physical exercises, moral education, language, science, mathematics, music, visual art. The objectives for these areas were specified for three age-groups in a program.

In the same year, the Ministry of Health also issued the National Care and Education Guideline for Children under Three. The guideline includes (1) The principles for the care and education of children under 3; (2) infant and toddler neuropsychological development milestones; (3) education in the daily routine; (4) infant and toddler language development; (5) infant and toddler motor development; (6) infant and toddler cognitive development; (7) infant and toddler interaction with adults and peers; and (8) teacher-directed activities for infants and toddlers. Education goals and teaching strategies were included within each learning area in the document.

The second National Curriculum Guideline was issued in 2001. (see the curriculum entry below for details). This guideline has been thought of as an important milestone for the reform of early childhood education, since the guideline reflects important changes in the understanding of the importance of education for young children, and in recognizing the place of children in the process of education in Chinese early childhood education history. One important change is that early childhood education has been treated as an important component of the basic education system in the nation, a foundation phase for formal schooling and the system of lifelong education. Another important change is that the child is treated as an independent person and an active participant in the process of education. Children's rights in play, education and development, children's needs, interests, and autonomy should be respected.

National Program Hygiene and Health Regulations

These regulations first came out in 1980, produced by the Ministry of Health and the Ministry of Education. In 1985 the regulation was revised and issued by the Ministry of Health. The regulation includes daily routines; food preparation; physical exercise; health checks for children and staff; hygiene and disinfection; disease prevention and safety.

National Regulation on Group Size and Staffing

The Ministry of Education issued a regulation for group size and staffing in full-day programs and boarding schools in 1987. Child programs in China are generally grouped by age, although mixed age classes do exist. Three age-groups were specified. the junior class (3–4 years old), middle class (4–5 years old) and the senior class (5–6 years old). The group size for each age should range from 20–25, 26–30, and 30–35 respectively. For each class, staffing is to include 2–2.5 teachers and 0.8–1 teacher assistants. The overall adult–child ratio is 1:6–1: 7 for a full-day program, 1:4–1: 5 for a boarding school.

In 1996, the National Regulations for the Qualification of Program Directors was issued. Directors are required to have at least three years of professional training, two to three years of child-center working experience and a title of first class teacher. The responsibilities of a director and the posting requirements are also specified.

Program Physical Design Regulation

The Program Architectural Design Regulation was issued by the Ministry of Environment Protection and the Ministry of Education in 1987. It proposed standards for the location, amount of inside and outside space, the room space required for different functions, such as classroom, bedroom, restroom, kitchen, etc.; the structure and quality of the building structure (availability of sunlight, lighting, sound insulation, water supply system, room temperature and air quality, electricity facilities). The space required for a classroom must be no less than 60 m^2, and the calculation formula for the space of the playground in a center is $M^2 = 180 + 20 (N - 1)$, where $N =$ the number of the classes in the program).

The Quality Control and Monitoring System

The quality of a program is monitored by provincial/city governments. The monitoring system includes two components: (1)inspector system; (2) program evaluation and ranking system. The inspector system has been set up by the Ministry of Education and organized by the provincial education committee. The professional and visiting inspectors in each city are supposed to inspect all programs once in a cycle of three years. The inspector group is usually composed of local teaching and research coordinators, center directors, experienced teachers, or other early childhood education professionals. Trainings are usually provided for the participating inspectors before the inspection visit.

The program evaluation and ranking system in most of the provinces was started in early 1990s. The evaluation is operated by the provincial and city education committee and under the leadership of the Office of Educational Monitoring and Guidance in the provincial and city education committee. Each province has developed a program quality standard and evaluation indicators based on the regulations issued by the central government and the local economic situation. Local standards, or lower quality standards may be set up by the local governments. Program quality is monitored more regularly in urban than in rural areas. In some rural areas the program may have never been evaluated at all. The most challenging quality issue in these areas is the lack of qualified teachers and physical environments that may not be able to meet the minimum requirement for children's safety and health.

The provincial quality standard is usually composed of the following indicators:

1. Physical environments and facilities, which include overall center space, classroom space, playground space, surrounding environment, classroom and playground facilities, teaching and learning materials.
2. Staff qualifications and professional development, which includes qualifications and position requirements for all staff members, adult–child ratio, teacher in-service training.
3. Program administration and management, which includes center size, group size, staff recruitment, program goals and department objectives, the establishing of program administration committee and staff participating in center policy decisions, program management regulation, rules and position responsibilities, program and department working plan and final report, regular evaluation, records keeping, finance management, the center's cooperation with the family and community.
4. Child care and education, which includes the establishing of children's records, regular health checking and disease prevention, hygiene and disinfection, safety, nutrition, daily routine, curriculum goals, content, organization, setting and learning materials, teacher-child interaction, child development outcomes, research projects and publications.

For the assessment of child development outcomes, children are observed in the classroom for their physical and emotional development, social interaction, initiative, curiosity and learning interests, and self-help skills and habits. The evaluation is not compulsory and the program must apply in advance for the evaluation. The procedure of the evaluation starts from the program's self-study of the evaluation indicators. After the self-study and self-improvement, the program applies to local education commission for the evaluation site visit. The evaluation group is usually composed of six to eight professionals including city and district administrators, teaching and research coordinators, experienced center directors, and teachers. The site visit usually takes two to three days. The program quality evaluation results in a total score and a ranking system. The ranking system is usually organized as follows: Provincial/city demonstration program, provincial/city first class program, provincial/city second class program, etc. Based on the score of the evaluation, the program is awarded a rank for the quality of the center. Centers with a higher rank can set a higher fee to be paid by parents for children's enrollment. The programs that received a ranking need to be reevaluated in two to three years. At present, data are not available for the percentage of the programs in different ranks.

Current Issues and Challenges

The importance of the quality at the system level needs to be emphasized. Universal and equitable access to education for all children has been a common goal for all the nations in the world. China has been making such an effort in the sector of compulsory education, but not yet in early childhood education. In the past decades, the early childhood programs in urban areas received more government financial support than did the programs in rural areas. In rural areas, both the quantity and the quality of the program have lagged behind and there are no programs at all in some remote and undeveloped areas. Education equity in early childhood education is a great challenge for the nation.

Another problem is that research on program evaluation is rare. Longitudinal studies are needed in identifying important contributors to the quality of an early childhood program, so the research information can be used as a solid base for the development of government policies, regulations, and the establishment of quality indicators. Child assessment measures and program observation scales need to be developed; efforts have been made in adapting some measures (such as the measure similar to ECERS) into the Chinese context.

Although the overall adult–child ratio in many programs is as high as 1:6, the actual adult–child ratio in the classroom is quite low. This is due to the substantial number of the adults who do not actually work in the classroom, and the fact that the three adults assigned to a class sometimes cannot all be present in the classroom for the whole day. The actual adult–child ratio may be as low as 1:30 at certain times during the day. This is a quality problem we need to solve.

Further Readings: Chinese Preschool Education Research Association (1999). *The collection of important government documents of the People's Republic of China on early education.* Beijing: Beijing Normal University Press; Jiangsu Education Commission (1996). *Indicators for the evaluation of a modern kindergarten*; Preschool Education Research Association, ed. (2003). *The century Chinese preschool education: 1903–2003.* Beijing: Educational Science Press.

Xin Zhou

Curriculum in Chinese Preschool Education

Introduction

Preschool education in China refers to the education for children from 3 to 6 (or 7) years of age, although in recent years it has been extended to include the education for children before age 3. Preschool education is considered an integral part of the basic education and the foundation for children's later school education, but it is not a part of compulsory education. The institute that provides education and care to young children for this age period in China is called *You Er Yuan* (kindergarten). (The English translation of both *You Zhi Yuan* [see below] and *You Er Yuan* is kindergarten. The term *You Zhi Yuan* was changed to *You Er Yuan* when the Communist Party took power in 1949.) The 2002 statistics indicate that there were 118,000 kindergartens nationwide with a total enrollment of 20,360,000 children.

The Social Historical Context and Early Education Curriculum Development

In 2003, China celebrated the one-hundredth anniversary of the first Chinese educational institute for young children. During the economic reform in the late Qing Dynasty, the first institute for young children was opened within an elementary school in Wu Chang in "Guang Xu Year of Twenty-nine" (1903 A.D.), called *Mong Yang Yuan*, meaning a public place where children were enlightened and cared for. In the same year, the provincial official Zhang Zhi-Dong, under whose jurisdiction the first *Mong Yang Yuan* was established, proposed the "Statute of Mong Yang Yuan and Family Education," which was made official by the Emperor Guang Xu in 1904. The first public establishment of an educational institute for young children, and the first relevant statute signified the beginning of a specialized education for the youngest age-group of its citizens in China. Before then, young children were cared for and sometimes educated at home. The development of Chinese early education and curriculum over the past century can be viewed in three periods.

Chinese curriculum: 1903–1918. The first period was from 1903 to 1918, during which the first early education institute, Mong Yang Yuan; was established and the first government statute was issued by the Qing Dynasty government. Although the initial Mong Yang Yuan adopted a Japanese model, including hiring teachers from Japan, the Statute of Mong Yang Yuan and Family Education specified Mong Yang Yuan to be housed in the social welfare institute for widows and the trained widows to serve as staff. After the Republic of China was established in 1911, the Education Ministry of the transitioning government issued another statute that included Mong Yang Yuan in the nation's education system, but it did not grant it independent education institute status. Mong Yang Yuan was affiliated within the women's normal school, or normal college instead of a social welfare institute. The curriculum included the following:
• Conversation on social conventions and physical objects
• Behavior and manners

- Reading
- Arithmetic
- Manual skills using Friedrich **Froebel**-inspired teaching materials
- Music and song
- Play

Chinese curriculum: 1919–1949. The second period was from 1919 to 1949. During these thirty years, China went through two civil wars (1927 to 1937 and 1946 to 1949), and the Second World War (1937–1945). Besides its war resisting Japan's invasion, China endured constant political struggles and military conflicts between the Communist Party and the Nationalist Party. During this period, the majority of China was under the government lead by the Nationalists, along with regions gradually lost to Japan's invasion, and some regions lost to the Communists.

A "School System Reform Plan" was issued as an education reform order in 1912. It abandoned the Japanese model and adopted the model from the United States for the nation's school system, called the "Six (elementary years)-Three (Junior High years)-Three (High School years)" system. The reform order started to use the name *You Zhi Yuan* (kindergarten) for children under 6, which was defined as an independent education institute for the first time in the Chinese history. The Ministry of Education enacted the first "You Zhi Yuan Regulations" in 1939 (revised in 1943) that defined specific goals for kindergarten education. The Ministry of Education also issued and revised the "Kindergarten Curriculum Standard" between 1932 and 1936. The Standard stated four education goals for children under 6 were as follows:

1. Promote children's physical and mental health.
2. Strive for the happiness children deserve.
3. Foster basic good habits for life including both physical and behavioral domains.
4. Support families in raising young children, and seek improvement in family education.

The curriculum standard described the curriculum content and the minimum objectives to be achieved in the following areas: music, story and rhyme, play, social knowledge, work, and rest.

During this second period various curriculum models were developed. For example, a kindergarten founded by Chen He-Qing, who studied John **Dewey** in the United States, developed a curriculum that based its content on the natural and social environment of young children. He implemented a "Wholeness Pedagogy" that included five kinds of activities: health, social, science, arts, and language. The contents in the five areas were organized in "units" based on the nature and society. Another curriculum model, the "Action Curriculum" was developed by Zhang Xue Men. Zhang believed that curriculum was experience, and the curriculum was to prepare the experience children liked and were capable of doing. The curriculum models during that time were influenced by the Western educators such as Froebel, Maria **Montessori**, and Dewey. Nevertheless, they were also intentional experiments and explorations of developing education models appropriate for Chinese children.

During the same period, some regions of China were under the Communist Party and its army's control. Although the material conditions for these regions were scarce, there were boarding child-care centers organized for children whose parents fought in the wars. Many of these child-care agencies, called *Bao Yu Yuan* (A place of protection and education), became famous kindergartens after 1949 when they moved to the big cities.

Chinese curriculum 1950–1954. The third period started in 1950 right after the Chinese Communist Party became the governing power in the nation. Between 1951 and 1954, several important government regulations and curriculum outlines regarding *You Er Yuan* (kindergarten) were enacted. They included the "Kindergarten Provisional Regulation," the "Kindergarten Provisional Teaching Outline," and "the Kindergarten Education Guide (Initial Version)." These documents clearly defined the goals, content, and principles of the preschool education. They went on to describe the age characteristics and educational focus for each of the three age classes: the junior class (3–4 years old), middle class (4–5 years old), and the senior class (5–6 years old). The Teaching Outline specifically defined the teaching plans for different classes such as weekly lessons and the number of assignments in each of the six subject areas. It also laid out the daily schedules for half-day and all-day programs. The six subject areas were physical education, language, knowing the environment, arts and crafts, music, and arithmetic. The lengths of lessons for each age-group were also specified, from fifteen minutes per session for the junior class to twenty-five minutes for the senior class. The Teaching Outline emphasized that education for young children should pay attention to their age characteristics, and that teaching needed to be systematic. These documents were developed under the theories and direct guide of educators from the Soviet Union. The changes in the curriculum content and pedagogy model comparing to those before 1949 reflected these influences. The governmental statutes set up a national curriculum model with clearly defined educational objectives, content, and pedagogy. The Ministry of Education and the central government not only enacted the regulation and the curriculum outline, they enforced the implementation nationwide as well. Over the next thirty years, until the 1980s, Chinese preschool education became an established system with a unified program setup and curriculum model. The number of kindergartens increased from 1,300 centers with a total enrollment of 130,000 children in 1949, to 170,400 centers enrolling a total of 11,507,700 children in 1980. It should be mentioned that from 1966 to 1976, the regular preschool education and curriculum development were interrupted because of the political chaos caused by the "Cultural Revolution," which affected every aspect of the Chinese society.

In sum, the development of the first eighty years of Chinese preschool education and its curricula were intertwined with economic reform and social changes. Despite political struggles and wars, the Chinese government and educators strived to establish and develop specialized education for its young citizens. The curriculum content and pedagogy integrated theoretical and practical influences from the outside world, especially from American progressive education and education in the Soviet Union.

The Current Curriculum Status: Reform in Progress

The Chinese preschool education curriculum has been undergoing changes since the 1980s as a part of education reform related to the national economic reform. The milestones are two important government regulations: Kindergarten Operation Regulations by the National Education Commission, (third version in 1989 and revised in 1996), and Kindergarten Education Guideline (Provisional) by the Ministry of Education in 2001. The former defines the national program standards for kindergarten; the latter defines the national curriculum standards.

Current curriculum guidelines. The current curriculum guideline has four sections: Preamble, Education Content and Requirements, Organization and Implementation, and Education Evaluation. It states that kindergarten education is an important component of the basic education, and the foundation for a child's later school experiences and lifelong education. It requires kindergarten to serve the following functions: create the best conditions for children's development in co-operation with the families, communities, and elementary schools; provide young children with a rich environment and experience that meets their needs; follow the natural laws of development and learning of young children using play as the basic activity media; and provide both education and care. In the preamble it states for the first time that kindergarten should respect children's integrity and rights.

There are five curriculum domains: Health, Language, Society, Science, and Arts. Each domain contains the objectives, content and requirements, and key guiding points. For example, in the section of Language, the following five objectives are described:

1) Be willing to converse with people, in the proper manner.
2) Listen and be attentive in a conversation, and understand daily usage of the language
3) Be able to express oneself clearly
4) Be interested in listening to stories and reading picture books
5) Be able to speak and understand mandarin.

In the "content and requirements," the Guideline further elaborates the content needed to achieve the objectives. For example, one item states, "Provide a mandarin language environment. Help children become familiar, understanding and speaking mandarin. Children in the minority regions should be helped to learn their ethnic language as well." Under Language, the "key guiding points" describe concepts from the language development perspective to guide the curriculum planning. For example, "Young children's language develops in close relationships with their development of emotional, experiential, thinking and social interactive competences. Therefore, language development should be integrated into other domains of education in order to enrich children's experience, so as to create conditions that promote language development."

The Organization and Implementation section describes underlying principles of curriculum implementation. For example, in the item "The selection of education content," it provides three "principles" in addition to what is stated in the Content section. The principles assert that the content should "Be appropriate to the children's current level, yet challenging; meet the children's current needs, yet promote long-term development; related to the children's immediate life experience and interest, yet help them to expand their experience and knowing." The section also describes the principles of organizing the daily schedule, working with families, and access to community resources.

The Education Evaluation section provides the underlying principles rather than concrete evaluation approaches and instruments. For example, item 7 states the key criteria for evaluation. They are: whether the education plan and the activity objectives are based on an understanding of the children currently enrolled; whether the content, method, strategy, and environmental setting motivate children to learn; whether the educational process provides the children with useful learning experiences and is appropriate to their developmental needs; whether the content and requirements pay attention to individual needs as well as group needs so every child feels successful and develops; whether the teacher's guidance promotes children's active and effective learning.

The current national education guideline. The current national education guideline reflects a drastic shift in the government's point of view, especially in terms of the focus of education, the curriculum content, and implementation. The guideline no longer prescribes specific weekly plans and "assignments" for each of the curriculum subject areas. It pays more attention to the areas of development rather than knowledge and skills in subject areas. Children and their developmental needs are acknowledged and serve as the base for curriculum planning. However, the current guideline only provides overall education objectives and general principles. It expects the local governments to further develop their interpretations and guides, and the individual kindergartens to decide their own curriculum under the guiding principles.

Flexibility in curriculum. The general curriculum guidelines defined by the government leave a great deal of flexibility for kindergartens in different regions, cities, and communities to develop a curriculum that fits the children they serve. There has been a great variety in ways individual kindergartens develop and implement curriculum. Meanwhile, a growing number of curriculum resources have been published. Many of these resources may be titled as a specific curriculum, for example, "Constructive Curriculum," and the activities in different curriculum books may overlap.

Another factor that contributed to the emergence of a great variety of curriculum models is the allowance of privately owned kindergartens as part of the economic reform under way since the late 1980s. Some kindergartens adopted curriculum models such as Montessori, models based on the Multiple Intelligences, etc. There is a greater autonomy for individual kindergartens, especially those privately owned to create their own curriculum model, as long as it complies with the governmental regulations and guidelines.

Current Issues and Challenges

The recent education reform and new governmental statutes brought opportunities for the development of the Chinese preschool curriculum. It brought challenges as well. Individual kindergartens and teachers who used to operate under a clearly and specifically prescribed curriculum can feel lost when they are expected to develop their own curriculum following abstract principles. The teachers and school administrators are not equipped in their knowledge and skill to undertake such a task without extensive professional development. One trend is to encourage individual kindergartens to develop a "kindergarten-based curriculum." However, what this means is not clear either theoretically or in practical terms. The focus on children's developmental needs rather than subject knowledge learning indicates a shift toward child-centeredness in the preschool curriculum. Yet parents and the teachers are concerned about how well the children are prepared when they go to elementary school since it is common that elementary schools expect the children to be prepared academically. Furthermore, many concepts and theories that originated in Western cultures have been introduced into the field of Chinese preschool education as resources for the ongoing reform. How such contemporary thinking and practices are examined in their own contexts, how they are authentically interpreted and adapted, but not copied into the Chinese culture, remains a challenge.

Further Readings: In Chinese: Ministry of Education (2002). Kindergarten education guideline. In The Basic Education Division of The Ministry of Education, ed., *The interpretation of kindergarten education guideline (provisional)*. Nanjing: Jiangsu Education Press; National Education Commission (1996). The kindergarten operation regulation. In Chinese Preschool Education Research Association (1999). *The collection of important government documents of the People's Republic of China on early education*. Beijing: Beijing Normal University Press; Preschool Education Research Association, cd. (2003). *The century of Chinese preschool education: 1903–2003*. Beijing: Educational Science Press; Zhu, J. (2003). *Kindergarten curriculum*. Shanghai: East China Normal University Press.

Wei Li-Chen

Play in the Chinese Context

Play is an important process that differentiates preschool education from primary school education. In China, play is regarded as the activity in which children may make fun freely. While playing, children are usually joyful, excited, and roused. They are absorbed in the imagined situation, with rapt attention, initiative, and creativity brought into full play. It is so often that young children want to put off mealtime again and again in order to continue playing, and even finally end up in sleeping beside their toys. So it is evident that play has great charm to children. They are immersed in the freedom and happiness of play and just play for play, without other aims, without considering other things (for example, reality, reward, or a particular reason to play, etc.). Play is the most important thing in children's lives, and makes a decisive contribution to children's physical and psychological development.

The Value of Play for Children's Development

Play meets children's needs for physical activity, cognitive activity, and social interaction. Children will continuously repeat all kinds of body movements such as running and jumping in play, thus the blood circulation and the development of bone and muscle can be promoted, and the needs of physical movement can be met. By playing with peers, children may accumulate the experience of social interaction; learn to solve problems by means of declining modestly, discussion, cooperation, or taking turns. They can also undergo different feelings, such as happiness, delight, sadness, or frustration, thus their emotional and social development can be promoted.

The surveys we have done indicate that the children with problems in personality and social development are usually those who are not interested in play or don't know how to play. Researchers and educators have increasingly paid attention to the value of play in children's healthy mental development. Various kinds of toys (blocks, ball, Chinese chess, dolls, etc.) and materials (water, sand, paper, paint, etc.) used in play can bring children various perceptual stimulations and intellectual challenges, thus arousing their interest in exploration and their desire for knowledge. In the course of repeated play and explorations, their needs for cognitive development are met.

Children learn through play. It is very difficult to ask young children just to sit and listen in the class, but interesting and funny play can deeply engage them. In relaxing and free play, children may explore actively and find out things and phenomena in which they themselves are interested. Free play not only meets children's desire to play but also increases their ability to learn while playing. Play is the principle learning approach for preschool children, and also the most enjoyable one.

The Place of Play in the Early Childhood Education Curriculum

Although theoretically play is regarded as a valuable and important activity for children's development and learning by Chinese professionals, this may not be evident in the actual practices found in Chinese kindergartens. For some teachers, less value is attached to play than to teacher-directed teaching and learning activities. Although the Kindergarten Education Guideline (Provisional) issued by the Ministry of Education in 2001 makes clear that "Play is the basic activity in kindergarten", in actual classroom practice, we may see phenomena such as "lessons are more valued than play" and "teaching games with a set of teaching objectives are preferred to the free play initiated by children themselves."

In the current kindergarten curriculum, play is more likely to appear in the following three forms:

1. As a leisure, free activity separated from teaching and learning activities. In this way play is treated as a means to meet the needs of children's social and emotional development, but the value of play to children's cognitive development is neglected. In

such play, teachers do not provide much support or provide appropriate materials for learning.
2. In overlap with the learning of specific knowledge. Under this condition the playful element of play is neglected and children's interest in learning cannot be maintained. As a result, play and learning (work) stand in opposition to one another. The idea of using play to provide an attractive situation for children's learning is not bad, but the challenge is how to create a playful situation for children's learning.
3. In integration with learning. This is the most ideal situation. That is, children do need free play, but teachers can also find opportunities in free play to facilitate children's learning by providing materials or scaffolding. If play is used in children's learning activities, then play should be really fun and engaging and children should participate in play actively.

The Types of Play

The two main types of play in Chinese early childhood programs are free play and play with rules.

Free play. This is the kind of play where children enjoy the freedom and happiness in choosing and deciding what to play, how to play, and with whom to play. Types of free play generally include role-play, construction play, and acting play. Role-play is the kind of play where children imagine and pretend, taking their living experience as the source. Construction play aims at creating something by using different kinds of constructing materials. While in acting play, children usually act the roles that are from fairy tales or story plots. This kind of play and other similar play activities such as "acting with flannel pieces," "puppet play," and "shadow play with story characters" are popularly used in language and literature activities in Chinese early childhood education programs. In the context of free play teachers in kindergartens usually leave children an acting corner called a "little stage" where all kinds of stage props are available for children to use and take roles freely. During the whole course of acting, teachers don't intervene or even pay attention to the children.

Play with rules. The second type of play involves a game with rules, which usually requires the participation of a group of children. Teachers usually take advantage of such games to bring children's interest in learning into play, or just use this kind of game as a means to teach knowledge. Therefore these are also called teaching games, which include quiz games, music games, and sports games. Teaching games are often created by teachers to reach their teaching objectives. Each game consists of its objectives, steps, and, of course, rules. The quiz game combines the purpose of developing children's cognitive abilities with the fun of a game, which enables children to exercise their skills and develop their intelligence. Puzzle games, maze games, and riddles are the typical examples of a quiz game. The sports game is used to develop children's basic movements. Many originated as Chinese traditional folk games; for example, "Hawk Catch Chickens," "Throw Handkerchief," "Bake Sesame Seed Cakes" (all are chasing games with certain rules). A music game is used mainly to enhance children's musical perceptive ability, accompanied by music or songs.

The Organization of Play in Early Childhood Education Programs

The play environment in early childhood education programs includes two settings: indoors and outdoors. The outdoor play environment mainly includes some large equipment for children to climb on and play, a sand box, and in some centers a water pool. A place with a natural lawn or covered with cement or plastic boards is for children to run, jump, walk, or ride a bike. A certain amount of outdoor space containing basic safety measures is required by government regulation.

The indoor play environment includes the following several areas:

1. those usually set up in the classroom, such as the house area, block area, and art area;
2. in addition to the classroom, many kindergartens in urban areas have special rooms for specific kinds of play or activities, such as a chess playroom, computer room, or music activity room. Children in each class usually take turns to go to these activity rooms during the week;
3. vacant place in the sleeping room (for napping) is sometimes used as additional play space. Some activities may be set up there. Chinese teachers are also encouraged to make toys or help children to make toys with a variety of materials such as packing boxes, bottles of soft drinks, etc.

Generally speaking, the typical playtimes occur in several segments during the day.

1. One hour of morning exercise, when children mostly play some traditional folk sports games outside, such as ball games, rope skipping, walking on stilts, etc.;
2. Thirty to fifty minutes of free play after the circle time, when children choose freely the play area or materials they prefer. Role-play such as house or hospital are popular themes for children's play;
3. Thirty to fifty minutes of free play in the afternoon, after the nap and the snack, when small manipulative toys or games are usually provided. Outdoor play may also be provided later in the afternoon.

The teacher's role in children's play is mainly to support and facilitate. The extent to which teachers actually do facilitate children's play depends on their training and working experience with young children. Generally speaking, many teachers regard the observation of children's play as a very difficult task. Without an understanding of children's play behavior it is difficult to facilitate children's play in an appropriate way. Therefore, training in observation and facilitating skills for children's play should be emphasized in teacher training programs.

Ideally, the teacher's role in children's play can be basically described in the following way. Teachers need to observe children's play behavior carefully and try to identify their problems and needs through their play. They may join children's play by taking either the role of a teacher or one of the roles identified by the children in their play. Teachers may facilitate children's play by setting up or changing the play setting, through provision of materials, and by taking roles or providing direct modeling or suggestions.

Current Issues and Trends

Most of the studies of play that have been done in China are observational studies, most of which have provided descriptive reports on the characteristics of children's play activities. The unique value of play to children's development cannot be fully recognized as research methods are limited to descriptions.

The low position of play in the curriculum in some classrooms is embarrassing. The value of play to children's development has been accepted by most of the professionals in the field, yet in real practice that value has not been translated into teaching practice. The position of play in the curriculum has also been caught between parents' high expectations for children's academic learning and the teacher's desire to respect children's right to play. Frustrated by the contradiction between theory and the practice, researchers have found it perhaps not enough to limit study only to the field of play. Only by focusing on both play and the curriculum can we do the justice to the educational value of play in early childhood education programs.

Chinese researchers and educators have paid close attention to the following questions: how to make use of play effectively to facilitate children's development; how to arouse children's enthusiasm and initiative in the learning process; how to find the source of the curriculum from children's life and play; how to make the teaching and learning activity more joyful like play; and how to integrate play with children's learning and teaching activities. Many Chinese early childhood education professionals are convinced that early childhood education programs should not only facilitate children's development and learning, but also provide a happy life environment for young children's childhood.

Further Readings: In Chinese: Feng, X. X. (December 2004). The position of play in the reform of Chinese kindergarten curriculum. *A lecture in the Second National Conference on the Relationship between Play, Curriculum and Teaching.* Xiamen, Guangdong; Liu, Y. (2004). *Children's play: A fundamental theory.* Beijing: Beijing Normal University; Ministry of Education (2002). Kindergarten education guideline. In The Basic Education Division of The Ministry of Education, ed., *The interpretation of Kindergarten Education Guideline (Provisional).* Nanjing: Jiangsu Education Press.

Xueqin Qiu

Creativity, Music, and Visual Art Curricula in China

In China, research on young children's creativity started about twenty years ago. Before the mid-1980s, Chinese early childhood educators paid less attention to children's creativity, and much of their attention was on the training of skills. In art activities, teaching was focused on how to help children learn to make a product. It was not important whether children were developing creativity. However, this situation has been changing in the past two decades. Many educators have begun to pay attention to the development of children's creativity and its effects on the harmonious development of personality.

New Curriculum Goals in the Arts

The Kindergarten Education Guideline (Provisional) issued by the Chinese government in 2001 specified the goals of development of children's creativity in art education for young children. The guideline stated that creative artworks and art activities are significant ways for young children to express their emotions and show their cognitive abilities. Teachers should guide children to get in touch with the beautiful things in their lives and environments. With guidance, children can enrich their experiences and aesthetic perception. Teachers should support children's ways of expression that are rich in character and creation. They should provide chances for children to express themselves freely in their activities, and be encouraged to express their emotions, understandings, and imaginations bravely by using different art forms. Each child's ideas and creations should be respected. Their unique aesthetic feelings and ways to represent should be appreciated and accepted. Finally, the happiness children exhibit when they create should be shared. In practice, the Chinese art education curriculum generally includes two parts: music and visual art.

Music Curriculum in China

Music is an important part of the social and cultural life of human beings. It is also indispensable in the development, learning, and lives of young children. Music education has taken an important place in the 5000 years of education in China, especially in the history of early childhood education.

Beginnings of music education in china. In the Zhou dynasty (1006 B.C.–476 B.C.), the mastery of six arts was required for all ancient scholars. The six arts included: rituals, music, archery, charioteering, reading/writing, and arithmetic. Among these, rituals and music were the most important, because the ancient Chinese believed that music was the thing wise men liked, and music could guide people to be nice. It was also believed that people's hearts could be deeply touched and social customs transformed by music. Because of these beliefs, ancient empires set up a special institution for music education.

Changes in music education. In more contemporary times, the development of music education for young children was influenced by changes in people's values for music. From the 1920s to the 1970s, people understood music as a kind of skill that must be learned, and a method to convey ideas. Music education for young children was mainly concerned with how to help children receive musical education happily and effectively. This continues to be a part of China's goals in music education today.

The traditional music education in early childhood education programs generally included singing, moving to musical rhythms, moving to musical feelings, playing percussion instruments, and musical appreciation. The curriculum was carried out through these formal activities. Music education was also provided in less formal formats, such as sing-and-movement play or games.

Children were attracted by the musical activities and got involved in them happily. For example, a traditional children's game, "Drop the handkerchief" begins with all the children sitting in a circle and singing. One child walks around the circle and drops a handkerchief anonymously behind a sitting child. The sitting child must notice the handkerchief, pick it up, and catch the circling child before he or she makes an entire lap and reaches the sitting child's place again. If sitting child does not reach the circling child, the sitting child will have to change roles and begin circling.

New trends. During the 1980s and 1990s, while the traditions described above were still practiced, the educators started to pay more attention to the effect of music education on children's musical and creative ability. This new trend was the result of the impact from many western philosophical, educational, and psychological theories introduced in 1980s. The early childhood music education now includes more creative activities, such as the following examples:
- Making new words for a familiar song
- Creating movements to match the given songs and tunes
- Creating different rhythms, movements, and instrumental-performing schemes for given songs and tunes
- Expressing feeling and understanding of the music freely by action images, visual art images, and language images
- Expressing the experience and emotions of daily life freely by action images, voice images, and music images.

To bring up children's aesthetic and creative awareness and ability, teachers are now expected to create a free, relaxing, and informal environment for learning. The musical materials teachers provide for children to play and explore should be easily understood by the children. Teachers are expected to respect every child for her/his ideas and efforts. Teachers are also to avoid, by all means, circumstances where children become unhappy or lose self-confidence.

Current conceptions of music education. In the last few years, Chinese educators have finally agreed that only on the basis of understanding children can teachers support and promote child development effectively. This has prompted Chinese educators to pay closer attention to the role of the teacher in musical education. For example, a series of researches has been done recently on the educational influence of music activities on the development of children's musical ability.

Besides developing children's musical ability and fostering children's sensitivity to musical beauty, music education is considered a significant means of facilitating the harmonious and healthy development of children. Music education is believed to foster a positive mental state in young children when they are emotionally involved positively in activities. By encouraging positive thinking, music also facilitates harmony that individuals can achieve between body and mind, the individual and others, and the individual and the environment. By feeling, experiencing, and expressing beauty in music education activities, children can reach harmony in their physical and psychological development. The educational activities that emphasize mechanical drill and installation may cause unharmonious development and should be avoided.

Music curriculum in practice. In kindergartens, there are usually planned group musical activities two times a week. But in most cases, musical activities are integrated into curriculum themes and daily routines. In language activities, scientific explorations, free playtime, or waiting for meals, music or songs will be played according to the atmosphere. A piano or an organ is required in every classroom in early childhood education programs in most of the areas in the nation. Art education such as singing, dancing, and instrument playing is emphasized in teacher training programs, so teachers are able to play instruments in the classroom.

According to the Kindergarten Education Guidelines issued by the Ministry of Education, the goals of the early childhood music education are to develop children's aesthetic perceptual ability for music, to enrich their aesthetic emotion, and to nourish their aesthetic awareness and creative ability. Teachers can achieve these goals through beautiful and fun musical activities.

Visual Arts Curriculum

In visual art activities, people possess the following essential abilities:
- To perceive and imagine the visual figures
- To see and understand visual models
- To master excellent technical skills
- To be creative

For young children, visual art may reflect their sensitive experience, their insight, and their ability to represent and create the beauty.

Aims and objectives of visual art curriculum. As described in the excerpt below, the Kindergarten Education Guideline, issued by the Ministry of Education in 2002, advances the following aims for children's creative visual art curriculum.

to experience the beauty in the environment, life and arts; to be fond of arts activities and freely express own feelings and experience; to be able to participate in the art representational activities through individual child's own way

The objectives for creative visual art curriculum are as follows:

1. To foster children's sensitivity and experience for beauty by exercising the key elements of visual images. Practice in lines, shapes, colors, etc., gives children initial experiences with these elements. Through understanding the elements of visual images, children develop the ability to appreciate the beauty of nature, social life, and artworks.
2. To develop children's interest in visual art. Children should be stimulated to express their ideas and feelings, and to represent and create beauty by means of visual, creative art activities.
3. To develop coordination and flexibility of children's fine muscle, and help them to learn to use art tools and materials.

The contents of the children's creative visual art curriculum include drawing, handicraft, and visual art appreciation.

Understanding children's creative acts. To some degree, children are born to act in creative ways. The ways they act are unique and are different from those of adults. Children usually treat painting as an activity of play and a perceptual activity for beauty. They feel happy through free scrawl and creation. In their spontaneous play, children constantly have new experiences and feelings.

Children's aesthetic interests and spontaneous abilities should be valued, and their creative ability should be encouraged. However, the development of children's art ability is the result of learning, not the result of maturity. Through creating and experiencing art, this ability can and should be learned. Visual art education should treat children as active learners. Teachers may use many methods to bring children's full potential into play, to develop their creative ability, and to help them reach the goal of self-realization.

Theories in visual art education. Art education at the kindergarten level focuses on the children's lives. Children can see and touch the shapes, colors, and materials in the classroom. These are applied when children imagine them as themes and images in art activities. Teachers often suggest themes for activities that introduce key elements for sculpture. Children participate in these art activities in a free and playful way. They make sculptures by drawing, playing with mud, and decoratively designing. A variety of materials are provided for designing, such as cardboard, iron wire, pieces of bamboo, wood, recyclable junk, tins, etc. We believe that simultaneous use of both hands and brain arouses children's independent and creative instinct.

These principles and methods are different from those of traditional visual art education, which emphasized modeling and imitation. The basic principle of modern childhood visual art education is to encourage the spirit of free creativity. Teachers choose methods that are appropriate for children and engage them to express themselves through activities with paint or sculpture. In planning activities, teachers consider the children's interest, the children's developmental level, and the basic elements of image design. Teachers guide children to start from basic expression of images, which gradually leads to free creation. Children may use activities in design to imagine a kind of play or perceptual activity for beauty. Children are expected to complete unique works through their own thought and action.

Furthermore, the new visual art education emphasizes children's own observation of and experience with artistic works to help them understand the use of shape, space, color, and material. In children's art creation, beauty is the center and also the starting point. Visual art education aims to encourage children's perception of beauty. Children are encouraged to create new conceptions through design.

Learning through process and play. When children practice creating new designs, their experiences are enriched. When children draw or make crafts, they reflect while they are working, and their plans constantly change. The pleasure children get from creating is not judged or altered by an idea of "well-done work" or successful product. The core philosophy of art education for young children is that learning occurs through the development of the child's creative instinct, and the process of exploration and creation.

Children may need to learn some necessary skills in art education and these skills can be connected to their play in art activities. This will eventually lead to conscious and planned representation. If children can constantly explore new themes and methods, the ways they represent and express themselves will be enriched. Children will then be able to follow their inner creative desire, and to freely explore different kinds of creative ideas in art activities. As a result, children develop creative dispositions and personalities.

Current issues in art curriculum. Chinese scholars and educators have worked together to develop a comprehensive art curriculum in recent years. They have combined three types of art curriculum—literature, music, and visual art—into one curriculum theme. These three types of art are integrated to stimulate and support each other. The activity in a curriculum theme may start with any one of the arts.

How It Looks: An Integrated Curriculum

A class may start with a literature activity. The teacher lets 3- or 4-year-old children appreciate a poem titled *Star*, which is dubbed in with the music *Träumerei* by Schumann. From this activity, children's rich experiences and emotions could deepen as both music and visual art are related to the activity. The teacher encourages the children to sing the song *Twinkle, Twinkle, Little Star* in a soft and happy voice. This activity is then followed by a visual art activity. Children are asked to paint pictures of *A Starry Night*.

Similarly, the theme could start from a music activity. The rhythm and melody may spark off children's passion in the creation of literature and visual art. In a visual art activity, the form and structure children perceived may be transferred to a musical creation or literary activities. Children may want to create music to represent a picture they have appreciated. A picture may make it easier for children to understand a piece of music, and the emotion experienced from the music and picture may be transferred to comprehend a fairy tale, relating back to literature.

Moving Forward in Practice

There are still many problems in art education remaining to be studied in terms of fostering creativity. In practice, teachers often oversimplify "creativity" into "being different from others." As a result, children's understandings of the basic elements and skills of art might be neglected. Educators need to improve the relationship between theory and practice so that teachers begin scaffolding children's development of art skills, and their artistic and aesthetic feelings.

Further Readings: Lou, B.S., and M. R. Tu eds. (1997). *The study of children's comprehensive artistic education.* Beijing: Beijing Normal University; Ministry of Education

(2002). Kindergarten education guideline. In The Basic Education Division of The Ministry of Education, ed., *The Interpretation of Kindergarten Education Guideline (Provisional)*. Nanjing: Jiangsu Education Press; Preschool Education Research Association, cd. (2003). *The century Chinese preschool education: 1903–2003.* Bcijing: Educational Science Press; Xu, Z. Y. (1996). *Music education for young children.* Beijing: People's Education Press.

Yunfei Ji and Meiru Tu

Social and Emotional "Curriculum" in China

The development of a Chinese social and emotional 'curriculum' in early childhood education has been closely related to the social and political change in the country over the past decades. Shortly following the founding of the People's Republic of China in 1949, the main purpose of early child education in China was defined as to "foster children's development in social dispositions such as patriotism, honesty, braveness, cooperativeness, friendship and proper social behaviors." Unfortunately the whole early child education system deteriorated along with the social turbulence that occurred from the middle of the 1960s to the late 1970s. Social and emotional education for young children was distorted and defined narrowly as ideology and morality education. Young children were asked to recite the national leader's quotations and political slogans, just as adults did at that time.

It was not until 1979, when the social reform and open society policy began, that early child education returned to normal. The subsequent national program regulations defined the education of young children's social and emotional development as "political and moral education." The contents of this curriculum were interpreted specifically into Five Loves—to love the country, to love the people, to love labor, to love science, and to love public properties. In classroom practice teachers tended to substitute moral education for the education of social cognition, behavioral habits, social behavioral skills, and social emotion. They attempted to reach their educational goals through such routine teaching methods as establishing model children and enforcing discipline.

Educational Objectives for Social and Emotional Curriculum

After the mid-1980s, with the introduction of educational theories and practices from Western countries and the publishing of a series of studies conducted by some Chinese scholars, the concept of social and emotional development became accepted by the professionals in the field. Thereafter, practitioners realized that there were shortcomings in the social and emotional education for young children. Young children's social and emotional education was for the first time set forth as an independent subject along with health, science, language, and arts in Kindergarten Education Guideline (provisional), issued by the Ministry of Education in 2001.

Social and emotional development for young children was interpreted in detail in this national curriculum guideline. It emphasizes the development of children's self-esteem, self-confidence, the disposition of caring for others, and friendship. These goals are further elaborated into five operational objectives. Children are to (1) be encouraged to engage in play and other beneficial activities happily and confidently; (2) be willing to interact with others in a polite, decent, and friendly manner; (3) be able to tell right from wrong on the basis of social norms of behavior; (4) be responsible and try their best to do what they can do; and (5) love their parents, teachers, and peers, and love their hometowns and the country.

Besides the five objectives, the Kindergarten Education Guideline (Provisional) also proposes specific recommendations for social and emotional education for young in four curriculum areas. For example, in health education, the teachers are required to keep children adjusted to the program with steady emotion and to help children feel safe and happy. In science education, children are encouraged to play and work together with their peers and to communicate with each other naturally. In language education, teachers are required to foster in children the ability to listen to others carefully, and to teach the children to talk with others politely.

For early childhood education teachers to realize all the social and emotional objectives in education, the Guideline specifically requires that the teacher should do the following:

1. Encourage children to engage in play and various activities and to experience the enjoyment of playing with peers;
2. Encourage children to interact with teachers and peers, and foster children's positive and friendly attitudes toward others;
3. Teach children some basic social skills such as learning to share with others, to take turns, to negotiate with others, and to be nice to others;
4. Provide opportunities for each child to show their strength and experience the feeling of success, thus to reinforce their self-respect and self-confidence;
5. Give children opportunities to explore freely, to support their autonomy in choosing and planning their activities, and encourage them to work hard to carry out their own plans;
6. Help children to understand and obey basic social rules in daily life and activities;
7. Teach children to take good care of toys, books, and other materials in the classroom, and learn to clean up after the activities.

Current Classroom Practice for Social and Emotional Development

Since the enactment of the Kindergarten Education Guideline, children's social and emotional education in China has been developing quickly. In educational practice, early childhood teachers are currently required to follow five principles in designing and organizing educational activities: (1) to establish specific objectives for the activity; (2) to adapt activities to children's life and experience; (3) to engage children in some kinds of activities to learn social skills; (4) to involve all children in the activity; and (5) to help children learn in an integrated way. The objectives of social and emotional learning may be accomplished through teacher-directed learning activities, in play and games, in field trips, in daily routines, or by some other social practice. Teaching methods may include explanation, conversation, discussion, demonstration, empathy training, and role-play. Social and emotional education for young children may take place in the program or through program–family cooperation. The effects of this education for social and emotional development are to be evaluated through observation, conversation, measurement, questionnaire, projection, or situation testing.

At present, education for social and emotional development has received much attention in China, with significant progress made in this field during the last decade. Early childhood teachers have generally accepted four conceptions regarding a social and emotional "curriculum." First, social and emotional development and education should be an integrative area that involves all other daily teaching and learning activities. Second, social and emotional education is different from the teaching of specific knowledge or a skill; it will take persistent efforts over a long period of time to see effects. Particularly for the learning of social attitudes and social emotion, children learn by their own experience as that is accumulated in their practical life and activities, it is not the result of teachers' direct teaching. Third, teachers and parents are the most important models in children's social learning. Imitation is an important way of social learning for children. Teachers' and parents' behavior affect children in direct and indirect ways. So adults should consciously do what they expect the children to do. Fourth, effective social and emotional education could not be achieved in early childhood education programs alone, it needs the cooperation of the family and even the whole society.

The four conceptions mentioned above are generally embodied in Chinese early childhood education. However, since social and emotional development in young children's education has just attracted attention for a short period of time and because the traditional Chinese educational philosophy still has a strong influence, there are still some challenges that need attention in the future. For example, the majority of Chinese parents and some early childhood teachers usually overemphasize academic preparation. Social and emotional development is often overlooked and distorted. Some teachers and parents may misunderstand and simplify social and emotional education by applying simple strategies such as talking or punishment. Other problems include the lack of sufficient playtime and play space for children in some programs, which may have negative impact on children's behavior and social and emotional development. There is much work to be done in these areas.

Further Readings: In Chinese: Liu, J. B. (1999). *Teacher-child interaction, what I saw in the kindergarten.* Nanjing: Nanjing Normal University Press; Ministry of Education (1952). Temporary Regulations for Kindergarten Education (Draft); Ministry of Education (1979). Regulations for Urban Kindergarten Education (Draft); Ministry of Education (2002). Kindergarten education guideline. In The Basic Education Division of The Ministry of Education ed.,. *The interpretation of Kindergarten Education Guideline (Provisional).* Nanjing: Jiangsu Education Press; Wang, Z. Y. (1992). *Children's socialization and education.* Beijing: People's Educational Press; Yang, L. Z., and W. J. Wu (2000). *Children's social development and education.* Liaoning: Liaoning Normal University Press; Zhang, W. X. (1999). *Children's social development.* Beijing: Beijing Normal University Press.

Jingbo Liu

Literacy in Early Childhood Education in China

Early literacy in the Chinese context focuses mainly on the development of basic reading and writing skills such as the understanding of the relationship between written and spoken language; the ability to recognize Chinese phonemic system *Pinyin* and some simple Chinese characters; the cultivation of an interest and a positive attitude for reading; the coordination between the hand and the eye and the development of fine motor skills, and so on. At present, it has been well accepted by the professionals that the early literacy education should start right after the child's birth. Since spoken language is the basis for the development of reading and writing skills, the development of spoken language becomes the first stage of early literacy education. Also, the cultivation of an interest and a positive attitude for reading is the central task for early literacy education. Through the rich experience of shared reading with adults children can have the opportunity to contact with books, learn the language, and grasp some basic ideas in reading and print.

The phenomenon of script is in nature a phenomenon of culture. The Chinese language, as an ideograph with its special characters, has countless ties and a harmonized connection with the Chinese culture. The implied meaning and the pattern of Chinese characters are imbued with the prototype of the Chinese people's human nature. The language conveys the messages of the history and the culture. With its character of pattern and meaning, Chinese has long been called the fossil of history and culture. And this characteristic of Chinese could definitely bring the atmosphere of culture, learning, and experience to children's early literacy beyond just cognitive and language training.

On the one hand, Chinese reading and writing research follows the cognitive psychology tradition, which focuses on information processing such as the storage of Chinese characters, the meaning extracted, the regulation effect of pictophonetic characters, the recognition of Chinese characters as influenced by the Chinese character pattern, the basic unit and the process of Chinese recognition, and so on. On the other hand, researchers have been making an effort to work from the cultural and psychological aspects of Chinese characters. They try to explore the culture and psychological archetypes in Chinese characters themselves and the cultural and psychological meaning in their patterns and structure.

The Historical Context in Early Literacy Education

As early as the 1920s, a Chinese early childhood education pioneer Heqin Chen proposed that young children should have the chance to learn written language through the activity of reading picture book stories, to recognize Chinese characters by drawing a picture, and to recognize Chinese characters that are used often in daily life. In 1960, based on the positive results of the study of children's early reading, the Ministry of Education issued a document to require early childhood education programs (kindergarten) to teach Chinese phonetics and characters. A variety of teaching methods and materials were recommended in the document, such as play, rhyme, story, music, movement, pictures, flannel piccces, puzzles, slides, etc. However, the implementation of the early reading education in Chinese early childhood education programs was short-lived because of negative results that soon appeared when the children entered the elementary school. Many first graders who had been taught early reading in kindergartens were found to acquire incorrect pronunciations for the phonetics and to be applying incorrect instructions for the strokes in Chinese characters. Kindergarten teachers were blamed for the lack of the ability to speak standard Chinese and to provide a quality teaching in early literacy learning. Therefore, early literacy education completely disappeared from the classroom soon after early 1960s. Although some scholars did studies of early literacy in the 1980s and 1990s, the official reestablishment of literacy education in the kindergarten came in the year of 2001, forty years after the abandonment of the teaching of the reading of Chinese characters in the kindergarten classroom.

Goals and Curriculum in Early Literacy Education

The goals for early literacy education are to foster children's interests in children's literature; to help children develop their ability to listen to others; to allow them to express their ideas; and to provide the opportunity to engage in early reading and writing activities. Specifically, literacy education should do the following:

1. Foster children's interests and positive attitudes in books, reading, and writing. Children should be interested in listening to the stories read by adults and be interested in the recognition and reading of Chinese characters.
2. Help young children to acquire some initial reading and writing skills. Specifically, this includes the following:
   (a) to help children understand the structure of a book, which means that children should know the book cover, the page, and the title on the book cover;
   (b) to learn the basic skills of how to hold a book, look over a book, and read a book. For instance, children should know how to read a book from page to page, and how to read line by line from left to right;
   (c) to recognize the people and the objects in a book. For example, they should be able to understand the basic ideas of a picture book and be able to tell the main content;
   (d) to recognize and read some common Chinese characters in the book, have an initial sense of the structure of Chinese characters, and be able to write some simple Chinese words.
3. Help children to develop interests in recognizing some simple signs and written symbols presented in their daily life and environment;
4. Help children to develop good reading habits, such as taking good care of books and not to tear or fold book pages. Children should learn to pay attention while they are reading and keep their eyes at an appropriate distance from the book. Also, children should be helped to learn the skill of pointing to the words while they are reading the story.
5. Help children to develop the ability to appreciate literacy works. Adults should read literature aloud to children. While reading books, children should enjoy the richness and elegance of literary expression, and therefore deepen their experience and understanding in the literacy works.

In the classroom, children may participate in various reading and writing activities. Picture books are displayed on the shelf in most of the kindergarten classrooms in urban areas. Children may choose to read a book during playtime, before or after the lunch, or at the end of the day, when children are waiting for their parents to pick them up. Teachers may read a book to the whole class or to a group of children during the day. Particular books may be recommended for children for the specific themes they are doing. Children are sometimes encouraged to make their own books, etc. Very often, children are encouraged to act out the stories they have read.

Current Issues and Challenges

The development of early literacy education in China faces five main problems:

1. Early literacy education in some kindergartens may be oversimplified as simply the learning of Chinese characters. Thus reading becomes just a tool for the learning of characters, and the number of characters children can read is pursued as the major objective of early literacy education. This trend sometimes may be encouraged by parents eager to prepare their children for the elementary school.
2. Reading activity may be treated only as a tool for children to acquire information and knowledge. In this case the important purpose of fostering children's reading interest and reading ability in early literacy education can sometimes be neglected.
3. High quality picture books for young children are extremely rare, and there is an especially great need for those functional reading materials that parents and children of different ages could share through reading. In recent years, some good English children's books have been translated and published in China, but these still cannot meet the need.
4. Parents lack effective education in understanding how important it is to help their children to read early or how to help children to learn to read. Besides, people in urban areas in general would like to spend money on books, but the time spent actually reading with children has been decreasing in the recent years.
5. Community libraries are almost nonexistent in many communities and it is hard to find good books for young children in most of the libraries in China. Social organizations for reading are not fully developed, due in part to funding shortages, and reading societies and interest groups are extremely rare. The year 2004 was the fortieth anniversary of the "World Literacy Day," but even now China has not become a member state of this association.

As a result of these factors and unfavorable conditions for learning to read early, many Chinese children do not learn to read until they enter into the elementary school. Particularly for the children who live in rural areas or live in urban areas with their migrant parents reading begins much later than for the children in urban areas, since books are not even available in many of those families. Projects have been undertaken in urban areas to ask for book donations for those children who live in rural areas. To provide those children with early literacy education is an urgent mission as well as a great challenge for Chinese educators as well as for the whole of Chinese society.

Further Readings: In Chinese: Preschool Education Research Association, ed. (2003). *The century Chinese preschool education: 1903-2003.* Beijing: Educational Science Press; Meng, X. Z., and H. Shu (1999). The study of Chinese children's reading disabilities. *Psychological Development and Education* 4, 54-56; Shu, H. (2002). The input and recognition of the components of Chinese characters by the children who were in different reading levels. *Acta Psychologica Sinica* 2, 133-136.

Web Sites: http://www.chinaeducationandresearchnetwork; http://www. chinaliteracyonline.

Lan Gao

Care and Education in China for Children under 3

Traditionally, Chinese families tended to have multiple children, many of whom lived with extended family members. During those years, children under the age of 3 often stayed home and were cared for by their mother, grandparents, older siblings, or a nanny. Beginning in the 1950s, women were encouraged to join the workforce for economic independence and in order to gain equal status to men. As a result, babies whose care was not provided by extended family members were usually cared for by child-care services provided by their mother's employer. This care was available for children before they could be enrolled in kindergarten at the age of 3. Babies might start going to such care as soon as the mother's fifty-six-day maternity leave was over. During the 1950s and 1960s, the development of such child care increased rapidly. Since many of these child-care centers were sponsored by workplaces, that is, factories and farm communes, the centers' hours were flexible to meet the mothers' working schedule. The care might be during the day, at night, on a boarding basis (day and night), or seasonal in rural areas, for example. It was common in some workplaces to provide nursing mothers a "nursing break" so they could go to the on-site child-care center to nurse or visit their babies. Sometimes the urban families might have paid individuals such as a neighbor or a baby-sitter to look after the baby. Regardless of whether or not the baby was looked after at home, or outside of home in an individual or group setting, the attention was focused on the baby's care rather than education.

Group child care has undergone many changes in the past twenty years. Since 1979, due to the great pressure from a continuing and rapidly increasing population, the Chinese government started enforcing the "only child" policy, which allows one child per family. As a result, government policies granted families benefits, especially mothers who promised to have only one child. One of the benefits, for example, was to allow the mother to stay home with the baby for one year, still being paid with a regular salary. This initiative greatly reduced the need of on-site child care. However, how this benefit is exercised now is less clear, because in recent years many formerly state-owned businesses have become privatized, and many private enterprises have been developed. In either of these situations, governmental policy may not have the same power it once had to enforce this benefit.

Types of Education and Care

There are several types of care and education arrangements for children under the age of 3. Many children before the age of 2 are cared for at home. The care providers can be the mother, grandparents, or a paid individual such as a live-in nanny or a daytime baby-sitter. The paid individuals are usually young women from poor rural areas. There are a couple of changes in group care. One is an extension of kindergarten, the preschool education setting that enrolls children above the age of 3. Many kindergartens start to enroll 2-year-old children in toddler class, while some others enroll children as young as $1^1/_2$ years old. Another type of care for children before the age of 3, which has gained popularity in recent years, is called a "Private Baby-Sitting Station." This care is usually a private business and enrollment may be as small as four babies or as large as eighty. The fee is negotiable and parents like this option for its low cost and convenience. When the child is 2 years old, the parents typically send her/him to kindergarten. However, some of these "Baby-Sitting Stations," especially those in the outskirts of the city, may not be regulated at all.

Parents' Awareness of Education for Children before Three

The adults who take care of children under the age of 3 focus most of their attention on the child's physical needs. The child's needs for emotional and cognitive development are sometimes met in nurturing spontaneous interactions or self-initiated explorations. Some parents, especially well-educated mothers, have started to pay attention to the educational needs of children at this young age. These parents actively seek out scientific resources that address how to rear and educate children under the age of 3, and they learn how to understand and respect the needs of their children. If the family's financial resources allow, some mothers even leave their job to stay home with the baby. This indicates that parents' values reflected in the education of young children are changing, specifically related to the first couple of years of children's lives. Their parenting is becoming more thoughtful and intentional.

Furthermore, when children started to enter the Toddler class in kindergarten, some parents become actively involved in the kindergarten. For example, they attend activities organized for both parents and their children; they organize "Parents Salon," they exchange information through the Internet, collect and provide resources for the school, write for the bulletin board, and so forth.

Resources for Parents

There are a variety of services for parents of children under the age of 3. For example, in some cities, there are agencies that organize group activities for both parents and the babies on the weekends. This type of service is sometimes referred to as an "Early Education Center" and it charges a fee for participation in its educational program. However, some parents are anxious about how to get their children "ahead." These parents may be tempted to use some commercially motivated "educational materials" claiming to know how to produce a child prodigy. These parents would start with training in reading, arithmetic, reciting Chinese classics, second language, and so forth for children under the age of 3. There are also programs that provide formal trainings for children under the age of 3.

Policy

In 1956, several ministries (Education, Health) of the central government decided that care services for children before the age of 3 belonged under the jurisdiction of the local health administrations and the central government. In contrast, kindergartens, the education settings for children between the ages of 3 and 6, remained under the jurisdiction of the Ministry of Education. In 1980, the Ministry of Health and Ministry of Education jointly issued a health regulation for children 0–3 (and 3–6), which defined specific regulations in group settings regarding daily schedules, nutrition, physical exercise, health screening, sanitation and quarantine, disease prevention and safety, parent communication, and so on. In the same year, the Bureau of Women and Young Children under the Ministry of Health issued a program regulation specifically for children under the age of 3. It required that group settings for children under 3 needed to use age as the guideline: less than 10 months old (Nursing Group), 10–18 months (Little Group), 19–24 months (Middle Group). The group size for children in these three groups range between fifteen and eighteen children. Groups of 2-year-old children are called the "Older Group" and might have twenty to twenty-five children per group. For the younger groups the adult–child ratio is 1:5-6, and for the older group it is 1:6-8.

In 1981, the Bureau of Women and Young Children of the Ministry of Health issued another important statute, "Education Guideline for Children before Three (Provisional)." This statute, for the first time, elaborated the educational objectives for children under the age of 3. It stated that the educational goal is to build a healthy, intelligent, and moral foundation for the new generation. Therefore, the educational task is to promote young children's development in physical, intellectual, moral, and aesthetic areas. The following education principles should be applied: use individualized education as a base, and integrate group activity into the daily routine; keep a balance between quiet and active activities, and indoor and outdoor activities; pay attention to both physical and behavioral development. The choice of educational content and method should be based on children's psychological, neurological, and physical developments. Likewise, education should be integrated through daily routines so that children can develop healthy habits in eating, sleeping, dressing, washing, and toileting. Their language development, cognitive competence, and social interactive competence with children or adults are to be enhanced. The activities and assignments of language, physical education, arithmetic, music, and arts and crafts can be implemented for the Older Group, that is, the 2-year-olds. They may have four to six lessons per week, and each lesson may last from five to ten minutes.

Trends in Development

Some recent government documents indicate development trends in the care and education for children under the age of 3. For example, the National Women's Federation proposed the "Chinese Children Development Outline" in 2001. This document, issued by the state council, suggests developing the education for children under the age of 3 and completing and improving the regulatory system for such education during the period from 2001 to 2010. Some local governments made regional plans to achieve better service for these children. For example, Shanghai Municipal Government requires that 95 percent of the parents and caregivers receive scientific guidance on child rearing by 2007.

Teacher Training

In responding to the demand for specialized care personnel for children under the age of 3, the Ministry of Labor and Social Protection developed and published a national vocational curriculum and certificate for *Yu Yin Yuan,* meaning "caregiver for infant/toddler" in 2003. It requires that people who provide care and education for children 0–3 must have such training and be certified. Even with this directive, there is still a lack of experienced and well-trained teachers in the all-day group settings for children under the age of 3. Although there are more diverse types of services due to more relaxed government policy on private business, the professional qualification of people in privately owned agencies for children under the age of 3 varies greatly. Sometimes the content of so-called "educational programming" tends to be commercialized rather than educational. There are more and more curriculum models for children under the age of 3, but there is a lack of research and assessment in terms of their appropriateness. Many parents, grandparents, and caregivers who are involved with children under the age of 3 still lack an understanding of scientific knowledge and appropriate practice.

At the government level, the Ministry of Health's distinctive role has diminished since the 1990s. In some regions, such as Shanghai, the leadership has been transferred to a joint effort by the Department of Education, the Women's Federation, the Birth Control Commission, and the Health Department. However, in many regions the regulatory and directive responsibilities and roles toward education and care for children under the age of 3, in group or at home, have not been clearly defined among the government agencies.

Access

The last point of concern is the rural areas. In all respects, the education and care for children under the age of 3 in rural areas has lagged behind, and not much attention, public or private, has been given to it. However, a recent report on a UNICEF project, "Early Childhood Care and Development Project" (ECCD) did identify some international and national joint efforts. One of the objectives of the five-year project was to have "70-80% of the parents of 0- to 3-year-olds in project areas receive parenting training." Six project provinces were in poor rural areas in western China. Various project activities, such as parenting information dissemination and community parent–child educational activity stations, were reported.

Further Readings: In Chinese: Chinese National Women's Federation (2001). *China child development outline.* Beijing: The State Council of China; Department of Labor and Social Protection (2003). *Yu Yin Yuan vocational training certificate and curriculum.* Beijing: China Women's Publication; Preschool Education Research Association, ed. (2003). *The century Chinese preschool education: 1903–2003.* Beijing: Educational Science Press; *In English:* Zhou, X., and L. Gao (2005). A report on the site visit for ECCD project. Reports to UNICEF and the Ministry of Education.

Bisheng Lou and Wei Li-Chen

Early Childhood Special Education in China

Introduction

As a populous nation, the People's Republic of China is home to a large number of persons with disabilities, as well as young children with special needs. In 1987 there were over 2.4 million children with disabilities from birth to six years of age in the following five categories in mainland China: physically disabled, visually impaired, hearing and/or speech impaired, mentally retarded, and mentally disordered.

In China, the origins of systematic early childhood special education can be traced back to the 1980s, when several hearing and speech training classes for hearing impaired infants, toddlers, and preschoolers were established in rehabilitation centers and hospitals. Since then, early childhood special education in China has developed relatively slowly in comparison to the development of special education in the compulsory education sector. In recent years, compulsory education has been a priority in China, consisting of six years of elementary education and three years of junior high school education for all children. Several policies and strategies have been applied to promote the educational service for children with special needs within this system. For example, the government provides financial support for educating children with special needs; curriculum standards have been established and special textbooks have been produced. In addition, special administrators in local governments have been assigned to facilitate the children's education. However, all these policies and strategies applied in compulsory education have not yet been applied to early childhood education.

At present, the information on the system of special education for young children in the nation is quite limited. In some urban areas, such as in Shanghai, Beijing, and Tianjing, there are several kinds of placements for young children with disabilities. First, these children may be placed in specific classes in special schools. For example, Shanghai School for the Blind and Low Vision is the first school to provide programs for young children. Since then, schools in Qingdao, Guangzhou, Beijing, and Chengdu have established programs for visually impaired young children. Now, both hearing impaired and mentally retarded preschoolers can enroll into specific programs in many special schools. Second, some rehabil-itation centers run by the government civil administration organizations provide special services for infants and preschoolers with mental retardation, physical handicaps, visual impairment, hearing impairment, and autism. Third, in recent years, some early childhood education programs have opened their doors to chil-dren with disabilities. The young children with special needs can enroll in regular programs and study in regular classes. The trend of inclusion, or "learning in the regular classroom," a term used in a Chinese context, is gradually becoming a sup-porting force in China's system of early childhood special education. Fourth, in some communities a home-visiting service is provided for the young children with disabilities who stay at home. The home-visiting service delivery program in China is basically child-focused. That is, the home visitors focus primarily on enhancing the child's development, while providing some guidance to the parents.

In sum, the development of early childhood special education in China is relatively slow when compared to the faster development of special education in the sector of compulsory education. However, in recent years, much more attention has been paid to the needs of infants and preschoolers with disabilities.

Policy

In the late 1980s and early 1990s, the government passed three important statutes regarding education for children with special needs. These statutes in-clude: the Compulsory Education Act (1986), the Law of the People's Republic of China on the Protection of Persons with Disabilities (1990), and the Five-Year Plan for the Disabled (1991). Since then, special education for children has developed rapidly in China. Although these laws focus primarily on school-aged children, in recent years, there has been an increase in attention to the needs of young children with special needs.

The Social Context of Special Education

Special education in China refers to the education provided for children with special needs in special schools, such as schools for the visually disabled, hearing disabled and mentally retarded children; in special classes in ordinary primary and secondary schools; or in regular school classrooms. Special education specifically aims at the physically and mentally disabled children who require special services. In 1951, the government issued a document called The Act on the Reform of School Systems, which stipulated that special schools should be established for school-aged children who were deaf or blind. Since then, special education has formally become a necessary component in China's national education system. But for a long time, neither special schools nor general early childhood education programs accepted children with disabilities under the age of 6.

Since the 1990s, the development of special education in China has entered a new phase. On the one hand, China established concrete laws and policies that focused on persons with special needs. In order to promote the develop-ment of special education, the People's Congress passed the Law of Compulsory

Education, the Social Security Law for Disabled Persons. These laws aim to protect disabled persons, ensuring their political and educational rights. As a result, special education is an important part of China's formal education system. At the same time, social attitudes toward children and adults with disabilities have changed significantly. For example, the number of special schools and institutions for children with disabilities has been increasing rapidly. Besides the schools for children with visual or hearing impairment, schools for mentally retarded children have been built all over the nation. In some provinces, rehabilitation centers, welfare homes, and day-care centers for disabled persons have been established for persons with different kinds of disabilities. Children receive different kinds of support in these schools and institutions, aimed at improving their cognitive and social skills and helping them gain a sense of self-reliance and confidence to socialize. Furthermore, these facilities help provide a more comprehensive system of special education. Presently, the central government is planning to construct a network for the education of children with disabilities, with special schools as the backbone of this network. The supporting force of this program includes special classes in general schools, as well as regular classes with children with disabilities. All these programs should follow the general guidelines, which are to enable each student to develop morally, intellectually, and physically. At the same time, the education provided should adapt to the children's unique characteristics and their special needs.

The System of Early Childhood Special Education

Current programs for young children with disabilities in China include (1) special classes in regular early childhood education programs, called kindergarten; (2) special classes for preschoolers in special schools such as schools for the visually disabled, hearing disabled, and mentally retarded children; (3) programs for children with relatively minor handicaps in ordinary kindergarten classes.

Curriculum. In China, teachers play an important role in planning the activities for young children with disabilities. Many special educators believe that curriculum has to be developed by each special class teacher, who then adapts to the conditions of the community, the young children's needs, abilities and aptitudes, etc. Yet there are no national curriculum standards for the education of children with special needs. Usually, the curriculum is planned with a focus on the training of children's independent living skills and basic academic skills, while the moral, cultural, intellectual, physical, and compensatory mental education are also included. An Individualized Education Program (IEP) should be developed for each young child with special needs as a supplement to the common curriculum. In order to develop the potentials of each young child with special needs, the success of IEP depends on the cooperation among the professionals and parents.

Although every teacher who teaches in an early childhood special education program has been required to develop IEP programs for individual children, it is not an easy task for many teachers and there is still a great need to raise the quality of instruction for young children with various conditions.

Current Issues and Challenges

There are a lot of issues and controversies in early childhood special education in China. The first problem is the assessment and referral system for the children with special needs. The enrollment of a child with special needs into the special education program is determined on the basis of an assessment and placement procedure. However, a standard assessment and referral procedure for the parents of young children has not been established, and the process for the identification of a child who needs special help is usually quite slow. As a result, a high percentage of young children with disabilities may not be able to get into the screening process on time. In urban areas, kindergarten teachers are usually sensitive, and sometimes may be oversensitive, to children who may have learning and communicating problems and are able to refer them to hospitals for testing. The second problem is the lack of appropriate assessment tools for the identification of young children with special needs. Tests developed in the western countries, such as the Wechsler Preschool and Primary Scale of Intelligence, Standfor-Binet tests, have been used to detect and identify disabilities. Although the assessment of cognitive and social functions by using these tools is a good starting point, the assessment of a child with mental disabilities requires a more comprehensive assessment for a wide range of skills. Third, teacher training for special education is still a great and urgent problem. Many educators who are working with young children with special needs have not received any pre- or in-service special training.

Further Readings: Chen, D. Z. (2001). *Early childhood special education.* Beijing: Beijing Normal University Press; Chen, Y. Y. (1997). *Integrated education reform in China: Theories and practices.* Beijing: Xin Hua Press; Tang, S., and X. X. Feng, eds. (2003). *The centenary Chinese preschool education: 1903-2003.* Beijing: Education and Science Press; Xu, Y., and Y. Y. Si, eds. (1990). *Symposia of special education on mentally retarded children.* Hangzhou: Zhejiang Education Press Co; Zhang, F. J., and H. Y. Ma eds. (2000). *History of special education.* East China Normal University Press.

Wen Qian

Early Childhood Teacher Education in China

Yinghua girl's school, founded by an American Methodist church in Suzhou, Jiangsu province in 1889, was the first educational institution that offered vocational training for Chinese preschool teachers. In the following years a number of women's schools and colleges were established by missionaries from the United States and other foreign countries, and quite a number of independent teacher training colleges began to set up training programs for preschool teachers. The training offered by these missionary schools and colleges had a strong religious component in the curriculum, and artistic education was also emphasized.

The first teacher training institute run by the Chinese was a women's school, which was set up by Hubei Preschool in 1903. This institute recruited and trained young women aged 15–35 to be preschool teachers. However, it was soon closed because of the official ban on women's schools at the time. With the emergence of private women's schools, some nursemaid training programs were also set up.

For example, Yanshi Women's School in Tianjin with its nursemaid-training class was quite well known at that time. These private institutes usually hired Japanese teachers or sent teachers to Japan to be trained in child care. The curriculum in these programs typically includes courses in child care, music, and gymnastics, games, handicrafts, English, child psychology, pedagogy, arithmetic, physiology, and chemistry.

From the 1910s to 1930s, teacher training programs were set up in many private normal schools (schools to provide teacher training at the secondary education level) or universities in the cities of Beijing, Tianjing, Shanghai, Hangzhou, Suzhou, Xiamen, and Nanjing. The government issued the Women's Normal School Regulation in 1907, which officially lifted the ban on women's schools. For the first time in Chinese history, education for preschool teachers was treated as a formal part of the teacher education system.

The first public normal school for preschool teachers in China was established in Jiangxi province in 1940 by Heqin Chen (1892–1982). Mr. Chen had studied with John **Dewey** at Columbia University in the United States and was the founder of early childhood education in China. In 1943, this school was upgraded to become a national normal school, which was supported by the central government. In 1946, Heqin Chen established the second normal school in Shanghai. These two modern normal schools have been regarded as milestones in the history of teacher education for young children in China.

Over the past century, and especially since the founding of People's Republic of China in 1949, an educational system for preschool teachers has been established in China to meet different needs in basic education. This educational system consists of independent teacher training institutions as the core, supplemented by other educational organizations. Currently, preschool teacher education in China is composed of two parts: preservice education and in-service training.

Preservice Teacher Education

Preservice preparation takes place at both the secondary school and higher education levels.

Programs in secondary education. These programs are offered in three different settings: independent normal schools, regular normal schools, and vocational senior high schools.

Independent normal schools. An independent normal school for preschool teachers provides a four-year or three-year full-time education for female students (male students occasionally) graduated from junior high schools. By the middle of the 1990s, such schools had become major educational institutions for the training of preschool teachers. The curriculum planning in these schools has been guided by the central government. The Ministry of Education has issued a series of versions of the Guidelines for the Curriculum Plan for Normal Schools for Preschool Teachers (1956, 1980, 1985, and 1995), which provides guidance in the curriculum planning, including goals and objectives, curriculum content and components, and the implementation procedures. The typical curriculum for these programs includes required courses, elective courses, practicum and extracurricular activities. Courses offered in those programs are basically composed of two parts. One part includes the basic courses in high school education; the other part includes the courses in teacher training, such as child care, child psychology, introduction to early childhood education, language, mathematics, science, music, and visual art education for young children. Artistic skill training in these schools has been also emphasized, such as singing, dancing, and piano playing.

In the recent years, the number of such independent normal schools for preschool teachers has been decreasing gradually and some of these schools have merged with the preschool education programs in the university, due to the raising of qualification standards for preschool teachers in urban areas. In some urban areas this standard has risen to at least an associate bachelor's degree. However, the teacher qualification in rural areas is much lower.

Programs in regular normal schools. Because of the shortage of independent normal schools for preschool teachers, starting in 1951 the Chinese government stipulated that all regular normal schools (schools for the training of primary school teachers) should set up training programs for preschool teachers. Such programs recruit graduates from junior high schools. The curriculum in these programs is similar to normal schools for preschool teachers.

Programs in vocational senior high schools. In the 1980s, the number of programs for preschool teachers in vocational senior high schools increased substantially to meet the increasing demand for preschool teachers. Students graduated from junior high schools were admitted for two to four years of training. Data indicate that in the year 2000 about 152,900 preschool teachers out of the total 900,000 had been trained by these programs nationwide. The majority of the preschool teachers currently working in rural China were trained in such programs.

Higher Education for Preschool Teachers. There are three levels of preschool-related preparation at the college and university level: associate bachelor's programs, bachelor's programs, and postgraduate programs.

Associate bachelor's program. Two types of institutes provide such programs: independent colleges for preschool teachers and departments in normal universities (universities provide the bachelor's or a higher level of teacher training). These programs admit students who graduated from senior high schools or normal schools for preschool teachers, or those with equivalent educational background. These programs last for two years.

Bachelor's programs. The Departments of Early Childhood Education at Nanjing and Beijing Normal Universities started this program in the early 1950s. The program ceased operations between 1966 and 1977 during the Cultural Revolution, and restarted in 1978. East China Normal University and a number of other normal universities established early childhood education programs in early 1980s. The students who want to enroll in these programs have to take the national college entry examination and get a score that meets the requirement set by the university. These programs are four years in duration.

Programs for early childhood education increased rapidly in 1990s. Typical training in this program is composed of courses in the field of child development; theories in early childhood education; children's development and education in the area of language, mathematics, science, visual art, and music. Student teaching and thesis writing are required. Many new courses have been offered through bachelor programs in recent years, such as education research methodology, preschool curriculum development, child nutrition, information technology and early childhood education, and remediation for children's abnormal behavior. Graduates from these programs used to work in normal schools for preschool teachers as instructors prior to the mid-1990s. However, in recent years many graduates have started to work as teachers of young children in urban areas, because of the decreasing number of normal schools for preschool teachers and the higher standards for teacher qualifications in the cities.

Postgraduate programs. In the mid-1980s Nanjing Normal University and Beijing Normal University started to offer master's programs in early childhood education. The first doctoral program in early childhood education started in Nanjing Normal University in the mid-1990s and now a doctoral program is offered in several universities. People with postgraduate degrees in early childhood education usually work as professionals at universities or research institutes, although some of them have worked in early childhood education programs as directors or teachers and research coordinators.

Continuing Education

Continuing education for preschool teachers operates at two levels: secondary education and higher education.

Secondary continuing education. Secondary continuing education, both degreed and nondegreed, has been offered to preschool teachers who did not receive formal training in early childhood education. Programs at this level include the following:

Certificate programs. In these programs teachers are able to get training to meet a minimum requirement for the teacher position. The training is usually composed of nine core courses such as child psychology, early childhood education pedagogy, child hygiene, language, mathematics, science, music, visual art, and physical education for young children.

Part-time programs. These offer in-service teacher training equivalent to that of secondary education at normal school. Such programs may offer either full-time or part-time training, night school, correspondence courses, or self-study examinations organized by the provincial government.

Specific theme-based training classes. Usually offered by universities, normal school for preschool teachers, provincial or municipal teacher training centers for preschool teachers, or some private educational organizations or individuals.

Center-based workshops. These workshops provide preschool teachers an opportunity to learn from colleagues. Teachers may also learn to do reflective teaching by participating in action research projects in the center that is able to provide such an opportunity.

Continuing Higher Education. Continuing education for preschool teachers at the higher education level includes the following degree and nondegree programs:

Degree education. Continuing degree education is similar to regular degree education, including programs at the associate bachelor's, bachelor's, and master's levels. The associate bachelor's program may offer one of the following options: a two-year full-time program, a three-year correspondence program, an evening school program, or an examination for self-study learners. The bachelor's program may take four years of study for high school graduates or an additional two years of study after preparation at the associate bachelor's level. Preschool teachers may also pursue master's or doctorial study, mostly done on a part-time basis.

Nondegree education. Nondegree education for preschool teachers is provided through training classes, teaching-related researches, academic workshops, conferences, or nondegree graduate courses. Recently a new type of nondegree education is to take certain graduate courses to earn a certificate. In addition, preschool teachers' professional development in China is also benefited from educational exchanges between China and international organizations as well as other countries. A variety of international educational exchanges, such as delegations and study tours have contributed greatly to the development of preschool teacher education in China in recent two decades.

In sum, teacher education for preschool teachers has made great progress in the past two decades in mainland China, particularly in urban areas. However, there is a gap between the urban and rural areas in terms of teacher qualification and teacher education. Policies and financial resources should be used to provide support for the development of teacher training in rural areas.

Further Readings: Jiangsu Provincial Education Department (2002). *Collection of documents for the enforcement of teacher's qualification in Jiangsu Province*; Preschool Education Research Association, ed. (2003). *The century of Chinese preschool education: 1903–2003.* Beijing: Educational Science Press; Tang, S., and S. H. Zhong, eds. (2000). *The history of Chinese early childhood education.* Beijing: People's Education Press.

Jingbo Liu

The Czech Republic

Early Childhood Education in the Czech Republic

Introduction

The Czech Republic came into existence in January 1993, when the former Czech and Slovak Federal Republic split into two states. It is still in the throes of the transformation from a socialist society with centralized administration and a planned economy to one operating according to the principles of a market economy and political pluralism—the process that was launched by the political revolution of November 1989. The type of government is a parliamentary democracy with a president elected by the Parliament, which exercises legislative power. Executive power is held by the national government.

Public administration has experienced an extensive reform and is provided by state administration and self-government. The territorial administration has two levels: municipalities that are basic self-governing units, and fourteen higher territorial self-governing units called regions. Municipalities and regions have a double sphere of authority—independent powers, including education, and transferred powers, with which they perform state administration.

In 2003, the Czech Republic had a population of 10.24 million and a population density of 131 inhabitants per square kilometer. The fertility rate is unfavourable, resulting in a low birthrate. There are 540,000 children under 6 years of age. Infant mortality was 3.9 per thousand children in 2003. The state is neutral on religious matters, and freedom of religion is guaranteed. The number of people practicing religion is low (32% of inhabitants declare themselves as believers). Over 83 percent of believers belong to the Roman Catholic Church (over 26% of the population).

The language of instruction is Czech. Pupils from ethnic minorities are guaranteed the right to education in their mother tongue to an extent appropriate to the development of their ethnic community. Schools for national minorities can operate up to the upper-secondary school level. The total employment rate among women is 73.7 percent; the rate of employment among women with one child is

72.3 percent and with two children 59.4 percent. The rate of employment among women with children under six years of age (255 thousand) was 36.4 percent. Only 4.0 percent of women work part-time.

The budget reserved for social expenditures is 20.1 percent of GDP; the child poverty rate is 5.9 percent after redistribution (OECD average is 11.9%). Funding of preprimary educational services is 0.5 percent GDP, corresponding to 10 percent of the education budget.

Early Childhood Education

Nursery schools (mateřská škola) have a long and special national tradition, influenced among others by the ideas of Jan Amos Komenský (John Amos **Comenius**) in the seventeenth century. Preprimary education was incorporated into the education system in 1948. The quality of preprimary education increased considerably in the postwar period. At the same time, however, it became an instrument for increasing the number of women in the country's labor force, while enforcing the principles of collective education and weakening the influence of the family over the children's education.

After the 1989 revolution a lively debate developed over the role of nursery schools, their new role in the education system and their educational function. The personality-oriented model of preprimary education was encouraged by new legislation (Act no. 390/1991). Nursery schools now must contribute to an increase in the level of sociocultural care for children and lay the foundations for their future education.

Early childhood education in the Czech Republic is regarded as part of the system of education and its objectives are defined by the Educational Act (Zákon, 2004), enacted in 2005 by the Ministry of Education, Youth and Sport. Early childhood education in the Czech Republic is almost entirely a public service. Some private and denominational nursery schools are now in operation, but only on a small scale.

Attendance is not compulsory, but 87 percent of children attend nursery schools (2002/2003), with attendance increasing in the last year of preschool education (98%). The basic age-group of children attending nursery schools is 3- to 6-year-olds. In exceptional cases, where parents have no other alternative, it is possible to accept younger children, for whom municipalities otherwise set up day crèches (for infants and toddlers). Currently there are also older children (about 20%) whose attendance at basic school has been deferred, usually at the parent's request. Fewer than 1 percent of applications for placement in nurseries are not met. Children in their last year before the start of compulsory school are enrolled in nursery schools preferentially. If a child cannot be enrolled in a nursery school for capacity reasons in his/her last year before the start of compulsory school, the municipality in which the child has a permanent address makes sure that the child is enrolled in another nursery school. The child may be enrolled for early childhood education at any time throughout the school year.

Classes are coeducational. Schools with fewer than 100 pupils prevail (92% in the school year 2002/2003). Some schools are attached to a basic school (základní škola). Their number increased in 2002.

Financing

Funding for early childhood education is drawn from multiple sources—the regional school authority (teachers' salaries, books, and equipment), municipalities (running costs and capital investments), and parental fees (capped at 50% of costs for the first two years and free for the final year). Funds to improve material conditions or purchase equipment and toys are often generated through sponsoring contracts with private enterprises. Parental fees are reduced or waived for families in need. There are special supports for low-income/ethnic areas and families. Parents also contribute to meals that are subsidized; however, some municipalities do not impose this charge.

Organization and Coordination of Services

Child care for children under 3. Almost all children aged 0–3 are cared for by their families or through informal care arrangements. Center-based crèches are scarce. Child-care services are a municipal responsibility. Government funding is directed almost exclusively to parental leave policies. Maternal and parental leave is as follows: twenty-eight weeks maternity leave paid at 69 percent of earnings, followed by a flat-rate, parental leave benefit paid until children reach their fourth birthday.

Crèches are administered by the Ministry of Health and therapeutic child-care centers are part of the Ministry of Social Affairs. In practice, there is no longer an organized day-care system for children from 0 to 3 years of age, compared to a coverage rate of 20 percent in 1989. The introduction of an extended period of maternal leave after transition reduced demand for public child care outside the home. Only sixty crèches (in 2004) have survived from the previous regime. Former crèche buildings have been sold or allocated to other purposes. However, children over 2 years of age can attend nursery schools (at the present time, about 20% do). Public child care for children under 3 is governed by no obligatory educational program. Children in crèches are cared for by children's nurses with high school education acquired at secondary medical schools.

Nursery schools. Nursery schools are administered mainly by municipalities, which also fund them (except for salaries and teaching aids). There are an insignificant number of private and denominational nursery schools. Usually open for ten to eleven hours a day, nursery schools are established as full-day (the majority) or half-day-care centers. They can also be established as boarding facilities or facilities with an irregular attendance schedule.

An amendment to the law on the state administration and self-government required all schools to become legal entities from January 1, 2003. This resulted in some cases in the merging of several nursery schools, and more often in the combining of nursery schools and basic schools under one directorate.

Classes should have a minimum of fifteen children and a maximum of twenty-five, but this maximum is currently being exceeded. Decisions on class sizes are taken by school heads after consultation with the school's organizing body. The average number of pupils per class is 22.3. One or two teachers care for each group of children depending on the number of children in the group and length of the day. The recommended pupil/teacher ratio is 12:1. Groups may be organized according to age, by the degree of adaptability or achievement, or with mixed ages and progress levels. Inclusion of children with disabilities is increasing, although many special nursery schools and schools still exist, even for children with relatively light handicaps. Disabled children make up 4.2 percent of the total number of children attending nursery schools; almost a half of these attend special nursery schools. A parent responsible for a chronically ill or long-term disabled or handicapped child is entitled to parental benefit until the child is 7.

Problems of poverty, social exclusion, and educational underachievement are most acute among Romany families. Romany is an ethnic group which originally came to Eastern and Middle Europe from India and which has a characteristic language, cultural traditions, and way of family life. It is estimated that the Romany community constitutes 0.7 percent of the population. High rates of unemployment are recorded among this group and levels of education are low compared to Czechs, 84 percent of whom complete upper secondary education. Since 1993, the government has invested in several pilot projects for Romany children, and preparatory classes for socially or culturally disadvantaged children of 6–7 years of age (whose entry into compulsory school had been delayed). In 2004, 126 preparatory classes with 1,779 children were in operation. The Ministry of Education provides grants to NGOs (nongovernmental organizations) to support work with Romany parents and schools to increase the inclusion of Romany children in nursery schools.

Nursery School Curricula

In 2001, the Ministry of Education published a General Curriculum for Early Childhood Education, which was made a binding document by the Educational Act in 2005. Each nursery school uses it as a basis for the development of its own school curriculum. Parents can significantly influence the orientation of the programs and participate in their implementation.

Early childhood education in the Czech Republic has the following main objectives: to develop the child's ability to learn, to teach him/her the basic values on which our society is based, to make him/her become independent and able to express him/herself as an individual in relation to its surroundings. It is possible to differentiate between different aspects of education according to the relations which the child gradually develops towards himself/herself, other people, and the world. The main components of the program are spontaneous games and physical activities, including outdoor activities and games, walks and excursions. Sleep is also an important element of the routine. Personal development and socialization are also supported by activities related to literary, artistic, and moral education. All activities emphasize emotional involvement and encourage a spirit of participation. Nursery schools are moving toward internal differentiation and individualization of their programs. Foreign language teaching, swimming courses, artistic activity, speech therapy, and programs for gifted children are also offered.

Teachers in Nursery Schools

More than 95 percent of teachers in Czech nursery schools have completed four years of training (15–19 years) in one of the seventeen upper secondary pedagogical schools in the country. Nursery school teachers obtain a full qualification from a four-year course with a standard school-leaving examination (maturitní zkouška) in secondary pedagogical schools (střední pedagogická škola). There is also the possibility of a three-year study at higher vocational schools with specialization in pedagogy at the tertiary level or three-year bachelor's or four to five-year master's degree course at pedagogic faculties (university level).

Since 1999, the workload for nursery school teachers has been decreased to thirty-one hours per week. Most work full-time. In 2004, the average wage of teachers in nursery schools was 76 percent of the average wage in the Czech Republic (the teacher wage in basic schools is 96% of the average wage). The status of a nursery school teacher is still lower than that of basic school teachers. Virtually all employees of the school are women, although the occupation is open to both sexes.

Further Readings: Národní zpráva o stavu předškolní výchovy, vzdělávání a péče o děti předškolního věku v České republice (National report on the state of early childhood education and childcare for pre-school children in the Czech Republic). Prague: MŠMT, 2000, p. 87; *Rámcový vzdělávací program pro předškolní vzdělávání (General curriculum for early childhood education).* Praha: MŠMT, 2004; OECD (2001). *Starting strong. Early childhood education and care.* Paris: The Organization for Economic Cooperation and Development Structures of Education, Initial Training and Adult Education Systéme in Europe. Czech Republic 2003. EURYDICE/CEDEFOP, 2003. Available online at http://www.eurydice.org, http://www.cedefop.gr; Zákon č. 561/2004 Sb., o předškolním, základním, středním, vyšším odborném a jiném vzdělávání (školský zákon). (Act No. 561/2004 Coll. on Early Childhood, Elementary, High-school, Higher Vocational and Other Education—Educational Act).

Milada Rabušicová

The Sociology of Childhood in the Czech Republic

Childhood, as a specific social category, is a social construct undergoing change at the levels of both approach and existential context. As Mintz writes, "Every aspect of childhood—including children's relationships with their parents and peers, their proportion of the population, and their paths through childhood and adulthood—has changed dramatically over the past four centuries." Ways of looking at childhood and handling children thus vary historically and culturally. The Czech Republic has recently emerged from relatively dramatic social change, and as some research suggests, these changes are also reflected in a shift in the discursive representation of childhood. While during the forty-year era of the building of socialism the child was perceived largely as a passive being, malleable and subject to the authority of adults, in the present it tends to be viewed as a "little adult". This trend offers the promise of partnership between children and adults on the one hand, but a risk of insufficient protection for the immature child on the other. In early childhood education, this shift in perceptions of the child has been reflected in individualization of the approach to children and a requirement that their individual needs be acknowledged and considered in the institutional care provided for them.

The social change in the late 1980s and early 1990s has also had a profound effect on the life space in which Czech children are growing up; above all, the family domain metamorphoses have largely been shaped by changes in social politics and in the labor market and the domain of institutional care provided for preschool children.

The Impacts of Societal Transformation

The Czech Republic is a country in which the birthrate has been decreasing consistently since the 1970s, with a significant intensification of this trend after 1989. The total fertility rate was 1.89 in 1990, but only 1.18 in 2004, a value ranking among the lowest in Europe. The drop is often interpreted in the light of the transformation of the Czech society from a totalitarian state into a western democracy, connected with a new plurality of opportunities for social self-fulfillment of women. A distinct shift in values has occurred. Rabušic writes: "While in 1991 63% of Czech respondents agreed with the opinion that a woman must have children if her mission is to be fulfilled, only 44% of respondents shared the same opinion in 1999." This reflects the fact that the demographic structure of society is changing; the Czech society is aging. This is also evident from the numbers of children in the youngest age categories: while there were 393,000 children aged 0–2 in the Czech Republic in 1989, that number was only 278,000 in 2003. In 1989 there were 405,000 children aged 3–5, while in 2003 this number had dwindled to 267,000.

The value of family as perceived by the Czech society remains very high, however. Research on family behaviour among the younger generation (24–34 years) shows that three-quarters of respondents still prefer marriage as the most appropriate alternative for organizing their marital/partnership relations. An overwhelming majority intend to have children, most often two. Despite the fact that a majority of people wish to live in a marriage-based family with children, the number of people living in incomplete families has been growing. This fact has a significant impact, especially on children. In 2001, 27 percent of all dependent children were living in incomplete families. These families, emerging most frequently as a consequence of divorce, were usually provided for by the mother. This means that over one-quarter of Czech children are growing up deprived of the permanent presence of a father in the family. While there were 38 divorces per 100 concluded marriages in 1990, the rate has increased to 48 in 2003. This trend is largely regarded as a risk factor with respect to the future of the Czech population.

Although provision of help by grandparents to young families with children continues to be a relatively common phenomenon, relations between generations are clearly loosening in the long run. Multigenerational homes are getting scarcer. As far as care of preschool children are concerned, it is characterized by the new concept of maternalization of childhood—disregarding the fact of whether the father or grandparents are part of the family, it is unequivocally the mother who is regarded as the primary person responsible for bringing up the children.

The State Role in Family Functioning

A number of original functions of the family have gradually shifted to the state. The family policy of the Czech Republic continues to be characterized by a high degree of redistribution of resources. The basis of this policy is the family allowance, varying in the amount of money according to family income and drawn by an overwhelming majority of families with dependent children. Each woman is entitled to a maternity leave of twenty-eight weeks after the birth of a child, drawing 68 percent of her previous wages during this period. Maternity leave is followed by parental leave, which can be drawn by the mother or the father up to 3 years of age of the child. The parent draws a fixed allowance of approximately 20 percent of the average wage during this period. If the parent does not insist that he/she be able return to her/his initial work position, he/she may draw this allowance until the child is 4 years old. Maternity and parental leave in combination in the Czech Republic are therefore very long compared with those in other European countries.

The national family policy also involves a system of public care of preschool children. Throughout the socialist era there was a very extensive network of crèches and nursery schools. In 1989 there were 7,328 nursery schools attended by 395,164 children and 1,313 crèches attended by 52,656 children. The network of nursery schools adjusted to the decreasing numbers of children after 1989, but their availability and popularity remained unchanged. During the school year 2002/2003, the total of 5,552 nursery schools were attended by 278,859 children. However, crèches were abolished, with only a few exceptions. There were only sixty crèches in the whole of the Czech Republic in 2003, with an overall capacity for 1,678 children aged 6 months to 3 years. While in 1989 crèches were attended by 13.4 percent of all children aged 0–2, the rate was only 0.6 percent in 2003.

The employment rate among Czech women has traditionally been very high. As the socialist Czechoslovakia stressed engagement of women in the work process, mothers often returned to work soon after giving birth, placing their children in crèches. An important changeover occurred after 1989, however. Mothers are taking advantage of the long parental leave offered by the state. Remaining home to provide the child with full-time care up to 3 years of age is currently the strongly dominant maternal strategy. As the demand for crèches decreased, these institutions were gradually closing down without being replaced by another alternative.

Ideologies Underlying Czech Family Policies

It may be said that in this respect the Czech Republic has recently undergone a kind of development contrary to that in most other European countries. The dominant ideology of family policies in postwar Western Europe was based on emphasizing the primary role of the mother, inspired by thinkers such as Sigmund **Freud** or Bowlby, and this resulted in the imperative that the woman stay at home with her children. It was only at the end of the 1960s that the need for women's right to professional life was voiced and resulted in an increase in the number of early childhood education institutions. In postwar Czechoslovakia, on the other hand, engagement of women, including mothers, in the workforce was encouraged, based on the assumption that children can benefit from collective education more than from individual education. This assumption was often motivated by political and economic arguments rather than psychological, pedagogical, or medical ones. The political change in 1989 then swayed the imaginary pendulum the other way.

The current situation nevertheless is coming under criticism, the argument being that the long period during which women stay home results in their being poorly positioned in the labor market and leads to a social risk. Sociologists call for harmonization of family and work life; research shows that establishing harmony between work and family obligations is made possible above all by work flexibility—the degree to which the employee may choose when and where he/she will perform his/her work. However, this flexibility is offered by only a few employers in the Czech Republic. Part-time work is rare as well: only 4 percent of women worked part-time in 2002. These circumstances, along with the negligible number of crèches and the state subsidies provided to mothers taking care of their young children, are the reasons why an overwhelming majority of children up to three remain at home with their mothers.

Maternal Entry into the Workforce

Most mothers, however, wish to return to the labor market as soon as their child reaches 3 years of age. This moment usually comes when the child enters nursery school. Seventy-six percent of children aged 3 enter nursery schools and nursery schools are attended by as many as 95 percent of 5-year-olds. Institutional education is regarded as something children of this age can profit from significantly. Nursery schools are very popular among Czech parents and considered to be providing good services. Parents are generally satisfied with them. Their existence has been part of a deeply rooted tradition of public care of children in early childhood in Bohemia and Moravia since the nineteenth century.

Other forms of nonmaternal care of preschool children are little developed in the Czech society, and very little empirical data is available on their actual distribution. Foreign research shows that mothers prefer babysitting by a family member (the child's father if possible) for times when they cannot take care of their children themselves. In reality, however, children are more often cared for away from home, mostly in group settings. Czech data suggests that childminding by family members is preferred ahead of crèches, reflecting the current reality. Childminding by paid private persons has been a marginal phenomenon in the Czech Republic so far.

At the same time, an actively developing sector of care for the youngest children is represented by maternal centers and mothers' clubs—facilities attended by mothers on maternal leave and their children, combining a joint program for mothers and children with childminding. This is an innovative compromise: the mother remains with her child while escaping social isolation and the child gets into contact with a larger peer group even before entering nursery school.

It may be said, in summary, that currently an overwhelming majority of children in the Czech Republic participate in institutions providing early childhood education. There is, however, a fundamental divide between créches and nursery schools. The network of créches is currently little developed; children up to three stay home with their mothers and parents are not too inclined to use crèche services. In contrast, nursery schools are viewed very positively and are attended by almost all children aged 3-6. Other forms of institutional and individual non-maternal child care have been a marginal phenomenon in the Czech Republic, but their dynamic growth may be expected in the future.

Further Readings: Hill, E.J., Ch. Yang, A.J. Hawkins and M. Ferris (Dec. 2004) A cross-cultural test of the work-family interface in 48 countries. *Journal of Marriage and Family* 1300-1316; Mintz, S. (2004) The social and cultural construction of American childhood. In M. Coleman and L.H. Ganond, eds., *Handbook of contemporary families.* Thousand Oaks, A: Sage, pp. 36-54; Nosál, I. (2003). Diskurzy a reprezentace dětství ve věku nejistoty. (Discourses and representations of childhood in the era of uncertainty) In P. Mareš and T. Potočný, *Modernizace a česká rodina (Modernization and the Czech family).* Brno: Barrister and Principal, pp. 177-188; Rabušic, L. (2001). *Kde ty všechny děti jsou* (Where are all the children gone). Prague: Sociologické nakladatelství; Riley, L.A., and J.L. Glass (Feb 2002). You can't always get what you want—Infant care preferences and use among employed mothers. *Journal of Marriage and Family* 2-15; Zaouche-Gaudron, Ch. (2003). Malé dítě uprostřed dvojí socializace rodina—jesle (The young child at the centre of the twofold socialization family—crèche). In L. Šulová and Ch. Zaouche-Gaudron, eds., *Předškolní dítě a jeho svět (Pre-school child and his/her world).* Prague: Karolinum.

Klára Šeďová

Theories of Early Childhood Education—Pedagogy

The theory of early childhood education in Bohemia and Moravia has a long tradition. Its development has reflected the changing approaches to children and the changing environment, both in the family and educational institutions.

Johannes Amos Comenius

The primary theoretician was Johannes Amos **Comenius** (1592-1670), who is regarded as one of the founding fathers of modern European pedagogy and is world renowned as author of a conceptual framework for early childhood education. In his treatise *"Informatorium scholae maternae"* (1633) Comenius proposed an integrated concept of early childhood education as a necessary stage preceding general education. He regarded early childhood education as an integral part of lifelong personal development. His concept of early childhood education was designed primarily for parents to improve family upbringing and he allowed for establishment of public education institutions later. The objective of education as he saw it was harmony, which he perceived as consonance of humans with nature, other people, and the God, that is, understanding the global picture of life and the world.

In Comenius' concept the child is a being entitled to care and protection and a right that others empathize with his/her needs, a right to a loving relationship providing him/her with a sense of safety, and a right to be respected. Implementation of these rights is a duty of the adults. The child is to be provided with all this as a basic and self-evident prerequisite of his/her further development. For the child's development to approach harmony, it must be based on Comenius' basic assumption—naturalness of children's development. This implies the need to create conditions so that the child may develop most naturally in parallel with natural development so as to uphold the principle "Let everything flow freely, let violence be far from things."

For Comenius nonviolence does not mean passive submission of the educator to evolutionary characteristics of the child; rather it means active but very sensitive guidance. The balance between freedom and guidance, spontaneity and discipline recommended by Comenius shows his refined pedagogical sensitivity. This also implies an emphasis on what educators should focus on. If the child is to be educated to achieve a certain goal, the educators, too, must strive to attain the goal. The relationship between an educator and a child is a result not only of the education, but also of the extent to which the educator understands the child. "Like a physician, a cultivator of the young is a mere servant, not a lord of the nature."

The child also is not merely a passive recipient of the efforts of the educator. He/she plays an important and active role, acknowledged to him/her by the emphasis on creativity and activity. The life experience of the child, associated with sensory perception in the beginning, is applied and developed in play. Comenius regarded play in early childhood as just as important as food and sleep. He recommended play based on movement and imitation as preparation for future work activities. He was opposed to violating children's naturalness by guiding children to artificial inaction and passivity. His curriculum is based on the specifics of children's development and respects these objectives, too. The stress is on the educational content as a whole, not just some of its components. It emphasizes (1) healthy physical development of the child, (2) development of his/her fine and gross motor skills, (3) sensory development, (4) development of cognitive processes, abilities, and skills, (5) systemization of knowledge in 6-year-olds, (6) gradual development and purity of children's language, (7) aesthetic education with stress on music, (8) religious education and elements of piety, (9) education in ethics with stress on discipline, obedience, morals and virtues, and (10) emotional education.

Comenius recommended free development of children, but under nonviolent and wise guidance. He also addressed the issue of dichotomy between learning/education and faith. The three sources of knowledge that are given to humans according to him—the Bible, the world, and ourselves—are mediated mainly by reason. This means that neglect or suppression of cognitive development constrains the use of these sources, which constrains the fullness of faith in its turn. Faith and education complement each other to create a fuller unity of the whole.

The Nineteenth Century

The foundations of Czech national tradition in early childhood education had been laid by Comenius almost 200 years before Czech public early childhood care started to be organized. The period of establishment of national school systems in the nineteenth century had an impact on how the youngest children were brought up, too. Care of preschool children ceased to be a matter exclusively of the family, and became a subject of interest for the whole society. Institutions implementing the concept of community child care and education of young children were initially designed for children from poor families, but the interest in public early childhood education grew among higher strata of the society as the nineteenth century proceeded.

The newly emergent institutions were called "childhouses" ("dětince" from "děti"—children) or "growhouses" ("pěstovny" from "pěstovat"—"grow"). They may be divided into nurseries, kindergartens, and maternity schools according to their character and history of development.

The oldest institution was a nursery, whose initial form in Europe may be characterized as a purely childminding, welfare institution. Czech nurseries, however, tended to differ from this description from the very beginning thanks to the efforts of Jan Vladimír Svoboda, who developed and implemented a new concept of nursery operation in his first Czech nursery "Na hrádku" in Prague in 1832, in which the educational characteristics prevailed. He went beyond the charitable nature of nurseries by bringing in children from well-to-do families so that they could learn the elements of the trivium (reading, writing, and arithmetic) in Czech before entering school, where the language of instruction was German.

The National Enlightenment (movement in support of the Czech language and culture that developed in response to Germanization pressures of the Hapsburg monarchy in Bohemia), in the beginning of the nineteenth century pursued from the very beginning the idea that Czech children should obtain at least the very basics of education in their mother tongue. A treatise by Svoboda called *Nursery or primordial, practical, self-explanatory, versatile teaching to the little ones for real perfection of reason and cultivation of the heart pointing to reading, arithmetics and technical drawing for teachers, fosterers and parents*, written in 1839, presents an entirely original concept, although it was influenced by Comenius. According to this idea, children are taught and educated adequately to their age, above all through a system of purposefully designed and systematically used games so that they obtain a body of knowledge based on immediate experience. Adequate procedures built around facts help children to acquire even the elements of the trivium. It may be said that Svoboda combines and develops Comenius' idea of maternity school and the idea of elementary school in the mother tongue. Each requirement from "Informatorium" by Comenius was methodologically elaborated by Svoboda in his "Nursery". The brain, the heart, and the hand were to be trained simultaneously and the whole concept of education was organically interconnected by education in ethics.

Svoboda's efforts to enhance national education represented an important milestone in early childhood and elementary education in Bohemia and Moravia.

Thanks to his influence a strong Czech school of methodologists of early child-hood education was established.

German Influence

In Bohemia and Moravia, where a significant proportion of the population spoke German, typical German-like early childhood education institutions were established, too—**Fröbel's** kindergartens (Fridrich Fröbel 1782–1852). The first German kindergarten opened in Prague in 1864. Kindergartens were first attended by children from well-to-do families and the poor were admitted later. These settings gradually attempted to attract Czech children as well. But because only German was spoken there, they were regarded as a tool of Germanization efforts and the Czech patriotic public opposed them fiercely.

The Pedagogy of the Czech Nursery School

The institution of the Czech nursery school emerged as a counterbalance to the system of German kindergartens. The first Czech *maternity school* was founded at St. James's in Prague in 1869. The number of maternity schools grew over time, reaching 249 by 1897.

Maternity schools were designed especially to play the national-awareness-raising task. They were based on the Czech system of education, but their authors took inspiration from three well-known concepts: Svoboda's, Fröbel's, and the French system. The application of the concept developed by Svoboda consisted mainly of taking over the global approach to early childhood education, leading to harmonization of the physical and psychic aspects in child development with stress on cognitive education and gradual preparation for reading and writing. Fröbel's methodology provided the Czech maternity school with inspiration in terms of children's handiwork activities, gardening, and an emphasis on play as the number one educational tool. The French tradition contributed the organizational structure of maternity schools, stressing the schooling nature of work. Apart from that, the importance of instruction in morals and the loving attitude of the fosterer to the child were emphasized. Although the concept of Czech maternity school was developed eclectically, the efforts that contributed to its formation can be evaluated as balanced since the individual sources were used to contribute those elements that had proved most vital.

The Imperial Education Act of 1869 granted all children the right to compulsory education in their mother tongue. The Act thus cancelled the necessity to teach Czech children the trivium in Czech prior to enrolling in schools where German was spoken. Individual types of early childhood institutions started to differentiate more markedly (maternity schools—educatory goal, nurseries—care-taking goal) and to deviate from the didactic goal of elementary school (compulsory primary school). A state directive specified the respective functions of maternity schools, nurseries, and crèches and their mutual relations in detail. Maternity school was presented as a public and free-of-charge institution, which made it possible to en-roll children from all income groups. The trivium was withdrawn from maternity schools and the curriculum was specified with more consideration for the early age of the children.

All in all, this period may be evaluated as a very important one for development of institutional early childhood care of children in Bohemia and Moravia, since early childhood education came to be understood as part of education as such and responsibility for it started to shift from the family to the nationwide context.

Reformist Tendencies in Pedagogy

The end of the nineteenth century and the beginning of the twentieth century were characterized by development of reformist tendencies in pedagogy, which among other things concentrated on the issues of early childhood education. These tendencies developed in reaction to the so-called fröbelism (a deformed version of the concept developed by Fröbel), the school-like character of maternity schools, and their excessive intellectualism. What became stronger were pedocentric trends emphasizing the child's personality as the central point of educatory activities, also termed as the "Copernicus turn" in education. This approach required that the goal of education be oriented to intellectual development as well as practical skills and development of personality traits. The curriculum was individuated and differentiated with respect to the child's personality. The approach to development was activity-centred, that is, the child participated in his/her education and development by his/her own activity. The need for imposing discipline externally was restricted and the relation between the adult and the child was based on trust and mutual respect. An atmosphere of joyful activity was to be a guarantee of progress and the success of each individual child.

This reformist spirit gained dominance in the newly emerged Czechoslovak Republic (1918) as well. Reformist efforts affected all types of school, including nursery schools. As in other European countries attempts to integrate nursery schools into the larger system of education, that is, to connect early childhood education with other stages of school education occurred in what was then Czechoslovakia.

The search for a new concept of nursery school in the period between the world wars culminated in the formation of two reformist trends: the radical one, accentuating especially the didactic point of view (including an attitude approving the teaching of reading and writing in nursery school) in the work of nursery schools, and the moderate one, emphasizing the preparatory and family-like nature of nursery school. These differing concepts coexisted until 1939, when the very lively and heterogeneous pedagogic activities were interrupted by World War II.

The approval of the Integrated School Act in 1948 (the first educational act after the coup) implemented the prewar requirement to make nursery schools a stage equal to other stages of education. The number of nursery schools grew rapidly, and almost 100 percent of the population of children attended them over the next forty years. As far as quality was concerned, the detailed methodological elaboration of individual aspects of education and the systemic planning and formulation of the target requirements in children's development were regarded as steps forward. However, negative consequences of this excessive "integration" became manifest as time passed. Implementation of an integrated nursery school—from goals, content, and forms to organization and methods—suppressed the personality and creativity of the teacher as well as the child and provided no scope for respect for the child's individuality. Moreover, strong ideological trends proscribed by the official Marxist doctrine were put through in nursery schools just as at other levels of education.

One absolutely essential requirement that was expressed by pedagogical approaches after 1989 was the one of "freedom, decentralization and removal of unification". The "Personality Developing Model of Early Childhood Education" (Osobnostně rozvíjející model předškolní výchovy) that began in 1993 was conceived along these lines. It defines nursery school as an open system akin to education in the family. The general atmosphere of nursery schools is to combine humanization with democratization. The attitude toward the child stresses his/her absolute uniqueness, with social roots. Nursery school is to be characterized by partnership between the teacher and the child, open communication, considerable scope for multifaceted activities of the child, and positive motivation.

The last stage of the transformation of Czech nursery school into its present shape is the approval of the General Curriculum for Early Childhood Education (2004) as a curricular document specifying the characteristics shared by early childhood education as well as the opportunity for differentiation and application of the specifics of individual institutions for early childhood education. It identifies the goal of nursery school as facilitation of further life path for the child, creation of prerequisites for further education, and maximum support to individual development of individual children.

In summary, during its history the Czech pedagogy of early childhood has coped especially with the issue of naturalness and freedom and the degree of their application to the education of young children. The current concept can be viewed as balanced in this respect.

Further Readings: Bartušková, M. (1948). *Mateřská škola v Československu (Nursery school in Czechoslovakia).* Prague: MŠ; Čapková, D. (1968). *Předškolní výchova v díle J.A. Komenského, jeho předchůdců a pokračovatelů (Early childhood education in works by J. A. Comenius, his predecessors and continuators).* Prague: SPN; Jarníková, I. (1930). *Výchovný program mateřských škol (Educational curriculum for nursery schools).* Zábřeh: Společenské tiskárny; Komenský, J. A. (1992). *Informatorium školy mateřské (Informatorium scholae maternae).* Prague: Kalich; Mišurcová, V. (1979). *Dějiny teorie a praxe výchovy dětí předškolního věku v 19. a 20. st. (History of theory and practice of bringing up children in 19th and 20th century).* Prague: SPN; Opravilová, E. (1993). *Osobnostně orientovaný model předškolní výchovy* (Personality-oriented model of early childhood education). Prague: UK; *Rámcový vzdělávací program pro předškolní vzdělávání (General curriculum for early childhood education).* Praha: MŠMT, 2005; Svoboda, J. V. (1958). *Školka (Nursery school).* Prague: SPN; Uhlířová, J. (1992). Komenského pojetí dětství. (Comenius' concept of childhood) In *Odkaz Komenského a předškolní výchova (The legacy of Comenius and early childhood education).* Prague: UK; Uhlířová, J. J. A. (1992). Komenský a jeho vliv na počátky předškolní výchovy v Čechách (J. A. Comenius and his influence on the beginnings of early childhood education in Bohemia). In J.V. Svoboda, ed., *Učitelé - šiřitelé myšlenek Jana Amose Komenského (Teachers—Propagators of Ideas by J. A. Comenius).* Přerov: Vlastivědné muzeum J.A. Komenského.

Jana Uhlířová

Public Policies for Early Childhood Education

The present form of early childhood education in the Czech Republic was significantly influenced by the political, economic, and social change that affected the whole educational environment after the revolution of 1989. Strategic goals for the global transformation of the Czech educational system started to be implemented based on the following principles:

- depoliticization of education;
- recognition of the civil rights of children, pupils, students, and their parents to choice of an educational path depending on children's individual skills and interests and their right to choose an appropriate school;
- abolishment of the educational monopoly of the state and establishment of private and religious nursery schools;
- quantitative expansion of the network of public schools and qualitative diversity of educational opportunities and formation of a competitive environment in education;
- implementation of funding in the educational system based on the normative method

The flow of full freedom in education, and application of market principles in satisfaction of educational demand and in funding, characterized by liberalism and deregulation, led to a gradual internal and external reform also in early childhood education. Pedagogic discussions yielded the following major topics that proved to be of key importance for further development of educational policies concerning child care and education of preschool children:

- importance and place of early childhood education within the system of education;
- early childhood education availability and funding;
- curriculum for early childhood education and quality of provision of education;
- qualification training for teachers involved in early childhood education.

Each of these topics has a fifteen-year history mirroring the fermentation of opinions and political accents in a society that was undergoing a transformation from a totalitarian regime into a democracy.

Importance and the Place of Early Childhood Education in the Educational System

Opinions about the importance and the place of early childhood education in the whole educational system were consolidating in the course of the 1990s. The opinion that early childhood education should become part of the Czech system of education and as such should be defined as level 0, that is, the preprimary level, in accordance with international classification (ISCED 97), gradually came to prevail. The existing Educational Act (2004) codifies this approach starting in 2005, specifying the goals of early childhood education as follows:

> Early childhood education enhances development of personality of the pre-school child, contributes to his/her healthy emotional, cognitive and physical development and acquisition of the basic rules of communication, basic values and interpersonal relations. Early childhood education prepares basic conditions for further education. Early childhood education helps to make up for irregularities in the development of children prior to enrolment to primary education and provides children with special educational needs with special pedagogic care.

The position of early childhood education in the Czech Republic has also been strengthened by the newly formulated general principles of Czech and European educational policies, especially the concepts of lifelong learning and equal educational opportunities. Both these concepts basically mean a paradigmatic transformation in the approach to the place and importance of education as such, including early childhood education, since they view them in the context of the whole life path and in the context of all opportunities that may be open to people.

Thanks to this shift, the opinion that early childhood education should be made compulsory from 5 years of age surfaced in the discussions. Since this opinion did not win in the end, the current solution is the following: each child has a right, not an obligation, to education in the last year before the start of the compulsory school attendance. And conversely, each municipality is obliged to provide early childhood education for all children whose parents apply for it.

Another much discussed topic was interconnecting early childhood education and compulsory primary education, or nursery school and primary school, at the level of subject matter and potentially also organization. Due to fears that nursery schools might adopt the "scholastic approach" excessively, this interconnection has not been implemented to any great extent. On the contrary, the stress instead is on making the first grades of compulsory school more like early childhood education by emphasizing natural individual differences in children's maturation and learning, more freedom in terms of learning content and the pace of learning, avoidance of classification, and so forth.

Early Childhood Education Availability and Funding

Thanks to the long tradition of building the network of nursery schools and crèches throughout the socialist era, availability of early childhood education was not generally viewed as a major problem. It is nevertheless a fact that the situation did diversify after 1989, for demographic, geographic, social, and economic reasons. Some regions experienced a shortage of nursery schools, and especially crèches, because some of the state-owned enterprises that had established and sponsored them failed to survive. The numbers of preschool children began to shrink as a consequence of demographic trends, which also led to the closing of crèches, and to a lesser extent nursery schools (see entry on child care for 0- to 3-year-olds). The number of nursery schools dropped by about 22 percent compared with the period before 1989; this trend was most significant in the countryside, where nursery school availability went down radically. The current availability seems more or less equal to the demand, with no major discrepancies. The potential solution is fully in the hands of local governments.

The situation in terms of the economic and social availability of early childhood education is somewhat different. Early childhood education in the Czech Republic is funded partly from municipal budgets and partly from payments by families; the existing financial participation of parents is generally regarded as acceptable. The charges are reduced for lower income families and some families do not pay at all. Despite this, in the words of OECD experts, "guaranteeing the general availability of early childhood education, especially for children from socially and socio-culturally challenged families, is a top priority for the future in the Czech Republic." It is turning out that parents from families challenged in these ways do not care for early childhood education for their children and do not send their children to nursery school on their own accord. There is no mechanism to make them to do so, only long-term education and motivation can be applied, but they have just started to be paid adequate attention. The fundamental argument is that children generally receive child care in early childhood education institutions comparable with child care within the family, and above all that children from socio-culturally challenged environments will undoubtedly profit from being in a crèche or a nursery school.

A Curriculum for Early Childhood Education and the Quality of Provision of Education

The beginning of the 1990s in early childhood education was characterized by making the curriculum for early childhood education entirely open. The syllabi valid up to that time were withdrawn, and a liberal approach was followed under which the headmaster in cooperation with the teachers was to set a curriculum for the particular nursery school. A whole array of alternative programs attractive to the Czech pedagogic public were offered (**Waldorf** pedagogy, **Montessori** pedagogy, Dalton Plan, Step by Step Program, and others). It nevertheless started to become evident that many nursery schools interpreted the openness and freedom they were given in curriculum selection as an opportunity to "do hardly anything" or, in other words, to abandon systematic and purposeful guidance of children and keep their educational efforts to a minimum. This compromised the quality of provision of early childhood education, which until then had been generally regarded as high.

The relatively turbulent pedagogical as well as political discussion finally settled down, and led to the opinion that a general curriculum must be developed—In terms both of a general compulsory educational offering, and of the setting of conditions (organization, personnel, material, mental health related, safety, etc.), adherence to which should be compulsory for nursery schools and for the municipalities establishing them. This opinion was also supported by the conclusions of the expert assessment of the standard of early childhood education in the Czech Republic organized by OECD (2000). According to these conclusions, development of a general curriculum at the national level would provide the grounding needed to guarantee the quality of provision of early childhood education, surveillance of how educational goals are met, and comparability of pedagogical processes and outputs.

These discussions and recommendations led to the development and implementation of the General Curriculum for Early Childhood Education (2004). Its fulfillment, allowing for diversified school curricula, has become an obligation for all nursery schools in the Czech Republic. The reservations of the lay and pedagogic public about this requirement have now been replaced by positive attitudes.

Qualification Training for Teachers Involved in Early Childhood Education

The increased demands of the work together with the higher responsibility and extended authorities of teachers in nursery schools have provoked the question of how their qualification training should change. Besides application of the curriculum for early childhood education, teachers are expected to use it as a basis for developing curricula adequate to the particular groups of children committed to their care, their individual needs, the requirements of parents, and conditions of the particular nursery school. Teachers are also expected to have diagnostic competencies and communicate with parents to a greater extent, being able to provide them with counselling support regarding the development of their child.

A desire that such demanding occupational requirements should be underlain by more demanding and longer occupational training, shifting the training of teachers for early childhood education from the present secondary level of education to the tertiary one (university or nonuniversity studies), emerged by the end of the 1990s. Again, this goal was supported by an OECD expert report on the state of early childhood education and child care for preschool children in the Czech Republic (2000).

However, this goal was not fully accepted. This was due, paradoxically, to disapproval on the part of nursery school teachers themselves, who feared they would have to complete another demanding program of studies. It was due also to opposition on the part of secondary pedagogic schools, who until then had a monopoly on the training of nursery school teachers. The situation resulted in a compromise acknowledging both types of education: at the secondary level (secondary pedagogic schools) and at the tertiary level (higher vocational schools and bachelor programs at universities) (see Teacher Preparation entry). The trend is toward preparation at the tertiary level, which should strengthen occupational skills of nursery school teachers, their social status, and their economic situation while making their status comparable with that of teachers at higher levels of education.

The upbringing and education of preschool children are currently regarded as one of the best developed areas of care for the young generation in the Czech Republic in terms of legislation, educational content, and organization. This does not mean that there is a shortage of topics needing further discussion. These topics include especially the availability of child care for children from 0 to 3 years of age, the availability of child care for socioeconomically challenged children, greater parent involvement, and better qualification of nurses in crèches and teachers in nursery schools.

Further Readings: Národní zpráva o stavu předškolní výchovy, vzdělávání a péče o děti předškolního věku v České republice (National report on the state of early childhood education and childcare for pre-school children in the Czech Republic). Prague: MŠMT, 2000, p. 87; *Rámcový vzdělávací program pro předškolní vzdělávání (General Curriculum for early childhood education)*. Praha: MŠMT, 2004; OECD (2001). *Starting strong. Early childhood education and care*. Paris: The Organization for Economic Co-operation and Development; Zákon č. 561/2004 Sb., o předškolním, základním, středním, vyšším odborném a jiném vzdělávání (školský zákon). (Act No. 561/2004 Coll. on early childhood, elementary, high-school, higher vocational and other education—Educational Act).

Milada Rabušicová

Family Involvement in Early Childhood Education

In the Czech Republic family is regarded the basic, natural, and the most crucial environment for a child at an early age. This is especially the case for children up to 3 years of age and the prevailing arrangement of things reflects this: a great majority of children remain at home, cared for by the mother or another member of the family. The family policy of the state makes this possible through a long maternity/parental leave lasting until the child is 4 years old. For this reason, there is no extensive network of crèches in the Czech Republic to provide infant and toddler care (see entry on child care for 0- to 3-year-olds). Various religious and private initiatives and activities of nongovernmental organizations offer parents, mainly mothers, different opportunities for spending time with their children within a group, with the support of experts. For example, parents may form various "mums' clubs," "work-out clubs for parents and children," "consulting rooms for healthy children's diet," etc. Beyond the different debates about the appropriateness of this "family" arrangement are discussions surrounding the issues of equal opportunities for women and men, support to family as such, and the development of the demographic situation characterized by a low birthrate. However, the prevailing opinion today in the Czech Republic is that a close bond between the child and the mother is the most crucial element for the development of a very young child.

The situation concerning children from three until the start of compulsory school attendance at six is radically different. Most Czech families with children of this age take advantage of public early childhood education institutions, that is, mainly nursery schools. The proportion of children attending nursery schools ranges between 67 percent for 3-year-olds and 98 percent for 5-year-olds. This number demonstrates that the nursery school attendance is close to universal in the last year before the start of compulsory school. However, families from some socially and economically challenged groups, especially Romany families, tend not to send their children to nursery schools. Various programs have been developed to motivate these parents. These programs include the so-called "preparatory classes" where these children are given special care and support and where Romany assistants help.

When parents delegate their caring and upbringing authority to experts in public early childhood education institutions to the extent found in the Czech Republic, the subject of the relations and cooperation between these two institutions—the family and the nursery school, or the parents and the teachers—must be addressed. For the most part, these relations had not been regarded as a problem or as deserving much attention until the 1990s, when political change was brought about by the "Velvet Revolution" of 1989. The prevailing attitude was straightforward: "There are experts in nursery schools, just like in other school institutions, who know best how to take care of a child; let parents respect their approaches and intents." Parents largely endeavored to satisfy the requirements of schools in the sense that can be summed up as "Take care of the child so that he/she comes to school or the nursery school on time and well-prepared." The (nursery) school took charge of the child and used its professional methods to enhance his/her intellectual and other development, but also his/her discipline and social integration. This "labour division" usually worked quite well and if not, the participants tended to regard it as an example of the uneven distribution of power between these two institutions. The model in which the state takes on responsibilities originally belonging to the family through its institutions was common and more or less accepted.

Just as in other spheres of life within Czech society, much changed about this model during the recent years. It may even be said that the situation changed radically, since parents have started to be referred to as partners, collaborators, clients, and even citizens, who—as follows from the principle of civil society—may actively participate in the life of any public institution, including schools/nursery schools.

Policy

This new approach to family involvement was also reflected in school legislation of the Czech Republic. The relation between early childhood education institutions and parents is currently defined by the General Curriculum for Early Childhood Education, which came into effect as part of the Educational Act of 2004. According to the General Curriculum, the purpose of institutional early childhood education is to *supplement upbringing in the family* and in close cooperation with the family, helping to provide the child with various and adequate stimuli for his/her active development and learning. According to this binding curriculum, the participation of parents in early childhood education is fully satisfactory if the following conditions are met:

- Relations between teachers and parents are characterized by mutual trust and openness, goodwill, understanding, respect and willingness to cooperate. The cooperation is based on the principle of partnership.
- Teachers respond to particular needs of individual children/families and try to understand them and meet their wishes.
- Parents can participate in the activities of the nursery school, take part in various events, and interact with their children as part of their play if they choose to. They are informed of all events and activities in the nursery schools regularly and to a sufficient extent. If they give an indication of interest, they may contribute to the process of program planning, help to solve problems that have occurred, etc.
- Teachers inform parents of the proficiency of their child as well as of his/her individual learning and development progress. They coordinate with parents for joint action in providing the child with upbringing and education.
- Teachers protect the privacy of the family and act discreetly as far as internal issues they are aware of are concerned. They behave toward parents with thoughtfulness and tact, realizing they are handling confidential information. They do not interfere in the life and privacy of the family, avoiding excessive ardour and the giving of unsolicited advice.
- The nursery school supports family care and helps parents by sharing the care of their child; it offers parents counselling services and all kinds of educational activities concerning upbringing and education of preschool children.

Research Initiatives

In the last fifteen years, several research projects have focused on exploration and analysis of the relations between parents and teachers, including teachers of nursery schools, and on parent involvement. Results from one of these research projects served as preparatory material for the National Report on the State of Early Childhood Upbringing, Education and Care of Pre-school Age in the Czech Republic, 2000, prepared within the Thematic Review of Early Childhood Education and Care Policy organized by OECD. A questionnaire survey was conducted with 164 nursery school directors, 733 teachers, and 1,433 parents of children attending nursery schools throughout the Czech Republic. It addressed, among other things, issues like parents' opinions on the functioning and program of their nursery school, satisfaction with teacher/parent cooperation, and the forms taken in these relations.

Parents' opinions about the functioning and program of the nursery school. The responses show a general satisfaction of parents with their nursery school (99% of parents), its organization and program, as well as how well the parents were informed of nursery school activities. Parents expressed their unequivocal trust towards nursery school teachers (99%) and saw the nursery school environment as appropriate and universally beneficial to their child (97%). Two-thirds of parents believed their child received enough individual care in the nursery school. The satisfaction of parents with nursery schools corresponds with the assessment on the part of teachers and directors. Teachers and directors (99%) believe that parents are unequivocally or largely satisfied with nursery school and the services it provides for them and their children.

Satisfaction with teacher/parent cooperation and forms of this cooperation. Parents were more satisfied than nursery school teachers with teacher/parent cooperation. This relationship was assessed as excellent or very good by 60 percent of parents and 51 percent of teachers. Teachers indicated that they expected parents to show more interest, openness, goodwill, and involvement. Parents primarily care about how their child feels in the nursery school, which is understandable. Leaving the program offered to their children in the nursery school aside, however, this is where their interest usually ends. Thus parents continue to leave all responsibility up to the nursery school, which may be interpreted as an assumption that their child receives good care during the day and as a sign of their full trust in the quality of care provided and the professional skills of the teachers. Other possible causes can be identified, however, including lack of time, little experience and skills in communication with nursery school teachers, a certain convenience, and a tendency to shift responsibility. The forms of cooperation and communication mostly include usual and traditional activities such as presentations for parents, parent meetings, and individual consultations. These are forms in which the role of parents is rather passive. Activities requiring more active participation of parents (e.g., an open house with a program, joint events for the whole family, parents as class assistants, etc.) are much less frequent.

Based on this research, it may be said that parents are largely satisfied clients receiving services offered by nursery schools in the Czech Republic. The situation seems not to motivate them enough to be active participants in the process of providing care, upbringing, and education to their children in nursery schools.

A very similar conclusion has been arrived at by another research project undertaken in 2002–2003, which used sophisticated methods to find out the position of parents with respect to school and nursery school. The research was based on established theoretical concepts characterizing parents as clients, educational and social partners, citizens, or "trouble-making parents." The results showed that with respect to nursery schools, the client role of parents prevails unequivocally (analogous to primary school), from the point of view of both school representatives and parents themselves. The role implies that parents are interested to such an extent as to choose the school for their child, desiring the best teachers and the best care possible for their child. Parents also want the school to provide an adequate amount of information to them. The parent activity usually does not go beyond this degree of interest. Parents are also perceived as educational partners (57%) in nursery schools, with more frequency than in other types of school (first and second stage of elementary school). This points to good potential for further development of cooperation between nursery school and parents as they are parents willing to participate, help, exchange information about the child with the teacher, and support the child in his/her development and learning. And finally, parents are perceived in nursery schools as "the trouble-making parents" (42%) if they act too independently, do not show enough interest in nursery school, and do not communicate much with teachers.

The research results described above present a largely positive image of relations between parents and nursery school teachers, testifying to satisfaction and perhaps even some balance of power. As far as parent involvement in the sense of active sharing, cooperation, and partnership is concerned, however, there is some scope for further development and improvement.

Cooperation between teachers in nursery schools and parents of children attending nursery schools has recently been considered one of the priorities of pedagogical work involving preschool children in the Czech Republic. It is generally believed that of all educational institutions, the focus, organization, and operation of nursery schools offer the most favourable formats for providing good communication and potential cooperation between parents and teachers. It is, nevertheless, important that both parties work collaboratively to achieve this cooperation.

Further Readings: Bastiani, J. (1993). Parents as partners. In P. Munn, ed., *Parents and schools. Customers, managers or partners?* London: Routledge, p. 182; Cullingford, C. (1996). The role of parents in education system. In C. Cullingford, ed., *Parents, education and the state.* Aldershot: Arena, p. 186; *Národní zpráva o stavu předškolní výchovy, vzdělávání a péče o děti předškolního věku v České republice* (National report on the state of early childhood education and childcare for pre-school children in the Czech Republic). Prague: MŠMT, 2000, p. 87; Rabušicová, M., and M. Pol (1996). Vztahy školy a rodiny dnes: hledání cest k partnerství (1), (2) (Relations between school and family today: Looking for paths to partnership). *Pedagogika* (Pedagogy), No. 1 (49–61) and No. 2 (105–116); Rabušicová, M., K. Šeďová, K. Trnková, and V. Čiháček (2004). *Škola a/versus/*

rodina *(School and/or family)*. Brno: Masaryk University, p. 176; *Rámcový vzdělávací program pro předškolní vzdělávání (General curriculum for early childhood education)*. Praha: MŠMT, 2004; Vincent, C. (2000). *Including parents?* Buckingham: Open University Press, p. 156; Wallace, T., and H. Walberg (1991). Parental partnership for learning. *International Journal of Educational Research* 15(2), pp. 131–145.

Milada Rabušicová

Quality of Provision of Early Childhood Education

The importance of improvement, monitoring, and assessment of quality of education has recently been increasing in the Czech Republic. This growing importance has to do with the introduction of the two-level (national and school) curriculum and therefore with the opportunity to choose an individual educational path, which is also associated with a great deal of responsibility on the part of individual nursery schools, or their teachers, for the quality of provided education. This involves not only *external quality assessment* performed by central or regional inspection. Because schools do not work on the basis of any normative document, but every nursery school develops a school curriculum of its own, there is a need for feedback on the functioning of the whole system inside the nursery school. It is therefore why *internal assessment* is used, the general goal being to make self evaluation gradually become a natural part of work of each nursery school.

Specification of Early Childhood Education Quality in Documents

The question of how to define and assess quality of early childhood education in the Czech Republic is currently addressed by legal regulations (the Educational Act, orders, directives) and the national curriculum (General Curriculum for Early Childhood Education, GC ECE).

Structural quality and availability of early childhood education. Legal regulations concentrate on defining the *structural quality*, which can be expressed in terms of objective and measurable variables (size and structure of children's groups, number of children per teacher, education of teachers in early childhood education, etc.), along with the *quality of services* provided for parents (availability, service hours, opportunity to choose from among different institutions, and curricula). The main indicators of structural quality of early childhood education in the Czech Republic are the following:

- Early childhood education in the Czech Republic is provided for children from 3 to 6 years of age. If a child is not mature enough, compulsory school attendance may be deferred.
- Nursery schools have three grades. Children from different grades may be assigned into a single classroom. A nursery school group may have up to twenty-four children. The limit is lower if children with special educational needs attend the group.
- Nursery schools providing daylong, part time, or around-the-clock services may be established. Service hours may be adjusted in line with the needs of the children

depending on local conditions or wishes and needs of parents. A child may enroll into a nursery school at any time throughout the school year.
- Nursery schools provide meals for children for a fee.
- Teachers working in nursery schools are mostly high school educated, some of them are university-educated (see separate entry on teacher preparation).
- Parents can choose from among alternative general curricula and different school curricula.

As far as availability of early childhood education is concerned, the intention in the Czech Republic is to guarantee each preschool child a legal right to early childhood education and a feasible opportunity to apply this right in practice. This is evidenced by the following legal provisions:
- Early childhood education is not compulsory.
- Each municipality is obliged to guarantee nursery school placement to all children whose parents apply for it.
- Nursery school charges may be lowered or waived for children from socially challenged families.

Process quality of early childhood education. The national curriculum (GC ECE) deals with issues of process quality and quality of results achieved. It is formulated so as to provide an integrated set of the main criteria, which are in line with valid legislation and define the desired quality of early childhood education in terms of forms and methods of work, educational goals, content, conditions, and results to be achieved. These are largely qualitative criteria, applicable in both internal and external evaluation of nursery schools and the education they provide.

GC ECE specifies methods and forms of work corresponding to the specific needs and possibilities of preschool children. It defines general educational goals to be met. It describes the level of key skills attainable during early childhood education. It identifies the subject matter to be offered to children, in terms of practical and intellectual activities and basic domains of elementary knowledge. GC ECE also specifies the expected outputs as the assumed results of early childhood education. It describes material, organizational, personal, psychic health-related, and pedagogical conditions affecting both the process and the results of education. GC ECE also specifies the main principles to apply when developing school curricula and, last but not least, the basic labor laws for teachers involved in early childhood education and their responsibilities toward children and their parents. GC ECE also specifies risks that may pose a threat to the success of educational plans of teachers and diminish the quality of education provision. This currently represents the basic framework for achievement and assessment of quality of the process of education in nursery schools.

Assessment of Provision of Education

The Educational Act and its implementing regulations (orders, directives) together with the General Curriculum sets a framework for evaluation and assessment of school curricula and of the quality of provision of education by individual nursery schools from the position of external supervision (inspection) as well as internal control (self-evaluation).

External quality assessment. Assessment of quality of early childhood education from the position of inspection is to be based on the rules inspectors apply when planning and performing their inspection activities. Inspectors monitor and assess school curricula and the process and results of education provision. They evaluate adherence to legal and implementing regulations, analyze and assess whether the school curriculum is in line with the requirements (formal and content-wise) of the General Curriculum. The inspectors check the correspondence between the planned curriculum and its implementation, observe and evaluate the course of education (methods and forms, quality of interaction and communication) as well as the achieved results. They check and assess the methods and effectiveness of planning, the methodological procedures used by teachers, evaluation activities, management and supervisory activities of the schoolmaster, etc. The school curriculum and its quality are evaluated as a whole.

Internal quality assessment. Rules for assessment of quality of provision of education from the position of the nursery school (self-evaluation) are set by GC ECE. The school is obliged to perform self-evaluation activities in a process of continuous self-regulation of its own educational work with a view to increasing its quality. These activities mediate a better understanding of the processes in the school and their regulation based on feedback (improvement).

A survey of the evaluation activities is a compulsory part of the school curriculum. The survey should include the following:

- a list of activities at the school level (especially conditions of education, goals and objectives of the school curriculum, and work of the pedagogic staff are evaluated);
- a survey of activities at the children's group level (the educational offerings, the proficiency of the group as a whole are evaluated, teachers contribute their self-assessment);
- a survey of monitoring and evaluation of results (developmental and learning progress of individual children is evaluated).

The concrete subject of self-evaluation is especially the implemented curriculum or the course of the process of education and its results. Self-evaluation may in this respect focus on many areas, e.g., on evaluation of the interrelationships between the school curriculum and the group curriculum, of the educational offerings, the material, health and mental health related, safety, organizational and other conditions, the pedagogical style and school climate, the forms and methods of work, cooperation with family, fulfillment of individual needs of children, supplementary program, or the offer of standard services. Practical evaluation consists of a continuous use of feedback on the part of the teacher. The teacher poses questions systematically and looks for answers to these questions, reflects on the ways of obtaining these answers, ways of collecting information and evaluating the monitored phenomena (which forms and methods and/or techniques to use). Commonly used methods include interviews, discussions, sessions, observations, class monitoring, educational plan, or class plan analysis, resulting in minutes from class observation, various kinds of questionnaires and survey cards, assessment reports, notes from observation, audio and video records, all kinds of artifacts by children (two- and three-dimensional didactic sheets, drawings, handmade products by the children etc.), notes and commentaries of teachers.

The basic criteria to apply during the process of evaluation and to use in assessment of a phenomenon under observation—certain criteria of comparison—are defined by GC ECE. This means that in practice a teacher compares the state of the phenomenon under observation (his/her findings) with GC ECE requirements, concludes whether and to what extent the situation is satisfactory or unsatisfactory, and decides how to proceed in light of these conclusions.

To specify the quality of provision of education more accurately, GC ECE uses the concept of risks. Risks identify phenomena posing a threat to the success of educational projects and diminishing the quality of the process of education and its results. Their presence is a sign of unsatisfactory quality of provided education.

Assessment of results of education in individual children. GC ECE brings some entirely new insights into the issues of assessment of quality of provision of education for children. The former focus on child's performance, its comparison and evaluation with respect to a specific norm has been replaced by continuous monitoring and assessment of individual progress achieved by children in the process of their education. The purpose of the assessment is not to compare children against one another and label them as successful or unsuccessful, but the assessment is a tool in the process of searching for optimum paths in education of individual children.

Regarding the criteria for evaluation of achieved educational results, GC ECE does specify certain outputs, referred to as expected results, but only for the stage at which the child finishes early childhood education. Even then, these criteria are very general and meant to be used as a benchmark only. It is to be borne in mind that each child attains different outputs at different times, in a different extent and a quality corresponding to his/her individual talents. This means that it is the optimum fulfillment of a child's educational potential and needs that is the indicator of the quality of educational results.

Good education is education in which the teacher stimulates the child adequately, noticing possible irregularities in his/her development at an early stage and providing him/her with adequate support and assistance. The teacher watches the child in natural and artificial situations continuously, observing developmental and learning progress purposefully, analyzes the results of these activities so as to find out about the child's needs and limits in order to be able to adjust the educational offerings accordingly. The assessment of the standard of educational results is not a one-time "survey" and state-of-the-art assessment, but a continuous process of feedback, whose results are continuously projected into further educational work of the teacher directed toward the child. Rather than levelling out children's performance forcibly, good early childhood education contributes to making the educational and life chances of individual children more even.

This approach to the development of quality of early childhood education provision and its assessment is an entirely new phenomenon in the Czech Republic, still awaiting an objective evaluation by all those involved: teachers, parents, and the general public.

Further Readings: (1996). Assessment in transition. Learning, monitoring and selection in international perspective. Pergamon Press: London; Bennett, J. (2000). *Goals, curricula and quality monitoring in early childhood system.* New York–Paris: The

Institute for Child and Family Policy, Columbia University–OECD; *Rámcový vzdělávací program pro předškolní vzdělávání (General curriculum for early childhood education)*. MŠMT ČR 2004; Smolíková, K. (2005). *a kol. Manuál k přípravě školních (třídních) programů (A handbook for preparation of a school (class) curriculum)*. VÚP; Vyhláška o předškolním vzdělávání, Sb. Zákonů č.14/2005, částka 4 (Order on early childhood education, collection of Acts No. 14/2005, part 4); Zákon č. 561/2004 Sb., o předškolním, základním, středním, vyšším odborném a jiném vzdělávání (školský zákon) (Act No. 561/2004 Coll. on Early Childhood, Elementary, High-school, Higher Vocational and Other Education—Educational Act).

Web Sites: www.vuppraha.cz; www.rvp.cz.

Kateřina Smolíková

Curriculum

Introduction

Currently, preschool institutional upbringing and education in the Czech Republic is a natural part of the system of education, and as such has a clearly formulated program of education, or curriculum. Curriculum formation has a rich tradition in Bohemia and Moravia, evidenced by the fact that the current curriculum has emerged from a dynamic process. A product of the Educational Act of 2004, the General Curriculum for Early Childhood Education (Rámcový vzdělávací program pro předškolní vzdělávání), was adopted as the national curriculum of the Czech Repubic.

Key Moments in Curriculum Formation

A look into the history of the early childhood curriculum and early public childhood education in the Czech Republic confirms that despite the fact that the development of Czech early childhood pedagogy has been influenced especially by both social processes and development of pedagogic thinking worldwide, there have been a number of attempts to develop an early childhood curriculum that is distinctively Czech in character.

The first integrated early childhood curriculum created in this country was *Informatorium scholae maternae* by I. A. **Comenius** (1592–1670). This curriculum specifies educational objectives (harmonious personal development), the teaching content (body of knowledge concerning nature and society), as well as a way of communicating it to children (by play). Many of these ideas are still alive today and are of interest even for a modern early childhood curriculum.

Another period that proved important for further development of the Czech curriculum was at the turn of the eighteenth century, when institutions providing exclusively social care (nurseries, kindergartens, and infant schools for children of working mothers) gradually evolved into educational institutions. The first program of upbringing called *Kindergarten* (created for the purposes of a nursery founded in Prague in 1832) was a relatively sophisticated program of elementary education. It emphasized instruction in morals, learning about the surrounding world, elements of writing and reading, and was supplemented with methodological guidelines and notes.

The development of the early childhood curriculum was regulated by *Educational Acts (1869, 1908)* at the end of the nineteenth and the beginning of the twentieth centuries. General rules for early childhood curricula, entirely distinct from the school curriculum, were formulated in the process. Nursery schools were charged with supporting and complementing family upbringing, preparing children for school and developing their physical, sensory, and psychic potential. Tools for educational work, namely play, occupation, light work, and observation were set also in legislation. The necessity to respect the needs of the child was stressed—methods of work used in school were prohibited explicitly. This trend later found support in a reformist pedagogical movement. What is worth stressing from that period is especially the *Program of Upbringing for Nursery Schools, 1927(Výchovný program mateřských škol)*, an integrated and systematic treatise on early childhood education, written from the theoretical and practical, conceptual and methodological points of view.

The period that followed was characterized by—unfortunately unsuccessful—efforts to legitimize early childhood education as the first stage of the school system. The function of an early childhood curriculum was played by syllabi and work plans still based on the reformist concept of educational work.

The number of nursery schools increased dramatically in the post–World War II period, due to the increased rate of employment among mothers of young children. The formation of national guidelines started at this stage. The first of them was still under the influence of reformist pedagogical movement but subsequent guidelines abandoned these reformist efforts, concluding with the Integrated School Act, 1948, which included nursery schools in the system of education (although with a curriculum very school-like in character). From this point on the function of the early childhood curriculum was played by school syllabi, that is, compulsory, detailed, and ideologically oriented guidelines. Segmentation into individual educational categories (physical, cognitive, moral, aesthetic, and labor-related) appeared for the first time as a counterpart to school subjects. Educational requirements were specified for two age-groups and a firm structure of the day as well as forms of educational work were defined, with primary attention paid to preparation for instruction in the integrated school environment.

With time the situation changed again. The marked school-like orientation of the early childhood curriculum was somewhat attenuated in the 1960s, thanks among other things to efforts to consolidate educational processes from birth to the entry in school. This made the curriculum a matter of concern for the Ministry of Health along with the Ministry of Education, because it included crèches for infants and toddlers as well as nursery schools. Due to the integration of the medical point of view into this platform, the program gave greater emphasis to the natural development of the child and the attenuation of social norms, despite the ideas of the contemporary, integrated, and collectivist-oriented school. The second version of the *Program of Educational Work in Crèches and Nursery Schools, 1978* was a failed attempt at making compatible what was essentially incompatible: deepening ideological-educational activities while at the same time respecting the age-related as well as individual needs of children sufficiently, and better preparing children for school.

Early Childhood Curriculum Development: The Current State of the Art

The period after November 1989 was characterized by a need to provide a new system for schools and education in the new political and social contexts. School reform preparation was launched. In line with new principles of curricular policy, formulated as part of the National Program of Development of Education in the Czech Republic, (the so-called White Book, 2001) and regulated by the Act for Early Childhood, Elementary, High School, Higher Vocational, and Other Education (2004), a new system of curricula was introduced into the system of education. The main objectives of the reform were to transform the educational environment by opening up educational offerings increasing the autonomy of individual schools and their teachers, and guaranteeing the quality of the education provided. The curricular documents were formulated *at two levels*—the nation and the school. The state level is represented by the National Curriculum (NC) and the General Curricula (GC). The NC formulates educational requirements pertaining to education as a whole, and the GC defines educational frameworks required for the individual stages (early childhood, elementary, and high school education). The school level is represented by the school curricula (SC) designed to provide guidelines for the process of education in individual schools. School curricula are formulated by individual schools in line with the principles set by the relevant GC.

This system of organization is especially significant for the early childhood curriculum because the new Educational Act appreciates the pedagogical importance of nursery schools and radically shifts the position of early childhood education within the system of education: early childhood education is regarded as an important part of lifelong education and is guaranteed and supported by the state in a variety of ways. There is a national early childhood curriculum (General Curriculum for Early Childhood Education, or GC ECE). This curriculum sets a compulsory, but sufficiently wide framework for development of different pedagogical concepts and trends as well as for development of school curricula suited to the particular conditions of individual nursery schools.

A Brief Description of The Early Childhood Curriculum

The recently instituted childhood curriculum (GC ECE) in the Czech Republic is based on the following principles:
- acceptance of natural developmental specifics of preschool children and their systematic reflection in the content, forms, and methods of their education;
- preservation of room for individuality of personality in children and enabling development and education of each individual child compatible with their individual possibilities and needs;
- orientation to creation of a basis for lifelong learning and social self-fulfilment, focus on creation of foundations for key skills attainable within the early childhood education stage (i.e., not only with a view to preparation of the child for school);

- creation of room for individual profiles of individual nursery schools (allowing schools to take advantage of different forms and methods of education and adjust education to specific regional and local conditions, possibilities, and needs);
- guaranteeing comparable pedagogical efficacy of curricula developed and offered by individual nursery schools;
- defining quality of early childhood education from the point of view of objectives, conditions, content, and results of education in order to provide general criteria for internal and external evaluation of nursery schools and the education provided by them.

The curriculum reformulates the pedagogical goals and content of early childhood education as well as the conditions in which it takes place.

Goals of the Early Childhood Curriculum

The goals and objectives of the early childhood curriculum were set in line with the goals and objectives of the curricula for further stages of education, but at a level corresponding to the age of the children. The main objective is to develop each individual child in his/her physical, psychological, and social aspects and guide him/her so that by the end of the preschool period the child is a unique and relatively independent personality, competent to handle—actively and to his/her personal satisfaction—those situations he/she will commonly encounter (especially in familiar environments, i.e., in family and at school), as well as those situations to be faced in the future. The general goals set by the curriculum are the following:

- development of the child, learning and getting to understand,
- internalization of the fundamental values this society is based upon,
- acquisition of personal independence and the ability to act as an independent personality affecting one's environment.

The process of fulfillment of these goals is directed at formation of elements of key skills (concerning learning, problem solving and communication, social and personal, activity-oriented, and citizen skills) to be further developed and deepened in the following stages of education.

Methods and Forms of Early Childhood Education

Methods and forms of early childhood education, too, are adjusted to the developmental, physiological, cognitive, social, and emotional needs of children of this age (3–6 years). Early childhood education offers children an environment that is welcoming, stimulating, interesting, and rich in content, in which the child can feel confident, safe, joyful, and satisfied and which provides him/her with opportunities to act, enjoy himself/herself, and be occupied in ways natural to children. Education is consistently associated with needs and possibilities of individual children differing on an individual basis, including specific educational needs. Each child is provided with assistance and support to the extent that the particular child needs and in the quality he/she finds adequate. Early childhood education is organized so that children, regardless of age differences or different abilities and learning potential, can be educated in the same class.

Methods of experiential and cooperative learning through play and activity are applied in education of preschool children. Training activities are organized above all as free play in which children participate on the basis of their own interest and by their own choice, drawing on situations presenting the children with comprehensible practical examples of contexts encountered in life. The activities used are spontaneous or directed, interlinked with one another and balanced, and are organized usually in smaller groups or on an individual basis. The didactic style is based on the principles of education, individual choice, and active participation of the child. Education is organized in integrated blocks not differentiating between "educational domains" or "components," but presenting the child with educational content in natural contexts, connections, and relations so that it is easier to understand for the child and the obtained experience can be used in practice.

Educational Content of Early Childhood Curriculum

The educational content of the early childhood curriculum is the main educational tool. It is formulated in a way suited to the integrated character of education and its activity-based nature. Consequently it is set only in general and applied to the whole age-group, that is, for children from 3 to 6 years of age. Formally speaking, the educational content is structured into five domains selected so that they respect the natural wholeness and development of the child's personality as well as his/her gradual integration into living and social environment. These areas are titled in the curriculum as follows:
- The child and his/her body.
- The child and his/her psyche.
- The child and the other.
- The child and the society.
- The child and the world.

The individual educational domains are treated in the curriculum so as to be comprehensible to the teacher and so that he/she can further develop the content (i.e., use the domains as a basis for formulating suitable integrated blocks of the school curriculum). Each domain includes the following interrelated categories: component goals (objectives), educational offerings, and expected outputs or results. Component goals express what the teacher should consider in the process of early childhood education, what he/she should support in the child. Educational offerings represent a set of practical and intellectual activities and opportunities, leading to goal fulfillment and output attainment. Expected outputs are component outputs of education that can be regarded as generally attainable at this stage of education (they are not compulsory for the child) and are formulated as skills and competencies. The curriculum also specifies potential risks to be avoided as they may pose a threat to the success of educational objectives.

The curriculum also identifies the conditions within which early childhood education is to take place, in the areas of material equipment, lifestyle and diet, psychic hygiene, organization and management, human resources and pedagogic qualification, and parent involvement. It identifies the optimum standard (quality) of these conditions, whose full provision should gradually be approached.

Development of school curricula by individual schools presupposes application of self-evaluation activities in each nursery school, including monitoring and evaluation of individual educational achievements by individual children.

Support for Curriculum Implementation

Currently, supplementary methodological documents are developed and other development projects are pursued to support implementation of the new curriculum into the practice of nursery schools. This is done not only to facilitate for teachers the techniques for development of their own school curricula, but also to provide practical examples, ideas, and illustrations as a means of enhancing the possibility of success. The responses to this new curriculum for early childhood education by the pedagogical community in the Czech Republic have in general been very positive.

Further Readings: Curriculum for pre-school, Lpfö 98. Ministry of Education and Science in Sweden. Stockholm, 1998; *Early childhood and care education (Basic indicators on young children).* (1995). Paris: UNESCO; *Rámcový program pro předškolní vzdělávání (General curriculum for early childhood education).* MŠMT 2001; *Rámcový vzdělávací program pro předškolní vzdělávání (General curriculum for early childhood education).* MŠMT 2004; Smolíková, K. (1998). *Kurikulum předškolní výchovy— základní východiska předškolní institucionální výchovy (Early childhood curriculum: Basic starting points for institutional early childhood education).* VÚP; Smolíková, K. (2005). *a kol. Manuál k přípravě školního (třídního) programu mateřské školy (A handbook for preparation of a school (class) curriculum in nursery schools).* VÚP; Národní program rozvoje vzdělávání v České republice (Bílá kniha) (National Program of Development of Education in the Czech Republic—White Book). MŠMT 2001; *Národní zpráva o stavu předškolní výchovy, vzdělávání a péče o děti předškolního věku v České republice. Studie OECD (National report on the state of early childhood education and childcare for pre-school children in the Czech Republic. OECD study).* MŠMT 2000.

Web Sites: www.vuppraha.cz; www.rvp.cz.

Kateřina Smolíková

Learning a Foreign Language as Part of Early Childhood Education

Learning (communicating in) a second language other than the mother tongue has always been regarded as one of the key skills (strengths) of a well-educated person in the Czech Republic. This requirement has recently been extended to all those undertaking compulsory education, and mastery of at least one foreign language has been considered a basic competence necessary for everyday life.

Foreign languages have been assigned more space in the school curricula. Within compulsory education one foreign language is taught starting in primary school and instruction in another one is defined as optional at the lower level of secondary education. Practice nevertheless indicates that the forms of teaching foreign languages used so far are not always efficient enough. One of the reasons is that foreign language teaching is started too late. As a number of studies in developmental psychology, social psychology, neuropsychology, psycholinguistics, and other disciplines show, the ideal age for starting foreign language learning is early childhood.

Why Start Second Language Learning Early?

Justification for starting early is mainly as follows. Language is a system consisting of five subsystems: the phonological, the lexical, the morpho-syntactic or grammatical, the pragmatic, and the discursive one. They are integrated within the general language system, enabling its harmonious functioning. Each of these systems, nevertheless, has a certain degree of autonomy, attributable to the diversity of their developmental calendars. Two of them, the phonological and the grammatical subsystems, develop most profoundly in early childhood. The period of sensitivity to them therefore lasts from birth (or even earlier) to approximately six years of age. The end of this period for phonological aspects of language is at 8 or 9, or maybe even earlier—our current state of knowledge in this area does not allow us to establish the time frame more accurately. After this period, the child begins to perceive phonemes of a foreign language systematically on the background of the mother tongue. The chances of mastering a foreign language to perfection therefore decrease dramatically from this age on despite the fact that the child keeps maturing as far as different domains of cognitive development are concerned. Although for morpho-syntactic aspects the period of sensitivity ends as late as at 14–15 years of age, many studies suggest that the capacity of the central nervous system and the neurolinguistic apparatus for construction of basic grammar starts to gradually decrease as early as when the child has reached 5 or 6 years of age.

Competing Needs and Interests

Although learning foreign languages in early childhood is mostly regarded as highly appropriate and efficient, one must take into account that early childhood is a crucial period for the development of many other skills and competencies in all areas of development of the child's personality. One must therefore ask the question of whether it is really so important to devote time and effort to foreign language acquisition as opposed to other things at this age. Moreover, at the present time, typified by the development of media and information technologies, a growing percentage of children are showing signs of speech disorders due to a lack of natural high-quality face-to-face communication in their first language. It is mainly for this reason that the attitude of many experts on early childhood education toward foreign language learning in early childhood is reserved. There has been no unequivocal comprehensive view on this issue yet.

The Impact of Political Change

Arguments in support of early foreign language learning have only slowly been entering the awareness of experts as well as the general public and parents of preschool children in the Czech Republic. The political and social change in 1989 in the Czech Republic and the associated opening to the surrounding world were followed by a growing awareness of the importance of the ability to communicate in foreign languages, both in professional and in personal life. Methods of foreign language teaching have become a field for modernization and efficiency improvement. Experience from western European countries became a starting point for a process in which foreign language teaching—to the satisfaction of parents—started to find its place within early childhood education.

Types of Foreign Language Learning

Types of foreign language learning in early childhood may be divided according to the criterion of whether the goal is to arrive at *bilingualism* or just a certain degree of *sensibility* to a particular foreign language. Definitions of bilingualism vary, from the one by Bloomfield defining a bilingual person as someone with "full competence in two languages" to the one by McNamara defining a bilingual person as someone "competent in a language other than the mother tongue in at least one of the following linguistic domains: comprehension, speaking, reading, writing." Bilingualism can be further divided into ambilinguism, equilinguism, and semilinguism, or to dominant as opposed to balanced bilingualism. Both bilingualism and sensibility can, with a varying degree of success, be achieved both through education in the family and through educational institutions.

Bilingualism in the family is the most natural way of acquiring two languages by a child. By a bilingual family we understand a family commonly using two languages (with a certain frequency). The growing number of foreigners who settle down to live in the Czech Republic is accompanied by a growing number of bilingual marriages. Because the Czech Republic has been a markedly monolingual country, the phenomenon of bilingual upbringing of children in the family has largely been a new one. Experts, like the lay public, still have some misgivings as far as bilingual upbringing of children is concerned. Nevertheless, as many researches currently demonstrate, bilingual or multilingual education does not have the negative impacts assumed by the scientists of the 1950s. However, it is appropriate to adhere to some rules. Romaine proposes six configurations of **bilingual education**. The best known one is the Ronjat principle "one person, one language," also known as the "Law of Grammont." This principle can be recommended in a situation when a child's family environment involves two parents whose mother tongues differ. It is based on the hypothesis that distinct language contexts enhance acquisition of bilingualism while mixed contexts tend to be a disturbing factor in this process of language acquisition. According to this principle, each parent should address the child in one language only, specifically his or her own first language. Bilingual upbringing of children is nevertheless attempted also by families whose first language is the same as the language of the environment the family lives in. It is advisable in this case that the foreign language is used by one parent only. This parent should be proficient in the language, and as close to bilingual as possible, especially in the phonological and grammatical aspects. Otherwise there is a risk that the child may acquire incorrect language structures, whose correction becomes difficult. It must nevertheless be borne in mind that the first language has an irreplaceable role in the general development of the child's personality. The definition of "first language" may be difficult in some ambiguous language contexts. One possibility is to define it as the language the child learns from his/her mother or the primary person taking care of him/her.

Bilingual Education in the Czech Republic

There are so-called bilingual nursery schools in the Czech Republic based (although it may be an unconscious choice in some cases) on the *immersion method* developed by the social psychologist Wallace Lambert in Canada in the 1970s, which try to simulate the situation of natural bilingualism. This method is proposed for the whole period of school attendance from nursery school to secondary school, the several first years being characterized by a total "immersion" of the children in the foreign language. This method expanded into a number of Canadian and North American schools very quickly. In the European context it was introduced as an experiment in the nursery school of the Léonie de Waha Coeducation Lycée in Lutych in 1989 in response to the incentive of the Association for Foreign Language Learning by the Immersion Method, and especially its founder Jacques Heynen.

When speaking of the immersion method, or other forms of foreign language learning in early childhood in general, a question arises regarding whether the child's knowledge of the first language deteriorates when the language is not used to the same extent as by his/ her peers living in a monolingual environment. Research dealing with this topic nevertheless shows that inclusion of a foreign language into the school curriculum does not delay the natural process of learning the first language in any way. Some studies conclude, moreover, that teaching by the immersion method may even be beneficial to progress in the first language to some extent, especially in terms of vocabulary. Also results recorded in classes of the nursery school of Léonie de Waha Lycée in Lutych confirm the hypotheses that the immersion method is harmless with respect to the first language.

Bilingual nursery schools in the Czech Republic are mostly private. Foreign language instruction is in most cases provided by Czech teachers who are highly proficient in the foreign language while their pedagogical qualification is not a necessary requirement. The ideal situation in which the teacher is a native speaker with pedagogical qualification is rare. The tuition fees in bilingual nursery schools are usually relatively high and therefore there is a great concentration of children from high-income families in these schools.

Foreign Language Teaching Pedagogy

Teaching whose goal is development of a sensibility to the particular foreign language takes place in nursery schools, language centres or schools, or other educational institutions or directly in the family environment where the teachers are the parents themselves. For class instruction the recommendation is to teach groups of five to six, but not more than ten children for ten to twenty minutes. Children should be taught every day in an ideal case or they should at least have an opportunity to revisit what they already have learned every day. The main principles for familiarizing children with a foreign language published in literature designed for Czech nursery school teachers are the following:

- To use comprehensible language,
- to speak slowly,
- to use short sentences and phrases,
- to avoid using abstract words while using pictures or distinct gestures with clear meanings,
- to maintain short breaks after every sentence or phrase,
- to come up with "clean and clear" demonstrations so that children can repeat them as accurately as possible, to show the reaction the teacher expects,
- to repeat and explain as many times as necessary,
- to check whether the child has understood what the teacher wanted to say,
- to arrange questions from the easiest ones to which children can answer "yes" or "no" to more difficult ones where the child chooses between two alternatives, to the most difficult ones with several alternative answers for which pictures or aids should be used in the beginning.

It is essential not to cheat the child of his/her first language. Therefore if he/she feels the need to speak it, the teacher should not prevent him/her from using it. When teaching children a foreign language the teacher should adhere to the principle that things should not be overdone and should return to previously introduced vocabulary and use it as a starting point. It is also recommended to tell children of the life and institutions of the country whose language they are learning, to teach them to respect the culture of another country and to have tolerance toward foreigners. This is where foreign language learning gradually merges with the multicultural education so needed in the traditionally monocultural and monolingual Czech environment.

Although the centralized curriculum for early childhood education (General Curriculum for Early Childhood Education) does not include instruction in foreign languages, a great many nursery schools in the Czech Republic currently offer optional foreign language instruction (mostly English, but German in some regions near the borders) in response to a demand on the part of parents, usually one or two lessons per week. Due to the lack of foreign language teachers even at higher levels of school these classes are often taught by persons without the necessary linguistic and pedagogical qualifications. They are mostly qualified teachers who, however, do not know the foreign language well enough, or teachers who know the foreign language well but do not have the pedagogical qualification. This problem has to do with the fact that most of the teachers currently employed finished their studies before 1989, when foreign language teaching (apart from teaching Russian) was a rather marginal affair. We may nevertheless predict a significant improvement in this area, to go hand in hand with an increasing language competence of the Czech population.

It may be said in general that the lay population in the Czech Republic is currently in favour of teaching foreign languages in early childhood, quite contrary to the opinion of many experts who regard it as a factor contributing to the growing number of speech problems in children. It is, however, evident that the whole business of foreign language learning in early childhood is very new in the Czech Republic and may be expected to receive more attention in the future.

Further Readings: Comblain, Annick, and Jean Adolphe Rondal (2001). *Apprendre les langues, où, quand, comment?* Sprimont: Masdaga, p. 136; Lietti, Anna (1994). *Pour une éducation bilingue.* Paris: Payot, p. 204; Marxtová, Marie. (2003). Cizí jazyky v mateřské škole (Foreign languages in nursery school). In Václav Mertin, and Ilona Gillernová, eds., *Psychologie pro učitelky mateřské školy (Psychology for nursery school teachers).* Prague: Portál, pp. 185–192; Šulová, Lenka, and Štefan Bartanusz. (2003). Dítě vyrůstající v bilingvní rodině. In Václav Mertin and Ilona Gillernová, eds., *Psychologie pro učitelky mateřské školy (Psychology for nursery school teachers).* Prague: Portál, pp. 171–178; Tabors, Patricia (1997). *One child, two languages: A guide for preschool educators of children learning English as a second language.* Baltimore: Paul H. Brookes, p. 195 s.

Lucie Kozáková and Milada Rabušicová

Teacher Education in the Czech Republic

Historical Background

Although early childhood pedagogy is one of the youngest among teaching professions, it has a history of dynamic development, characterized by efforts for professional quality and specialization.

In the Czech context, as in other European nations, the first public educational institutions for early childhood education started to emerge in the 1830s in the form of nurseries, sanctuaries, and kindergartens. These settings were designed for children aged 2 and up, who required care while their mothers were away from home for work. There was no special training for childminders working in these institutions. The children were cared for by experienced women, selected in line with contemporary criteria of civil integrity.

The dominating social-charitable focus of these institutions was altered by the Prague nursery founded in 1832, where a qualified male elementary school teacher was employed in order to prioritize the educational function over the nursing function of preschools. The institution also served as a centre for preparation and education of male teachers for work in other nurseries. This marked the beginnings of the approach to early childhood education as qualified work, requiring formal training.

The subsequent development of social-charitable public institutions for early childhood education, characterized by considerable numbers of children per group, led to the development of a staff position known as "lady minder." Her crucial role involved being a kind and helpful person to stand in for the mother, providing the child with necessary care, and helping the child to acquire good manners. Starting in 1868 only single women were allowed to work in nursery schools, and this emphasis on unmarried teachers lasted until 1919.

The Imperial Act of 1868 defined nursery schools as educational institutions. This act called for teacher qualification specialization, and the Statute of Training Colleges was subsequently issued to serve as a conceptual basis for theoretical and practical instruction at one-year (later two-year) training colleges. Graduates of these courses were referred to as nursery school teachers from 1934 onward.

Two theoretical camps began to form, with differing views on the role of early childhood teachers and the training that they should receive. One group viewed the early childhood educator in a classic teacher role, and aimed to integrate professional training for teachers of the preelementary and elementary stages. The other group prioritized simple practical training focused on nursing care, thus reflecting the status of the early childhood educator as nurse childminder. This dilemma had legal and occupation-statutory consequences, which have been reflected in professional training of teachers during the twentieth century.

Starting Points for Occupational Transformation

In the first half of the twentieth century, the nursing (care) approach to early childhood education still prevailed. The low occupational and social status of the nursing profession became a subject of criticism by employees of early childhood education institutions. Together with elementary school teachers, they requested the opportunity to improve their occupational qualifications through university education. Although their request was not recognized by legislation, nursery school teachers organized remarkable self-help educational activities (they, for example, organized university courses, established a resource and record-keeping centre, implemented research projects in experimental schools in collation with experts, published books, and journals). These spontaneous self-educatory activities were interrupted by World War II, after which they were not fully resumed.

Occupational training of nursery school teachers shifted to the university level with the creation of pedagogical faculties in 1946. Nursery school teachers trained together with teachers of other stages of education between 1948 and 1950.

The year 1948 was marked by a radical political and social turn in what was then Czechoslovakia, resulting (among other things) in increased political pressure calling for a broad engagement of women in the labor market. This pressure led to an increased demand for early childhood institutions such as crèches and nursery schools, as well as for adequate human resources. Crèches were established for children between 3 months (six months later) and 3 years of age. These institutions, largely with round-the-clock operation, were run by the Ministry of Health. Child care was delegated to children's nurses, who trained at medical (high) schools, which marked the beginning of the medical accent in care of the youngest children that has later been criticized.

During this time, pedagogical faculties failed to produce enough teachers for nursery (as well as primary) schools. Occupational training for these two types of teachers was subsequently demoted to the level of a four-year high school in 1950. While training of primary school teachers soon returned to the university level, high school training of nursery school teachers still remained, and was the basic type of their occupational training until the mid-1990s.

In 1970, the preparation of a dual system of nursery school teachers' training was launched. This system involved a choice between training at specialized high schools, concluding in a standard graduation exam (higher secondary level of education, ISCED 3) or training at the tertiary level (ISCED 5). Most teachers in training elected the former option, while the latter tended to be viewed as training for potential nursery school headmasters.

Perspectives on Staff Training Programs

The social situation after 1989 has brought new challenges in training in early childhood pedagogy. The dominant belief that attendance at an early childhood education institution is an important investment for life and lifelong learning has increased requirements for occupational training of this staff rather dramatically.

Programs for infants and toddlers. Childminders in crèches represent a special category of qualified staff for the youngest children; they are referred to not as "teachers", but "nurses." This is because the model of their training has remained unchanged since the socialist era: they study at high schools with medical specialization. Crèches, the settings for which they train, remain under the surveillance of the Ministry of Health. The contemporary emphasis on the importance of the family and individualized care of the youngest children, together with the legal right to a 36-month maternity leave, has decreased the need for public educational institutions for children below the age of 3. Crèches served about 20 percent of the under 3 population prior to 1989. Since then, the rate has dropped to less than 1 percent today. Along with the decline in the number of crèches, the care of children under 3 is characterized by private efforts and contracted services, which are not subjected to public control or regulated by requirements for licensed occupational services. Their distribution tends to be marginal.

Teacher training programs. There are currently three paths to the nursery teacher occupation. A general shift to the tertiary level of training and conceptual relatedness between training of nursery school and primary school teachers, who have trained at the tertiary level since the beginning of the 1950s, is envisioned for the future.

Legal unification of requirements for training in early childhood pedagogy (Teacher Training Standards), specification of content-level requirements and skills (the National Curriculum), and a general increase in the occupational status of nursery school teachers (requirement for full occupational training at national and accredited institutions and wage equalization with other teacher categories) are expected to take place.

High School Specialization

High school education with specialization has been the prevailing qualification attained by 95 percent of nursery school teachers. Graduates of these programs pursue work mainly as nursery school teachers, preceptors in schools and other educational institutions (after-school centres, school clubs, centres organizing leisure-time activities for children, children's homes), or in welfare centres for children with special needs.

There are currently seventeen high schools with pedagogical specialization in the Czech Republic. The program of studies is designed for students who have completed nine years of compulsory school attendance. Enrollment is contingent upon passing entrance exams in the student's first language successfully, a personal character evaluation, and demonstrating talents in music, sports, and the arts. The course of study lasts for four years, and graduates receive a certificate of full high school education with specialization. The degree is completed with a satisfactory score on a standardized exam (level 3A according to international standard classification ISCED).

Vocational School Training

An amendment to the 1995 Educational Act has enriched the portfolio of nursery school training to include studies at higher vocational schools. There are currently twenty-one state-run higher vocational schools with specialization in pedagogy and teaching, six of which include specialization in early childhood pedagogy. Graduates of these programs are generally seen as overqualified to be nursery school teachers, and frequently pursue a broader—in terms of both age and domains—spectrum of activities organized for children and the young.

In order to enroll in the vocational programs, a student must have completed a full high school education (general or with specialization) and received a passing grade on the graduation exam. Applicants must prove their personality qualifications and talents in aesthetic disciplines. Students graduating from the vocational school receive a graduation certificate at level 5B according to international classification ISCED.

University Training of Nursery School Teachers

There are currently seven state universities offering programs with specialization in pedagogy in the Czech Republic. These institutions organize three-year bachelor study programs referred to as "Pedagogy for Nursery Schools". These programs may include intramural, combined, or extramural studies. The first program to receive accreditation was launched in 1993 at the Faculty of Pedagogy of Charles University in Prague. Students must have passed the high school graduation exam in order to enroll in this program.

The university program of studies includes general and specialized training, as well as intensive theoretical and practical training for early childhood educators. This program is in accordance with European standards in early childhood pedagogy (ISCED 5).

University studies are concluded with a state bachelor examination consisting of a defence of a bachelor thesis and an oral exam. The graduates are granted the academic title "Bachelor" (abbreviated as "Bc").

Occupational skills obtained by a graduate of this program include the following:

- respect the personality of the child, develop it, and be able to create an atmosphere of trust, safety, and understanding for the children;
- identify specific characteristics of individual children and make these a basis for one's educational activities;
- structure activities based on the needs and skills of preschool children;
- choose adequate methods with respect to the particular conditions and the developmental level of the children, select pedagogical processes correctly, analyze and justify one's decisions;

- plan one's activities and create conditions for the development of the individual and the group, including children with specific needs;
- be proficient in basic musical, artistic, and dramatic activities appropriate to early childhood and use one's talents in these areas.

Graduate Studies

A more advanced training in theory and methodology or early childhood pedagogy can be obtained in the program of studies "Early Childhood Pedagogy," also organized by the Faculty of Pedagogy at Charles University in Prague. The program is organized to combine the intramural and extramural form and lasts for ten semesters. It is concluded by a state examination consisting of a defence of a diploma thesis and an oral examination. Graduates are granted the academic title "Magister" (Master) abbreviated as "Mgr."

Within the program of studies, occupational skills are extended by analysis of theoretical problems from the domain of early childhood pedagogy, reflection and generalization of pedagogical experience, training in empirical research methods, and presentation of research results.

Future Possibilities and Social Repercussions

A program of two-level training in early childhood pedagogy consisting of co-ordinated successive bachelor and graduate studies is currently being developed. The bachelor studies portion of this program is regarded as a general compulsory qualification for nursery school teachers, while the second, gradate level should involve a more advanced theoretical understanding and occupational specialization.

Occupational training within the nursery school teacher specialization is currently available to both women and men. It has not always been so. Until the mid-1990's, only women were admitted to the high school specialization programs. The existing percentage of male teachers in nursery schools remains close to zero.

The occupational and social status of a nursery school teacher is comparable with that of primary school teachers, although wages are lower. The average monthly wage of a nursery school teacher in the Czech Republic in 2004 was CZK 16,146 while the average wage of an elementary school teacher was CZK 20,227. These wages are comparable to those of other professions, as the average wage in the Czech Republic lies somewhere between 18,000 and 20,000 CZK (roughly $800–$1,000 USD).

Nursery school teachers are relatively in demand in the market. However, demographic trends signal a decline in birthrates in the future, which is likely to result in decreasing numbers of children in nursery schools.

Nursery school teachers currently represent the second-most numerous teacher category in the Czech Republic, working with over 90 percent of the population of preschool children attending nursery schools. The importance of high-quality training for a demanding job is no longer in doubt and is generally recognized.

Further Readings: Comenius, John Amos (1992). Heritage and education of man for the 21st century. Section 4. In John Amos Comenius, ed., *Heritage and early childhood education.* Prague: Charles University—Comenius Institute of Education; General Teacher Education. Network Norway Council, 1999; Opravilová, E. (2002). Příprava učitelek mateřských škol na úrovni vysoké školy (Nursery school teacher training at university level). In *Retrospektiva a perspektiva předškolního vzdělávání a příprava předškolních pedagogů. Sborník 3.celostátní konference profesních organizací předškolního vzdělávání (Retrospectives and perspectives of early childhood education and training of teachers for pre-school education. Papers from the 3rd National Conference of Professional Organizations in Early Childhood Education).* Prague: APN; Opravilová, E. (2004). Vzdělávání učitelek mateřských škol: Vývoj, současné proudy a perspektivy (Education of nursery school teachers: Development, current trends and perspectives). In *Spilková,V. a kol.: Současné proměny vzdělávání učitele (Contemporary Transformations in Teacher Education).* Brno: Paido.

Eva Opravilová

Child Care for Children from 0 to 3

Child care for children from birth to three years of age is a topic involving a great variety of possible viewpoints and approaches. The most common approach considers the youngest children in terms of their medical safety and psychological development, including cognitive and social development. To be able to do this, we need to understand the optimum conditions and environment for this development.

Background

Traditionally, the family has been responsible for creating favourable conditions for child development, and has been regarded as the most appropriate "instrument" for fostering this development. Historically, in both the Czech and the wider European cultural spheres, this approach was advanced by the well-known pedagogical treatise *Informatorium scholae maternae* written by John Amos **Comenius** in 1632. This document contains advice and recommendations to mothers taking care of their infants and toddlers.

As the traditional society transformed into a modern one, new approaches and arguments considering a broader social, economic, and cultural context started to emerge. In the second half of the nineteenth and the first half of the twentieth centuries there was a boom in institutions providing early childhood education in the Czech Republic. These institutions were almost exclusively nursery schools catering to children ranging from 3 to 6 years of age. However, the period of the communist regime in the late 1940s brought a huge expansion of public care institutions (crèches), first for children above 3 months of age and then for those 6 months to 3 years of age. The main reason for this expansion was that during the communist period, child care was primarily used as a tool for obtaining a new labor force. This was especially evident in the 1950s when the government initiated a policy of intensive female employment. During this initiative, the preference was to build collective crèches, which were governmental and state enterprises that at one point served some 20 percent of children of preschool age. This trend continued in the following decades. The government controlled the accessibility, quality, and even the pedagogical programs in these institutions.

Immediately following the political change at the end of the 1980s, the number of crèches was dramatically reduced. The reason for this reduction was the argument that children under 3 feel best with their families. This argument was provoked especially by the negative experience of previous generations of Czech children and parents, who remember crèches as one of the worst oppressions of the communist regime. A saying from those times goes: "Old people's homes are children's revenge to parents for crèches."

Child Care for Infants and Toddlers

Currently, child care for the youngest children in the Czech Republic is a highly controversial topic, reflecting both the unhappy experience from the recent "socialist" past and the new up-to-date requirements attributable to the acceptance of the Czech Republic into the European Union (in 2004). The main arguments in general for extending institutional child care for children from birth to three years of age include participation of women in the labor market, equal opportunities for women and men in terms of their personal development, support to families in a broader sense of the word, and enhancement of the birthrate. These arguments have also started to gain weight in the Czech Republic.

At the same time, the strong traditional argument emphasizing the importance of a close bond between the mother and the child still exists. This argument has shifted public opinion away from institutionalized child care, in support of an arrangement of care within which the child grows up in the family, cared for by the mother, usually until the child is at least 3 years old.

Policy Initiatives

At present, Czech social policy in relation to the youngest children and their families seeks to find links between the interests of the children and parents, especially mothers. Policymakers are trying to approach the new philosophical and political bases of the social and family policy in the Czech Republic. As can be expected, this rather discrete discussion involves some strongly differing attitudes, depending on the political orientation of their advocates.

Briefly, the three main strategies of social policy in relation to the family are as follows:

1. *Market-oriented strategy:* Accentuates the role of the market, while provisions for families are minimized. In this strategy, the state helps to find solutions for only extreme cases. The family is perceived resulting from how people arrange their lives. As a result, this strategy emphasizes the need for a variety of available options.
2. *General support to families:* Emphasis is on marriage, cohesiveness of the family, and education of children within the family, particularly by means of child benefits and tax allowances related to the absence of mothers' economic activities, and

by means of public institutions such as nursery schools providing day care for children.

3. *Support for double incomes:* Aims at equality of opportunities for men and women in the labor market, enabling men to share the duties related to upbringing of children with women. In particular, this approach emphasizes public care and education, by means of public day care or residential care, emphasizing a rich and long parental leave.

The current policy in the Czech Republic seems to be a combination of the first two strategies. Especially in the beginning of the 1990s, a tendency towards a market-oriented type of family policy (at least supporting the argument in favour of everyone's personal responsibility for themselves, and in the system of family benefits) was noticeable. Alongside this, elements of the traditional model of general support to families became evident: a maternity grant increase, extension of the period of eligibility of parental allowances from 3 to 4 years of age (maternity plus parental leave) aimed at providing women (or men, with children aged 6 months and more) the opportunity to leave the labor market for a relatively long time. According to surveys of public opinion (ISSP), the Czech population prefers this traditional model, which is obviously one of the reasons for the low demand for crèches. Besides, Czechs prefer a traditional division of roles in the family duties and responsibilities. They see the woman's role, first of all, as that of giving birth.

Reduction of Crèches

The number of public institutions providing child care for children up to 3 years of age (crèches) was reduced drastically at the beginning of 1990s. This social change was followed by a radical ideological shift away from public child care. Many families found the idea of public child care for children from birth to three years of age undesirable. Instead of institutional child care, the traditional concept, based on the idea that "a child feels best home with his/her mother," was embraced and crèches closed down in huge numbers. Diminishing parental demand for crèches, combined with a drop in the birthrate, has led to the beleaguered state of public services for children of 0–3 years of age. The government has drastically reduced its monetary support of such institutions. In fact, the organized day-care system for very young children has disappeared. What was once a child-care system supported by crèches is gone, leaving only a few centers from the previous regime, administered by the Ministry of Health. The physical premises of former crèches have been sold or rebuilt to be used for other purposes. At present there are a total of fifty-eight crèches in the country, with a capacity of 1,674 children. To illustrate the change, there are now only three crèches in Brno, a city with a population of 450,000 which contained 115 such settings in the 1980s, In the rest of the South Moravia region (Brno being its centre), there are currently no crèches at all.

Some nongovernmental (private) initiatives are emerging, aimed at providing parents (mothers) immediate assistance if they need respite from their children for a particular period of time. Private care (by female students or seniors) is also expanding. Yet both these options are expensive and many people doubt the quality of such services. In addition to this, there are services by civic associations or churches focused on the care of mother and child, such as centers where they can spend time together (mother's clubs).

In contrast to this reduction in creches is very generous maternity and parental support, consisting of a parental leave of twenty-eight weeks, 69 percent of the previous salary, plus a four-year-leave at a flat rate (until the child's fourth birthday).

Financing

Crèches are administered by the Ministry of Health. They are established by the Municipalities (regional administration), through which they are subsidized. Yet their operation is expensive (at some CZK 7,500 monthly), resulting in the fact that parents must contribute approximately 13 pecent to 19 percent toward the costs (CZK 1,200 to 1,500; between 50 and 65 USDper month). So the service is not cheap, although the fee is adjusted to family income. A new bill has been drafted that proposes making crèches private enterprises instead of being regarded as health care institutions.

Accessibility and Quality

Even though the number of crèches in the Czech Republic has reached an all-time low, their availability still exceeds their demand. For instance, the three above-mentioned crèches in Brno can serve 100 children but are only used to 60 or 70 percent of their capacity. This demonstrates that even such a small supply exceeds the demand. On top of that, the crèches are used mostly by lower income parents.

The main argument of the opponents of public care for the youngest children is the low quality of crèches. Those in the generation brought up in communist crèches have expressed their discontent with the quality of care, and their experiences are quite sad—nurses dressed in white, and hygiene standards given much more importance than a creative environment for children. The focus was on care, not on development. Such opinions still prevail in the general public and among politicians. Unfortunately, the structure of the current (public) crèches still gives this impression, although some improvements are evident. Nurses who work in crèches typically attend four-year secondary schools of nursing. Pedagogy and psychology are part of their curricula.

Research Findings and Conclusions

The previous paragraphs provide the basic facts concerning child care for children from 0 to 3 years of age in the Czech Republic, and the corresponding political background and interpretations. What is needed at this point is research-based empirical evidence regarding the benefits and risks of each particular alternative for the development of the child. Systematic research in this area has been absent. However, there are isolated research projects that provide some useful information, and relevant research in other areas. Some conclusions on the quality and conditions of child care for the youngest children can be inferred from this information. In summary, the following facts are evident regarding the current situation in child care for children from 0 to 3 in the Czech Republic, placed in a broader context:

- There is a decreasing birthrate (currently 1.17), which may be a cause or could be a consequence of the present child-care situation;
- Mothers are getting older (more frequently giving birth in their thirties), which means fulfillment of the "biological role." Mothers more often want to take care of their "ardently desired" child at home;
- The public has a generally negative attitude, resulting in a low demand for crèches;
- The quality of the care is usually regarded as low or not corresponding to the modern state of knowledge on the development of young children;
- Crèches are health care institutions, which implies that their priorities are hygiene, health, surveillance, and good food;
- There are no alternatives to crèches from which to choose;
- Crèches are costly, the government has cut the subsidy so that parents must contribute;
- The prolonged parental leave is also of importance;
- Finally, under pressure from the authorities, some kindergartens accept children aged 2 (although this seems to be the case in some regions only).

What is the consequence to young families? Families themselves have to care of their children in the long term, very much so through jobs available in the labor market. The society would only intervene if poverty becomes a serious issue, but even then this help would be rather limited. Women can stay out of the labor market for a relatively long period of time and devote themselves to the care of their children, and marriage is seen as advantageous. No significant support with housing or in the compensation of expenses related to upbringing can be expected.

What is needed, however, and what state policy and legislation in affairs of the society, the family, and employment should contribute, is to create conditions for families in which parents, and especially women, are able to make carefully considered choices, based on individual and family priorities. Currently there are no such choices or options regarding child care for children under the age of 3 in the Czech Republic.

Further Readings: Brannen, J., and P. Moss, eds. *Rethinking children's care.* Buckhingham: Open University Press; Child care in changing world—Conference report. Available online at http://www.child careinachangingworld.nl/downloads/conference_report.pdf; Moss, P., and F. Deven (2002). Leave arrangement for parents: Overview and future outlook. *Community, Work and Family* 5(3), pp. 237–255; *Národní zpráva o stavu předškolní výchovy, vzdělávání a péče o děti předškolního věku v České republice (National report on the state of early childhood education and child care for pre-school children in the Czech Republic).* Prague: OECD, MŠMT; , 2000OECD (2001). *Starting strong. Early Childhood education and care.* Paris: The Organization for Economic Co-operation and Development; Šulová, L., and Ch. Zaouche-Gaudron (2003). *Předškolní dítě a jeho svět (Pre-school child and his/her world).* Prague: Karolinum.

Milada Rabušicová

France

Early Childhood Education in France

Introduction

In France, compulsory school begins at age 6. In this centralized country there are national guidelines aimed at insuring the equity of early childhood policies. Care and education are implemented separately, by local authorities (regions, *departements,* municipalities). Under the auspices of the Ministry of Education there is a strong public investment in the education sector, which provides one unique and universal provision: the *école maternelle*. The care sector for children under 3 and for leisure time outside school is provided under the auspices of the Ministries of Social Affairs, Health, Youth and Sports. Various kinds of services are provided to these two age-groups.

The École Maternelle for 2- to 6-Year-Olds

The first *écoles maternelles* were charity institutions created during the nineteenth century to allow women to work in factories and to protect young children of these poor families. Their number increased quickly within the public system of education when the first laws of the French Republic defined, in 1881, *école maternelle* for the 2- to 6-year-olds as voluntary, free, and nonconfessional. The status and working conditions of the preschool teachers were aligned with those of elementary teachers in 1921. Since 1945, the increasing number of children from more advantaged backgrounds largely influenced the educational models, emphasizing progressively creativity and self-expression. During the 1970s, new national orientations included two main goals: socialization and learning, and, little by little, the *école maternelle* came to be valued as the first step toward school success.

Main characteristics. Nowadays, almost 100 percent of the children over 3 years of age and about 35 percent of 2-year-olds attend *écoles maternelles*. These free public institutions (12% are private) are organized like elementary schools: similar hours (8:30–11:30 AM; 1:30–4:30 PM) and holidays, similar separation into groups of about twenty-five children by age, and located in the same group of buildings. Curriculum, teachers' salaries, training, and evaluation are the responsibility of the National Ministry of Education, but buildings, furniture, materials and assistants' salaries, training, and evaluation are the responsibility of local municipalities. At present the preschool teachers have the same training and job title, *professeur des écoles*, whether they are working in *écoles maternelles* or in elementary schools. Their salaries are the same as *professeurs* of secondary education. By contrast, teaching assistants are required to hold only a one-year certificate in early childhood, and their salaries are very low.

Current policy for École maternelle. In 1989, the Law of Education specified that primary school must include both *école maternelle* and elementary school. *École maternelle* constituted cycle 1 (cycle of "early learning") for the 2- to 5-year-olds. Continuity with the elementary school was emphasized at the beginning of cycle 2 (cycle of "basic learning") by having the last year of *école maternelle* linked with the two first grades of the elementary school. The Law defined the right of access for all 3-year-olds, and gave priority to 2-year-olds living in high-need education areas (ZEP). Parents were officially recognized as members of the education community. In 1995, a curriculum for the *école maternelle* was published, to be included in the curriculum for primary school, which reaffirming republican ideals emphasized early learning within five domains. In 2002 the new curriculum reaffirmed this focus, and an absolute priority was given to mastering the French language.

Implementation. With the exception of some fruitful local experiences, teachers have resisted this new pedagogical reform that requires particularly strong team-work and the development of new practices. At the present time we are seeing an "elementarisation" of *école maternelle*. The parental participation remains relatively weak in the field, as well as the inclusion of handicapped children.

Although middle-class families express a strong desire for early schooling for their 2-year-olds, this is controversial: children are too young or the *école maternelle* is unsuited to caring for their emotional needs / supporting children's early competencies. Emphasizing equality or calling for transformations of preschool practices to accommodate younger children is important. Studies indicate that participation by 2-year-olds results in some reduction, but not a complete removal of social inequalities. In high-priority zones (ZEP) 45 percent of 2-year-olds attend *école maternelle*. Better results at age 12 are observed in ZEP with the highest rate of early schooling (60% and more): early schooling is considered as one of the effective means developed in ZEP.

Child Care for the Under Threes

A very old practice of nonmaternal child rearing in the countryside explains the strong tradition of childminders in France. The first centers for very young children, called *crèches*, appeared in the middle of the nineteenth century, but unlike the *écoles maternelles,* they remained without official recognition for many years. As a result, their number grew slowly, providing very inferior conditions of care to the poor children who attended them. In 1945, personnel from the hospital sector replaced the existing staffs in order to reduce child mortality. A negative view of the *crèche* persisted until the late 1960s, when the arrival of both new professionals (early childhood educators and psychologists) and parents of the "1968 generation" led to a new outlook. Crèches became more attractive to middle-class parents in a period when more mothers' participation in the labor force was on the rise and while a growing concern for emotional security, autonomy, and creativity developed within the new staff training program.

Main characteristics. The French care policy is aiming the parent's free choice between different settings. The Ministries of Social Affairs and Health develop the regulations and, with the national family allowance fund (CNAF), define the goals and resources of the regional family allowance funds (CAFs) which carry out, in each *département*, the policy decisions. Currently, care provision remains insufficient for children under age 3.

After the maternity leave (sixteen weeks paid and job protected) and the paternal leave (eleven days), half of the children under 3, and particularly those from modest backgrounds, stay at home. Some of these children, however, attend part-time provisions (*haltes-garderies*) or free centers for children and parents (*accueils parents-enfants*) run by municipalities or nonprofit associations. Most of these parents receive a parental leave allowance.

The remaining children are cared for in various settings that are heavily financed by public authorities. Parents have to contribute financially and are helped by allowances and tax reductions, including upper-class families who hire an in-home caregiver (1% of the under threes).

Many of the under threes (20%) are cared for by licensed childminders in the homes of those caregivers (three children authorized). The majority of them are employed by parents. These independent childminders may attend a network of childminders generally coordinated by an early childhood educator. Some others are employed by community family centers. Salaries are regulated by law at a rate of 2.25 times the national minimum wage per child per day.

Other children (10%) attend a *crèche* (for infants and toddlers), run mostly by municipalities but also by nonprofit organizations, parent cooperatives, or public companies, and very recently by the private sector. These centers are open all day and operate year-round. The head is generally a pediatric nurse; the staff includes a majority of pediatric nurse assistants and some early childhood educators, plus part-time pediatricians (compulsory) and psychologists (not compulsory). Salaries vary greatly according to the different categories of professionals. The ratio in crèches is one adult for every five babies, and one adult for every eight children who are able to walk.

About 10 percent of under threes, mainly from disadvantaged backgrounds, are cared for by grandparents or by nonlicensed childminders (illegal in France), without any public financial assistance.

Current policy. A comprehensive national policy was designed in the early 1980s to improve the quantity and quality of these programs, and to encourage decentralization. Thanks to early childhood contracts between the regional family allowance funds (CAF) and the municipalities, the number of crèches doubled and of *haltes-garderies* tripled. In order to reduce the isolation of both mothers and childminders (and more recently in-home caregivers), innovative forms of care developed: first parent-child centers and then childminder networks, providing these adults with social support opportunities and children with group activities. During the 1990s "multicare" services (including several kinds of arrangements) developed as a response to parents' increasing irregular work schedules and atypical working hours. The aim of these early childhood contracts is to increase quality by supporting in-service training, financing cultural projects, and recruiting municipal early childhood coordinators.

In 2000, a decree on collective care services updated and harmonized requirements: at least half of the personnel are required to have a diploma of pediatric nurse, early childhood educator, or pediatric nurse assistant; a quarter need to have qualifications related to health or social work; and a last quarter is exempted from any qualification. Paramedical professionals remain the majority but early childhood educators are now authorized to be heads of small *crèches* (less than forty places).

Curriculum. There is no curriculum in this sector, but the 2000 decree recognizes the educational role of these services in terms of well-being and development. No concrete content about play and "awaking" activities are specified but a pedagogical plan is required, as well as individualized plans for handicapped children and a social plan, aimed at parental participation and support, as well as prevention of social exclusion.

Implementation. Despite France's policy of neutrality toward the type of child care chosen by parents and a positive evolution of the early childhood education (ECE) system during these last decades, real choice is highly limited both by local provision and financial constraints, particularly for families of modest means and living in rural areas. Crèches concentrate, in fact, in the Parisian area and big cities, and childminders remain too expensive for low-income families.

Except in the case of the cooperation between families and professionals existing within parents cooperatives, child-care staff are not involved in a real partnership with families, despite an important focus on welcoming parents and supporting parental competencies ("parentality"). These professionals are now calling for better training in how to work with parents, and particularly with those in social difficulties.

Leisure Time Services for After-School-Hours

The first leisure time services, called *patronages,* were created simultaneously with the republican school; nonprofit associations began to run these programs at the beginning of the twentieth century, and municipalities took over in the 1950s. This sector has been regulated since the 1970s.

Main characteristics. Preschool children generally eat at the *école maternelle* (between 11:30 AM and 1:30 PM) and some of them also attend out-of-school-time services (before 8:30 AM or after 4:30 PM). Lunch time and out-of-school-time services are run by municipalities or not-profit associations, staffed by *animateurs* (low salaried) and a director qualified in out-of-school activities.

These very inexpensive services are regulated by Ministries of Health, Social Affairs, Youth and Sports. They are attended by children from all backgrounds, and particularly by lower income and poor families.

Recent legislation stresses the educational dimension of these services, which are to be approved by the child and maternal health services and have to develop educational projects. Thanks to local educational contracts between municipalities and local partners, leisure time services now are developing various cultural and sports activities, particularly in disadvantaged zones. Research on leisure time services is very recent. Further documentation is needed.

Conclusion

Despite the separation between the education and care sectors within ECE, a number of innovative projects and experiments are striving to improve access, quality, and equity for parents and children, offering interesting perspectives for the future. Based on teamwork and partnerships with other professionals, they enrich the children's experiences and increase the professionalism of early childhood personnel. Teachers transcend their didactic perspectives and become more aware of the children's learning processes, and medical orientations decrease among care professionals as leisure time teams begin to reinforce educational perspectives. Examples include the following:

- cooperation between teachers, assistants, and early childhood educators in *classes-passerelles* ("bridge-classes"), which aim to connect families and schools by enrolling 2-year-olds cared for at home and particularly those from disadvantaged backgrounds;
- cooperation between professionals from the health, social welfare, and school sectors in centers for children and their parents, which also aim to facilitate the transition to *école maternelle* (in addition to supporting parental competencies and social links in disadvantaged areas);
- cooperation between early childhood staffs and culture professionals (artists, librarians, etc.) within various cultural projects, sometimes linking the care and education sectors, and stimulated by the Ministry of Culture with the aim of democratizing French culture and preventing social exclusion.

But the development of a "common culture" of early childhood needs, in fact, a stronger policy in order to go beyond the traditional cleavage between the different sectors. Will the recent creation of departmental early childhood commissions (not yet implemented in all *departments*), which include representatives of all sectors, contribute to this change?

Further Readings: Baudelot, O., S. Rayna, S. Mayer, and T. Musatti (2003). A comparative analysis of the function of coordination of early childhood education and care in France and Italy. *Early years: An International Journal of Research and development* 5, 32–48; Dajez, F. (1994). *Les origines de l'école maternelle.* Paris: PUF; Lebon, F. (2003). Une politique de l'enfance, du patronage au centre de loisirs. *Éducation et sociétés* (11), 135–152; Neuman, M., and S. Peers (2002). *Equal from the start: Promoting educational opportunity for all preschool children. Learning from the French experience.* New York: French-American Foundation; Rayna, S. (in press). Some issues and problems of France's crèches and école maternelle. In M. Takeuchi, M. Shigeru, and R. Scott, eds., *New directions in early childhood education in the 21st century: The international perspectives.* Waverly, IA: G & R Publishing.

Sylvie Rayna

Culture, Race, and Ethnicity

Issues of culture, race, and ethnicity are different in every country. The notions of diversity, **immigration**, citizenship, nation, and public services education are linked to one another and must be examined when considering the issue of multiculturalism. This discussion begins with a short history of the French context and values, followed by a description of the role played by early childhood settings in France's strategy of integration. Next comes a presentation of some cultural projects and policies in early childhood, including their goals of democratization of culture throughout these early interventions. Also highlighted is the prevention of children's school failure and reduction of social exclusion, including content and strategies, and effects on children, families, and professionals. The entry concludes with a discussion of other initiatives.

The French Context

The issue of immigration. As in other countries, early childhood services are partly for young children of parents who have come from other countries. For many families, these services are the first time in which they meet the public culture of their new country. Most immigrant children are born in France and become French citizens when they reach adulthood because the French laws of naturalization consider anyone born and living in France to be a French citizen.

Immigration has a long and important history in France. France's immigration can be linked to its colonial past, with high rates during the 1970s and 1980s and a current flow of illegal immigrants (the borders are now officially closed). Following an older wave of immigrants from Italy, Poland, Spain, and Portugal, immigration shifted to North Africa and Black Africa, Turkey, Asia, and Eastern Europe. Immigrants represent about 11 percent of the French population (not including those born elsewhere but having French citizenship), and are overrepresented among disadvantaged families living in the neighborhoods of big cities.

The issue of ethnicity. In France one does not use the notion of ethnic minorities. Communities created around a common origin, religion, or culture are not officially recognized. The values of the French Republic (Liberty, Equality, Fraternity) are supposed to transcend the particularities of individuals, and its laws are based on a strict separation between the religious and the political spheres. It is forbidden to distinguish people according to their national or cultural origins. Cultural, ethnic, and religious identities have meaning only in the private sphere. Avoiding the notion of communitarianism and multiculturalism, the goal of France's policy of integration is to provide everyone a place within the nation. Within a context of increasing social problems and poverty, France is currently searching for a new model of integration, no longer referring to the former goal of assimilation.

The Role of Care and Education Settings

Early childhood services are key sites for enacting national goals for integration and the creation of new citizens.

Écoles maternelles. In France, 3-year-old children, both citizens and immigrant children (about 8%), attend *écoles maternelles* (see earlier). Play is seen as an important component of the *écoles maternelles* because it provides an opportunity for children to share a common language and values. The *écoles maternelles* and elementary schools are also known as "schools of the Republic," a term used since the end of the nineteenth century and constructed in opposition to the power of Catholicism. Today, many believe that secular policy provides protection for minority religions by calling for the absence of religious signs in public life. This law has recently been an issue for Muslim families, related to their wish to have their girls wear veils.

However, the central objective of *écoles maternelle*s, as the primary place of integration, is to provide all young children with an equal opportunity and with an equal chance to succeed in school, through a focus on French language which is a priority in the preschool curriculum. At the end of this curriculum, there is an initiation to other cultures through traditional songs, but mother tongues other than French are not promoted. The role of parents is traditionally limited, but some innovations toward more inclusion have been developed, particularly in priority education areas (*Zone d'éducation prioritaire [ZEP]*) where immigrant populations concentrate, in the suburbs of some cities around Paris or in the provinces.

The care sector. A smaller number of immigrant children attend crèches and other care services because a smaller number of these mothers work. However, this is changing as more women from these communities are entering the workforce. Efforts are made to encourage them to use part-time crèches or parent and children centers, not as immigrants but as disadvantaged families. The goal is to introduce important early socialization to their young children and prepare them for entry into *école maternelle,* as well as to help the entire family integrate socially. When the young children of these families attend crèches, some attention is paid to cultural diversity, based on psychological ideas encouraging enhancement of the continuity of care between families and centers. For instance, in a recent French-Japanese comparative study, it was observed that in French crèches babies, mostly from immigrant families, who are rocked to sleep at home, are also rocked in the center, while generally the other babies are put to bed rapidly with their pacifiers. In-service training contains some introduction to the maternal practices of other cultures and includes discussion of the kinds of cultural projects described in more detail below.

More generally, including and supporting parents is one of the main issues. Although working with parents is important, analyses of institutional practices often reveal contradictions, infantilizing and stigmatizing parents while at the same time demanding too much from them. However, there are some fruitful innovations, empowering poor families (including immigrant families) in some cooperative crèches that are working specifically on diversity issues. These initiatives are carried out by their national association of cooperative crèches *(Association des Collectifs Enfants, Parents, Professionnels—ACEPP)*—within the European network called Diversity in Early Childhood Education and Training (DECET), where various modalities of parental participation are being tested.

New Partnerships between Early Childhood and Culture Professionals

In the early 1980s, two main associations initiated innovative projects based on new partnerships between early childhood and culture professionals, which led to an incentive policy launched by Ministry of Culture in 1989. The first of these, *ACCES* (Cultural Association against Exclusion and Segregation), was created by three children's psychiatrists and psychoanalysts. These psychonalysts developed prevention projects, within a Winnicottian and Piagetian theoretical framework (see Jean **Piaget**), that were based on providing babies with books in the places where they are found: the waiting rooms of pediatric centers, places were childminders meet, etc. The second association, *Infance et Musique* (Childhood and Music), created by a pediatrician and a musician psychologist, developed musical projects, including multicultural projects, in crèches and other places in disadvantaged areas.

A cultural policy of early childhood. With the aim to democratize culture, to improve quality in early childhood services, and to reduce social exclusion, The Ministry of Culture, in cooperation with the Ministry of Social Affairs, developed a new cultural policy toward young children and their families. Beginning in 1989, subsidies were given for cultural projects proposed by early childhood services, cultural or training associations, or municipalities for children under the age of 6. These projects, supported for two- or three-year periods, have to promote close cooperation among early childhood professionals, culture professionals (artists, librarians), and parents in order to ensure continuity between services and families.

However, continuation of these projects has also been sustained by other mechanisms of financing, such as early childhood contracts (*contrat-enfance*) between municipalities and Family Allowance Funds (CAFs). The goal of this financing was not only to increase the quantity of services but also their quality. These types of projects can also be initiated by schools and sustained by other types of contracts, for instance between schools and municipalities.

Implementation and effects of the cultural projects. Through the implementation of this policy, important subsidies were given for cultural projects linked to the work of the two pioneer associations and others created later. The most common projects involved books (particularly for crèches), which were and are still largely developed in cities in the north, west, and southwest of France. Some other programs have led to interesting experiments, such as theatre projects for a young audience. The introduction of early childhood professionals to new cultural and artistic approaches (and the artists discovering new perspectives) have contributed much to the enrichment of play activities in care services as well as learning activities in *écoles maternelles*, reducing some of the more questionable practices and improving the atmosphere of the settings. When culturally focussed training sessions included both preschool teachers and care professionals (center professionals as well as childminders) the results were particularly fruitful. Beyond the local transformations they produce, they contribute to the emergence of a common professional culture of early childhood (for children aged 0–6), which is dramatically missing in France.

Today, when cultural associations offer animations and training for all the children, the focus is on children from disadvantaged backgrounds, including immigrant families. For instance, in Paris, the association *LAP* (*Lire à Paris*: Reading in Paris) focuses its projects in waiting rooms of pediatric centers attended primarily by these populations, in social centers along with literacy classes for their parents or the mothers, and more recently in full-time centers where children, for social or health reasons, are waiting to be adopted or cared for in other families (if they cannot be returned to their parents). Books are read both from the French repertoire as well as from other cultures. There are no quantitative assessments of the effects of such projects on children and their families, but qualitative data (testimonies of teachers, etc.) converge to show significant impacts of strong and coherent projects, carried out in some cities. One example is a small city in the north where mothers from disadvantaged backgrounds tell stories to the children and are progressively involved in the project. There is a strong partnership in this city between an association and the *ZEP*.

Other Initiatives

Among other initiatives related to the issues addressed here are the *classes* and *actions passerelles* (bridging classes and projects), where the cultural projects described above often develop. These programs, based on institutional partnerships between municipalities and departmental administrations of education and health, and with cooperation between teachers and professionals of the care sector, aim to facilitate the transition to *école maternelle* of young children cared for at home, including many children from disadvantaged and immigrant families. Until recently these settings, which are also based on a mixed professional culture of care and education, were not receiving enough support at the national level. Despite a lack of studies showing how diversity is taken into account in these programs, several examples in some cities suggest the richness of such innovations.

Further Readings: Bonnafé, M. (1994). *Les livres, c'est bon pour les bébés* Paris: Calman-Levy; Caillard, M., and Ch. Attali-Marot (1999). Des pratiques culturelles et artistiques pour le jeune enfant et sa famille : quinze ans d'expérience. In O. Baudelot and S. Rayna, eds., *Les bébés et la culture: Petite enfance, éveil culturel et lutte contre les exclusions.* Paris: INRP-L'Harmattan; Lorcerie, F. (2003). *L'école et le défi ethnique. Éducation et intégration.* Paris: INRP-ESF; MRIE. (2003). *Prévenir l'exclusion dès l'enfance.* Lyon; Ott, L. (2004). *Travailler avec les familles. Parents-professionnels: un nouveau partage de la relation éducative.* Ramon St Ville: Erès; Rayna, S. (2004). Professional practices with under ones in French and Japanese day care centers. *Early years* 24(1), 35–48.

Sylvie Rayna

Family Involvement in France

This discussion of family involvement addresses relations with two types of centers: crèches for children under 3 and *écoles maternelles* for 2- to 6-year-old children. As described earlier, *écoles maternelles* are free and open to every child, whether their parents are working or not. Crèches are not free, and although the decree on care services (August 2000) no longer requires parents to work, in practice children attending crèches have working parents. Due to the history of these institutions, parents are considered more as recipients of public and professional services than as real partners, except in the case of parent cooperatives (crèches *parentales)* run by nonprofit associations. However, recent writings in both the care and education sectors recognize parents as the first educators of their children and coeducators with the centers, and tend to promote family participation.

The Background: Imposing Moral Values on Working-Class Families and Keeping Parents at a Distance

During the nineteenth century, crèches and *écoles maternelles* provided services for economically disadvantaged children. The relationships with parents were strongly influenced by the sociopolitical context: industrialization, child labor, poverty, infant mortality, political troubles, and religious conflicts. The first *écoles maternelles* (1826) and crèches (1845) emerged out of social utopian ideals and charitable policies. Since this time, the aim of social control and normalization of the working-class families has partly conditioned the relationships with parents. Different reasons led *écoles maternelles* and crèches to close their doors to parents: Republican principles and the fight to reduce infant mortality.

Republican principles. The Republicans set out to break loose from monarchical ideas and the power of Church. In 1881, the goal of uniting the French population within Republican values was implemented throughout the republican schools, which included *école maternelle*. When this integration took place within the public system, the principle of egalitarian treatment of all the children kept parents at a distance.

Combating infant mortality. Fighting infant mortality became the first goal of crèches. Linked to Pasteur's discoveries, the objective of crèches shifted from charity toward health and medical aims. Maternal education became more and more influenced by hygienist prescriptions. In 1945, the child and maternal health centers (PMI) were created, from which the first the regulations for crèches appeared, requiring medical personnel (child nurses and child nurse assistants) as staff. Due to fear of health contamination, parents' presence was prohibited in the crèches, and they were assigned inferior status relative to the professionals, who came from the hospital sector.

Opening the Doors to Parents: Rationale and Results

Two factors led crèches and *écoles maternelles* to open their doors to parents during the 1970s: the increasing attendance of children from middle- and upper-class families and the widespread dissemination of a psychological discourse about the importance of parent-child bonding. Starting around the events of the May 1968 student revolution, and due to the interest of "new parents" in a collective education for their children under the age of 3, the concern about the parent-professional connection resurfaced. These parents from middle- and then upper-class families expressed new expectations and made new claims (antiauthoritarian education, coeducation, etc.). Groups of students created the first parent cooperatives within university campuses. These cooperatives (which were officially recognized in 1980) brought to the forefront the value of parent involvement and cooperation with professionals.

Psychoanalytic studies on the effects of early separation and maternal deprivation disseminated beginning in the 1950s were also influential. I. Lézine, a pioneer who defended the idea of the complementary role of family and *crèche* and who developed an early childhood psychopedagogy, trained the first psychologists employed in crèches during the 1960s. Their critical approach gave support to the claims of the "new" parents, and contributed to the reopening of crèches to parent involvement.

As a result, in 1975, an official government document again allowed parents to enter the rooms where their children lived in the centers. Home-to-center transition practices requiring mother's presence were implemented, as well as the first conferences with parents. However, parents were still far from becoming partners. This document underlined simultaneously the importance of exchanges with mothers, during which a health education should take place. In 1983, another document instituted *crèche* councils, which were to include parent delegates. These councils never developed because parents were generally not informed of their right to this involvement, due to worries about what might result from their actual participation.

The pressure of upper-class parents in école maternelle. In the 1970s, the increased number of children from higher socioeconomic backgrounds attending the *école maternelle,* which occurred earlier than in *crèche,* led to the progressive transformation of the pedagogy from the prevailing productive model to an expressive one. Aiming at the development of the child's personality through the implementation of expressive activities and a more liberal attitude of the teachers, this new model reflected the influence of a psychological perspective on the young child. In 1977, the official texts supported these values and recognized parental involvement. School councils were created and, unlike with crèches, were developed successfully. Parents elected their representatives every year, and on the national level the voice of the two main federations of parents, which were concerned with the whole school system, became stronger. In 1986, a new text provided the parent delegates with the possibility of participating in educational issues, but the teachers resisted this sharing of the educational territory. In fact, parents' involvements were generally focused on material issues, like supporting the local educational team's requests to ministerial or local authorities for more resources. Among the delegated parents, lower class parents were (and are) rarely represented, and the opportunities organized by the schools to meet all the parents (formal parent-teachers conferences once a year, etc.) are not very attractive to them. The cultural and social distance between these parents and professionals increases misunderstanding and exclusion.

Toward a Partnership?

Today parental participation is officially encouraged both in *écoles maternelles* and in crèches, but practices change very slowly. The Law on Education (1989) reaffirmed parents' involvement with their children's school life. Parents were defined as "permanent partners of the school." The main role of teachers was to inform parents about their ways of working and the children's progress in order to increase parents' involvement in their children's early learning. However, parents' involvement in school generally remains punctual and limited (taking the children to the swimming pool, organizing the annual fete, etc.), and mainly concerns elected parents. The parent–teacher relationship still consists of individual exchanges, varying according to the families' social position. The new status of the teachers ("school professors") tends to increase the cultural distance with disadvantaged families. Moreover, the current focus on early learning tends to limit the presence of the parents in the schools and the informal exchanges. However, the general use of life notebooks, making the children "messengers," mediates the communication with the families, providing them an important support. These notebooks usually focus on a significant event in the daily life of the child. Some schools, however, develop interesting projects, which include strong parental participation, notably in priority education areas (ZEP) where the quality of the relationships with the families favors both children's school integration and adults' social inclusion.

Since 2000, all care services, including crèches, are required to develop a "project of establishment." These projects must include the definition of the families' place in the program and of their participation. The interior regulation also needs to include examples of parents' participation within the services. But there are no minimum requirements, or a clear definition of such participation. No evaluation is required. Therefore, changes in practices are very limited at the moment. Parents' involvement is expected principally during morning and evening exchanges. Their presence at social events is appreciated, but except on rare occasions, their effective participation in crèches is practically nonexistent. Nevertheless, parents seem generally satisfied, but the relationships with the professionals present a variety of configurations for several reasons. Qualifications and status vary greatly among professionals: some have no diploma, whereas others have a child nurse, assistant child nurse, or early childhood educator diploma. Professional values and representations of children's needs differ among these different types of staff. Moreover, there is no national curriculum, so educational attitudes and projects can vary from one *crèche* to another one. Parents belong to a range of socio-professional categories, and although they share some common expectations concerning the *crèche* (children's blossoming and preparation for the *école maternelle*), some of them are willing to totally delegate their educational role, whereas others refuse any kind of educational delegation. Typologies of parents and of their relationships with crèches have been established (Bouve, 2001; Moisset, in press) but, in spite of a strong influence of the social background on these relationships, parents cannot be reduced strictly to their social standing: identical models of representation can be partly shared among individuals from different social backgrounds. In any case, it is the confrontation of educational and pedagogical practices between parents and institutions that underlies these relationships.

Supporting Parent's Competences

In 1998, a new idea appeared in the political and professional discourse supporting parental competences, which, in fact, goes well beyond the field of early childhood and is implemented throughout networks aiming at supporting parental functions. These networks include various kind of services, such as centers for children and parents (play centers that children can attend with their parents in order to reduce the isolation of the families) or centers for parental mediation (in case of parental conflicts). Crèches are considered to contribute to this effort, as are schools, where the necessity to "remobilise parents and to encourage families to exercise all their responsibilities" is officially mentioned (1998).

The articulation between parental support and parental involvement is ambiguous. Parental support may represent a modern version of the previous parental education within a framework with a background in social assistance and control, rather than promoting the emergence of new models. The notion of parental support is not explicitly linked with a notion of reciprocity, which is needed in order to bring equity and balance to relationships between parents and professionals. The question of the parental responsibility is often used to denigrate the supposed uninterested and uninvolved parents (and particularly those living in a precarious situation: single parents, immigrant families, etc). This raises the issue of the need to question the historical permanence of such suspicion about parents' competences.

The current orientation of the association of parent cooperatives (ACEPP) is, however, important to underline. This association supports projects based on parental participation, including families from lower and intercultural backgrounds, and is carrying out an analysis of parental and professional competences within the European network DECET (*Diversity in Early Childhood Education and Training*), with the goal of promoting early childhood services "free of any kind of discrimination" and supporting the participation of service recipients "as active citizens."

Finally, it is important to mention that a gender issue underlies the issue of parents–professional or family–institution relationships. These relationships refer essentially to relationships between mothers and female professionals. An important task is to encourage more significant father involvement both in their own children's education and in early childhood services. Could such a change induce a different configuration within parent–professional relationships?

Further Readings: Bouve, C. (2001). *Les crèches collectives: usagers et représentations sociales*. Paris: L'Harmattan; CRESAS (1984). *Ouvertures: l'école, la crèche, les familles*. Paris, INRP-L'Harmattan; Francis, V. (2005). Le partenariat école—famille: le rôle de l'enfant messager. In S. Rayna and G. Brougère (coord.) *Regards sur les relations entre parents et professionnels de la petite enfance*. LYON: INRP; Moisset, P. (in press). La diversité des rapports parentaux à la crèche et ses déterminants. In S. Rayna & G. Brougère (coord.) *Regards sur les relations entre parents et professionnels de la petite enfance*. Paris: INRP; Plaisance, E. (1986). *L'enfant, la maternelle, la société*, Paris, PUF.

Catherine Bouve

Early Childhood Education Pedagogy in France

The division that separates the child-care system from the education system in France is reflected clearly at the level of pedagogical orientations and practices. The term "pedagogy" is standard usage in *école maternelle*, because it is considered a school. But this term is sparingly used in child-care centers, where the terms "education" and sometimes "psychopedagogy" are preferred. The assumption seems to be that "pedagogy" refers to school learning and not to child development. However, pedagogical models do underlie the practices of the different care and education services, linked to their own traditions.

Pedagogical Models in the Care Sector

In the care sector, pedagogical models follow those that developed within crèches and have then spread throughout the whole field. For about a century these models were based on the maternal models imposed by the dominant discourses. They were then replaced by professional models, based currently on dominant psychological orientations.

Maternal models. Since they were first established, crèches have had a primariy social function (baby care and assistance to mothers from the working classes). The educational function, also present, was based on Rousseau's educational philosophy, centered on gentleness and persuasion. This informal model was popularized by F. Marbeau, a magistrate and municipal councillor who set up the first *crèche* in 1844 in Paris.

However, this model fell out of favor with the coming of *puériculture* (specialized infant care and nursing), when the battle against high infant mortality rates in crèches was launched. But the hygienist principles popularized by doctors from the 1870s onward were accompanied by moral prescriptions (rocking babies in one's arms was forbidden, and the child's access to different kinds of objects was restricted). Such choices marked a new conception where early training of infant behavior was the priority. What had originally been an open pedagogical model in the crèches turned rigid with the adoption of more and more rules.

The sharp drop in infant mortality in the 1950s marked a turning point coinciding more or less with the expansion and popularization of psychological studies and knowledge concerning child development from the 1960s.

Specific professional models. The rise of interest in the social and educational role of child-care institutions owes much to the work of I. Lézine (1964) who insisted on the doubly positive aspect of the crèches, not only a "help to parents" but also an "educative setting for children," and encouraged the entry of psychologists in these services. Studies conducted by psychoanalysts in nurseries also gradually relieved concerns about emotional deprivation among young children raised in a collective context.

After 1968, models of *Éducation Nouvelle* spread due to the influence of the new education movements. A significant voice heard in defense of the "cause of children" was that of F. Dolto, psychoanalyst and "educational doctor" who, in her writings and radio interviews, addressed professionals and parents, urging them to adopt an approach based on respect, attentive listening, and confidence in children. This conception was echoing the expectations of new parents' (from more upper-class backgrounds) who were beginning to invest in crèches at this time.

The introduction in France of the pioneering work conducted in Hungary at the Loczy nursery contributed to a new outlook on young children and important changes in practices (autonomy, continuity of relationships, etc.).

Gradually, with the introduction of training programs inspired by all these new orientations plus some innovative programs based on cultural activities (music, books, plastic art), crèches achieved their own place and identity, by distinguishing themselves from the maternal model and maintaining a certain distance from the school model.

From the 1980s on, many initiatives developed, favoring relational stability and continuity (same-age or heterogeneous groups of children in the charge of adults acting as stable points of reference). The importance given to play and verbal and nonverbal communication in social and emotional development led to a diversity of proposals to enrich the children's experience. Fieldwork showed the surprising social and cognitive capacities of the children as well as the creativity of the staffs.

Without supposing that all crèches develop the same pedagogical approach (due to the decentralization of the care sector), one can assume that their past and present evolutions as well as their current official objectives (well-being and harmonious development of children) make their pedagogy very different from that of the *école maternelle*.

Pedagogical Models in Écoles Maternelles

Historical overview. The pedagogical function of the *salles d'asile*, ancestor of the French *écoles maternelles*, had been clearly asserted since its creation in 1826. Brought under the charge of the Ministry of Public Instruction in 1837, these centers provided assistance to children between the ages of 2 and 6, while teaching basic literacy. Archives mention the use of teaching material, like tables of letters and numbers, abacuses and other counting machines, linked to the curriculum (focused on reading and writing, arithmetic, science, history and geography, religious education, drawing, music, and gymnastics). The strictly controlled organization of these centers favored "mutual education." This made possible the acceptance of a very large number of children. More than a hundred children were sometimes grouped together where some older children taught the younger ones.

These centers became *écoles maternelles* in 1881. Interest in childhood and in the education of young children grew further. P. Kergomard marked a turning point in pedagogical options. From about 1875 onward this inspector denounced the regimental training of children. She insisted on the need to abandon the repetitive and rigid collective techniques, and progressively introduced play, in line with Rousseau's ideas but also with Fröebel's German kindergartens. Two sections were set up, one for younger children between the ages of 2 and 4, and the other for those between 4 and 6. Numbers were limited to fifty per class. Although the curriculum mentioned the distinctiveness of the *école maternelle*, which is "*not a school in the ordinary sense of the word,*" it remained attached to the division of the school timetable according to subjects, though reduced at Kergomard's initiative. The distribution of subjects over the school day was based on a pedagogical model alternating lessons with play situations.

The professional corps of female inspectors for *écoles maternelles*, officially set up in 1910, played a decisive role in the spread of new pedagogical models thanks to the introduction of pedagogical lectures (in-service training). Their role was progressively strengthened by a professional association, the general association of preschool teachers, founded in 1921. The new pedagogical orientations advocated by the *Education Nouvelle* movement contributed to the growing interest in approaches centered on the activities of the child and the social life of the group. Contributions of the Italian Maria **Montessori** and of the Belgian O. Decroly contributed to the spread of a pedagogical model including planning of activities around "centers of interest" and stimulating learning materials adapted to children's activities.

The dynamism of the general association of preschool teachers, its national congresses and regional meetings, grew during the 1960s, favoring reflection around a pedagogy of expressivity and creativity. "Children's art," encouraged by C. Freinet, came to be widely represented in teaching practices. The demand of families from the upper classes strengthened this "expressive model" based on the expression of the child's personality, which became predominant in the late 1970s.

Current pedagogical options. Since the end of the 1980s, along with classroom furniture and materials for play and learning (including children's literature, usually abundantly available in schools), work materials have been a concern among teachers. Widely published and distributed through professional journals and by a rapidly expanding sector of school publishing, photocopiable work sheets as well as workbooks are used as learning material for children's individual work. Used in many classes of the middle or older group, sometimes even for the youngest children (2- and 3-year-olds), they suit the pedagogical specificities of a newly defined preelementary model. Introduced with the 1986 curriculum they include, nowadays, an evaluation of the learners' skills.

The *écoles maternelles* today are specifically attuned to the development of early skills defined in the curriculum, which is linked since 1995 with the elementary school curriculum. Simultaneously the same initial preparation is given for teachers in *écoles maternelles* and in elementary schools, and the separate corps of specialized inspectors has been done away with. While these measures aim to ensure easier transition between *écoles maternelles* and elementary schools, and despite the fact that the curriculum recommends maintaining a distinctive and separate pedagogy in the *écoles maternelles*, the risk of an overly rigid approach cannot be ignored. However, debates around different pedagogical options are regularly triggered as each school is required periodically to reflect upon its own pedagogical project.

Classrooms are usually composed of several play areas, a space reserved for artistic activity, a library, and an area where all can gather as a group. A separate room is usually reserved for physical activity and a dormitory allows the youngest group a nap.

The distribution of activities is based on a timetable set at the beginning of the school year. Along with the activities corresponding to the five areas of learning, defined by the curriculum, time is devoted to receiving the children every morning, to meals and refreshments, recess and rest.

The school day usually opens with a morning ritual using a variety of pedagogical resources: calendars, timetables, class lists for marking attendance and tables for distributing tasks amongst children, weather information, etc. Some teachers choose to vary these resources over the year to keep up interest and involvement.

Practices are far from uniform, but a general pattern is established: on the one hand, individual activity alternates with small-group activity or whole-class activity, and on the other, activities chosen by children alternate with others structured by the teacher, sometimes in collaboration with his/her assistant (ATSEM). The idea that play, action, experimentation as well as structured activities ought to be integrated together into learning seems to lack acceptance in the classrooms, where, in fact, activities often seem to be split into distinct parts. The organization of activities in small groups itself is rarely used to stimulate cooperation among children.

Pedagogical Models in Leisure Time Centers

Regulated in the 1960s within a care perspective, the legal framework of the leisure time centers, which operate during out-of-school hours, now includes an educative role. The staff of *animateurs* base their approach on an educational project using leisure time activities. School holidays are most suitable to more ambitious projects carried out in partnership with local institutions like libraries, museums, play centers, sport associations, etc. Particularly in urban settings, the variety of activities offered to the children calls for the regular use of the culture and sports infrastructure. These options are also likely to familiarize their parents with these local resources. This obviously brings up the question of equitable access to such resources in different rural and urban settings.

Mutual Interactions to Be Strengthened in the Future

Despite their specific pedagogical characteristics, professionals of the different sectors point out the advantages of their mutual interactions when they are involved in some common local projects. Innovative experiments, developed in the cities within local educational contracts (CEL) and particularly important when carried out within deprived areas provided with additional resources (ZEP), tend to stimulate organizations toward practices more suitable to the needs of children and families. Pedagogical experiences such as transition classes (between families and school), where professionals from both education and care work together, have allowed the emergence of new blends in professional practice. But mandates from administrators concerned with security and with aligning practices with those of the elementary school limit the development of such evolutions in practice.

Acknowledgments: The contributor thanks very much Akshay Bakaya for supervision of the English version of this paper.

Further Readings: Bréauté, M., and S. Rayna, eds. (1995). *Jouer et connaître chez les tout-petits*. Paris: INRP-Ville de Paris; Lézine, I. (1964). *Psychopédagogie du premier âge*. Paris: PUF; Luc, J.-N. (1997). *L'invention du jeune enfant au XIXe siècle. De la salle d'asile à l'école maternelle*. Paris: Belin; Plaisance, E. (1999). L'école maternelle française entre accueil et apprentissages. In G. Brougère and S. Rayna, eds., *Culture, Childhood and Preschool education*. Paris: UNESCO-University Paris 13-INRP; Rollet, C. (1990). *La politique à l'égard de la petite enfance sous la Troisième République*. Paris: PUF/INED.

Véronique Francis

Curriculum

The French system of the early childhood education and care is characterized by a significant contrast, from a curricular standpoint, between the domains of child care and early education. On the one hand, the *école maternelle* has a national curriculum that defines a set of school learnings. On the other hand, child-care services do not yet have precise official educational orientations.

The Curriculum of the École Maternelle: A Brief Historical Overview

The *écoles maternelles* (and still earlier, the *salles d'asile*) curriculum was established from the beginning. Between 1855 and 1921 these programs were reproducing the curricula of elementary schools. With exception of the transmission of the republican values, the content of these encyclopedic curricula changed very little from 1881, when the *écoles maternelles* were integrated into the French system of education. Thanks to dynamic female inspectors of *écoles maternelles* such as Pauline Kergomard, who introduced new ideas about early education and play activities, a specific preschool education progressively emerged over time.

After 1921 this deep transformation went on for more than fifty years without any new official curriculum. The national association of preschool teachers, created in 1921, has played (and continues to play) an important role in the dissemination of this specific preschool culture. However, for half a century a "productive" pedagogical model was dominant. This model changed after World War II along with the changes in the social makeup of the *écoles maternelles*, including the presence of more and more children from middle- and upper-class families. During the 1970s, the dominant model became an "expressive" one.

In 1986, national guidelines were established. Three main goals were defined for the *écoles maternelles* as follows:
• "schooling" (the child must get used to this new environment)
• socializing (socialization is acculturation)
• learning and practising (developing abilities)
   Physical activities, communication, oral and writing expression activities, artistic and aesthetic activities, technical and scientific activities are the main domains supporting these goals.

In 1989, the Law on Education integrated these orientations, placing the child "in the heart of the educational system," and organized the primary school, including both the *école maternelle* and the elementary school. Three cycles of learning (three years each) were conceived in order to bridge the two schools:
• Cycle 1, the "cycle of early learning," covers the first years of *école maternelle* (children from 2 to 5 years);
• Cycle 2, the "cycle of basic learning," includes the last year of *école maternelle* and the first two years of elementary school (children from 5 to 8 years);
• Cycle 3, the "cycle of reinforcements," concerns the last three years of elementary school (from 8 to 11 years).
In 1995, this primary school was granted a curriculum based on this new organization into cycles of learning. Currently, the curriculum for the *école maternelle* (including cycle 1 and the beginning of cycle 2) is the first part of the one designed for the primary school as a whole. This curriculum was reaffirmed in 2002.

The Current Curriculum for the École Maternelle

The current curriculum is defined in terms of competencies within several domains of activities that children should have acquired by the end of the *école maternelle*. In this curriculum, republican values are reaffirmed with the challenge of offering equal opportunities from the very beginning of school, linked with an objective of excellence for all.

The following five domains of activities are presented in the 1995 national curriculum:
• Living together
• Learning to speak
• Acting and expressing emotions and thoughts with one's body
• Discovering the world
• Imagining, feeling, and creating

Teachers are to develop their educational projects and organize the children's activities within this framework. Teachers are encouraged to evaluate each child in order to guide their individualized support for the learning progress and validate a satisfactory level of competence for entering elementary school.

This curriculum, focused on learning, does not give much space for play. The only reference is to a limited amount of playtime in the courtyard (thirty minutes), in the morning and in the afternoon.

Mastering the French language became an absolute priority in the new curriculum published in 2002, under the title *What Do We Learn in the École Maternelle?* Thus language, "at the heart of learning," is now the first domain. The aim is to develop various language activities within effective communicative situations, providing each child with numerous opportunities to speak, and to learn and use language, not for evoking current events (previous, future, or imaginary events) but to be familiar with writing French and building the beginnings of a literary culture. When French is not the native language of the children, immersion is advocated. More opportunities to communicate are to be provided to these children. A first contact with a second language (foreign or regional language) is encouraged for the 5-year-olds. Competencies to be acquired in the language domain are the following:

• Communicative competencies
• Competencies related to description of action (language in situation)
• Competencies related to evocative language
• Competencies related to writing: writing functions, familiarization with literature and writing language, discovery of sounds, drawing activities and writing, discovering alphabetic principles

However, the curriculum mentions the necessity of a specific pedagogy for young children, as follows: "the child builds, following his own way, his acquisitions through play, action, autonomous research and sensory experience."

The Implementation of the Curriculum

French teachers generally follow the main principles of this curriculum, although among older teachers there is some nostalgia for the *école maternelle* of the 1970s, which was characterized by greater liberty and creativity. This was the preschool the younger teachers experienced as children.

The curriculum provides teachers with a range of references to guide their educational planning, including the following:

• the regular use of audio and video recording equipment, in a specific corner of the classroom and in every classroom of the school, will foster the development of listening, attention, and expression skills; or
• "from the very first paragraphs to a full text writing meaning," a school project based on the enrichment of graphic activities, the discovery of a real sense of writing and the use of children's' cultural diversity; or
• the theme of the year, on water, for instance, designed in numerous activities inducing oral and written language.

The different parts of the day seem to be conceived according to the aims of the curriculum. Thus, the daily sequences of collective morning rituals are oriented by at least two domains of activity: "language" and "living together." Children are supposed to

- acquire a sense of time by anticipating events,
- acquire the sensation of belonging in a social group,
- recognize each other as individuals,
- recognize their names and the name of a friend.

French children's experience within the *école maternelle* is a student experience based on a wide range of exercises that are considered and referred to as "work." Play (pretend play with dolls, constructive play with blocks, etc.) is possible, but only after having finished the different individual tasks linked to the curriculum, as proposed by the teachers, generally organized within small groups.

Crèches: The Hidden Curricula of Care Services

There is no national curriculum for children under 3 years of age in the care sector. However, hidden curricula are underlying the practices of a wide range of professionals in these settings, who are not teachers but instead belong to the social and health sectors.

A brief historical overview. Crèches, created in the middle of the nineteen century, had charitable missions (see earlier). During the twentieth century these settings were dominated by a strong health orientation. Until recently the educational nature of crèches was not officially recognized.

Toys, and consequently play, were introduced into crèches first by psychologists who began to work in these services in the mid-1960s. During this same period a new kind of professional, the early childhood educator, was integrated into the paramedical team. In the 1970s, under the influence of these new professionals, due to expanded research on early development, and through pressure by parents from more privileged backgrounds, the crèches became attractive "places of life and education."

In contrast with the *écoles maternelles'* orientation toward learning, crèches are focused on development. Adults do not expect formal results, but guide children in the acquisition of autonomy. Starting in the late 1980s, cultural activities with very young children (books, music, etc.) developed, supported by the Ministry of Culture. While official texts concerning care services remained focused on sanitary dimensions (health and security), over the past twenty years most of the crèches have developed a "life project" or an "educational project," even though it may not be formalized or written down. Several psychological and pedagogical sources of ideas and information have informed the professional practices through the initial and in-service training of staff.

The new legislation (2000). In 2000, the new decree on care services recognized the educative nature of care services for the first time. One mission consists of taking care not only of health and security, but also of the development and well-being of the children. The decree requires that each care service must now write an "educational plan." This plan defines the objectives and resources used to provide care, sustain the development, early learning, and well-being of children, ensure individualized relationships, and take into account the interdependence of the children's physiological, psychological, and affective needs. A "pedagogical project" must translate this plan into the day-to-day practices of the center. A "social project" is also required, situating the service within the local political, economic, and social context.

In contrast with *école maternelle* teachers, who are provided with a national curriculum, no ministerial direction is given to professionals of the care sector regarding education in care services. The aim of the care sector, the "blossoming" of the children, is sometimes explicitly referenced in municipal or departmental regulations where, beyond play and learning, "awakening activities" are mentioned.

The implementation of the educational and pedagogical projects. So far, we do not know the extent to which crèches have designed such plans according to the new regulation. There are difficulties in the field, linked to the lack of national guidance and to insufficient resources devoted to the educational dimension in the initial and in-service training of staff. Within this void dominant medical discourse, including current psychological and psychoanalytical notions, continues to shape professional practices.

The childrens' experiences in crèches are based on play: free play for the youngest, and more directed play for the older. Often initiated by the early childhood educators who now have a major role in the staff, this play aims at the development of the whole personality. Although the professionals in these settings share a common reluctance to speak in terms of learning (defined as the *école maternelle's* school learning), despite the fact that they recognize the important social learning included in the process of socialization of the children, they tend to use the word "activity" more frequently than "play."

Conclusion

Curriculum in French early childhood settings reflects two different universes: the "school learning" world of the *école maternelle* and the health and social service world of the *crèche*. In the absence of greater national leadership these two universes will continue to exist, although there is some movement in the direction of greater emphasis on promoting child development for the youngest children.

Further Readings: Brougère, G. (1997). Jeu et objectifs pédagogiques: une approche comparative de l'éducation préscolaire. *Revue Française de Pédagogie* (119), 47–56; MEN (2002). *Qu'apprend-on à l'école maternelle?* Paris: CNDP; Mozère, L. (1992). *Le printemps des crèches*. Paris: L'Harmattan; Plaisance, E. (1986). *La maternelle, l'enfant, la société*. Paris: PUF; Rayna, S. (2003). Play, care and learning: Curriculum for early childhood education in France. *Researching Early Childhood* 5, 127–142.

Marie-Laure Vitali

Assessment

In France there is a strong culture of evaluation, which has an older and more formal tradition within the education sector, but is now emerging within the care sector. On one level, ministries and public agencies regularly carry out studies contributing to the evaluation of the French early childhood system of care and education. They also regularly put out calls for research that is carried out by universities and research organizations. Researchers inform policymakers through their own research projects on the implementation and effectiveness of care and education policies. On another level, the staff and quality of early childhood education (ECE) services are assessed by inspectors and other professionals responsible for oversight. On a third level, children's accomplishments are now supposed to be evaluated by teachers in *écoles maternelles*. This is not expected in care services.

Assessment of Systems

The education sector. Evaluation is carried out through the general inspection of national education (IGEN), which publishes yearly thematic reports. Other services within the Ministry of Education also contribute to the evaluation of the evolution and characteristics of the educational system. Regular statistical surveys are thus carried out and published in various documents. Evaluation of primary school policies (including both *école maternelle* and elementary school) is also conducted by these ministerial services or by researchers (universities, National Institute of Pedagogical Research, etc.). Since the 1980s this assessment has addressed primarily those mechanisms and programs aimed at prevention of school failure.

Studies on the functioning and impacts of the priority education zones (ZEP), which receive supplementary resources, have shown the positive effects of this positive discrimination policy, implemented since 1981 in France, on students' school results, class environment, and teaching conditions. Studies on the time management of children's lives within school hours and leisure time (ARVE), a policy implemented during the 1890s in partnership with the Ministry of Youth and Sport, have shown an expansion of the interface between schools and local communities, despite a lower level of involvement of the *écoles maternelles* than of elementary school. The implementation of the learning cycles, the pedagogical reform included within the Law on Education (1989) in order to improve continuity of learning (conceived in the frame of three-year cycles), has also been studied. These studies document the important practice changes required (including teacher cooperation related to each cycle) and difficulties encountered.

Some studies are specific to the *école maternelle*. Since the early 1980s most of these have focused on the schooling of children aged 2–3, and have examined the policy decision to give priority with funding to early schooling within the ZEPs. A recent study focused on the effectiveness of the ZEP has shown that those ZEPs in which high proportions of children receive *école maternelle* at age 2 (average

60%) have better long-term educational performance than those ZEPs with low *école maternelle* rates for their 2- to 3-year-olds (average 33%).

A report on *classes passerelles* ("bridging classes" including professionals from both the care and the education sectors) by both Ministry of Education and Ministry of Social Affairs, concluded that these interesting experiments need further evaluative studies before being expanded.

Care sectors. Numerous studies have been carried out to see whether and how the current objectives of care policies are being met: policies offering parents free choice of an individual or collective care; those favoring children's health, safety, development, and blossoming; those preventing exclusion and inequality. The Ministry of Social Affairs conducts statistical surveys on the care services and routinely issues calls for research projects. The National Family Allowance Fund (CNAF) also conducts studies and launches calls for research projects. In the late 1990s, CNAF prioritized analyses of the quality and effects of the different kinds of care services on child development (including, for the 2-year-olds, comparison with *école maternelle*). Despite the methodological difficulties encountered, these studies, based on various criteria and tools, converge to show the positive role of nonfamilial care and education provision on the social and cognitive development of the children. Although not favoring one type of setting over another, the studies show that crèches play a compensatory and preventive role for children from disadvantaged backgrounds.

Some studies have shown the importance of policies contributing to improving the quality, equity, and coherence within the care sector, for instance those concerning coordination mechanisms implemented at the municipal level, or in partnerships supported by the Ministry of Culture within an early childhood policy framework.

In 2002, the Directorate of Research, Studies, Evaluation and Statistics (DRESS), within the Ministry of Social affairs, together with the CNAF and with the Council on Employment, Incomes and Social Cohesion (CERC) conducted a large survey of child care in order to provide a precise picture of the different solutions adopted by parents. Five studies focused on the rationale for and process of choosing child care have been selected for a secondary analysis of the data. Within this general framework on reconciliation of work and family responsibilities, several other studies are currently focused on local innovative care solutions, taking into account the evolution of the parental needs (e.g., atypical hours of work, etc.), particularly those of lone-parent families, of families with precarious jobs, and of poor families.

Further studies on leisure time services for children attending *écoles maternelles* are to be carried out, due to the high use of these services by children of disadvantaged backgrounds.

Assessment of Personnel and Services

Education sector. Education offices at the departmental (regional) level are in charge of the management of primary school teachers (promotions, transfers, etc.). The pedagogical oversight of these teachers is assigned to inspectors (IEN), who are no longer specific to the *écoles maternelles,* but rather are in charge of both the *écoles maternelles* and the primary schools. In France, directors of schools have no position in the evaluation hierarchy and do not participate in the teachers' evaluation.

The aim of the inspections is to assess the quality and conformity of the teaching practices related to the national goals and curriculum as well with the goals of the school. Official texts summarize these objectives, as well as the methods and criteria of the inspection. Teachers are first inspected during their second year of teaching, and then every four years, on the average. Generally, this assessment is based on direct observations of the pedagogical practices, and discussions with the teachers. Despite a negative perception of this kind of control by the trade unions, inspection sometimes provides some teachers with opportunities to demonstrate the value of their work and to receive support and guidance. However, the integration of the inspectorate for the *écoles maternelles* with that of the elementary schools is often conceived as contributing to the loss of the specific professional identity of teachers working with children under 6 years.

An informal evaluation is made by pedagogical counsellors and teacher trainers (IMF) who regularly meet and observe novice teachers. Assistants (ATSEM), who are municipal employees, are assessed by municipalities. Due to their proximity within the school, some directors of schools would like to participate in their evaluation.

Care sector. The care sector is monitored, on a departmental level, by child and maternal health services (PMI), which is responsible for licensing and monitoring care and leisure time services. Within PMI, doctors, nurses, psychologists, early childhood educators, and social workers are in charge of the monitoring of these services and of the training of the licensed childminders. The PMI's technical advice, required for all services before opening, and then later assessments, aims at insuring conformity with the national regulations (2000) concerning ratios, personal qualifications, etc. Despite the diversity observed from one department to another, controls are generally made on three levels: hygiene and safety, protection of childhood, and quality of care. Some documentation is currently required (pedagogical and social projects, internal evaluation, quality charter, communication tools with families).

Within the care services, evaluation of the professionals is part of the work of the directors (pediatric nurses or early childhood educators), who also have to coordinate the program of service and evaluate it in cooperation with the staff. On the municipal level, evaluation is one of the early childhood coordinator's missions, often conceived as a professional accompaniment.

Assessment of Children

Education sector. Linked to its main objective of preparation for school, assessment of children is to be done in *écoles maternelles*. Most of the required competencies, according to the goals of the national curriculum, are evaluated by direct observations of child behaviors (for example, concerning the youngest children: speak spontaneously; feel comfortable in elementary actions such as running, jumping, climbing; autonomous during moving, dressing, or in the bathroom). The Ministry of Education has provided teachers with evaluation tools, but the practices of child evaluation vary from one school to another. Teachers often construct grids, more or less inspired by these official documents. The aim of assessment is to get a precise appreciation of each child's progress and use this to shape the teacher's actions. The results are used for information to families and during the cycle councils (teachers meetings within cycle 1, involving all the teachers of the *école maternelle,* and within cycle 2 including teachers in charge of the 5-year-olds and teachers of the two first grades of the elementary school). From 1990, a school report book is required for each primary school student. Although many teachers are convinced of the necessity of regular, but flexible, evaluations of child learning, many also fear negative effects and risks of an early stigmatization of school failure.

Detection of serious difficulties leads to intervention by the networks of specialists (psychologists, etc.) linked to each school. Oversight of children's health in *écoles maternelles* is the responsibility of PMI.

Care sector. There is no curriculum and no assessment of children in the care sector. A detection and prevention role is nevertheless assigned to PMI and to the professionals who are sharing the everyday life of the children.

Conclusion

Evaluative researches and practices can be considered as efforts to highlight and support the main current social and political issues. They are profoundly shaped by French values (republican values) and traditions of care and education sectors (health vs instruction), as well as of disciplines (psychology, sociology, etc.).

Evaluation is generally conducted separately within each sector. In order to reduce territorial disparities, however, early childhood departmental commissions were created in 2002, mixing representatives of the different sectors. They are just beginning to develop. Their missions include the evaluation of the needs of care and education within each department.

Further Readings: David, T. ed. *Researching early childhood: European Perspectives.* London: Paul Chapman; Florin, A. (2000). *La scolarisation à 2 ans et autres modes d'accueil.* Paris: INRP; Paquay, L. (2004). *L'évaluation des enseignants. Tensions et enjeux.* Paris: L'Harmattan; Plaisance, E., and S. Rayna (1999). Early childhood education research in France. In Sauvage, O. (in press). Intervention within the panel: Débat contradictoire. In SRED, *Scolariser la petite enfance?* Geneva: University of Geneva; Thélot, C. (1993). *Évaluation du système éducatif.* Paris: Nathan.

Alexandra Moreau and Sylvie Rayna

Infant and Early Childhood Education

French Traditional Norms and Values

Working mothers with young children are now the norm in France. Women's work and the care of very young children outside the family are generally accepted, despite the fact that half of the under threes continue to be cared for at home. Crèches have been very popular during the past twenty years, despite the fact that parents are more likely to employ a childminder (*assistante maternelle*) than use a crèche for their child-care needs. Nevertheless, traditional values remain perceptible on different levels, leading to a number of contradictions and paradoxcs.

Gender issues and professionalization. Currently there is some tension in French society between the care of young children on the one hand and gender equality on the other. Although the new norm of parenthood, based on the sharing of children's care, contributes to reduce the gap between the traditional roles of fathers and mothers, and to propose new definitions of fatherhood, the traditional cultural notion of motherhood is not fundamentally questioned.

In child-carc scttings, a paradoxical "sacred worship" of the maternal role is still visible. Men, whose knowledge in this field is not linked to any maternal competencies but is acquired, are very rare in crèches. They appear to threaten female professionals, whose status and salaries are generally low compared to teachers in *écoles maternelles* (partly explaining the current recruitment difficulties). Within the hierarchical organization of the French crèches, the pediatric nurse's assistants (*auxiliaires de puericulture*) who are working under the direction of a pediatric nurse and often under one or two educators, receive strong (often contradictory) demands. Psychologically oriented demands, having replaced the previous medically based ones, inhibit the expression of their own voices. Despite this, these caregivers can still develop effective professional competencies. For this to happen the context must favor agency and serendipity. Unfortunately these caregivers are often required simply to execute the prescriptions of the dominant discourse, due to their low positions in the status hierarchy.

At the same time, despite the important evolution (since the mid-seventies) of the institutionalization of the status of the childminders, which has regulated the market, the process of professionalization of these practitioners seems to be limited by a tacit maintenance on the *status quo* among childminders, those services in charge of licensing them, and parents. This is due to the belief that their work is a kind of extension of their role as mothers. Childminders, who have historically been the traditional carers in France, currently remain the dominant care arrangement. Nowadays, parents tend to choose childminders for practical reasons—they offer more flexible hours than crèches. However, some parents, mostly from advantaged backgrounds, prefer crèches for educational reasons, and others choose them for their natural dispositions and experience with young children, with this legitimacy being more based on their reputation than on a professional certification.

Parents as first educators. Another tension exists between the myth of an ideal family as the best carer of the young child, and the caring institution's attitudes toward parents as inadequate. If parents are officially recognized as their children's first educators, the relationships between the child-care professionals is often paradoxical. And if a number of settings develop fruitful projects based on a positive outlook toward parental competencies, including those living in poverty, this new task of supporting parenthood (linked to the increase of social difficulties) is being asked of early childhood professionals whose training does not prepare them for these two contrasting roles (child-care expert and supporter of parenting competence).

Neonates and Infant Care

Concerning neonates and infants, if they are not cared for by their parents (usually, by their mothers), they are cared for by other carers (either individual arrangements or crèches that accept 3-month-old infants). Parents who need to find care for an infant often use various solutions (holidays, assistance of family members, etc.) delaying for some weeks or months the beginning of the external care of the baby (sometimes waiting until September when a majority of children leave the *crèche* or the childminder and enter the *école maternelle*, at 2 or 3 years of age).

Maternal and Paternal Leave

In general, French people think that maternal leave is too short (sixteen weeks allowed for the first two children, then twenty-six weeks for the third child and more in case of twins). However, most appreciate the recent paternal leave that lasts for two weeks. The subsidized parental leave (an allowance allowing mothers to stay out of the workforce for up to three years) is not an option for all families, rather it is often "chosen" by a majority of relatively uneducated mothers. Among the reasons explaining this are the relatively low allowance paid for this leave, the relatively high cost of a childminder (for families with modest incomes), and the lack of crèches. Additionally, these mothers have more difficulty rejoining the workforce. To facilitate the transition back to employment, they can now receive both their allowance (parental leave) and an income during the last six months of the leave.

Studies show that the reduced work week in France (thirty-five hours per week) and the two most frequent modalities for this reduction (regular days or half days) have contributed to a reconciliation of family life with professional life (most women with young children using this time to care for them). However, many families would argue that these modified working hours have not shifted enough for families with infants and young children. Under economic pressures, many families piece together several care arrangements, despite the fact that crèches are generally opened eleven or twelve hours per day. Often parents who work far from their homes employ an additional babysitter and may use the adaptations of the care services supported by the public policies described below.

Policies: Recent Trends and Experiments

Diversification of child care. Beginning in the 1980s policies of diversification of care services, which assigned an important role to numerous decentralized service systems and providers, were implemented with the aim of increasing the choices available to families. These policies were also implemented to serve the families' diversified needs, which were linked to changing work conditions (flexibility, atypical working hours) and family forms (single parents). As a result, the number of part-time and full-time crèches and individual settings (childminders) increased. Innovative services developed, with nonprofit associations (including parental cooperatives) playing an important role in the creation of these flexible and proximity arrangements. Such services were facilitated by providing standard funding for care regardless of parental employment status and the number of hours the child attends.

Multi-accueils (multicare settings), more likely than traditional crèches to be located in small cities (half of the cities with more than 30,000 residents in the provinces have developed this type of setting compared to a third in the Parisian region), combine different collective and individual arrangements (including extended hours and occasional care). Today about 70 percent of parent cooperatives offer multicare.

Itinerant services have developed in rural areas, allowing early socialization of the children and provided time for their parents. Thus, minibuses with play and care material travel each day from one municipal building to another, according to a regular schedule. The cost of the equipment, functioning, and staff is shared between several villages. Financial help is also provided by CAFs (Family Allowance Funds—see financing entry) and sometimes by foundations and private sponsors.

Following French psychoanalyst, F. Dolto's experiments, parent–child centers, mostly run by associations and financially supported by municipalities and CAFs, aim to support parent–child relationships, strengthen social links, foster children's autonomy, reduce parent isolation, and prevent child neglect. Many centers created in disadvantaged areas combine psychology and social work. Networks, for childminders (*Relais Assistantes Maternelles—RAM*) and more recently for in-home care providers, have been created to provide children and adults in these individual types of care arrangements with socialization opportunities.

However, local policies are often not coordinated enough (due to the different traditions and aims of a number of the decentralized authorities) to face the new challenge of social cohesion. Despite the presence of significant institutions and financing in the care sector, as well as efforts made in cities that are financially supported by contacts (*contrat enfance*) with regional family allowance funds (*Caisses d'allocations familiales, CAFs*) social cohesion is still missing. The choice, for many parents, remains limited by the geographical disparities of the care provision and, for the poorest of them, by the costs.

Atypical Hours Arrangements

Within this context, recent national policies focused on parents who cannot use the traditional official settings and thus turn without any public help to several types of informal arrangements (unlicensed childminders, family, friends) are encouraging the development of local initiatives welcoming children during atypical hours. Since 2000, recognition of these innovative settings is included in the official care regulations, and subsidies are provided toward more flexible functioning of individual and collective settings (opening earlier and closing later). Some services are open twenty-four hours, including crèches (although rare) and services employing childminders. Experiments with new care arrangements are supported by the interministerial services of cities' affairs and women's rights. These experiments, initiated by associations, often complement the traditional settings, with some professionals working both in a *crèche* and in a parent's home, for instance. The development of crèches provided by private companies, which were not numerous in the past, is now also being promoted.

Studies show that single-parent families are interested in centers that provide atypical hours and that cover a variety of configurations of work: variable, regular, or irregular hours as well as scheduled and unscheduled hours. Some experiments seem to contribute to a certain stabilization of the care of the children of these families, but these new arrangements remain flimsy at the moment. They affect the conditions of work and the work itself of the care professionals (childminders as well as, in crèches, pediatric nurses, assistants, and educators). The strategy of complementarity contributes to opening the frontiers between collective and familial settings, and the extension of the recruitment to other types of professionals (such as psychologists or social workers), linked to the specific projects of these innovative arrangements, contributes to reducing the segmentation of the social and health fields. Contrasts in the points of view of these different sectors are nevertheless noticed. Although a number of professionals working in crèches, where hours are atypical but regular, may be relatively satisfied, childminders working on irregular atypical hours feel more difficulties. Despite the satisfaction linked to the innovative aspects of these arrangements, and to the training and the additional supports that often accompany them, their views vary according to their own personal family situations.

Further Readings: Abalea, F. (2005). La professionalisation inachevée des assistantes maternelles. *Recherches et Prévisions* 80, 55–65; Eme, B., and L. Fraisse (2005). La gouvernance locale de la diversification des modes d'accueil: un nouvel enjeu de "cohésion" sociale. *Recherches et Prévisions* 80, 7–21; Eydoux, A. (2005). les métiers de la petite enfance à l'épreuve des horaires atypiques. *Recherches et Prévisions* 80, 41–53; Fagnani, J. (1999). Parental leave in France. In P. Moss and F. Deven, eds., *Parental leave: Progress or pitfall? Research and policy issues in Europe*. Bruxelles: NIDI/CBGS Publications; Le Bihan, B., and C. Martin (2004). Atypical working hours: Consequences for childcare arrangements. *Social Policies and Administration* 8(6), 12–28; Murcier, N. (2005). Le loup dans la bergerie. Prime éducation et rapports sociaux de sexes. *Recherches er Prévisions* 80, 67–75.

Sylvie Rayna

Special Educational Needs and Inclusion in France

Introduction

Currently in France, as in most European countries, there is a move toward increasing the participation of children identified as having special educational needs in mainstream education. This marks a change in direction, following a period in which a large network of special education establishments were developed, and raises issues regarding the coexistence of the two educational systems (ordinary and special) and the need for the transformation of educational practices.

The notion of special educational needs has only recently been introduced in France and refers to children whose development has been affected by an emotional or physical difficulty or impairment. It also refers to children whose development has been impacted as a result of some other cause that is not necessarily apparent. The term special educational needs is not used, as in some other countries, to refer to children whose problems arise as a result of socioeconomic conditions, and terms such as "handicap" and "impairment" continue to dominate when referring to disabled children.

In the following sections we will begin with an overview of French legislation and then analyze the barriers to integration for young children in reception and education services (*écoles maternelles* or nursery school for children from 3 to 6 years of age, and day-care centers for the under threes). We will conclude with some key perspectives.

Legislation and the Organization of the Education System

There has been a gradual introduction and implementation of legislation supporting the educational development of children with special educational needs in mainstream settings. This legislation defines the principles and conditions governing such integration in legal terms.

The 1975 law regarding people with disabilities declared that children with special educational needs have the right to the medical care they require and, like other children, the right to education. Preferably, this education should be provided in a mainstream environment. If this does not seem possible, owing in particular to the seriousness of the impairment, education should be provided in special education establishments. When this situation arises, children are placed in special institutions based on impairment type. These special institutions will provide medical care and education, and most will accept children from the age of 6.

For children under the age of 3, the law envisages the creation of early intervention services, whose purpose is to prevent and detect difficulties related to sensory, physical, and mental impairment. These services incorporate various professionals (speech therapists, physiotherapists, specialized teachers) who intervene to support the children and sometimes visit them in their homes. These children may also attend day-care centers (crèches and *haltes garderies)* on a full- or part-time basis. One of the missions of the care services, as summarized in the recent regulations, (2000) is to "contribute to the social integration of children with special needs or with chronic illness."

For school-aged children (i.e., those who attend *école maternelle* and elementary school), special education committees have been created to examine each child with special educational needs and determine the nature of his or her difficulties. These committees are able to arrange the payment of benefits to the family and recommend placement in an appropriate special education settng. When the children are admitted to mainstream schools, they may attend school on a full-time or part-time basis.

However, integration in regular schools does not depend solely on the children's ability, but also on the educational conditions available. To facilitate the education of disabled children, numerous legislative guidelines have been introduced to improve professional practice, educational structures, and organization. Examples of those guidelines include the following:

- The legislation takes into account the importance of coordinating therapeutic and educational work. It also encourages the implementation of individual education plans based on consultation with all the partners including specialized professionals, teachers, and parents (1982 and 1983 laws).
- The integration mission falls within the general organization of both special and mainstream settings. The 1989 Education Act recommended the development of pedagogical approaches able to respond to pupil diversity, individual interests, and differences in family background. The law emphasizes the belief that such approaches facilitate the participation of children with special educational needs.

In the same year, new regulations gave special education establishments a mission to provide pupils with support for their education in regular schools. In theory, schools must accept children with special educational needs if they live in their catchment area. However, this is only possible if the establishments themselves consider that they have adequate provision in terms of teaching resources and the necessary staff.

Expansion of Resources

An expansion in human resources is planned in order to provide therapeutic and pedagogical support to children with special educational needs, and information and support for the teachers. These human resources include the following:

- Professionals in medical care and special education who provide pupils with special educational needs and support in school.
- Learning support assistants who provide the child with support under the guidance of the teacher. These assistants do not have a professional qualification and are paid by parents' associations or, at present, more often by the Ministry of Education.

Evaluating Education Policies

It is difficult to evaluate the effects of policies on integration in early years of education. Data provided by the different ministries (Social Affairs, Education) are not collected on the basis of common criteria. In general, the population of children from birth to six years of age is not treated separately from the whole population of children.

For a long time, evidence from numerous studies concerning the effects of integration policies in schools reflected the minimal impact of these efforts. For the school year 1989–1990, only 7 percent of the disabled children between 2 and 11 years old (i.e., children attending *école maternelle* and elementary school) benefited from education in a regular class. Many parents of disabled children were dissatisfied with these results and felt that they are being poorly represented by traditional associations. As a result, these parents have developed their own organizations and are demanding additional resources in support of integration.

During the ten years following the 1989 legislation, there was a steady increase in integration. Ministry of Education's statistics for 1999–2000 showed that 12 percent of disabled children aged 2–11 attended mainstream schools on a full- or part-time basis.

Evaluations have examined the nature of the difficulties encountered and found that these arose principally owing to a lack of resources, too few specialized professionals and learning assistants, as well as a reluctance on the part of professionals. Other results of the evaluations include the following:

- Teachers of regular classes feel unprepared to take care of children with special educational needs. They fear becoming isolated and being expected to solely solve the problems associated with pupils with special educational needs.
- Professionals working in specialized settings fear losing their jobs or are concerned about the possibility of having to take care of only the most seriously disabled children.
- Collaboration between regular schools and special schools remains difficult. Historically, the two educational systems have developed along two distinct pathways in which different professional cultures have evolved. In most cases, contact between the two sectors is rare.

Crèches and Children with Special Educational Needs

It is generally considered that crèches and *haltes garderies* are more open to children with special educational needs than are schools. Listed below are the two reasons for this:

- The younger the children, the more tolerant the establishments.
- In crèches, a high proportion of the staff have some medical training; therefore, there is less reluctance than in schools to take the medical aspects of care into account and cooperate with specialists.

In general, the main problem is that there is a serious lack of care and educational provision for all young children compared with what is required.

The education of children with special educational needs in the mainstream environment is still insufficient in terms of responding to demand. Despite numerous legislative measures, the government has not succeeded in bringing about the necessary transformation in educational practice necessary for the successful integration of children with special educational needs. There is an urgent need, therefore, to develop a new direction in educational policy making.

Integration Philosophy and the Way Forward for Improving Practices

For a long time in France, the notion of integration has been linked to the notion of normalization. According to this notion, integration consists of providing the individual child with special educational needs with all the support he or she needs in order to benefit from the education provided in regular schools for other children of the same age. However, education policies are now beginning to take into account the concept of inclusion, which involves the transformation of the whole social and educational environment in education, so that schools become more open to diversity. Inclusion presupposes an acceptance and consideration of all pupils as they are, as well as a commitment to supporting their progress through participation in a shared culture. One of the aims of educating children with special educational needs in a mainstream environment is to foster social understanding for all children based on nondiscrimination and the acceptance of everybody. From an inclusive perspective, partnership between the mainstream and special education sector is essential, as is collaboration between the professionals of these sectors.

Concerning the future, the state has confirmed that it is ready to provide greater financial support to mainstream schools, particularly by increasing the number of learning support assistants. However, legislation advances slowly. The new law regarding disabled people (2005) emphasizes the right of children with special educational needs to attend the school nearest to their home. However, special educational committees have the power to decide whether education in a mainstream school suits a child's individual needs.

Teacher Preparation

As in most countries, professional training is considered to be one of the essential factors in the development of inclusive education. It is necessary, however, to define the aims, the content, and conditions of an appropriate training. It seems particularly important that professionals in mainstream schools develop skills in terms of their educational practices to take into account pupil diversity. These professionals also need information so they can understand the nature of the difficulties experienced by children with special educational needs. It is often through discussion with professionals in the special education sector that the necessary supportive approaches are developed. Therefore, it is necessary to train all professionals to collaborate so that the specific skills developed in the special education sector can become a resource for the mainstream sector. In order to encourage understanding between the different professional cultures, training sessions providing opportunities to work collaboratively and share teaching practices between professionals from the different sectors could be organized.

Acknowledgments: The contributors thank Felicity Armstrong and Morgane Prevost for supervising the English version of this entry.

Further Readings: Armstrong, F., B. Belmont, and A. Verilon (2000). Vive la différence? Exploring context, policy and change in special education in France: developing cross-cultural collaboration. In F. Armstrong, D. Armstrong, and L. Barton *Inclusive education: Policy, contexts and comparative perspectives.* London: David Fulton Publishers; Belmont, B., and A. Vérillon (2004). Relier les territoires par la collaboration des acteurs. In. D. Poisat, (coord.) *Éducation et handicap. D'une pensée territoire à une pensée monde.* Ramonville St Agne: Éres; Lessain-Delabarre, J. M. (2000). *L'adaptation et l'intégration scolaires: innovations et résistances institutionnelles.* Paris: ESF; Plaisance, E. (2005). *Petite enfance et handicap. La prise en charge des enfants handicapés dans les équipements collectifs de la Petite Enfance* (Dossiers d'études n66). Paris: CNAF; Vérillon, A., and B.

Belmont (1999). Integration of disabled children in French schools. *European Journal of Special Needs Education* 14(1), 1–11.

Allette Vérillon and Brigitte Belmont

Current Trends in Early Childhood Care and Education Policies

France is well known for the longevity and the strength of its family and education policies, as promoted and implemented by the Ministry of Social Affairs and the Ministry of Education. These take several forms: (1) tax measures to reduce the fiscal pressure on families, based on the number of children in the family; (2) a whole range of financial aids and allowances to the parents of young children, both to help them vis-à-vis the burden caused by their children (family allowances) and to allow them to care for their children themselves or to have them looked after by another person (while they work outside the home); (3) a publicly financed range of services to care for the young children and educate them—*crèches*, *halte-garderies* (see earlier), and especially the *école maternelle* (which is free and open to children as soon as they reach 2, "provided that they are physically and psychologically ready to attend it," in the words of the Ministry of Education).

Today France understands the importance of this effort as it supports a key demographic indicator—one of the strongest birthrates in Europe. But there is also awareness of the persistent insufficiency of ECE provision (for the under threes). For these reasons the French government continues to intensify its efforts in this arena, which is coupled today with an increased search for coherence and clarity in the mechanisms of parental assistance and of childhood care and education.

The Intensification and Simplification of Subsidies to Families: The PAJE

This intensification of support for early childhood and the effort to simplify the system can be seen in the establishment of the PAJE (*Prestation d'Accueil du Jeune Enfant*) which replaces various preexisting allowances. The PAJE is composed of a basic financial allowance intended for all the families on arrival of a new child. To it can be added the following:

- A "supplement for free choice of the young child's care" for those parents wishing to resort to external care. To a certain extent this supplement increases the financial aid available for the use of an *assistante maternelle* (licensed childminder) particularly for the families of the lower and middle classes, who would not otherwise be able financially to reach this mode of care.
- A "supplement for free choice of activity" for the parents wishing to stop working for a while in order to look after their children. This supplement increases the financial aids granted previously to these parents. What is new is the fact that it is available directly with the first child, for parents who have held a job previously and for a period of six months.

This increased financial support for the parents on arrival of a child is coupled with an effort to promote and adapt the collective services and individual arrangements to make real the concept of "free choice" for the families.

The Promotion of the Provision Guaranteeing Free Choice

Adapting and developing collective services: the FIPE and the PSU. Since 2000, with the establishment of the FIPE (*Fonds d'Investissement Petite Enfance*), the effort to expand collective services has intensified. This fund, renewed in 2001, made it possible to plan the addition of 20,000 new places between 2001 and 2005. At the time of the Conference on the Family in 2003, a fund was again mobilized, aiming for 20,000 additional places. Within this effort to create additional places, company crèches are supported and, in a new development, provision is opened to the private sector.

But it's not only a question of creating new places; it is also necessary that they meet the present needs of parents. Also, beyond the emphasis on flexible and innovative efforts to create new places using the FIPE, measures have tended for several years to adapt the collective provision to the new needs of parents resulting from the greater flexibility in working hours and the new legal length of the workweek (thirty-five hours): the increased need for part-time services, for shifted or changing schedules, etc. Thus, the CAFs (*Caisses d'Allocations Familiales*) set up the PSU (Prestation de Service Unique) at the beginning of 2002. This new and unique financing measure prioritizes the public financing of services according to the importance of their operational innovations.

1. The acceptance of the parents' needs, including those that are not determined by professional activity and may be part-time;
2. The development of emergency services (for instance, to help unemployed parents to attend training courses);
3. Payment based on actual use of the services (by the hour and no longer by the day). This measure encourages program managers to understand and meet precisely the real time needs of the parents by establishing contracts with them. But it encounters difficulties in its implementation precisely because of the challenge of defining with the parents the hours their children will be present in the setting.

Promoting the provision of individual arrangements. Thanks to the PAJE, the use of licensed childminders (*assistante maternelle*) is accessible to a greater number of families. Therefore the question of the development of this kind of arrangement (which has already doubled since 1992) and of the increasing attractiveness of the childminder's occupation arises today with growing strength. To address it, a law was adopted at the beginning of 2005. Progress was made on several significant elements, including the following:

• a preoccupation with the improvement of the quality, through the installation of a preservice training course and the reinforcement of this training once the childminder is employed
• an improvement of the statute, increasing access to professional rights and protections
• a better legal framework for the relationships between childminders and parent-employers

This promotion of individual arrangements has the advantage of rebalancing the provision at the national level. Indeed, the geography of these arrangements is relatively complementary to that of collective services, with childminders popular in the countryside, balancing the center-based services in urban areas.

The Early Schooling

Since the late 1980s the *école maternelle* has been regarded as a tool to struggle against school inequalities. Centered on an academic approach to the young child, the most recent reforms keep going in the direction of a "scholarization" of this institution. The "fundamental missions" of the *école maternelle* are reaffirmed with a particular stress laid on the learning of the French language.

Today, the question of early school for 2-year-olds is still bitterly discussed. After a series of reports underlining its advantages, particularly in those geographic areas with high poverty, high concentrations of immigrants and school failure (ZEPs), other reports have called into question its real effectiveness in the child's school performance.

In fact, the treatment of the 2-year-old children in this educational institution is completely at odds with the other care services, where the adult–child ratio is very small and the focus is more on child development than on school learning. With little exaggeration one can say that the *école maternelle*, protected by the strength of the academic institution, acts with young children from the age of 2 with great independence regarding the primary questions that stimulate the field of early childhood in France. The Children's Defender (*défenseur des enfants*), Claire Brisset, even called in her 2003 annual report for a halt in the development of schooling for 2-year-olds and the setting up of an in-depth reflection on how to promote better conditions for 2- to 3-year-old children. (The Children's Defender is an independent authority charged, since 2000, with defending and promoting the rights of the child).

Toward More Coherence: The Departmental Early Childhood Commissions

Vis-à-vis the multiplicity of stakeholders in the field of early childhood (communes, departments, CAF, nonprofit associations, etc.), in 2002 the government decided to set up departmental (regional) early childhood commissions. The aim of these commissions, "reflection, council, proposal, support and follow-up," is to support the development and the coherence of provision at the departmental level. A new element deserves mention: *école maternelle* and school-age leisure time services are integrated in this effort toward more coherence. These commissions must also disseminate information to the families, promote equal access for every child, and insure the quality of the provision within the department. After some initial difficulties these commissions have made great strides, and by 2004 were functioning in half of the departments in France. It is, however, still too early to know the extent to which this measure will bear fruit.

Supporting Parental Competencies

An interdepartmental policy since 1997 has aimed at supporting parents with and through the care and the education of their children. This very fuzzy concept conveys, in political speech, uncertainties born both of changes in living conditions of families (precariousness, modification of working conditions) and of internal modifications within family relationships (increasing individualization resulting in an increase in divorces, blended families, and new kinds of relationships with children). There is concern that these transformations generate or encourage the weakening of parental authority and explain the increasing incivility of young people. This new tendency toward concern for parental competence seems to induce a change in the child-centered definition of the early childhood professional occupations, leading them to integrate into their competencies and their concerns another character: the parent.

Difficulties and Questions

The slow development of the collective services. In spite of the current efforts, the development of collective services remains too slow to meet the needs. There are several reasons for this. Departments and municipalities are encouraged and supported financially, but currently are not required to participate. Moreover, the operational costs of these services often make them falter. In addition, the occupations associated with these services suffer from great difficulties in recruitment. Even when the means are there to open these services, it may be very difficult to recruit adequate staff. A number of the *puericultrices* who are heads of crèches are retiring and these professionals, who are trained to work in crèches or in hospitals, often prefer this latter sector. There is a growing shortage of early childhood educators, who are more and more likely to become the heads of new services such as networks for childminders, and the *auxiliaires de puéricultures* are also in short supply, due to unappealing salaries and professional development.

The question of "free choice." Beyond the efforts carried out to ensure—through a sufficient provision—a true free choice for families among the various options, this policy raises a question in itself. Indeed it puts forward a number of alarming social tendencies. The incentive toward in-home care (with the increased support for parents making this choice) causes a drop in economic activity among women with two children (including one under 3), and especially for relatively young and uneducated mothers. This fact brings an overall slowdown in the equalization of positions between men and women and leads more particularly to the maintenance of lower class families within a traditional model of parental roles, with only the families of the middle and upper classes finding a means for greater male/female equality. Confronted with this situation, the policies designed to help women return to employment still remain too weak.

This disadvantage in the policy of free choice could find a partial solution by devising a formula for a shorter and better paid parental leave (one year), which would keep women out of the labor market for a shorter time period and thus have less of an impact on their professional careers.

Further Readings: Caille, J. P. (2001). Scolarisation à deux ans et réussite de la carrière scolaire au début de l'école élémentaire. *Éducation et Formation* 60, 7–18; Fagnani, J. (1998). Helping mothers to combine paid and unpaid work or fighting unemployment. The ambiguities of French family policy. *Community, Work and Family* 1(3), 297–312; Neyrand, G. (1999). Savoirs et normes sociales de la petite enfance. *Recherhces et Prévisions* 57-58, 3-16; Plaisance, E. (1999). L'école maternelle en France: normes éducatives et socialisation après la seconde guerre mondiale. *Recherches et Prévisions* 31-43, 57-58.

Pierre Moisset

Financing

There is a strong system for financing early childhood education and care in France. National and local actors contribute to this financing, which is largely a public system. The main actors are three Ministries (Education, Social Affairs, and Youth), the National Family Allowance Fund—CNAF—(at the head of 125 Family Allowance Funds—CAFs supervised by the French state), departments, municipalities, and parents. The contributions of these different players vary by sector (care or education) and within one of them (the care sector), while the costs vary according to the different kinds of setting.

How Much Does Early Childhood Care and Education Cost?

The costs are higher in the education section than in the care sector.

Écoles maternelles. In *écoles maternelles* (see earlier entries) the current average annual cost of a child is almost the same as for an elementary school pupil, that is about 4,000 Euros. There are no parental fees, so this high cost, partly due to the salaries of the teachers, is supported by a very strong public investment. Since 1981, within a positive discrimination policy, more money was provided to *écoles maternelles* (as well as elementary schools) situated in priority education areas—the *Zones d'Éducation Prioritaire (ZEP)*.

Care services. Concerning out of school activities for school-aged children, the cost varies by municipality or by the nonprofit associations that organize them. Access is generally not free but the fees are low and are adjusted to parental incomes, guaranteeing access for disadvantaged families. As an example, in Paris the cost of the two hours after school in 2005 was between 0.40 and 1 euro per day.

Concerning the other care provisions (full time), the costs are lower than those of *écoles maternelles,* but parents assume an important portion of them. For crèches, attended by the under threes, the average annual cost for a child (full time) is estimated at about 1,200 Euros. For a childminder (*assistante maternelle*), it varies between 700 and 900 Euros. For in-home care, it is estimated at 1,700 Euros. In the care sector, these costs are shared by numerous actors (differently according to each kind of provision).

Who Pays for Early Education?

Two actors are sharing the costs of public *écoles maternelles* while the source of financing is more complex in the care sector.

Écoles maternelles. The cost of public *écoles maternelles* is shared between the Ministry of Education and municipalities, even the few private *écoles maternelles* (12%) are heavily financed by public funds. The Ministry of Education supports the main cost (teachers' and inspectors' salaries), while municipalities pay for buildings, furniture, pedagogical materials, and teacher assistants' salaries.

Care services. The Ministry of Social Affairs, which defines the CNAF program, partly finances the initial training of the professionals (pediatric nurses, assistants, and early childhood educators) while the Ministry of Youth finances the training of the personnel for leisure time centers.

CNAF supports the development of the care sector with funds covered by social contributions and taxes (9.6 billion Euros). Beginning in 2000, two types of additional grants, an Early Childhood Investment Fund (*Fonds d'Investissement Exceptionnel pour la Petite Enfance*—FIPE) and a Special Investment Support (*Aide Exceptionnelle à l'Investissement*—AEI) were funded annually (about 200 million Euros each). These allowed an increase in the number of places for children in collective settings.

CAFs also partly finance the functioning of care centers (which contract with the municipalities for the rest of their funding). This support was recently redesigned so that municipalities and nonprofit associations are not penalized by serving children from low-income families. This introduction of a single benefit sustains the development of *halte-garderies* (part-time centers) and *multi-accueils* (centers including various kinds of provision and flexible functioning) in order to meet the new needs of families stemming from recent constraints of the labor market.

Municipalities play a central role in the care sector. They partly finance full-time and part-time crèches and leisure time services (about a billion Euros). In the absence of requirements, they develop local early childhood policies that vary considerably in strength. Contracts with CAFs (*contrat-enfance),* created by the CNAF in 1988, provide financial incentives to increase both the quantity and the quality of care services. The CAFs subsidies cover up to 50–70% of new planned expenses for traditional care and leisure time provision, as well as for innovative settings. These contracts also help to coordinate the different settings, disseminate information to families, and train professionals. The number of such contracts continues to increase at the present time, involving more municipalities.

Departments (regional entities) are in charge of financing the childminders' training. They can also expand local policies in order to promote the development of early childhood services by financing the creation or the functioning of services and particularly networks of childminders or services for parents and children. Recently, CNAF experimented with contracts to departments with the aim of improving individual care (childminders), local coordination, information to families, and innovations.

Private companies are also involved with care arrangements. Some of them provide or finance places for their staff's children. They have recently been allowed to create services.

Parents have to pay for care, but if they use an official provision (i. e. not an unlicensed childminder), they receive subsidies to offset the costs of their care arrangements and also benefit from tax reductions. They pay the salary of the childminder or the in-home caregiver they employ, but if they use a *crèche* (run by municipalities as well as nonprofit associations which follow the same parental fee scale), they pay according to family income and size (one does not know what happens today for private crèches, recently created). On the average, parents pay 27 percent of the cost of crèches (municipalities and departments: 43% and CAFs: 30%). However, the range in family expenditures is large, from less than 1,000 Euros (40% of families) to more than 5,000 Euros (10% of families). For low-income families the public subsidies are inadequate, although they make an important contribution.

Subsidies to Families and Tax Benefits

Subsidies. The current national aim is to encourage the free choice of parents, who are facing not only a disparity of provision from one municipality to another but also the different costs from one care setting to another. Subsidies are offered to them by CAFs in order to offset these differences and to support the choice between a childminder, an in-home caregiver, or a *crèche*, as well as to help those (generally the mother) who choose to care for their own young children at home.

Until 2003, parents were provided with several types of subsidies, according to their choices, including an allowance for young children (*Allocation pour Jeune Enfant*—APJE), which was received by about 80 percent of families from the fifth month of pregnancy until the child's third birthday (159 Euros per month).

A parental education allowance (*Allocation Parentale d'Éducation*—APE) helped parents, who were not working (or in part-time employment) and with at least two children, until the child's third birthday (485 Euros per month).

Parents who employed a licensed childminder were helped for this employment (*Aide à la Famille pour l'Emploi d'une Assistante Maternelle*—AFEAMA). This allowance covered social contributions to the state plus an additional amount to offset the cost, based on family income (203 Euros for those with annual incomes under 12,912 Euros, 160 Euros for incomes between 12,912 and 17,754 Euros, and 133 Euros for those with incomes over 17,754 Euros).

Parents who employed somebody in their homes received an allowance for an in-home caregiver (*Allocation de Garde d'Enfant à Domicile*—AGED), which varied according to family income (up to 1,548 Euros per trimester when the family income is less than 34,744 Euros).

Studies of the use of these different subsidies (Bonnet and Labbé, 1999; Guillot, 2002) found that family income and the mother's employment status (plus the type and amount of the local provision of care) continue greatly to determine parents' "choice" and thus the type of subsidy they receive. Important differences were noticed between households receiving AGED (very high-income families), AFEAMA (middle- and high-income families), and APE (mainly unqualified mothers). For low-income families crèches are the less expensive setting, but crèches are concentrated in the Paris region and in other big cities. Some working parents, mainly from disadvantaged backgrounds, use no official provision and thus receive no financial help to care for their children (this includes about 10% of the under threes).

At the present time, in order both to reduce inequities and to simplify the system of family allowance, a unique family subsidy (*Prestation d'accueil pour jeune enfant*—PAJE) has replaced all the previous subsidies. It is determined by the number of children and family type, varies according to household income, and includes specific help for the employment of an in-home carer or a childminder (the financial help for the employment of a childminder is upgraded) or for caring his/her own child (also upgraded).

Tax deductions. In addition, parents can benefit from tax reductions for care expenses. The maximum tax reduction is 575 Euros per year, except for the employment of an in-home carer (the maximum tax reduction is 3,450 per year). About 545 million Euros is the total fiscal benefit related to early childhood care, provided through tax reductions.

Future Needs

We agree with other authors who have urged the continuation of family policy efforts that would make it easier to provide access to care services for all families. Efforts should also be made to increase the recruitment of professionals by upgrading their status and training, thus reducing the salary differences between these caregivers and the teachers in the *écoles maternelles*.

Further Readings: Bonnet, C., and M. Labbé (1999). L'activité des femmes après la naissance de leur deuxième enfant *Recherches et prévisions* 59, 18–25; Guillot, O. (2002). Une analyse du recours aux services de garde d'enfants. *Économie et statistique* 352–353, 213–230; Legendre, F., R. Lorgnet, and F. Thibault (2004). Les aides publiques à la garde des jeunes enfants. *Recherches et Prévisions* 75, 5–20; Leprince, F. (2003). *L'accueil des jeunes enfants en France: État des lieux et pistes d'amélioration.* Rapport Haut Conseil de la Population et de la famille; Perier, L. (1999). Le contrat-enfance. *Recherche et Prévisions* 57–58, 91–92.

Sylvie Rayna

Teacher Preparation in France

Introduction

In France, early childhood education is partitioned into two separate areas, with distinct provision for each sector. The crèches (centers) and childminders (home-based) provide care services for children under age 3, and leisure time activities for children attending from two years of age. The *écoles maternelles* are preschools for children over age 2. This distinction by sector is found, too, in the status and training of personnel in early childhood. The differences between these two sectors are numerous, especially with regard to the level and the length of the training, and the program orientation. There is also considerable diversity in preparation within each sector.

The Education Sector

Several kinds of personnel are working in the *écoles maternelles*. University-trained teachers, called *professeurs des écoles*, are national civil servants qualified to teach 2- to 11-year-olds in *écoles maternelles* or in elementary schools. In *écoles maternelles*, they are assisted by staff who are municipal workers.

Training of professeurs des écoles. Until the early 1990s, teachers were trained in the École Normale (teacher training college), which included specialized training in early childhood education for working in *écoles maternelles*. At the end of the 1980s, a crisis in the vocations and an increase in teaching requirements drove the authorities to upgrade the image of the teaching occupation. This was accomplished by significantly raising the wages of the teachers and increasing their level of qualification by providing them with a university level of training.

University Institutes for Teacher Training (IUFM; Institut Universitaire de formation des maîtres) have now replaced École Normale, providing within the same institution training for both primary education (*école maternelle* and elementary school) and secondary education (Robert and Terral, 2000).There is no longer a separate preparation for preschool teachers, but instead a common training for primary education.

A national exam is required in order to graduate from the IUFM. Candidates first have to pursue a *licence* (a three-year college degree) at the university (maths, biology, literature, science of education, or any other subject). They can then prepare for the national exam during one year in IUFM or independently. The exam includes written papers in French, math, science and art, a practical exam in physical education, and an oral exam on workplace experiences. Those who pass the exam then complete one year of professional training in IUFM (about 450 hours). This component includes eight to twelve weeks of supervised work placements in schools, where the novice is responsible for the class and teaches.

The teacher education curriculum, approved by the Ministry of Education, is focused on broad education-related courses, such as psychology, sociology, history of education, philosophy, and studies in education. Subject-based courses are also included, such as French, math, music, art, etc. Despite a high level of qualification, there is an obvious lack of specialization in early years education within the current teachers' training program (Oberhuemer and Ulich, 1997). This is also visible in practice; for example, inspectors may not specialize in *écoles maternelles*, but must control and provide professional development sessions to all primary school teachers.

During their careers, teachers are entitled to thirty-six weeks of in-service training, which is organized on a departmental level. Unfortunately, the sessions concerning early years and the available places are not numerous enough to meet teachers' needs. Fortunately, there is a well-established professional association for preschool teachers that organizes an annual conference and other forms of training and support for its members. After gaining some work experience, teachers can pursue further training to become a specialized teacher, educational psychologist, trainer, principal, or inspector.

Assistant teacher training (agent territorial spécialisé des ecoles maternelles).
These municipal employees assist the teachers in the *écoles maternelles*, particularly those in charge of the youngest children. Their functions vary from city to city and even from school to school. Officially they belong to the educational team, but their role is focused on care (hygiene, meal, nap) and is often limited to domestic tasks, including the cleanliness of the classroom and preparation of the material needed by the teacher.

Until 1992, these assistants were regarded as custodial workers. Since then the status of the assistants has risen, due to the introduction of a mandatory training called CAP Petit Enfance that takes place over a period of twelve to eighteen months and leads to a certificate in early childhood. However, this preservice (in a professional school after the age of 16) or in-service training is focused on children's care and classroom hygiene. Assistants also have limited access to in-service training and career mobility. Yet in practice, when cooperation with teachers exists, training takes place throughout the preparation and sharing of activities carried out with the children.

The Care Sector

The care sector includes both home-based and center-based caregiving and teaching. Childminders provide care in their own homes, and in-home caregivers work in the child's home. Centers are staffed by pediatric nurses, early childhood educators, and assistant pediatric nurses.

Home-based caregivers. There are several different types of home-based caregivers.
Childminders (assistantes maternelles). Childminders need licensing approval to care for children in their own homes. This approval is granted by departmental authorities after assessment of the quality of the home environment and the health, mental health, and moral character of the applicant. The license is authorized for a five-year period, and is renewable on the condition that the childminder participate in a sixty-hour in-service training, including twenty hours during the first two years. This training, financed and organized by mother and child health centers (PMI), includes general notions on child development, individual rhythms, and needs; educational aspects of childcare; relationships with parents; and institutional and social frameworks. In addition, PMI provides in-service support by children's nurses and social workers. Training opportunities are available when childminders are employed in a crèche familiale, generally directed by a pediatric nurse (puéricultrice:see below) or participate in a network of independent childminders, generally directed by an early childhood educator (*relais assistantes maternelles*: see below). But childminders often complain about the lack of recognition (Blosse-Platière and *al,* 1995). A reevaluation of their status and prestige are presently at the center of a national debate.

In-home caregivers. No training is required for in-home caregivers employed directly by the parents. However, some municipalities offer in-home caregivers some training opportunities. This occurs, for instance, via childminder networks (*relais assistantes maternelles*). In those settings an early childhood educator can provide childminders and in-home caregivers with educational opportunities, both for them as well as for the children they care for. When parents recruit in-home caregivers through private organizations, some training may be provided by these organizations prior to recruitment.

Center-based services. In center-based services, which consist of full-time or part-time centers for children and part-time centers for parents and children (*pouponnières, crèches, halte-garderies, accueils parents-enfants*), two kinds of professionals have tertiary-level professional qualifications. Pediatric nurses (*puéricultrices*) are the heads of these services. Early childhood educators (*éducateurs de jeunes enfants*) can be heads of part-time services and are allowed (since the year 2000) to be heads of small crèches (less than forty children). The training programs for these two kinds of professionals differ from that of other professionals with lower qualifications.

In this sector, initial training is provided by public or private colleges and in-service training by various centers. A national center and several associations are responsible for the in-service training of the municipal and departmental employees.

Pediatric nurses (puéricultrices). Pediatric nurses may work in hospitals or in mother and child health services (PMI) or in crèches. After gaining at least five years of professional experience as an assistant, a pediatric nurse may assume a leadership position within a crèche.

Initial training for these nurses is provided by public or private colleges approved by the Ministry of Health. After three years (general training to become a nurse), the training for working with children takes place over a period of twelve months (1,500 hours), with a nationally defined curriculum. The program includes 650 hours of theoretical and practical work centered on the knowledge of the child (physiology, psychology, psychopedagogy, diet and nutrition, child pathology, care), its environment (health policy, sociology), and the profession (roles and functions, administrative, social organization, management); 710 hours of field placement; and 140 hours of directed study and evaluation.

Experienced pediatric nurses can become early childhood coordinators on a municipal or departmental level. No mandatory training exists for this relatively new professional role, except for some in-service training sessions proposed by several universities and public training centers.

Early childhood educators (éducateurs de jeunes enfants). Early childhood educators work with groups of children or direct staff. Created in 1973, this profession has evolved over time (Verba, 2001). Early childhood educators, formerly called kindergarten educators (*jardinières d'enfants*), were once viewed as welfare workers with an educative function for young children. Currently, they receive training over the course of twenty-seven months in centers approved by the Ministry of Social Affairs.

The curriculum for the early childhood educator program is defined at a national level. The 1,200 hours of both theoretical and technical training are composed of seven units: pedagogy and human relationships (160 hours); pedagogy of the expression and educational techniques (160 hours); knowledge of young children from birth to seven years of age (240 hours); group life (160 hours); health, health education and medical-social protection (160 hours); law, economics, and society (180 hours); professional culture, methodology, and technique (140 hours). The initial training includes nine months of fieldwork. Early childhood educators may work toward a higher diploma in social work. They can also become early childhood coordinators.

Assistant pediatric nurses (Auxiliaires de puériculture). In center-based services the bulk of the staff is assistant pediatric nurses. These caregivers have completed a one-year vocational training in public or private schools, approved by the regional authorities and open to candidates who are at least 17 years old. The training includes ten months of field placements. Since 1994, part of the training has been carried out together with that of assistant nursing staff. It is composed of six modules focusing on hygiene, care, relationships, communication, ergonomics, and public health; and four field placements in hospital, medical, and maternity wards. The other part of the training is more specific to early childhood education (ECE), and includes modules (nine weeks) on the child and his environment: the prenatal period and birth, the development of the healthy child, the sick child, the handicapped child, and palliative care. This second phase of training also includes six field placements (seventeen weeks) carried out in different sectors of health (pediatrics, maternity ward, child psychiatry, bottle-feeding, diet), and day-care settings. In all, this training lasts 1,575 hours (including 630 hours of theoretical work and 845 hours of practical fieldwork). Career opportunities for these professionals remain very restricted.

The Leisure Time Sector

This sector, organized by municipalities and associations, is a part of the care sector devoted to children during after-school hours, on Wednesdays, and during holidays. These services may be located within or outside of the school buildings. The leisure time staff are not necessarily qualified. Nevertheless, most hold a diploma, the BAFA (*Brevet d'aptitude aux fonctions d'animateur*), which consists of twenty-eight days of training related to out-of-school activities and is administered by the Ministry of Youth and Sports. This certificate qualifies a person to work in the leisure-time sector. The diploma required in order to become a director of a leisure-time center is the BAFD (*Brevet d'aptitude aux fonctions de directeur*). Provision of and participation in in-service training is voluntary. Cooperation with teachers within global school projects provides these staff members with training opportunities.

Conclusion

Although in general considerable heterogeneity and separation characterize teacher and caregiver initial training in early childhood care and education, in-service training sessions can be offered in some cities to professionals of both the care and the education sectors, based on a partnership between the different institutions in charge of early childhood. For example, training sessions on cultural activities toward young children and their families (books, music, etc.) are being offered simultaneously to preschool teachers and crèche staff. These efforts, which need further development and expansion, open interesting perspectives by providing trainees with opportunities to know each other, to confront their own views on young children and education, to develop a mutual respect, and to take the first step toward a common culture of early childhood (Rayna and Dajez, 1997).

Further Readings: Blosse-Platière, S., A. Dethier, C. Fleury, and N. Loutre due Pasquier (1995). *Accueillir le jeune enfant: quelle professionnalisation?* Paris: CNFPT-Erès; Oberhuemer, P., and M. Ulich (1997). *Working with young children in Europe. Provision and staff training*. London: Paul Chapman; Rayna, S., and F. Dajez (1997). *Formation, petite enfance et partenariat*. Paris: L'Harmattan; Robert, A., and H. Terral (2000). *Les IUFM et la formation des enseignants aujourd'hui* Paris: Presses Universitaires de France; Verba, D. (2001). *Le métier d'éducateur de jeunes enfants*. Paris: Editions La Découverte et Syros.

Alexandra Moreau

Italy

Early Childhood Education in Italy

In this profile we begin by describing Italy in demographic terms, from an early childhood perspective. Attention then shifts to the historical and cultural underpinnings of Italian early care and education. This is followed by introductory discussions on pedagogy, curriculum, and the staffing of early childhood education (ECE) settings, all topics addressed in greater detail in later entries. We conclude with an overview of several topics currently challenging the ECE field in the Italian context.

Demographics

In 2005, fifty-seven and a half million people lived in Italy. The birth rate in 2004 was about 1.22 children per woman of childbearing age, well below replacement. The employment rate for women with children under 6 years was 50 percent, ranging from 67 percent for high-qualified women to 12 percent for those with low qualifications.

Italy, though small, is a very diverse country in geography, from the Alps and the influence of France on the western border, Switzerland and Austria to the northeast, to the Mediterranean and insular Sicily and Sardegna, including the full range from small rural traditional areas to metropolitan and industrial settings like Milano, Torino, and Genova. Lombardia, the region in the north with Milano as its capital city, is the most populated area of Italy (about 10 million inhabitants). This is the region with the highest per capita income in Europe and one of the highest rankings on school results by international comparison, whereas other regions are at very low levels of employment, income, and school results. Regions like Tuscany and Emilia-Romagna (where the municipal tradition of average sized cities like **Reggio Emilia**, Modena, Parma, Pistoia, Florence, and Bologna is strongest) have invested highly in early childhood education in the past thirty years and can offer full time, full coverage for children from 3 to 6 (*scuole dell'infanzia*, formerly called *scuole materne*: i.e., "maternal" schools) and places for over

30 percent of children under the age of 3 (*asili nido* or *nidi*, "nido" meaning "nest"). Some cities and regions of the south, although they are now reaching 80 percent of full-time coverage for children between three and six, can offer little more than 1 percent of their resident children a place in *nidi*. Overall averages in Italy are, therefore, highly misleading and analyses should be made at the regional or even municipal level.

Today (2006) over 90 percent of children between 3 and 6 attend schools (over 95% of five-year-olds), including children with special needs. City and state schools are free of charge and the time schedule varies between twenty-seven and forty hours per week. Only 10 percent of the children between three months and three years attend *nidi*, but figures range from 40 percent in some cities of Emilia Romagna to 1 percent in some areas of the south. *Nidi* are not considered a fully public service, but rather a so-called "service at individual demand," and families pay according to income ranging from a symbolic fee to full cost. *Nidi* are also in general full time (eight to nine hours per day, five days a week), meals are provided to the children and the menu is set by health authorities, with special diets for health or religious reasons in general guaranteed.

The Culture and Tradition of Early Childhood Educational Services

Italy has only been a nation since 1861. Since the Middle Ages the city-states (municipalities or *Comuni*) have been the level of government with which Italians identify. Civic traditions, the influence of the church, and the socialist movement are the three major factors that have determined the development of early child-hood educational services and are necessarily the cultural lens through which the existing panorama of policies should be examined.

Traditionally preschool services have been promoted by city governments (primarily in traditionally socialist ruled cities like Reggio Emilia, Bologna, or Florence but also in other big cities like Milano, Torino, Genova, Rome, and Palermo) or by parishes of the Catholic Church. There is also a tradition of mutual help among women in the North, where women's leagues in rural areas have organized shared care since the beginning of the twentieth century. State involvement came much later—in the late 1970s. The first kindergartens or *scuole materne* date back to the end of the eighteenth century, established in the large cities of the North following the influence of enlightened thinkers like Ferrante Aporti and inspired by Friedrich **Froebel** and Johann **Pestalozzi**. In the first two decades of the twentieth century most average and big municipalities of the North and the Center had developed their own systems of schools for children between 3 and 6, along with network of social services for children aged 0–3 directed to mothers in need (ONMI—*Opera Nazionale Maternità e Infanzia*). In that same period, the first **Montessori** schools opened in public housing sites in Rome, promoted by the municipality. Not long after that the sisters Agazzi opened their first school in Mompiano, where some decades later the *Centro Nazionale per la Scuola Materna* (National Center for Maternal Schools) was founded, supported by the northern city of Brescia, the national government, and the church.

After World War II, most cities of the Center and the North invested in *scuole dell'infanzia*. Reggio Emilia was an example, with the women physically building schools for their children. When the State became involved in 1968, by passing Law 444 stating that state schools for young children would be built where they did not already exist, over 50 percent of the Italian children between 3 and 6 were already regularly attending a full-time service. This service was generally free, with only the meals to be paid for on a sliding scale based on income. Just three years later, in 1971, national Law 1044 was passed that promoted *nidi*, which were to be planned at a regional level and run by municipalities. It is within this tension among strong civic tradition, impulses from the state, and interaction with the church that the development of the Italian early childhood education systems can be understood. The tensions and coexistence of these three main actors accounts for the continuous growth of early educational services across years of continuous political change. It appears evident that only a common feeling and a widespread consensus about public funding of early childhood education, about sharing responsibilities for raising children, and about education as a community endeavor could account for the expansion of educational services for children even in years of economic stagnation and decline.

The ideas of children as an important investment, of shared responsibilities in education, and of the tradition of civic engagement metaphorically visible in the *piazza* ("public squares")—the central gathering place in every *scuola dell'infanzia* or *nidi*—is widely shared across the country. But it coexists with a strong feeling of the importance and role of the family. This is expressed both in the legislation that guarantees maternal leave (five compulsory full-paid months to be used before or after childbirth, three more months without pay, the possibility of staying home longer without losing the job in public employment), and in the legal right to stay home without salary if the child is ill up to the age of 6. It is interesting to note that the first bill introducing maternity leave was issued contemporaneously with the *nidi* law. At that time, in the early 1970s, the Catholic culture advocated for longer maternity leaves, and the socialist Unions for more *nidi*. Today all parties promise more services for all children, and the differences are in the *forms* of education and care for the very young (municipal care versus company crèches or family networks). We can say that over the last decades, issues associated with the education and care of young children have been increasingly seen as public concerns rather than as exclusively women's issues or family problems.

The following three dimensions mark the development of *scuole dell'infanzia* and *nidi*:

- the progressive inclusion of these settings within the educational system (*nidi* were previously conceived as social services) and the development of their own pedagogy, which is considered to be rooted in a developing "culture of childhood" rather than in a standard curriculum;
- the inclusive character of the educational services, conceived potentially for *all* children as an expression of a subjective right of the child herself;
- the tradition of *partecipazione*, a concept that encompasses both civic engagement and its expression in organized form of participation and control—the so called *gestione sociale* of the 1970s. This tradition was later sustained by a Law that regulates families' representation and responsibilities in schools. In reality this links the daily life of children, family, and school together through practices such as

gradual transition from home to school, parental engagement in school activities and planning, projects expanding the school life by bringing children out into the community and community members into the school.

Pedagogy and Curriculum

Nidi have, over the years, gained an educational and pedagogical quality highly concerned with the emotional well-being of the children, marked by strong links between family and center, with attention focused on organizing spaces, groups, and activities in order to foster a strong relationship with one or two significant caregivers, child–child interaction, progressive autonomy, and general well-being in an appropriate and warm environment. The approach is holistic and there is no such concept as a zero-to-three curriculum, although symbolic play, manipulative and expressive activities and storytelling, and documentation are common features. The emphasis is definitely on relationships and on creating a "good," "pleasant," aesthetically and convivially attentive context through spaces, materials, carefully thought out routines, and social activities. The pedagogy of early childhood, or rather the "culture of childhood," has developed in cities and across cities through a constant networking (especially through the *Gruppo Nazionale Nidi-Infanzia* and two professional magazines, *Bambini* e *Infanzia*). It has been strongly influenced not only by Piagetian (see Jean **Piaget**) and Vygotskian (see Lev **Vygotsky**) thought (Vygotski had been translated from Russian into Italian since the early 1960s, long before his writings were known in the Anglo American context), but also by Maria **Montessori**, authors like Henri Wallon and Iréne Lèzine, by psychoanalysis and attachment theory and by the Hungarian experience of Loczy. Since the responsibility of *nidi* at the national level is not yet in the Ministry of Education, whereas at the local level in most cases *nidi* are run from educational authorities in continuity with the scuole dell'infanzia, there are no common National Guidelines. Regions and cities, however, have developed standards and instruments to assess quality and guidelines.

Scuole dell'infanzia had developed rich and significant experiences long before the State came onto the scene in 1968. They now follow National Guidelines called *Orientamenti*, *Nuovi Orientamenti*, and *Indicazioni* because the term "program" or "curriculum" is not considered appropriate to describe the pedagogy that informs the school system. These guidelines have traditionally been drawn through a wide national consultation with researchers, administrators, and practitioners. Even the new *Indicazioni* included in the 2004 reform bill do not radically reconceptualize the early childhood pedagogy established over the past thirty years. This reform reconfirms the achievement of a sense of identity, of autonomy, and of competence as main educational goals left to each school, with substantial freedom to schools to interpret the guidelines and to design their own curriculum. Project work, emphasis on children's multiple symbolic languages, documentation, and a holistic approach are still dominant features in most Italian *scuole dell'infanzia*; but a stronger pressure toward a more structured curriculum and measurable performance outcomes has been emerging recently.

Although Reggio Emilia *scuole* and *nidi* are the most striking and widely known, many other towns deserve attention not only because they share some of the characteristics of Reggio schools that are widely recognizable as a general Italian frame, but also because they have developed their own original systems, deeply rooted in the tradition of the community. Middle-sized cities like Pistoia, Modena, Parma, and Trento provide good examples, as do small municipalities like San Miniato in Tuscany and big cities like Milano, Torino, Genova, Bologna, and Ancona.

Staff

The staff of *nidi* and *scuola dell'infanzia* are called *educatrici* or *educatori*, words different from caregiver and teacher, which convey a meaning of educationally oriented care. The minimum required training for *nidi* staff is a diploma obtained from a teacher-training-oriented secondary school (*Istituto Magistrale*). Regular in-service training that can range between 100 and 150 hours per year, along with thirty to forty hours for group work and meetings and interviews with parents, is built into the contract as paid time. Nowadays a widely shared opinion is that basic training should be raised to a three-year postsecondary (university) degree in educational sciences or psychology, and many *educatrici* are already so qualified. Since 1998 the requirement for *scuole dell'infanzia* has been a four-year university course, and this will be raised to five years. *Nidi* and *scuole dell'infanzia* are coordinated by professionals called *coordinatori* or *pedagogisti*, who combine administrative and management responsibility with the task of pedagogical supervision and implementation of the educational offering and of teacher development.

Current Issues

The recent 2003 Law allows families to enrol their children in *scuole dell'infanzia* at age $2^1/_2$ and also to anticipate primary school at age $5^1/_2$. This puts *scuole dell'infanzia* under pressure because of the growing demand of care for under threes, and challenges a long established system that has always resisted acceleration and insisted on respecting the child's pace. Teachers share what has been for many years a common feeling—namely, that early childhood years are precious and should not be quickly "consumed." The conviction is that the experience in settings especially designed for children, rich and free of pressure, is by no means a waste of time. It is rather an important training ground for consolidation of the sense of self, of social competence, of exploration and of research attitudes. Many families, nevertheless, ask for more and want it faster. This pressure forces *nidi* and *scuole* to rethink, redefine, and renegotiate shared ideas about children with families, their common responsibilities, and the schools' mission. It does not necessarily mean that the pedagogy of early childhood education will have to yield to the acceleration pressure, but that it is necessary, at the beginning of a new millennium, to rethink, redefine, and retune fundamental educational goals.

A second emerging issue is intercultural education. Italy, for decades a country of migrants, is now a host country. Over 25 percent of the children who attend early childhood services are born in families of non-European origin. If, on the one hand, the traditional inclusiveness of the early childhood education system accounts for a generic welcoming attitude, on the other hand the idealization of the child, the scarce knowledge of different cultures, and the resistance to activating special activities for any child (the compensatory model has always been rejected as stigmatizing) may prevent early childhood education services from fully exploiting the opportunity provided by the preschool years to foster active integration and prevent later exclusion and school failure.

Further Readings: Gandini, L., and C. Pope Edwards (2001). *Bambini: The Italian approach to infant/toddler care.* New York and London: Teachers College Press; OECD (2001). *Starting strong, early childhood education and care.* Paris: The Organization for Economic Cooperation and Development.

Web Sites: www.istruzione.it; www.cede.it.

Susanna Mantovani

Pedagogy

Pedagogy is the general framework within which we think about education; it is the science, the epistemology where we reflect about education, its means, methodologies, and goals. The objects of pedagogy are educational relationships, situations where the educational processes occur, and educational practices and how the subjects involved experience them. Pedagogy is reflection about educational experiences that are characterized by values, goals, intentionality, intrinsically relational (or intersubjective), situated in culture and in time, and asymmetric. Pedagogy is at the same time a theory (of education) and a practical science, and is therefore both philosophical and political. It is a social science, one of the "human sciences" because the educational process can only take place in situations where human beings interact within specific and evolving cultural and political contexts. In order to be regarded as a science, pedagogy needs to be intentional, to make the ideas that it produces explicit, and to orient and give meaning and significance to the educational events and processes with which it deals. Educational events, experiences, and processes, as oriented around, studied, and interpreted by pedagogy, are social, socializing and inclusive, marked by different forms of cooperation and participation, constructivistic, and culturally situated.

Early childhood is a crucial focus for pedagogy because it is the period of life where the underlying assumptions related to the processes and the experience of growing, interacting, learning, being taken care of, and being educated can be observed at their origins; within the family and in other educational contexts less formalized and defined than school or other instructional settings. This includes the ideas of educating and caring adults within the family and in other contexts intentionally prepared for young children, and the social policies toward children, families, and working mothers. It also involves as one of it core interests *participation*; that is, how the persons involved in the educational process interact, share and take responsibilities, and *the places (loci)* where child development and education occur: family/home, neighborhoods, early childhood services, day care, preschools, and so forth.

Early childhood pedagogy is founded on perspectives, approaches, and general categories rather than by specific frameworks and processes of teaching and learning activities (curricula). Curricula are the *hic et nunc* translation of broader theories and ideas about education. Actually the word curriculum does not appear in official Italian documents concerning preschool. At present we can, therefore, try to sketch a pedagogy of early childhood where on the one hand a few general ideas are widely debated and shared across many cultures, and on the other hand some specific approaches, rooted in specific communities (local communities or communities of researchers and decision makers) flourish, interact with other approaches, and eventually contaminate them.

Early childhood pedagogy is, in fact, both a very vivid expression of cultural niches and local particularities and the continuous contamination or *métissage* or crossfertilization of paradigms and practices. It is, therefore, a good example of the tension and dialectics between cultural identity and universal goals that characterize the contemporary world: thinking about children, their families, and the practices and goals of their education emphasizes both the personal and local and the general and universal values and choices.

Early childhood pedagogy is not a specific theory (and even less *one* theory); it reflects critically on the educational processes that take place locally and on the theories developed to interpret and orient them. This pedagogy operates in two directions. One is the "bottom up" direction. This involves the discussion and interpretation of already existing educational experiments, policies, and practices, when community or local experiences meet theories. The other, more traditional, and less active, constructive, and culturally conscious direction is where pedagogy inspires and directs the planning and conduction of policies, practices, and local experiments. This is the "top down" direction, where a community or a group of educators or researchers is "doing" or experimenting (e.g., a Vygotskian or constructivistic or **Reggio Emilia** or **Head Start** approach, or in earlier times when they were "doing" **Montessori**, etc.).

The pedagogy of early childhood education in Italy is currently oriented around the following:

- A broad and holistic approach, and more specifically the idea of an active, constructive, competent, and social child, interacting in culturally situated environments with adult, peers, and cultural artifacts, learning through a "guided participation in social activities."
- The idea of multiple intelligences and languages (Gardner, Jerome **Bruner**, Reggio Emilia) and therefore of a necessary integration of languages, art, science, social interaction, etc.
- The consideration of the importance of the situations and environments in which the educational process takes place (physical environment i.e., the location of institutions and the significances conveyed by the organization of space, safety, and aesthetics of the environment).
- Attention to participatory processes (at a socioemotional, community and political level) in the definition of institutions and services in the engagement of families, decision makers, and citizens.

- Inclusion and therefore attention to diversity as a challenge and effort to develop respectful and deep transactions between all individuals, groups, and educational approaches.
- A striving for universal access to educational and care services as an opportunity to experience diversity, to negotiate meanings, and to develop a broader self.

The following are some key words connected with the term "pedagogy" often found in Italian literature on early childhood education:

- *"la pedagogia del benessere"*—a pedagogy of well-being or well feeling, indicating the need to connect educational opportunities with a deep sensitiveness to the child's personal needs (bodily well-being, conviviality, links between family and school, times and spaces to play, rest, and share pleasure) and to the attention to the well-being of adults as well as children
- *"la pedagogia del gusto"*—a pedagogy where the aesthetics, the quality of the materials, the environment of the objects, and images the child encounters are considered crucial for the forming of a full personality and identity and of a young citizen that learns to like, love, and respect the environment. Space and materials made available to children are considered "the third educator" as well as the first form of **documentation** that gives a message to the community about the value of childhood.
- *"la pedagogia delle relazioni"*—a pedagogy where interpersonal and social relationships are seen as a fundamental means for sustaining autonomy, enhancing the development of a strong sense of self, eliciting curiosity, and sustaining attention though dialogue, discussion, fun, and stability in partnership.
- *" la pedagogia della continuità"*—the very high degree of continuity that characterizes the Italian school system. Children stay with the same group of children and team of teachers for three years. This organizational and cultural choice explains the developing of long-lasting projects and the strict link between peers, their families, and teachers.
- *"la pedagogia della partecipazione"*—this concept, which is difficult to capture within the framework of home–school relationships, describes the community character of schools for children and the consciousness that for parents and children the school of the early years is often the first experience of getting in touch as citizens or future citizens with the communities, its rules and its opportunities. It encompasses both the ideas of control and cooperation of citizens of the community in establishing and running the early childhood education system and the daily practices connecting school with family and with the outside community, such as transition practices, meetings with group of parents, and common initiatives.
- *" la pedagogia della documentazione"*—documenting what children are and do through observation, listening, recording, and organizing with them and among teachers the projects in their doing, allowing children and adults to reread the past experiences, to renew memories and to rethink. This is both a form of evaluation and a way to illustrate and extend the culture of childhood that is developing in the educational context. This process has a long tradition and has been enriched and diffused in cities like Reggio Emilia, Pistoia, and Milano. It has strongly influenced the new form of evaluation (portfolio of competences) recently proposed by the new guidelines for nursery school.
- *"la pedagogia culturale"*—the consciousness of the cultural nature of ideas and practices concerning children and education, which is becoming more acute today

now that Italy is faced for the first time with a relevant **immigration** wave and needs to develop ways to reorganize, redefine, and expand the boundaries of the pedagogy of childhood without disregarding traditions and roots in the community. The need is to incorporate practices where the recognition of other identities and stories and the dialogue between children and adults coming from different backgrounds can become a first opportunity for new forms of socialization in the community.

All these ideas point to a way of considering the education of children as a shared social responsibility and the early childhood years as a very precious time in one's life, a time that should be tasted, explored, and experienced without haste. "Where is the hurry?" is a question posed in early childhood pedagogy in Italy today. This orientation is strongly challenged by the urges and trends of globalization, and by an imported trend based on a so-called "scientific" way to look at learning and curriculum, which is preoccupied with anticipating and accelerating the acquisition of specific knowledges and skills rather than supporting and protecting children's interest in researching, exploring, and playing around with new ideas and curious problems. This trend emerges with some contradictions in the National Guidelines (Indicazioni Nazionali, 2004). It will be interesting, over the next years and decades, to see how the Italian early childhood pedagogy will react or adapt to these trends.

Further Readings: Bertolini, P. (1988). *L'esistere pedagogico*. Firenze: La Nuova Italia; Bruner, J. (1996). *The culture of education*. Cambridge, MA: Harvard University Press; Dewey, J. (1972 [1929]). *Le fonti di una scienza dell'educazione*. Firenze: La Nuova Italia; OECD (2001). *Starting strong, early childhood education and care*. Paris: The Organization for Economic Cooperation and Development; Ministero Istruzione Università e Ricerca (MIUR), (2004). *Indicazioni Nazionali per i Piani Personalizzati delle Attività Educative nelle Scuole dell'Infanzia (2004)* Rome: Miur; Rogoff, B. (1990). *Apprenticeship in thinking: Cognitive development in social context*. New York: Oxford University Press; Zimmer, J. (2000). *Das Kleine Handbuch Zum Situationsansatz*. Berlin: Broschiert.

Susanna Mantovani

Play

Play is a multifaceted phenomenon that eludes clear-cut definitions. However, theorists who studied play agree on the fact that it is an aimless, freely chosen, pleasant, and "uncertain" activity. Play has no other goal than the pleasure that it offers. It is voluntary and freely initiated and its outcomes are unpredictable. Furthermore, play is a human activity whose value and function depends strictly on the social and cultural context in which it takes place. Different cultures attribute different social meanings to play and offer different sets of traditional play settings and forms (games) to players.

As Jean **Piaget** underlined and as broadly recognized, play is considered typically—if not exclusively—a behavior of children, characterized by pleasure, positive affection, and emotional engagement. It develops during infancy and takes different forms: from sensory motor activities such as running, jumping, object manipulation, rough and tumble play to games with rules (hide and seek, football and so on) passing through "pretend" play, a form of play in which objects, people, and spaces assume meanings different from those assigned in ordinary life. Initiated by the adult (especially by the mother in some typical forms as peekaboo play), who acts as the first play trainer and partner for the child, play is one of the most important interactive and social behaviors of young children; it is a way to dialogue and share positive emotions with caregivers and peers. It also represents a way to approach the world that minimizes the consequences of one's action, allows learning in a less-risky situation, and provides a place where it is possible to express emotions and feelings freely (particularly in symbolic and sociodramatic play).

For these reasons play is considered an essential part of every child's life and vital to the process of human development. In order to play, children must be able to express themselves and use their best capabilities. Play contributes to elaborating identity, exercising abilities, reinforcing development, and enhancing learning.

How Does Play Relate to Children's Learning and Development?

From a psychodynamic point of view play, especially "pretend play," is seen as an arena of children's self-expression; a context in which it is possible to experiment with different identities and relationships, to develop a broad range of feelings and emotions, and to explore social meanings and roles. By representing affects and feelings in play, children can satisfy inner desires, experiment with different solutions to relational problems in a simulated way, and come to master anxiety and aggressive drives. From a cognitive point of view, play is seen as a primitive form of world representation that marks the distinction between objects and their meanings. It is characterized by combinatory freedom and prompts the process of finding new relationships and arrangements. But most of all, play in its social forms definitely promotes social learning. When playing together, children learn to take into account other people's points of view, to negotiate and respect rules, and to cooperate in order to create a shared setting. In its sociodramatic form, play also helps to test social and imaginative roles, particularly related to family and gender. Language development is also fostered by play, especially when play assumes a narrative character as in telling a story and if children, playing together and negotiating roles and plots, develop some form of metacommunication.

Thus play *per se* is neither synonymous with learning nor has it learning aims. But it can contribute to the fostering of what **Vygotsky** calls the "zone of proximal development" if it stimulates and exercises emerging capacities. For these reasons all children should have access to good quality, safe, and affordable play opportunities, with supervision provided where appropriate, in accordance with age and need.

In Italy, play is recognized as a right for all children, which has to be sustained by opportune policy interventions. The educational settings of the best Italian day-care centers and nursery schools give broad space to play in daily activities. They support play mainly by offering toys and furniture *ad hoc* (blocks, "pretend" play furniture, dolls, dresses to disguise, toy cars and trucks, etc.) organized in centers of interest where little groups of children can interact together. It is in fact also recognized that the social context of play is crucial because of its implications for children's development and that to play with a small group of close friends is an important opportunity for social learning.

The Role of Adults in Play

The role of adults in fostering children's play, mostly with children from three to six years of age, is less emphasized in Italy. Caregivers and teachers give more relevance to peer interaction in play than to adult–child interaction. Adults offer material and toys, propose or suggest activities and then take mainly the role of supervisors without playing with children. There is, however, solid research evidence and a theoretical basis in support of the idea that, in order to foster children's development, teachers should promote children's abilities by actively and playfully interacting with them. Particularly an intervention based on tutorial strategies could offer a scaffold for promoting more developed forms of play and correlated abilities.

Play and Work

Another popular idea is that play is the opposite of work; that is, in educational contexts, the opposite of didactic activities. So in many Italian educational settings—although more in nursery schools than in day-care centers—the time span daily dedicated to play is called "free play" to distinguish it from that dedicated to didactic activities, which take place mainly in the central part of the morning. The practice of separating play from "work" has negative consequences: play is considered nonacademic, nonlearning time, and only valued as leisure activity. Didactic activity, on the contrary, aimed at fostering capacities and the acquisition of learning, is seen as an assigned, obligatory (*versus* voluntary) situation that cannot last beyond the limited span of attention of children.

Play is sometimes considered as a pleasurable way of learning and working. Such an idea, which is also present in official documents such as *Orientamenti* issued by the Ministry of Education as a guideline for nursery school education and curriculum, is often misinterpreted by teachers, who tend to present imposed didactic activities as playful and pleasant ones. Play can instead be really integrated with learning activities by orienting it toward socioemotional developmental goals. In this case great importance is often given to peer interaction and to sociodramatic play, which can be facilitated by offering opportune play spaces, time, and props, and by arranging children in small playgroups. Alternatively it can incorporate cognitive goals. In such cases (e.g., Pistoia and Modena nursery schools) spontaneous children's activities, such as exploratory and symbolic play, are fostered and oriented toward more developed and culturally valued activities by offering *ad hoc* material (books, images, scientific props) and through an adult–child interaction aimed at coordinating and expanding children's proposals and ideas.

Italian preschool caregivers and teachers have different understandings of how to incorporate play and work in early education: whether as peripheral to learning or as disguised academic work, whether as integrated with socioemotional development or as integrated also with intellectual developmental goals.

The importance of play for physical development is also recognized in Italian day-care centers and nursery schools, where there is almost always an indoor large space arranged with equipment for gross-motor activities and an outdoor garden furnished with a sandbox and props for physical activities. Due to parents' and teachers' preoccupations, outdoor play is limited by weather conditions and takes place mainly in the warm season (late Spring, beginning of Summer, and early Autumn).

Research on Play

Research on children's play in Italy shows a prevailing ecological and qualitative approach founded on observations of children in their daily life contexts, especially outside the home. The following aspects of children's play have been explored over the last decades: parents' ideas about the importance of play and its effective relevance in children's life; toddlers' interactions in exploratory and symbolic play; the role of gender in children's interactions; developmental stages in symbolic play; the role of the adult in enhancing children's play; how childhood culture is expressed in play; and how sociodramatic play affects children's narrative competence.

New challenges to play research come from multicultural experience in day-care centers and nursery schools, where attendance by nonnative children increases every day, and from children's play experience in educational contexts different from the traditional ones, called "play centers," whose ecological variables and their effects on children's play behavior and interactions have not yet been explored.

There are many open questions about how to incorporate play in educational curricula, which will be hopefully answered by further research: the link between play and academic activities (such as narrative, counting, reading, reasoning, etc.); the role of furniture and toys to enhance different kinds of play; and, last but not least, the adults' strategies to help children share play and become more and more expert players. An ecological approach, which interprets children's play behaviors as affected by contextual variables, is needed to know which situations better elicit children's developed forms of play. It would be desirable that teachers as researchers answer these questions by verifying the effects of their play practices and by reflecting on their ideas about play and education.

Further Readings: Bateson, G. (1956). *The message "This is Play.* In B. Schaffner, ed., *Group processes: Transactions of the second conference.* New York: Josiah Macy Jr. Foundation; Bondioli, A. (1996). *Gioco e educazione.* Milano: FrancoAngeli; Bondioli, A., ed. (2004). *Ludus in fabula. Per una pedagogia del narrare infantile.* Bergamo: Edizioni Junior; Bondioli, A., and D. Savio (1994). *SVALSI, Scala di valutazione delle abilità ludico-simboliche infantili* Bergamo: Edizioni Junior; Bondioli, A. (2001). *The adult as a tutor in fostering children's symbolic play.* In A. Goncu, and E. L. Klein, eds., *Children in play, story, and school,* pp. 107–131. New York: Guilford Publications; Bruner, J. S. (1972). Nature and uses of immaturity. *American Psychologist* 27(8); Camaioni, L. (1980). *L'interazione tra bambini.* Roma: Armando; Corsaro, W. A. (1994). Discussion, debate and friendship: Peer discourse in nursery schools in the US and Italy. *Sociology of Education,* 61, 1–14; Fein, G., and M. Rivkin, eds. (1986). *The young child at play.* Washington DC: NAEYC; Garvey C. (1977). *Play.* London: Fontana/Open Books; Livolsi, M., A. De

Lillo, and A. Schizzerotto (1980). *Bambini non si nasce*. Milano: FrancoAngeli; Musatti, T. (1985). *I bambini nel gruppo: in asilo nido*. In E. Catarsi (ed.), *Il nido competente*. Bergamo: Juvenilia; Piaget, J. (1951). *Play, dreams and imitation in childhood*. New York: Norton; Vygotsky, L. (1937). *Play and its role in the mental development of the child*. In Bruner, J. S., A. Jolly, and K. Sylva, eds. (1976). *Play*. Harmondsworth: Penguin.

Anna Bondioli

Quality

In Italy during the past two decades the issue of quality has mainly been addressed in connection with the definition and the planning of educational services for children between 0–3. The quality of services for children between 3 and 6 is conceived within the general national Guidelines and within the debate of how to evaluate the school system in general, which is just beginning to work through INVALSI (National Institution for the Evaluation of the School System) according to the 2003 reform bill. In some instances municipalities have developed their own guidelines and taken some initiative to define their local model and to control quality, but the newest and most interesting development of the definition of quality has taken place regarding the services for 0- to 3-year-olds, within a general conceptualization widely shared for all age 0–6 services. Issues like school readiness are not yet on the scene, and have in fact always been strongly resisted by the early childhood education world. But this issue is coming along, will inform future debate and the discussion and conceptualization of quality in ECEC might well become an important contribution for the discussion of quality in general.

The debate in Italy about quality in early childhood education started in the 1980s, and was informed by the following perspectives:

• The cultural organizational projection of a service ultimately conceived as an educational service for young children and their families, implying the idea of care but putting the pedagogical goals front and center.

• A shared understanding of scientific knowledge regarding children's competences and potentials, as well as of the benefits children could draw from an educational service in the early years of their lives.

• A new social representation of childhood and of the opportunities inherent in educational strategies based on the relationships between families and educational services, rooted and disseminated in those areas of the country where the development of crèches has been stronger.

The years during which the discussion and definition of quality was developed are the very same years that marked the beginning of a stagnation phase in national policies aiming at the development of the educational service system for young children. This was undoubtedly a time when, due to research and to practices successfully implemented, Italy was finally in a position to conceptualize quality, using this concept as a "comprehensive semantic container" of the different qualifying aspects of the system, including the following:

• theoretical assumptions,
• the subjects involved,
• relational structures,
• organizational and functional standards,

- strategies for designing and documenting experiences,
- coordination, monitoring and supervision, and
- rules and regulations and related control processes.

These are elements that may tell us how "good" a project or experience is, both from the point of view of the conditions which may determine its quality and from the point of view of evaluating its effectiveness.

Within this framework, when defining the elements that contribute to the quality of an educational service for early childhood, broad consensus seems to emerge in relation to the following areas:

- focusing on children and their competence/experiential construction in the design of the service;
- acknowledging families as having an active role as chief partners in the design of the service;
- building, over time, the relationships among children, educators and parents, with full recognition of identities and of active and constructive contributions from each of the three partners;
- considering the impact of the physical organizational context of the service and the need to determine quantitative and qualitative standards, as well as to identify acceptable adult/child ratios;
- focusing educational planning on the environment and organization of the physical contexts surrounding children, valuing local and original taste and traditions, emphasizing an educational style centred on listening, tutorial support, and respect which may help value individual differences rather than direct intervention deriving from preset goals, using observation, documentation, and evaluation strategies to outline individual profiles, strategies, and personal styles connected to a process- and discourse-oriented representation of children's experience;
- attaching strong importance to organizational managerial structures and educational coordination structures in order to meet the need to ensure adequate and continuing "caring" management. Coordinators are a key figure to act as an external eye, to share reflections upon the project, to perform a supervising function on the educators' work in order to guarantee consistency between the educational project, the resources and the organization;
- defining rules and regulations which may give substance to and set limits for the governance of the system, together with the related regulation and control strategies/procedures.

Although the debate around quality and related issues has been inspired initially by contributions and tools previously worked out in non-Italian contexts (see documents by the European Network and tools like the Italian versions and adaptations of Harms, Cryer, and Clifford, 1990; Ferrari and Livraghi, 1992), a number of specific action/research processes has led to the development of evaluation tools constructed locally with coordinators and caregivers and therefore more directly tailored to specific experiences in Italy (see the cases of Toscana, Emilia Romagna, and Umbria, in Cipollone, 1999; Bondioli and Savio, 1994; Bondioli and Ghedini, 2000).

However, the issue of quality—conditions to achieve it and strategies to evaluate it—is strongly linked to a multidimensional approach toward quality in order to protect and value the idea that, within some common standards, quality has to be defined locally; that it is strictly linked to the local culture, traditions, and situations. Within this general frame of reference it can be understood why little attention is devoted to investigating the relationship between quality of educational services for early childhood and subsequent success in learning on the part of children, the so-called longitudinal effects. This is a theme in which Italian preschool and early education services have never shown much interest, because the cultural, political, and educational reasons to invest in early education and to define and evaluate quality are rooted in the correspondence and compatibility of the services with the community, and with the ideas and representations of children, rather than projected in a more "product-" or performance-oriented perspective that gains strength only when the compulsory school years begin. A "good" service is a service open to all children and good for them in the present, rather than a service that produces good students in the future.

Another feature of quality that has received attention is "perceived quality," a factor that has contributed to but has not determined the definition of instruments and processes of quality control. Even less meaningful has been use of the concept "quality certification" (used in the corporate world), owing to its lack of attention to relationships and processes within educational services.

Some contributions have linked the issues of "quality" and "costs" from two different perspectives.

- to identify "threshold values"—functional and financial at the same time (in terms of number of square metres per child or maximum ratio educators/children) which should be taken as reference in order to make quality possible;
- to understand how, apart from those standards, quality basically depends on the quality of use of available resources;

Some developments within the educational service system over the last two decades have recently drawn attention to the need and potential connection between measuring quality and regulating/controlling a more pluralistic and diversified "market" of educational services for children and families. This has especially been the case with new services (part-time services, mother/toddler groups and company-based crèches) and new providers (cooperatives and other nonprofit organizations). These circumstances have alerted municipalities and regions to the need for the following:

- better defining rules and standards of reference;
- developing new tools to evaluate quality; and
- identifying procedures for regulation and control.

In regions of the country where services are widespread, interesting experiences have already been developed which identify the conceptual area of quality as the point of balance between the following:

- the development/evolution of regulation and standards (e.g. regions like Emilia Romagna and Tuscany have developed a system of regulations encompassing types of services, space standards, staff training requirements, adult/child ratio, etc.);
- the development of specific experiences of traditional and new services;
- the increase in the awareness and professional development of the subject (professionals) involved.

On the other hand, at the national level, the high diversity in the diffusion of early childhood services—the national average of infant–toddler services is around

10 percent, but it ranges from 1 percent to 40 percent—does not encourage a consistent effort to link together the extension of services and the conceptualization of quality standards. In other words, where the quantity of services is very low and far from the demand, both the lack of early childhood "culture" and experience and the pressure for quantity slow down the development of a serious conceptualization about quality.

The process of conceptualizing quality practiced within early childhood services has nevertheless become one of the most important dimensions in professional development and can also contribute to stimulate and update the national choices and policies to develop and qualify the ECEC system.

Further Readings: AAVV (2006). *La qualità dei servizi educativi per l'infanzia in Toscana. Uno strumento per la valutazione della qualità dei nidi e dei servizi integrative.* Firenze: Istituto Degli Innocenti; Bondioli, A., and P. Ghedini, eds. (2000). *La qualità negoziata: Gli indicatori per i nidi della Regione Emilia Romagna.* Azzano San Paolo: Edizioni Junior; Bondioli A., D. Savio (1994). *SVALSI, Scala di valutazione delle abilità ludico-simboliche infantili.* Bergamo: Edizioni Junior; Cipollone, L. (1999). *Strumenti e indicatori per valutare il nido.* Bergamo: Edizioni Junior; Harms, T., D. Cryer, and R. M. Clifford (1990). *Infant/Toddler Environment Rating Scale.* New York: Teachers College Press. (Italian translation and adaptation Ferrari, M., Livraghi, P., *Scala per la valutazione dell'asilo,* Angeli, Milano, 1992); U.O.C. Infanzia ed Adolescenza, Istituto degli Innocenti, ed. (1998). *Manuale per la valutazione della qualità degli asili nido nella regione toscana.* Bergamo: Edizioni Junior. [Handbook for assessment of quality of the infant toddler centers in the region of Tuscany.]

Aldo Fortunati

Curriculum

Italian nursery schools have accepted the idea of a curricular framework with ambivalence. In fact, the very concept of curriculum has emerged long after establishment of the nursery school system and its basic identity defined and shared at local (municipal) and central (state) levels. In a sense many of those involved as coordinators, administrators, researchers, and theorists consider the Italian experience too important to define its educational significance merely in curricular terms. The development of a strong educational model for nursery schools took place well before the idea of curriculum became widespread in the United States and Europe, and educational experiments were in most cases first practiced, and only then diffused from the "bottom up." The need for theoretical justification and a systematic formalization developed later, progressively and over decades, following from widespread community experiments.

Two different interpretations of the word "curriculum" coexist within the nursery school world in Italy. The first is an extensive connotation, where curriculum is intended as "fundamental architecture" of the nursery school system. This involves the established principles and the basic philosophy that inspires the educational model, the results of which are the methodological and didactic choices. The second is an intensive interpretation, according to which curriculum means the contents of knowledge and/or experiences and the methodology adopted to put them into practice.

Curriculum in Extensive Terms

The extensive meaning of curriculum can be traced to the original tradition of Italian nursery schools, where attention was focussed on experience and on practice. For a long time a definition of the schools' pedagogical, methodological, and didactic statutes in formal curricular terms was not deemed necessary or even sought. The nursery schools were established as a local community experience organized around the church or the municipality. The first nursery experiences date back to the beginning of the nineteenth century, and much development took place at the beginning of the twentieth century, sponsored by the large city municipalities in the North and the Center (e.g., **Montessori**'s Children Houses located in city public houses in Rome started in 1912). State nursery schools were first established much later, in 1968. Only then did it become necessary to define guidelines, called orientations and later indications to emphasize their open and flexible character in contrast with the stronger word programs used for compulsory school levels. We can say that in the Italian tradition, the "doing" and "finding solutions" in relation to concrete problems posed by children and community prevailed for many years over any definition of a preventive theoretical "source."

Nursery school has always been a full day experience and the need of working families for care has been always considered and strictly linked to the aim of creating an educational environment. Diverse local experiments of education and care, although inspired by some shared ideas and theories, were the basis on which national guidelines were drawn. These guidelines were defined broadly enough to allow established experiments to accept them and new experiments to flourish, guaranteeing both a common ground and the possibility for local community interpretation of the educational offers for children. Specific methods or locally developed outlines continue to coexist within the national framework. The attempt to devise an official national curriculum can therefore be considered the result partly of the merging of different experiences and partly of research in education and development.

Without using the word curriculum, the famous educators who influenced the nursery schools movement traced outlines for environment, organization, methodology, and content on which the educational offerings could be based.

• Rosa Agazzi (1866–1951), one of the educators who most influenced the Italian system after establishing the school in Mompiano (Brescia) with her sister Teresa, wrote many instruction books on how educators in the *giardino d'infanzia* (kindergarten) should work. Agazzi did her best to achieve an "alive school," and along the route traced by Friedrich **Froebel**, anticipated the "competent child" of later research as an active and creative being who has within himself the potential to grow and educate himself in an environment where daily life experiences become organized in a pedagogical perspective. The pedagogical heritage of Agazzi is in fact the awareness that every educational project must be based on children's real experiences and on their authentic and specific need to grow within their own community. The main task of the kindergarten, therefore, is to promote the child's educational development through action. From Agazzi's perspective competence is essentially linked to doing or acting in an organized way, without the need of special materials but rather with well organized material and objects that could be found in the surrounding environment (the so called museum of little things).

- Maria **Montessori** (1870-1952) was also deeply convinced that each child could command a human potential that only needed an appropriate environment, adequate materials, and respectful and observing teachers to bloom. The environment she proposed was more organized and structured, strewn with stimuli that the child has to find and accommodate to while always following its own rhythm. Montessori assumed that the child already has inside potential and instruments waiting to be practiced and put to good use. Therefore the teacher is not there to "teach" but to allow and promote various intellectual occasions to help the potential to come out, be practiced, and become firmly established. In her words, "... knowledge can be given in the best way when there is a burning desire to learn ... because the mind of the child is like a fertile field, ready to receive what will later sprout in the form of culture. But if the mind of the child ... is neglected, or frustrated in its needs, it becomes artificially dulled and will later oppose the teaching of any notion."

- Directly and indirectly Agazzi and Montessori inspired innumerable other experiences, especially in the north of Italy. The most famous and original in its reinterpretation of part of their tradition is that of **Reggio Emilia**, where **Loris Malaguzzi**, the director and inspirer of the nursery schools that developed from a strong community effort right after the Second World War, turned his attention in particular to the constructive creative child. Children "think," they have ideas, they construct projects and try to fulfil them. From the beginning Malaguzzi wanted the school to be wide open to the parents and to the city. The school is deeply rooted in the area; it "belongs to" and represents the local community. The teacher must be capable, well qualified, and cultivated, and the children's competence and creativity become visible through long lasting cooperative projects and art. Malaguzzi, drawing from Agazzi, Montessori, Freinet, and Bruno Ciari, from his own cultural and artistic experiences, and from the numerous experiments that were popping up in many cities in the 1970s, sketches children who are the following:

1. *Expressive*—endowed with ample creative capacity. It is important to propose expressive activities, such as painting, graphic expression, drama, dressing up, storytelling, etc. With their imagination, and through constant dialogue and interaction with other children and with listening and provoking adults, children focus on their ideas, think them over, elaborate and reformulate them. Children have the right not only to appropriate but also to beautiful environments, painting, music, and everything that is expression at the highest level.

2. *Constructive*—endowed with minds capable of observing, gathering information, discussing that information and assembling it in original ways, with curiosity and with a strong inclination toward exploration. This can happen when children are placed in conditions encouraging them to be protagonists and active participants.

3. *Manual and visual*—children's minds are strongly connected to the body, hands, and eyes, and it is necessary to give precedence to the practical abilities that are both essential for the solving of everyday problems and also useful for checking hypotheses and ideas, choosing and finding solutions etc. The hand guides the mind and is guided by the mind.

4. *Social*—expression, creativity, and learning happen through interaction, dialogue, and continuous negotiations between children, between children and adults, and between school and community.

Curriculum in Intensive Terms

The intensive meaning of curriculum can be found by following the progressive political engagement at State level, official documents, and scientific literature on early childhood education.

The following three steps mark the national nursery school system:

- The institution of State Nursery Schools in 1968 and the subsequent *Orientamenti per la Scuola Materna* (1969).
- The revision of these Guidelines, which took placc in 1991 rethinking the pedagogical framework (*Nuovi Orientamenti per la Scuola Materna*). The revised text was widely discussed at the community level and in the academic and professional networks before being issued, and therefore contributed to a considerable cultural relaunching of nursery schools. It is based on three main educational goals or key words: reinforcing the child's identity, supporting the acquisition of autonomy, and the recognizing and sustaining of the child's competence.
- The third National document subsequent to the school reform bill issued in 2004 (*Indicazioni Nazionali per i Piani Personalizzati nella Scuola dell'Infanzia*) does not substantially change the general framework of 1991. The novelty in this document is that the general objectives of the educational process are spelled out in specific objectives of learning and broad areas called *campi di esperienza* (experience fields): self and others, body, movement and health, message fruition and production, exploration, knowledge, and planning. The criteria for documentation and evaluation (Portfolio of individual competences) are illustrated through many items and examples.

The *Indicazioni* are a move toward curricular organization in a perspective closer to a great part of the American and European debate. But they are perceived by many teachers and experts in the Italian early education field as a rigidifying and impoverishment of the nursery school experience, in its variety and developing culture. They can be regarded as a compromise (not very good but not too bad) between the "good practices" developed in many communities, the theories currently at hand and the need for specific orientation of schools and areas where the *cultura dell'infanzia* (the culture of childhood) and the *servizi educativi per l'infanzia e la famiglia* (educational services for children and families) have not yet developed.

Good Practice

The concept or principle of good practice refers on one hand to a model (a conceptual scheme in which different aspects of educational life can be connected and ordered in relation to a teleological principle that insures organic unity and coherence), and on the other hand to the structure of the experience (all the forms that the model assumes or can assume practically, in relation to possible or historical and social situations). The structure is the visible variable distinguished by the things that are done, by the everyday situations, by the choices made at the moment. The model is the hidden variable that indicates the principles that inspire and infer the structure and are often implicit.

Two different outlooks, holistic or molecular, can be retraced in the different local experiences. They correspond broadly to the extensive and intensive approach to curriculum. The holistic perspective prefers a global form of guidelines in which attention to the overall context of the child's life prevails. The molecular perspective generally prefers to identify specific steps to reach knowledge and competence. The holistic experiments prefer wide-ranging aims that incorporate daily life, the caring aspects, and social and community experiences into the curriculum. They see the nursery school as a place in life where global experiences such as constructing one's identity, attaining self-sufficiency, making relationships with peers, interaction with the community culture and the attention to processes are a priority. The molecular perspective pays more attention to problems regarding teaching methodology and the contents of learning, with specific performance goals and a stronger preoccupation with results.

One perspective does not exclude the other. They are trends. In Italy, broadly speaking and with many exceptions, the first dominates in the municipal schools (e.g., Reggio Emilia) and the second in state and private schools. In many schools the two perspectives actually coexist due to the way the system has developed in a single city or school or to the influence of local experts.

The Domestic Child and the Apprentice Child

Finally, two further polarized concepts influence the thought and the practices connected with nursery school curriculum: the idea of the domestic child and that of the apprentice child. The school for the domestic child is the school that places more emphasis on everyday aspects, which recalls the idea of home, proposes global contexts, and focuses primarily on experiences lived by the child. Routines and caring aspects (i.e., common meals) are considered important and built into the curriculum, and when activities are proposed, including cognitive ones, this is done within a global approach. The child's day is full of activities that have much to do with everyday life, organization, symbolic play, relationships between peers and between children and adults. Evaluation is also a global concept and not a priority in its traditional formulation.

The apprentice child's school, on the contrary, sees itself as real school, with the main goal to enhance knowledge. It aims at a precise educational and teaching program, and it articulates its activity in more classic curricular terms. It looks at evaluation as a means of keeping a check on the teacher's work.

The Searching Child

The idea of the domestic child is clearly no longer enough if the apprentice's complementary dimension is missing. At the same time, the idea of the apprentice child exposes the nursery school to the limits of an institution aimed only at results, which can fail to recognize the intrinsic value of childhood, and which risks transmitting an established body of knowledge while overlooking the importance for the child of gaining confidence and producing knowledge himself. The capacity to progressively discover, face, and solve problems seems linked to being given the possibility and having the time needed to mature internally and to work socially. The searching child, offered an environment rich in social, cognitive, and aesthetic opportunities together with the time to explore, play, discuss, and think at his own pace, expressing himself in a hundred languages and evaluated using practices centered on documentation, seems to be an appropriate synthesis of the two current Italian traditions for looking at curriculum as an evolving concept.

Further Readings: Agazzi, R. C. (1960). *Lingua parlata.* Brescia: Editrice La Scuola; Bertin, G. M. (1973). *Educazione alla ragione.* Armando Armando Editore; Battista Borghi, Q. (2001). *Coro di bimbi a Mompiano.* Bergamo: Junior; Edwards, C., L. Gandini, and G. Forman, eds. (1998). *The hundred languages of children: The Reggio Emilia approach-advanced reflections.* 2nd ed. Stamford, CT: Ablex; Ministero della Pubblica Istruzione, Servizio per la Scuola Materna (1991). *Nuovi orientamenti per la scuola materna.* Rome: Ministero della Pubblica Instruccione; Montessori, M. (1992 [1943]). *Come educare il potenziale umano.* Milan: Garzanti.

Battista Quinto Borghi

Literacy

In Italy, as in many other places, the term "literacy" entails multiple meanings: from a general and vague familiarity with the written language to the ways through which people gain their abilities to read and to write. In English literature we find the terms of "emergent literacy" or "early literacy" related to the initial and noninstitutionalized approaches to written language. The corresponding Italian words "alfabetizzazione" and "alfabetizzazione iniziale" are slightly different from the English terms because they mainly refer to the mastery of the notational system used for writing, that is, the ability to say and write the letters of a word in the correct order. In fact, these terms are actually acquiring a wider meaning concerning both the children's ideas and hypotheses about the structure and function of their system of writing and the ways cultural, educative, and familiar contexts promote these processes.

As regards the ways that early childhood education addresses literacy practices in Italy, the situation is very variegated: ranging from direct instruction perspectives, which offer scripted, teacher-directed lessons (charts, guides, assessment handbooks), to child-initiated approaches, which view young children as active constructors of knowledge who are not dependent on didactic instructional cues from a teacher. The historical, intellectual, and cultural conditions that formulated our early childhood curriculum guidelines are based on a holistic approach in which children are seen as social beings who acquire a framework for interpreting experiences through social life. In fact, because the tradition of Italian early childhood education considers the sphere of social interaction between children as the basic learning context for the construction of knowledge, the following statements characterize approaches to written language teaching:

• the development of the individual cannot be understood without taking into account his or her interaction with other people, that is, child learns to write by interacting with people in very different situations and contexts;

- the social environment is itself influenced by the wider culture, that is, the nature and uses of written language are related to specific and varied social conditions and practices.

Considering the first statement, early childhood education has emphasized the importance of social interactions within learning to read and write. This approach leads to the following two concerns:

a. *Adult-child interaction* in the classroom, in particular the support and stimulation that teachers provide to pupils. In fact, throughout different kinds of techniques, as for example, repeating, reformulating, or asking for an explanation, teachers can encourage pupils to specify and evaluate their working hypotheses, as well as to develop their hypotheses and to find counter examples to test their conclusions. Further, teachers can help their students to approach written language by acting as readers and writers themselves. Teachers who do not write or read cannot sensitively help others learn to write and to read. In this sense particular importance is given to story telling during early childhood, since pleasure in reading is built throughout an affective relation with a meaningful adult. Libraries in preschool, reading spaces in nurseries, and reading activities and proposals for young children in town libraries, have therefore increased in the last years. As regards the role of the teacher as a model of writer, some studies show how writing in front of the pupils is useful for them in order to discover some of the writing system proprieties (such as the direction of writing, the segmentation between the words, the punctuation, etc.), and some of the written language aspects (such as the different kinds of genres). Besides, in the dictation situations, according to the type of text the group is producing (narrative, instructional texts, or letters), pupils develop different kinds of interventions, and this confirms children's textual awareness or sensitiveness.

b. *Peer interaction.* Several studies report that peer interaction facilitates children's learning in the classroom by delineating those aspects of cooperative learning that are involved in successful arrangements. In general, research suggests that cooperation is most useful for the kind of learning that involves conceptual change. Because learning to write is considered a conceptual learning, the research in this field has showed how the exchange of ideas among children is particularly effective for planning and writing a text, so as to understand the sense of a text when it's read. Construction of knowledge is facilitated when a child tries to put his or her knowledge into relationship with ideas that are at a similar level, because children have points of view that are more or less alike.

Regarding the idea that the social environment is itself influenced by the wider culture, most of the Italian studies conclude that literacy practices should be proposed within authentic communication situations and through the use of real texts. The first point is based on the importance that is assigned to the fact that children should discover the utility, the power, and the pleasure that reading and writing give them. In other words, school should contribute to the development of adults who are linguistically competent, in order to be able to produce an adequate and effective text according to the communication context, that is, citizens of the written culture. Therefore, in classroom approaches the emphasis is put in writing and reading text with clear proposals and real addressees, rather than writing exercises and skills that are usually not contextualized. The second point is based on the importance that is assigned to exposing children to different genres and types of text and text containers, to encourage them to discover their proprieties and characteristics.

In summary, literacy in Italian preschools is mainly connected with activities related to children's knowledge construction processes, to invented or spontaneous spelling and to spontaneous reading throughout the exchange of ideas among peers and the adults. In these contexts teachers have a significant role because they have to encourage children to exchange points of view among themselves, in order to promote either the revision, the consolidation, or the transformation of their hypothesis without imposing the adult vision of the writing system. At the same time, teachers have to represent the written culture throughout, offering a variety of genres and types of texts, encouraging authentic reading and writing practices and acting as an expert in the written language.

Regarding the research about how children move toward literacy prior to any schooling, most of the Italian studies have looked at how children construct the principles of their writing system within educational contexts. This linked relationship between research and school contexts has provided teachers and curriculum planners with the voice of children, which helps them to understand the possible reasons underlying a particular difficulty in order to clarify the role of errors in the learning processes. The research findings in this field have important educational implications, not only for the design of activities but also for evaluating children's linguistic knowledge.

It was considered central to study the interplay between children's hypotheses about the writing system and the conventional rules of correspondence between phonemes and graphemes or between oral, signed, and written forms in the Italian language. Other studies have noted that young children are content-sensitive, that is, they do not write all the words when they are asked to write down sentences dictated to them. In fact, most young children do not write marks for articles, qualifiers, or even verbs when asked to write full sentences, nor do they "read" or anticipate these categories of words separately when they are asked to "read" a written sentence. They only consider the full nouns, a fact that indicates that children in some moments of early literacy develop sensitivity to the referential meaning of what they represent through writing. In the same direction, a sort of "semantic phase" was demonstrated in response to the request that they write some words and their diminutives (in Italian they are formed by using suffixes that generate words that are always longer compared to the base word although the object referred to is smaller) and plurals (that, although representing a more numerous set, only require a change in the final vowel in spoken and written Italian). The researchers found out that about one-third of the children tried to keep in their writings the similarities of the semantic field of the base word in diminutives and plurals, while changing the dimensions or the order of the marks used in the first case or repeating marks for the plural.

Another dimension studied concerns the children's awareness of or sensitivity to the type or genre of texts they were asked to write down or to read. Two main methodologies have been used within this approach: either the child is asked to dictate his/her text to the researcher, or after the child has written his/her text, the researcher, hearing what the child verbalizes, rewrites it in conventional writing. The textual awareness was shown in the former approach throughout the content of the text they had just dictated and in the latter approach throughout the differences in the graphic layout children produced as well as in the content of the oral text they elaborated when reading what they had written. These studies have demonstrated that long before children read and write in a conventional way, they are sensitive to certain grammatical, rhetorical, and lexical devices for written language and distinguish between different genres.

These findings suggest that the distinction between the knowledge of the writing system and the knowledge of written language cannot be strictly maintained from the point of view of the child writer. They encourage future approaches that are undertaken within a more integrated vision about both types of knowledge and a more integrated vision about the ways in which genre and writing conventions interplay not only in writing but also in reading.

Further Readings: Ferreiro, E. (2003). *Teoria e pratica dell'alfabetizzazione*. Milano: Raffaello Cortina Editore; Pascucci, M. (2005). *Come scrivono i bambini*. Roma: Carocci; Pontecorvo, C. (1995). Iconicity in children's first written text. In R. Simone, ed., *Iconicity and language*, pp. 55-76. Amsterdam: John Benjamins; Pontecorvo, C., ed. (1997). *Writing development*. Amsterdam: John Benjamins; Pontecorvo, C., ed. (1999). *Manuale di psicologia dell'educazione*. Bologna: Il Mulino; Pontecorvo, C. and C. Zucchermaglio (1988). Modes of differentiation in children's writing construction. *European Journal of Psychology of Education* 3(4), 371-384; Pontecorvo, C. and R. M. Morani (1996). Looking for stylistic features in children's composing stories: Products and processes. In C. Pontecorvo, M. Orsolini, M. Bruge, and L. Resnik, eds., (1996). *Children's early text construction*. Hillsdale, NJ: Lawrence Erlbaum Associates, pp. 229-259; Pontecorvo, C., M. Orsolini, M. Bruge, and L. Resnik, eds. (1996). *Children's early Text Construction*. Hillsdale, NJ: Lawrence Erlbaum Associates; Simone, R., ed. (1995). *Iconicity and language*. Amsterdam: John Benjamins; Tolchinsky, L., ed. (2001). *Development Aspects in learning to write*. Dordrecht, The Netherlands: Kluwer Academic Publishers; Zucchermaglio, C., and N. Scheuer (1996). Children dictating a story: Is together better? In C. Pontecorvo, M. Orsolini, M. Bruge, and L. Resnik, eds., *Children's early text construction*. Hillsdale, NJ: Lawrence Erlbaum Associates, pp. 83-99; Zucchermaglio, C. (1991). *Gli apprendisti della lingua scritta*. Bologna: Il Mulino.

Lilia Teruggi

Socioemotional Development

In Italy, the socioemotional aspects of children's experiences in early childhood educational settings are considered an important educational dimension. This attention is due partly to the cultural context within which the early childhood educational services were expanded in the 1960s and 1970s.

Historical Antecedents

First the expansion of the *scuole dell'infanzia* and then the establishment of the *nidi* later was achieved under pressure from the trade union and women's movement, aimed at reconciling child care with women's participation in the labor market. This historical process has left important traces in the organization of the services managed by the local authorities—and later also by the national authorities—in which different forms of parent participation in the services were introduced, such as their involvement in management aspects (*gestione sociale*) and other social events, such as parties, outings, or discussions regarding educational topics. This historical origin of these educational services also contributed to stimulating discussion of their significance in the life of families and on their impact on the development of the child–mother relationship. In opposition to a psychoanalytical approach, which predicted negative consequences on the establishment of an attachment bond deriving from early separation of the child from the mother, early childhood educational practices stressed the importance of guaranteeing significant relationships between teachers and each child and children's early social experiences with their peers. These goals translated into some good quality educational practices that spread widely throughout the country and were aimed at sustaining children's socioemotional development. These practices contributed to characterizing the new services in an innovative perspective compared with previous forms of child care, and to giving them a different educational identity from that of the primary school, which aimed essentially at knowledge acquisition.

The Child–Teacher Relationship

Early childhood pedagogy has had to match itself with two different existing models of the relationship between teachers and children. One model repeats at an early age a type of relationship designed to have the child acquire the social norms or cognitive behavior and motor abilities required for later formal learning. This model has long predominanted in the *scuole dell'infanzia*. According to the other model, more widespread in the *nidi*, adults were given a function essentially involving the control and promotion of the physical well-being of the children and substituting for their mothers' care. In actual educational practice, within both types of service a conception of the adult's role different from either of these models emerged, according to which the teacher aims at encouraging the children's process of discovery of the physical and social environment and at supporting them on both the affective and the cognitive levels. Within this perspective, the educational context has to be set up to allow teachers to intervene in the children's activities in a nondirective way—with concern to communicative style and content. The teacher's intervention aims to enter the children's ongoing social and cognitive processes without disrupting them, as well as to guarantee that each child will benefit from her exclusive attention, particularly during physical care. The importance of constructing significant stable relations between children and teachers was also stressed. Both in the *nidi* and in the *scuole dell'infanzia*, the teachers themselves accompany the same group of children throughout the years of their attendance. In the *nidi*, which have a larger teacher's team, there is a widespread practice of identifying a specific teacher for each child as a reference person for both the child and her/his parents. Discussions and practices involving the relations between children and teachers have contributed to showing that in the educational settings the children have to cope with a complex social context, which differs from that experienced at home and involves a plurality of adults and children.

Social Contacts with Peers

The attention focused on social contacts with peers received strong support from studies carried out in Italy and other countries in the 1970s and 1980s on children's competence in interacting with peers at an early age. These studies showed that as early as the middle of the first year of life, if children are seated near each other on the rug, they succeed in soliciting reciprocal attention and then in exchanging objects. In the *nidi* it became common practice to place the younger children on a rug with their toys in a position that would favor visual and physical contact among them. Research also showed that toddlers are able to direct social behaviors toward their peers (glances, smiles, motor acts, and utterances), to respond to behavior directed toward them, and to produce relatively long interactive sequences. However, such phenomena can vary greatly according to the quality of the relations between the children and the organization of the context.

Social familiarity, defined as the mutual knowledge of the children based on their repeated meeting, was found to be a basic factor in determining the quantity and quality of children's interactions. In the *nidi* educational practice, this involved providing the children with opportunities to gain knowledge of their reciprocal identities, characteristics, and preferences. Care is taken that, at the time of their first entry to the *nido*, newcomers are introduced to children already attending, and that each child will learn the names of all the other children (e.g., by means of various forms of daily roll call, during which they repeat the names of all the other children, showing interest in the reasons for the absence of certain children, involving telephone calls to the latter's home). When talking to children, the teachers take care to call out the name of each child, to speak of a specific emotional mood or the preferences or requests of an individual child and to make their reasons explicit also to the other children. This support given to mutual knowledge of the peer's identity and emotions has positive effects on the socioemotional climate in the educational context. Even in *nidi* it is frequently possible to observe the development of significant relations among children.

The Importance of Context

Research has also indicated that the frequency and quality of the interaction among children vary as a function of contextual variables such as the number of children present, the number of toys available, the activities prompted by these objects. These findings, together with **Montessori**-based educational suggestions, are strongly echoed in educational practice of both Italian *nidi* and *scuole dell'infanzia*. Two procedures in particular are widespread. The first is that of the arrangement of play areas characterized by a specific theme. These areas are spatially limited and contain materials suitable for performing specific exploration and play activities. They have a two-fold function: of encouraging the gathering of a small number of children, and of orienting their activities on the same topic, thus favoring sharing among the children. The second procedure, partially related to the first, is to arrange the educational contexts in such a way that the children may often find themselves in small groups during the play and exploration activities. This educational goal affects the service organization at various levels. It is necessary, for instance, to arrange teachers' work schedules so that a greater number of them will be present during the hours of play activity, to organize the environments and play materials to allow and/or favor the division of the children into small groups. A large variety of solutions have been found according to the type of service—*nido* or *scuola dell'infanzia*, its architectural structure, and the number of children attending. It must be stressed that all the solutions are based on the idea that the ratio between the number of teachers and number of children must be evaluated with reference to the quality of the social contexts set up for children. In some cases, as in the educational practice of Pistoia and **Reggio Emilia** services, teachers aim also to support children's shared activities over time, encouraging their repetition, and the maintenance of their products or other outcomes.

Parent Interests and Attitudes

Parents have also paid increasing attention to the socioemotional aspects of the children's experience in the educational services. Surveys conducted over the past decades in different sites concerning parents' satisfaction with *nido* experience have always shown that they pay particular attention to the relations between teachers and the children. However, providing the children with social experiences with peers has been found to increasingly motivate parents' demand for educational services for toddlers. This demand also includes services that offer only social experiences with peers for just a few hours per day and in the company of the parents. It has been argued that this demand stems from both the large number of only children in Italian families and the positive social experience gained by a growing number of children in the educational services.

Further Readings: Mantovani, S., and T Musatti, eds. (1983). *Adulti e bambini: educare e comunicare. La ricerca in asilo nido 1.* Bergamo: Juvenilia; Musatti, T. (1986). Early peer relations: The perspectives of Piaget and Vygotsky. In E. Mueller and C. Cooper, eds., *Process and outcome in peer relationships.* New York: Academic Press, pp. 25–53; Musatti, T., and M. Picchio (2005). *Un luogo per bambini e genitori nella città. Trasformazioni sociali e innovazione nei servizi per l'infanzia e le famiglie.* Bologna: Il Mulino;.Rullo, G., and T. Musatti (2005). Mothering young children: Child care, stress and social life. *European Journal of Psychology of Education* XX (2), 107–119; Stambak, M., M. Barriére, L. Bonica, R. Maisonnet, T. Musatti, S. Rayna, and M. Verba (1983). *Les bébés entre eux: inventer, decouvrir et jouer ensemble.* Paris: Presses Universitaires de France; Verba, M, and T. Musatti (1989). Minor phenomena and major processes of interaction with objects and peers in day-care center. *European Journal of Psychology of Education* IV, 215–227.

Tullia Musatti

Infant/Toddler Care

Infant/toddler care is provided in Italy mainly by *asili nido*, also called *nidi d'infanzia* (*nido* in Italian means nest). These are educational services for children between the ages of 3 months (when compulsory maternity leave for working mothers generally ends) and 3 years, when nursery school starts. Since 1971 *asili nido* have been run at the city level and planned on a regional basis. They offer a full-time service. The normal school day ranges from 8:00 A.M.–9:00 A.M. to 4:00 P.M.–5:00 P.M. Monday through Friday. Some children attend only part time and leave after lunch, and extended hours are usually provided at family request between 7:30 A.M. and 6:00 P.M. In the public settings families pay according to income on a sliding scale.

Italian *asili nido* should not be considered either a "program" for infants and toddlers or mere "day care," but rather as *educational services for children and families*, where education and care are built into a full daily experience for children that includes routines (meals, sleep, toilet), extended social experiences with peers and adults, and educational opportunities for the development of a child with a strong sense of identity, a progressive autonomy and articulated social and expressive skills.

In recent years many cooperatives, other nonprofit organizations and profit-oriented companies have entered the infant/toddler care scene as a consequence of a steadily growing demand among middle-class families (who were traditionally organizing early childhood care within their homes), the increasing number of working mothers, and the growing number of immigrant families with young children (who are currently about 25 percent of the users of these services in big cities).

Demand for Infant–Toddler Services

National data indicate a figure of 10 percent of children attending this type of care, but the percentage rises to 20–25 percent in the cities of the North and the Center of the country and reaches 30–40 percent in some regions. Demand usually greatly exceeds supply, and therefore in the past five years a growing number of companies has opened *asili nido* for their employees, encouraged by tax cuts and some direct state funding, and many private for-profit settings are popping up. It is generally agreed, however, that public *asili nido* set the quality standards, offering more than the minimum standards required by regional regulations concerning staff qualification, adult/child ratio, space, health, and safety requirements. Adult/child ratio is in general 1/5–1/6 for children between 3 and 12 months and 1/8–1/9 for children between 12 and 36 months. Six/eight square meters are at an average required for each enrolled child as well as special bathrooms, sleep spaces reserved for children, and open playgrounds. Only centers serving less than twelve children are allowed, in some regions, to meet more flexible standards. Centers are usually organized in two or three age groups unless they are very small. Children with special needs and disabilities have priority and their access as well as some regulated forms of parent participation are requirements for public recognition and funding. Centers that obtain public funding cannot deny access to any child because of family background, ethnicity, religion, or special needs. In the case of special needs the city usually supports the center with extra staff. *Asili nido* are, therefore, conceived as potentially for all children whose families wish or need them.

Staffing

At present (2006), staff is not required to have a postsecondary (college or university) degree. They have either to have attended a high school oriented toward the education and child-care professions or to have an undergraduate degree in education, but the number of well-qualified caregivers is steadily growing and it is likely that the three-year postsecondary degree will soon become compulsory. In-service training is provided on a regular basis—in general 150–200 paid hours per year are foreseen for further training, team meetings, and work with parents. This probably accounts for the widely recognized quality level many city systems of infant/toddler care have attained. At this time infant/toddler centers are usually included in the education department of the municipality and are run in continuity with the municipal nursery schools. In most cities the direction, professional development, and educational planning is under the responsibility of a *coordinatore pedagogico* or *pedagogista*, an expert in education with a postgraduate degree who is generally in charge of a number of centers in the area. These coordinators act as a team in the city or inter-city area, and also supervise private settings that receive public funding, creating a so-called *integrated* system.

Other Types of Services

Since the mid-1980s other forms of infant/toddler care have been first tested and then widely established (law 285, 1998), including mother/toddler centers, part time services, play libraries, family centers with some day-care provision attached to other health or social services, centers especially focussed on immigrant mothers, "bridge" classes for 2-year-olds located in nursery school annexes, etc. The first of these "new" services was *Tempo per le Famiglie* (Time for Families) established in Milan in 1985, then rapidly followed by a number of other experiments in Pistoia, Modena, Rome, etc. A peculiar feature of these flexible services, created to meet a wider range of families with young children and to support early education and parenting in various ways, is that they have appeared and grown as a development of city public services. This has often involved the experienced staff of traditional infant/toddler centers, and thus has contributed to the development and enrichment of the educational network for children and families.

Changing Attitudes Toward Infant/Toddler Care

As in many other countries, ambivalent attitudes greeted the development of full-time educational services for the very young. The question of possible negative effects of attending out-of-home care was raised in the 1970s when infant/toddler centers were still meant only for working mothers or mothers in need. Gradually, however, the trust of families in the choice of sharing the rearing and education of infants with professionals grew, influenced by the development of an educational concept for early childhood education and expansion of the nursery school experience, by clinical psychology and ecological approaches, and by emerging practices of constant connection between centers and home (the attention given to transition processes and in general to the emotional *benessere* (well-being and well feeling) of children and adults). The increasing attention to the child's emotional and social needs as well as to the parents' needs, doubts and anxieties was a stimulus to the testing and establishment of a very particular set of practices for encouraging and ritualizing a gradual transition into the care setting called *inserimento* or *ambientamento*. Transition lasts in general two weeks, based on the needs of the child and his /her parents, and is officially specified as a routine practice in all municipal guidelines for infant/toddler services.

Whether or not infant/toddler care is good for children is no longer a debate in contemporary Italy, and the extensive research carried out in the United States and in other countries on the topic is viewed with scepticism. First, "effects" seem correlated in many studies with day-care variables not well defined in terms of the quality of the care itself. Which day-care centers produce such effects? How are their transition practices and parent involvement practices designed to build participation and relationships? What is the quality of peer interaction, significant relationships between infants and caregivers, daily routines, space and environment? Scores obtained with different assessment instruments (e.g., Harms, Crycr, Clifford, 1990-tr.it.1992), although interesting as an analysis and training tool for staff, do not seem to be sensitive enough to account for crucial variables in quality. Second, there is a widespread mistrust for research paradigms which emphasize the interest in the longitudinal effects of an experience as complex as daily life in an infant/toddler center ahead of the analysis of the quality and value of childhood *hic et nunc*; that is, which do not take into account context variables such as the alternative choices available to families, the link between centers and community, and the attitudes of parents toward this educational choice. It is felt that these studies are biased and not likely to have a constructive impact on policies.

Demand for early education and care is growing together with the trust toward existing municipal services. Infant/toddler centers are now considered to be well-balanced "daily life contexts" where the children can find a more extended social experience than within the family. The Italian birthrate, at 1.2 children per woman of childbearing age, is one of the lowest in the world, and "only children" are in the majority. With the potential to facilitate development, to foster autonomy and to encourage parents to find advice and support from peers and professionals, infant/toddler centers are increasingly considered the best solution for the care of children under the age of 3. Even middle-class parents declare that they prefer this setting to other forms of private care because it enhances social development and because they trust good professionals. They are prepared to pay rather high fees even in public centers, which can become much higher in the case of private provision even when time schedules are not fully compatible with their working hours. Leaving children in centers for more than eight to nine hours is in fact strongly discouraged. Parents feel secure about leaving their children in well-supervised, healthy, and safe environments where professional adults have as their specific focus enhancing the well-being of the child, supporting and involving parents, and offering and documenting rich, social, and educational experiences.

Changed and positive attitudes of families and experts toward infant/toddler care outside the family are the result of many factors, including the following:

- the development of the caregiver into a professional and educator and a support and consultant for parents;
- the attention to routines as fundamental opportunities for relationships, sense and control of the bodily functions and opportunity for progressive autonomy;
- the increased knowledge and sensitivity toward the emotional and intellectual needs of young children, the importance of peer relationships and of educational opportunities where exploration and long-lasting cooperative projects are made possible and can be carried out;
- the continuity of care that allows caregiver, children, and parents to invest in relationships that can extend over three years;
- the encouragement and possibility of parent involvement;
- the refinement and flexibility of transition practices;
- the attention to the safety, richness, and aesthetics of the environment;
- the accurate choice and development of diverse materials;
- the importance given to symbolic play and storytelling and the first approaches to art through manipulation of different materials, music and rhythm, and movement;
- documentation as a tool for tracking progress, supporting memory, and making visible children's culture and potential.

Each setting develops its own identity, projects, and materials, but practices, processes, materials, and documentation are widely shared through the contacts within and across the city systems of services. The main network systems are two magazines for professionals (*Bambini, Infanzia*, etc.) and the *Gruppo Nazionale Nidi Infanzia*, an association which had Loris Malaguzzi as first president, which networks through conferences, seminars, publications, and researches but has also developed in an advocacy agency recognized at a national level.

In the past decade the debate over quality and about how to define, assess, and guarantee has stirred the system of early childhood education, and several regions and cities have activated processes of discussion, analysis, and development of instruments and criteria (see the Quality entry, below). National Guidelines setting standards exist only at a local level, accounting in part for the diversity found across settings and municipalities.

Challenges

The current challenges for the system of *asili nido* are numerous. The most critical is pressure for expansion and the high costs push local authorities toward outsourcing and "buying" places from cooperatives or profit centers. Therefore the coordination, control, and guarantee of the same levels of quality is at risk. The development of competent staff requires time and higher qualifications at a time when a strong generational change and turnover is expected. The increasing number of immigrant children challenges the capacity of the system to face this new form of inclusion and emphasize the crucial role of early childhood services in supporting them as they first approach the community and become active within it. New parents are in a good position for reciprocal recognition, interaction, and the overcoming of prejudice and mistrust if they share with their children a good educational and care experience and are supported by open and experienced staff. This opportunity should not be missed. Italian infant/toddler centers have grown in thirty-five years to be looked at as "good places" potentially for all children. It will be interesting to see whether they can keep the pace with the demands, conflict, and changes of contemporary times.

Further Readings: Harms, T., D. Cryer, R. M. Clifford (1990/tr. 1992). *La Svani: Scale per la valutazione dell' asilo nido.* Milan: Franco Angeli. Mantovani, S., L. R. Saitta, and C. Bove (2000). *Attaccamento e inserimento. Stili e storie delle relazioni al nido.* Milano: Franco Angeli; Mantovani, S. (2001). Infant toddler centers in Italy today: Tradition and innovation. In L. P. Gandini, and C. P. Edwards, eds., *Bambini. The Italian approach to infant toddler care.* New York: Teachers College Press, pp. 23–38; Musatti, T. (1992). *La giornata del mio bambino.* Bologna: Il Mulino, Bologna; OECD (2001). Starting strong, early childhood education and care. Paris: The Organization for Economic Cooperation and Development.

Web Sites: www.minori,it www.istitutodeglinnocenti.it

Susanna Mantovani

Parent Involvement

History and Changes Over Time

Home-school relations and parental involvement have been conceptualized in Italian early childhood education as *partecipazione*—a term that implies parents, teachers, children and other members of the community take an active part in the life, culture, and decisions concerning children and the educational services created for them. At its origins, in the late 1960s and early 1970s, *partecipazione* was strictly connected with another term *gestione sociale*, meaning "community-based management." *Gestione sociale* is the practice of sharing responsibilities in managing institutions and services between caregivers, educators, parents, and other community members. Interpreted as a political principle, it was initially aimed at organizing forms of democratic control of public services by their users. *Gestione sociale* originated in Italy in early childhood services, and then spread and transformed into a more specific but unfortunately an often more bureaucratized form of parent engagement in school life regulated in 1974 by a national law.

Today each infant/toddler center or preschool has a committee or council where families are represented though elections, but the spontaneous participation that was at the origin of many early educational services in the 1960s and 1970s has faded and is only alive in municipal services and in cities where civic and political engagement is strong. Early childhood educational services often emerged from a bottom-up movement. As they became strongly rooted in the community, educators and caregivers began to experiment with various different strategies for involving parents. *Partecipazione* was transformed into a civic and educational engagement, and involvement of parents in a series of practices that connect home and school and are now a main trait of Italian early childhood education. Originally political, *partecipazione* is still a community matter. It is often the first step of young families into the public and social life of the community, the first contact with public services and their rules, and a potentially effective "playground" for becoming integrated and active community members.

After some years of disengagement and of a stronger demand for more individualized relationships and support, parents seem today to value the opportunity offered by early childhood educational services to meet and built social and friendship networks and to become active in advocating for quality services for their children. Over the years, after the first decade where engagement was at its strongest and early childhood education a hot political issue, *partecipazione* has been spelled out in a more personal sense. This has involved developing the transition practices, individual interviews, parent groups, daily encounters, and common initiatives which can be important opportunities for families, often isolated after the birth of their child, for sharing and discussing the educational issues. Today it can be considered both a pedagogical and a social concept, referring to any process designed to construct a web of human relationships between the family and the school and encompassing practices of communication and sharing responsibilities and practices enacted by caregivers and teachers to involve parents and support them.

Contributing Factors

Early childhood education in Italy is a system with a high degree of continuity in relationships. Children stay in the same preschool with the same caregivers/teachers group for three years, and this encourages a high investment in building and cultivating relationships inside and outside the school (see Infant/Toddler Care entry). When asked, parents and teachers say that the family has the fundamental responsibility for educating children in terms of orienting them to the most important values—moral and/or religious—but school is seen as an important partner and has the fundamental task of creating a context where children can experience and learn sociability and where adults are socialized too and can offer a consistent model. Parents feel that social experience and creative self-expression in play and other languages come first as the most important achievements early educational services should pursue, and cognitive performance ranks only as third priority at this age level. Welcoming children into infant /toddler groups and schools, attuning the transition from home to school, fostering autonomy without interrupting attachment bonds, and creating and supporting a network of relationships among children and parents is therefore considered one of the most important tasks of early childhood educational service, especially for the very young.

The tradition of family participation and involvement which marked the origins of municipal infant–toddler care generated times and spaces and the conceptual basis for developing partnership with parents. Parental involvement is therefore not only one of the major pedagogical axes of the best experiments in early childhood education—in cities like **Reggio Emilia**, Modena, Pistoia, Parma, Trento, San Miniato, etc.—but also one of the important criteria used today in assessing the quality of early childhood services and in the professional development of teachers. At least four hours are usually devoted by staff per month to meetings and interviews with parents, and it is considered as paid time just as the hours worked with children.

Forms of Parent Involvement

Parental involvement takes the following several forms:

- participation on the elected board (*comitato di gestione*) which participates in decisions about access, waiting lists, and expenditures;
- daily communication between parents and teachers during drop-off and pick-up time. Most infant/toddler centers have a special place where parents can sit with their children or among themselves when arriving and before leaving;
- practices and rituals for gradually transitioning the child and his /her parents into the center (*inserimento*);
- regular interviews and group meetings to share ideas on education, life with children, and school projects;
- informal meetings on special occasions (Christmas, Carnival, end of the year, open days, etc).

The relationship with the family begins even before the real entrance of the child into child care. Once the child has been accepted, parents are invited to visit the center in the presence of other children so that they get familiarized with the center's environment by observing them go through their daily schedule. Meetings with other new and old parents are then organized and this is the first opportunity for interaction among families, children, teachers, and the environment of the center. Before the child enters the center individual interviews with parents are carried out to establish a dialogue between parents and teachers, so that they begin to know each other and set the basis for mutual trust. Parents narrate their child's daily life and provide the caregiver with basic information regarding the child's habits. Taking care of a baby or a young child is a very intimate matter. Emotions and ambivalences involved in the first experiences of parting and sharing can be very strong and the parents should feel that teachers are aware of their natural anxiety, accept it, and are at the same time experts and in control. The underlying message is: "This is your child, you know how she/he is, we need your knowledge and experience to understand who he/she is and create for him/her the best opportunities." Before the beginning of the school year, there might be another meeting to decide the organization and the plan for the gradual transition process, which lasts generally two weeks in infant/toddler centers and one week in schools for children aged 3–6.

Inserimento consists of a set of predictable strategies for getting to know each other that involves teachers, parents, and children. It is a gradual process of becoming familiar with a new community for the child along with his or her accompanying parent, the caregiver, other parents, and their children. It serves two primary goals: facilitating an active adjustment of the child in the new setting and a strong connection or alliance with the families; and fostering parents' involvement and participation in the early experience of the child in the center as a first important step for further involvement.

Inserimento is aimed at giving children the opportunity to explore the new environment with their parents, to practice brief separations, to get gradually in touch with new adults and to feel secure. Parents, for their part, have a chance to know the environment where their children will spend so much time, its routines, and convivial moments. Teachers have the rare opportunity to observe children in interaction with their parents, discovering the interactional styles of each pair and to getting to know the child without the strong protests of sudden separations. This privilege will not last forever, but it gives young children an initial feeling of familiarity and emotional security that usually carries over when the parent is no longer present. While the caregiver gradually takes over responsibility, the parent is personally involved in facilitating and supporting his/her child and feels active and useful.

Inserimento is a common practice in infant/toddler centers and in municipal preschools and parents are seriously invited to spend as much time as possible in the center on the occasion of the first entrance of their child into the new community. As the child will gradually experiment with an increasing distance (both physical and emotional) from his parents, parents will benefit from the opportunity to observe their child's exploration of the new setting and they will also take their time to get to know the teacher and other parents.

Daily communication is also considered important and it develops through encounters that occur every day between teachers and parents. Informal communication between parents and teachers takes place daily. Individual interviews and meetings relating to the specific experience of each child can be requested either by the school or by the family. Family members are involved in decisions about their children and are encouraged to be active protagonists of their child's life at the center. Documentation and display on the walls shows what children can do and elicits more questions and active interest from the parents.

There is no doubt that friendly and balanced relationships between parents and teachers improve the child's well-being and his or her growth. Teachers are also aware that welcoming a child into the child-care setting also implies an important investment in the relationships with parents and can become a significant way to support parents in their responsibilities and apprenticeship as educators, making them feel active, important, and empowered. This task takes maturity and specific professional development, which is fairly well established in most municipal infant/toddler centers but still not fully developed in preschools, especially where an exclusive focus on curricular matters can hide the strong emotions and the need for support involved in the first sorties of the child out of the family circle.

Continuity of care in educational services and in school and links between school and families are basic assumptions in the Italian interpretation and practices of early childhood education. This idea of continuity works together with the notion of complementarity between the experience of growing and being educated at home and in the out-of-home settings. The interpretation of "good practices" in the education of young children is seen as resulting from dynamic interactions between all the adults involved in this process. Finally, infant toddler/centers and preschools are interpreted as relational systems where both children and adults are formally initiated into an organized community and where parents and teachers can practice shared responsibilities in a society that tends to isolate families.

Challenges

Whether or not involving parents in the child's growth ensures high quality early childhood or good experiences for children in early childhood settings is not in question. Research and experience give evidence of the importance of these practices and attitudes in working with young children. The fast changing educational models and representations of children, their development in an accelerated and global society, and a growing pressure for early performance are forces that might erode the good, relaxed time to practice and experience new relationships. Intimacy and distance are new challenges threatening a thus far balanced model. It is also a challenge figuring out how best to engage the growing number of families from different cultural and national backgrounds. These families bring with them, within the universal expectations of the best for their youngsters, different ways of understanding and experiencing educational responsibilities, interdependence and autonomy, and community life. Early childhood educational services can thus be a crucial opportunity either for a feeling of belonging or a first experience of exclusion. Cultural understanding, communicational skills, and a strong professional commitment need to be developed in early childhood educators in order that they be able to face these challenges and to conceive, propose, negotiate, and make possible renewed forms of *partecipazione*.

Further Readings: Bove, C. (1999). L'inserimento del bambino al nido (*Welcoming the child into infant-care*): Perspectives from Italy. *Young Children* 54(2), 32–34.; Bove, C. (2001). Inserimento. A strategy for delicately beginning relationships and communications. In L. Gandini, C. P. Edwards, eds., *Bambini: The Italian approach to infant/toddler care*. New York: Teachers College, Press, pp. 109–123; Mantovani, S., and N. Terzi (1987). L'inserimento. In A. Bondioli, S.Mantovani, eds., *Manuale critico dell'asilo nido*. 1st ed. Milano: Franco Angeli, pp. 215–130; Mantovani, S., L. R. Saitta, and C. Bove (2000). *Attaccamento e inserimento. Stili e storie delle relazioni al nido*. Milano: Franco Angeli.; Mantovani, S. (2001). Infant toddler centers in Italy today: Tradition and innovation. In L. Gandini, C. P. Edwards, eds., *Bambini: The Italian approach to infant/toddler care*. New York and London: Teachers College Press, pp. 23–37; New, R. (1999). Here we call it 'drop off and pick up'. Transition to child care, American Style. *Young Children* 54(2), 34–36; New, R. S., B. Mallory, S. Mantovani (2001). Adult relations in Italian early care and education. *Innovations* 8 (2), 1–13; Spaggiari, S. The community-teacher partnership in the governance of the schools: An interview with Lella Gandini. In C. P. Edwards, L. Gandini, and G. Forman, eds., *The hundred languages of children: The Reggio Emilia approach-advanced reflections* 2nd ed. Stamford, CT: Ablex, pp. 99–112.

Chiara Bove

Teacher Training

In Italian the concept and the word used for teacher's "training" is *formazione*. This word conveys a very different meaning from the English word "training." The concept comes from *forma* (structure, to shape) and is intended in the sense of taking form rather than being given a form. The concept underlying the word training is better translated with the word *addestramento,* a series of practices that can be operationalized as used in sports or in training animals, or in the technical part of the preparation of an artist or a professional. Italian teachers would resent the very idea of being "trained" instead of "formed."

An Evolving System

The qualification of teachers for *scuole dell'infanzia* (schools for children aged 3–6) and of caregivers for *asili nido* (infant and toddler centers), both called *educatrici* (educators) rather than *insegnanti* (teachers), changed very little until 1998. These students attended special high schools for teachers or, for professionals who intended to work only in the infant and toddler centers, a high school for caregivers (*puericultrici*) oriented on health and care rather than education.

Beginning in the 1980s many caregivers attended universities after their high school and obtained a four-year degree in *Scienze dell'educazione* (Educational Sciences), often while working. Although this degree was optional for caregivers, it was required for directors and coordinators of social and educational early childhood services (often called *pedagogisti*).

Since 1998, the requirement for teachers of *scuola dell'infanzia* is a four-year degree in *Scienze della Formazione Primaria*, a course preparing both preschool and primary school teachers with a common curriculum in the first two years and a specific curriculum in the following two years.

In 1999, the University system was reformed in accordance with European agreements, and is now organized in a three-year level (*laurea*) and a two-year postgraduate level (*aurea magistrale*). At present (2006), at the national level *educatrici* for infant and toddler centers are not required to have postsecondary training. But in many cases educators in service have attended a three-year course in educational sciences, which in some cases gives them priority in the "point basis" hiring system common in public services. Coordinators of early childhood services are now always required to have at least a three-year degree (for infant and toddler centers) and a four- or five-year degree for *scuola dell'infanzia*.

Beginning in 2007 the four-year course for preschool teachers should be extended to five years—the so called 3+2—as will be the case for all teachers at every school level. The trend for *educatrici* in charge of children under the age of 3 is to require the three-year course that is the basis for the further training of preschool teachers, thereby reestablishing the possibility of continuity and career development. Some cities and regions resist this trend for fear that it will lead to higher salaries and to keep the staff of infant toddler centers at the same level as family day-care staff.

The Professional Profile

The basic ideas underlying the training processes activated by the new courses provide a profile of a professional capable of translating multidisciplinary knowledge (*cultura generale*) into teaching practices that can be adapted to different environments, changing social features and family patterns, specific attitudes, and the cognitive styles, characteristics and cultural backgrounds of the children. Teachers should aim to make children capable of learning how to learn. The teacher is expected both to integrate within herself/himself and to activate in the children emotional, cognitive and social resources, and curiosity and pleasure in learning. The proposals for the new curriculum emphasize the following five areas of competence:

- *Disciplinary*: well grounded in general and specific knowledge and the capacity to translate them in inspiring teaching;
- *Methodological*: the capacity to observe, document, and support the progression of learning through specific teaching strategies;
- *Communicational*: the capacity to involve children in their work through group work, active participation, mutual help, coconstructed practices including new languages, and the new communication technologies;
- *Managerial and organizational*: specifically related to the creation of the interpersonal and learning environment;
- *Ethical*: the capacity to face the many dilemmas of the teaching profession, coconstructing common rules, working to overcome prejudices and discrimination, trying to develop in the school community a sense of responsibility, solidarity, and social justice.

The Curriculum

This first experiment at university courses for early childhood professionals is characterized by the following:

- a *multidisciplinary approach*;
- a curriculum where theory and practice are *integrated*; and
- a *partnership with schools*.

The curriculum is *multidisciplinary* in several different respects. First, the school systems containing preschool and primary school-teachers are in continuity with one another—with an extra year a preschool teacher can also get a degree valid for primary school and vice versa. Second, there is a balance in the teacher preparation program between human sciences (education, psychology, sociology, anthropology) and curricular disciplines (languages, history, geography, mathematics, sciences, art, music, etc.). Third, in *scuola dell'infanzia* and in primary school the Italian system foresees a teacher that stays with his/her class for several years (three years in *scuola dell'infanzia*, five years for at least one teacher in primary school) and who can teach all subjects. Even teachers who are going to work with children with special needs first have to go through the basic four-year course.

The curriculum is *integrated* in the sense that traditional lecturing is combined with laboratories where students are split into small groups (lectures have enrollments ranging from 30 to 200 students). In these smaller groups, starting in the first year, students practice experiential learning and simulations of what they will be doing in the child-care settings and in schools. During the field practice (called *tirocinio*), which are supervised in small groups, the students observe in a first phase, cooperate with the class teachers in a second phase, and take direct responsibility in the third phase.

The curriculum is carried out in *partnership with the schools* because each university to which the Ministry of Education assigns teacher training programs—one or two in each region according to resources and number of teachers needed—is supposed to get in touch with schools in the entire area. These universities can count on the fact that some teachers and school principals, temporarily detached in the university and in collaboration with university faculty, will work part time for the program to supervise the laboratory and *tirocinio* activities.

At the end of the program the students take a final exam where they present and discuss a research paper they have written under the guidance both of their supervising school-teacher and of a member of the faculty in front of a committee appointed by the university and by the Regional Bureau of the ministry of education and this qualifies them to teach in any public or private school. Public schools are required to hire qualified teachers, and private or municipal schools must do so if they want to be considered *scuole paritarie*, that is, schools recognized by the ministry and thus eligible for financial support.

This experiment is the first ever organized in Italy on a large basis where university and schools are systematically working together. Preliminary findings indicate that it is being received with mutual satisfaction and mutual advantage. There are of course problems. First, many think that a jump from no postsecondary training at all to four and soon five years is too abrupt and maybe even too much. Second, a certain mistrust needs to be overcome on both sides. On the one hand, schools think universities are too distant and too abstract from the daily problems and challenges of real teaching. On the other, universities are not so familiar with working on an equal basis with teachers and getting "hands dirty" in the field beyond "clean" research practices. But the first eight years of the experiment are in general considered satisfactory, and many unexpected practices have come about. These include courses offered by universities for the teachers in the schools agreeing to assist with the *tirocinio*, themes of interest to the schools proposed for the documentation or research work leading to the final papers by the students, regular meetings to discuss school reform and new programs, and coconstructed in-service training activities. For all these reasons the upcoming change that will transform the now well-established four-year program into the five year—three plus two—curriculum, where the activities in partnership with the schools will be mainly concentrated in the last two years, is looked at with a certain apprehension.

Training Teachers for Children with Special Needs

Teachers who intend to work as an extra teacher in classes with children with special needs have to complete their four-year course, which includes special education and at least one other course on disabilities, and then take an additional program, lasting from one semester to one year, which qualifies them for this specialized task. The Italian system is inclusive, and all children with special needs, no matter how serious, are included. The special teacher is supposed to be a support to the class, and specific rehabilitation takes place, if necessary, out of school. One drawback is that because positions for teachers trained for special needs are numerous, many students specialize and get into the job primarily as a way of entering the profession rather than as a real choice.

Professional Development

Before the 1998 program started, the main training responsibilities for early childhood educators were carried out by municipalities, and to a lesser extent by the state system (*Servizio Nazionale per la Scuola Materna*) through in-service training. This accounts for the large amount of time (150 to 200 paid hours per year) that has traditionally been built into the contract for training, teamwork and work with parents. This training has usually been planned on a yearly basis, combining activities and courses offered in response to specific staff requests with other activities planned at city level to foster specific skills, or to give a common foundation to staff, or to pursue special projects. Group work and supervision, action research experiences monitored by researchers, and altogether a strong focus on the context, combined with considerable freedom in choosing courses linked to the specific talents of individual educators (in art, photography, drama, science, etc.) have characterized the best known high-quality experiences like **Reggio Emilia**.

The new regulations for teachers training encourage the link between universities, local authorities, research and training centers such as INDIRE (*Istituto Nazionale per la Documentazione e la Ricerca Educativa*) specialized in e-learning and e-training, INVALSI (*Istituto Nazionale per la Valutazione del Sistema Scolastico Italiano*) for evaluation and assessment, and the various regional institutes (*Istituti Regionali per la Ricerca Educativa*). This will be advantageous for cities which did not have the resources or the expertise for organising professional development activities, but it might encourage other municipalities with histories of being strongly engaged in fostering professional development reduce that investment when resources become scarce. The outstanding Italian experiences such as Reggio Emilia, Pistoia, Modena, Parma, Milano, Bologna, and Trento have always been grounded in a strong community-based training, which probably accounts for the richness and creativity of these programs, so it would be a great loss if the local efforts and resources to implement ECEC services should be reduced or totally reshaped.

Challenges

The past decade has brought about deep changes—not yet well understood and evaluated—in the standards, expectations, and rationale of the training process for teachers and caregivers. If on the one hand they give greater dignity to the preschool teachers, on the other hand they exclude the educators of the very young from the public education school system, contradicting a well-established tradition of continuity and exchange between *asili nido* and *scuola dell'infanzia* and exposing *asili nido* to the risk to be pushed back to mere care.

Even if everybody agrees that the cultural background of the preschool teacher has to be stronger, the risk is that this professional comes to look at the school for the children from 3 to 6 in a more formalized and schoolish way, and in so doing denies the best tradition of the holistic approach that characterizes the Italian tradition (see Pedagogy and Curriculum entries). Having a curriculum in common with primary school-teachers might orient new ECE teachers in a different way and interrupt the continuity and exchange with the professionals working with the 0- to 3-year-olds.

The Italian system for the very young children has grown over the years with a continuous professional development because of the poor basic training of these early childhood professionals. This huge investment by local authorities has brought about habits of group work, active learning processes, action research experiences, contacts and exchanges with universities and research centers, and a constant adjustment of the professional tools to the community and the changing society. It would be a pity and a loss if the new university curriculum (which certainly strengthens the professional self-image and social role) would have as a consequence a strong reduction of time and resources for professional development.

Italy was confronted with the paradox that the level of its school system considered the best in international comparisons—early childhood education—was the one where the teachers had the lowest basic and academic training. We still do not know if the new system will be able to provide the professionals needed for ECEC with the knowledge, the attitudes, and the skills necessary to maintain and extend the good job done so far by dedicated teachers, who are child, family, and community oriented and always ready to learn more and in new ways. A new balance between basic training and professional development is crucial; good educators have to be well formed and cultivated. But they are not specialists or experts on single subjects or problems: rather they are professionals of everyday life, capable of interacting with parents, to support them by sharing the responsibilities of growing and educating their children, to look at the children as whole persons in specific and changing environments or ecological niches, to help them find many ways and languages to express themselves and develop. Early childhood education is a profession too complex and too delicate to be confined within a standardized and centralized curriculum, and too important for establishing a culture of childhood not to deserve a strong societal investment right from the beginning.

Further Readings: Dalle Fratte, G. (1998). *La scuola e l'università nella formazione primaria degli insegnanti. Il tirocinio e i laboratory.* Milan: Franco Angeli; Galliani, L., and E. Felisatti (2002). *Maestri all'università.* Lecce: Pensa Multimedia; Luzzatto, G. (1999). *Insegnare a insegnare. I nuovi corsi universitari per la formazione dei docenti.* Rome: Carocci; Moscati, R. (2002). Implementation of comprehensive reform in Italy. *International Journal of Higher Education* 26: 3–5; Nigris, E. (2004). *La formazione degli insegnanti. Percorsi, strumenti valutazione.* Rome: Carocci; OECD (2001). *Teachers for tomorrow's schools. Analysis of the world education indicators.* Paris: OECD (Organization for Economic Cooperation and Development).

Web Sites: www.indire.it; www.cede.it

Elisabetta Nigris

Public Policies

Public policies aimed at the development of educational institutions for early childhood were specified for the first time in 1968 for *scuole dell'infanzia* (3–6) with Act 444, which instituted state schools on a national level where these services were provided by the church, by municipalities and, on a very small scale, by private organizations. The national policies for services to younger children, *asili nido* (0–3), began with Act N.1044 in 1971; previously the only state intervention was confined to crèches for children in need through an organization set up during the fascist years in the 1920s called ONMI (*Opera Nazionale Maternità e Infanzia*).

Since 1968 *scuole dell'infanzia* have been progressively expanded and built within the general educational system. Although not compulsory, they are now attended by the large majority of children (over 90% of five-year-olds in 2005). Recent law reforming the school system (Act 23, 2003) states that *scuole dell'infanzia* will be guaranteed to all children. The 1968 bill ruled that the State should intervene where the municipal or private system was not sufficient, and foresaw state support for municipal and private schools. Since then state direct involvement has grown, especially in the South and in rural areas where the municipal and church traditions were weaker. Today (2006) about 50 percent of all *scuole dell'infanzia* are state schools. There is little or no discussion about policies to expand and support these schools and it is assumed by all political parties that it is a state responsibility to complete the coverage quickly and to maintain good standards.

Policies Related to Services for 0- to 3-Year-Olds

Public policies for *asili nido* (0–3) have always been more controversial, and although today there is a strong consensus about the educational character of these services and a general request for more of them, their development is still far from being satisfactory. The 1971 law was mainly conceived to provide women easier access to work within the framework of a broad welfare system where long maternity leaves were also granted. The 1044 law was undoubtedly the first step in orienting public policies toward the development of educational services for young children. These services were identified as social services of public interest, which involved providing for financial support from the state to regional and municipal authorities to cover both investment costs and a large portion of management costs.

The plan, involving the development of a nationwide network of 3,800 *asili nido* over five years, faced a social context in which sharing educational responsibilities between families and educational services was not yet generally felt as natural and positive. Perhaps chiefly for this reason, the plan met with different levels of acceptance depending on the different local cultures in the country.

Thus, while the development of services in the different areas provided a highly differentiated picture, with a strong concentration in the northern-central parts of the country, two general events took place that were of critical importance in view of further developments in the service system:
- the potential drive to development provided by the national fund set up at the beginning of the 1970s came to an end by statute (Act n. 448) in December, 1988;
- starting at the end of 1983 crèches were no longer qualified as "services of public interest," and instead, they were usually included in the so-called "services on individual demand," with part of the cost to be charged to users.

Starting in the mid-1980s a long cycle began, which still continues, in which shaping a broad political scheme *on a national level* for the development of educational services for young children has proven consistently difficult. Over the same period, the efforts of many families and many municipalities toward updating national rules and regulations and reactivating the development of an educational system for children has led to the advancement of a few legal policy proposals originated at the grassroot level *(leggi di iniziativa popolare)*, which have, however, never managed to capture enough attention on the part of the Parliament to be approved.

General Policy Trends

Despite the lack of attention on a national level to the issue of policies for children, the service system has followed a number of recognizable developmental trends in those northern-central areas where higher levels of development have been recorded. These trends are as follows:

- the longer-established experience of crèches has generated "new types" of services meant to welcome children or children with parents/with relatives for regular attendance more than once a week (see Infants and Toddlers entry);
- connections and synergies between municipal authorities and cooperatives and other nonprofit organizations have led to a progressive differentiation of the human resources involved in the system as activators and/or managers of educational services.
- the responsibility, and the cost, of development for this growing service system, which has gone from 2000 facilities at the end of the 1980s to the 4000 currently operating, has increased its potential for coverage from 6 percent to about 10 percent of potential users nationwide.

Distinguishing National, Regional, and Municipal Roles

The increase in coverage and quality is largely to be ascribed to the policies developed at a municipal level, partially with the financial support of Regional Authorities and in synergy with the cooperative movement. The very "regional" and "local" character, that had been negatively characterized during the partial and highly differentiated implementation of the National Plan put forward with Law 1044-1971, is pivotal to local and/or regional experiences, which have, over time, reached meaningful quantitative targets (with local peaks of over 40% coverage), getting at the same time very deeply rooted into the public policies of local communities and regional governments.

The very synergy between Municipalities and the cooperative movement in jointly supporting the development of an educational service system—often simplistically interpreted in the past as a mere money-saving device for public authorities—has taken on the connotation of a general strategy, which has further substantiated and strengthened the role of the public player. This has resulted in a fuller recognition of public responsibility for system governance and regulation, and enhanced the value, through adequate orientation and control strategies, of private contributions, which already fall within the framework of public interest, coming as they do from nonprofit organizations pursuing social goals.

Today we are in a position to evaluate how other functions concerning system governance and regulation as well as advanced design and management skills can be—and in fact are—the ground upon which Municipalities and the cooperative movement can meet and jointly lead the development of an integrated service system offering children and families greater access and quality.

At this stage it is worth mentioning that in more recent years there have been a few central measures aimed at the development of service policies:

- Law N. 285 (August, 1997) provided financial support to actions addressed to children and adolescents, limiting its scope to additional services for crèches (play areas and centers for children and parents) in the field of educational services for early childhood.
- State Financial Laws for 2002 and 2003 (Law N. 448 of December 21, 2001, and Law 289 of December 2002) provided for financial support "to build and manage crèches and micro-crèches in working environments."

These provisions, although they have contributed to a local extension of services, lack a general view of a national integrated system.

The debate on the constitutional organization of the State oriented to strengthen federalism and decentralized action defines a new profile for national rules and regulations, which is supposed not to clash with the broader powers ascribed to regional parliaments. Although the emphasis on regional responsibility corresponds to the development of early childhood services, the diversity of the country in terms of resources, municipal traditions, and effectiveness of management experiences worries associations and other parties who advocate for early childhood education, which try to promote a concept of "federalism in solidarity."

The present political scene is confused. It is widely felt that some kind of new balance needs to be pursued among:

- state competences concerning the basic level of services, relating to civil and social rights, which have to be granted in any part of the country;
- adequate measures to ensure that the required resources for achieving and maintaining such "basic levels" are identified;
- the possibility, above those levels, to design implementation based on local and regional needs and experiences.

Recent statements on the part of the Supreme Court (*Corte Costituzionale*), in highlighting the above perspective, state clearly the educational character of crèches and other services for early childhood, and suggest that these should fall within the area of education in terms of government competences (thus confirming the prevailing trends on a regional and local level that emerged in the previous decades).

Major emphasis is being placed on working out an updated framework in terms of rules and regulations—integrated with consistent ongoing development plans supported by adequate funding—which may foster the growth of the service system in the medium/long term. Only by taking this perspective will we be able to consolidate basic service levels in the whole country while confirming and enhancing the relevance ascribed to regional and local levels in planning and implementing educational efforts.

Further Readings: Fortunati, A. (a cura di) *I nidi e gli altri servizi educativi e integrative in Italia*. Quaderno 36, Centro Nazionale di Documentazione e Analisi per l'Infanzia, Istituto degli Innocenti; Law 1044 (1971). *Piano quinquennale per l'istituzione di asili-nido comunali con il concorso dello Stato*. Rome: Gazzetta Ufficiale. (December 15, n. 316); Law 285 (1997). *Disposizioni per la promozione di diritti e di opportunità per l'Infanzia e l'adolescenza*. Rome: Gazzetta Ufficiale. (September 5); OECD (2001). *Starting Strong, early childhood education and care*. Paris: The Organization for Economic Cooperation and Development.

Aldo Fortunati

Japan

Early Childhood Education in Japan

Introduction

In some sixteenth- and nineteenth-century essays, European authors remarked that Japanese society was paradise for young children. Young children were cherished, full of energy, and free. Although the authors neglected the tragedies of children living in poverty and a patriarchic family system, it was true that many children were cherished by members of extended families and looked after by people in their community. Traditional views of children supported the belief that the child was the gift of gods, born with good nature, and in the realm of gods until the age of 7. Adults needed to protect children from evil influences so that they could develop their own innate good nature. Mothers were responsible for raising their children to become respectable adults. A mother's role was important in another sense, especially in the upper class; she was responsible for raising the first boy to excel as the successor in the patriarchic family system.

Transmission of Traditional Culture

Early childhood education has taken over the family's role regarding cultural transmission. Japanese people had many traditional festivals following each season, from New Year's Day to the end of the year. Children have prominent roles in many festivals originated in Shintoism, because they have been thought to be children of gods. In many festivals originating in agriculture, there have been special events for children. These ceremonies have been celebrated in both families and communities. Today, while most of these customs are lost in families, kindergartens and day-care centers celebrate these customs and apply them in educational practices. Some traditional play activities that are no longer popular in families are also practiced in preschool education. Thus, kindergartens and day-care centers have assumed the role of transmission of traditional culture (see also the Cultural Characteristics of Japanese Preschool Education).

Brief History of Japanese Early Childhood Education and Care

The first kindergarten was founded in the late nineteenth century for children of the upper-middle class. Teachers were women of upper-middle class who had been trained at the first teacher training school for women. This training school, Tokyo Women's Teacher's College, was founded in 1874, opened its kindergarten in 1876, and established the training course for kindergarten teachers in 1878. Its educational theory and practices were established by Sozo Kurahashi, a professor at the College.

The first day-care centers were also opened in the late nineteenth century in the countryside for children of farmers and workers. Several years later, the first day-care center in an urban area was created in Tokyo for poor children of working-class mothers. Teachers at this center were also graduates of the Tokyo Women's Teacher's College— highly educated women with progressive ideas. As a result, the development of day-care centers became a social movement to save poor families. Intellectuals, volunteers, educators, and child psychologists played an active role in improving the educational practices of these programs.

These historical streams show that, from the beginning, both kindergartens and day-care centers had professionals of high quality and people contributing to their creation and improvement. After complete destruction in World War II, the dual system was reconstructed in 1948 with establishment of its legal basis. Since then, the education guidelines for kindergarten have been revised four times, providing an historical record of the changes in national policy about early childhood education and care during the second half of the twentieth century (see Pedagogy in Japan).

Characteristics of Japanese Early Childhood Education and Care

Sozo Kurahashi's theory has always been one core of Japanese preschool education. (see Pedagogy entry, below). Some characteristics of modern early childhood education and care can be traced directly to him, while others are the outcomes of social changes.

"Hoiku"—care and education for humanity. The expression "education and care (*hoiku* in Japanese)" is usually used in Japanese kindergartens and day-care centers. The meaning of "Hoiku" includes fostering personality, sensibility, emotion, motivation, human relationships, and health; that is, the basis of humanity rather than the teaching of knowledge and skills. This principle is presented in Kurahashi's theory of "education by inducement." The word "hoiku" is distinguished from education in school ("*kyoiku*"). While the word "kyoiku" is rarely used in day-care centers, it is used as "preschool education (*yoji-kyoiku* in Japanese)" in kindergartens, which legally belong to the school system. The use of kyoiku in kindergarten is controversial. In one aspect, kindergarten education has a uniqueness that distinguishes it from school education. On the other hand, continuity with preparation for elementary school is stressed. This contradiction contributes to the diversity of educational practices found among kindergartens.

Social change after world war II. The political and social contexts greatly changed after World War II. As a relatively monocultural society, this change was mainly caused by the innovation of social systems and economic growth. Social systems changed family and community. Both traditional extended families and neighborhood community disappeared. Today, mothers raise their children in a nuclear family without the help of grandmothers or their neighbors. Economic development has dramatically decreased child mortality (infant mortality rate is 3.2 and mortality rate under age 5 is 4 per 1000 births). The most drastic change is the decline of fertility.

Early Childhood Development Programming

Today, many Japanese children under the age of 3 are looked after by their mothers during the daytime. The enrollment rate of children under 3 years old in day-care centers is 21 percent (1999). Nine percent of 3-year-old children attend kindergartens and 30 percent of them attend day-care centers. At age 5, 83 percent of children participate in collective education (48% at kindergarten and 35% at day-care centers). Almost all 5- to 6-years-old children receive preschool education (60% at kindergartens and 39 % at day-care centers) before entering elementary schools. Elementary school is obligatory for children from 6 to 12 years old.

Early childhood education in Japan has two systems, kindergarten and day care. Kindergartens are operated under the School Education Law, and accept children from 3 to 6 years of age for four hours a day more than 39 weeks a year. The kindergarten education guidelines (National Curriculum Standards for Kindergartens) issued by the Ministry of Education, Culture, Sports, Science and Technology (MEXT) regulate the objectives and contents of kindergarten education, although private kindergartens are not required to follow them completely. Parents can choose either the two-year course (from 4 to 6 years old) or the three-year course (from 3 to 6 years old), and more and more parents choose the three-year course. The teacher/child ratio is at most 1:35. Kindergarten teachers are trained for more than two years after high school to get the kindergarten teaching license. Of the 13949 kindergartens countrywide, 60 percent are private and 40 percent are public (2005, MEXT).

The second system is the day-care center. In Japan, day-care centers are legally a social institution based on the Child Welfare Law and operated under the auspices of the Ministry of Welfare and Labor. Day-care centers accept children from three months (after maternity leave) to 6 years of age whose parents cannot take care of them during the daytime because of work or illness. Day-care centers are normally open from 7:30–8:30 in the morning until 6:00–7:00 in the evening. The Day Care Education and Care Guidelines provide the framework for the curriculum, although for children 3- to 6 years old the kindergarten guidelines are applied. In order to obtain a license professional day-care providers also must receive training for two years after high school. The adult/child ratio is 1:3 for children less than 12 months old, 1:6 for 1 and 2-year-old classes, 1:20 for the 3-year-old class, 1:30 for classes of 4- and 5-year-olds. There were 22,490 centers with 2,028,045 places in 2004 (Ministry of Health and Labor). Fifty six percent of all the day-care centers are administrated by local government and the remainder are private.

Although unification of these two systems for children aged 3 to 6 has been discussed several times since 1945, the two systems remain separate and each belongs to a different ministry. Recently, however, a third system, the "comprehensive educational facility," has been created. This system combines the day-care center and the kindergarten and allows various styles of care and education in one institution.

The Five Content Domains of Early Education

Japanese preschool education focuses on five areas of study: health, language, expression, human relationships, and environment. The objectives of preschool education are not to attain goals but to encourage motivation or inclination. In the Guidelines, for example, we see emphasis on objectives such as "a child *enjoys*," "a child is *interested* in," "a child *tries* to . . . ," " a child *feels*" etc.

Education Through Play and Environment

Indirect instruction is one of the particularities of Japanese early childhood education. The Japanese believe that the best way to accomplish the objectives of preschool education is through play, where teachers support children so that they can develop by themselves. This is called, "education through the environment," "education through play," or "child-centered education" (see Curriculum and Play entries, below).

The theory of "education through the environment" has been accepted not only in collective education but also in family education. Literacy provides an example. Japanese language has three systems of characters: abundant Chinese ideograms (*Kanji*), and phonemes such as 55 *Hiraganas* and 55 *Katakanas*. It looks complicated, but in fact, it is not so difficult to engage young children in literacy initiatives. In fact, young children are easily attracted by letters, because simple ideograms look like drawings and phonemes have one-to-one correspondence between letter and sound. Children are often motivated to ask adults how letters can be read and what they mean. If adults are responsive to their questions, children can acquire basic literacy by themselves. Parents who emphasize this indirect education motivate their children by making use of their surroundings.

Since the 1960s, with Japan's growth as a worldwide economic power, a social trend valuing the advantages of intellectual learning has prevailed. Parents expect their children to obtain an advantageous position in society, and insist that kindergartens teach intellectual skills directly. It is not surprising that many kindergartens and day-care centers, especially private ones, respond to parental pressure by giving instruction in, for example, literacy, numeracy, physical training and exercise, and instrumental music. Even though "education through environment" is thought to be an ideal theory, parents prefer practical outcomes that prepare children directly for elementary school studies. Many other kindergartens and day-care centers are wavering between these two modes of education.

Early Development and the Family

Some studies show that many young mothers who are isolated in a nuclear family feel that their child-rearing is a burden. These women receive abundant information on child-rearing from TV, magazines, or books, but they often have no one with whom to discuss their concerns or ask for advice. Many young mothers confess that they want to be excellent mothers but feel guilty that they are not achieving this goal. Despite this concern, social support systems to replace traditional community have not been organized until recently, when local governments have attempted to address this lack of support with a new system of services for mothers. These services offer advice, opportunities to meet and talk with other young mothers, and provide facilities or interaction with other parent and children (see Family Involvement and Infants and Toddlers).

Children as Targets of Commercialism

Japanese economic growth has brought an increase in child-targeted industry. Family education has been impacted by this increase in commercialism. With one or two children in a family, a child has "six pockets" (two parents and four grandparents). Various child-focused industries promote the message that parents should spend money on their children. These industries encourage parents to take their children to various lessons (English language, computer, piano, swimming, dance, etc.), and claim to give the children intellectual training through the sale of educational materials, including computer games. These children are often too busy attending extra lessons to find time for playing with other children.

Risk Avoidance

In a society of low fertility, a child's life is extremely precious for parents. Parents are nervous about their child's safety, and careful to avoid risks in order to prevent accidents. Kindergarten and day-care teachers are also very careful to make sure that children have little risk of hurting themselves, for fear that parents will blame them for an accident. This tendency leads to overprotection of children both by parents and teachers. Because both teachers and parents are trying to avoid any possible accidents, children are deprived of adventurous activities, struggles with other children, and the use of dangerous tools. As a result, children are likely to miss the opportunity to acquire the skills needed to manage challenging situations.

Children and Outdoor Play

Children used to play in the neighborhood with other children of different ages, where they learned social rules and skills from older children. Today, there are few occasions for children to play outdoors with their peers. In urban areas little outdoor space is available where children can play safely without paying attention to the cars. Older children are often busy after school and are not able to take care of the younger ones while they play. As a result, children prefer to play with computer games instead of playing outdoors. When a crime against a childis committed somewhere in Japan and is then reported on TV, parents feel afraid to let their child play outdoors. These phenomena prevent children from acquiring necessary social skills for their development.

Social Pathology and Children

In every society, young children are most likely the victims of social pathology. Although the number of reported cases in Japan is less than that of many other developed countries, there is an increasing problem of mothers mistreating their children. Japanese mothers feel pressure to be good mothers. Their feelings of discrepancy between the ideal and reality, both about themselves and their children, cause anxiety and lead some mothers to neglect their children.

Another topic often discussed is the increase of children with behavioral disorders; for example, an increase in the number of schoolchildren who cannot stay calm in classrooms, children who become aggressive without good reason, or children without concern for others.

In contemporary Japanese society children are valued in the sense that parents spend more time and money on their children with greater interest and concern than parents did in 1950s (when they had many children and spent most of their time working to support their families). However, children today are treated more as possessions of parents, objects of marketing, and future participants in the worldwide competition called globalism. Children are encouraged to adapt themselves to the outside world, but are less sensitive either to their own or others' inner world. Children are not isolated from today's world of war and discrimination, and they are certainly influenced by a world in which power and violence dominate, even if they are not its immediate victims. We adults face the challenge of cooperating in an international context to provide children with societies in which they can lead happy and productive lives.

Further Readings: Japanese National Committee of OMEP (1992). *Education and care of young children in Japan*; Hoshi-Watanabe, M. (1999). Play or learn? Inside and outside of preschool in changing Japanese society. In G. Brougère and S. Rayna, eds., *Culture, Childhood and Preschool Education*. 85-100, UNESCO-Universite Paris Nord; Ministry of Education, Culture, Sports, Science and Technology (2005). Annual Report on Basic Statistics of School Education. MEXT; Sekiguchi, H., and N. Teshima, eds. (2003). *Hoiku Genri—Jissenteki Yoji-Kyoiku Ron (Principles of early childhood education)*. Practices of early childhood education. Tokyo; Edition Kenpaku-sha (in Japanese); Shwalb, D. W., and B. J. Shwalb, eds. (1996). *Japanese childrearing*. New York: Guilford Press.

Miwako Hoshi-Watanabe

Cultural Characteristics of Japanese Preschool Education

Japan is not an obviously multiracial or multicultural society, confronted with problems of maintaining the ethnicity of minority groups. Although it is not, in reality, a country of homogenous race, the preoccupation with the "homogeneity of Japanese culture" evident among Japanese is found in Japanese education.

Japanese cultural characteristics penetrate various aspects of early child education. Also, the transmission of Japanese traditional culture is seen in educational programs.

The Traditional Concept of Children

There is an old saying in Japan that children under the age of 7 are still in God's hands. This means that children under the age of 7 are not considered the objects of purity or impurity. Their souls should be placed in the territory of God and should be free from every constraint to resurrect their soul. Ethnological religions do not believe it is a good idea to place children under 7 years old in the control of Buddhism. The 7-year-olds celebration is considered to be a ceremony celebrating the first step in the process of transition into adulthood.

The Celebration of 7, 5, 3

There still remain many traditional events commemorating the children's growth according to their age. The most popular one is known as the celebration of 7, 5, 3. This celebration involves a festival day for children ages seven, five, and three. As part of the celebration, girls at age seven and three and boys at age five visit a Shinto shrine with their family wearing traditional dress. The actual birthday celebration is carried out much as in Western countries. But in child care and educational institutions, birthdays are celebrated on a monthly basis. That is, children who share their birthday in the same month celebrate together. In Japan, group activities are common and considered a typical educational method.

The Japanese Group Orientation

In a study of how children are educated in Japanese kindergartens, using an ethnographic method, a difference was found between United States and Japanese ways of teaching. In identifying the "Japanese group-oriented tendency" the author described how Japanese children might belong to ten different groups simultaneously within the classroom. It is true that many groups exist in the kindergarten. Each group has its own name and /or color. For example, one particular child belongs to the kindergarten, the grade, the class, the group, the bus route, the locker, the uniform, the smock, the hut, the outdoor cap, and the shoes shelf. Each girl in the orange group, for instance, is called Miss Orange Group. By calling a child by his or her group name instead of his or her own name, a teacher intends to help the children become aware of the responsibility to the group (not as an individual). In part, Japanese children belong to many groups because one teacher has to take care of more than twenty to thirty children in her class without an assistant.

Group Behavior and Discipline

The sense of group belongingness helps children behave well not only for themselves but also for their peers. It also provides children with close human relationships with their peers. To not make trouble for others comes ahead of all other things.

At the same time, group solidarity may cause some negative impacts on children who are isolated from the group. Although Japanese early childhood education has insisted on the importance of child's individual development, it may be difficult to develop a child's individuality within such group-oriented educational conditions.

"Omoiyari" or Altruism

"Omoiyari" may be called altruism in psychology. It is defined as behavior initiated based on the understanding of other people's situations and feelings. Although Japanese children experience group-oriented education, this doesn't appear to take away their sense of themselves as individuals. In Japan, young children are often encouraged to express their own thoughts. However, being nice, friendly, and sympathetic to others is the ultimate educational goal during the preschool days. Cooperating with peers promotes many dynamic activities; for example, building a big structure with large blocks and performing dramatic play helps promote an understanding of how to participate in group activities. Through this process, most teachers encourage children to make friends with their peers. Therefore "omoiyari" must be the keyword in Japanese education of early childhood.

Bokasi—A Gradation of Color

The word "bokasi" (which means gradation or obscure or vague or ambiguous) is also a key factor in understanding Japanese culture, thinking, language, human relationships, and view of nature and social structure. In artistic terms "bokasi" is an unlimited gradation of color. It is a beautiful technique used for traditional clothing. Japanese Empress Michiko frequently wears a "bokasi" designed dress. Psychologically, "bokasi" is thought to be an expression of an ambiguity. One expresses ambiguity in order to avoid showing independence from the group. Thus one identifies oneself as a member of the group and makes one's individual position congruent with that of the group.

Special Programs

Another important characteristic of Japanese early childhood care and education involves special programs, which are introduced in day-care centers and kindergartens. Those special programs are defined to be activities carried out on a certain day for a certain educational purpose. According to the purpose of education, each special program is planned appropriately for children. There is an entrance ceremony, the parent meeting, a home visit, children's day, mother's day and father's day (parent day), festival time, memorial day, good teeth day, July 7 festival (Tanabata), pool open day, summer festival, lodging with peers away from families, moon viewing, elder people's day, sports day, excursions, sweet potato digging, autumn festival, Christmas, New Year days, "Setsubun" bean scatter (to drive out bad luck), girl's festival and the graduation ceremony. It is not necessary to carry out all these programs in one institution, but it is often heard that teachers are forced to host these events even in daily programs, which results in a very busy schedule and insufficient time allocation for daily care.

Why do we have so many special events? Most are traditional social events that have been carried out in the community. With the economic growth that occurred in the 1970s many community-initiated traditional events or festivals were replaced by commercialism. Communities and families no longer play a major role in such annual events. Consequently, preschool teachers are encouraged to provide opportunities for children to experience those annual events. This has led to concern regarding allocating enough time for children's free play in daily activities.

Cultural Differences

Japan is not strictly a homogeneous society. There are aboriginal people in the northern part of Japan. In the western part of the country there has been mixing and interacting with people from China, Korea, and South East Asia for centuries. Recently, many students have expressed an interest in multicultural education. More children from abroad are involved in Japanese preschools. Japanese teachers tend to treat foreign children equally; however, foreign children are encouraged to accept Japanese culture and life just like their Japanese counterparts. Behaving similarly with others might be stressful for some foreign children. Japanese educators sometimes lose sight of the fact that foreign students have their own individuality and their own culture, in favor of cooperation and harmonization with Japanese culture. But multicultural education in preschool settings is a growing concern among those who study early childhood education in Japan.

Further Readings: Hendry, J. (1986). Kindergartens and the transitions from home to school education. *Comparative Education* 22(1), 53–58; Hisatomi, Y. (2004). A study on communication between teacher and foreign children in Japan. *Resarch on Early Childhood Care and Education Japan* 42(1) (in Japanese); Hoasi, A. (2005). Study on Omoiyari. Presentation at the 58th Conference of Japan Society of Research on Early Childhood Care and Education (in Japanese); Iwata, K., T. Ayabe, and N. Miyata (1985). Original Image of Children's Culture, Tokyo; Nihon Housou Shuppan Kyoukai Press (in Japanese); Kanda, E. (2004). Event. *Dictionary on Child Care and Education*. Tyoto; Minerva Shobo Press; Kanda, T. (2003). The present situation on multi-cultural education in Japan. Presentation at the *56th Conference of Japan Society of Research on Early Childhood Care and Education* (in Japanese); Mori, M. (1999). Theory and practice on multi-cultural education in Japan. Presentation at the *52nd Conference of Japan Society of Research on Early Childhood Care and Education* (in Japanese); Nakayama, O. (1982). Japanese culture of Bokasi, Tokyo; Arufah Shuppan Press; Nakura, K., and J. Nakazawa (2002). International Exchange Committee: Special Symposium at the 55th conference of Japan Society of Research on Early Childhood Care and Education (in Japanese); Sato, Y., S. Shinzawa, C. Teshi, E. Nakamura, and N. Hatanaka (1994). Interactive support between preschool and families of foreign children. *Research on Early Childhood Care and Education Japan* (32) (in Japanese); Yuhki, M. (1998). First group-life in Japan—ethnographic studies of a kindergarten Tokyo; Yuhsindo Press (in Japanese).

Junko Enami

Family Involvement in Japan

History

Japanese education has some characteristics that differentiate it from other countries in terms of family involvement. School/kindergarten events are seen as family life events that include whole extended families, many school/kindergarten supplies are individual personal possessions, and the educational curriculum encompasses social manners. Why this is so can be looked at from a historical perspective.

During the Edo period, when Japan was isolated from other countries for over 200 years, each social class in Japan had its own separate educational system. The Samurai class had their own clan schools for their sons to be taught Confucianism, the Chinese philosophy of politics and morality, and martial arts, reading, writing, and arithmetic. For the lower classes of farmers, merchants and craftsmen, there were small schools called "terakoya," literally meaning small temple room, where Buddhist monks taught small numbers of students the specialized skills of basic literacy and the math skills they would need to function successfully in their designated profession.

However in 1868, the Meiji Restoration took over the Edo Shogunate, and the new government abandoned the old popular educational system, promulgating a new system adopting Western educational approaches. Although over the years this educational system has been reformed, its top-down nature and strong centralization under government control have not been altered.

The first kindergarten in Japan was established for aristocrats in 1876. This government-led education system continued after World War II and was successful in achieving high enrollment and literacy rates for the Japanese. Using the same curriculum all throughout Japan, this system created a meritocracy, whereby social success was determined by academic achievement based on one's academic resume, without relation to the social class in which one was born. With educational success having become the key to social success, schools and teachers have gained relatively high social positions and garnered widespread respect. Therefore, school ceremonies are almost family events in which every member should participate. Community members attend other school events like sports days or performances, thus becoming the glue that holds a community together as communities' traditional festivals diminish in cities.

The morality of Confucianism has had a great influence on the Japanese mentality. The principle that government, not citizens, should have the responsibility for education leads to the concept that morality and social manners also belong to school education. As a result, schools have internalized the idea that it is their role to teach social manners. One example of this is: at elementary and junior high schools, lunch time and overseeing the classroom cleanup by the students are also matters for teachers to control. During lunch, the teacher encourages the children to try a variety of foods, encouraging them to not take what they cannot eat, and to use good table manners. She/he is actively monitoring and teaching during lunchtime. In early childhood education its tendency is the same as that found in school.

Early Childhood Education

Two separate streams make up the system of preschool education in Japan (see earlier). One component is the day-scare center, which is under the control of the Ministry of Health, Labor and Welfare. Day-care centers give education and care to babies and children from 0 to 6 years old whose parents are both working; as a result they are open more than eight hours a day.

The second stream is for children who are cared for by someone (almost always stay-at-home mothers) at home and who attend kindergartens from 3 to 6 years old. These kindergartens are under the regulation of the Ministry of Education, Culture, Sports, Science and Technology (MEXT). Although there have been two separate systems, the two functions of care and education are merging together and the education of all 3- to 6-year-olds at day-care centers falls under the same guidelines that kindergartens have followed and is overseen by the Ministry of Education.

Family Involvement

Two aspects regarding family involvement in early childhood education will be discussed. The first will explain how Japanese kindergartens and day-care centers traditionally involve parents. The second will explore the new concept developing in day-care centers and kindergartens regarding family services for all child-rearing families, as well as in the communities and nonprofit organizations.

Parental involvement in kindergarten and day care. Shortly before a child begins kindergarten, parents are requested to prepare all the supplies that he/she will need for kindergarten life. Parents either purchase or make between ten and twenty items such as uniforms, bags, and lunch bags. For day-care centers, the list is even longer, expanding to include sheets for sleeping on during nap time, pajamas, diapers, futon covers, etc. Traditionally, the kindergarten recommended that the mother make these items by hand as an expression of her love of her child. Recently, many kindergartens have lessened the emphasis on homemade items. A further expectation of parents is that they write their child's name on all the new items. This is quite a time-consuming task as kindergarten supplies are almost always personal possessions.

A typical supply list would include a box of crayons, a clay case, scissors, a drawing notebook, and colored pencils. Marking each item goes beyond simply writing the child's name on the top of a crayon box. Individual items such as each of the 12 crayons, the top of the crayon box and the bottom of the crayon box would have the child's name written on it. Although this labeling is time consuming, it is through this patient work that parents and children mutually cultivate their expectation of attending kindergarten. This feeling is passed down over generations in a Japanese family.

Entrance and graduation ceremony and other events. Entrance and graduation ceremonies have special meaning for families with kindergarten children. Parents and children, and sometimes grandparents, come in their proper and rather formal clothes, usually a dark color and navy suits or dresses. Grandparents sometimes join in this event by presenting new clothes for the entrance ceremony. Even though these ceremonies are held on weekday mornings, most fathers would not consider missing such an important event. Events like sports day, drama performance day, art exhibitions and musical concerts at kindergartens and day-care centers are also important to family life. These are held as big events lasting the full day and are open to all families in the community. Often grandparents, uncles, aunts, cousins, and community members attend, as this is a focal point in the life of the neighborhood as well and an opportunity to meet each other.

Activities for parents. During the two or three years of kindergarten, parents are kept informed of their child's life through parent/ teacher class meetings, open observation days, and one-on-one parent/teacher interviews. Parents do not usually participate in daily kindergarten activities (such as reading stories or helping put together art work). However, when teachers request volunteers to accompany field trips, parents are often willing to sign up and assist. Kindergartens also serve as a social outlet for parents. For example, many kindergartens have parents' circles for cooking, chorus, and arts. Library groups and puppet theater classes may perform dramas and storytelling as part of the kindergarten activities.

Curriculum

Life skills are also taught in day-care centers and kindergartens. Life skills are seen as important educational objectives and they stand equal with other academic objectives in early childhood education. Day-care centers and kindergartens both emphasize greetings, washing hands, mealtime manners, brushing teeth after lunch, and other social manners. Teachers feel responsible for fostering the child's development of a proper daily routine, and actively promote and expect that the family cooperates and supports the development of this discipline. In an effort to assist parents during summer break, many kindergartens send newsletters recommending appropriate behavior during the long summer holiday. Examples include not drinking too many cold drinks in the hot summer, being careful to avoid traffic accidents, going to bed early and getting up early, and not watching too much TV.

Parent–Teacher Communication

There are special message notebooks that encompass the majority of communication between teachers and parents and are exchanged back and forth between them. At day-care centers these are particularly important and are written in daily, with teachers communicating detailed information such as the frequency, timing and condition of bowel movements, appetite and consumption at mealtime, and observations at nap and play. Reciprocally, parents are required to write the child's physical condition, body temperature, food consumption, bedtime and wake-up time, etc. Kindergartens also use notebooks to communicate how a child is relating to his peers, how he is participating in class activities or other relevant details from his time there. It is taken for granted that parents check the class newsletter and also the kindergarten newsletters, because they contain important notices, such as changes in pick-up timings, lists of items to be brought for arts and craft activities in the following week or for upcoming field trips.

Involving Fathers

Although child-rearing traditionally has been the mother's role, day-care centers and kindergartens have recently invited fathers to play with the children and established meetings just for fathers to share their child-rearing experiences in comfortable situations.

New Family Services and Early Childhood Education

In the past, new parents looked to their parents, extended family members, and neighbors as child-rearing mentors, who would provide examples of child-rearing. Given the declining birthrate and aging society, young Japanese parents have little experience with child care, and nuclear families have no one in the neighborhood to advise them. Therefore, child-rearing neurosis and child abuse have become a greater concern in the past few years. To counter this, day-care centers and kindergartens are now offering their child-care resources to families in their communities, regardless of whether their child attends the kindergarten or not. Examples of this support are playgroups for parents with babies or toddlers, opening up the playgrounds or indoor play spaces for play, teachers counseling on child-rearing concerns, etc. The centers offer a gathering place for parents to drop in and meet other parents in the neighborhood, helping to develop friendships and alleviate feelings of isolation.

There is also a simultaneous push to establish family support services within the broader community. Local governments and nonprofit organizations also are offering drop-in activities, chat lounges, and space for counseling in their facilities. Although they are not early childhood education institutions per se, these settings function to help young parents by providing places to gather and play, with facilitators who are public health nurses or child-care workers. They also maintain groups for young parents to get together, setting up their own organizations or study groups to discuss child-rearing or their own problems. Sometimes these places provide supervision or babysitting services for children in order to give parents a short respite. The goal of these services is to prevent parents and children from feeling isolated, to help them make friends, and to alleviate some of the pressures and troubles of child-rearing.

With family support services for parents in the early childhood years the government is taking steps to counter the declining birth rate, which reached an alarmingly low number of 1.29 in 2005. Having children is felt to be an exceedingly heavy burden on mothers. Family support in Japan should have a dual role of not only offering day-care centers for children of parents rearing children, but also of preventing child abuse and poor environments for mothers and children. The concept of prevention is new to early childhood education in Japan and it will be more important in the future in family services.

Further Readings: Benjamin, G. R. (1997). *Japanese lessons: A year in a Japanese school through the eyes of an American anthropologist and her children.* New York: New York University Press; Tobin, J. J., D. Y. H. Wu, and D. J. Davidson (1989). *Preschool in three cultures, Japan China and the United States.* New Haven, CT: Yale University Press.

Kazuko Matsumura

Pedagogy in Japan

The current *National Curriculum Standards for Kindergartens* (the guidelines for Japanese preschool education, revised in 2000) describes their basic principle as education through use of the environment, taking account of traits of early childhood. This principle of "education through environment" has three axes of practices: the importance of all phases of daily kindergarten life appropriate for early childhood, comprehensive guidance through play, and individual guidance based on understanding of each child. The approach can be summarized as "child-centered education." The pedagogy of the Japanese child-centered preschool education has its origin at the dawn of kindergarten.

The Establishment of Kindergartens and the Introduction of Froebel's "Gabe" Method

In the late nineteenth century, after Japan had been reformed from feudalism to a modern regime, the Meiji government introduced western policies and systems, including educational systems. In 1886, the government promulgated the "Order of School Education," by which modern school education systems were started.

Masanao Nakamura (1832–1891), who was famous for his translation of "Self Help" of the British pedagogue Smiles, insisted that individual independence was indispensable for the modernization of Japan. He devoted himself to the establishment of educational systems for women and for young children. In 1876, when he was the president of the Tokyo Women's Teachers College, he created an attached kindergarten, the first kindergarten in Japan. He introduced Friedrich **Froebel**'s theory to this kindergarten, asserting that under adequate conditions of collective education, young children should be assured their full development through play activities and interaction with peers. Ms. Clara Matsuno, who had graduated from the Froebelian teacher training school in Germany, had become the first head teacher of this kindergarten. Based on Froebelian ideas and methods, she introduced Froebel's "Gabe" method. Within several years this "Gabe" method was spread into many kindergartens that had been opened in all parts of Japan at that time. However, this application of the "Gabe" method lost sight of Froebel's original philosophy and became too formalistic.

The Beginning of Child-Oriented Education

In 1899, the "Act of Content and Facilities of Kindergarten Education Guidelines," the first guideline for kindergarten education was enacted by the Ministry of Education. The guideline identified four contents of education: play, song, speech, and handicrafts. Although "Gabe" includes just a part of the category of "handicrafts" in the guideline, the fact was that in many kindergartens most handcraft activities were collective handworks with "Gabe" objects under teachers' instruction. By the early twentieth century, however, the "Gabe" method was being criticized as inflexible and too teacher oriented. Instead, child-centered theories were proposed. For example, Motokichi Higashi (1872–1958), an assessor at the Kindergarten attached to Tokyo Women's Teachers College, emphasized the importance of free play. He systematized play-centered educational programs and published *The Method of Kindergarten Education* (1904). This was the first systematic theory of early childhood education by a Japanese author.

At the same time, the reform of teaching programs was proposed by two educators, Goroku Nakamura, the principle of the Kindergarten, and Minoru Wada, a teacher at Tokyo Women's Teachers College. They insisted on a change from teacher-oriented programs to child-oriented or play-centered programs. However, this proposal was too progressive to be accepted widely at that time.

Sozo Kurahashi and the Progress of Child-Oriented Education

Early in the twentieth century, along with the tide of Taisho democracy, child-oriented approaches inspired by the American new educational movement of John **Dewey**, Kilpatrick, and others had a strong impact on kindergarten education. Fostering spontaneity, creativity, and individuality of children was valued.

The educator who created a child-oriented theory that was suitable for Japanese sociocultural conditions and traditional values was Sozo Kurahashi (1882–1955). He had been interested in early childhood education since his high school days. After majoring in child psychology at a university, he taught at Tokyo Women's Teachers College. At its kindergarten, he played with children, observed them, and discussed them with teachers. In 1917, when he became the head of the kindergarten, he put all the "Gabe" materials together in a basket so that children could play with them freely and voluntarily. He practiced his child-centered education based on Froebel's theory, instead of the formal education of "Gabe" method. To develop his own theory, he tried to integrate western theories with his practices at his kindergarten and the traditional Japanese view of education and children. He had studied the ideas of John Amos **Comenius**, John-Jacques Rousseau, and Johann **Pestalozzi**. Later, when he visited European countries and the United States, he studied **Montessori**, the theory of the Progressive Education, and especially Froebel. He knew that in the Japanese traditional view of education parents would have just observed their children and provided them with good environment, because the child was born good and had potentiality to grow up by himself. He integrated all these into his theory, not only practicing it in his kindergarten but also described it in his three books *The Preschool Education* (1932), *The Essence of Kindergarten* (*Youchien Shintei*, 1934, revised in 1953) and *The Mind of Bringing up Children* (*Sodate no Kokoro*, 1936). Almost all the basic ideas of the present national curriculum of kindergartens and day-care centers have already been shown in these works. His theory has been the pillar in the history of Japanese preschool education and still has a great effect on present education both theoretically and practically.

Promulgation of "the Kindergarten Act" in 1926 was followed by the increase in the number of kindergartens and improvement of their education. The model of the improvement was the education of the kindergarten attached to Tokyo Women's Teachers College.

Kurahashi described his theory most systematically and comprehensively in *The Preschool Education*. Three purposes and eight methods of preschool education were introduced. The purposes are as follows:

1. *Kindergarten as a place of fundamental education.* Preschool education is fundamental to all education, because it cultivates the humanity and the potentiality of self-development that are the basis of further development.
2. *Fostering physical strength and health.* To foster children's physical strength and health, teachers should give children opportunities to enjoy their moving bodies. Outdoor play is an example. These experiences would motivate them to maintain their health by themselves.
3. *Fostering a good nature.* "Good nature" in Japanese means gentleness, sympathy, and intimate feelings toward others, and is highly valued in Japanese society as a fundamental trait of humanity. It should be cultivated with deliberate and delicate care by adults in early childhood.

The eight methods of preschool education are as follows:

1. *Daily-life oriented education.* To encourage the development of children's minds and bodies, educational programs should be based on consideration of all aspects of their own daily lives. This means that it is important to respect their spontaneity, not to interfere in their natural stream of life, and to assure them that they be able to lead their lives voluntarily.
2. *Respect for play.* It is through play that children show the essence of their nature. Play gives children the power of future development, and so must have an essential role in development of young children.
3. *Encouraging social relationships.* Preschool education cannot consist only of the one-on-one teacher–child relationship. It is also important that children have opportunities to encounter and relate with one another in order to establish social relationships.
4. *Preparing a good environment.* A desirable kindergarten environment is one in which children feel free, behave voluntarily, get rich stimulation from their surroundings, and thus accomplish self-fulfillment in their everyday lives. Kurahashi's idea of the emphasis on environment was maintained later in the national guidelines as the concept of "education through environment."
5. *Grasping opportunities for intervention.* To guide children in respecting their own stream of life, it is important for teachers to seek appropriate chances to intervene and support them.
6. *Supporting the motivation for achievement and self-satisfaction.* A teacher expresses his/her appreciation for the children when they devote themselves to their activities, and supports them until they have deep satisfaction. This brings them a sense of self-fulfillment and further motivation to achieve.
7. *Inducement in life.* The concept of "inducement" in Japanese is that a good environment guides children in a desirable direction for educational purposes. The

teacher has a role of "inducing" children, because he/she is one of the elements of the environment. The method of inducing is, above all, to be vivid and active and to invite children to share in that life. Children are inspired by example, and lead their own lives voluntarily and actively.

8. *Interacting with children with a warm heart ("Kokoro-mochi"). Kokoro-mochi,* a Kurahashi term, means having a sympathy or resonance for others' feelings. When children lead full lives, they should have a warm heart and kokoro-mochi. Teachers should be sensitive to each child's kokoro-mochi, express appreciation for those feelings, and recognize those feelings as positive attribute, rather than simply to encourage the child's intellectual interests. This also enhances respect for individuality.

In *The Essence of Kindergarten*, Kurahashi also explained "self-fulfillment," one of his central concepts. Children have the potentiality of self-fulfillment innately and develop it in free and spontaneous play activities. Teachers can support them by preparing adequate "arrangements" that guarantee children feel free. His theory was widely accepted by kindergarten teachers and researchers and has become the basic principle of early childhood education.

Pedagogy since World War II

Following complete destruction during World War II, the new educational system was mandated in 1948. Kindergartens were included in the educational system operated under the Law of School Education. New guidelines of care and education (both for kindergartens and day-care centers) were enacted in that year. Kurahashi's ideas were retained as the theoretical basis of these guidelines.

Since then, the guidelines have walked along a winding path to the current version. The first revision of guidelines (*National Curriculum Standards for Kindergartens*) in 1956 established six domains of educational content; health, social competence, nature, language, music and rhythm, and drawing. In 1966 the Ministry of Welfare created the guidelines for day-care centers, in which the kindergarten guidelines were applied for children older than 3 years old.

Emphasis on continuity with elementary school education in these guidelines reinforced the inclination toward direct instruction that grew along with Japan's economic growth in the 1960s and 1970s. Kindergartens appeared that were explicit in giving young children an intellectual education and preparation for success in school. These trends raised various controversies. In 1989, a third revision of the guidelines validated child-centered education as the essence of preschool education. Once again, "education through environment" was declared, as well as Kurahashi's three purposes; education in the stream of daily life under suitable conditions for early childhood, comprehensive education through play, and guidance appropriate to each child's traits. The educational contents were revised to five domains; health, human relations, environment, language, and expression.

The pedagogy of preschool education since World War II has often been challenged by those who proclaim the importance of the early instruction of intellectual abilities such as numeracy and science. They look at children as future technocrats or eminent experts who will contribute to our economic growth. However, Kurahashi's successors all over Japan have cherished his theory because they believe that the essence of preschool education is to foster humanity. For example, Makoto Tsumori, who focuses his research and practices on children's inner development, expressed this thought in his work *Horizons of Early Childhood Professionals* (1997): "Taking care and educating children [For Tsumori, care and education are a set and equally important.] in preschool is the work of supporting the development of human beings. When children through their challenges discover themselves in interaction with teachers, they can make their way forward with self-confidence. The major concern of teachers should be whether children behave according to their own will: that is, whether they bring up themselves."

Further Readings: Holloway, S. (2000). *Contested childhood: Diversity and change in Japanese preschools*. New York: Routledge; Ishigaki, E. H. (1991). The historical stream of early childhood pedagogic concepts in Japan. *Early Child Development and Care* 75, 121--59; Ishigaki, E. H. (1992). The preparation of early childhood teachers in Japan (Part 1): What is the goal of early childhood care and education in Japan? *Early Child Development and Care* 78, 111–38; Japanese National Committee of OMEP (1992). *Education and care of young children in Japan*. Tokyo: Japan Committee of OMEP, Kurahashi, S. (1965) *Kurahashi Sozo Zenshu (Complete works of Kurahashi Sozo)* Tokyo: Froebel Kan (in Japanese); Ministry of Education, Culture, Sports, Science and Technology: (MEXT) (1998). National Curriculum Standards for Kindergartens. Available online at http://www.mext.go.jp/english/news/2001/04/010401.htm; Peak, L. (1991). *Learning to go to school in Japan: The transition from home to preschool life*. Berkeley, CA: University of California Press; Tsumori, M. (1997). *Hoiku-sha no Chihei (Horizons of early childhood professionals)*. Kyoto: Minerva Shobou (in Japanese); Tsumori, M. (1998). Education and care for children with special needs. *International Journal of Early Childhood*, 30(1), 79–82.

Nobuko Kamigaichi

Curriculum in Japanese Early Childhood Education

An Experience-Based Curriculum

In Japanese kindergartens and day-care centers, the central part of the curriculum is children's experiences in play. Play is highly valued, because it is an autonomous activity of children. The Japanese concept of curriculum is not one that has children acquire knowledge and skills by systematic teaching programs. Rather, it is a type of curriculum in which a teacher picks up and focuses on an aspect of a child's experience, gives suggestions about it, and accumulates these occasions in various activities within children's play. We call it experience-based curriculum. For example, if a child is interested in insects and hunts them during the playtime, a teacher, respecting the child's interest, could plan programs about insects. The teacher could ask the child to draw a picture of an insect, and also to prepare picture books such as the life of insects or how to keep insects. It is likely that the child would be fascinated with such activities. These experiences nurture in him or her a scientific mind, expression of feelings, and/or respect for the life of other creatures. We consider this concept of curriculum desirable for early childhood education for it builds the basis for development over the lifespan.

Early childhood is the period of life where children enrich their sensibilities, acquire positive attitudes toward various matters, and become aware of concepts of objects and events, through concrete and immediate experiences. Education in kindergartens and day-care centers sets out to fulfill these aspects of development, and play is a process central to accomplishing this goal. However, play does not mean "laissez-faire." The subjects of play are the children themselves. Teachers, while respecting children's autonomy and their own will, should think about what the necessary experiences are for each individual at every moment, reflect on what activities and environmental conditions can provide them optimal circumstances, and then plan and construct the actual (concrete) environment.

An experience-based curriculum is more difficult for teachers than a goal-oriented curriculum in which achievement goals are set, planned to be attained, and put into practice. In Japan, we believe that it is better that teachers, while respecting children's autonomy, carefully insert desirable factors into the play environment, and allow children to have additional useful experiences with them. However, this demands more competence of planning and a deeper understanding in children than is required in goal-oriented instruction. For these reasons, it is not always successful in practice.

Policy Background

The concept of this type of curriculum has a basis in law. Japanese kindergarten is one of the school institutions that operates under the Law of School Education. Article 77 of that law states that "the kindergarten aims to give education and care to young children by providing a suitable environment and to encourage their development of minds and bodies." More concrete criteria for curriculum are found in Article 76 of Rules of the Law of School Education, called the National Curriculum Standards for Kindergartens. The curriculum for children from 3 to 6 years of age in kindergartens as well as day-care centers is based on these guidelines. Here the discussion will be limited to the application of the guidelines to kindergarten education.

National Curriculum Standards for Kindergartens

First, the guidelines regulate the time conditions of kindergartens. In principle, kindergartens should be open no more than thirty-nine weeks a year and four hours per day. In fact, due to recent flexibility in the application of this regulation, more and more kindergartens accept children for a longer time.

As for education, the guidelines indicate that kindergartens should think about the children's future learning, so that the aims of education will be accomplished by all aspects of children's lived experience in kindergarten, from entrance to departure and at every moment in the daily life of the child. In keeping the whole kindergarten life appropriate to developmental stages of early childhood, teachers foster the development of children mainly through play. In other words, the aims of education should not be pursued primarily by guiding children with a teacher's initiative. The principles of education contained in the Guidelines, curricular aims and contents, and the multiplicity of developmental aims with each activity are discussed in more detail below.

Principles of Education

There are the three principles of kindergarten education: that the lived experience be suitable for early childhood, that a comprehensive education be provided through play, and that education be carried out in accordance with the specific developmental traits of the individual child.

Young children can develop and widen their world when feeling that they are affirmed and loved by adults. In constructive kindergarten life, built on the feeling of trust with teachers, children have interest voluntarily in various things and engage themselves in play, in which they have positive relations to others and events. Teachers have to provide curriculum experiences that assure these aspects of development.

In each kindergarten curriculum is developed according to age level. Although one curriculum is applied to all children of the same age level, individual difference is also taken into consideration. Teachers have to prepare different paths and means according to the developmental stages of each child.

Aims and Contents

What should be nurtured in play, the central process in Japanese early childhood education? The National Curriculum Standards for Kindergartens formulate "contents" and "aims of education." "Contents" describe necessary practices to accomplish the aims. "Aims" do not mean goals to be achieved, but rather are orientations of development; that is, sentiments, attitudes, or motivations that are to be fostered in the course of development. There are five areas of developmental orientation: health, human relationships, expression, environment, and language. The concepts in these areas should not be confounded with those of subjects in school learning. For example, "health" does not simply mean physical activities, and the curriculum in health should not only be related only to physical activities. The orientations of these five areas are as follows:

- *Health*—to foster a healthy body and mind; to encourage keeping healthy and safe through self-care.
- *Human relationships*—to foster cooperative relationships and empathy for others; to foster independence and autonomy.
- *Expression*—to foster the ability to express one's feelings and opinions; to enrich sensibilities and creativity.
- *Environment*—to foster explorative interest in surrounding objects and events, and to apply these experiences in life.
- *Language*—to foster and to express verbally one's feelings and thoughts with one's own words; to listen to others' speech; to nurture sensitivity to language and to verbal expressions.

Comprehensiveness of Aims and Orientations

The curriculum should be developed so that children have comprehensive experiences of these five aims in one activity. Teachers expect that the accumulation of various experiences within each activity, which interrelate these five orientations in a comprehensive way, will be fruitful for each child's development. An example follows:

> Some 5-year-old children are going to organize a relay race. They make a course by tracing it with line-marker on the ground. In planning the race, the children find that they need more runners. The children invite their friends to join them. Then they make two teams and begin the race.

This sequence of behavior is totally self-governing, and contains many elements. A relay race is a physical activity; it contains the "content" of "play voluntarily in outdoors" in the "health" area. Making a course together and appealing to friends demonstrates a realization of the "content" of "think by oneself, behave in one's own initiative" and "cooperate with friends, have sympathy toward others" in the area of "human relationships." And it also represents "have a pleasure of self-expression" in the area of "language." In this process, teachers should observe children attentively, interpret comprehensively what the children are experiencing, and grasp how the experiences are accumulated. In this example, if a teacher thinks that this is an opportunity to regulate the number of runners, he/she may give the children pieces of cloth (or badges) with numbers so that they find an equal number more easily by themselves. Thus, after interpreting the children's experience in play and extracting important elements from it, teachers add further necessary elements to enrich or modify their play situation. This is the process of making and practicing curriculum in a kindergarten. Evaluation of curriculum examines what aims were realized in their activities and what aims could not be activated. Further planning will be carried out on the basis of the evaluation.

Educational Practices

Teachers make two sets of curricular programs. The first of these is short-term, including daily and weekly plans and activities. The second is the long-term program, containing monthly, semester, and annual plans and activities. Both programs have the same sequence: (1) understanding the children's reality by observation, (2) setting aims for the education, (3) planning of the supporting environment, (4) modifying the aims or reconstituting the environment by observation and evaluation. What is most important for teachers is to understand children both in the long term and in the short term. It is not easy for a novice to make a short-term program in the perspective of a long-term program. Without it, however, it is difficult to really understand children's actual states.

What is the best kindergarten life for development of a young child? It may be one in which, under human conditions that affirm all his or her existence, time, space, and other physical conditions allow the child to do try-and-error as he or she wishes. The competence acquired through play is a kind of basic living force. It is implicit, and its effect is hard to see immediately. It becomes explicit only in later life. However, due to recent social trends demanding immediate visible effects of education (i.e., a child becomes capable of something that can be demonstrated), an increased number of kindergartens adopt a goal-oriented curriculum. A variety of possible interpretations of the National Curriculum Standards for Kindergartens allows for diversity of curriculum in kindergartens. We have to reexamine what sorts of curriculum are most appropriate and needed for early childhood education, given that this is the period for construction of the basis of personality.

Further Readings: Kawabe, T. (2005). *Asobi o Chushinnishita Hoiku (Education and Care through Play)*. Tokyo: Hobun-Shorin. (in Japanese); Ministry of Education, Culture, Sports, Science and Technology: (MEXT) (1999). Explanations of The National Curriculum Standards for Kindergartens. Tokyo; Froebel-kan; Toda, M. (2004). *Hoiku o dezain suru (Designing Education and Care)*. Tokyo; Froebel-kan (in Japanese).

Takako Kawabe

Play in Japanese Early Childhood Education

Definition of Play in Early Childhood

Playing is one of the most important activities in early childhood. Playing is voluntary and is in itself an objective, rather than just being a method of adjusting to reality. Playing has a lot of freedom, with high changeability. Because of this, playing is perceived as being fun and comfortable, and children will regard playing as something that would give them pleasurable feelings. Children can develop many functions through playing, which enables them to adapt more adequately to reality. At the same time, they will develop their ability to use imagination. Imagination may help them overcome difficulties they face in reality. Playing in early childhood also encompasses learning. This is because children learn the feeling of wanting to play—the will to play—and play nurtures behavior that enables them to develop curiosity, the basis of learning throughout life.

The Place of Play in the National Curriculum

In the national curriculum for early childhood education in preschools in Japan importance is placed on "promoting proactive activities of children so they will be able to lead a preferable life as a child," and "comprehensive teaching through play which is a voluntary activity conducted by children." This shows that play in early childhood education is considered very important. Teachers are asked to come up with ways to enable children to proactively participate in play, while at the same time inserting teachers' ideas into the school environment structure. In the preschools that follow this national curriculum children are able to spend two thirds of a day doing things that they have proactively selected. As mentioned in the definition, the foundation of this is the notion that play encompasses learning.

Types of Play in Early Childhood

Sensory motor play. An infant becomes aware of the world around him using his body, and develops many functions through the interaction with his surroundings. The younger the child, the more important the role of the body. Jean **Piaget** (1951) called use of the body in play sensory motor play.

One of the most popular sensory motor play activities among Japanese children is playing in the sand box. Children at preschool never get tired of sand boxes. They touch the sand, mix it with water, make dumpling shapes with it, dig a hole in the sand, or create a mountain in the sand box. They utilize all their senses, including touch, sight, and movement, feeling the coldness of sand or water, its weight, hardness, and softness, looking at the colors and shapes. They also make use of their cognitive ability and mental capacity during their adventures in the sandbox.

Symbolic play. The characteristics of symbolic play or make-believe play are "awareness of oneself and others" and "awareness of reality and fiction." Through children's development, this play tends to include larger and larger numbers of children, developing into mass symbolic play such as "playing house."

In Japanese preschool education, teachers support further enhancement of make-believe play by creating corners for playing house and providing large-sized or regular-sized building blocks to stimulate children's imagination. Importance is also placed on developing relationships with others through collective symbolic play. Children aged 4–5 engage in sophisticated symbolic play with stories and fictive human relationships. As their play becomes more deepened, teachers should support the children to establish relationships among each other through these activities.

Game play. During early childhood, children tend to pursue playing games with various rules, through which they learn that "everyone is equal under the rules." They also acquire the foundation of a sense of ethics such as fairness and equality.

Let's take playing soccer as an example. Today 4-year-old children are often playing soccer in the playground of kindergartens. At the beginning, they play alone, kicking the ball toward the goal. Then they begin kicking the ball among them. At the age of 5, they play soccer games by dividing themselves into teams. However, as they have no rules whatsoever for establishing a team, it often happens that one team wins because of a larger number of members. Children may get frustrated by this, and the game may end spontaneously just as it started. As they repeat this process, children realize that teams would work better if both teams had the same number of players, and that games wouldn't be fun if they cheat. Children learn through trial and error that games would be more fun with rules. In Japanese preschools, teachers don't impose rules on children at the beginning. What teachers try to accomplish is for the children to figure out who and what they are through self-generated games. By respecting children's learning process, adults hope that they learn "morality" as well.

Expressive play. Expressive play has many cultural elements that lead to the nurturing of artistic qualities in children. This includes musical play such as listening to music and playing to musical rhythms, plastic play such as molding, and word play such as listening to stories, reading picture books and playing "first and last" the word game *shiritori*. Compared to other types of play, adults tend to support children actively with more cultural background, so that children can create a higher level of expressive activities using the techniques and knowledge of the teacher.

For example, when a teacher shows "The Three Billy Goats"(a Scandinavian story of three goats and trolls and one of the favorite books for Japanese children) and tells the story, children listen intently to it and cheer at the climax. They beg to have it read over and over again. While the teacher reads the story to them every day, he/she also encourages them to create "The Three Billy Goats Play." The teacher proposes that they make a scene for the story. Using large-sized blocks, the children build a bridge. They themselves play the roles of goats and trolls, and this goes on for days. During this sequence of play over several days, children improve the way of constructing the bridge, or of creating costumes from clothing. Sometimes they add music. If one child is playing both the big goat and the small goat, he invents ways to change his face expressions and voices. By allocating responsibilities the relationships among children will deepen through this play.

Challenges Facing Play in Japanese Society

Through play, a child repeatedly goes through the process of "thinking while taking action," which constitutes a basis for abstract thinking for the future. However, play environments that enable children to come up with voluntary playing activities have decreased dramatically. Playing, which was originally "natural," has become part of "education." In other cases, children are given a "culture for children" created by adults, rather than creating their own culture through play. The deterioration of environments for play also makes it difficult to nurture children's abilities to interact with one another and to be aware of others' feelings and thinking. Keeping in mind today's Japanese social circumstances, the following requirements for play in early childhood become more and more important. Play should be proactive, creative, fulfilling, comprehensive, expose children to diversified experiences, and nurture cooperation among children. Finally, it should be experienced through the body.

As for teachers' role, this involves grasping the challenges faced in the children's development and supporting them in adequate manner. Teachers must observe children from the child's perspective, while at the same time having expectations for them. They should consider the play environment carefully, ensuring that it is designed so that children can discover by themselves that learning is fun.

Further Readings: Nishimura, K. (1989). *Asobi no genshougaku (Phenomenology of play)*. Tokyo; Keisou-shobou (in Japanese); Piaget, J. (1951). *Play, dreams and imitation in childhood*. London: Routledge; Uchida, N. (1986). *Gokko kara Fantaji he (From make-believe to fantasy)*. Tokyo; Shinyo-sha. (in Japanese).

Reiko Irie

Imagination and Creativity in the Early Childhood Classroom: Current Issues in Japan

In Japan, nurturing imagination and creativity is an important basis of early childhood education. Activities intended to nurture children's imagination and creativity involve not only artistic activities such as music, dance, drawing, and craft, but also other experiences including communication with other people and interaction with the environment. Among these, artistic activities are given special emphasis. These activities enrich children's emotions, cultivate their aesthetic sensibilities and cultural consciousness, and develop their relationships with others, as well as developing their cognitive skills and intellectual abilities. These effects cannot be realized by any other activities.

National Curriculum Standards for Kindergartens

The National Curriculum Standards for kindergartens show five areas corresponding to several aspects of children's development. Among them, the area of *Expression* is particularly concerned with artistic activities.

The aims of expression at the kindergarten-level are the following:
* To develop enriched feelings toward beauty
* To enjoy expressing what one feels and thinks in individual ways.
* To understand expression enriches images and experiences in life.

The contents of expression are as follows:

1. Children recognize and enjoy the various kinds of sounds, colors, forms, texture, and movements in life.
2. Children come into contact with beauty and things that move people emotionally in life, and create enriched images.
3. Children express joy when impressed by an act of expression.
4. Children express thoughts and feelings freely through sounds, movement, drawing, painting, and other media.
5. Children are familiar with various materials and making use of them creatively in play.
6. Children are familiar with music. Students enjoy singing and using simple rhythmical instruments.
7. Children enjoy drawing, painting, and creating. Students use what they create in play and as decoration.
8. Children experience expressing their own images in words and movements, performing, and playing.

The following points for dealing with the contents are mentioned in The National Curriculum Standards:

1. Children's feelings will be enriched if they encounter beautiful and fine things. The images and objects that move children emotionally should have a rich connection with their surrounding natural and physical environment. A strong interaction between environment and experience can be fostered if children share their

impressions with other children and teachers, and express their impressions through the arts.

2. Children's self-expression is unique to childhood, but may seem simple. Teachers should encourage children to express themselves in their own ways, by being receptive to children's expression and by acknowledging the willingness of children to express themselves.

3. Teachers should provide developmentally appropriate play equipment and apparatus that allow children to fully express their intentions.

It is noted in the National Curriculum Standards for Kindergartens that artistic activities should not be considered as opportunities for domain-specific trainings, or as preparation for elementary school learning. They should be intended as a part of children's daily experiences.

According to the National Curriculum Standards, art activities in kindergarten are planned to help children develop wholly, by providing experiences in their everyday lives. Kindergarten teachers carefully refrain from forcing children into specialized drills or training, but instead encourage them to express their ideas and feelings freely. Artistic and aesthetic programs are more often related to children's interaction with nature and their play than to intentional instruction designed to improve their skills or to increase their knowledge.

Imagination and Creativity in Musical Activities

Singing, playing instruments, and listening to music are familiar musical activities in Japanese kindergartens. Music curriculum is related to seasons, annual events, and children's daily lives. Music is often integrated with drama, dance, and the visual arts. One activity may involve singing, playing instruments, dancing, and making crafts. A comprehensive overall view of these activities is shown in The National Curriculum Standards.

The National Curriculum Standards for Kindergartens were revised in 1989, when the area "Expression" was introduced for the first time. Music educators and researchers who are engaged in early childhood education have come to realize that the experiences suggested in the National Curriculum Standards can build the foundation of children's musical knowledge. Music education researchers do not expect kindergarten teachers to provide children with specialized musical training, nor a musical program that is to prepare for the elementary school music learning. Children's musical activities in kindergartens include making sounds with objects around them and listening to sounds in the environment, as well as singing, playing instruments, and listening to music.

Integrating Sounds in the Environment

Children live surrounded by the sounds of their daily lives. They listen to sounds such as falling raindrops, blowing wind through a bamboo grove, singing birds, and other sounds from nature. When children listen to these sounds, they associate them with images and engage their imaginations. For example, children may take turns putting a spiral seashell up to their ears, and have different reactions.

Some may say there is "a lion," "sea sound," or "running water" in the shell. In experiences such as these, sounds provoke imagination, and children make meaning through symbol and expression.

Children also make many sounds themselves. These sounds do not necessarily come from musical instruments. Children enjoy the exchange of sounds, which sometimes develops into what we can call musical improvisation. In musical improvisation, children communicate what they feel and think through the sounds they make. Experience with sounds motivates children to establish intersubjective relationships with others, enrich their imaginations, assign meanings to sounds, and sometimes organize sounds into a composition.

There are many cases in which a clear distinction between "participating in musical activities" and "being involved in sounds" cannot be made. In other words, children may participate in musical activities such as reproduction of musical pieces, but may also give musical meaning to ordinary sound situations around them. Sometimes listening to sounds around them and listening to music can be equally aesthetic. Making sounds and playing instruments can also be respected as imaginative and creative. In planning musical activities, it is necessary for kindergarten educators to integrate sounds in the environment with sounds produced by musical instruments in children's everyday experiences.

Other Japanese Musical Programs

In addition to the principle ideas laid out by the National Curriculum Standards, there are several musical programs that are familiar in Japanese kindergartens. These imported methods are combined with Japanese traditional and modern repertoires and have taken root in Japanese kindergartens. The Jacques-Dalcroze method was introduced into Japanese early childhood education in the 1920s. K. Orff's *"Music for children"* and Koday's method both became popular in the 1960s. In most cases, these methods intend children's musical activities to contribute to their development as a whole. Nurturing children's imagination and creativity parallels the contents of the National Curriculum Standards.

Imagination and Creativity in Plastic Arts Activities

Art activities in Japanese kindergartens are currently called "plastic arts activities." Visual art was once called "picture painting" in kindergartens, "arts and crafts" in elementary schools, and "fine arts" or "arts and crafts" in junior high schools and high schools. Historically, the aim of art education was to achieve realistic, adult-level art. The conception that "realistic art is good art" affected the content of art activity in the classroom. The lower the age of a child, the simpler the content of the art activity.

Approaches and philosophies in plastic arts curriculum. Humans' innate senses are stimulated by their immediate environments. From this stimulation, humans actuate and express images. Young children often develop the ability to draw a circle without guidance. The skill develops through spontaneous representation. A young child assigns meaning to his/her image of the circle, and adds lines or other circles to further define his/her image. The teacher can support this spontaneity through a "bottom-up process" in which teachers understand children's potential. In this process, teachers encourage and assure children as they explore materials. A counter approach would be the "top-down process," in which teachers give children goals to reach and guide them.

Japanese curriculum currently recognizes that when children are creative and imaginative, they are fully sensitive, stimulated, and motivated by their own initiatives. We cannot expect children be creative and imaginative by following instruction. It is important that art curriculum in early childhood respects the minds and spontaneous will of children. This type of early childhood art activity plays an important part in the development of young children.

Plastic arts activity in practice. "Plastic arts activity" is the act of interaction with objects. Interaction with familiar objects allows children to understand and transform the objects' shapes, colors, or textures. Transforming the shapes and colors of familiar objects opens up the imagination. In kindergarten, children also combine one object with other ones to make new objects. Teachers provide encounters with these new shapes and colors that widen the possibilities of creation. In art made by both children and adults, objects are the media of expression that stimulate expression and are then manipulated. When we express our emotion on objects, they respond to us through transformation. Sometimes objects we make have the power to heal us by their transformed colors or texture. These qualities are true in professional artists' work, but some assert that children can be artists as well. However, we do not agree with this assertion. We do not identify children's art activity with artwork by artists who have more mature awarenesses of spirituality and intention.

Understanding plastic art activity in early childhood. Young children's art activity has its own world. Children do not reproduce what they see. They try to represent what they are interested in. They focus interest on their own lives, and not on the objective world. Because their art activity reflects their experiences, the richer their experiences in life are, the more imaginative and creative their plastic arts activity. However, as children develop through elementary school, they will become more objective and their plastic arts activity will change its nature.

There is an assertion that the aim of art education is to bring children out of their own world of experience and teach them how to reach adult's plastic activity. Some educators teach children "how to draw a person." Some instruct them to paint an object with its original color. Some give them a theme of a picture to draw. These types of instructions neglect children's subjectivity and fail to enrich their imagination and creativity.

Further Readings: Schafer, M. (1992). *A Sound Education*. Tokyo: Shunjusha; Ooba, M. (1996). *Hyougen genron (Principles of expression)*. Tokyo: Hobun-shorin (in Japanese); Saeki, Y., H. Fujita, and M. Sato, eds. (1995). *Hyougensha to shite sodatsu (Growing up as expressive individuals)*. Tokyo: Tokyo University Press (in Japanese).

Kyoko Imagawa and Tomohisa Hirata

Infant and Toddler Care in Japan

Where are Japanese Infants and Toddlers during the Day?

Most Japanese infants under the age of 1 are at home, and as they get older, the percentage of enrollment at day-care centers increases. The table below provides an overview of the settings containing infants and toddlers nationwide.

Where Japanese children under three years spend their days

Age	Home	Day-care center	Other child care facilities
0	92%	4%	3%
1	81%	17%	2%
2	74%	22%	4%

Source: Ministry of Social Welfare and Labor, 2003.

Most of these children are looked after by their mothers full time, regardless of age, until they are three years old. Among the many reasons why so many mothers have left their jobs to devote themselves to child-rearing has been a strong child-rearing belief, prevailing since the late seventies, referred to as the "legend of three-year-old child." Influenced by the theory of attachment, it asserts that to assure a child's healthy personality development, a mother has to be totally responsible of bringing up her child until he/she becomes three years old. Therefore, many mothers prefer to take care of their children by themselves before sending them to kindergarten at the age of 3.

However, since the 1990s, the number of women with infants who continue to work has rapidly increased. These working women prefer day-care centers rather than grandmothers or babysitters. In the last fifteen years alone, places at day-care centers have increased 1.8 times for infants under one (71,000) and 1.6 times for toddlers of 1 and 2 years of age (500,000). Often, demand exceeds supply; infants account for 10 percent and toddlers comprise 58 percent of the waiting lists at public centers. Local governments are trying to respond to this increase in demand for day care centers for children under the age of 3. Other childcare facilities such as family care and small day-care rooms are concentrated in big cities where supply for day-care centers is far from satisfactory.

History

The first Japanese day-care center was created at the end of the nineteenth century in the countryside, where children of agricultural families were accepted while their mothers were working in the field. Day-care rooms were also established in some elementary schools for the younger brothers and sisters of school children, because otherwise the school-aged children had to baby-sit for their siblings within their own classrooms while their parents were working. These early facilities were as basic as open schoolrooms staffed with caretakers. At the beginning of the twentieth century a day-care center was opened in a popular area of Tokyo for families of the lower class. This center was staffed with teachers who were specialists, educated at the first teacher training school for women. These teachers gave both care and education to children. These private centers were funded by charitable persons and social activists, and public centers soon followed. The aim of helping mothers and children of lower socioeconomic classes continued until World War II. After the war, new systems were introduced through both educational and welfare policies. Since 1948, day-care centers have been controlled by the Ministry of Social Welfare. The first national guidelines were established in 1952. Nevertheless, it was private day-care centers and day-care rooms that continued supporting working mothers and their children under the age of 3. These facilities varied in quality of the care they provided. Some were run based on educational principles, while others just babysat the children. Mothers had to wait until 1972 for the first public care of infants. Since then, private facilities have chosen different approaches; many have established approved centers, while others have decided to remain unapproved.

The Day-Care Center System

In Japan, a day-care center is legally under the control of the Ministry of Social Welfare and Labor, and operates under the Law of Child Welfare. It accepts children from infancy to 6 years of age, from parents who are unable to take care of them because of work or illness. Although it depends on the individual center, legally a child must be at least two months old in order to be placed in a day-care center. In 2005, there were 23,000 centers with 2,000,000 children from 0 to 6 years of age. Thirty percent of these children ranged from 0 to 2 years of age. There are public day-care centers (56% of all centers in 2003) that are operated by local governments, approved private centers, which are run under the same conditions as public centers, and non-approved private centers. As for public and approved private day-care centers, minimal standards of physical and staff conditions are set by the Ministry of Welfare and Labor. According to the authorities, a baby room should have at least 1.65 m^2 per child and for crawling babies, 3.3 m^2 per child. A center is open for more than twelve hours a day, including eight normal hours and then extended hours. The teacher/child ratio is 3 children for 1 teacher for a baby class, 6 children for 1 teacher for a class of toddlers of 1 and 2 years of age. Besides nursery teachers and the director, a center should also have a nurse if it has baby classes, a nutritionist and cooks.

Nonapproved centers are free from control of standards but are not subsidized by the government. Some centers accommodate mothers' needs not met by normal centers. For instance, there are "baby hotels" for children of mothers who work for long hours or at night.

Programs of Care and Education

The Japanese name for day-care center—"hoiku-en"—means "facility for care and education." It offers both care services and education to even the youngest children. The Ministry of Welfare and Labor provides guidelines that give an overview of development, principles and objectives, and the teachers' roles and practices for children of each age level. For children under 3 years old, the guidelines have four chapters according organized around the following age levels; under 6 months old, 6–15 months old, 16–23 months old, and 24–35 months old. Care of infants and toddlers addresses health, physical cleanliness, nutrition, rhythm of life, and security. As for education, following the guidelines of kindergarten by the Ministry of Education, five domains of education are applied: health, human relations, interest in the surrounding environment, language, and expression.

According to the guidelines, when caring for infants under 15 months of age, day-care centers are responsible for promoting health, physical cleanliness, and nutrition. Centers are also responsible for establishing a rhythm of life, as well as security and emotional bonding between the teacher and each child under her/his care. Establishing and maintaining this affective bond with the teacher is believed to be of particular importance for a child's psychological security. Therefore, adult–infant interaction is very frequent, with physical contacts such as touching, holding, and playing in physical intimacy. The Japanese believe that play with adults stimulates curiosity which in turn promotes cognitive development.

Baby foods are cooked in different ways depending on children's age in months (from four to seven steps until 18 months old). Even during the weaning period the meal is meant not only for nourishment but also is also an occasion for enjoyment and having aesthetic sensory experiences. Cooks prepare various plates with different tastes and colors so that children of each age level can enjoy eating them. Because sleeping and emotional security are valued, a teacher accompanies a child until he/she falls asleep. Diaper changes are frequent, so that a baby becomes accustomed to being clean and develops a sensitivity to uncleanliness. Additionally, nature is an important component of Japanese day-care centers. Going outdoors is seen as indispensable for promoting health. For example, even in winter, babies "take a walk" in a baby carriage, as it is believed that outdoor activities help children get in touch with nature.

Training children to be autonomous begins between the ages of 15–23 months. It is believed that children can acquire autonomy through emotional security and attachment to teachers. Care is taken not to destroy the important bond the child has with adults. The first stages of this training entail having the child eat by him/herself, using a spoon, and toilet training. Physical movements such as going up and down steps, and manipulation with the hands are encouraged in play and in outdoor activities. Also, listening to a teacher telling a story or singing stimulates the child's interest in language and expressive activities.

Two-year-olds have more autonomous tasks; taking off clothes, washing hands, going to the toilet by oneself, and eating by oneself are introduced with support from the teachers. Relationships with other children are respected. Developing conversations with teachers, looking at picture books and theater are seen as opportunities to enjoy speaking. Materials such as water, sand, mud, flowers, leaves, and seeds are incorporated in outdoor play to help children begin to have an understanding of nature.

Family Day Care

Family day care is a system of day care where an approved caregiver, often called a "day-care mom," cares for not more than three children under the age of 3 at her home. Local governments organize and control this system of care. These governments give subsidies to day-care moms and also introduce parents to them. Since their creation in Kyoto City in the 1950s, these centers have played the role of "waiting rooms" for day-care centers. The number has been limited (1400 caregivers in 120 local governments in 1999) and concentrated in urban areas. Recently, however, this system has been reexamined due to a growing diversity of needs. Parents who want their babies to grow up in family circumstances rather than in a collective setting prefer this mode of care. The task for local governments is how to assure a professional quality of care by these moms and a satisfactory quality of the settings in which they provide care.

Recent Trends in the Public Care of Infants and Toddlers

We are now in transitional period for public day care. There are four big trends surrounding day care of children. The first point is diversification of needs. With the increase in working mothers, the variety of working styles demands diverse forms of day care; acceptance of children at night, care rooms for children while they are ill, creation of day-care centers in front of subway stations for the convenience for parents, and so forth.

The second trend relates to how Japan can best support full-time mothers. Urbanized lifestyle has contributed to young mother's feelings of isolation. Some investigations show that many mothers find child-rearing painful work. The drastic decline in the fertility rate (1.29 in 2005) has shocked the government. Partly as a result, the Ministry of Welfare and Labor and local governments have instituted various child-rearing support policies. However, with insufficient budgets and without long-term perspectives, these policies are not always effective. Day-care centers are given additional tasks for providing various supports to full-time mothers. Examples include temporary day care, group activities for mothers, and consultations with mothers (face-to-face and by telephone). However, these are often carried out without additional specialized staff, which brings teachers nothing but more work. These supports need to be improved in order for the day-care centers to function well.

The third trend, which has begun in some big cities and is going to extend to other areas, is the privatization of public day-care centers. This privatization policy contains "freedom from minimum standards," which may lead to the decline of quality of care. Some privatized centers are run by enterprises that follow "market principles." While they aim to respond to "users' needs," they think the users are mothers and not children.

The fourth trend is the transformation of present kindergartens and other facilities into new organizations called "comprehensive facilities of care and education," which have been created through collaboration between the Ministry of Education and the Ministry of Welfare and Labor. This system places various modes of care and education in one facility: kindergarten, day-care centers, temporary day care, playroom for parent-child, etc. Although this system looks like an ideal care place because of its availability and flexibility, it was initiated without sufficient preparation; for example, kindergarten teachers without training are working with infants.

In the day care of infants and toddlers, we are facing a situation that raises the question, "which is important, mothers' needs or children's happiness?" The social trend has been toward mothers. However, we have to look at children to ask, "what are the best conditions of care and education for infant and toddlers in day care?" To answer this question, in addition to our long history of past experiences, we need more useful theories based on sufficient scientific data.

Further Readings: Hoshi-Watanabe, M. (2000). Mode de garde et éducation des enfants de moins de trois ans au Japon. In G. Brougère and S. Rayna, eds., *Traditions et innovations dans l'éducation préscolaire*. Paris: INRP (in French), pp.65–94; Ministry of Welfare and Labor. (1999). Guidelines of care and education at day care centers. Revised version in 1999 (in Japanese); Morikami, S. (2004). Recent documentation on education and care in Japan. Kyoto; Minerva shobo (in Japanese).

Miwako Hoshi-Watanabe

Inclusion, Care, and Education for Children with Special Needs in Japan

Introduction

In Japan, special education has been serving children with disabilities since the end of the Second World War. The educational practices designed for these children are based on the kinds and the degrees of the disabilities. However, several changes have occurred in the special education field during the last decade. Some of these changes are: increased social interests to normalization; increased severity and variety of disabilities among children; and an increased awareness of mild developmental disabilities of children who are enrolling in regular schools. To respond to these changes, Japan's special education program is facing a crucial turning point, prompting it to review its mission and its methods of practice.

To develop new concepts and systems, an Advisory Committee on Future Directions for Special Education in the 21st Century was organized in 2001. The committee's final report was submitted to the Ministry of Education, Culture, Sports, Science and Technology (MEXT) in March, 2003. According to the report, basic concepts for developing special education for the future were stated as follows: "In line with the government policy for enhancing normalization in our society, a lifelong support system shall be developed through cooperation among every sector in society to promote children's autonomy and participation in all aspects of society."

The 2001 report indicates that the kinds and the degrees of disabilities are no longer the main focuses of special education; rather the specific needs of children with disabilities are the focus. In other words, special education in Japan is moving away from separated/integrative education and shifting toward an inclusive education model. Along with this change, MEXT has shifted the term from "Special Education" (*Tokushu-Kyoiku*) to "Special Support Education" (*Tokubetu-Shien-Kyoiku*).

Since this conceptual change, Special Support Education is in a transitional period. Therefore, these new concepts have not yet been fully implemented in the Japanese school systems.

The Special School System

Children with severe or profound disabilities are eligible to attend the special schools (*Yougo-Gakkou*) for the blind, the deaf, children with intellectual disabilities, children with physical disabilities, and children with health impairments. Distinctive programs are prepared to meet each child's needs in special schools. There are four levels of schools in the special school system: kindergartens, elementary schools, lower secondary and upper secondary schools. For children who cannot attend schools, special schoolteachers are provided through a home-visit program. Socialization is an important component of the special school system. In order to promote the children's participation in society, children in special schools are encouraged to be involved in activities in regular classes with their peers (*Koryu-Kyoiku*) and activities in the community.

Special Classes

Special classes (*Tokushu-Gakkyu* or *Shinsho-Gakkyu*), which are located in elementary and lower secondary schools, are available for children with moderate and mild disabilities. Children who participate in these special classes join their peers in regular classes in some subjects and school activities. Children with mild disabilities enrolling in regular classes are eligible to attend resource rooms (*Tukyu*) depending on their special needs. MEXT provides the Course of Study (*Gakushyu-shido-yoryo*) and national curriculum standards for schools. Each school develops distinctive curricula according to the needs of the children.

The Road to Inclusion

Although the actual implementation of inclusive education has not yet been accomplished, the 2001 Advisory Committee provided several concrete proposals based on the earlier mentioned concepts, such as; (1) the possible amendment of The Order for Enforcement of the School Education Law regarding placement of children with disabilities; (2) Establishment of special support services in regular classes for children with special educational needs such as Learning Disabilities (LD), Attention-Deficit Hyperactivity Disorder (ADHD) and so on; (3) Establishment of new functions of special schools as local Special Education centers; (4) Reconsideration of the classroom management system of special classes and resource rooms; (5) Promotion of enrollment to upper secondary schools and enrichment of life-long learning of people with disabilities; (6) Encouragement of professional development for Special Education personnel.

Some efforts in line with these proposals were already underway. For example, in 2001, the Advisory Committee on the "National Agenda for Special Support

Education" was established to help clarify the future role of special schools and search for better support for children with mild disabilities including LD, ADHD, and high functioning autisms who were attending regular classes. The committee suggested five objectives: (1) To make Individual Education Programs (IEP) for each child; (2) To place a Special Support Education coordinator in each school (including special schools as well as elementary and secondary schools); (3) To organize a committee to coordinate local administrative departments of Special Support Education; (4) To transform special schools to local Special Support Education centers; and (5) To integrate special classes and resource rooms into Special Support Education rooms.

The objectives appear to facilitate the development of an adequate environment for promoting inclusive education. However, as mentioned above, implementation in schools has only recently begun and educators are struggling to develop Special Support Education in their schools. It is expected that the objectives listed above will take time to implement and will be achieved in the near future.

Support Services for Children

Regarding children before school age, various types of social welfare services are available to support children with special needs. Since the 1960s, pediatricians, public health nurses, and psychologists have performed health examinations for all children from infancy to 3 years of age. Follow-up programs, or early intervention programs, are available for at-risk children and their parents. These programs involve specialists in local Child Guidance Offices (*Jidou-soudansho*), Health Care Centers (*Hoken Center*), Centers for Handicapped Children (*Shougai-Fukushi Center*) and the like.

After the follow-up programs, most of the children who need Special Support Education attend *Yochien* (Kindergartens for children from 3 to 6 years old), *Hoikuen* (Day-care centers for children from infancy to 6 years old) and/or facilities for children with special needs.

In facilities for children with special needs, specialists such as early childhood educators/caregivers, doctors, psychologists, physical therapists, and speech therapists guide individualized programs in a small group setting. However, these facilities may differ, as the availability of the specialists and programs varies among local governments.

In recent years, an increased number of children with special needs have been integrated into the public *Yochien* and *Hoikuen*. It is very common for public *Yochien* and *Hoikuen* to accept two or three children with special needs. In many provinces and cities, the local government provides additional financial support so the program can employ an extra educator or a caregiver for children with special needs. However, there is a lack of trained special needs educators/caregivers. Although children who attend *Yochien* or *Hoikuen* are able to continuously receive periodical checkups and guidance at the local Child Guidance Offices, Health Care Centers, and Facilities for Children with Special Needs, professional supports are still needed in *Yochien* and *Hoikuen*.

To solve this problem, outreach programs *(Junkai-Soudan)* by consulting staff members, who are mostly psychologists, are becoming popular among public

Yochien and *Hoikuen*. Such programs provide professional support for educators/caregivers and parents, along with suggestions on how to plan an individualized program for the children. These outreach programs help facilitate inclusive education and care in early childhood education. Unfortunately, these services are not available for most of the private *Yochien* (about 60% of all *Yochien* are private) and the private *Hoikuen* (about 45% of all *Hoikuen* are private) in Japan. Thus, it is essential to build a system that extends outreach programs to private *Yochien* and *Hoikuen*.

Teacher Training

Another way to solve the problem is to provide educational opportunities for early childhood educators and caregivers, helping them learn about special support education. Some efforts are already made, for example, caregivers in *Hoikuen* are required to complete a subject "Caring for Handicapped Children (*Shougaiji-Hoiku*)" as it is part of the national curriculum. To improve the quality of special support educators, the National Institute of Special Education (NISE) and local Special Education Centers are assisting the government by offering specialized training programs for educators.

Fostering Inclusiveness and Cooperation in Schools

It is also crucial to facilitate collaboration and cooperation among teachers/caretakers, parents, and schools. Without fostering an inclusiveness, their educational initiatives will be ineffective. As discussed above, special, elementary, and secondary schools hope to place a coordinator of Special Support Education in each school. However, few discussions have been officially initiated for facilitating collaboration and cooperation among them in *Yochien* and *Hoikuen*, with most efforts stemming from individual educators or caregivers.

Partnership between the families with and without handicapped children is another key to promoting inclusive education. Partnerships among the families with handicapped children have been increasing in the last decades. A number of parents with handicapped children have organized groups and are taking active roles in our society. On the other hand, not enough attention has been paid to partnerships between the families with handicapped children and the ones without them.

The present situation of Special Support Education in Japan, particularly in early childhood education and care, calls out for improvement in a number of areas. The new concepts of Special Support Education and their implementation are expected to become established practice in the near future.

Further Readings: Ministry of Education, Culture, Sports, Science and Technology: MEXT (2002). Special Support Education in Japan-Education for Children with Special Needs; Ministry of Education, Culture, Sports, Science and Technology: MEXT (2005). Special Support Education. Available online at http://www.mext.go.jp/english/org/formal.

Keiko Gondo

Public Policies in Japan

Today, the child-rearing environment and education have become important issues for several reasons: the declining childbirth rate, the trend toward nuclear families, the lessening of the importance of education in the community, the increasing numbers of working women, and the trend toward academic competences. The political movement supporting early childhood education and care is changing rapidly. This section focuses on the main issues facing Japan: the future of early childhood education, establishing connections between early childhood and elementary school education, and improving the quality and expertise of kindergarten teachers based on the recent policy trends set by the Ministry of Education, Culture, Sports, Science and Technology (MEXT).

The Future of Early Childhood Education in a Changing Environment

Recently the Central Council for Education (2004) published a report titled "The future of early childhood education based on the changing environment surrounding children," in which early childhood is regarded as a critical growth period for cultivating the very basis of human development. Several directions for the future of early childhood education were proposed. The first was the "overall promotion of early childhood education by the home/community/institution." Early childhood education should insure the healthy growth of children, with a balance of educational responsibility among three areas: the home, the community, and institutions such as kindergarten, which is seen as enriching early childhood education. However, the power to educate at home and in the community has decreased with the rapidly changing social environment, affecting education in institutions such as kindergarten. Accordingly, one current focus is the "enrichment of early childhood education based on the continuity of children's lives, development, and learning," which encompasses such areas as the reinforcement and improvement of the continuity between early childhood and elementary school education, and assurance of a smooth transition for prekindergarten children who are under three years of age to kindergarten.

Key Issues and Related Policies

The following three issues and seven policies for enriching early childhood education were listed in the report. The key issues are as follows:

1. Reinforcing and expanding the function of education.
2. Regenerating and empowering the home and community.
3. Reinforcing the foundations that support early childhood education.

The related policies are as follows:

1. To provide all children the opportunities for early childhood education.
2. To improve early childhood education, focusing on developmental needs and the continuity of learning from preschool to elementary school.

3. To foster the professional development of kindergarten teachers.
4. To regenerate and empower home and community education by preschool institutions.
5. To regenerate and empower home and community education by strengthening a policy that supports both lifelong learning and work.
6. To utilize human resources in the community.
7. To reinforce the support base for early childhood education in the community.

From Early Childhood Education to School Education

Emphasis must be placed on a curriculum, environment, and a support system based on child development and learning continuity, focusing on the transition from learning through play during early childhood to learning set subjects in elementary school. During early childhood, children encounter many people, things, and events, and accumulate experiences through play and everyday life experiences. These experiences foster "sprouts" that contribute to a base for further learning about life and study in school, self-development, and morality. Teachers must recognize the sprout within each child, and construct an appropriate environment for its growth. Continuity in the preschool and school curriculums is needed, and it is especially important to consider the transition period prior to starting elementary school. The 2004 Report of the Central Council for Education proposed an interchange of personnel, a program that connected and led to collaborative activities between kindergarten and elementary schoolteachers, and encouraged the implementation of model schools. Based on these proposals, the Curriculum Research Center of the National Institute for Educational Policy Research published a guide called "From early childhood education to elementary school education" (February 2005).

Quality Improvement and the Expertise of Kindergarten Teachers

The Central Council for Education has indicated that to improve the quality of teachers and their expertise, there is a need for the improvement of training, the promotion of participation in training, and a study of measures to increase the number of teachers possessing a bachelor's degree. In response to the "Early Childhood Education Promotion Program" by the Ministry of Education, Culture, Sports, Science and Technology, a study of improving the quality of kindergarten teachers was conducted. The report in 2002 presented the following points as expertise required of kindergarten teachers:
• The ability to understand children's thinking and to comprehensively instruct them.
• The ability to make and implement plans.
• The fostering of teachers' own speciality, cooperativeness as a member of the teachers' group.
• The ability to respond to children who need special educational consideration.
• The ability to promote collaboration between elementary schools and day-care centers.
• The ability to build relations with guardians (parents) and the community.
• Leadership displayed by executive officers, such as a principal.
• An understanding on human rights.

One approach to improving the quality of teachers has been voluntary in-service training efforts. In particular, the importance has been stressed of enriching training both within and outside kindergartens, of designing training based on amount of teaching experience (newly appointed teachers, young teachers, mid-level teachers, executive officers), and of focusing training on a diverse set of needs (for example, instruction of disabled children, consultation on child raising, attitude and mentality needed for counseling, etc.). Collaboration between the field of early childhood education and universities engaged in the preparation of kindergarten teachers is very important, and the role of such universities is significant.

Further Readings: Ministry of Education, Culture, Sports, Science and Technology: (MEXT). (1998). National Curriculum Standards for Kindergartens. Available online at http://www.mext.go.jp/a_menu/shotou/youji/english/youryou/index; Ministry of Education, Culture, Sports, Science and Technology: (MEXT). Available online at http://www.mext.go.jp/; Oda, Y. (2004). Tracing the development of Japanese kindergarten education—Focusing on changes of contents and curriculum. *Bulletin of National Institute for Educational Policy Research* 133, 77–84; Research Center for Child and Adolescent Development and Education: (RCCADE) (2004). Early Childhood Education Handbook. Tokyo; Ochanomizu University.

Takako Noguchi

South Africa

Early Childhood Education in South Africa

Introduction

In South Africa, early childhood development (ECD) is the term used for "the processes by which children from birth to nine years grow and thrive, physically, mentally, emotionally, morally and socially." According to the 2001 Census there are approximately 8.3 million children in this age group: 5,418,204 from 0–5 years, and 2, 872,254 from 6–9 years.

South Africa still faces formidable challenges in addressing the rights and needs of her children. Racist colonial and apartheid policies have left socioeconomic imbalances between black and white and rural and urban South Africans. There is high unemployment and many households live with the stresses of hunger, the lack of formal housing, and high levels of crime and violence including sexual abuse. Many children die of preventable diseases, with the under 5 mortality rate averaging 59.4 per 1000 in 1998. The revised projection for 2002 was 100 per 1000, attributed to the toll of the rising HIV/AIDS pandemic. The migrant labor system and rapid urbanization have eroded traditional family structures, and poverty-stricken female-headed households are common. At an overall prevalence of 29.5 percent, HIV/AIDS is a serious threat impacting on the livelihoods and family structure, with the burden of caring for children in badly affected regions falling upon the elderly and increasingly on older siblings. Many caregivers have low levels of literacy, making it difficult for them to fully support their children's early education.

History

In South Africa, provision for the care and education of young children outside the home was initiated last century by the community, parents, and welfare organizations. By 1940 there was limited state support, with per capita subsidies paying for full day centers under the auspices of social welfare and approved nursery schools from education departments. *Crèches* (day-care centers) were seen as custodial and nursery schools as primarily educational. Because subsidies did not keep up with inflation, centers had to rely more and more on fees to cover costs. Nursery schools with trained teachers became privileged middle-class institutions, while crèches serving working-class children could only afford basic custodial care. This reinforced white privilege and black disadvantage.

When the apartheid Nationalist government came to power in 1948, they were not in favor of provision for young children before school. Until 1969 government policy discouraged the development of early childhood services except for limited service provision for poor white children through differential per capita education subsidies based on parent income and the introduction of parent income limits for a welfare subsidy.

Provision for white children expanded considerably in the 1970s and there was some development in other communities in response to the Head Start movement in the United States and Non Governmental Organization (NGO) initiatives funded by international foundations.

Because of the lack of state involvement in ECD the community and a variety of NGOs shouldered most of the burden of providing ECD services. During the 1980s and 90s a substantial number of NGO providers were set up to provide in-service training for community-based ECD teachers.

After their election in 1994 the democratic African National Congress (ANC) government identified children's rights, which included ECD, as a key area in the process of reconstruction and development. The last decade has seen the evolution and ongoing development of new policies aimed at promoting the rights of young children and career paths of ECD teachers. These policies are excellent, but the challenge to find resources and capacity to support implementation on the ground is great.

Coordination of Services

Government departments with key responsibility for the provision of services to children in this age group are education, social development (welfare), and health. The health and welfare departments focus on children up to five years. While education is concerned with the full 0–9 years and its policies reflect this, its priority has been to provide a Reception Year for children from 5 years, mostly within public primary schools. An integrated plan for servicing 0- to 4-year-olds has recently been developed by the three departments. This provides for a range of health, social support, and stimulation programs focusing on children at home as well as those in centers.

Policy

Democratic government policy in South Africa needed to address decades of racially discriminatory policies affecting the majority of children in South Africa. Values underpinning our policies include access, redress, equity, quality, and democratic governance.

Education White Paper 1 in 1995 defined government's commitment both to working interdepartmentally and to young children, starting with the phasing in of a Reception Year as part of compulsory schooling. An Interim ECD policy followed in 1996, and a National Pilot to investigate the phasing in of a reception year, accreditation of teachers and training providers. Recommendations from the pilot were the basis for the 2001 Education White Paper 5 on ECD. This provided for the phasing in of the reception year for children turning 5, prioritizing the poorest of the poor. It is intended that all 5-year-olds will be in Grade R classes by 2010. For children younger than this, the White paper prioritized the development of the strategic plan for intersectoral collaboration, with education focusing on program curriculum and quality. Education policy includes a focus on very young children with disabilities to allow for early identification and intervention but children with disabilities make up as little as 1.4 percent of children attending ECD facilities. Children from 5 and a half to 6 years are eligible to attend compulsory primary schooling, which is governed by the South African Schools Act of 1996.

Within welfare policy, provision of appropriate early childhood development services, including day care, parent education and support, is considered to be an important measure, which facilitates the optimum development of children and their families. The White Paper for Social Welfare (1996) prioritises services for disadvantaged children under five years and they are the targets for receipt of child-care subsidies. Though the subsidies are well targeted to the poor, given the total numbers of young children likely to be at risk, the number of children receiving subsidies is very low. A child support grant for children up to 14 years in poor families is another support mechanism.

The Child Care Act of 1983, which will be replaced by the Children's Act (currently before parliament), provides that regular care and partial care services for more than six children not in a school should be registered with social services. Registration is contingent upon meeting the Guidelines for ECD services which define minimum standards for the physical facilities, health and nutrition, educational and management aspects of a day-care program. A health clearance certificate is required from local authorities.

The Department of Health provides free health care for pregnant women and children under 6 years and for older children whose carers earn below a certain threshold. Young children are a priority in the Integrated Nutrition Policy. This includes food fortification, nutrition education and growth monitoring, parasite control and food supplementation to malnourished children and pregnant and lactating women. Food support is available to children in public primary schools through the Primary School Nutrition Program.

Access and Supply

ECD services can be a significant support to children in difficult circumstances but in South Africa there are vast disparities in access to provision on grounds of race (population group) with African children having the lowest access overall. Rural areas, where 70 percent of poor children live, have only 40 percent of all ECD facilities. (Under the apartheid state, people were classified by race—white, colored (persons of mixed origin), Asian or African, which was further categorized by ethnicity. These politically imposed terms were used to socially mark people for a variety of purposes. The term "black" is used in this entry to refer collectively to all population groups other than white.) Overall enrollment in approximately 23,500 ECD centers audited nationwide in 2000 was 16 percent. This ranged from 8 percent and 10 percent in two of the poorest, rural provinces to 25 percent and 26 percent in the wealthiest and most developed Western Cape and Gauteng provinces. Access to services increases with age with only 5 percent of children under 3 in centers compared to 15 percent of children aged 3–5 and 21 percent aged 5 to 7.

Teacher Preparation

In the past the majority of ECD teachers were trained by NGOs and their qualifications were not formally recognized. All accredited education and training now falls under the South African Qualifications Authority (SAQA). This was set up in 1995 to develop and implement a National Qualifications Framework (NQF). The NQF is the framework on which qualifications and courses are registered and against which learner achievements are recorded. ECD qualifications can be obtained from a range of providers—private, nongovernmental, further education and training colleges as well as universities—who are accredited by a quality assurance body appointed by SAQA. A challenge is crediting the prior learning of the many experienced teachers who did not have access to accredited training in the past. Qualifications have been registered at several levels but there is little specialized ECD training at the higher levels, especially postgraduate. Teachers training for primary schooling require a four-year degree as a minimum but there are many under-qualified black teachers from the apartheid era who require upgrading.

Financing

Most ECD provision for all ages is run by welfare organizations, NGOs, community-based organizations, and private providers. Parental fees are the primary source of income for many centers, which in poor communities puts ECD facilities in a precarious position. Due to lack of resources, the quality of much of the provision is less than optimal as many of the centers are poorly equipped, teachers are untrained, and conditions may be unhygienic. The nearly 53,000 teachers of children prior to Grade 1 earn very low salaries; 44 percent earn less than R 500 per month (approximately $77) and another 30 percent between R 500 and R 1500 ($230).

Provincial departments of social development subsidize children from 0 to 4 years in some registered centers on a per capita basis per attendance day and this varies from R 2 to R 6 ($0.31 to $0.92) across the provinces. In 2004/5 these subsidies were paid to about 20 percent of centers in South Africa. Provincial education payments are made also on a per capita basis of R 3 ($0.46) per day for up to 200 days per annum to learners in registered Grade R classes. There are also a small number of Grade R teacher posts funded in some provinces. The numbers of Grade R children subsidized will increase substantially starting with poor schools as Grade R rolls out until there is universal coverage. National norms have been recommended for increased per capita subsidies for both education and social development.

Early Childhood Development Programming

Principles for programming include holistic development of the child, contextually and developmentally appropriate activities, a focus on human rights and values in the curriculum, and opportunities to play and learn informally through experience in a nurturing environment.

There is no prescribed curriculum for children under five years though the Department of Education plans to test and introduce curriculum guidelines for under fours. There are concerns in both the government and NGO sector that the requirements and delivery may be overly formal for such young children. ECD service guidelines reflect the need for stimulating activities as well as provision for health and nutrition.

Curriculum for 5-year-olds forms part of the Revised National Curriculum Statement for the Foundation Phase (Grades R–3 or approximate ages 5–9 years). The focus is given to literacy, numeracy, and lifeskills programs. South Africa follows an outcomes based education (OBE) system that clearly defines the outcomes to be achieved at the end of the learning process with grade-related assessment standards. Outcomes for each learning area are based on achieving a set of critical and developmental outcomes that focus on producing learners with knowledge, skills, and values for productive engagement in the workforce and a democratic and caring society.

Early Childhood Development and the Family

Building partnerships between home, preschool, and the early years of primary schooling is recognized as important in supporting children's development. However, there are challenges in establishing partnerships. Many parents lack the time, confidence, or understanding to be involved in their children's early education. Many teachers do not value parent input or are uncertain how to involve parents. For these and other reasons parents, especially those living in poorer communities, are not generally involved in the schools their children attend. When they are they are most often involved in fundraising and maintenance rather than the educational program.

The other aspect of partnership with families is to reach the majority of children who are not accessed by center-based services. Programs targeting primary caregivers and supporting them in their role as educators and providers for their young children have been developed and run by NGOs for many years. In poor communities the outreach workers involved in these programs play an essential role in linking parents with resources such as clinics, social grants, and income generation as well as focusing on developing their knowledge of how to support early learning. Recently, as part of extension of government programs to children under 5, the departments of health, social development, and education are planning a strong focus on parenting. But this is still at the planning stage.

There has also been a focus on educational media programs for young children, of which Takalani Sesame, the South African version of Sesame Street, an initiative of the SABC, Department of Education and Children's Television Workshop, is the best known. As well as television and radio components it has an outreach arm that trains parents and teachers to use the programs to enhance the development of their young children.

Further Readings: Biersteker, L. (2001). Early Childhood Development—A Review of Public Policy and Funding. Cape Town: Children's Budget Unit, IDASA; Biersteker, L., and A. Dawes (forthcoming). Early Childhood Development. *The Human Resources Development Review 2006.* Cape Town: Human Sciences Research Council. Will be available online at www.hsrc.ac.za; Department of Education (2001). The Nationwide Audit of ECD Provisioning in South Africa. Pretoria. Available online at http://www.Education.gov.za/DoE_Sites/ECD/early_childhood_development.htm; Department of Education (2001). White Paper 5—Early Childhood Development. Pretoria. Available online at http://www.education.gov.za/DoE_Sites/ECD/early_childhood_development.htm; Short, A., and P. P. Pillay (2002). Meeting the Challenges of ECD Training in South Africa. Paper presented at the Omep World Council and Conference, Durban.

Linda Biersteker

Poverty and Young Children in South Africa

Many of the roots of child poverty in South Africa were firmly planted by the Apartheid government in its disenfranchising policies of underdevelopment and poor education.

The 2000 South African Income and Expenditure Survey was used to quantify the extent of child poverty from a monetary point of view. Two poverty lines were used to calculate child poverty at national and provincial levels. These are slightly higher than the international standard of $1 and $2 per person per day. Using the higher line, 74.9 percent of children aged 0 to 17 in South Africa are poor—more than 13 million children. With the lower poverty line, 54.3 percent of children across South Africa are ultrapoor—some 9.7 million children.

Poverty is not evenly distributed across the nine provinces in South Africa. The provinces of KwaZulu-Natal, the Eastern Cape and Limpopo together were home to 60 percent of South Africa's income-poor children. These provinces all include the previous "homeland states," entities established by the South African government under apartheid to deny South African citizenship and rights to the black majority. They were overcrowded, and had bloated and corrupt administrations. These rural areas are significantly underdeveloped.

The biggest single contributor to household poverty is the very high rate of unemployment, which has been on the increase since South Africa opened its economy after the end of Apartheid. The official unemployment figures of September 2004 show that 26.2 percent of the economically active population was unemployed. Given the Apartheid legacy of racial discrimination, employment levels are highly differentiated by race. Black South Africans who make up 79 percent of the population have a 31.3 percent unemployment rate, whereas the same rate for white South Africans is only 5.4 percent.

These unemployment statistics are only a partial reflection of the work situation in South Africa. A more useful expanded definition of unemployment includes those people who would like to find employment but are discouraged work seekers. On this calculation, unemployment levels are at 41 percent in South Africa.

While there are large numbers of children living in absolute poverty, South Africa, a middle-income country, is also marked by stark inequalities. The United Nations Human Development Report 2004 includes a range of indicators of inequality. South Africa is ranked 119th out of 177 countries reflected in the report with a Gini coefficient of 59.3. (The Gini coefficient is a commonly used measure of how evenly or unevenly income is distributed within a nation). The poorest 20 percent of South Africans have access to only 2 percent of income.

The extent of the HIV/AIDS pandemic as well as the government's weak response to it, have deepened poverty. While there is a comprehensive plan for prevention campaigns and to provide medication to those infected, a lack of political will and weak health services infrastructure have hampered delivery, particularly of Antiretroviral therapy. The best data on the impact of HIV/AIDS comes from the Actuarial Society of South Africa (ASSA) model. Estimates of the spread of HIV/AIDS for 2004 derived from this model are that 5 million South Africans of a total population of 44.8 million are currently infected. An estimated 63,000 children were infected at birth or in the course of breastfeeding in 2004. This is in contrast to some one million babies born uninfected. The model also estimates that in the same year some 245,000 children from birth to fourteen years were HIV positive or had AIDS defining illnesses. AIDS has made a substantial difference to infant mortality with 40 percent of child deaths (IMR) attributable to HIV/AIDS.

A useful indicator of the impact of the pandemic is that of maternal orphans, defined as children from birth to eighteen years who have lost either their mother or both parents. Currently there are some 1.2 million such children in South Africa, more than 600,000 of whom were orphaned by the AIDS pandemic. Projections are that, without significantly increased access to treatment for adults with HIV/AIDS, this number will increase significantly, rising to nearly 2 million by 2015. There can be no doubt that many of the gains made since the advent of democracy are being reversed by the ravages of the HIV/AIDS pandemic.

The Impact of Poverty on Young Children

According to calculations made from 2001 census data, in that year there were 8.3 million children from birth to eight years in South Africa, comprising some 18.5 percent of the total population of the country. The most basic manifestation of poverty and inequality is the lack of household food security. The best source of information on food security and hunger is somewhat out of date—the 1999 National Food Consumption Survey in children aged 1 to 9 in South Africa. The situation of children in terms of hunger was not good in 1999. This study found that at the national level, 52 percent of children aged 1 to 9 cxpcrienced hunger.

A further 23 percent were at risk of hunger. Only 25 percent appeared to be food secure.

Poor households that are characterized by greater numbers of very young or school-going children also have less access to essential services such as water and sanitation, communications, roads and energy sources, particularly in rural areas. They also have long distances to travel to access health facilities. A vigorous government program to upgrade access to basic services such as water and sanitation has increased the percentage of people with access to a safe water supply from 60 percent in 1994 to 91 percent by March 2004 and basic sanitation from 49 percent to 64 percent.

Poverty impacts on the very structure of children's lives. As well as material poverty, poverty has social and power manifestations. Family life is most fragmented for the poor. In many poor households fathers are absent or children live apart from their parents. There is evidence that protracted physical poverty leads to social isolation of families. Poor children are more likely to grow up in communities wracked by crime and violence.

Government Strategies to Combat Poverty and Ensure Development

The South African government is acutely aware of the problems of poverty and joblessness, and antipoverty rhetoric is prominent in public life. The years of democracy have seen a number of strategies to combat poverty—some of which specifically focused on children.

In 1994, the Reconstruction and Development Programme announced a series of lead projects aiming to extend the reach of the public service into previously neglected communities. In 1996, the African National Congress government introduced the Growth, Employment and Redistribution policy (GEAR) policy. Its primary objective was to stimulate growth by opening the economy, reducing public expenditure and attracting foreign direct investment, and by that means, reducing poverty. The majority of the targets of the strategy were not met. GEAR projections ended in 2001, and since then, no other unified national strategy around trade or expenditure has been announced. There has however been a substantial shift toward increased social expenditure since the end of the GEAR period.

While these macroeconomic policies were being put into place, a wide range of programs aimed at developing communities that were without housing and services were initiated, and massive institutional reform took place to unify and standardize education, health, and municipal services.

In 1998, the state introduced the Child Support Grant, a small noncontributory poverty-targeted cash grant paid monthly to the primary caregiver of the child. Initially, children from birth to six were eligible. Since 2000, this grant has been rolled out to older children so that children under 14 are now eligible. Some 5.5 million poor children now have access to some measure of income support in this very successful program.

Since 1994, there have been large-scale programs aimed at improving the living conditions of children and others. One of the first policy announcements was the introduction of free public health care to children under 6 and pregnant women.

This has since been extended to free primary health care for all children and adults, and free secondary and tertiary care for children with disabilities. There have been similarly large-scale interventions in housing, with over one million new houses built for low-income families. There are however problems with the quality of these houses, their location, and their tiny size.

With respect to education and early childhood development services, the record of government in addressing the needs of children to the age of 9 is mixed. In the formal schooling sector including primary school and the recently introduced Grade R, a number of interventions have been inadequately financed and managed. Although school enrollment is high in South Africa, in the region of 95 percent at the primary school level, attendance is much lower. Efforts to support learners to attend school include the School Fee Waiver policy and the Primary School Feeding Scheme.

Initiatives to support children before their schooling years have been very weak and have not been a significant component of the government's poverty alleviation strategy, though plans to expand the system and make more resources available are before Cabinet. Outside the primary school environment under the Education Department, all services to children fall under the Department of Social Development. The expansion of the social safety nets to children and adults has squeezed out funding for social services, which have received very little attention. There is an almost total lack of family support interventions for parents with young children. Those early childhood development (ECD) services that do exist are facilities based but poorly supported in the poorest communities. Some facilities that are able to register receive a per child per day allocation based on parental income levels which varies in different provinces. This is a contribution toward staff salaries, educational activities, and nutrition. The majority of ECD facilities are however, unable to register because of norms and standards that do not take the living conditions in rural areas, informal settlements and inner-city areas into account. Lack of funding can mean poor or no nutrition offered to the children and lack of educational equipment but more seriously impacts on the wages earned by the educators leading to high attrition from the sector, and in many cases low motivation. Facilities in poor communities have significantly poorer infrastructure in the form of buildings, water, and sanitation and this is especially so of facilities serving African children. Because many ECD facilities operate as small businesses the need to make them financially viable can lead to overcrowding.

Local government's constitutional mandate for ECD provision is ambiguous but there are some signs that ECD is beginning to get more prominence at local government level in some areas, both metropolitan and rural, with priority to young children being seen as a social upliftment and poverty alleviation strategy.

Further Readings: For official statistics including population demographics and employment levels, contact Department of Health (2000) National Food Consumption Survey 1999. Available online at http://www.sahealthinfo.org/nutrition/foodconsumption.htm; Dorrington R. E., D. Bradshaw, L. Johnson, and D. Budlender (2004). *The Demographic Impact of HIV/AIDS in South Africa: National Indicators for 2004*. Cape Town: Centre for Actuarial Research, South African Medical Research Council and Actuarial Society of South Africa, pp. 1–28; Statistics South Africa. Available online at www.statssa.gov.za;

Streak, J. (2004). Child poverty in South Africa and implications for policy: Using indicators and children's views to gain perspective. In Erika Coetzee and Judith Streak, eds., *Monitoring child socio-economic rights in South Africa: Achievements and Challenges*. Cape Town: IDASA, pp. 9–49.

Annie Leatt

Early Childhood and Violence Exposure

First it is appropriate to provide some definitions. The key concepts are structural, political, and interpersonal violence. Each impacts significantly on early childhood.

Structural violence refers to a political and economic system that excludes people from full participation in society, either by law or by the nature of the economic system. In South Africa under apartheid adults and children were excluded from full participation in society on the basis of color. Education and all other services were racially discriminatory. Community life was segregated. The limited educational opportunities of blacks compromised their life chances in very fundamental ways. It also shaped the young child's perception of those of "other" groups entrenching racist attitudes.

Structural violence can continue in a democracy if the society is highly skewed in terms of a small wealthy group and a very large population living in long-term poverty (as is the case with Brazil and South Africa). In this form of structural violence, the survival, development, protection, and opportunities of the poor child are likely to be severely compromised, particularly when there are inadequate welfare provisions.

South Africa has a strong child rights tradition. The Constitution has a special section (28) that grants children nonderogable rights to social security, protection, shelter, health care services, and education. These provisions provide powerful tools that can be used to advance children's rights. They have led to the provision of child grants for parents who have less than a certain level of income. All children under six are entitled to free health care, as are all older children whose carers earn less than a certain threshold. Free nutrition is provided at means-tested schools and some registered early childhood development (ECD) centers. While there is much that still needs to be done, these provisions certainly offset some of the major threats to early development that are part and parcel of societies that have high Gini coefficients—a commonly accepted marker of a structurally unequal society (see Poverty and Young Children in South Africa).

Political violence is a form of intergroup conflict. In some instances the state is in conflict with a group or groups who use violence against it. It can refer to the violent actions of state forces used to oppress citizens (regardless of whether there is violent opposition or not). Political violence usually refers to intrastate conflict. Classical examples include that between the South African state and liberation forces during the apartheid years; the Irish nationalist—British loyalist conflict in Northern Ireland; and the Palestinian-Israeli conflict. All have affected children very deeply in a range of ways.

In South Africa, from the late 1970s through the mid-1990s, thousands of young people were engaged in violent political conflict against the regime. Many more suffered under the lash of political oppression. There were an estimated 51,000 detentions of adults and children without trial between 1984 and 1988. About 24,000 children (the vast majority adolescents), were held in detention without trial in the period 1985 to 1989. Children experienced the terror tactics of the state, including threats, misinformation, smear campaigns, harassment of kin, intrusion into domestic space, as well as teargassing and closure of schools. It was not only the adolescent political activists who were affected by the invasion of schools by the police and the army. Children under the age of 9 were also affected. Their education was disrupted by school closures for long periods. Particularly traumatic, family members disappeared, and were killed. As the political struggle in South Africa intensified, it became ever more public. Teenagers would often lead the assault against the soldiers and police. They would participate in the murder of officials in public places accompanied by large crowds singing and cheering them on.

Generations of South African children therefore grew up in a context of political violence coupled to the structural violence of apartheid racism and poverty. They learnt that violence was an acceptable approach to the resolution of conflict, they lost years of education, and for many the emotional costs of seeing their parents and families suffer were very significant. Nonetheless, it is also true that the majority of these children showed enormous strength under very difficult conditions.

Interpersonal violence refers to that between individuals rather than groups. For children it takes many forms. Direct exposure to direct violence includes bullying in the playground, fights with siblings, and being subjected to violence by those who are charged with their protection and development (caregivers and their teachers). Indirect exposure involves witnessing violence to others (in real life or screen media). Many children witness violence at home and on the streets. While direct exposure has negative outcomes for children, particularly when repeated and severe, witnessing violence, particularly in domestic settings, is deeply disturbing, particularly to young children whose ability to process such events is not yet mature.

Young children in South Africa have suffered exposure to child abuse, and violence and alcohol abuse by their caregivers for many generations. Recent studies have shown that many live in communities in which violence is endemic. Rather than unanticipated, isolated events, the violence often consists of multiple, traumatizing events. For example in one survey conducted in a poor area of Cape Town, 70 percent of 8-year-olds had witnessed violence including murder and domestic violence and other forms of assault, and 47 percent had been victims of assault. A major problem is the chronic shortage of clinical services to deal with these children.

Despite the high levels of violence, it is essential to stress that the majority of young children exposed to violence do not show evidence of major psychological difficulties. This finding is in line with studies conducted elsewhere. While these children are remarkably resilient, this does not mean there is no effect. Many children may be deeply distressed and harbor traumatic memories. However, they have sufficient internal resources and external supports that prevent the development of psychopathology.

Child abuse is a major source of violence exposure for South African children. Due to the nature of the problem it is not possible to derive accurate figures. Nonetheless it is reasonable to estimate (based on several data sources) that some 20 percent of children experience contact sexual abuse. While police crime statistics are not accurate representations of sexual abuse, they can provide a rough guide. A South African Police Services study of recorded rape indicates that in 1998, 15 percent of South African rape victims were below the age of 12 (prevalence: 130/100,000 of female children under 12 years). These are shocking figures. Again services are limited to a few treatment centers in some major cities.

Partner violence is another serious threat to the well-being of young children. It is well known that their emotional development is compromised by exposure to violence between their carers. A recent representative South African national prevalence study found that at least 20 percent of adults were involved in violent relationships.

While many do not consider physical punishment of children to be "violence," it is. When adults hit one another it is called "assault." When parents hit children, it is called "discipline." The UN Committee on the Rights of the Child has consistently argued that physical punishment is a violation of the Convention of the Rights of the Child and lobbied that it be outlawed to protect young children. A recent South African household survey showed that 59 percent of parents use corporal punishment and that the most vulnerable age is between 3 and 5.

Exposure to media violence should not be omitted from this discussion. It is worth noting the impact of media violence, particularly television, on the development of violent orientations in the young child. Children under the age of 6 are most likely to mimic screen violence as they are less conscious of fantasy/reality distinctions, and because it is a period in which children can identify with screen heroes in a manner that makes them feel strong and able to overcome difficulties in their own lives.

Implications for the Protection and Development of Young Children

Exposure to violence provides many opportunities for the young to learn violent behavior. At the same time, repeated traumatization is also likely to result in psychological states that are associated with aggressive behavior, particularly in young males. If we are serious about youth violence prevention, young children and their developmental contexts require our focused attention.

One has to start at the level of legislation to create appropriate constitutional and legislative mechanisms for the protection of the most vulnerable in society, in particular the establishment of individual rights and also social rights and protections. In South Africa this has been addressed through the Constitutional process, which includes key protections for the young. At the level of implementation, South Africa has a long way to travel.

Large-scale policy initiatives are not enough however. Many communities, schools and homes remain unsafe for young children. A key intervention is to introduce peace education and nonviolent conflict resolution in schools and ECD settings. We first have to ensure that they develop and use policies of nonviolence that operate between *all* persons and at all levels. Teachers and other staff need to buy into the policy and model nonviolent conflict resolution for children. Then we need to actively teach children these skills and see that they employ them in the playground. South Africa has moved forward to some extent with such initiatives in the formal primary school setting, but not in preschool settings. Reducing violence in schools and ECD settings lowers the opportunities for the young to learn the acceptability of violence from peers. In addition, if school safety and nonviolence is coupled with training in nonviolent modes of conflict resolution, the young have the opportunity to learn pro-social problem solving, to which they would not otherwise be exposed. Even though it is probable that these interventions do not contribute massively to a reduction in violence, they will in all likelihood provide better outcomes for a proportion of youth.

Finally, it is important to intervene with young children who are at high-risk for violent conduct due to the nature of their temperaments and their family settings (e.g. boys in dysfunctional families in high crime neighborhoods). We know that if a preschool child with a history of persistent aggressive behavior is not assisted in early childhood, the odds are that the pattern will persist. This is particularly likely if the child is troubled and has a dysfunctional parenting situation.

There are a number of well-tested interventions for children in this position. A South African example of an early preventive intervention is Petersen and Carolissen's (2000) early school-based child and parent intervention program for aggressive preschool children. They are intensive programs and therefore are not cheap to implement. However, the cost to society of *not* intervening early and not assisting these children *and* their families is far higher in the long run. This is because these children are likely to develop antisocial behavior, have school problems, and eventually drop out.

In sum, as with other aspects of early childhood intervention, we need to prevent threats to development due to violence while we promote positive nonviolent development. Prevention of violence in the ECD setting and the school are priorities for South Africa. These must be complemented with interventions in the home that have been shown to make a difference. Home visiting programs have been shown to work in improving infant emotional outcomes. The work of Cooper and colleagues (2002) is a South African example. Again those that work are labor intensive and don't come cheap. But that is what it takes if we wish to address the impact of both structural and interpersonal violence in developing country settings. Early investment pays long-term dividends.

Further Readings: Bierman, K. L., M.T. Greenberg, and Conduct Problems Prevention Research Group (CPPRG) (1996). Social skills training in the FAST TRACK program. In R. D. Peters and R. J. McMahon, eds., *Preventing childhood disorders, substance abuses, and delinquency*. Thousand Oaks, CA: Sage Publications, pp. 65–89; Bushman, B., and C. Anderson (2001). Media violence and the American public: Scientific facts versus media misinformation. *American Psychologist* 56, 477–489; Cairns, E. (1996). *Children and political violence*. Oxford: Blackwell; Cooper, P. J., M. Landman, M. Tomlinson, C. Molteno L. Swartz, and L. Murray (2002). Impact of a mother-infant intervention in an indigent peri-urban South African context: A pilot study. *British Journal of Psychiatry* 180, 76–81; Dawes, A, and G. Finchilescu (2002). What's changed? South African adolescents' racial attitudes between 1992 and 1996. *Childhood: A Global Journal of Child Research* 9(2), 147–165; Dawes, A., Z. de Sas Kropiwnicki, Z. Kafaar, and L. Richter. (2005). Partner violence. In U. Pillay, B. Roberts, and S. Rule, eds, *South African Social Attitudes: The Baseline Report*. Cape Town: HSRC Press; Dawes, A., Z. Kafaar, de Sas Kropiwnicki, Z. R. Pather, and L. Richter (2004). Partner violence, attitudes to child discipline & the use of corporal punishment: A South African national survey. Report for Save the Children Sweden. Cape Town: Human Sciences Research Council; Eyber, C., D. Dyer, R. Versfeld, A. Dawes, G. Finchilescu, and C. Soudien (1997). Resisting racism: A teacher's guide to equality in education. Cape Town: IDASA; Huesmann, L. R., J. Moise-Titus, C. Podolski, and L. D. Eron (2003). Longitudinal relations between children's exposure to TV violence and their aggressive and violent behavior in young adulthood: 1977–1992. *Developmental Psychology* 39, 201–221; Olds, D. L. (1990). Can home visitation improve the health of women and children at risk? In D. L. Rogers and E. Ginzberg, eds., *Improving the life chances of children at risk*. Boulder CO: Westview Press, pp. 79–103; Petersen, H. J., and R. Carolissen (2000). Working with aggressive preschoolers. In D. Donald, A. Dawes, and J. Louw, eds., *Addressing Childhood Adversity*. Cape Town: David Phillip, pp. 94–112; Richter, L., A. Dawes, and C. Higson-Smith, eds. (2004). Sexual abuse of young children in Southern Africa. Cape Town: HSRC Press; Straker, G. (1992). Faces in the revolution. The psychological effects of violence on township youth in South Africa. Cape Town: David Philip; Van der Merwe, A., and A. Dawes (2000). Prosocial and antisocial tendencies in children exposed to community violence. *Southern African Journal of Child and Adolescent Mental Health* 12(1), 19–37; Villani, S. (2001). Impact of media on children and adolescents: A 10-year review of the research. *Journal of the American Academy of Child and Adolescent Psychiatry* 40, 392.

Andrew Dawes

Child Health and Well-Being in South Africa

Children's right to nutrition and basic health care services is guaranteed by the South African Constitution, and young children up to the age of 5 are prioritized in health policies. Targets are guided by international agreements such as the Millennium Development Goals and World Fit for Children. High poverty rates impact negatively on the survival and health of young children in South Africa and the HIV/AIDS crisis has severely worsened the situation.

Current Indicators of Child Health in South Africa

According to the Demographic and Health Survey in 1998 the infant mortality rate (IMR) was 45.4 per 1000 and under five mortality rate 59.4 per 1000 live births. The national figure conceals wide geographic differences with far higher rates in the poorer rural provinces (urban 43.2 and rural 71.2) and population group differences with African children having the highest mortality rates (white children 15.3 and African 63.6). Between 1998 and 2002 estimates are that IMR increased by 14 per 1000 almost exclusively because of mother-to-child transmission of HIV. The under 5 mortality rate almost doubled to 100 per 1000.

Leading causes of death include intestinal infection, lower respiratory infection, unnatural causes, and HIV. Malnutrition accounts for about 6 percent of child deaths. In 2003 the Department of Health reported immunization coverage of 82 percent for one-year-olds, but here too there is regional variation with lower rates in poor rural provinces. For children 12–23 months cover drops to 63.4 percent.

Stunting is the most common form of malnutrition. The 1999 National Food Consumption Survey showed that 21.6 percent of children aged 1–9 are stunted compared with 10.3 who are underweight for age. Younger children aged 1–3 are most severely affected as well as those living on commercial farms (30.6%) and in tribal and rural areas. Obesity is a growing problem for about 7.5 percent of children aged 4–9, predominantly in formal urban areas.

There is a serious tuberculosis epidemic that is increasing at about 20 percent per annum as a result of its association with HIV infection. In the more northerly and north-east provinces such as KwaZulu Natal, Limpopo, and Mpumalanga malaria rates are high.

HIV and AIDS are a dire threat to the survival and well-being of very large and growing numbers of young children in South Africa. In 2004, 29.5 percent of pregnant women tested at public facilities were HIV positive. An estimated 6 percent of babies are infected peri-natally through mother-to-child transmission. Far greater numbers of children have their survival and well-being compromised through growing up in houses where breadwinners and caregivers are infected or have died. Young children are most developmentally vulnerable to deprivation of consistent, responsive care, adequate nutrition, and interpersonal and environmental stimulation. Children from households perceived to be HIV/AIDS affected are often stigmatized impacting negatively on their self-esteem and other factors that promote resilience.

State Initiatives to Address the Health of Young Children

Child health and nutrition are high on the list of the government's priorities. The new government has introduced a number of significant policies to redress inequities in the allocation of health resources and to improve maternal and child health care. These include the Primary School Nutrition Programme (PSNP), more recently, the national Integrated Nutrition Programme (INP) for South Africa, Free Health Care for pregnant women and children under six years, the Expanded Programme of Immunisation, and Integrated Management of Childhood Illnesses (IMCI).

The INP includes fortification of staple foods, promotion of exclusive breast-feeding, community-based growth monitoring, developing community food gardens, and nutritional supplementation. For children in public schools the PSNP provides a nutritious snack. This is not available to Grade R classes in community schools or for younger children and there are difficulties accessing nutritional supplementation and emergency food aid in many districts.

In response to HIV/AIDS the Department of Health launched its strategic plan in 2000. This framework for responding to the epidemic has four priority areas including Prevention; Treatment, Care and Support; Research, Monitoring and Surveillance; and Human Rights. Of particular relevance for 0- to 8-year-olds are Reduction of Mother-to- Child HIV Transmission and Expanding the Provision of Care to Children and Orphans.

In the same year the Departments of Health, Social Development and Education, the major social service deliverers in prevention and management, developed a national integrated plan for children infected and affected by HIV/AIDS. The intervention includes poverty relief, life skills education, and home and community-based care.

A Prevention of Mother-to-Child Transmission (PMTCT) of HIV program started in 2001 and operates at a number of public hospitals and community health centers throughout the country. Services include voluntary counseling and testing, advice on infant feeding and use of milk formula as well as general education and support. Prevention of vertical transmission is, however, only one aspect of preventing vulnerability. Providing treatment and support to children's mothers and other caregivers, so they can provide good care for as long as possible, is as important. In April 2004, a national Antiretroviral Therapy treatment program started. However, it has faced numerous challenges, especially in the poorer provinces, and is not rolling out rapidly enough to meet the demand for treatment. Midway through the first year only 11, 000 of a target of 53, 000 people were involved in treatment.

Important aspects of a safety net for all children affected by HIV include improving access to child support grants, which requires children's births to be registered and adults to have identity documents. Securing foster care grants for caregivers of children not their own by birth is a slow statutory process requiring fast tracking.

Apart from the specifically age targeted PMTCT programmes there is little focus in programs on the particular vulnerabilities of very young children affected by HIV and AIDS. Problems of keeping children in school, supporting child headed households and prevention programs aimed at older children and youth have been most common.

The Early Childhood Development Services Response to HIV/AIDS

A number of service responses are emerging to address the situation of young children made vulnerable by HIV. An obvious target group is those children in early childhood development (ECD) centers and the early grades of primary schooling, but there is a need also for broader outreach to the majority of young children not reached by these services

Early childhood development center programs. There are many training courses to teach ECD teachers and caregivers to deal with affected children in their centers. These involve information to dispel myths about HIV, training about universal precautions, and how to provide emotional support to children coping with trauma. Some of these can be credited to a national qualification in ECD. However there are many recorded cases of reluctance to accept children suspected of being HIV positive into centers because of fear and stigma. Practitioners could play a far more strategic role in identifying children at risk and linking them with resources if they had additional information and support. ECD centers could provide safe care, security, and stimulation for young children traumatized by sickness and death. When young children attend ECD programs parents and caregivers are released to attend to survival needs, and older children who are caring for the young ones to go to school. This would only be possible with greater subsidy support for children attending ECD centers.

Outreach programs. Young children made vulnerable by poverty or household illness are among those least likely to attend preschools centers or schools. A number of programs are attempting to reach these children, who are outside of the service loop. The family and community has traditionally been the safety net for young children but is stretched to breaking point, with elderly caregivers and child heads of households particularly in need of support.

Common principles on which these programs are based include a rights-based approach to programming, a broad focus on vulnerable children, as targeting of orphans or HIV affected children can increase stigmatisation, and building on the capacity of communities to care for affected children and link them with resources. The value of combining academic knowledge and more traditional knowledge bases in addressing the impact of the pandemic is recognized.

The Training and Resources in Early Education's (TREE) Integrated ECD Projects in areas of KwaZulu Natal provide an example. These aim to promote the physical well-being of children as well as strengthening their resilience through psychosocial support and linking them to all support services available to them. This involves providing information and support to all adults who interact with young children and may include assistance in getting identity documents, accessing grants and nutritional support as well as initiating stimulating play activities for young children. The program aims to build community-based management to support the needs of vulnerable young children by doing the following:
- Strengthening families
- Lobbying local leadership and local government
- Linking with ECD practitioners
- Establishment of community child care committees with representation of major stakeholders and responsible for identification and monitoring of particularly vulnerable households in their community
- Use of volunteer family facilitators to build caregiving capacity at household level
- Linking with a wide range of public services for children and people in the community: for example, welfare, health, agriculture, policing.

Media programs. Media projects have great potential to influence attitudes as well as providing information. Takalani Sesame, which has radio, television, and outreach materials, has introduced an HIV positive Muppet, Kami, as a member of the cast. It aims to provide age-appropriate messages for children aged 3–7 years assisting young children, parents, and caregivers with knowledge and skills to deal with the pandemic.

Meeting the rights and needs of South Africa's young children in the face of the enormous and devastating effects of HIV/AIDS requires the dedication of South Africa's human resources to fighting a full-scale war against the pandemic. Sustainable initiatives to identify, support, and monitor vulnerable children in communities must include the people, leaders, and government, have a common focus to which all partners are committed, access to resources and be strongly driven over a sustained period of time.

Further Readings: Biersteker, L., and L. Rudolph (2003). Report on Phase One: South African Action Research Programme: Protecting the rights of orphans and vulnerable children aged 0–9 years. Cape Town: Early Learning Resource Unit; Biersteker, L., and N. Rudolph (2005). Protecting The Rights of Orphans and Vulnerable Children aged 0–6 Years. A South African Case Study. Cape Town: Early Learning Resource Unit. Available online at www.elru.co.za; Department of Health (2000). HIV/AIDS/STD strategic plan for South Africa 2000–2005. Pretoria: Department of Health; Department of Health (2002). South African Demographic and Health Survey 1998. Pretoria: Department of Health. Available online at http://www.doh.gov.za/fcts/1998/sadhs98; Department of Health (2005). National HIV and Syphilis Antenatal Survey in South Africa—2004. Pretoria: Department of Health Available online at www.doh.gov.za; Department of Social Development (2001). National guidelines for Social Services to children infected and affected by HIV/AIDS. Pretoria; Dorrington, R.E., D. Bradshaw, and D. Budlender (2002). HIV/AIDS profile of the provinces of South Africa–indicators for 2002. Center for Actuarial Research, Medical Research Council and Actuarial Society of South Africa; Labadarios, D., ed. (2000). The National Food Consumption Survey (NFCS): Children aged 1–9 years. Pretoria: Department of Health. Available online at http://www.sun.ac.za/nutrition/nfes.html; Picken, P. (2003). Orphans and Vulnerable Children—Challenges and Approaches in ECD Programming. Durban: TREE.

Linda Biersteker and Victoria Sikhakhana

Family Involvement in Early Childhood Development in South Africa

South African children grow up in very diverse family and household structures. South African society includes a multiplicity of religious and cultural beliefs, kinship patterns, and economic structures. Traditional family structures of black South Africans have been profoundly altered by the institutionalized state racism of the apartheid era and colonial past. Labor policies often separated black fathers and mothers from their families, leaving grandmothers, aunts, and older sisters in parenting roles. Increasing urbanization of young adults and the impact of HIV and AIDS are also creating different family structures. Many households are in a constant state of flux, with children moving between relatives most able to care for them at particular times in their lives. Female-headed households are increasingly common with less than half of African children living with both parents.

Parent education levels are strongly associated with the well-being of children, their survival rates, and capacity to support children in their schooling. The 2001 Census revealed that 18 percent of the population was categorized as functionally illiterate and this group included more women, who are most often primary caregivers, than men. Many parents lack the knowledge, confidence, and material resources to support their children's education even in the preschool years; therefore, many children do not attend school or drop out in the early grades.

A National Indicator Project for the Department of Education showed that very large numbers of children are living in families that lack resources, including food and educational materials. Recent studies and newspaper reports have indicated that even in urban areas, literacy is a peripheral activity in the home and that most children from disadvantaged homes start school with no experience of books or word play.

Policy towards Families and Early Childhood Development (ECD)

Within a short period of time, South Africa has moved toward the incorporation of a human rights and child rights approach to early childhood development policy formation and programming, as embodied in the South African Constitution.

Early childhood development (ECD) policy from the Department of Education stresses the importance of continuity between the home, preschool, and early years of schooling. It also recognizes the importance of parental involvement as seen, for example, in the composition requirements for School Governing Bodies and is committed in the Revised National Curriculum to support learning by the use of local content and building on the child's own experience. The Department of Social Development policies and programs for ECD also contain a commitment to education of parents as part of a range of strategies to prevent children becoming "at risk." New ECD related programs, such as the Integrated ECD Plan, include a focus on parent education. Additionally, the Expanded Public Works Program includes a provision for training parents.

Different Types of Parent and Family Services

While training for ECD practitioners incorporates components for working with parents, only one in twenty young children in South Africa is in preschool facilities or Grade R classes. The challenge for parent and family services is to reach those children outside of provision. Therefore, family programs for ECD include those servicing parents of children in schools and preschools, a number of programs that directly target the primary caregivers of young children who are not in any ECD facility, and more general awareness and media programs for parents.

The Challenges in Forming Links between Home and School

Parents who have low levels of schooling themselves often lack understanding of ECD and are uncomfortable with the play-centered learning activities associated with ECD programs, feeling more at ease with rote-centered learning practices. Those parents who received more formal education often associate school with formal instruction where teachers set the rules. It is likely that these parents have never experienced a productive and interactive parent–teacher relationship.

Experience of a Parent Support Program in a rural township in the Free State province showed that teachers who regarded themselves as "experts" tended to alienate poor parents. A well-designed short training program, incorporating sensitivity to social realities and cultural norms for both teachers and parents, led to improved relationships between the two groups. The program increased the parents' awareness of the role of early stimulation and the links to later schooling.

Involvement of parents as governing bodies for community-based preschools is well established, as is the teacher's expectation that parents should be involved in fundraising events and maintenance. Involvement as a support in the classroom is less common, though it has been used very effectively to promote diversity in some programs.

In low-income urban areas, teachers often struggle to secure parent attendance at meetings. This is often a result of time pressures on parents, safety issues in attending meetings in the evenings and a lack of understanding of the importance of their role as parents, something to which teachers often contribute.

In rural areas, where preschools exist, parents are often more involved in the preschools because of the strong social networks where people know one another. However, parent interest and involvement in the education program is more common for parents in more affluent communities.

Awareness Programs

The South African Broadcasting Corporation Educational TV and radio programs include parent education as part of the strategy for educating parents about support for very young children. An estimated 84 percent of South Africans have access to radio and daily radio programs. Some programs, such as Takalani Sesame, include an outreach component with training and print materials targeting primary caregivers as well as ECD teachers. Many local and community radio stations feature parent information or phone-in advice programs for parents of young children. The Department of Education has recently undertaken a media campaign to raise awareness of the importance of supporting early childhood development.

Donor sponsored newspaper supplements, especially for the early years of primary school, are a regular feature in the press. In addition, health and social grant related information in the form of posters and pamphlets are distributed at public places where parents are likely to gather—clinics, social work offices, NGOs, libraries.

Programs Aimed at Primary Caregivers

In an attempt to provide supportive programming for the primary caregivers and parents of young children, and to offer early childhood information that is sensitive to sociocultural differences, a range of programs are available. Unfortunately, most of these programs are only available in urban areas. Program strategies include toy libraries, library programs, mother–child groups, play in the park programs, ECD sports programs and support for informal playgroups. For-profit parenting training programs and parent support groups such as moms and tots groups are common in more affluent communities.

The greatest need addressed here is to reach the parents of children who are very poor, or in areas that are poorly resourced. In response to this need a number of good practice examples have been developed in the NGO sector. These services have a holistic focus, helping parents access resources such as social security, food, and a component that brings them information about early childhood development. However, budget constraints continually limit access for large numbers of vulnerable families and children.

The *family motivator*, the foot soldier in ECD strategy, is gaining momentum as a mechanism for reaching young children in areas that lack a developed physical infrastructure. This approach has been pioneered by NGOs and most often relies on facilitators and volunteers from communities who visit households to provide support and information. Primary caregivers may be brought together for ECD-related workshops. These events help build a network of social support. A related program, known as the ECD hub, involves either a preschool, community, or health center and it strives to become a one-stop shop by bringing together a range of services that include social welfare (access to grants), safety, and protection.

An example of the integration needed is a family outreach program in seven villages in the Northern Cape (an area of deep poverty, violence, and crime). To be successful, several important components needed to be incorporated. First, there needed to be a solid family support service within the community structures, as this facilitated increased access to health services, child support grants, and pensions. Secondly, dialogue and problem-solving approaches to learning and teaching strengthened ECD understandings and practice among primary caregivers, ECD, health and community development practitioners.

Communicating the Early Childhood Development Message to Parents

Linking ECD with other family development programs is one strategy for communicating the ECD messages to parents. For example a Family Literacy program in the KwaZulu Natal Province offers rural women literacy and English and key early childhood development messages, particularly around child early literacy and HIV/AIDS. In other projects, a child-care and education component has been linked to income generation projects targeting women, including a national public works program called Working for Water.

Library services, where such services exist, sometimes include toy lending and lap programs, designed to encourage parents to read to their young children. Projects that encourage a culture of reading include the development of indigenous language books for young children. These books focus on South African themes and have been distributed to parents, preschools, and libraries. However, the majority of children are growing up in an environment where print material is not available.

Child-to-child programs have worked well in certain areas. For example, primary school-aged children in an area of KwaZulu Natal were guided to take key health messages back to the homes and to check young children's clinic cards. This initiative significantly improved the immunization rates in their villages. In Cape Town, older children have been trained to make play materials from waste and shown how to use these with younger children in their homes.

Challenges

ECD parent/family programs often lack both the capacity and the resources for systematic data collection and analysis; therefore, the opportunity to influence government policy and programming is lessened. ECD seldom shows up in Integrated Development Plans and budgets at the local government level. Advocacy efforts need to be strengthened and gain wider support in order to ensure the place of a truly holistic ECD on the national agenda. Parent and family services, provided mostly by the nongovernmental sector, remain hard pressed to deliver widely without systematic and sustained government and donor support.

Further Readings: Biersteker, L. (1997). An assessment of programs and strategies for 0-4 years, the South African Case Study report. World Bank/Africa Regional Integrated Early Childhood Development Services Initiative. Cape Town: Early Learning Resource Unit; Biersteker, L, and K. van der Merwe (2004). Final report on a Grade R pilot training program designed to strengthen home/school and Grade R/Grade 1 transition. Cape Town: Early Learning Resource Unit. Available online at www.elru.co.za; Bozalek, V. (1999). Contextualising caring in Black South African Families. *Social Politics International: Studies in Gender, State and Society* (Spring Issue), 85-99; Desmond, S. (2003). Making reading a shared pleasure and a valuable skill: The Family Literacy Project in the southern Drakensberg. *KwaZulu Natal Innovation* (June 26, 2003). Available online at www.familyliteracyproject.co.za. University Library, University of Natal; Mptlhaolwa, M. P. (1999.) Searching for other mechanisms for helping families and parents to find solutions for their problems. Paper presented at the International Conference on Early Childhood Care and Development. Uganda (6-10 September 1999). Available online at www.dedi.co.za; Newman M., T. Uys, and T. Noko (2003). Implementers' Report: A Re Direng. Cape Town: Early Learning Resource Unit.

Mary Newman

Human Rights, Inclusivity, and Social Justice

South Africa has a rich diversity of culture, language, and religious traditions. However, we come from a history of oppression where one culture was viewed as superior to others. For decades a minority white and Western culture dominated and was institutionalized as the norm. Other cultures were practiced in local segregated communities.

Since the beginning of our democracy in 1994, the South African Constitution and the Bill of Rights have been the guide for national and provincial laws and policies across government departments, civil society structures, and organizations. Both the Constitution and the Bill of Rights have been a means for the transformation of our society. To develop an understanding of human rights issues, there is a strong emphasis on human rights awareness and education in South Africa. As a result, government institutions, corporations, nongovernmental organizations, and community-based organizations have developed visions, missions, and policies to align themselves with the South African Constitution. Over the last ten years national pride has also emerged as our society celebrates its diverse cultures, languages, and traditions. Increasing numbers of Africans from all over the continent have migrated to South Africa, bringing many different traditions. Unfortunately, these new immigrants have become the targets of xenophobia.

Human rights relate to a wide range of diversity, which includes race, gender, culture, ethnicity, class, ability, and language. Transformation also means leveling the playing fields of the past, which is why the focus of the South African government's laws and policies is human rights, inclusivity, and social justice.

A decade is a very short period of time in any country's history. We face and grapple with many challenges when it comes to looking at issues of diversity in the education of young children. These challenges include the following:

- More than 80 percent do not have access to child-care facilities and come from the poor section of our communities;
- Lack of qualified teachers and facilities;
- Educational stimulation by and large in the hands of families and our poor communities;
- Development and empowerment of our communities in advocacy around issues related to the education of young children.

As duty bearers, across all levels of our South African society, we are responsible for early childhood education. We need to continue to work toward ensuring all our children are included and reap the benefits of our democracy.

Winds of Change

Nongovernmental organizations (NGOs) have been involved at the forefront as agents of change even before 1994. NGOs actively challenged discriminatory policies and practices, which excluded the majority of the children in South Africa. The Early Learning Resource Unit (ELRU) in Cape Town pioneered antibias work for the early childhood sector and has been involved in antibias work since 1990. At the time, formerly all white schools were starting to enroll African, colored, and Indian children. In the changing of our history, this was the right thing to do, if you could afford it. It was a very assimilationist approach and in practice it was a challenge.

Faced with this more diverse enrollment, teachers identified language as a major issue. Children from other cultures and racialized groups battled with English, the medium of instruction at these schools, and many did not speak the language at all. For some learners, English was their second, third, or fourth language. Teachers recognized that while the language issue was a reality, it was very closely connected to issues of culture, race, and class. These learners came from different backgrounds and experiences than those of the teachers and many of their classmates. In the words of one author, "the education system treated black children like foreigners in their own country, tending to reflect English or American culture."

The approach ELRU adopted, which drew on the work of Louise Derman Sparks at Pacific Oaks College, California, was to provide skills and support to teachers in implementing an antibias approach. This approach challenges oppressive beliefs, attitudes, behaviors, and social and institutional practices. Antibias training does not have an exclusive cultural focus—believing that all forms of bias, discrimination, and oppression need to be challenged and that these intersect in many ways. However, as a result of our history and experiences of apartheid and transformation, racial discrimination still remains a major focus. An antibias approach requires that teachers are aware of their own biases, reflect on these limitations, and find ways of moving forward by changing attitudes and behaviors.

Teacher Training

The transformation of South African society over the last decade has brought about many changes. Laws and policies have been put in place at government, corporate, organizational, and community levels. We have discussed, debated and implemented processes, systems, and policies to develop our democracy. Early childhood education is intertwined with our transformation. As a result, as South Africa grapples with issues related to our past and creates our future, we have elected to view cultural appropriateness in broad terms of a human rights approach.

In response to these challenges, one of the many initiatives taken by the Education Department is a pilot project to train teachers on Values and Human Rights in the Curriculum. This involves a group of teachers in the same district, in each province. These schools come from diverse historical experiences, backgrounds, and situations, use different languages, and include both private and state schools. All grades are included. The training is short but focuses on a process of personal reflection on attitudes on issues of diversity and how those attitudes can influence the interactions in the learning environment. The project also provides each school with a kit of grade-appropriate materials that focuses on values and human rights and can be used across the curriculum. A further departmental pilot involves an Advanced Certificate in Human Rights and Values, offered for teachers at the tertiary level.

The Role of Education Policy

Educators of young children strive to help them develop a positive self-image. Culture is central to this identity. In South Africa, the approach to diversity is developing a culture of human rights and inclusivity that promotes the affirmation of all children, their families and experiences irrespective of difference. It is about recognizing and respecting similarities and differences. From an early age, young children are influenced by societal norms and biases. Often, these children will respond to differences according to the prevailing societal norms they experience in their environment.

The South African government sees education as a key vehicle for achieving real change in our society. Human rights and inclusivity issues are firmly on the National Education Department's agenda as part of the transformation and the infusion of human rights and values in education. In the years since democracy, the antibias approach first tested in the NGO sector, which aims at affirming all of South Africa's children and making education truly inclusive, found expression in several education policy documents. These documents include the South African Schools Act of 1996 which allows instruction in the language of choice, the Language in Education Policy (1997) which promotes additive multilingualism, and White Paper 6 on Inclusive Education (2001) which sets out policies to facilitate inclusion of all children in schools. National standards for accredited training of early childhood teachers include a focus on an inclusive antibias curriculum. Another initiative of the Education Department has been the development of the Manifesto on Values, Education and Democracy (2001). This initiative examined what values would reinforce and confirm the learners' critical skills of communication and participation, in nurturing the democratic values of the constitution. Following this, human rights, inclusivity and social justice are highlighted in the Revised National Curriculum Statements (RNCS) of 2002 and integrated across all learning areas for all children. The aim is to develop a culture of democracy, human rights, and peace. Developing this involves learning about human rights within a human rights environment and critically engaging issues related to human rights, inclusivity, and social justice—basically putting human rights into practice.

A Culture of Human Rights and Inclusivity in the Classroom

Creating an inclusive human rights approach in education is integral to the program, not simply an add-on. To do this, educators must recognize that we live in a society with prejudices from our past and that we should actively encourage children to challenge their bias and discrimination, to ask questions, to notice unfairness and to challenge it. We need to create learning environments, at home and at school, that provide an alternative to the biased messages that society provides. We need to model that we value diversity and difference in the friends we choose or where we shop, to be positive about each child's physical characteristics and cultural heritage. Educational materials should reinforce the value of different cultures and people that can make children proud of their heritage. Sensitivity to local contexts and interests of children is a key aspect of this orientation. The RNCS is not prescriptive of what should be taught, but rather aims at general outcomes that can be realized through a variety of learning content.

Teachers are urged to provide books, dolls, pictures, posters, stories, songs, and art activities that show different images that the children might not otherwise see. This helps children understand and value differences, and to challenge stereotypes. These may include the following:

- Black women in leadership roles such as chairing a meeting, and white men in laboring jobs such as digging a road.
- Men and women in nontraditional roles for example, a man cooking, a woman in charge of a shop, a man bathing a baby, girls playing with cars, boys feeding baby dolls.
- A variety of different family types that we find in our society: single parent families, large extended families, etc.

Children should have opportunities to play with other children who are different from themselves, for example, children with disabilities, with different religions, who speak different languages. Language diversity is encouraged. Given that many previously oppressed parents view the English language and Western culture as key to the road to economic success, as well as the inevitable inroads of globalization, developing a society which values difference is not without challenges.

Challenges and Opportunities

One of the challenges facing South African teachers is including and infusing human rights knowledge, skills and values into education. This requires a particular focus and understanding on the part of teachers, for they are responsible for creating a human rights environment in their classroom and in the school. This whole school approach includes the learners, parents, and the community, as active partners in the education of our children. Like many of the parents, the majority of our teachers were educated and trained in an extremely authoritarian, oppressive, and divided era. Transformation requires change or making paradigm shifts through a process of unlearning old and familiar ways of doing things, and creating new ways and democratic perspectives in our interactions with one another as members of our society.

Further Readings: Department of Education (2002). Revised National Curriculum Statement—Policy Overview. Pretoria: Department of Education. Available online at http://www.education.gov.za; Department of Education (forthcoming). *Values and Human Rights in the Curriculum—A Guide*; Derman Sparks, L. (1989). *Anti-bias Curriculum: Tools for Empowering Children*. Washington DC: National Association for the Education of Young Children; Early Learning Resource Unit (1999). *Teaching Young Children to Challenge Bias: What Parents and Teachers Can do*. Cape Town: Early Learning Resource Unit; Koopman, A. (1997). *Shifting Paradigms*. Cape Town: Early Learning Resource Unit; Ministry of Education (2001). Manifesto on Values, Education and Democracy. Cape Town. Available online at http://www.education.gov.za; Robb, H. (1995). Multilingual preschooling. In K. Heugh, A Siegrühn, and P. Plüddeman, eds., *Multilingual education for South Africa*. Johannesburg: Heineman, pp.15–22.

Beryl Hermanus

Early Childhood Education Curriculum in South Africa

In post *apartheid* South Africa, "curriculum" carries with it connotations of liberation, social change, and transformation in education. *Curriculum 2005* is the new plan for school education. It specifies the "knowledge, skills and attitudes" that children are expected to attain, on a year-by-year basis, from age 5 to 15, in their journey through the formal schooling system. Importantly, as policy, it declines to prescribe either specific content or pedagogic process, deeming these to be the professional responsibility of educators. Instead, policy specifies a range of general ("cross-field") and subject specific outcomes that can, in principle, be attained along any number of different learning pathways. In this situation, consideration of curriculum is often highly politicized. Besides the usual features that one would consider—subjects, programs, pedagogy, assessment—any analysis of curriculum in South Africa must reflect on the following: its symbolic role in transforming the contents of the racist past, the implementation problems associated with pressures for rapid change, and the question of the right of access to a new curriculum.

Transformation

In 2002, the Department of Education published the Revised National Curriculum Statement (RNCS), specifying learning outcomes and assessment standards for learning areas in schools. The first four years of formal schooling are known as the Foundation Phase (Grade R or "reception year," Grade 1, Grade 2, Grade 3).

Grade R is not yet but is in principle compulsory, as it is for children aged 6–7 to 8–9 to be enrolled in Grades 1, 2 and 3. The RNCS specifies three learning programs to be followed over the four years, namely Literacy, Numeracy, and Life Skills. Each has a number of specific learning outcomes associated with it. For reasons of limited space, these cannot all be spelled out here, but the examples provided in the table below will portray the current South African curriculum policy.

The Revised National Curriculum Statement

Learning Program	Learning Outcomes (LOs)
Literacy	LO1: *Listening* LO2: *Speaking* "The learner will be able to communicate confidently and effectively in a spoken language in a wide range of situations." LO3: *Reading and viewing* "The learner will be able to read and view for information and enjoyment, and respond critically to aesthetic, cultural, and emotional values in texts." LO4: *Writing* LO5: *Thinking and reasoning* LO6: *Language structure and use*
Numeracy	LO1: *Numbers, operations, and relationships* "The learner will be able to recognize, describe and represent numbers and their relationships, and to count, estimate, calculate and check with competence and confidence in solving problems." LO2: *Patterns, functions, and algebra.* LO3: *Space and shape (Geometry)* "The learner will be able to describe and represent characteristics and relationships between two dimensional shapes and three dimensional objects in a variety of orientations and positions." LO4: *Measurement* LO5: *Data handling*
Life skills	In the Foundation Phase, the RNCS requires integration of outcomes from a number of different, distinct learning areas studied in later years of schooling, For example, LO3 from History: *Historical interpretation* "The learner will be able to interpret aspects of history." LO1 from arts and culture: *Creating, interpreting, and presenting* LO1 from life orientation: *Health promotion* (which includes *inter alia* that the learner has an appropriate knowledge of HIV and AIDS).

The entire RNCS document may be viewed at Department of Education (2005).

In addition to such outcome statements, there are specified Assessment Standards associated with each Learning Outcome (LO). For example, one of three assessment standards for Grade R for Literacy LO2 reads, "We know this when the learner uses and responds appropriately to simple greetings and farewells, and thanks people." One of seven assessment standards for Grade 2 for Literacy LO3 reads, "We know this when the learner recognizes the silent 'e' in common words such as 'cake'." And one of six assessment standards for Grade 3 for Numeracy LO1 reads, "We know this when the learner performs mental calculations involving addition and subtraction for numbers to at least 50, and multiplication or whole numbers with solutions to at least 50."

Important Aspects of the RNCS

The overall RNCS—the official national curriculum—is clearly an extensive and complex document. There are a number of things that one needs to notice about it when considering the transformative aspects of curriculum in South Africa:

- It employs distinctive terminology. "Learning areas" rather than "subjects," "numeracy" rather than "mathematics," "learners" rather than "pupils," and so on. A number of commentators have recognized how this in itself is an assertion of a new curriculum against the prevailing political order, distancing it from the language of the past.
- It does not specify any particular content. This is very much a reaction to the *apartheid* order, in which content tended to be narrowly specified in ways that were blatantly racist, colonial, sexist—white histories, the absence of African perspectives, patriarchal gender stereotyping, etc. For example, one *apartheid* era Grade 1 textbook characterizes "black homes" as being either grass or mud huts and "white homes" as brick and mortar structures. Currently, there is an important debate in South Africa about whether or not this tendency has gone too far, losing sight of what Lee Shulman terms *pedagogic content knowledge*, not least in relation to the particular knowledge that teachers of young children must have regarding the way their learners think about language and mathematics.
- It is driven primarily by assessment criteria. There are well-known "design down" imperatives in outcomes-based education to prioritize assessment in the curriculum process. In South Africa, the leveling of the playing field that "transparent" assessment criteria brings gave impetus to the policy decision to opt for an outcomes-based curriculum and, ultimately, the RNCS. However, there is now a concern that this emphasis on assessment may entail too much surveillance of children, too much of a "check list" mentality on the part of teachers, that detracts from the school's ability to provide the well-rounded learning process that children require.

Implementation

The RNCS, then, is the major plan for curriculum as it affects children in South Africa. But what of another important perspective on curriculum, that which would view curriculum as practice rather than as plan? Conceived as a plan, a curriculum is understood as official documents from a recognized authority that prescribes what should be taught and achieved in the classroom; conceived as practice, it is a set of guidelines used unevenly by teachers and experienced in different ways by learners. In South African policy debates, this lived experience of curriculum has been characterized as the "curriculum-in-use." Here, one considers children's experience as organized by teachers and caregivers, in a focus on the actual implementation of curriculum.

Challenges Associated With Implementation

As pointed out, the RNCS is an enormously complicated document. Unfortunately, South African teachers have often struggled to understand its complex terminology, or have tended to be confused about the design and implementation of the new curriculum. A 2000 commission appointed by the Minister of Education found that "all available evidence [suggests] that although Curriculum 2005 has generated a new focus on teaching and learning, teachers have a rather shallow understanding of [its] principles" (Chisholm 2000, p. 20). In the Foundation Phase, recent research has suggested that teachers tend to have insufficient time for the development of effective reading skills, foundational mathematics, and core concepts in life skills. Other studies have identified the poor conceptual knowledge base of teachers, even in relation to the basic mathematics taught in early primary school years (place value, shape, measurement). There is now widespread agreement amongst educators that curriculum implementation was initially too rushed, and was founded on inadequate teacher training, monitoring, and support for teachers. The upshot of this is that there is a renewed focus on the fundamentals of reading and writing instruction and mathematical computation in the early primary school curriculum in South Africa. This "back to basics" emphasis is perhaps not as dramatic as that in some other countries, notably the United States, but it is nonetheless a significant contemporary trend in curriculum policy.

Innovative Practice

Nonetheless, despite these discrepancies between curriculum as plan and curriculum as practice, there are numerous examples of innovative practice being developed by teachers in Foundation Phase classrooms. Curriculum 2005 has brought about a shift in the understanding of what constitutes good education for young children—an emphasis on the totality of listening, speaking, reading, and writing, without losing sight of the importance of phonemic awareness, for example, or a concern to ensure that children are given the opportunity to construct their own solutions to arithmetic problems, without losing sight of the need to instruct them in certain basic algorithms. The implementation of the new national curriculum continues to inspire various interesting initiatives on the part of many teachers of young children throughout the country.

Access

The RNCS does not engage questions of curriculum for children under the age of 5. A recent national consultative conference on Early Childhood Development (ECD) (March 2005) has put the question of a curriculum for 0–4 year-olds-back on the national agenda. However, the government has been frank (and controversial) in declaring that, at this stage, it cannot afford to fund such educational provision. It has called for partnerships with communities, NGOs, and industries to address the curriculum and broader educational needs of these children. As is the case in most developing countries, there has been a concern to ensure universal primary schooling in South Africa over the past decade. By 2000, the country had a net enrollment ratio of 87 percent in primary schools, still short of its goal. In 2001, it made a move to formalize Grade R education for children aged 5, and declared that its target was to "universalize coverage of the Reception Year, whilst maintaining a significant coverage in earlier years" (Department of Education, 2001, sect 4). Children aged 0–4, however, remain on the outside.

One consequence of the government recognizing Grade R as a formal part of the school curriculum was a renewed sense of the integrity of a curriculum for young children. Demarcating the first four years of schooling as an integrated learning pathway in the RNCS consolidated educational thinking in this area. Ironically, however, a broader sense of curriculum integrity regarding ECD as a whole (ages 0–9) was undermined.

This situation has led to considerable criticism of government and advocacy for improved ECD provisioning on the part of government. NGOs that train caregivers and teachers and that provide various kinds of education and care for young children have been prominent in these efforts. In fact, it is such organizations that have kept alive a concern with curriculum for young children. Their role in South African ECD must be acknowledged. Three examples will make the point, although these are by no means the only significant contributors in the field:

- Since the 1970s, The Early Learning Resource Unit (ELRU) in Cape Town has developed contextually appropriate curricula for children in resource poor communities, emphasizing an inclusive antibias approach. ELRU provides for babies, toddlers, and 3–6-year-olds, and offers nationally recognized training for practitioners in an extensive community of ECD centers and Grade R classes in public schools.
- The well known High/Scope program delivered by Khululeka in the Eastern Cape has been adapted to meet the unique needs of local community contexts and specific groups of children. Khululeka offers teacher training for basic and nationally recognized certificates in ECD.
- The Woz'obona organization in Johannesburg has since the 1980s developed an adapted **Montessori** curriculum, utilizing sensorial materials fashioned from waste materials. It too trains teachers and caregivers for nationally recognized certificates.

Curriculum for the Under Fives

The "curriculum for the under-fives" in South Africa is concentrated in the hands of twenty or so different NGOs, and straddles a large range of "philosophies" and methodological approaches. This leads to many innovative approaches, but it also means that the overall provisioning for young children remains small in relation to the overall need. A national sense of curriculum in this area, which can go to scale, still seems some way off. There is wide expectation of government that it will, at some point, take the initiative in driving a national agenda in this regard. If it can tap into the wide pool of established curriculum knowledge in South African NGOs, it may well be able to do this. But it requires money, trained people, and political will.

Further Readings: Chisholm, L. (May 31, 2000). *A South African Curriculum for the Twenty First Century: Report of the Review Committee on Curriculum 2005*. Presented to the Minister of Education, Professor Kader Asmal. Pretoria; Department of Education

(May 2001). *Education White Paper 5 on Early Childhood Education. Meeting the Challenge of Early Childhood Education in South Africa*. Pretoria: Department of Education; Department of Education (2002). Revised National Curriculum Statement. Pretoria. Available online at http://www.education.gov.za/; Hoadley, U., and J. Jansen (2002). *Curriculum: From plans to practices*. Cape Town: South African Institute for Distance Education & Oxford University Press; Shulman, L. (February 1986). Those who understand: Knowledge growth in teaching. *Educational Researcher*, 4–14. (Presidential Address at the 1985 annual meeting of the American Educational Research Association, Chicago); Taylor, N., and P. Vinjevold (1999). *Getting learning right: Report of the president's education initiative research project*. Johannesburg: JET.

Ian Moll

Foreign Language Learning in South African Early Childhood Education

Historical Context

South Africa, like most countries on the African continent, is multilingual. Although a minority of children grow up in monolingual English homes, for the vast majority it is usual to speak one or more indigenous African language at home and to learn to understand and communicate in other languages at some point during childhood in more or less formal ways. One or more of these languages, although they may be variously termed "2nd" (L2), "3rd," or the more generic "additional" languages, are often in effect, foreign for many children.

The following table gives the breakdown, based on the 2001 Census, of the home languages of the approximately 45 million South Africans.

Percentage of First Home Language Speakers

Language	Percentage of First Home Language Speakers
IsiZulu	23.8
IsiXhosa	17.6
Afrikaans	13.3
Sepedi	9.4
English	8.2
Setswana	8.2
Sesotho	7.9
Xitsonga	4.4
Siswati	2.7
Tshivenda	2.3
IsiNdebele	1.6
Other	0.5

English is the language of high status and power in South Africa. Under colonial rule, most African countries came to "choose" a foreign language (such as English,

French, or Portuguese) as the official language. The legacy of this has prevailed and has contributed significantly to a complex and often problematic linguistic situation in society, particularly in the domain of education. In South Africa during the Apartheid years, English and Afrikaans (a language which developed from seventeenth-century Dutch) were enforced as the two official languages. African languages were only used as languages of instruction for the first few years of primary schooling and were the medium through which "Bantu education" (an inferior system of education aimed at keeping black people in lowly positions in society) was initiated. For this reason, many African language speakers still associate the notion of mother tongue education with inferior education.

Post-Apartheid Language in Education Policy

Since the demise of Apartheid, South Africa has 11 official languages and since 1997 a Language in Education Policy (LiEP). The LiEP follows the constitutional obligation to recognize cultural diversity as a valuable asset and to promote multilingualism, the development of African languages and respect for all languages used in the country. On the basis that it assumed its written standard form in South Africa, Afrikaans is now considered to be an African language. In terms of a language in education approach, the LiEP supports and promotes "additive approaches to bilingualism." Based on research evidence about the benefits of mother tongue learning and bilingualism this implies that learning is most effective when strong foundations in the mother tongue are established to which one or more languages are then added (rather than replacing). Official government policy in early childhood is thus mother tongue education up to (at least) Grade 3, with the learning of at least one additional language as a subject from Grade R.

Language Learning in Early Childhood

For most young South African children, learning English constitutes learning a foreign language. Many African language speakers live in rural areas, where they have little, if any exposure to English as part of their daily home and community activities. Because English, as the language of power, continues to be regarded widely as the "open sesame" language in South Africa, it is commonly understood that most parents want their children to learn English. Often it is assumed that this should necessarily involve their children learning through the medium of English in order to learn it. This assumption has some credibility in South Africa through research studies on the success of the L2 "immersion" ("sink or swim") models in countries such as Canada. However, these studies are limited, and relate to middle-class situations, where families generally use the child's mother tongue at home, both orally and for literacy. In most South African home and community settings, the situation is very different: the mother tongue is cherished and in constant use in oral form. However, owing to the low use and status level African languages have as written languages in society, mother tongue literacy is not significantly used or valued at home. Children thus have had few opportunities to explore or develop significant insights and understandings about print in any language before entering school.

Since 1994, this "sink or swim" situation is common for a small but significant number of African language speaking children who live in towns and cities and attend former "white" or "colored" preschool and primary schools. Generally speaking, these children must come to survive in an English medium environment despite the cautionary evidence that early exposure to the L2 should not be done at the expense of the L1 as this can harm cognitive development. One of the consequences of this approach is that by the end of Grade 3, many children neither learn to read and write effectively in their mother tongue, nor in English.

In African language speaking communities, the general trend in terms of language learning in preschool and the Foundation Phase (Grades R to 3) is toward the earliest possible introduction of English, despite the fact that usually those who teach English are often themselves poor speakers (and role models) of the language and few have been trained in modern methods of L2 instruction.

The emphasis is generally on an informal introduction to the language through songs, rhymes, and chanting of common functional phrases. In preschools and schools located in African language speaking communities, throughout the Foundation Phase, English instruction accelerates with an initial emphasis on oral language skills development, but with the gradual introduction of reading and writing. Grade 3 literacy test results in the Western Cape province provide an example of the lack of effectiveness of this approach: children have not learned to read and write in either their mother tongue or English, nor do they know English well enough to use as a medium for successful learning.

Unpublished research conducted for the Pan South African Language Board indicates that the majority of parents would like the home language to be maintained throughout education as long as this does not jeopardize the learning of English. However, the situation still prevails that in Grade 4, the beginning of the Intermediate Phase, a "switch" is made to English as a medium for teaching and learning. At this point, children are expected to be able to read and write using English, all teaching and learning materials are in English, and assessment is carried out in English.

In English and Afrikaans speaking communities, the desirability of introducing children to an African language is increasingly being acknowledged. Informed by the understanding that children learn languages best when very young, many private and some government assisted inner city preschools offer lessons in a predominant African language of the area. Generally, communicative approaches that are playful and focus first on rhymes, songs, and stories are preferred.

Further Readings: Bloch, C. (2004). Enabling effective literacy learning in multilingual South African early childhood classrooms. PRAESA Occasional Papers no. 16 PRAESA, UCT; Department of Education (1997). *Language in Education Policy*. Government Notice No 383. Pretoria: Department of Education. Available online at www.education.gov.za; Many Languages in Education. *Perspectives in Education* [Special Issue] 20(1; March 2002).

Carole Bloch

Early Intervention and Education for South African Children with Special Education Needs

Although many young children with disabilities are still hidden away from society and/or neglected (also known as backroom children), there are heartwarming stories of young children with disabilities who have been successfully included in mainstream schools and early childhood education (ECD) centers. Early identification and intervention is often the crucial factor that paved the way for successful inclusion.

Educators believe that it is important to identify any impediment to growth or learning as soon as possible. Early intervention should be available to minimize the effects on the learning process and to prevent secondary problems from developing. South Africa is a country in transition; as a result, despite progressive legislation and policy, actual implementation of systems and practices regulating early intervention and education for children with special education needs is not yet adequate.

Policy

Under the pre-1994 dispensation, a small percentage of children with disabilities (from the age of 3) were admitted to preschool sections of special schools where they received early intervention services. However, the specialized education was provided on a racial basis and white children benefited the most from this program. In 1990 the National Education Policy Investigation revealed that of the 2,015 children aged 3–6 in state supported special education classes, 52 percent were white. There were virtually no facilities for African children. The special schools that existed were available by category of disability, leaving children who did not fit the categories or who had multiple disabilities without access. The majority of children with severe disabilities were simply excluded from the education system. Some of these children had access to custodial programs in daycentres. Such resources fell under the auspices of the Department of Health. Children with moderate or mild disabilities were sometimes included in mainstream schools by default, but received little specialized intervention once they actually entered school. Private therapy and early intervention programs were available for those children whose parents could afford them. Parent support groups were an important source of information and informal support. Some groups such as the Disabled Children's Action Group, an organization for parents of children with disabilities, provided access to informal day care and playgroups for children with disabilities.

Under the new dispensation after 1994, the following steps were taken to improve the situation:
- The Constitution (1996) founded our democratic state and common citizenship on the values of human dignity, the achievement of equality and the advancement of human rights and freedoms. Everyone has the right to basic education and discrimination against anyone, including people with disabilities, is not allowed.
- This was reinforced by the South African Schools Act (1996) stating that
  - All learners should have access to learning and to equal education opportunities and support where necessary.

- ○ State resources must be provided to ensure this.
- ○ Parents have a right to choose where they want to place their children in school.
- ○ Schools are not allowed to refuse access to children with special needs.
- In 1996 the National Commission on Special Needs in Education and Training and the National Committee on Education Support Services were appointed to investigate and make recommendations on all aspects of "special needs and support services" in education and training. These led to the promulgation of Education White Paper 6 in 2001, presenting an eagerly awaited paradigm shift in the thinking on children with special needs. The resulting twenty year plan envisaged new strategies including:
  - ○ A new approach toward organizing support within a single, integrated education system in contrast to the previous separation of "normal" and "disabled or special needs" children.
  - ○ A move away from a learner deficit model that organizes all support on the basis of the category of disability/learning difficulties of the learner without attempting to understand the intensity and the nature of support that the learner really needs.
  - ○ A move beyond the notion of "Special Needs" Education to understanding the various barriers to learning. These barriers go beyond disability and also include, amongst others, negative attitudes toward differences, poverty, language, gender, disease, inappropriate pedagogy, and particular life experiences.
  - ○ Special schools will be transformed and recreated as resource centers, catering to children with severe needs and providing support to children experiencing barriers to learning in ordinary schools.
  - ○ Disabled and other vulnerable children not attending schools will be identified and placed in suitable school settings.
  - ○ There needs to be an acknowledgement of the importance of assessment and intervention during early childhood, even before children enter the school system. Additionally, it is necessary for there to be an understanding of the importance of collaboration between the departments of education, and health and social development. There is a promise of a legally binding National Strategy for Screening, Identification, Assessment and Support to be put in place throughout the education system with the main purpose of facilitating access to schools and to additional support as needed. Partnerships need to be established between community-based health clinics, the parents, and other social services. These relationships will help plan and implement ongoing intervention, and enable teacher support teams to prepare support programs for identified learners on entering school.
  - ○ Support should be redefined, shifting the focus away from supporting individual learners and toward addressing systemic barriers that prevent the system from responding to children's learning and other needs. An overemphasis on "special needs" has the tendency of labeling and inadvertently marginalizing children.

The Impact of Policy Initiatives

How do these positive policy developments impact young children with special needs in South Africa in 2005? Children with special needs still encounter many of the same barriers, but their journey may be easier because of the strong human rights foundation in the New South Africa. There has been a strong move away from institutionalization and a stronger focus on empowering parents and their communities to support children with special needs. Although no official procedures are currently in place to identify these children, or to help make them eligible for coordinated state supported early intervention programs, more community-based rehabilitation workers, health visitors, community development workers, etc. are being trained and deployed in rural areas to assist parents of children with special needs. Health Clinic nurses in many areas have been trained to identify children experiencing, or at risk of experiencing, barriers to learning and development. Screening instruments developed by the Health Department are used to screen babies and children visiting the clinics for their routine immunization appointments. Parents are alerted if there is reason for concern and nurses may give advice to parents on activities to enhance the development of the children.

Early Childhood Education for Children with Disabilities

There are more preschool centers that admit children with disabilities. ECD training organizations include modules on special needs/inclusion in their curriculum and it now forms part of the South African Qualifications Authority's accredited qualifications and standards. Barriers to fuller inclusion are a lack of resources, space, and training, as well as negative attitudes. However, ECD teachers often play a pivotal role in the identification of special needs that were previously overlooked. Teachers have an important role to play in the implementation of intervention strategies. Their knowledge of child development, strong appreciation of individual differences, and a commitment to viewing parents as partners in their children's education, equip them to form sound judgments on the child's potential and to have a positive impact on the development of these young children.

Admission to a mainstream school still proves difficult for students with disabilities. Due to the many changes in the education system and the inability of the new support systems to cope with the enormous barriers experienced by "normal" learners, mainstream schools are hesitant to welcome children with disabilities. However, this ineffective response may change within the next few years because of developing initiatives that focus on providing resources to mainstream schools. These initiatives also address the importance of providing intensive teacher training and district-based support teams to support inclusion. Tertiary institutions are offering teachers in-service and preservice courses about inclusion. The University of Pretoria is offering a postgraduate multidisciplinary course in Early Intervention.

Systemic Problems

Unfortunately the system is not working well in all areas, including the following:
• In rural and overcrowded peri-urban areas, social services are limited due to economic and geographical factors.

- Not all health clinic staff are trained to provide special needs screening. The workload at most clinics/hospitals is formidable, with no time available for screening and intervention activities. There is resistance to identifying relatively minor barriers to development because of the lack of follow-up intervention services.
- Health personnel are often not aware of organizations offering early intervention services and give little information or hope to the parents for the child's development.
- Negative attitudes toward disabilities still exist and many parents would rather hide their children than bring them into public. Children with disabilities might miss the initial screening procedure or might get lost in the system even though they have been identified at an early age.
- During the nationwide audit of ECD provisioning in 2000 only 1.36 percent of all children enrolled in ECD services including specialist services were disabled. Nearly two-thirds of these children were between 5 and 7 years of age. These findings suggest that ECD centers were admitting children who should have been in the public schooling system.

The Roles of NGOs, Parents, and the Community

The government's acknowledgement of the importance of nongovernment organizations (NGOs) and the vital role that parents and community members play in the education is a move in the right direction. In South Africa, many NGOs continue to provide advocacy and intervention services for children with "special needs." These include disabled people's organizations such as Disabled Children's Action Group and organizations for specific disabilities, for example, League of Friends of the Blind, Down Syndrome South Africa, DEAFSA, and Epilepsy South Africa. Other NGOs and nonprofit organizations work in the educational field to strengthen and supplement government provision and enhance the implementation of their policies, for example, language, aids, and inclusion policies. Active Learning and Leisure Libraries exemplify how nonprofit organizations providing early intervention services through the establishment of toy libraries at hospitals and in underprivileged areas can make a positive impact in South Africa. The Sunshine Center (Transvaal Memorial Institute) has developed an early intervention training program with manuals widely used by professionals, paraprofessionals, and parents in all sectors of the South African society.

Further Readings: National Department of Education (ELSEN Directorate) (2001). Education White Paper 6. Special Needs Education—Building an Inclusive Education and Training System. Pretoria. Available online at www.education.gov.za; National Department of Education (October 2005). Directorate Inclusive Education: Draft National Strategy for Screening, Identification, Assessment, and Support. Pretoria. Available online at www.education.gov.za.

Web Sites: Sunshine Center Association for Early Intervention, http://www.sunshine.org.za; http://www.thought.co.za/allsa—Active Learning and Leisure Libraries—South Africa, http://www.thought.co.za/allsa; University of Pretoria Early Childhood Intervention Programme, http://www.caac.up.ac.za.

Laetitia Brümmer

First Home Language Speakers

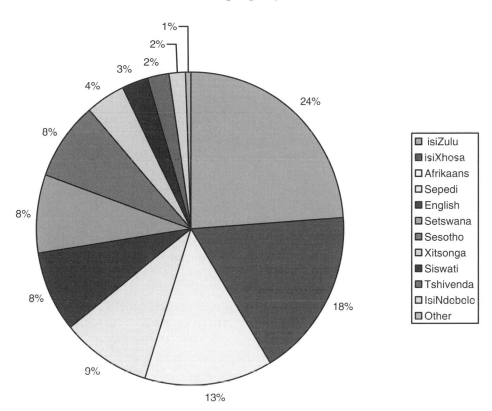

Legend:
- isiZulu
- isiXhosa
- Afrikaans
- Sepedi
- English
- Setswana
- Sesotho
- Xitsonga
- Siswati
- Tshivenda
- IsiNdebele
- Other

Financing of Early Childhood Development in South Africa

Prior to the change to a democratic dispensation, the financing of early childhood development (ECD) in South Africa was characterized by a system that was racially discriminatory and inadequate. The finance available for early childhood development was inversely proportional to need, with those in greatest need receiving the least. Children classified as "white" were eligible for some state support, children classified as "colored" received less, and children classified as "African" received minimal state support.

With the advent of a democratic government, the discriminatory nature of early childhood development financing disappeared. However, the inadequacy of financial support to early childhood development centers and programs continues. The issue of who provides the financing and bears the costs of early childhood development is extremely important as the sustainability of the majority of South Africa's early childhood development centers and programs is dependent on funding. In early childhood development centers and programs the most common sources of financial support are the following:

• Parents, families, and communities;
• Teachers and early childhood development practitioners;

- Government through provincial and local government;
- Private sector (philanthropists, foundations, the National Lottery and business social investment programs);
- Civil society (NGOs, churches, and others); and
- International donor organizations.

Parents, Families, and Communities

Parents, families and communities finance ECD in a number of ways. Most often, this occurs through the payment of fees, however modest, toward the operating costs of a center or program. Fees account for between 75 percent and 85 percent of the operating income of many community-based center and home-based programs. Parents in many cases support programs through the contribution of their labor to build and maintain a facility, through making toys and equipment and through caring for children. Parents may also contribute food that children bring to the program each day.

Although parents and families provide the bulk of the income for programs, it is unrealistic to expect that low-income families and communities will be able to bear all the program costs or sustain programs over time. As a result, many ECD programs in poor communities are of poor quality with poor infrastructure, untrained staff, and a lack of equipment. These often do not meet children's nutritional requirements.

For the more wealthy sections of the population where children are placed in privately owned, early childhood development centers and programs, fees will make up 100 percent of the operating income of such centers.

Teachers and Early Childhood Development Practitioners

Teachers and early childhood development practitioners indirectly finance early childhood development centers and programs through the acceptance of low salaries and, in many cases especially in rural communities, through not receiving payment at all. In instances where parents and families are not able to contribute toward the cost of the education and care of their children, practitioners are unpaid. In other cases, practitioners earn a fraction of a "reasonable salary." In a sector where at least ZAR 3,000 per month would be considered reasonable, 44 percent of practitioners earn less than ZAR 500 per month, these by making a "contribution" that has not been quantified but is clearly substantial.

Government Financing

In South Africa, government funds early childhood development through the provincial departments of Education and of Social Services. Each takes responsibility for a different age grouping. Education is responsible for financing the Grade R program. These are children turning five and Grade R is the first of ten years of basic education. The Social Services departments are responsible for the financing of children aged birth to 4 years.

Government's financial support is based on the premise that the social and education benefits of participation in an early childhood development program contribute significant benefits to society. Government also realizes that because the inability of parents to pay the full costs of ECD services, government has the responsibility to provide additional funding to support young children and their families.

Grade R. funding. Two principal mechanisms exist for funding Grade R in South Africa. Firstly, provincial governments fund grants to community-based ECD centers on a per-learner basis. These grants are expected to provide ECD in areas where other funding opportunities are not available. Provision financed by this mechanism was planned to reach a peak of approximately 135,000 children by 2004, and then grow no further.

Secondly, provision of Grade R in public primary schools is financed via a direct grant-in-aid from provincial departments of education to school governing bodies. These grants flow on a per-learner basis and are only for children in Grade R. The grant-in-aid is poverty targeted. The grants flow directly to the school governing bodies in terms of the South African Schools Act.

The grant-in-aid amount varies between provinces from R 2 per learner per school day to R 6 per learner per school day, based on 200 school days each year for up to 30 learners. Therefore, a class of 30 learners would receive R 12,000 per annum. This money is spent on part of the educator costs, learner support materials, training, furniture, nutrition, and educational equipment. For 2005/06 the nine provincial education departments have allocated R 489 million to Grade R grants-in-aid.

Government is of the view that this combination of poverty-targeted subsidies to children in Grade R in public schools, managed by school governing bodies, and the subsidization of some community-based sites will contribute to creating a vibrant and varied ECD sector. Grade R funding however lags substantially behind funding for other grades in the same school. For example, about R 4,243 is spent on each Grade 1 learner compared to only R 390 on each Grade R learner—–11 times less.

In 2005/06 ECD will receive only 0.7 percent of the total education budget. Clearly more funding is needed for improving ECD infrastructure, education programs, training, and personnel. If the current funding allocations are not increased substantially then parents in poor communities will continue to have to bear the costs of early childhood development, resulting in reduced quality in some centers and the closure of others.

The Minister of Education announced in May 2005 that a Norms and Standards policy for Grade R would be introduced in 2006. This would bring early childhood development for children upto 5 years into the formal funding program of government.

Funding for children aged birth to 4 years. Funding for children aged birth to 4 years takes the form of a provincial ECD subsidy. This subsidy varies according to province and ranges from R 2 per child per attendance day to R 6 per child per attendance day. A means test applies that disqualifies families who earn above a certain level and varies province to province. In total R 234 million was disbursed to 4,612 early childhood development centers (20% of the total number of ECD sites) in 2004/05. How the subsidy is used is not regulated but it is expected that it be used for staff salaries, children's food, educational equipment, and general expenses.

Before an early childhood development center or program can qualify for a subsidy it must be registered with the Social Services department in the province in which it is situated. To qualify for registration a center must meet the following criteria:
- Be legally constituted;
- Be a non-profit organization;
- Be able to show that it owns or leases the premises that it occupies;
- Meet health regulations of the local authority;
- Provide an educational program for the children.

Once a subsidy is approved the center or program has certain financial and program reporting responsibilities.

Local authorities generally do not fund early childhood development programs on a per capita and/or regular basis. In recent years some local authorities have taken to funding programs from their social development budgets. This funding usually supports the training of teachers and practitioners and equipping of early childhood development centers.

Private sector. Under the term "private sector" are included philanthropists, foundations, the National Lottery, and business social investment programs. Although private sector investment in education in South Africa is substantial at R 864 million in 2004, early childhood development only receives about 13 percent of these contributions. Of this most goes to training and service providers and not to community-based early childhood centers and program that work directly with young children.

Civil society. Civil society, including NGOs and churches, supports early childhood development centers and programs financially through contributions in cash and kind. All the main church denominations have social responsibility programs that include early childhood development.

International Donor Organizations

As with the South African private sector, international donor investment in education in South Africa has been substantial although it is decreasing rapidly. A portion of this support is through technical assistance and/or products. Again, early childhood development receives only a small percentage of this funding. Most of the international donor funds go directly to the South African government or to training and service providers. Community-based early childhood centers and programs that care directly for young children receive a miniscule portion of such funds.

Conclusion

South Africa has come a long way in early childhood development policy and practice. The new democratic government has done more for early childhood development than any previous government. However, young children still hover on the margins of the education system. The early childhood sector is under-resourced and it does not appear that this will change significantly in the decade ahead. It appears that the responsibility for financing the sector will continue to be borne by the nonprofit sector, parents, families, and communities.

Further Readings: Atmore E. (2005). Putting Young Children First—A briefing on Early Childhood Development in South Africa. Cape Town: Center for Early Childhood Development. Available online at www.cecd.org.za; Department of Education (2001). Education White paper No 5—Early Childhood Development. Pretoria. Available online at .www.education.gov.za; Wildeman R. (2004). Reviewing Provincial Education Budgets 2004. Budget Brief No. 143, Budget Information Service, Idasa 23 June 2004. Available online at www.idasa.org.za; Wildeman R., and Nomdo, C. (2004). Implementation of Universal Access to the Reception Year (Grade R): How Far Are We? Budget Information Services, Idasa. Available online at www.idasa.org.za.

Eric Atmore

Early Childhood Development Professional Development in South Africa

One of the most important indicators of quality early childhood development (ECD) programs is the quality of training received by the practitioners working with young children. A National ECD Audit conducted in May/June 2000 showed that the vast majority of ECD practitioners were underqualified (58%) or untrained (23%). The numbers of centers and children in provision were considerably greater than anticipated, but while provision for children has increased, training opportunities for practitioners have decreased considerably.

The opportunities provided through the development of the National Qualifications Framework (NQF), accreditation procedures and some new initiatives for funding training need to be fully explored to generate creative solutions for meeting training needs as cost effectively as possible.

Early Childhood Development Qualifications

After 1994, the South African Qualifications Act was passed. The Act aimed to design a national learning system, and established the South African Qualifications Authority (SAQA) as a statutory body responsible for the development and implementation of the NQF. The Act embodied the government's integrated approach to education and training. The principle of lifelong learning also underlines the progressive education policies of South Africa.

The NQF framework comprises eight levels, grouped in three bands. Level 1 (and below) comprises the General Education and Training band, levels 2 to 4 comprise the Further Education and Training band, and levels 5 to 8 the Higher Education and Training band (tertiary). The levels are defined by level descriptors that allow for equivalencies between different courses. For example, Level 1 on the NQF comes at the end of ordinary, compulsory schooling up to Grade 9, but can also be reached through ECD training for adults who had limited educational opportunities in the Apartheid era.

ECD standards and qualifications have been registered by SAQA at Level 1 (basic certificate equivalent to Grade 9), Level 4 (national certificate equivalent to a high school leaving certificate or Grade 12) and at Level 5, where there is a post-school higher certificate (one year) and a diploma (two years). Each of these qualifications prepares teachers to work in infant and toddler care (0–3 years) or the preschool phase (2–6 years), with various specializations such as the reception year (Grade R). A 4-year bachelor of education degree is required in order to teach at the foundation phase (Grades R–3, or 5–9 years). This is recognized as a Level 6 qualification.

Some tertiary institutions offer a specialization in preschool education. Postgraduate opportunities include an honors degree and higher diplomas (Level 7), masters and doctoral programs (Level 8), but very few tertiary institutions offer higher degrees in ECD.

Current Situation

In the year 2000, there were around 1.1 million children in some form of care. Provision has continued to expand with the Department of Education's policy to provide a reception year program (Grade R) in primary schools and financial support in some community-based classes. However, the quality of ECD care and education provided remains a major challenge.

Based on the National ECD Audit commissioned by the national Department of Education and conducted in May/June 2000, it was estimated that 53 percent of practitioners had completed schooling (Grade 12) while 16 percent had less than Grade 9. With reference to teaching qualifications, only 23 percent had a degree or diploma, while 54 percent would have been considered underqualified by the education department, mostly practitioners with in-service NGO training; 23 percent had no training at all. Of those with a degree or diploma, only 12 percent had professional ECD qualifications (at least 3 years tertiary study). In terms of training opportunities, it has been estimated that less than 10 percent is provided by formal tertiary institutions and the bulk (80%) of training is provided by the NGO in-service training providers.

Challenges in Early Childhood Development Training Provision

There are major training needs among ECD practitioners already working with young children in different forms of provision. Of particular concern are those who had no training in 2000 and the largest group who have had in-service training and need to get recognized qualifications—now possible for the first time through the establishment of the NQF. Furthermore, the statistics on training needs do not include the need to train new ECD practitioners to replace those leaving the system, to improve adult–child ratios, and the needs of growth in provision.

The challenges in meeting these needs are enormous in view of the existing training places available. There are a number of issues that complicate the provision of high-quality training services. These can be grouped into issues related to the delivery of quality training and issues related to providing training.

Challenges in training delivery (quality issues). There are various challenges to the provision of quality training.

Training of trainers. Perhaps the most urgent need to ensure quality training is upgrading the qualifications of the trainers, assessors, and moderators. Many experienced ECD trainers working in NGOs providing training have received only in-service training. Their knowledge and skills need to be verified through the recognition of prior learning and top-up training provided where necessary so that they can be assessed for valid current qualifications. This also applies to trainers working in the formal sector, especially in Further Education and Training institutions (which offer Grades 10–12).

For training providers to be accredited, the quality assurance body requires that trainers are qualified at a level higher in the field of practice (i.e., ECD) than that they are training. They also need to have adult education skills that are incorporated in the level 5 ECD qualifications. At this stage, however, there are very few ECD training providers that have the capacity to provide this training.

Career paths and leadership capacity. Opportunities for career advancement in the ECD sector in South Africa are extremely limited. This is because of the lack of funding available and limited promotion posts, either in higher education or in government departments. There is a major need to develop leadership capacity, especially in course design, materials and curriculum development, and research. More ECD practitioners with higher education qualifications (at Levels 7 and 8) are essential to create a more vibrant academic/ research-orientated climate.

Key issues in course design. The recognition of prior learning (RPL) is a key principle in the new outcomes-based education and training system, and it is a requirement for accreditation of training providers. In the ECD sector RPL is essential for the thousands of practitioners who have received NGO training over the last twenty years or more. RPL, however, is a new concept and training providers, in general, are struggling with it.

All ECD qualifications are made up of three components: fundamental learning (communication and mathematical literacy) required to improve the capacity for learning, core learning (compulsory subjects), and elective learning for specialization. There are three core areas: healthy development, provision for active learning (including activities and teaching methods), and a management component. Electives include specializations on curriculum areas such as literacy, numeracy, art, music, inclusion for children with barriers to learning, antibias curriculum, HIV and AIDS, and managing an ECD facility.

Most of the NGO training providers have focused on the core areas at Levels 1 and 4. Providing fundamentals training, as well as a range of electives in specialization areas, is a challenge for most NGOs, primarily because the training institutions are too small to offer specialist tuition.

Training delivery. State training providers are often in a better position to offer fundamental learning, while the NGO providers are very experienced and skilled in providing the in-service training that is most needed in the field now. One means of meeting this challenge would involve organizing consortiums among NGO providers. This would allow for a chance to "share the load" and also give students access to a wider variety of electives. Partnerships between state and nongovernment training providers should also be established.

Challenges in training provision.

Challenges in training provision. There are approximately 60–70 NGO training providers offering a variety of training to practitioners. Sixty-eight percent of the practitioners are African women, the majority of whom have received training from the NGO sector and are regarded as unqualified by the national Education Department. Half of the practitioners earn less than a living wage. Most training providers charge training fees but the NGOs rely heavily on donors and fundraising efforts to subsidize the training they offer.

Costs of training. Practitioners tend to choose training providers based on proximity and according to the training fees charged. Given the changes in terms of providing accredited training, NGOs face further costs related to training staff as well as reviewing training and assessment manuals and practice to meet the standards required by the quality assurer.

Funding. Government funding for ECD remains very limited (less than 1% of the education budget is spent on ECD). The Education Department subsidizes tertiary training institutions at a high level, but only for students who will work in the formal school system (from Grade 1 upward) following their training. There is also some subsidization for secondary colleges that provide full-time training for ECD practitioners on a small but increasing scale. As indicated above, most of the ECD training is provided in the shrinking NGO sector.

Due to the downscaling of foreign funding and the reality that available funding often goes directly to the government, a number of NGO providers have closed in the past five years. Others have downsized, often losing skilled staff to better paid jobs in other sectors. Many donors have specific funding policies that exclude training because this is seen as a government responsibility. A fee-based training service is not viable due to poverty and low wages in the ECD sector.

Government departments occasionally subsidize NGO training through special projects on a tender basis. A national skills levy also provides limited funds for ECD training, but the subsidies (per trainee) do not cover a substantial part of the costs.

Conclusion

Clearly the South African government needs to prioritize ECD, and budget for this area accordingly. Inter-sectoral collaboration will need clear objectives and dedicated staffing to be effective. Current government planning has a strong focus on improving ECD quality. As civil society, both NGOs and other ECD stakeholders will need to develop a strategy, part of which should be to engage the government on the promises it made to the children of South Africa.

Further Readings: Department of Education (2001). *The Nationwide Audit of ECD Provisioning in South Africa*. Pretoria: Department of Education.; National Education Policy

Investigation (NEPI) (1992). *Early Childhood Educare*. Final Report of the Educare Research Group (written by A. Short and L. Biersteker). Cape Town: Oxford/NECC; Short, A., and P. P. Pillay (2002). *Meeting the Challenges of ECD Training in South Africa*. Paper presented at the Omep World Council and Conference, Durban.

Ann Short and Patsy Pillay

Sweden

Early Childhood Education in Sweden

Introduction

Sweden spreads over a relatively large area, 450,000 square kilometers, making it comparable in size to California or Spain. Of the 9 million people in the population, 85 percent live in the southern part of the country, many in the three large metropolitan areas of Stockholm—the capital on the east coast, Göteborg on the west coast, and Malmö in the south. The northern part is a sparsely populated area with mountains, forests, and rivers, but the mining, lumbering, and water power available in this area have long represented important cornerstones of the Swedish economy, producing much of the raw materials and energy for the processing industries further south.

Increasingly the population is becoming more heterogeneous. Today people from more than 170 countries live in Sweden, and an estimated 18 percent of the population in Sweden today are first or second generation immigrants. These families came in the 1960s or 1970s, mostly from southern Europe or Finland to find factory jobs in the Swedish industry, or in the 1980s or 1990s mostly as refugees from conflict areas in Africa, Eastern Europe, or the Middle East.

Family Size and Structure

Several recent social developments have shaped modern childhood in Sweden. Most families (85%) have only one or two children, so growing up in a small family is common. Cohabitation is today a normal social phenomenon, and while most Swedish children experience growing up with both a mother and a father, one in every five families with children is a single-parent household. Most women continue working when they have children; 78 percent of mothers with children aged 0-6 years are active in the labor market. In Sweden, gender equality is based on the principle that each individual should be able to achieve economic independence through gainful employment.

Swedish Early Childhood Education and Care (ECEC)

The systematic expansion of the Swedish child-care system dates back to the early seventies. In particular, the following six goals hallmark Swedish preschool services: (1) stimulating and developmental activities for children, which combine education and care, (2) close cooperation between parents and service providers, (3) service provision for all children, with an emphasis on children in need of special support, (4) service provision designed to permit parents to combine parenthood and work, (5) public funding complemented by reasonable parental fees, and (6) municipal responsibility for full coverage.

Between the years 1970 and 2000 the number of children in full-time care increased tenfold. In 2002, 81 percent of all children aged 1–5 attended preschool activities, that is, 370,000 children had a place in preschools or family day-care homes. Of all school-aged 6–9-year-old children, 73 percent had a place in a leisure-time center before and after school hours. The vast majority of these ECEC settings are run by the local municipalities, but nonmunicipal, although publicly financed, settings have been more common during the past ten years.

Types of Settings

Swedish children start compulsory schooling at the age of seven. However, 98 percent of all six-year-olds attend the voluntary preschool class, which is typically a half-day service. Children in the 1–5 age group are found in the *preschools* (until recently named "day-care centers") or in the *family day-care homes*. Infants younger than one year of age are cared for in the homes by their mothers or fathers, who use their right to stay home with pay to take care of their babies from birth to thirteen months, hereby removing the pressure on municipalities to provide public ECEC outside the homes for these children. School-age child care is provided for 6–12-year-old children in *leisure-time centers* or family day-care homes.

Preschools offer full time care and education for 1–5-year-olds whose parents work or study, or if the child is judged to be in need of special support. Most preschools are located in the neighborhoods where the children live. They are open weekdays throughout the year, with hours adjusted to meet the needs of working parents. As of 1998, preschools have their own state-established national curriculum. In 2002, 72 percent of all children aged 1–5 were enrolled in preschools ("day-care centers").

In *family day-care homes*, the municipal family day-care mother takes care of children in her own home The curriculum of the preschool does not apply to family day-care homes, but should serve as a guide. In 2002, 8 percent of all 1–5-year-olds were enrolled in family day care homes. The number of children attending family day care homes in this age group decreased from a peak of 156,000 children in 1990 to 37,000 children in 2002.

Leisure-time centers for the 6–9-year-olds is the type of child care that has increased the most during the past ten years. Children enrolled spend those parts of the day when they are not in preschool class or primary school in the leisure-time center, which is often located in the primary school building. They might also attend during school holidays.

Since 1998 the municipalities have been obliged to provide all six-year-olds with a place in the *preschool class* for at least 525 hours. The preschool class is a voluntary school form for children and free of charge. Education in the preschool class is aimed at stimulating each child's development and learning and to provide a basis for further schooling. The nationally applied curriculum for compulsory schools (Lpo 94) has been adjusted to include the preschool class. The main reason for introducing the preschool class as a voluntary part of the school system has been to facilitate integration between preschool and compulsory school. In principle all six-year-olds attend the preschool class.

In addition, *open preschools* offer part-time activities for children who are not enrolled in other services. Open preschools require children to be accompanied by their parents. In this way they provide an opportunity for parents and caregivers to get together on an informal basis, with the result that some of the open preschools are functioning as *family resource centers*. In the period 1990–2002, the number of open preschools has decreased from 1,600 to 708, a drop largely explained by the fact that most children today are enrolled in other preschool activities.

Privately run, publicly funded ECEC became more common during the 1990s. In 2002, 17 percent of the children enrolled in preschools attended a private preschool. Forty percent of these children attended a parent cooperative and 30 percent attended a company-run preschool.

The distribution of various types of services differs between different types of municipalities. Family day-care homes are considerably more common in rural areas and other smaller municipalities than in big city regions, while the opposite applies for preschools and leisure-time centers.

"Full Coverage"

In relation to existing legislation, *full coverage* was basically achieved at the end of the 1990s, to the extent that places in ECEC settings were made available to those parents who worked or studied, or to children in need of special support, in 276 of Sweden's 289 municipalities. Some children were still excluded from services, however, and during the past five years new reforms have entitled parents staying home on parental leave to retain the place for their older children in preschools. In addition, children of unemployed parents now have the right to preschool activities at least three hours per day or fifteen hours per week. In January 2003, universal preschool was introduced for all four- and five-year-olds. All children are now offered at least 525 hours per year in preschool activities, starting in the fall of the year they turn four.

Staffing

The personnel in the Swedish ECEC settings are well educated. Very few of the personnel lack education for working with children. There are four types of personnel working in the preschools, family day care homes, and leisure-time centers.

The educational background and training of these four groups of staff members vary, as do the settings they work in and their professional responsibilities:

Preschool teachers complete a three-year university-level educational program that combines fieldwork and theoretical work. Courses focus on child development, family sociology, and teaching methods. Courses in research methods and evaluation skills are also part of this program. Studies are free of charge to the students.

Child minders receive their education in Swedish secondary schools. Three years in length, this program provides students with basic skills in child minding and developmental psychology.

Family day care providers are not required by the state to obtain any training, although it is recommended that they complete the child minder training course. Many municipalities, however, have instituted special training of about hundred hours, as an introduction to the family day care occupation.

The education and training of the *leisure-time pedagogues*, working with children in school-age child care, are rather similar to that of the preschool teachers—often the two groups of students take courses together at universities and university colleges. In 2002, the number of employees (full-time equivalents) amounted to 63,000 in preschools and 19,000 in leisure-time centers. Only about 5 percent of these employees have no training for working with children, whereas more than 50 percent have completed higher education university programs.

Salary differences between different categories of personnel working in ECEC settings are comparatively small. Whereas a child minder and a family day care mother might earn an average of SEK 15,000 per month (EUR 1,550), the salary of a preschool teacher or a leisure-time pedagogue after a few years employment might be about SEK 18,000 per month. (Teachers in the compulsory school system—grades 1–9 might be earning an additional SEK 2,000 per month).

Gender distribution among employees is very uneven. Only 6 percent in preschools and leisure-time centers are men, the same proportion as throughout the 1980s and 1990s. The highest proportion of men is found at leisure-time centers (16%) and among supervisors (20%).

A New Integrated Teacher Education Program

Through the transfer of responsibilities for preschools from Ministry of Health and Welfare to Ministry of Education and Science that took place in 1996, preschool became the first link in a broad and integrated education system covering the ages 1–19, from preschool to the end of upper secondary school. In 1998, the first preschool curriculum for children aged 1 to 5 years was issued.

These changes have also recently been followed by radical changes in the teacher education programs at Swedish universities and university colleges. In the new integrated teacher education programs, students planning to work in preschools, primary schools or secondary schools work together during several of the study terms. Students specializing in the early years will in the future be qualified to teach in preschools (ages 1 to 5), preschool classes (6-year-olds), the first years of the compulsory school (ages 7 to 11) as well as in school-age child care.

Funding and Financing

The total gross costs for the Swedish ECEC system amounted in 2002 to SEK 44,000 millions (EUR 4,500 millions). Preschool accounts for 68 percent of the expenditure, leisure-time centers for 23 percent, and family day-care homes for 8 percent. Staff costs make up about 75 percent of the costs, and costs for premises about 15 percent. Per child average costs amount to SEK 60,000, with average costs for children in preschools almost three times higher than costs for children in leisure-time centers. To cover the costs of ECEC the municipalities might combine the general government block grants with income tax revenues and parental fees in various ways. In 1999 a flat rate set fee was introduced by the government. Parent fees for one child are now maximized at SEK 1,260 per month, and municipalities are compensated for loss of income. This reform substantially lowered the fees for 80 percent of the families and eased difficulties caused by income-related and time-related fees.

The National Curriculum for Preschool

As mentioned above, the first national curriculum for preschool (Lpfö 98) came into effect in 1998, making the preschool a first step in the Swedish educational system. Overall, the educational system is now comprised of three curricula, one for the preschool, a second for the compulsory school (grades 1–9) also covering the preschool class for 6-year-olds, and a third for the upper secondary school (grades 10–12). The three curricula are linked by a shared view on knowledge, development and learning, and cover the first 20 years of the life-long learning philosophy of the Swedish society.

Philosophically, the preschool curriculum builds on the idea of the child as a competent learner, active thinker, and involved doer. Swedish theories about child learning can be briefly summarized by the following values:

- *Continuous learning and development*. Children learn continually in all places over time. Children use all their senses, so specific times for "learning" cannot be specified.
- *Play and theme oriented ways of working*. Play is the basis of preschool activity in that it fosters thinking, imagination, creativity, language, and cooperation. Theme-oriented learning fosters children's opportunities to understand contexts and relationships, and heightens their ability to develop their own learning theories.
- *Linking to the child's own experiences*. Children must be able to relate what they are learning to what they already know.
- *The pedagogical importance of care*. Care provides the experience and knowledge young children need to get to know themselves and the surrounding world.
- *Development in groups*. Children need other children from whom to learn; other children cannot be replaced by adults or toys.

The national curriculum for the preschool is based on a division of responsibilities, where the State determines the overall goals and guidelines for ECEC, and the 289 municipalities are responsible for implementation of these goals. Goals and guidelines for preschools are provided in the following areas: (a) norms and values, (b) development and learning, (c) influence of the child, (d) preschool and home, and (e) cooperation between preschools and the preschool class, the school, and the leisure-time centers. The goals in the preschool curriculum are defined as goals to be aimed at rather than explicitly achieved in terms of the individual development and learning of the child. Individual child outcomes will not be formally assessed in terms of grades and evaluations, since children might attend preschool at different ages over varying periods of time. The curriculum transfers over entirely to the professionals the responsibility for choosing and developing methods to achieve the goals.

Quality Controls

The School Act of 1998 stipulates that the municipalities are obliged to provide preschool activities of high quality. In ECEC settings, there should be personnel present with the appropriate educational background or experience to satisfy children's need for care and education. The size and composition of the groups of children should be appropriate and the settings should be suitable for their purposes. Activities should be based on the individual needs of each child.

According to the Ordinance on Quality Reports in the Education System, each municipality and school is to prepare written quality reports each year as part of the continuous follow-up and evaluation of the educational system.

Since 2003, the National Agency for Education is divided into two authorities: The National Agency for Education and The National Agency for School Improvement. The National Agency for Education is, through its Educational Inspectorate, responsible for educational inspection, national follow-up and evaluation, and reviewing curricula. The task of the educational inspectorate is to determine whether and how well an activity is functioning in relation to the regulations set out in the Education Act, school ordinances, and national curriculum. This involves auditing and assessment at the municipal and individual school level, focusing on both the quality and legal aspects of the activities under inspection. Educational inspection, a prioritized activity of the National Agency for Education, also provides an underlying basis for quality development in preschool activities, child care for school children, and the school system as a whole.

Current Issues of Concern

It is quite clear that the very rapid expansion of the child-care system, combined with severe cutbacks in municipal budgets during the 1990s, has led to larger groups of children and to lower adult/child ratios in preschools, family day care homes, and leisure-time centers. Even though the number of children increased by 185,000 between the years 1991 and 1997, total municipal costs for child care remained the same. On the one hand, these data may be considered as an increase in productivity, if productivity is measured in costs per hour. On the other hand, these changes do not necessarily bode well for children whose development and learning are nurtured by close interactions with playmates and adults, a condition that is reduced when the number of children per group increases, while the number of adults decreases. In 2002, the National Agency for Education carried out an intensive study of group sizes in preschools, preschool classes, and leisure-time centers. The results show no change in the size of preschool groups during the past year—the situation seems to be stabilizing, but at a historically high level. The average group size for younger children (1–3-years-old) is now 14.6 children, and for groups with older children (3–5-years-old) 19.7. The average adult/child ratio was 5.3 children per annual employee. These figures, and their consequences for the daily activities in Swedish preschools, are causing major concern among parents, personnel, and researchers, and (hopefully) among administrators and politicians involved in ECEC decision-making.

In 2002, 44,600 children aged between 1–5 years enrolled in preschool or family day care homes had a different first language than Swedish. Of these, only 5,800 received first language support, which might be compared with the situation in 1990 when 57 percent of children with another first language than Swedish received additional attention in their first language. The goal of the preschool for children who have their roots in a culture other than Swedish is to provide the foundation for active bilingualism and a dual cultural identity. Special government funds have been set aside for municipalities to improve the conditions of children and families in "neighborhoods in need of special support," that is, segregated urban areas with large proportions of immigrants. Some of these funds have been used to hire mother tongue teachers in the preschools, but support for language development in early years needs to be considerably strengthened, a point also stressed in the General Advice and Comments on Quality in Preschool published in 2005 by the National Agency for Education.

A somewhat different concern emanating from the launching of the new, integrated teacher education programs at universities in Sweden is linked to the fact that many of the students now specializing in Early Childhood Studies seem to have their focus on working with children in the 6–12-year age group, rather than the 1–5 year group. The new education gives students, following graduation, a chance to choose either of these groups and to work as teacher in preschools, preschool classes, or grades 1–5 in primary schools. Recruiting enough qualified teachers for the preschools might be difficult during the next decade, according to concerned school leaders all over the country.

Further Reading: Curriculum for the Preschool—Lpfö 98, Swedish Ministry of Education and Science, Stockholm; Curriculum for the Compulsory School System, the Pre-School Class and the Leisure-time Center—Lpo 94, Swedish Ministry of Education and Science, Stockholm; Gunnarsson, L. (1993). ECEC in Sweden. In Cochran, M., ed., *International Handbook of Child Care Policies and Programs*. Westport, CT: Greenwood Press; Gunnarsson, L., B. Martin Korpi, and U. Nordenstam, (1999). *Early Childhood Education and Care Policy in Sweden*. Background report prepared for the OECD Thematic Review on ECEC. Stockholm, Swedish Ministry of Education and Science; OECD (2001): *Starting Strong: Early Childhood Education and Care*. Final report of the OECD Thematic Report on ECEC; Swedish National Agency for Education. (2003). *Descriptive data on childcare, schools and adult education in Sweden 2003*. (Report no. 236); Swedish National Agency for Education. (2004). *Pre-school in transition—A national evaluation of the Swedish pre-school*. (English summary of report no. 239).

Lars Gunnarsson

Cultural Access and Respect for Differences

The Swedish preschool has from the very beginning been inclusive and has accepted children regardless of gender, class, language, and ability. Although small-scale state subsidies were allocated as early as in 1945, the preschools were still few in number, however, and not many children attended them. During the 1970s when preschool expanded and the first official state guidelines were issued, democracy and equality were stressed even more. When the first national curriculum was passed in 1998, it only confirmed what tradition, previous documents from the Government, and the curriculum of the teacher training had established as the fundamental values of inclusion and equality.

The National curriculum states that

> Democracy forms the foundation of the pre-school. For this reason all preschool activity should be carried out in accordance with fundamental democratic values. Each and everyone working in the pre-school should promote respect for the intrinsic value of each person as well as respect for our shared environment. An important task of the pre-school is to establish and help children acquire the values on which our society is based. The inviolability of human life, individual freedom and integrity, the equal value of all people, equality between the genders as well as solidarity with the weak and vulnerable are all values that the school shall actively promote in its work with children.

Thus, the Swedish preschool promotes diversity and acts against any form of exclusion or discrimination, in the official documents as well as in its practice.

Immigrant Children

Immigration to Sweden constituted no real problem regarding the integration of children before the Second World War, at least according to the official discourse. The Finnish children arriving during the war without their parents were quickly dispersed throughout the country and went to the same preschools or playgroups as the children of their new foster families. Not until the post-war years did Italian and Yugoslavian industrial workers to any observable extent bring their families to settle in Sweden. These children were accepted in the preschools of their new neighborhoods and the language was Swedish from the beginning. Children were supposed to assimilate Swedish values, the Swedish language, and the traditions. Their first language was seldom acknowledged as an asset but more as an obstacle to be quickly overcome.

For the immigrant families, preschool was often seen as the first contact with Swedish society and Swedish culture. In the guidelines issued by the National Board of Health in the 1970s the immigrant children were mentioned as a possible concern. The preschool constituted a moral dilemma for the individual child, who had to choose between different systems of norms and values. However, the general view was also that the Swedish children accepting an immigrant child in their playgroup had something to gain from the encounter.

As immigration increased in the late twentieth century, and as the whole preschool sector expanded, the focus concerning the children with "foreign background" was more on the language issue than on differing norms and values. Even though Swedish was to be the new common language for these children, there was a risk that the children's mother tongue was neglected. Many bilingual preschools, Turkish/Swedish, Serbo-Croatian/Swedish, staffed with bilingual teachers addressed this issue of double language proficiency. There was an imminent danger of children loosing their language of emotion, their mother tongue, as well as a risk of not being able to communicate with the relatives of their first nation, the country of their parents and grandparents. Growing up as a bilingual child was synonymous with being a child at risk.

In the last decade of the twentieth century many refugee families arrived in Sweden and the children were included in the Swedish preschools as part of the integration policy. The language issue transformed from bilingualism into multilingualism. In preschools with children of 15–20 nationalities and languages, and with children with Swedish as their first language as a minority, Swedish became the lingua franca common to all children and staff. Many children also speak at least two native languages, for instance one maternal and paternal, along with Swedish with their friends and teachers at preschool. As the situation is now in the early twenty-first century, multilingualism is seen as an asset rather than as a problem. Children who grow up in a multi-linguistic environment acquire a meta-linguistic competence necessary in a global world.

The national curriculum also stresses the future world that children will inhabit. In the words of the curriculum

> The internationalisation of Swedish society imposes high demands on the ability of people to live with and understand values in cultural diversity. The pre-school is a social and cultural meeting place, which can reinforce this and prepare children for life in an increasingly internationalised community. Awareness of their own cultural heritage and participating in the culture of others should contribute to children's ability to understand and empathise with the circumstances and values of others. The pre-school can help to ensure that children from national minorities and children with a foreign background receive support in developing dual cultural affiliation.

When Sweden became a member of the European Union, new light was directed toward the national minorities and their right to their first language, their culture, and traditions. In Sweden, these languages are Sami, Finnish, Meänkieli, Romani-chib, and Yiddish. In this policy, the first language identity is more accepted than it has ever been before.

The language issue has also to a large extent been overshadowed lately by the issue of cultural identity, in the fundamental values of democracy and equality. Again as stated in the national curriculum

> Increasing mobility across national borders creates cultural diversity in the pre-school, which provides children with the opportunity to build up respect and consideration for each individual irrespective of background. All parents should be able to send their children to the pre-school, fully confident that their children will not be prejudiced in favour of any particular view. All who work in the pre-school should uphold

the fundamental values that are set out in this curriculum and should very clearly dissociate themselves from anything that conflicts with these values.

Children with Special Needs

Children with special needs have the same right to preschool education as any other child. The national curriculum states that

> Pedagogical activities should be related to the needs of all children in the pre-school. Children who occasionally or on a more permanent basis need more support than others should receive this in relation to their needs and circumstances. The skill of the staff in understanding and interacting with the child, as well as gaining the confidence of parents is important, if the period in the pre-school is to provide support for children facing difficulties.

However, since the 1990s, the local councils are responsible for providing the necessary resources for preschool, with an attendance of more than 80 percent of children in the age group 1–5, as well as language support in first language proficiency, and support for children facing difficulties due to physical and psycho-developmental impairment. In a recession, when economic resources have become scarce, this means that the process of providing support has become more cumbersome to staff and parents, as well as to the officials.

In a government bill on the quality in the Swedish preschool this setting is characterized as the most important arena of integration. Nearly 14 percent of children in preschool speak a foreign first language. The proposal implies that the local authorities responsible for preschool allocate more resources to support these children. The current problem, though, is that resources allocated from the local councils are far from adequate for meeting the requirements of the national curriculum and the official policies. This conflict between national aims and local resources mostly affects children who need support in language development and in their daily lives. The decrease in resource allocation has led to an increased child/teacher ratio and to larger groups, although the variation in group size is high. Group sizes are higher in the urban areas where attendance is higher among immigrant and special needs children. There is also a general view among teachers and other staff that the number of these children has increased lately. Again, the children who need more support are less likely to get it.

Further Reading: Johansson, G., and I.-B. Åstedt (1996) *Förskolans utveckling. Fakta och funderingar (The development of preschool. Facts and thoughts)*. 2 uppl. Stockholm: HLS Förlag.; Regeringen. (2004). *Kvalitet i förskolan: Regeringens förskoleproposition (Quality in preschool. The government bill for preschool)*. Stockholm: Riksdagen, 2004.; Swedish National Agency for Education. (1998). *Curriculum for the preschool.* Available online at http://www.skolverket.se/pdf/lpfoe.pdf; Swedish National Agency for Education. (2003). *More Languages—More Opportunities.* A summary in English of Report 03:790. Available online at http://www2.skolverket.se/BASIS/skolbok/webext/trycksak/DDD/1111.pdf; Swedish National Agency for Education. (2004). *Preschool in transition. A national evaluation of the Swedish preschool.* A summary in English of Report 239:2004. Available online at http://www.skolverket.se/pdf/english/preschool.pdf; Swedish National Agency for Education. (2004). *Education for students of non-Swedish background and recognized minorities.* Available online at http://www.skolverket.se/pdf/faktablad/en_utlandsk.pdf.

Maj Asplund Carlsson and Johannes Lunneblad

Parental Involvement in Child Care in Sweden

Relations between parents and child care in Sweden may mean just a feeling that everything is all right and that their child is in good hands. Many parents find this quite satisfactory. On the other hand, there are parents who want to be part of the activities, to run the center, and to have full control and influence. And somewhere in between you find most parents.

Background

In public child care in Sweden, the importance of good relations with the parents is stressed. Child care is supposed to be a complement to the family and therefore a close cooperation between parents and staff is required. Parent cooperation is a constant theme in discussions about child care, but effects in practice are more difficult to document.

Official documents concerning school, preschool, and school-age child care state that parents have a right to be informed about, have influence upon, and take part in the activities that their children are attending. The official documents also state the staffs' obligation to make this possible in different ways.

Additionally, documents related to parental involvement and the importance of cooperation between staff and parents can be found at the local or school levels.

Parents are Different

Parents are different from one to another. The causes for these differences may be social, economic, and cultural. Consequently, parents' views show a wide range of variation. Different parents have different views of cooperation between home and child care or school, about the distribution of work at home, and about the territory of the parents and the territory of the staff. Parents also differ when it comes to the concept of knowledge—what is knowledge, what is important to know and to master? There are also different views on which roads to take to help children reach and master this knowledge.

Parents may also have different views of child development, how to raise a child and meet that child's needs, interests and behavior. The differences between the views of the personnel and the parents can be small or nonexistent, or there can be a gap that is difficult to manage. This gap can be troublesome for all parties concerned.

Contacts between Parents and Staff Members

In Sweden there are different kinds of contacts for parents to use. The first contact is when a child has secured a place in child care. Usually parent/s and child visit the preschool to become acquainted with the premises, children, and staff. When the child begins child care, a specially designed adjustment period, usually two weeks in length, is scheduled. During this period, parents spend time with their child in the preschool setting. Parents might also visit the preschool setting after the adjustment period is over in order to develop a deeper understanding for the preschool and its activities.

Group meetings for parents are scheduled 2–3 evenings every year. The goal of these meetings is to exchange information and to give parents a chance to get to know other parents and the personnel. There is also a special kind of meeting known as the drop-in-coffee. Typically offered one afternoon a month, parents are invited to the preschool to have a cup of coffee or tea and to meet the children, staff, and other parents. There is no program or timetable and parents can stay for as long as they would like when they pick up their child, or they can choose not to stay.

Other informal get togethers are picnics, field-trips, or "work days" where parents, children, and staff do things together; for example, paint a room or replant the garden. Participating in excursions, picking mushrooms, going fishing, or barbequing are examples of other joint activities.

More structured meetings include the individual developmental conversations that are usually arranged twice a year. During these meetings, which typically take about 30 minutes, parents and staff members have a chance to discuss matters inside or outside the preschool in more detail. They also talk about the child's development and learning.

Sometimes parents are elected to be members of the preschool board, which includes the director and representatives for the staff. Together they manage the preschool and make decisions. In parent cooperative centers, parental participation is often a prerequisite for enrollment. Parents are the employers, and have direct influence over activities. Parents often spend one or two weeks per year in the centers, actively involved in the daily activities.

Parental Perspectives on Involvement with Early Childhood Education Institutions

In a recent study we asked more than 200 parents of children in various early childhood education (ECE) settings about their views on the relations between the family and the child-care settings. Questions about relationships between jobs and child care, parental expectations, and cooperation and influence were included. Parents are also asked about other aspects of their lives, such as the family economy, household work, leisure time activities, and informal social supports. Key questions included the following:

- How do the parents' interactions with child care and school relate to the picture of their total life situation (family, work, housework, leisure time activities, and so on)?
- What are parents' conceptions of and attitudes toward child care? What information do they want and in which ways would they like to receive it?
- How actively involved do parents want to be? Which expectations do parents have concerning cooperation? What influence do they want to exert?

The Meaning of Child Care in Parents' Lives

We asked the parents what it meant to them to have their child in child care. The answers show the relation between the parents' efforts to cope with their whole life situation and their views of preschool. A large group of parents answered "It means everything." By this they meant that child care allowed them to have a job, earn a living, and use their education. Another thing that many parents stressed was that they could go to work without a bad conscience because they knew that their children were in good hands.

The Importance of Being Greeted in the Hall

Fathers and mothers stated that they have all had "experiences in the entrance hall." The entrance hall is often the place where parents and staff discuss the child's day, and it provides an opportunity to build a relationship between both parties. Mothers as well as fathers have opinions about how the staff meets parents at the time of arrival. One of the most crucial elements in the parents' total view of a particular preschool is based on whether a member of the staff comes out into the entrance hall to meet the parent and the child. If a parent wants to be met but seldom is, then that parent's disappointment tends to impact and affect his or her attitude toward the whole preschool environment.

Information about Goals

Few of the parents in our study were familiar with the social and educational goals of their particular day care center or school. Many parents stated that they had probably read about these goals or even heard about them, but could not remember the content of such goals.

To judge from the parents' answers, it is uncommon that teachers in Early Childhood Education settings explain to parents *why* they do what they do. Parents are often informed about *what* the children do, their routines and activities, or the schedule of the school, but seldom why. Sometimes parents ask questions about this, and are responded to in different ways by the staff members. Some staff see this as a serious question and explain the pedagogical or psychological reasons behind activities and routines. Others, however, might feel threatened by the question and might consider the parent to be troublesome.

To exert real influence, parents have to know about child care and school. It is not enough to have used the right to visit the child a few days a year. Not all parents are interested in obtaining this knowledge or have the time and energy to do so.

Parental Interests in Influencing Activities in Early Childhood Education Settings

An interesting, controversial, and complicated question concerns influence and how it is linked to parental involvement. Over the years, there have been many attempts to increase parental influence. For the most part, this has been done by practical measures such as increased number of meetings, parents participating in daily activities, questionnaires to parents about preferred activities, and so on.

In exceptional cases, a particular group of parents might become extremely active in trying to have influence and to effect what is going on. The cause of this activity is often a decision by local authorities to cut or even close down some provision. It may also be some negative change in the number of children or staff. When such incidents occur, most parents become deeply engaged, spending much time in meetings, searching for and presenting support for protests. In our study we tried to understand what kind of influence the parents really *wanted* to have on their child's particular preschool. The results from a questionnaire answered by parents in several different preschools, shown in the table below, can serve as an illustrative example.

	Want to participate	Actually do participate
Planning ECE activities	6%	1%
Putting forward views	44%	20%
Discussing ECE activities	34%	16%
No need for influence	16%	

As the table shows, when we compared what the parents wanted or wished for with what they perceived was the case in the present situation, we found that there was a clear gap between their wishes and their actual experiences. In addition, 27 percent of parents indicated that "I don't know how my points of view are treated by the staff," and more than one-third (36%) responded that they had no influence at all over what happened in the center.

Few parents wanted to have influence regarding activity planning. Some parents stated that they lacked sufficient knowledge to manage activities, the pedagogical framework, or the written documents. Several parents said something like "Goodness gracious! That is the job of the staff. They are trained for that. I would not like the staff to come to my job to tell me how to run that."

It as appears that as long as everything works well and the child gets on well and wants to go to preschool in the mornings and the parent doesn't see or feel discord, many of the parents don't want to or have time for extensive contact with the preschools. Instead, parents are free to use their time and energy to master their own jobs. An effect of this might be a lower level of perceived stress, which in turn might make parents feel more comfortable at home with their children.

A somewhat different form of influence that parents prefer is *cooperation*. The parents in our study wanted to have opportunities to discuss what they perceived to be the needs of their particular child, and they expected that the personnel try to provide for these needs as much as possible. In return, in order to make the whole group of children function together, the parents could accept the staff's demands and expectations.

Our analyses revealed that the concept of cooperation seems to be less problematic or threatening to parents than the concept of influence. Considerably more parents wanted to cooperate with the staff than wished to exert influence.

This last finding highlights the importance of knowing and paying attention to the fact that the use of particular words and concepts might affect parents' views and perspectives in different and unintended ways.

Further Reading: Cohen, B., P. Moss, P. Petrie, and J. Wallace (2004). *A New Deal for Children? Re-forming education and care in England, Scotland and Sweden.* Bristol, UK: The Policy Press; Macbeth, A., and B. Ravn, eds. (1994). *Expectations about Parents in Education. European Perspectives.* Scotland, UK: University of Glasgow; Smit, F., H. Moerel, K. van der Wolf, and P. Sleegers (1999). Building bridges between home and school. ITS/Nijmegen.

Lisbeth Flising

Gender Equity and Early Childhood Education in Sweden

Introduction

For some decades gender equity issues have in different ways been salient features in the arguments for and development of preschool services and early childhood education in Sweden. When the strong expansion of child-care services started in the 1970s, one major argument was that public child-care services are needed in order to give mothers and fathers equal opportunity to combine parenthood with employed work or studies. This goal for preschool is also mentioned in the 1997 government bill concerning a national curriculum for preschool.

The national curriculum for preschool specifies the values, norms, and educational goals for early childhood education. One highlight is on gender issues.

The ways in which adults respond to boys and girls, as well as the demands and requirements imposed on children contribute to their appreciation of gender differences. The preschool should work to counteract traditional gender patterns and gender roles. Girls and boys in the preschool should have the same opportunities to develop and explore their abilities and interest without having limitations imposed by stereotyped gender roles.

Early childhood education (ECE) settings have two different essential purposes to serve for gender equity, one concerning the parents and adult society and the other concerning the children and their conditions and development.

Early Childhood Education and Gender Equity among Adults

The parents. In combination with other public gender-reconciliating measures (e.g., parental leave periods for mothers and fathers to share) the rapid expansion of public preschool services over the past two decades may be the primary reason why Swedish mothers show one of the highest levels of labor force participation in the world, and Swedish fathers take more time off to be with their children than did their own fathers or fathers in most other countries. Early childhood education in the form of full day preschool service has undoubtedly contributed to more equal opportunities and greater gender equity for Swedish men and women.

The staff. When given greater opportunities to join the workforce many women have gone to work in the sectors of health, care, and education. The expansion of child-care services opened up a large new area of work, but a strong majority of those who went into this field were women. Nearly 98 percent of the staff in preschool services is women. This is not a new situation. Historically, the care and rearing of young children have been considered to be the responsibility of mothers, in Sweden as in most other countries. From the beginning of the history of early childhood education it has with few exceptions been women who have worked in this field and have created the scope of ideas and developed the activities and working methods.

Different measures have been taken, on national and local levels, to try to increase the proportion of men working within early childhood education and care. These measures have not been very successful thus far, but the work continues. The recently appointed national Delegation for Gender Equality in Pre-school is one such measure.

Approximately 1,700 men are employed in preschool institutions in Sweden. In the settings where these men work children might experience men and women working together on an equal basis. But in groups where all staff members are women, fewer resources and opportunities exist for meeting the stated goal of the curriculum "to counteract traditional gender patterns and gender roles."

Thus although in Swedish families nowadays fathers are increasingly engaged in the care of their children and in sharing more of household tasks and other family obligations with the mothers, in most preschool settings the care, upbringing, and education of young children are still almost entirely the responsibility of women.

Early Childhood Education and Gender Equity for Children

Most groups of children in preschool settings have a fairly even distribution of boys and girls. The national curriculum states that they "should have the same opportunities to develop and explore their abilities and interest without having limitations imposed by stereotyped gender roles."

When talking about gender issues, preschool staff often argue that they do not think about the children in terms of girls and boys, but see and meet every child in an individual way according to the needs and interests of that child. Hence they claim to be gender neutral in their interactions with boys and girls. But researchers observing the play and other activities of children in preschool settings usually find clear gender-related differences in the activities and social interactions of boys and girls. To generalize, girls often keep close to the staff, engage in rather peaceful activities like drawing, playing with dolls, or various forms of role-play. Boys often go to places where members of the staff are not present. They engage in physically active play like running, climbing, biking, pillow fighting, and in constructive play in the sandbox or with toy bricks. Both boys and girls engage in constructive play, but girls more often construct social settings and roles while boys construct physical things like roads and huts. Both boys and girls engage in role-play. Boys are often heroes, warriors, and different kinds of craftsmen, while girls more often play the roles of mothers or babies, nurses, models, and women-friends.

Lots of individual exceptions to these behavioral patterns do of course exist, but at a group level findings usually suggest that boys and girls do separate and different things, and often engage in play inspired by traditional male and female activities and patterns common in the surrounding society and culture. This might be said to be in opposition to the goal in the preschool curriculum that "The preschool should work to counteract traditional gender patterns and gender roles."

Gender Issues—A Confusing Mixture of Facts, Theories, Ideologies, Values, and Attitudes

There are several different theories and assumptions in operation when issues concerning similarities and differences between men and women, and boys and girls, are being addressed. This is not the place to review such theories or assumptions. But obviously facts and experiences may be understood in very different ways. Gender issues concern deep and basic aspects of personality and identity. Gender issues also concern power, influence, and opportunities, and they are important factors in social and cultural structures and discourses. Discussions concerning gender issues often evoke strong emotions and "everyone" has an opinion about what is "normal" and how it should be. Many people consider these matters to be private values and personal beliefs that should not be questioned or imposed on others. A starting point for educational awareness and development of methods to promote emancipating equal opportunities is to realize and be sensitive to the cultural and social constructions of gender, to recognize gender norms, and be aware of how they restrict the scope of action for boys and for girls and their possibilities to develop their full capacities.

Recent and Current Developments within Early Childhood Education and Care

During the last 30 years of substantial expansion in access to public ECEC various efforts have been made to develop more equal opportunities for boys and girls. The efforts often have dealt with educational methods and activities, usually in the form of supplying girls with more "technical" and constructive material, activities, and guidance. There have also been efforts to break up ingrained opinions and habits among the children. These have included systematically organized joint activities to get boys and girls to cooperate, respect, and appreciate each other, and separate activities for girls and boys designed to stimulate them to try new activities and to practice abilities other than those "gender-labeled" activities typically found in the early childhood settings.

This kind of development work has raised the awareness of equal opportunities, but there is still a question of the extent to which such working methods are operating in the everyday activities of early childhood settings. In many places it is "business as usual," and a large proportion of the staff members express the opinion that due to their individualistic approach to meeting the needs and interests of every single child, they do not differentiate based on gender and so do not see the need for special attention to be given to gender equity issues.

In more recent research, focus has actually been placed on how staff members act in relation to the children. In general terms, the results quite clearly indicate that the teachers do interact with boys and girls in different ways. There is an obvious risk that an individualistic approach conceals the fact that girls and boys as groups are treated differently and that these conditions effectively contribute to conserving traditional gender patterns.

In the last few years much attention has been paid to self-evaluative methods for teachers to observe and analyze their own actions. One focus has been on gender issues. The staff members often realize with astonishment how they respond to and deal with boys and girls in quite different ways without being aware of it. This growth in awareness often leads to an interest in identifying the ways in which the physical design of the ECE settings, as well as materials and activities, constrain the childrens' construction of identities and abilities, and how changes might give the children opportunities to develop a wider range of their personalities.

To reveal ingrained gender behavior may also give gender-mixed groups of staff reason to examine their interaction patterns and division of labor and help them avoid getting stuck in traditional gender roles. Actions taken to get more men to work in early childhood education and care have not thus far shown any great results. It is not, however, only a question of getting more men interested in preschool work, but also of analyzing and, to a certain degree, changing traditional female-dominated patterns concerning how work with children "normally" should be done. To achieve the goal of finding a substantially higher proportion of men working in preschool settings, there is a need for a change in attitudes and gender order in the whole society. This will probably take a long time. If early childhood education and care is successful in reaching the curriculum goal of counteracting traditional gender patterns and gender roles, this might help prepare the ground for the next generation of men to be more open to work with children, care, and education.

A specific initiative on a national level to promote gender equity in early childhood education is the attempt to train so called "gender educators." A gender educator is usually a preschool teacher who is offered specially designed university-level courses on gender issues. The idea is that every municipality should have some "gender educators" employed, to supervise groups of staff in their efforts to raise gender awareness and to develop their preschool activities in a more gender equal direction.

The previously mentioned government committee titled The Delegation for Gender Equality in Pre-School is another initiative at the national level. This committee is commissioned to compile the present knowledge and experiences concerning work for gender equity in preschool, and analyze different factors that have an influence on gender issues in that setting. In order to test ideas and collect experiences the committee is providing financial support for development work at a number of preschools. The work of the committee started in the beginning of 2004. In summer 2006 results and recommendations for changes and developments will be presented in an effort to strengthen gender equity and equal opportunities in preschool.

Further Reading: Flising, Björn. (1997). *Rekrytering av män till offentlig barnomsorg (To recruit men for work in public child-care)*. Rapport TemaNord 1997:567.

Copenhagen: The Nordic Council of Ministers; Ministry of Education and Science in Sweden. (1998). *Curriculum for pre-school*, Lpfö 98. (Stockholm, Fritzes); Owen, Charlie, Claire Cameron, and Peter Moss, eds. (1998). *Men as Workers in Services for Young Children: Issues of a Mixed Gender Workforce*. London: University of London, Institute of Education; SOU 2004:115. *Den könade förskolan—om betydelsen av jämställdhet och genus i förskolans pedagogiska arbete (The gendered preschool—concerning equal opportunities and gender in the educational activities of preschool)*. (Report from The Delegation for Gender Equality in Pre-school)

Web Site: Delegation for Gender Equality in Pre-school, Web page in English. Available online at http://www.jamstalldforskola.gov.se/show.php/17920.h.

Björn Flising

Quality in Swedish Early Childhood Education

Introduction

The Swedish School Act stipulates that the municipalities are obliged to provide preschool activities of high quality. In preschool settings, personnel should be present with the appropriate educational background and experience to satisfy children's need for care and education. The size and composition of the groups of children should be appropriate and the settings should be suitable for their purposes. Activities should be based on the individual needs of each child.

Issues linked to quality and equivalence in Early Childhood Education and Care (ECEC) have received an increased importance in Sweden during the past decades. One reason for this has been the changes in steering and supervision mechanisms that have taken place on national as well as local levels. The model previously dominant within the public sector was based on centrally formulated rules, regulations, and guidelines aimed at guaranteeing ECEC programs of high and uniform quality, and enforced through the system of state grants. The past twenty years have seen an increase in decentralization of decisions from national to local level, manifested in the 1991 Local Government Act, which provides a framework to strengthen local democracy.

Different Types of Quality Definitions

There are many different ways of defining (and measuring) quality within the ECEC arena. One of the most common definitions might be referred to as *structural quality*, and takes as its point of departure the frameworks and prerequisites of ECEC activities, often expressed in objectively measurable variables such as size and composition of children's groups, adult/child ratios, or educational level of the personnel. Factors linked to physical design of settings or outdoor environments might also be included among structural variables of interest. In Sweden, annual statistics, gathered systematically at the national level, give a good picture of changes over time in group sizes, adult/child ratios, personnel education, etc. Such statistics have been available since the 1960s.

During the 1990s, productivity in Swedish ECEC (measured in costs per hour) increased substantially. The number of children in ECEC settings increased by about 30 percent, whereas total costs remained the same. During the same period, changes in a number of structural variables were observed. The number of children in an average preschool group increased from 13.8 in 1990, to 16.6 in 1998. There was also an increase in the number of children per adult, from 4.2 to 5.6, during the period. In 2003, the average group size had increased to 17.2.

These negative changes have raised the issue of whether municipalities are able to maintain a quality level which meets the requirements stipulated in the School Act, in relation to good care and education based on the needs of each individual child. In the 2004/2005 Bill to the Riksdag, the National Government did include an extra three-year grant for the municipalities to employ an additional 6,000 preschool teachers and child minders, and make possible the decrease in the number of children in the preschool groups and a more favorable adult/child ratio.

Research has shown that there is no clear-cut relationship between costs and quality. However, studies investigating these relationships have also shown that socially disadvantaged groups of children are suffering more from a deterioration in ECEC structural quality than children from families with more resources. Solidarity goals and equal rights to good quality ECEC are issues highlighted in these types of quality discussions.

A different way of defining quality takes as its starting point the parents using the ECEC system, in their roles as citizens, clients, or "customers." *Quality of services* now becomes the main focus of interest. In measuring quality of services, issues like full coverage, efficient administration and distribution of places, access, opening hours, or parental freedom to choose among different ECEC alternatives might be at focus. National and local child-care surveys, conducted regularly, have until recently provided politicians and administrators with information on parental needs and preferences in these respects. During the past decade, municipalities have also systematically been using "consumer surveys" as ways of measuring parental level of satisfaction with existing ECEC activities, thereby relying on subjective quality ratings based on parental norms or preferences of what might be important aspects of ECEC programs.

High level of access or availability of alternative forms of ECEC programs might be defined as high *quality of results* linked to service level. Other result-focused quality definitions might be more geared toward measuring effects of education and care activities on children's development and learning. The goals presented in the Swedish National Curriculum for Pre-school specify the desired quality targets in the preschools. In the curriculum, goals and guidelines are being specified for the following areas: norms and values; development and learning; influence of the child, preschool and home; and cooperation between the preschool class, the school, and the leisure-time center. The goals specify the orientation of the work of the preschool and set out the qualitative development desired. The goals in the curriculum are formulated as *goals to strive for*, rather than *goals to be attained*. Thus they describe processes rather than final outcomes from preschooling.

Evaluating capacities, competences, or developmental progress of individual children are responsibilities to be carried out by ECEC personnel in cooperation with the child's parents.

Quality might therefore also be defined and evaluated in relation to pedagogical processes. *Process quality* refers to the quality of activities and relationships in the ECEC settings. High process quality calls for well-functioning relationships among personnel and children, and carefully planned activities, systematically analyzed and evaluated. Mutually trusting relationships among personnel and parents have also been found to be important. Measurement of processes has been conducted, for example, with the use of the internationally well-known ECERS scale, adapted to Swedish circumstances. Swedish research has found high quality, as defined by the ECERS scale, to be closely linked to parental feelings of trust, involvement, and understanding of the norms, values, and working methods of the personnel in the ECEC settings. In many Swedish preschools, there has been a growing interest in recent years in using pedagogical documentation as a tool for developing pedagogical work. In this context, the municipal preschools in **Reggio Emilia** in Italy have served as important sources of inspiration.

To improve process quality, resources might be well spent on the continuing education of ECEC personnel. One example of such an attempt to indirectly improve pedagogical processes is the ongoing, nationwide program to implement the new curriculum, financed through the National Agency of Education. Preschool teachers, primary school teachers, and leisure-time pedagogues meet to discuss fundamental values, goal definitions, and guidelines presented in the curriculum in cooperation with university teachers and researchers. In the basic university level teacher training, courses on research methods and evaluations have recently been added to the program to meet the increased demands for systematic analyses and evaluations of activities in the ECEC settings.

"Correct" vs "Incorrect" Definitions of Quality

There is an ongoing discussion among the various ECEC stakeholders in Sweden as to definitions and measurements of ECEC quality. Researchers and ECEC professionals might address the issue of quality from the perspective of expert groups that are likely to know what constitutes an optimal environment for children's development and learning. *High or low* quality is related to absolute standards and goals as defined in this way. Parents might look at quality from a different angle, including flexible opening hours, affordable fees, and particular personal interests in the equation. Municipalities, trying to adapt a "consumer perspective" or a cost reducing "lowest acceptable quality" perspective, might prefer a more subjective and relativistic *right or wrong* quality definition.

Political decisions made by elected representatives on the national level in the Riksdag, based on the principles of a multi-party democracy such as Sweden, are representing the collective sharing of responsibilities. In discussions around quality criteria in ECEC, some people have seen a danger in a situation when the individual, subjective goals of the parents, as specified in "consumer surveys," are given higher priority than, for example, the collective goals defined in the preschool curriculum, creating a situation where ideologically shared values and norms at the macro level, linked to solidarity and sharing of resources, might be overruled at the micro level, when quality in an individual ECEC setting is to be defined.

Present Development

In 2004 the Swedish National Agency for Education published a report presenting the first national evaluation of the preschool after the reform of 1998, when the preschool received its own curriculum and became the first step into the overall education system. The aim of the evaluation was to examine how the preschool has developed in different respects after the reform, and also to provide a progress report on the consequences of the reform. The evaluation also indicates the important choices confronting the preschool in its future development. Overall the results show that preschools have differing opportunities to carry out their task in a satisfactory way. Factors such as size of child groups and the catchment area of the preschool can explain a large part of these differences. Preschools in stable areas, as a rule, face better conditions for adapting their activities to the individual needs of children, to satisfy children in need of support, and to work together in good ways with parents. The report makes clear that certain preschools face inadequate conditions to carry out their tasks. In many of the multicultural, segregated, urban areas in Sweden the need for more resources linked to language and language development has been stressed. There is a need for educated mother tongue teachers, and for the inservice training of ECEC personnel in creating learning situations for children with Swedish as their second language. In the 2004–2005 Legislation, the government stressed the importance of clarifying in the national curriculum the multicultural responsibility of the preschool to strengthen childrens' language and identity development, and to make clear that one of the goals for preschools to strive for is to give every child with a mother tongue other than Swedish support to develop the competence to communicate in Swedish as well as in the home language.

Further Reading: Curriculum for the Pre-school. Lpfö 98, Stockholm: The Ministry of Education and Science; Gunnarsson, L., B. Korpi, and U. Nordenstam (1999). *Early Childhood Education and Care Policy in Sweden*. Stockholm: The Ministry of Education and Science; *Pre-school in Transition—A national evaluation of the Swedish pre-school*. (2004). (Summary in English of Report 239) Swedish National Agency for Education. Available online at www.skolverket.se; *Quality in Pre-school*, Swedish Government Bill 2004/05:11.

Lars Gunnarsson

Democracy: The Curriculum Foundation for Swedish Preschools

The focus here is on "the democratic project" to develop and come to a resolution about a Swedish national curriculum for preschool—how the perspective in the curriculum is formed and what this means for both pedagogues and children in preschool. How can the approach to children, their development, and learning be related to the culture and to theories about children? And how can pedagogues, parents, and children be implicated in the intentions of the curriculum?

The Swedish Early Childhood Education and Care System was already a strongly regulated sector in the 1960s. There were guiding principles for the area per child, the security, the number of children per adult and in relation to the children's different ages, and so on. During the past 20 years, however, the movement has been toward a deregulated and goal-guided system. This means that the goals for different public sectors are made explicit, while the responsibility for carrying out, or working toward, these goals becomes a question for the people involved—in this case, parents, pedagogues, and children. One could claim that behind this way of guiding the education lies a democratic strategy to make people implicated and engaged in their own lives. During the 1990s both the preschool and the school system in Sweden underwent more extensive changes than ever before.

A breakthrough in the change of preschool activities was established through "The pedagogic program for preschool" developed by the National Board of Health and Welfare in 1987. *Learning* as a conception was brought into view and became, step by step, accepted within preschool. Earlier, *development* had been the leading notion.

In 1996, the responsibility for the preschool was taken over by the Ministry of Education, which can be seen as a first indication of the inclusion of preschool within a "life-long learning" approach, and concretely within the educational system.

In a 1997 governmental declaration it was settled that preschool, school, and after-school centers should be integrated, in order to improve the first, important year in compulsory school. As a first step in this work, a unified goal document for the six-year-olds in preschool, the compulsory school and the after-school centers was composed. When this first step was completed it was decided that the preschool class (the six-years-old in school) should be regarded as a specific school form—the beginning of the next step beyond preschool. A committee was appointed to draft a proposal for a new goal document for preschool (1–5-years-old). To strengthen the pedagogic dimension of preschool, facilitate the long-term planning for the work in preschool, and make it easier to follow up and evaluate the goals, great importance should be laid on the goal document's structure and content. During the work in the committee a number of consultative groups, including the teachers' union, different interest organizations, people responsible for public education, and the Association of Local Authorities were involved. All this led to a strong political agreement and support for the curriculum proposal.

The Curriculum as a Regulation and as Goals to Strive Toward

The fact that the curriculum for preschool was given the same status as the curriculum for public schooling is viewed as a guarantee that the work and the activities in preschool will be equal for all children. At the same time it could be said that as a result of this change the preschool teachers' freedoms are going to decrease. Earlier, a preschool might state that "Here in our preschool, we are interested in music and therefore we mostly work with music." The goal statement might also say: "We do not work with mathematics, because children will have to deal with that in school soon enough." Of course it will still be possible to have preschools with special interests and aims, but it will not be possible to exclude certain goals, expressed as *striving goals*.

When you think about the concept "curriculum," it is important to take into consideration that it should be a plan for learning, in which the *values* for the work in the preschool as an institution, and what the *mission* of the preschool is, have been stipulated. The goal document for preschool is founded on the same principles and values as the curriculum for school, and partly follows the same structure. The individual child's development and learning are in focus, and the goals are intrinsically qualitative rather than quantitative, with focus on changing children's knowledge and their way of making sense of the world around them.

What is comparatively special with the Swedish curriculum is that the goals, with reference to the perspective on learning, have gained a supreme and central role. However, there is practically nothing written about *how* the pedagogues should work with the children. Still there are guidelines for how they should work or act in specific ways with children, in order to promote children's development toward the goals.

The Five Goals of the Swedish Curriculum

There are five groups of goals: (1) norms and values, (2) development and learning, (3) children's influence, (4) preschool and home, and (5) cooperation with school. One or two examples for each of these goals are presented below—

1. Norms and values
   Preschool shall actively and consciously influence and stimulate children to develop an understanding of the common democratic values in our society, and help them understand that in the future, they can be part of these. Preschool should strive to ensure that each child develops
   • his or her ability to discover, reflect on, and work out their position on different ethical dilemmas and fundamental questions on life in daily reality, and
   • respect for all forms of life as well as care for the surrounding environment.
2. Development and learning
   Preschool shall form a unity where the education is built on care, nurturing, and education. The activities shall stimulate play, creativity, and joyful learning, and use children's interest for new experiences to learn knowledge and skills. The flow of ideas and diversity should be explored.
   Preschool should try to ensure that children develop
   • their identity and feel secure in themselves,
   • their ability to listen, narrate, reflect, and express their own views,
   • a rich and varied spoken language and the ability to communicate with others and to express their thoughts, and
   • their vocabulary and concepts, the ability to play with words, an interest in the written language, and an understanding of symbols as well as their communicative functions.

Interrelated in the development and learning goals are "everyday life skills." These are corresponding to a number of qualities (in terms of properties and skills) like cooperative skills, responsibility, initiative, flexibility, reflectivity, active attitudes, communicative skills, problem solving skills, critical stance, creativity, as well as the ability to learn how to learn. These different qualities are seen as general and part of all school subjects, and form a central dimension of preparing the children and students of today for the society of tomorrow. There are also goals focused on making sense of the world around the child, and aspects relating to culture, natural science, reading and writing, mathematics, and so on.

3. Children's influence

To develop a base for understanding democracy, children must be deeply involved. Children's social development presupposes that they, according to age and capabilities, be given responsibility for their own actions and for the environment in preschool. Preschool should try to ensure that children develop

- the ability to express their thoughts and views and thus have the opportunity of influencing their own situation, and
- the ability to understand and act in accordance with democratic principles by participating in different kinds of cooperation and decision making.

The idea is that democracy should be treated both as a content and as a method in every day life with children.

4. Preschool and home

The person(s) having the legal guardianship of the child are responsible for the child's upbringing and development. Preschool is meant to be a complement to the home, which provides the best possible conditions for every child to develop richness and many-sidedness. The preschool should

- maintain, on an on-going basis, a dialogue with parents on the child's well-being, development, and learning, both in and outside the preschool,
- take due account of parents' viewpoints when planning and carrying out activities, and
- make sure that parents are involved in assessing the activities of the preschool.

5. Cooperation with school

It is important that there be a trusting cooperation between preschool and school (including after-school care). The cooperation should be based on the national and local goals and on directions valid for each activity. When the time comes to transfer from preschool to school it is the preschool staff's responsibility to find appropriate ways of rounding off and concluding the preschool period.

Curriculum Content

From the point of view of content, the most overriding theme in the curriculum is *democracy*. This not only shows in the perspective on learning, both of values and norms, but also in the emphasis placed upon children's participation and codetermination, as well as upon the cooperation with other participants in the home and in school.

The curriculum is now a regulation, which means that every public preschool has to work in accordance with these goals. This is expected to raise the quality of preschools all over the country. Privately organized preschools are not legally obliged to follow the curriculum, but it can be assumed that it will play a major role also in these settings, since quality is one of the factors for obtaining state money.

Curriculum Methods

In the national curriculum very little is mentioned about methods, or ways of working with children to reach the goals. Delegating methods, organization, etc., to the pedagogues is part of the decentralization efforts, and also a move away from earlier guidelines. The pedagogues are expected to have learnt about the methods during their own educational preparation, and there is also the assumption that there are several ways to work in order to reach the common goals.

The curriculum is mirroring an openness when it comes to teachers' methods and ways of organizing the work. Most of all, it becomes important that the pedagogue covers a wide range of methods, since children learn in different ways, and the pedagogue is expected to be able to meet each individual child in its efforts to understand the world and to master its own life.

What could be claimed more specifically is that content and form are related to each other and consequently have to be integrated. In other words, to use good methods without providing an engaging content, and the other way around, to provide an interesting content without good methods for making children engaged, will not be sufficient.

Even if the goals are formulated in this way, there are still several obvious connections to the school's subjects. For example, preschool should strive to insure that children develop the following:

- their ability to discover and use mathematics in meaningful contexts and situations,
- their appreciation of the basic characteristics of the concept of number, measurement, and form, as well as an ability to orient themselves in time and space.

One can imagine that it takes much thinking and great participation to implement the national goals within the specific age group or child group with which the pedagogues are working. It is most important that the goals direct children's attention toward the surrounding world, which can be interpreted and described by using mathematics, scientific conceptions, and so on, and not toward the school subject as such.

In conclusion, it can be said that there are goals to strive toward, but how to get along in this striving becomes a pedagogic challenge.

Further Reading: Alvestad, M., and Pramling Samuelsson, I. (1999). A comparison between the National Preschool Curricula in Norway and Sweden. *Early Childhood Research and Practice*, 1(2), http://www.ecrp.uiuc.edu/v1n2/index.html (Elektronisk tidskrift); Doverborg, E., and Pramling Samuelsson, I. (1999). *Förskolebarn i matematikens värld (Preschool children in the world of mathematics)*. Stockholm: Liber; EU. (1996). *Council for cultural co-operation*. Strasbourg: Education Committee. *Curriculum for pre-school, Lpfö 98*. Ministry of Education and Science in Sweden; Pramling Samuelsson, I., and Asplund-Carlsson, M. (2003). Det lärande barnet. På väg mot en teori (The learning child. Towards a theory); Socialstyrelsen. (1987:3). *Pedagogiskt program för förskolan (Curriculum for preschool)*. Stockholm: Allmänna förlaget; SOU. (1997:157).

Att erövra omvärlden. förslag till läroplan för förskolan (*To conquer the world*). Stockholm: Fritzes.

Ingrid Pramling Samuelsson

Early Childhood Teacher Education in Sweden

Introduction

The personnel in Swedish preschools and school-age child-care settings are comparatively well educated. Less than 5 percent of the more than 100,000 employees lack education specific to working with children, and more than 50 percent have a university-level education as preschool teachers or leisure-time pedagogues. Gender distribution among the personnel is very uneven, however. Only 6 percent are men, which has remained the same throughout the 1980s and 1990s.

In addition to preschool teachers and leisure-time pedagogues, childminders educated in the Swedish secondary schools make up about 40 percent of the work force in Swedish early care and education (ECE). Formerly, the program for childminders included (in addition to compulsory courses in mathematics, language, and social sciences) a combination of theory and practice to provide the students with the basic skills in childminding and developmental psychology. The program has recently been extended from two to three years of schooling, and broadened to include a wider range of options in the area of children and leisure-time activities (out-of-school time care).

There are also more than 8,000 *family child minders* in Sweden, providing child care in their own homes. A large majority of this group has completed the childminder training program, or 50–100 hours of mandatory course work provided by the municipality as an introduction to the family day care occupation. In recent years, a new one-year training program, with a national curriculum, has been arranged by the municipalities as part of their adult education program. This education is intended for students who have graduated from programs in the upper secondary schools and want to be qualified as childminders, or students who want to upgrade their existing (for some, rather short) childminder training. The entire program is practicum oriented; students spend extensive time in placements under qualified supervision.

Historical Background

In 1898, the first training course (four months of duration) was created for those who wanted to become teachers of young children. This educational initiative grew out of and supported the charitable work performed by unmarried middle class women in the early institutions for young children that developed during the second half of the 1800s. Two years later this initial course was extended to two years and given the name *Froebelseminariet*.

In 1996, federal responsibility for the preschools was transferred from the Ministry of Health and Welfare to the Ministry of Education and Science. Thus preschool became the first link in a broad and integrated education system covering the ages 1–19, from preschool to the end of upper secondary school. In 1998, the first preschool curriculum for children aged 1 to 5 years was issued. Two other national curricula exist: one for the preschool class (age 6) and compulsory school (ages 7–16), the other for upper secondary school (ages 16–19). In combination these three curricula unified the education system under a common educational philosophy. This unification process has had significant implications for teacher education.

Recent Developments

Toward the end of the 1990s, a new Teacher Education Commission was appointed by the government to set up goals for a completely new form of teacher education. This group suggested a comprehensive reform of all seven existing teacher education programs, including the one for preschool teachers. Their work resulted in a proposition put forward by the government to parliament, which was passed in the year 2000.

Basic principles. The reform discussed above is one of the most radical reforms in the entire history of Swedish teacher education. It implies a shift in the teaching profession from teaching to learning, from giving courses to enhancing competencies, and from being curriculum implementers to curriculum makers. The following are some of the basic principles for the new integrated teacher education:
- Formal education starts in preschool.
- The notion of life-long learning is emphasized.
- Learning is a social as well as an educational process.
- School provides an arena for social and cultural encounters.
- Teachers are mentors who are expected to scaffold and support children's overall growth and development.
- Education should support and stimulate children's creativity, imagination, flexibility, and problem-solving ability.

Program requirements. Three closely linked areas of education make up the new initial training program (see Box 1 below). The first comprises a unified interdisciplinary curriculum focusing on professionally relevant areas. This should preferably be offered to all prospective teacher students, regardless of specialization, and be spread over the entire length of training. For teacher candidates wishing to work with young children, the total requirement covers at least 140 credit points, or 3.5 years of full-time studies. Each credit point equals one academic full-time week of study. Each semester comprises 20 credit points. Completion of this program qualifies a student to teach in preschools (ages 1 to 5), preschool classes (6-year-olds), and the first years of the compulsory school (ages 7 to 11), as well as in school-age child care and programs for mother tongue teachers. (Children in Sweden start compulsory school in the autumn of the year they turn seven.)

Box 1. Integrated Teacher Education Program in Sweden since 2000
General Education Studies
- 60 credit points (at least 10 in work placements). These studies should comprise both areas of knowledge central to the teaching profession, e.g., education, special education, child and youth development, and interdisciplinary, cross-cutting themes such as socialization, democracy, and basic values/principles.

Subject Studies (subject enrichment)
- At least 40 credit points (10 in work placements). These studies should correspond to age-related subject areas, e.g., language, maths.

Specialist In-depth Study
- 20 credit points, building on previous knowledge, deepening a previous specialization, broadening an area of competence, or introducing a complementary perspective, e.g., integrative pre-school, sociology, adult education, international perspectives.

Program organization. Each university or university college in Sweden organizes these three elements in different ways. As a general principle, the structure should be such that students first begin to choose a specialization when they are well into their teacher education program.

For students aiming to specialize in early education, the program could have the following structure:

Semester 1: General Education Studies, 20 credit points
Semester 2: Subject Studies, 20 credit points
Semester 3: Subject Studies, 20 credit points
Semester 4: General Education Studies, 20 credit points
Semester 5: Specialist In-depth Studies, 20 credit points
Semester 6: Specialist In-depth Studies, 20 credit points
Semester 7: General Education Studies, 20 credit points

Within the framework of these three areas, students will be required to produce a dissertation accounting for at least 10 credit points. The belief is that this will help students to reflect systematically on the knowledge they have acquired in relation to their future profession. Furthermore, to prepare students for both the municipal preschool and the compulsory school sector, as well as for work in schools with specific pedagogical and methodological profiles, the new integrated teacher education should include different pedagogical approaches and methods. A new dimension of this teacher education model is that it will give practicing teachers the opportunity to take part in the undergraduate programs as part of their in-service training, and link them to proposed research programs.

Reflection, scientific knowledge, and integration are distinctive features of the new teacher education program, both separately and in combination. Another important aspect is the freedom of choice for the individual student to design his or her own program from a wide selection of elective courses. The program aims to support the students as they become reflective practitioners, and to include training in research methods to enhance their scientific knowledge base. Integration is desired during the general education studies, where students aiming to specialize in different levels of the education system will be given a common shared foundation of knowledge in the theory and practice of teaching.

Evaluation of the New Structure: Emerging Issues

Shortly after introduction of the new teacher education program several issues of concern emerged, recently highlighted in an evaluation of all existing teacher education programs throughout Sweden conducted by the National Agency for Higher Education (2005). These concerns include integration, the impact of general education studies, and recruitment issues.

Integration. Integration of teacher preparation across early education, primary education, and secondary education has not been altogether easy to achieve. Previous studies indicate that one of the problems related to integration has to do with the fact that different students seem to have different views of knowledge needs in teacher education, and therefore their investment in the various components of the teacher education program vary distinctly (Beach, 2000).

General education studies. Some students perceive the general education studies to be too general in character, and therefore hard to apply to their prospective teaching profession. Problems are also related to the far-reaching freedom of choice for students throughout the new program. That is, when students shape their own education through course selection, there are distinct implications for recruitment and teacher retention for the early childhood years. Previously, recruitment issues were solved by sorting students ahead of time into various programs aiming at a distinctive sector of the teaching profession (i.e., elementary school teaching or preschool teaching). Now this has become an internal matter for the individual student, who is expected to find his or her own unique path through the education system. The national evaluation indicates that students need much more guidance to insure that they design their education in such a way that they become attractive to prospective employers.

Recruitment and retention. Furthermore, the number of students aiming to become teachers of young children has dropped considerably following the new reforms. There are several possible explanations for this. Students may perceive that the working conditions are better in the compulsory schools, due to more desirable working hours and more planning time. Additionally, salaries and status of teachers working in the compulsory school system might be perceived to be higher. Finally, in the "old" integrated preschool teacher education program, which was well grounded in practice, the students in each teacher education program may have had a better chance to grow and develop a collectively shared teacher identity. In the new structure, developing a teacher identity has become much more of an individual responsibility.

Further Reading: Beach, D. (2000). Continuing problems of teacher education reform, *Scandinavian Journal of Educational Research* 44 (3); Högskoleverket. (2005).

Utvärdering av den nya lärarutbildningen vid svenska universitet och högskolor, del 1–3 [National Agency for Higher Education (2005) Evaluation of the New Teacher Education](Högskoleverkets rapportserie 2005:17 R); Ministry of Education and Science in Sweden. (1998). *Curriculum for pre-school*, Lpfö 98. (Stockholm, Fritzes); Swedish National Agency for Education. 2003. Descriptive data on child care, schools, and adult education in Sweden 2003. Report no. 236; SOU. 1999:63. *Att lära och leda. En lärarutbildning för samverkan och utveckling. Slutbetänkande av lärarutbildningskommittén (To lead and to learn. A teacher education for cooperation and development)*. Stockholm, Utbildningsdepartementet.

Maelis Karlsson Lohmander

Play and Learning—An Integrated Wholeness

In this discussion of the dimensions of learning in play and the dimensions of play in learning, we use the playful interaction between children and teachers as a starting point. We want to illustrate and discuss the didactic aspects that can possibly promote, or alternatively prevent, interactions between play and learning dimensions. We begin by briefly describing some characteristics of play and learning, respectively, that are of interest for this study. The starting point for our discussion of the conception of play as well as learning concerns experiencing and creating the meaning of the surrounding world. By using an empirical example of playful interactions between teachers and children, we will try to illustrate what happens between children and teachers in terms of play and learning.

It could be said that play is an important part of children's lives and their creation of meaning. In play, communication, creation and experiencing of meaning, reciprocity, and a feeling of solidarity between children take place. The worlds children create in play as well as learning are built upon children's experiences and are created within an interaction and reciprocity, but also involve aspects such as power. It is also conceivable that play challenges creativity and problem solving. In play children can experience their rights, participation, and influence. As children are "forced" to negotiate about play, test the quality of their arguments, and encounter other perspectives, their experiences become visible, both to themselves and to others. In play children learn from each other, and since the children's age and experiences often vary in the play groups, the learning will be challenged. These differences also give the children opportunities to experiment with, expand, and change their play worlds, and in that way develop new understanding.

Play as well as learning is considered to be a question of making sense of the surrounding world. In this process the idea of "as if" has been strong within play research, but we will point to the fact that the same idea applies to learning. It is in the situations where the child can go beyond the here-and-now situation and experience something else that new learning comes about.

Let us now look at an example from preschool praxis and search for dimensions of learning and play. How do the teachers and the children approach or deal with these dimensions?

Example

This preschool consists of 16 children aged between one and three-and-a-half years. Seven of them have an ethnic background other than Swedish. During the mealtime everyone is gathered in one room, sitting at three tables placed next to each other in a row. It is cramped around the tables, and everyone can see and hear what happens in the room. At this particular lunch there are fifteen children and four teachers at the table.

> Suddenly Yani (3yrs., 6 mo.) discovers how the sun is reflecting off his bib, making a pattern in the ceiling. Yani laughs and looks up at the ceiling. He points and says delightedly: "giraffe." He turns his body back and forth, making the pattern in the ceiling come and go. All the children watch; the teachers laugh. "Look," says one of the teachers excitedly. Adela (2yrs., 8 mo.), Amir (2yrs., 5 mo.), and Marga (1 yr., 6 mo.) cry out loudly and laugh. "It's amazing that he saw this. Such fantasy, to see a giraffe," says the teacher delightedly. "Children, did you see that Yani can do tricks?" she continues. Yani smiles happily and looks proud. "Giraffe," he repeats. It is lively around the table, the children point excitedly, and both children and teachers laugh.

What we first of all could ask ourselves is whether the situation described above could be defined as play. If we accept the fact that a play situation is characterized by "such as" and fantasy as our starting point, it becomes obvious that both these aspects are involved. The sun reflection in the ceiling represents something, and to the participants it looks like a giraffe. The play allows the discovery of this reflection to be something else. Also excitement seems to be involved, which we can see in the eagerness and the liveliness expressed by everyone around the table. Something unexpected has happened that everyone takes an active interest in. For a moment time stops and everyone follows the reflections in the ceiling. A common creation of meaning seems to become possible.

We can also see how the teacher gets involved in the children's play. Spontaneously the boy's curiosity and experiencing are being utilized. Jointly everyone takes some time to examine the boy's discovery and the children and the teachers share the joy. In spite of all this happening during mealtime, which makes the situation somewhat confused, free scope is given to the occasion and all children are allowed to be involved. Most of all it seems that it is the joy of discovery that is made apparent in this situation. One single child's discovery becomes a collective act in which all participate and direct their attention toward the pattern on the ceiling created by the bib. The teachers show their appreciation of the boy's discovery. They focus on his interest and encourage his initiative as well as the meaning he gives to the reflection on the ceiling. When he happily exclaims that it is a giraffe, the teachers share his joy and the other children are invited to take part in the joyful discovery. The teachers name his discovery and confirm his competence. *It's amazing that he saw this. What a fantasy.* They also point out to the other children that Yani can create something, *Yani can do tricks.* The situation could be interpreted as a moment of play, containing spontaneity, joy, social interaction, and symbolism, in which the process of interplay is important. We could, perhaps, say that there is a common ownership of the play.

We can also look upon the situation as a joyful process of learning. The children are encouraged to observe, discover, and imagine. Probably children's taken-for-granted way of experiencing the world is affected; they become fascinated and their interest is directed toward the reflection in the ceiling. The children become occupied by the pattern in the ceiling, and their joy is evident. The children's consciousness (and life world) focuses on an advanced phenomenon in their surrounding world. The sun's reflection is discerned as a pattern, which forms a picture and represents a symbol for something else in the world. The situation also takes place beyond here and now. Starting out from the actual situation at the dining table, both the children's and the teachers' interest is moved and becomes focused on the picture in the ceiling and its movements. Furthermore, the situation consists of communication, experiencing, and giving meaning. The teachers and the children identify the occurred phenomenon and give it a meaning. Regardless of what this meaning might be and what occurs to the individual child, we believe that the occasion has potential for learning, which is also full of joy and reciprocity. The teacher has an active role in her permissive and open attitude and the way of encouraging and sharing focus of interest with the children.

Discussion

The example we have been analyzing is a common situation in the world of the preschool. Let us start with what children spontaneously, or with the aid of teachers, direct their attention toward in this observation. We notice that the children are striving for an understanding of different phenomena in their own world. It is the child himself who spontaneously experiences and creates meaning by discovering the reflection in the ceiling. In this observation, it is through the child's initiative that the teachers and the other children notice the reflection of the sun. The child's attention is captured by, and becomes absorbed by, a phenomenon in the surrounding world. The child is permitted to stay in his experience and the teachers and the other children, sharing his joy, join him in his experiencing. The teachers contribute to the mutual experience, both by sharing it and by naming it. In this situation we find that play and learning are integrated. The children experience something new, which they create in the situation. They go beyond what they normally do at the dining table—have a meal, and they are permitted to be playful and to fantasize. There is something beyond here and now—a "such as."

In our example, the act of play and learning is to follow the child, and encouragement, imitation, and communication become prominent in the situation. What we have tried to illustrate with this observation is the importance of the adult when it comes to the development of a situation of interplay, and how this situation will appear to the children. We claim that teachers integrate play and learning, both in spontaneous situations and in situations in which the teacher might have taken the initiative.

Further Reading: Johansson, E. (1999). *Etik i små barns värld. Om värden och normer bland de yngsta barnen i förskolan (Ethics in the small child's world. Of caring and norms among the youngest children in preschool).* Göteborg Studies in Educational Scienccs, nr 141. Göteborg: Acta Universitatis Gothoburgensis; Johansson, E. (2003).

Möten för lärande. Pedagogisk verksamhet för de yngsta barnen i förskolan (Meeting for learning, quality for the youngest in early childhood education). Stockholm: Skolverket; Piaget, J. (1962). *Play, dreams and imagination in childhood*. New York: W. W. Norton; Pramling Samuelsson, I., and Asplund Carlsson, M. (2003). *Det lekande lärande barnet- i en utvecklingspedagogisk teori (The playing learning child—A developmental pedagogical theory)*. Stockholm: Liber; Williams, P. (2001). *Barns lär av varandra. Samlärande i förskola och skola (Children learn from one another—Cooperative learning in preschool and school)*. Göteborg Studies in Educational Sciences, nr 163. Göteborg: Acta Universitatis Gothoburgensis; Williams, P., Sheridan, S., and Pramling Samuelsson, I. (2001). *Barns samlärande—en forskningsöversikt (Children's cooperative learning—Research review)*. Stockholm: Fritzes. Studies in Educat

Eva Johansson and Ingrid Pramling Samuelsson

Early Childhood Literacy in Sweden

Introduction

During the 1990s, the Swedish Early Childhood Education and Care system changed from being more of a concern of family policy to being more a part of educational policy. This was manifested in the shift in government responsibilities from the Ministry of Health and Social Affairs to the Ministry of Education and Science, and in the presentation of the first national curriculum for preschools, which came into effect in 1998. There are also changes in society at large connected with communications technology, with home PCs, the Internet, and being able to send text messages via mobile phones. The discussion here will focus mainly on the intersection between preschool and school. Do these institutions share the same view of literacy, play, and the importance of learning, and of the use of digital learning environments as tools for playing and learning? By the concept *early childhood literacy*, we mean various creative ways of using the written language, corresponding to the concepts "broader textual concept" and "multimodality."

Our point of departure is that every child learns to read and write in his or her own way, depending on the child's opportunities, experiences, interests, the circumstances in which the child is involved, and the people with whom he or she is interacting. What you learn depends on the context. The historical and cultural context to which you belong determines the value of different types of competences. In the Western culture, formal linguistic writing and reading skills are highly valued, and considered essential competences. Expressing oneself in writing is a cultural activity, which develops as a result of the human need to communicate and keep records. Written language and written communication are in a period of change; their tools have changed in recent years with the advent of virtual and digital environments. New concepts are being used, such as a broader concept of language including other forms of expression than the verbal one, for instance, the language of music, art, and movement. One also speaks of multimodality as a broader textual concept, meaning that several ways of expressing and addressing, apart from text, are used in communication.

Theoretical Framework

Our didactic starting point, that children's learning should be understood from the perspective of the learner, has its roots in a phenomenographical and variation theory perspective. The phenomenographical research approach addresses questions that influence learning and understanding in a pedagogical environment. The learner's perspective is in focus. Researchers Marton and Booth describe the world as constituted as an internal relation between the learner and the environment. Individuals experience the world in different ways, and this affects their behavior in different situations. If you wish to understand how an individual handles a situation or a problem, you also have to understand how she/he experiences the situation or problem. Then some of the conditions of learning that are connected with the development of certain capacities will become apparent.

On the basis of many years of phenomenographical research, in which the learner's perspective has been central, Pramling Samuelsson and Asplund Carlsson have developed ideas leading to a theory of learning in the context of preschool—a developmental pedagogical approach. The theory has evolved in close collaboration with preschool teachers in different research projects. This theory states that playing and learning are inseparable in the world of the child. Children's interests and experiences cross the boundaries between subject areas. The teacher is challenged to direct the child's attention and interest to the learning object in a way that creates meaning for the child.

The sociocultural perspective also serves as an important theoretical base in understanding children's literacy, since we believe that becoming a literate person is learning to express oneself in writing as a communicative process and in the light of social and cultural conditions for children's knowledge and learning.

According to Lev **Vygotsky**, language and written language are the primary tools for learning. He writes about the external and internal functions of language. The external function is communicative, and the internal one is a tool for thinking. Written language has the same function as verbal language, but its external function is more concrete and observable. Its internal function is a tool for reflection and learning at a metacognitive level.

Kress states that children as well as adults create their own language and their own symbols on the basis of their own experiences and previous knowledge—quite contrary to many other theories and traditions in which man is seen as a user of an accepted language, signs, and symbols. Kress also claims that speech and writing are a form of communication designed to be maximally intelligible to the participants in a communicative situation. In an initial phase, children's early writing can only be understood by themselves.

For teachers in preschools and schools to be able to encourage, react to, and contribute to developing early childhood literacy, it is of vital importance for them to understand how children can learn to read and write and what role the teacher has in the development of early childhood literacy. Research is showing that children adopt an approach to learning to write at an early stage, and that this tends to be stable.

But because of different traditions and educational backgrounds, teachers in preschools and schools might not have a common approach to children's learning to write. The process might be interrupted when children move up from preschool to school. Here they might not meet teachers who will continue to support the learning process started in the preschool. The writing and reading process that take place in the classroom might not proceed from the perspective of the participant, and learning might not be seen as a communicative and social process in which the children could take part and construct their own knowledge and understanding of expressing themselves in writing. If the teachers and the children are approaching the learning object in different ways, this might affect both children's learning and their future. Two characteristic text environments have been identified in the process of recent research—the narrative one and the passive one.

The following three criteria stand out in the *narrative* text environment:
- A message is communicated;
- Communication is clearly related to children's experiences and the contexts in which they are involved.
- Communication linked to literacy learning is used in a natural way in daily interaction.

In a *passive* text environment, one or more of these criteria are missing, and the form of the written language is more prominent than the communicative aspects. Methods and material are mixed, but there is no obvious communication or interaction between the text, the children, and the teachers.

From the results of the latest Swedish studies on children's literacy learning, we might conclude the following:
- Children establish an understanding and an approach to literacy learning at an early age, and that this tends to be stable.
- In preschool and school there are traditions and things that are taken for granted with regard to children's literacy learning that should be rethought in order to realize the goals of the curricula.
- If preschool and school fail to collaborate and if the teacher does not take the perspective of the learner/child in learning to express themselves in writing, the individual child will be affected negatively.
- It is a challenge for teachers in preschool to create an environment that stimulates early childhood literacy, an environment with rich opportunities for functional literacy.
- It should be possible to utilize and develop the multi-modal opportunities, such as pictures, colors, shapes, design, etc., that have been a tradition in preschool.

The results of our own research demonstrate the importance of the adults collaborating with the children in a literate environment. One of the most important development areas that we can observe in our studies is that, when encountering children, the teacher in preschool should draw their attention to the learning objects identified in the preschool curriculum. To collaborate with children in this way there must be a special emphasis on developing the particular competencies involved. This competence development could be built into the organization, using the approach exemplified by "practice-close" research, where the teacher trainer and the practicing teacher work together in the classroom to strengthen the teacher's capacity to "take the perspective of the learner."

Learning to write and using a written language are complex processes that take place in complex contexts. Researchers and practitioners are abandoning the view that learning to write is a formal skill that the child acquires through instruction and practice. The written language experienced by children is changing all the time; what applies to one generation does not apply in the same way to their children and grandchildren. This makes it difficult for the one who is guiding children in the world of the written word. You have to take the child as your starting point—not your own childhood, but the child you are facing here and now.

From recent research we know that there is a considerable variation in how and what children think about learning to write and why they are good at writing, a variation in what they actually do. The role of the teacher and the environmental conditions then become important to analyze, that is, how the teacher in preschool arranges the textual environment. Observations indicate that the ability to interact in such an environment and with the preschool child that has not yet developed any understanding of the alphabetical system varies among teachers. The communicative function of written language as a learning object is a challenge for the teachers in preschool, as it requires an insight that they themselves lost when they acquired the skill of handling written language as a communicative system. Adopting the perspective of the learner in this area is a great challenge, but it is precisely what is needed when assisting a small child to become a person who can read and write.

Further Reading: Gustafsson, K., and E. Mellgren (2005). *Barns skriftspråkande—att bli en skrivande och läsande person (Early childhood literacy: Becoming literate).* Göteborg Studies in Educational Sciences 227. Acta Universitatis Gothoburgensis; Gustafsson, K., and E. Mellgren (2002). Using Text in Pre-school—A Learning Environment. *Early Child Development and Care* 172(6), 603–624; Kress, G. (1997). *Before writing. Rethinking the paths to literacy.* London: Routledge; Kress, G., and T. Van Leeuven (2001). *Multimodal discourse. The modes and media of contemporary communication.* London: Arnold; Marton, F., and S. Booth (2000). *Om lärande. (On learning)* Lund: Studentlitteratur; Myndigheten för Skolutveckling. (2004). *Early Effective Learning—Effetivt lärande i de yngre åldrarna—Om att förbättra kvaliteten i pedagogisk verksamhet för yngre barn.* Available online at www.skolutveckling.se 2004 09 30; Pramling Samuelsson, I., and M. Asplund Carlsson (2003). *Det lekande lärande barnet—i en utvecklingspedagogisk teori.* Stockholm: Liber; Utbildningsdepartementet (1998). *Läroplan för förskolan.* Stockholm: Fritzes.

Karin Gustafsson and Elisabeth Mellgren

Ethics and Morality in the Swedish Preschool

One important aim in Swedish preschool is to encourage children to develop moral standards. Children are to learn to respect others' integrity, to help others in need, and to understand one another's feelings. The study described below is presented to illustrate present discussions, positions, and reflections on social, moral, and ethical development in Swedish early childhood education and care. Its aim was to investigate young children's experiences of values and norms concerning treatment of and behavior toward each other in every day life in the context of preschool.

Theoretical Background

The theoretical basis for the study is the concept of lifeworld. The lifeworld is related to a perceiving subject, a subject that experiences, lives, and acts upon the world. The child creates meaning and is able to understand other people through its bodily being in the world. Thus we can understand that the child experiences and expresses morals through her/his body.

In international research, we find three main traditions for moral research: cognitive, emotional, and cultural. However, none of these traditions are internally homogeneous; they emphasize different aspects of children's morality and deal with different research questions.

The cultural *interactive* approach regards the interconnections among individual, contextual, and cultural aspects as the base from which morality develops. It also stresses that the child is active in interpreting and giving meaning to the world. Children, individually and with others, give their morality a specific character, shape, and meaning. This tradition lays closest to this investigation.

The Study

Nineteen children, ten boys and nine girls, one to three years of age, participated in the study. The children were part of a day-care group, in a small Swedish town. The daily interaction between the children was observed and video recorded for three days a week during a period of seven months. The analyses aimed to interpret and describe meanings from the children's perspective as expressed in their actions: What ethical values do children experience and express through their interaction? What norms do the children express and value? Values are positive or negative qualities (good or evil) that children express and experience in their own and in other children's behavior, acts, and attitudes. Norms refer to rules for behavior that children may express in their interaction.

Results

Two directions in the children's lived morality emerged from the data. The children defended and valued their *rights* and cared for *others' well-being*.

Rights. The children defended their rights to things and to share worlds with peers. They appeared to experience a type of compulsive attraction to things and thus experienced what is here called *a right to things*. Even from the youngest child's point of view, the children seemed to take for granted that things in preschool were waiting for them, *for* their inquiry. They protected their right to explore and play with things. But this self-evident relation to things was challenged by other children's demands for the same things. The children realized that things can be captured and held and as a consequence become another child's privilege. Thus the children saw that their rights must be justified. They developed norms that described how to act and what conditions gave rights. The norms concerned *control*, *time*, and *power*. These norms were relative to the situation and to each child's interpretation. Usually the child with control, whether through playing with the thing or keeping it in sight, had a right to it. In other words when the children experienced that things were under their control, they claimed their right to them. Time was also an important factor. The child that had had first control of the thing had the right to it. Thus previous control was a justification for maintaining the right to the things. Sometimes, however, power was an effective way to defend and gain the right to things. The strongest child often gained such rights.

The right to things also gave power, that is, the right to decide about conditions for using things, what to do, and with whom to play. In addition, the children defended their rights to things in different ways according to which other children were involved. This suggests that children made inferences from previous experiences with other children in similar situations. The children developed a "tacit understanding" for moral rules between themselves and others.

The children expanded their experience of their self-evident right to things and they connected this right even to others. This does not mean that the other child's wishes were always satisfied or that one's own right was reduced. On the contrary, it seemed that a condition for the children to defend another's rights was that they did not experience that their own rights were questioned. When the children shared worlds, the right to things sometimes became shared. A further step in the expansion of the children's rights was the experience that things can be shared equally. The children came to value justice, they compromised, and offered compensations to each other, and showed that they had an idea of equality.

The *right to share worlds* concerned shared meanings and activity and developed from projects that children created together. When others made claims to these projects, the value of shared worlds became evident. The children defended their worlds and took for granted their right to decide about them. They expected other children to respect this right. Other children might be permitted to join but the right to decide this belonged to those children who started the project. Just as power is a way to get the right to things, it can also help children win the right to a shared world.

Participating in a shared world gave children added strength. In addition the children created hierarchical structures that could influence the right to share worlds. In this regard, to be alike was important. This likeness was based upon size, age, and interests. Children also preferred to create worlds with children whom they defined as playmates and those with more influence.

The well-being of others. The value of others' well-being was expressed in two ways: *caring* and *not harming others*. Care for others was shown when children tried to do what was good for others and contribute to their well-being. They helped others, created situations of pleasure for them, and gave them advice. This behavior was more usual toward children that were smaller and younger, but was also sometimes expressed to those of the same age whose need for assistance was clear. The children seemed to find smaller children vulnerable. Toward younger children, good actions were embodied in the entire manner of behaving. Children used cautious gestures. Their acts were careful and gentle. But the results also showed that children seemed to claim that adults had the prime responsibility for the well-being of others. The children often looked for adults in such situations and asked them for help.

The value of not harming others means that the children tried to stop actions that harmed others or blamed the children doing them. They supported others when they found that they needed comfort, defense, or protection. Children were sensitive to others' pain, sadness, and anger, and tried to comfort them.

They gave physical and psychological support. The children also showed that they were concerned for others' well-being by explaining and making excuses for their own acts, and by referring to the norm of not harming others. The fact that children alternated between strategies of kindness and of harm could also be an indication of the fact that they knew or had a vague idea that the harmful acts violated the value of not harming others.

Discussion

In the study just described, two features were found to be of importance in children's morality in preschool: a commitment to their rights and a responsiveness for others' well-being. The values of rights to things and to share worlds with others are interpreted as existential, as children's way of being. First, things talk to children and inspire them to act. Children in this study were engaged with things seriously, with joy, and with curiosity. They were absorbed by things and took them for granted, as if the things were there for them, to be explored and examined. Second, another way for children to exist was by creating worlds with others. These worlds consisted of common meaning and shared activities. They were physical and psychological, inspired by the room and the things in it, but could reach far away in time and space.

Children are compelled to explore things and to share their worlds. When someone threatens or stops a child's inquiry about things or their shared worlds, this also threatens their very existence. The children expressed anger, sadness, and a feeling of being wronged when this happened. Out of this emerges an existential and lived ethical value of rights. This way of describing children's rights differs from previous research. Previous researchers mainly described this phenomenon in terms of children's defense of possessions, ownership, space, or interactive space. Even though conflicts over toys are well documented in research, this is mainly discussed as children's capacity to share and as a beginning of their emerging sense of justice.

The right to things and to share worlds with others is intertwined with life in preschool. In preschool things have a prominent place. Things are chosen and arranged to inspire children to play and to learn. Life in preschool is also built upon a feeling of community. For every child it is of existential importance to be a part of the common life with peers, to have friends to play with. This is something that children are confronted with every day.

Another part of children's morality is their interest in the value of others' well-being. They care for and defend others. The value of others' well-being actualizes a concept of "responsiveness" developed by Blum (1994). Responsiveness means that children are touched by other children's predicaments and try to do something to change the situation for them. In addition, when caring for others they sometimes show a concern for the other child's reactions. The children carefully look for the other's response and can change their own behavior in accordance with the other's experiences.

The value of others' well-being has an existential character. Since children are parts of each other's lives, they are concerned with each other's well-being. However, while the value does have existential character it differs from the value of rights. The value of others' well-being demands a focus upon the other. In this way it makes a greater demand on the child. This value becomes visible when children defend their rights, share worlds with others, and investigate the boundaries for other children's integrity. The discovery of others' well-being seems to be related to others' reactions, helplessness, vulnerability, and physical closeness.

Even if children's ethics cannot be separated from their lifeworlds and the grown ups included there, still they show that they discover values in their own relations with other children. In their life in preschool, things and friends are parts of their lifeworld and thereby highly valued. Out of these concrete relationships emerge values of rights and others' well-being.

Further Reading: Blum, L. A. (1994). *Moral perception and particularity.* Cambridge: Cambridge University Press; Johansson, E. (1999). Etik i små barns värld. Om värden och normer bland de yngsta barnen i förskolan (*Ethics in small children's worlds. Values and norms among the youngest children in preschool*). (Göteborg Studies in Educational Sciences, no 141). Gothenburg: Acta Universitatis Gothoburgensis, pp. 296; Johansson E. (in press). Children's morality—Perspectives and research. In B. Spodek and O. Sarachov, eds. *Handbook on the education of young children.* Mahwah, NJ: Lawrence Erlbaum Associates; Merleau-Ponty, M. (1962). *Phenomenology of perception* (C. Smith, trans.). New York, London: Routledge; Utbildningsdepartementet. (1998). *Läroplan för förskolan.* (curriculum for the preschool). Stockholm: Fritzes.

Eva Johansson

United Kingdom

Early Childhood Education in the United Kingdom

Introduction

The United Kingdom consists of four constituent countries: England, Scotland, Wales, and Northern Ireland. The unrolling of domestic policy is determined within each country, and early years provision takes slightly different forms in each. This account focuses primarily on England rather than on the United Kingdom as a whole. Specific aspects of policy and provision are dealt with in more detail in the ten topic items elsewhere in the volume. Across all of the United Kingdom, however, there is an active debate about the regulatory role of government, and about the sustainability of the welfare state. In particular there are conflicting views about the impact of the for-profit sector on social cohesion. Inequality and social exclusion are regarded as undesirable, but there is not a consensus about how they might be addressed. These debates underwrite the delivery of various aspects of early years education and care.

The profile of early years education and care in the United Kingdom has changed considerably since 1997, when the Labour Government took office. From being a political backwater it has become a popular campaigning issue. The Government has sought ways to coordinate and increase the provision of early education and care, and to improve its quality. It has taken these steps for three reasons: to improve educational attainment; to help parents of young children into employment, especially single mothers in receipt of state benefits; and in order to combat child poverty. Provision has substantially increased, although the biggest percentage increase has been in the development of the for-profit (private) sector, which was previously very small.

Despite their new prominence, developments in services have been erratic. There have been many new initiatives superseding one another, and various changes in strategy. Costs have also risen substantially during this period, and the sustainability of provision is threatened by high staff turnover. There have been a number of major reviews of UK policy and provision of early education and care in the last few years (OECD Country Note, 1999; Inter-departmental Review, 2002; Every Child Matters, 2004; National Audit Office, 2004), which have documented these changes.

Supply and Access

There are 2.9 million children in England below the compulsory school age of 5. (Children usually start primary school in the year in which they are 5). Different types of provision are available and/or most commonly used for different age groups. Typically a child will have two or three (or more) experiences of care and education arrangements before starting school at 4 years. These are summarized in the table below:

Age of child	Type of provision	Hours provided	Cost and subsidy if available
0- to 2-year-olds	For-profit day nursery;	Full time/flexible	Av cost £150–200 per wk.
		Full time/flexible	Tax credit if parental
	Childminder	Full time/flexible	income below £58,000.
	Nanny (in house	Full time/flexible	Ditto
	care)	Full time/flexible	Ditto
	Relative care		None
	Sure Start or		Variable
	Children's Centre if available		
3-year-olds	As above	As above	As above
	Preschool	10–15hrs per wk	Small fee
	(playgroup)	12–15 hrs per wk	Free
	Nursery class	12–15 hrs per wk	Free
	Nursery school		
4-year-olds	As above Reception class in primary school	As above 25 hours per wk	As above Free

Children from ethnic minorities, especially those whose home language is not English, and children with disabilities, are less likely to access early years provision than other children (National Audit Office, 2004). Most 4-year-olds are in reception classes in primary school. This means that if their parents are working, they will have to make additional arrangements for their children for out-of-school hours, often at considerable inconvenience. Many for-profit and nonprofit organizations offer out-of-school supplementary care, either on school grounds or in separate facilities. Out-of-school provision has grown rapidly, but it is also the least stable form of provision, with a high turnover of providers, partly because expansion has been based on short-term start-up grants.

Registered child-care providers and places in England: December 2004

	Providers	Places
Childminders	71,000	318,100
Full day care: (extended-day preschool groups and day nurseries)	12,000	507,700
Sessional care: (playgroups and private nursery schools)	10,500	256,300
Out-of-school day care: (including holiday schemes)	9,700	341,500
Creches	2,500	42,800
All types of provision	105,600	1,466,300

Source: *Nursery & Childcare Market News*, February 2005, Vol 3, Issue 8.

For profit and out of school provision has increased, but some kinds of provision have decreased. The biggest casualty has been nursery schools. Since the 1920s the United Kingdom has had an internationally admired tradition of free-standing nursery schools. In 1997, there were some 500 of these nursery schools. They offered free part-time or full-time (school year) places for children aged 3–4, and a curriculum, delivered by trained teachers, which valued free play and outside activities. (The regulations for child-care provision do not require outside playspace!) Under a separate initiative, now phased out, the best of these nursery schools were designated as "centres of early excellence," and subsequently, under yet another short-lived initiative, as "neighbourhood nurseries." But nursery schools, in their various guises, have proved too expensive to run, mainly because of their insistence on employing trained teachers led by head teachers. Nursery schools have either been closed, or have had to try to adapt, chameleon-like, into whichever government initiative currently offers funds. At the time of writing most of the remaining nursery schools which are able to do so are becoming children's centers.

The other category of provider that has suffered has been childminding or family day care. Between 1999 and 2003, 188,000 new childminder places were created, but 193,000 closed. This is partly because of the very stringent inspection requirements under OfSTED and partly because of the lack of demand for childminding places compared with other forms of provision.

Organization and Coordination of Services

There have been a series of moves to streamline the administration of services, at national and local level. In 1997, provision was piecemeal. Education provision (free nursery schools and classes) was controlled by the then Department for Education and Employment (DfEE) and provided on a discretionary basis. Welfare provision was regulated by the Department of Health (family day care, family centers, and various other types of nonprofit and for-profit care) under the terms of the 1989 Children Act. This Act specified staff child-ratios (a minimum of one adult to three children under two at all times), set safety requirements, and for the first time introduced guidance on equality issues.

In 1997, the Labour Government tasked the DfEE to extend free part-time nursery education to all 4-year-olds and for 3-year-olds with special needs. At the same time the Department of Health launched its National Childcare Strategy to increase child-care provision for working parents. The Childcare Strategy proposed tax credits for working parents, to try to enable low-income working parents to purchase child care in the for-profit sector. The Treasury developed a separate and unrelated antipoverty initiative, Sure Start, for children aged 0–3. This was intended to be a community-based initiative, spanning health, education, and social services, offering a range of home-visiting and center-based services for young children and their mothers in disadvantaged communities.

Some attempts were made to provide a coherent framework for these separate initiatives. The Government set up Early Years Development and Care Partnerships (EYDCPs), semivoluntary, semiautonomous, stakeholder organizations, to coordinate initiatives at a local level and to oversee the expansion of nursery education and child care. They received short-term funds for their work (at one point more than twenty-six different streams of funding!). In particular they were required to generate more for-profit child care through start-up grants, training, and business advice (Penn and Randall, 2005).

However, it became evident that many of the new initiatives were confusing and time-wasting. An interdepartmental report in 2002 recommended a "rebranding" and streamlining. The EYDCPs are being phased out in favor of direct local authority control. The "Sure Start" initiative, a central plank of the Government's antipoverty strategy, is also now being phased out or transformed because of slow implementation, poor take-up, and disappointing results. Funding will go to 3,500 local authority regulated multipurpose "children's centres" (subsuming all other service initiatives including Sure Start local programs) for the most disadvantaged communities. These centers, set to become on stream by 2012, are intended to provide integrated care, education, health, and family support services for children 0–5. At a national level, responsibility for *all* types of education and childcare provision (although not Health) has now been relocated in the Department for Education and Skills (DfES). A Minister for Children was appointed in 2004, and a Children's Commissioner in 2005.

Curriculum and Teacher Preparation

A common curriculum or "Foundation Stage" was introduced for all center-based care, including for-profit care. All regulatory and inspection activities were handed over to the national Education Inspectorate (OfSTED) although the actual inspection regimes for educational and child-care provision remain distinct (Penn, 2002). Training was also streamlined, and a minimum vocational qualification has been set for a proportion of staff in all center-based care.

Financing

In England, the Government spent £3.6 billion in 2002–2003, and has spent in total some £14 billion on early years services since 1998, mainly on early education rather than on childcare (National Audit Office, 2004).

Despite these well-meaning initiatives, and the considerable amount of money spent, early education and care in the United Kingdom is still piecemeal. It has not reached the levels of provision of most European countries, despite pressure from within the EU (European Childcare Network 1997) and from the OECD (2001). The children's center program is a belated attempt to redress the situation, but many problems remain. A key issue is whether the demand for universal, equitable services can ever be addressed within a market led system.

Further Readings: Department for Education and Skills (2004). *Every child matters: Change for children*. www.everychildmatters.gov.uk; European Commission Childcare Network (1995). *Quality targets in services for young children*. Brussels: European Commission Equal Opportunities Unit; *Inter-departmental review of childcare: Delivering for children and families* (November 2002). London: Cabinet Office Strategy Unit; National Audit Office (2004). *Early years: Progress in developing high quality childcare and early education accessible to all*. London: HMSO; OECD (1999). *UK Country Note*. Paris: The Organization for Economic Cooperation and Development; OECD (2001). *Starting Strong: Thematic review of early education and care*. Paris: The Organization for Economic Cooperation and Development; Penn, H. (2002). Maintains a good pace to lessons: OfSTED inspections of maintained nursery schools. *British Educational Research Journal* 28(6), 879–888; Penn, H., and V. Randall (2005): Childcare policy and partnerships under labour. *Journal of Social Policy* 34(1), 79–97.

Helen Penn

Sociology of Childhood and Children's Rights

Four interwoven strands in policy and thinking together make UK ideas about children and childhood distinctive. First, the United Kingdom is a wealthy country, but it has very high rates of poverty; when the Conservative party left power in 1997, their social policies ensured that one-third of children lived in poverty, and lone mothers and children were especially affected. The current New Labour government aims to reduce the proportion of children in poverty, and a principal method is to encourage mothers into paid work. Though early childhood services have expanded to meet this policy, in both quality and quantity they are inadequate.

Second, during the 1980s and 1990s, in explanation of high rates of poverty, politicians and right-wing media encouraged a culture of victim blaming, in which parents were blamed for children's failings. Children were described both as vulnerable to abuse by adults and as threats to the social order. These ideas persist today.

Third, as compared to other northern European countries, the United Kingdom has traditionally heavily emphasized parental responsibility for children's welfare and socialization, with the state playing a relatively minor role. Fourth, a linked point, there is general acceptance of the view that childhood is a presocial period; children are socialization projects for adults, especially for parents and, later on, early years preschool and school staff. Children are not generally recognized as citizens. Instead they are seen through "welfarist" spectacles as incomplete beings with a complex array of needs, whose welfare depends crucially on parental capacity and willingness to care.

The Rights of Children

Given this social context, the last fifteen years have seen increasing attempts to redress the balance, to do justice to children (and their parents), to rethink childhood: to think of children as people, as citizens who participate in social life. The 1989 UN **Convention on the Rights of the Child** (CRC) was ratified by the UK government in 1991, but not incorporated into UK law. Essentially the CRC lays out children's rights as citizens, under three main headings: rights to protection (since they are a minority social group in the power of adults); rights to provision (since as weaker than adults they cannot provide for themselves); and rights to participate in decision making on matters that affect them.

The UK government has found protection and provision rights readily accept-able, since they fit with a welfarist model of services and with children as a com-plex of needs. But within a strongly patriarchal society, governments and other policymakers have found participation rights more difficult to accept. However, the importance of listening to children and taking account of their knowledge and experience has been demonstrated through many research studies, including work with some of the youngest children, in early years settings. Government policy documents now acknowledge that children have the right to be consulted on a wide range of topics that affect their lives. But thoroughgoing reforms to procedures for planning and implementation are still needed to ensure children's voices are seriously attended to.

Childhood as Socially Constructed

In addition to moves toward listening to children, there has been increased interest in the idea that childhood is socially constructed. Sociologists, historians, and anthropologists have provided masses of evidence that adults define child-hood, and the children who inhabit childhood do so differently in differing times and places. This idea leads on to critiques of the ways in which childhood is commonly presented. Thus UK commentators note that the media and also pol-icy documents commonly present deficit models of children—emphasizing what they lack rather than their strengths. Children are routinely described as incompe-tent, vulnerable, ignorant, and needy; whilst an alternative set of words might be competent, strong and resilient, knowledgeable and capable. An important part of the social constructionist approach is that it draws attention to ways in which childhood relates to adulthood. Thus if adults define children as incompetent (and so on), then adults will feel bound to protect and provide for children in order to meet and remedy these defects. If children are vulnerable, then mothers must be extra vigilant. Early childhood services in the United Kingdom have long been affected by the concept of children's needs, and also by the idea that an important part of the role of staff is to compensate for parental failures in socializing their children.

However, there is general agreement that ideas about childhood and indeed services for children are changing. The CRC has been important, with nongovern-mental organizations (NGOs) such as Save the Children taking up a principled stance for children's rights. Also important are changes in early childhood courses and the huge increase in university childhood courses, drawing on anthropology and sociology. Although some of these courses still also draw on developmental psychology, they have built on and developed the work about listening to children, and further explored the social construction of childhood. The children's rights movement has brought strength to consideration of children's interests. The Open University BA in Childhood is already reaching out to thousands of students. These new strands in thinking are leading to debate on questions about the institutionalization of young children in nurseries (in the interests of decreasing family poverty) and about the character and quality of services for young children, and the appropriate training of those who work alongside them.

Deficit Models and Alternatives

However, the distinctive character of UK ideas about children makes it hard to obtain clear recognition of children as citizens with rights. Deficit models still prevail, rather than an understanding that children are not presocial recipients of adult socialization efforts. Sociologists concerned with childhood are attempting to move to a more structural understanding of childhood and to view children as constituting a social group that contributes through their labor to the maintenance and advancement of society. Just as in the past children used to work alongside adults in households, fields, and factories, so now their principal contributions are at school and at home. It is argued that children should be regarded not as objects of the education system, but as workers, who use their brains, bodies, and feelings to acquire knowledge and to help other children to do so. Staff in education settings should therefore think of their work as a partnership with children. This is probably easier for staff working with the youngest children, than for those gripped by the stringencies of the National Curriculum (see Curriculum entry, below)

At home, as every mother knows, children are not just the recipients of protection and provision; they are active participants in maintaining the household as a going concern. They engage in household work from their earliest months, they build and develop relationships; they comfort tired mothers and help their younger and elder siblings. In other words, they engage in people-work. One of the barriers to recognition of children's economic and social contributions is the long tradition whereby education staff define themselves as in authority over children; another is that children's people-work takes place mostly in private. It is only visible to another minority social group—women, and not to those who hold the power to change ideas about childhood.

Nevertheless, there are indications that policymakers on schooling are beginning to recognize that only if children actively participate in and engage with learning will they learn. The notion that children should enjoy learning is creeping back into policy statements. Some of this thinking may be a reaction to the straitjacket of top-down curricula and testing imposed from the 1990s onward. The new local authority controlled "children's centers" appear to emphasize a greater prominence for children's participation as key to good services. Perhaps the influence of such ideas will move upward through the school system?

Further Readings: Clark, A., and P. Moss (2001). *Listening to young children: The mosaic approach*. London: National Children's Bureau; Mayall, B. (2002). *Towards a sociology for childhood: Thinking from children's lives*. Buckingham, UK: Open University Press; Qvortrup, J. (1994). Childhood matters: An introduction. In J. Qvortrup, M. Bardy, G. Sgritta, and H. Wintersberge, eds., *Childhood matters: Social theory, practice and politics*. Aldershot, UK: Avebury Press; Woodhead, M., and J. Maybin, eds. (2003). *Understanding childhood*. Chichester, UK: John Wiley and Sons.

Berry Mayall

Culture, Race, and Ethnicity

Introduction

The United Kingdom has been a country of **immigration** and refuge for many years. However, in the 1960s and 1970s, the number of immigrants grew substantially, particularly from the countries of the New Commonwealth. The range of countries of origin and languages spoken broadened considerably in the 1990s due to refugees arriving from new conflict zones, economic migration, and the enlargement of the European Union. Current statistics show that currently 10 percent of all school pupils in England originate from black and ethnic minority communities. However this population is very unevenly distributed throughout the country, with the greatest concentrations in the major industrial cities and London in particular. It is currently estimated that 300 languages are spoken in the greater London area by school children.

Definitions

Providing definitions of terms such as "multiculturalism," "race," "ethnicity," or "identity" in the UK context is a challenge. There is little consensus and debate is lively. The Runnymede Trust, in a report on the future of multiethnic Britain, defined a broad concept of multiculturalism based on social justice for individuals. It also recognized that, as individual citizens belong to particular religious, ethnic, cultural, and regional communities, account has to be taken of these differences and affiliations if genuine equal treatment of citizens is to be achieved.

However, multiculturalism, by encouraging the concept of multiple and developing identities, has also been considered to be a divisive force in society. This concern rose to the surface in the aftermath of community unrest in the north of England in 2001 and the terrorist bombings in London in 2005 and led to calls for "integration" to replace multiculturalism and for the development of a concept of Britishness.

Developments in Policy

In the 1960s, as families with young children who did not speak English arrived to join working fathers in the major industrial cities, they posed a problem for an education system which was totally unprepared to receive them. Educational policies since that time have shifted between advocating integration, multiculturalism, equal opportunity and antiracist approaches, or indeed ignoring the issues altogether.

In 1966, the Home Office allocated funds to local authorities in areas where substantial numbers of new immigrants had settled to support any additional expenditure they may incur, in particular the cost of teaching English. The goal was assimilation. Children were initially taught in reception centres or in withdrawal units attached to mainstream schools. The expectation was that new immigrants would learn English and assimilate culturally into the mainstream society. Little interest was expressed in the children's cultural experiences and deficit models of bilingualism were common and teacher expectations low.

The concept of multicultural education developed in recognition that the school population in major urban areas had changed and that diversity of culture and language was an asset that needed to be recognized and valued to ensure equal educational opportunity. The Swann report, a major investigation into the education of children from minority ethnic communities, advocated a multicultural education for all children. It also reported on the effects of racism on black pupils and recommended that all pupils be taught in mainstream classrooms and have full access to the whole curriculum. The report was much debated but generally sidelined as the Education Reform Act of 1988 initiated government control of the school curriculum: the National Curriculum was statutory, assimilationist in its philosophy and eurocentric in its content. It was also overloaded, leaving little opportunity for teachers to work beyond it.

The new Labour Government of 1997 expressed a commitment to the development of early years education and childcare and to improving equality of opportunity for all children. The Curriculum Guidance for the Foundation Stage (QCA, 2000) acknowledged the different ethnic, cultural, linguistic, and religious backgrounds of children. Practitioners were expected to provide appropriate resources and encourage use of home languages.

Following the McPherson report of 1999 into the racist murder of a black teenager, which mobilized public opinion on the issue of institutional racism, the Race Relations Amendment Act (2000) gave institutions a duty to eliminate discrimination through auditing their practices and outcomes in all areas of their work. Educational institutions were required by law to have a Race Equality Policy and an action plan for implementation.

The Experience of Young Children in the Classroom

Multicultural education at its best in early years settings incorporates elements from the cultures of all pupils into the every day practice of the school. Teachers understand the benefits of bilingualism and seek staff who speak the children's home languages. They build partnerships with parents and communities and draw on their cultural expertise and community knowledge to incorporate language, cultural and religious events, and creative arts into the curriculum. The whole environment of the school, the displays, the books, the resources (utensils, dressing up clothes, dolls, food) reflect the home experiences of the children. Early years settings rise to the challenge of reflecting the very many different cultures that can be represented in one place. While acknowledging the importance of reflecting the experience of children in a particular setting, many educators feel that all children, especially in areas of low diversity, should experience different cultures on their way to becoming global citizens.

However, multicultural education has made little impact on the curriculum of schools. It does not generally address issues of economic and political power and their impact on the lives of children from black and ethnic minority communities. Neither has it had any significant impact on children's achievement in school.

The concept of antiracist education developed in response to the growing evidence of discrimination and the devastating effect this has on the lives and educational opportunities of children.

A curriculum for racial equality focuses on issues of social justice and combating racism. In the early years it recognizes that children learn their attitudes to race and social hierarchies from the environment and the adults around them at a very early age. Young children's experiences of racism (through name calling, ridicule, social rejection, etc.) seriously damage their self-esteem, their sense of personal identity and their educational achievement. An effective setting is a safe place for young children in which they learn to value differences, respect their peers, learn to be confident about themselves, and collaborate with others. It is a setting in which all staff, in partnership with families and communities, address negative behavior and support children who have suffered from racism.

Organizations such as the Early Years Trainers Anti-Racist Network have produced detailed guidance on these issues (EYTARN, 1998), as has the Commission for Racial Equality in relation to auditing equal opportunities in schools (CRE, 2000).

Issues in Practice

While good practice exists in relation to educating young children to value cultural differences, to respect others, and to develop a strong and confident sense of personal identity, this practice is not supported by a concept of entitlement and is a long way from being universal. The lack of consensus in relation to issues of culture, race, and ethnicity means that policy can change its focus as attitudes swing, governments change, politicians respond to shifts in public opinion, sometimes fuelled by sensational and negative press campaigns.

Government legislation since 2000 and the restructuring of services for young children have focused on quantifiable aspects of equal opportunities. Schools and early years settings are required to have policies and action plans, to analyze test results by ethnicity, to seek solutions to the underachievement of identified groups, some of which has been persistent and well documented for over thirty years.

Policies can be written and statistics collected. The skilled and sensitive practice required to translate equal opportunities into meaningful educational experiences for young children requires equally sensitive and skilled teacher education. New teachers feel they have been very poorly prepared to work with children from a range of cultural backgrounds (NQT survey) and there is a shortage of courses for experienced teachers in these issues.

In the absence of a consensus, how issues of social justice, racism, cultural, linguistic and ethnic diversity are addressed in practice in the classroom is often down to enthusiastic individuals who make full use of the legislative and policy framework, but go far beyond it in a commitment to developing the best practice for the young children in their care and organizing to influence policy. The extent to which educational experience is tailored to the cultural traditions of children and their families still varies greatly at the time of writing.

Further Readings: Baker, P., and J. Eversley (2000). *Multilingual capital: The languages of London's schoolchildren.* London: Battlebridge Publications; Commission for Racial Equality (2000). *Learning for all: Standards for racial equality in schools.* London: CRE; DES (Department for Education and Skills) (1985). Education for All, Report of the Committee of Enquiry into the Education of Children from Ethnic Minority Groups (the Swann report). London: HMSO; Early Years Trainers Anti-Racist Network (1998). *Planning for excellence.* London: EYTARN; Modood, T. (2005). Remaking multiculturalism after 7/7. Open democracy. Available online at http://www.opendemocracy.net/debates/article.jsp?id=2&debateId=124&articleId=2879#; Qualifications and Curriculum Authority (2000). *Curriculum guidance for the foundation stage.* London: QCA; Race Relations (Amendment Act) (2000). Available online at http://www.opsi.gov.uk/acts/acts2000/20000034.htm; Rynnymede Trust (2000). *The future of multi-ethnic Britain. The Parekh Report.* London: Profile Books; Siraj-Blatchford, I. (1994). *The early years, laying the foundations for racial equality.* Stoke-on-Trent: Trentham Books.

Raymonde Sneddon

Poverty

In the middle of the 90s, Britain ranked third from the bottom in an international comparison of relative child poverty rates in rich countries (UNICEF, 2000). Up to 1997 it also had the worst EU rates. Indeed, during the twentieth century's last decade, child poverty had become widespread, as demonstrated by the following excerpt from a major survey of children's access to necessities (Gordon, Adelman, Ashworth et al., 2000):

A third of British children go without at least one of the things they need, like three meals a day, toys, out of school activities or adequate clothing. Eighteen percent of children go without two or more items defined as necessities by the majority of the population.

After the 1995 Copenhagen World Summit for Social Development, Britain and 116 other countries agreed to adopt a two-tier approach to the measure of "absolute" and "overall," or "relative," poverty. They agreed to try to eradicate the former and reduce the latter. Relative poverty relates (a) to lack of access to basics and (b) to participation in decision making and in civil, social, and cultural life. The term "social exclusion" is generally used to refer to the second component of this poverty definition.

In accordance with European practice, the relative poverty line was set at 60 percent of median income level, that is, after deduction of taxes and benefits and adjusted for household size. The Poverty and Social Exclusion Survey (Gordon, Adelman, Ashworth et al., 2000) explored necessities deprivation and the distribution of poverty across households and argued for a long-term measure of poverty focusing on living standards, to provide a more comprehensive picture of the effects of poverty.

Child poverty was found disproportionately in minority ethnic families, in large and lone parent families, in families with younger children, in families in the social rented housing sector, and where families with children included a disabled member. General poverty in the United Kingdom, compared to that in other OECD countries, was also characterized by persistent, rather than transient poverty rates, high rates of workless households with children, of low-pay households and of low-employment levels and rates of pay among lone parent households, all factors with a direct bearing on children's life chances. Incontrovertible evidence confirms poverty's effect on children's present quality of life and later development.

When the Labour Government took office in 1997, these emerging general and child poverty data, coupled with Britain's ranking in terms of relative poverty among industrialized nations, caused official concern. While recognizing the complex and multidimensional nature of child poverty within robust economies, the UK government decided that tackling child poverty should be a key policy goal. In 1999, Prime Minister Tony Blair announced the government's intention to eradicate child poverty within a generation, that is, by 2020, and to halve it by 2010.

This announcement placed children center stage in the government's antipoverty strategy. Policies included the introduction of a minimum wage, increased child benefit packages and tax credit reforms, including the introduction of a child tax credit. The annual *Opportunity for All* surveys were established as a mechanism for monitoring general and child poverty levels. A Minister for Children was created in 2003, and Children's Commissioners were appointed in Wales, Northern Ireland, Scotland and England in 2001, 2003, 2004, and 2005 respectively.

The main focus of the new antipoverty measures was firmly on the under fives and their families. The "Welfare to Work" principle constituted the foundation for the Government's antipoverty strategy and was translated into the 1998 *National Childcare Strategy*, reformatted in 2004 as the *Ten Year Strategy for Childcare*. Its aim was to encourage a mixed market of child-care provision to support maternal employment, in particular the return to work of 70 percent of lone mothers by 2010.

The aim of improving long-term educational attainment, and hence a more highly skilled workforce, underpinned the provision of universal part-time free early years education for all 3- and 4-year-olds, a target achieved by 2004.

In addition, the government chose to address child poverty with targeted area-based initiatives such as *Education* and *Health Action Zones*, *New Deal for Communities* and an expensive, multiagency family support program *Sure Start* for under threes and their families. Yet the Government's own statistics confirmed that targeted policies would miss out many children, by showing that half of poor children lived outside geographically disadvantaged areas.

As far as poverty in early childhood was concerned, it soon became obvious that there were significant interface problems between the supply side subsidy provided to providers of early education, and the demand side subsidies provided to parents in the form of child-care tax credits, which was meant to encourage the operation of the child-care market. There simply was not enough money in the system to ensure day care growth, sustainability, and accessibility to poor children.

This "market failure" was behind the government's 2004 changes to the child-care strategy, including an increase in child-care tax credits limits and women's entitlement to a full-year paid maternity leave by the end of the present parliament. No robust measures were announced to encourage universal child-care provision for 1- and 2-year-olds. The reformatted child-care strategy was to continue its heavy reliance on market mechanisms for its success.

The Sure Start programs, originally the lynchpin of the antipoverty strategy, were integrated with a range of other center-based family support initiatives into a nationwide program of children's centers. By 2010 there should be 3,500 of these "in every community," offering access to integrated early years activities, child-care and family services, including some health services. As far as measuring the impact on child poverty of the government's early years strategies is concerned, the Sure Start initiative is subject to an extensive national evaluation. However, this has so far yielded few significant findings.

The government does appear to have achieved its main target for 2004, namely lifting some 700,000 children out of poverty since the late 1990s. But while gains have been made, some key indicators pertinent to child poverty have worsened significantly since the late 90s, including a doubling of the number of households with children in temporary accommodation. Gender, ethnicity, and disability continue to characterize child poverty in Britain and gains made in terms of children's healthy development and later life chances remain at risk.

The evidence justifies the conclusion that even under conditions of full employment, child poverty will not simply disappear, as low pay remains a significant problem. Investing in early education and care cannot on its own address child poverty significantly. Two parents in paid employment may be sufficient to keep a household with a couple of children above the poverty threshold, but lower levels of parental employment provide no guarantees in this respect. In an era that has witnessed the disappearance of the family wage, an over-reliance on paid work as a route out of poverty for households with children, and a rigid adherence to the "welfare to work" principle, may eventually prove counterproductive in achieving the Labour Government's aim of eradicating child poverty within a generation.

Further Readings: Adelman, L., S. Middleton, and K. Ashworth (2003). *Britain's poorest children: Severe and persistent poverty and social exclusion*. London: Centre for Research in Social Policy for Save the Children UK; Bradshaw, J., ed. (2001). *Poverty: The outcomes for children*. ESRC Occasional Paper 26. London: Family Policy Studies Centre; Department of Social Security (1999). *Opportunity for all: 1st annual report*. London: The Stationary Office; Department for Work and Pensions (2003). *Measuring child poverty*. London: The Stationary Office; Gordon, D., L. Adelman, K. Ashworth, J. Bradshaw, R. Levitas, S. Middleton, C. Pantazis, D. Patsios, S. Payne, P. Townsend, and J.

Williams (2000). *Poverty and social exclusion in Britain*. York: Joseph Rowntree Foundation; Hills, J. (2004). Poverty challenges and dilemmas for the next 20 years. In H. Glennerster, J. Hills, D. Piachaud, and J. Webb, eds., *One hundred years of poverty and policy*. York: Joseph Rowntree Foundation; H.M. Treasury (2004). *Child poverty review*. London: The Stationary Office; Lloyd, E. (in press). Children, poverty and social exclusion. In D. Gordon, C. Pantazis, and R. Levitas, eds., *Poverty and social exclusion: The millennium survey*. Bristol: Policy Press; Melhuish, E. (2004). A literature review of the impact of early years provision on young children, with emphasis given to children from disadvantaged backgrounds. In NAO, *Early Years: Progress in developing high quality childcare and early education accessible to all*. London: National Audit Office. Available online at www.nao.org.uk/publications; National Audit Office (2004). *Early Years: Progress in developing high quality childcare and early education accessible to all*. London: National Audit Office. Available online at www.nao.org.uk/publications; Palmer, G., and P. Kenway (2004). *Monitoring poverty and social exclusion 2004*. York: Joseph Rowntree Foundation. Available online at www.npi.org.uk/reports; Ridge, T. (2002). *Childhood and social exclusion: From a child's perspective*. Bristol: Policy Press; UNICEF (2000). *A league table of child poverty in rich nations*. Innocenti Report Card 1. Florence: Innocenti Research Centre.

Eva Lloyd

The Concept of Quality in the United Kingdom

"Quality" is a central concern for policy and research in early childhood education and care in the United Kingdom. It is seen by government to be a necessary condition to reduce the possibility of bad effects of attending child care and to ensure the best outcomes. In its recent *Ten Year Strategy for Child Care* document, the UK government speaks of its vision of a child care system where "child care services are among the best in the world; and all families are able to afford high quality child care services." Ensuring that "pre-school child care is of high quality will improve outcomes for children, particularly the youngest children, as well as creating wider benefits for families and society." It bases this statement on research interpreted as showing that "quality pre-school experiences can have clear positive effects on children's social, emotional, and cognitive development . . . [and that] early exposure to quality pre-school is more effective . . . the higher the quality of the education provided."

Recent research in the United Kingdom has been dominated by two large-scale government-funded longitudinal studies, one focused on the Labour Government's flagship Sure Start program, which targets young children and families in poor areas; the other examining the consequences of attendance at different forms of provision—*The Effective Provision of Pre-School Education* (EPPE). Much quoted by government, EPPE concludes that "high quality provision" has a positive effect on children's intellectual and social/behavioral development: the better the quality, the better for the children's development. Quality has been assessed using a standardized rating scale based on the Early Childhood **Environmental Rating Scale**, developed by Clifford and Harms in the United States.

The EPPE researchers further conclude that quality is associated with various staffing features, including staff with higher qualifications, leadership skills, and longer years of service: "having qualified trained teachers working with children ... had the greatest impact on quality, and was linked specifically with better outcomes in pre-reading and social development" (Sylva, Melhuish, Sammons et al., 2003, p. 2). In other words, structure (in particular staffing) and process (the environment of the service) are presented as closely connected. At the same time, in policy statements, government distinguishes access from quality, but presents them both as necessary and complementary goals.

However, given current policies it is difficult for government to meet these goals. A great part of early childhood services, those referred to as "child care," are delivered by private providers (mostly businesses) in a private market, and parents are expected to pay for these services as consumers needing to purchase "child care." Public funding is focused on parents unable to access the market because of low income, through targeted policies, in particular tax credits. Most of the costs of these child care services are, therefore, carried by parents, and this funding base has proved incompatible with developing a well-qualified workforce; levels of qualification are low, as are pay and related conditions.

Even within its own terms, government policy faces a contradiction: how to achieve "quality" in a market system. It faces a further problem. Parents as consumers may be unable to afford the conditions for good quality but they are also thought to lack the necessary knowledge to make informed choices: in the words of a government Treasury report, "although the quality of child care experience is vital to child outcomes, there is evidence to suggest that parents do not accurately observe the quality of the child care they use."

This discussion on quality in the United Kingdom today forms part of a wider discourse on quality, with its origins in the United States in the 1980s. The United States is seen as a reference point by UK policymakers and researchers, who draw heavily on the disciplinary perspectives, methods, and results of American research. The observation by Bloch (1992) about the United States could apply equally to the United Kingdom, at least when it comes to government-funded research: "early childhood educators who fail to frame their research or research methods in the largely positivist traditions and theories of child development or developmental psychology find themselves marginalized."

As part of the wider Anglo-American discourse about early childhood, the discussion and practice of quality in the United Kingdom is inscribed with the values and assumptions of liberalism and modernity. Quality is understood in terms of identifying and assuring certain conditions that will promote particular results or outcomes, usually defined in developmental terms. As such, it is a normative concept. It assumes the possibility of identifying stable, objective, decontextualized, and therefore generalizable criteria or norms, against which a service can be assessed: in a nutshell, quality is about conformity to norms. Moreover, the outcomes which quality is intended to promote are also normative, in the form, for example, of developmental or educational standards, and being normative they are also predetermined; quality, therefore, promotes and values an environment that ensures predictability.

This approach has been subject to some criticism, which has extended to problematising the concept of quality, and its attendant values and assumptions, and seeking an alternative approach to evaluation. During the 1990s, among some UK and other European researchers there was a growing awareness of the importance of, and impossibility of avoiding, context, complexity, plurality, and subjectivity. Attention was paid to the process of defining quality and to how that process might be made more inclusionary and participatory, involving a wide range of stakeholders. This introduced the possibility of multiple perspectives or understandings of what quality is, and that quality might be subjective, value-based, relative and dynamic, never reaching a final and objective statement. In its ground-breaking proposals for "quality targets in services for young children," the European Commission Child Care Network (1995), an expert group drawn from the then 12 member states of the European Union, summed up the search for a new approach to quality when it concluded that "quality is a relative concept based on values and beliefs, and defining quality should be a dynamic, continuous and democratic process." Further, it argued that "defining quality is a process ... [which] should be participatory and democratic, involving different groups including children, parents and families and professionals working in services ... [T]he needs, perspectives and values of these groups may sometimes differ." By adopting this approach, the Child Care Network implied that quality was as much a political as a technical issue, and a matter for citizens as much as experts.

It would be misleading to suggest that this approach to quality, or indeed other work which has questioned the very concept of quality and suggested that there are other concepts for evaluating early childhood services, has gained widespread currency in the United Kingdom. These are marginalized perspectives. The discussion—in government, services and research—remains dominated by a model of quality as conformity to expert-defined and neutral norms, a statement of fact rather than a judgement of value, and a way of coping with the complexities and uncertainties of the modern world. This model is accompanied by a prescriptive, centralized, and normative system of regulation of early childhood services, including national service standards, a detailed curriculum framework, early learning goals and a national system of inspection by a powerful agency (OfSTED), which originally covered schools and has now had its responsibility extended to cover early childhood services and, indeed, all other services for children. The chapter on "building quality" in the latest government policy statement focuses on two broad areas: improvements to the workforce and "a reformed regulatory framework and inspection system."

In this respect, early childhood services in the United Kingdom can be summed as a "quasi-market and an evaluative state," with a strong public rhetoric of choice and diversity combined with the actuality of a centrally regulated system.

Further Readings: Bloch, M. (1992). Critical perspectives on the historical relationship between child development and early childhood education research. In S. Kessler and B. Swedener, eds., *Reconceptualizing the early childhood curriculum.* New York: Teachers College Press; Dahlberg, G., P. Moss, and A. Pence (1999). *Beyond quality in early childhood education and care: Postmodern perspectives.* London: Falmer Books; European Commission Child care Network (1995). *Quality targets in services for young children.* Brussels: European Commission Equal Opportunities Unit; HM Treasury (2005). *Choice for parents, the best start for children: A ten year strategy for child care.* London. The Stationery Office. Available online at www.hm-treasury.gov.uk; Sylva, K., E. Melhuish, P. Sammons, I. Siraj-Blatchford, B. Taggart, and K. Eliot (2003). *The effective provision of pre-school education (EPPE) project: Findings from the pre-school period. Summary of findings*. London: Institute of Education.

Peter Moss

The Early Years Curriculum—United Kingdom

Introduction

The United Kingdom is made up of four distinct countries, each of which has jurisdiction over education: England, Northern Ireland, Scotland, and Wales. Though broadly similar, there are also some significant differences. In Wales, for example, the Early Years curriculum has taken shape in the form of the *Desirable Outcomes for Children's Learning*, which serves as a national guide for the Early Years. The Welsh educational model is also distinctive in its Welsh language policy, where Welsh is taught as part of the curriculum.

In England, most children enter primary school in the year in which they become 5 years old, either in nursery classes attached to primary school, or in the reception class. Children are taught the National Curriculum, which is based on a combination of subject divisions, learning stages, and attainment levels. Children's ability to meet the levels of attainment specified in the curriculum is monitored by national testing procedures in the form of Standard Attainment Tests (SATs). The SATs focused on attainments in reading, writing, and mathematics and the results of SATs are aggregated for all schools and presented in the form of league tables. Teachers in primary schools therefore face the pressure of teaching to these tests and keeping to a subject-based, direct teaching approach. In 1999, the National Literacy Strategy was introduced and in 2000, the Numeracy Strategy. These prescribed the content and duration (one hour) of special literacy and numeracy sessions for all pupils in state primary schools. They further reinforce the emphasis on a subject-based and target-oriented curriculum, despite the more holistic approaches to children under 5 years described below.

The English Curriculum: Birth to Three

As a precursor to the curriculum for 3 to 5-year-olds, the Government also introduced a curriculum model for under threes. This curriculum is intended as guidance for all those working with young children, in whatever type of provision is locally available.

The *Birth to 3 Matters* Framework (2003) consists of four aspects: a strong child, a skillful communicator, a competent learner, and a healthy child. The main aim of the Framework is to provide support and guidance for all those involved in the care and education of babies and children from birth to three years. The Framework "recognizes that all children from birth have a need to develop, learning through interaction with people and exploration of the world around them" and acknowledges the "individuality, efforts and achievements" of children. Indeed, the Framework emphasizes the child as an individual and makes a concerted effort to steer clear of subject divisions and curriculum headings. The Framework focuses on the skills and competences of the child.

The table below illustrates the four aspects and components of the Framework:

Aspects	Components			
A strong child	Me, myself and I	Being acknowledged and affirmed	Developing self-assurance	A sense of belonging
A skillful communicator	Being together	Finding a voice	Listening and responding	Making meaning
A competent learner	Making connections	Being imaginative	Being creative	Representing
A healthy child	Emotional well-being	Growing and developing	Keeping safe	Health choices

The English Curriculum: Foundation Stage

As part of a more general reorganization of early education and care, the government has made provision for all 3- and 4-year-old children to receive state-funded (but not necessarily state provided) part-time early education with a good quality curriculum.

The foundation stage. In September 2000, the *Curriculum Guidance for the Foundation Stage* for children aged 3–5 was launched by the Qualifications and Curriculum Authority (QCA) in England. The *Guidance* generally advocates the need for a holistic curriculum that takes into consideration the needs of the individual child and encourages children to be active learners. In contradistinction to the National Curriculum, the *Guidance* proposes Early Learning Goals (ELGs), as follows:

• Personal, social, and emotional development
• Communication, language, and literacy
• Mathematical development
• Knowledge and understanding of the world
• Physical development
• Creative development

The metaphor of "stepping stones" is used for each learning goal to describe a range of learning experiences, which all children need in order to achieve the ELGs. So for instance, within the area of "Personal, social and emotional development," the stepping stones include "show curiosity," "have a strong exploratory impulse," and "have a positive approach to new experiences." These "stepping stones" chart the progress of the children toward the ELGs and help to identify the kinds of knowledge and skills that children should have by the end of the Foundation Stage.

The six principles. Accompanying the ELGs is also a set of six principles that underpin the *Guidance*. These principles stress the importance of meeting the needs of children, the role of parents as partners, and the importance of play as a tool for learning. The six principles encompass the following:
* Putting the principles into practice
* Meeting the diverse needs of children
* Children with special educational needs and disabilities
* Children with English as an additional language
* Learning and teaching
* Play

The main purpose of the principles is to guide practitioners to assess and to plan for the children in their settings, and to ensure that all children are given an equal opportunity to develop and progress during the foundation stage. In the guidance notes for practitioners, the principles are also promoted through examples from real life settings and recommendations for practitioners.

Teacher observation and assessment. In an attempt to chart the progress of the children through the Foundation Stage, the curriculum is also accompanied by a handbook of assessment tools for practitioners, entitled the *Foundation Stage Profile*. The aim of the *Profile*, as the introduction states, is to provide a form of evidence-based report for parents of their child's development, and "for information to be passed on to the child's next teacher." The handbook is very much built on the use of observations as a tool for assessing and monitoring children's learning and development. It involves the practitioner carrying out regular observations on each child, and accumulating a record of the child's progress within the six areas of learning. In addition, embedded within the *Profile* are assessment scales, where the six areas of learning are matched against a set of 13 assessment scales, each of which has 9 points. So for instance, in the area of "Personal, social and emotional development," three of the points include, "shows an interest in classroom activities through observation or participation," "dresses, undresses and manages own personal hygiene with adult support" and "displays high levels of involvement in self-chosen activities." The practitioner records each point that the child achieves in each scale and collates it in the form of a Foundation Stage Profile booklet.

However, the introduction of the *Foundation Stage Profile* raises pertinent questions about the role of assessment, especially for this age group. The use of assessment scales and a system of points serve to drive the curriculum toward an outcome-driven and assessment-led approach, even as both the principles of the *Profile* and *Foundation Stage Guidance* claim to achieve the contrary. The assessment scales reinforce the "downward pressure" on Early Years settings to adhere to a "tick-chart" list of developmental achievement and render the curriculum more formal. The ambiguity in the descriptions of some of the assessment points also makes it difficult to quantify or qualify the achievements of the child. The progress and development of children are often uneven, as they do not fit neatly into separate compartments nor can they be checked against a definitive list of points.

The *Guidance* was developed in response to lobbying from practitioners for a less formal approach to learning and to some extent it has addressed some of those concerns. Prior to the *Foundation Stage Guidance*, there was no formal recognition of the value of play for this stage of learning, and this was in part due to the content-driven National Curriculum.

Curriculum philosophy. The underpinning philosophy and values of the *Guidance* are rooted in the notion that all children are entitled to a curriculum that reflects the needs of each child. However, while the introduction of the *curriculum* can be seen as a step forward in bringing about a legislated curriculum, it remains to be seen how its implementation impacts on teaching and learning within Early Years settings. Much has been left to the intuition and professionalism of practitioners to make sense of the document, and to make sense of the transition between the two age groups: between the *Birth to 3 Matters* Framework and the *Foundation Stage Guidance*. Especially with the latter, the challenge that practitioners face is to put the curriculum into practice. Ultimately, the true strength of the curriculum lies in the hands of the practitioner; in the appropriateness of her training and in her ability to make sense of the curriculum, and implement it in a way that also reflects the child's social and cultural context. In this light, it remains to be seen if the *Guidance* lives up to expectations, in realizing the more liberal vision of policy makers and professionals concerned with early years, and in meeting the aspirations of parents and practitioners.

Further Readings: Qualifications and Curriculum Authority/Department for Education and Skills (2000). *Curriculum Guidance for the Foundation Stage*. London: QCA/DfES; Qualifications and Curriculum Authority/Department for Education and Skills (2003). *Birth to 3 Matters*. London: QCA/DfES; Qualifications and Curriculum Authority/Department for Education and Skills (2003). *Foundation Stage Profile*. London: QCA/DfES.

Lynn Ang

Early Childhood Services and Children Under Three in the United Kingdom

Introduction

Early years policy concerning children under the age of 3 in the United Kingdom has turned 180 degrees in the last sixty years. In post war Britain, the Government and leading advocacy groups were unequivocal in their advice to mothers of children under the age of 2 that they should stay at home. Now, there is exhortation backed by some financial assistance to support parents' participation in the labor market.

In particular, the Labour Government, over two terms from 1997 to 2004, has introduced policies on the under threes which are based on the assumption that the first 36 months of life represent a critical opportunity in which to address the roots of lifelong disadvantage and inequality. In making this shift, the Government has drawn heavily on the American longitudinal research, especially the Perry High Scope study. Policy development for the youngest children has also been reinforced by emerging evidence from neuroscience, although the interpretation of this as meaning the first thirty-six months are an exclusively critical period has been disputed.

Policy

Compared to the long period of public policy neglect of the under threes, policy development in the last ten years has been dramatic and in three directions. The first of these is a major emphasis on compensatory intervention aimed at reducing disadvantage, through a program known as Sure Start. Sure Start initially prioritized families with children under the age of 4 in the 20 percent most disadvantaged wards (administrative districts). It focused funding on the development of services with a broad range of social and health intended outcomes. For example, it developed services to reduce the rates of smoking to improve birth weights and increase the rates of breast-feeding. However, while one of the goals of Sure Start is to help counter poverty, it has been estimated that even extending the program to 30 percent of the most disadvantaged wards would still leave 30 percent of the poorest children unreached.

The second policy goal has been to improve the quality and availability of nursery provision in order to improve educational outcomes for all children, including the under threes. The main approach here was the generous funding of a national network of nurseries (Centres of Early Excellence), designated on the basis of their capacity to work with children from three months and their families. In addition to the "excellence" of their educational provision, these centers have been expected to demonstrate how social (family support and child care for working parents) and educational provision can be integrated. Centres of Early Excellence also had a "beacon role" and they were intended to act as models of good practice for other local providers. However, both these and Sure Start Centres are being phased out or "rebranded" in favor of new, amalgamated "Children's Centres," which offer wider coverage, but which provide less per capita funds. The most recent proposal is the establishment of 3500 Children's Centres by 2010.

Funding

There has been a major push, primarily through economic incentives to the private sector and tax credits to parents, to expand the number of child care places for under threes for working parents. This has been almost entirely taken up by middle income rather than low-income families, as intended (see Finance entry, below). This primarily market driven approach to provision through demand side funding (money given to parents rather than directly to services) means that there is a continual sharp pressure to drive nursery costs down (meaning a poorly paid, poorly qualified, and high-turnover workforce) while actual nursery fees for working parents are disproportionately high in relation to most incomes.

This mixed economy of private and public provision, while being seen politically as the fastest route to expansion of places and reductions in inequality, has generated its own tensions and inequalities. Until 1990, early years services in practice meant mainly part time nursery education for 3- and 4-year-olds. Despite the rapid developments in policy to enable under threes to "catch up," in many respects, the "bolting on" of services for children under three to historically well-established educational provision for 3- and 4-year-olds has led to major philosophical and organizational tensions.

Training and Quality of Care

Organizational tensions have included the inevitable difficulties of bringing together the different professional groups that have been involved in the care and education of young children, mainly nursery nurses and nursery teachers. These groups have very different trainings, pay, conditions of service and status. Historically, they have been subject to different inspection arrangements, the former to do mostly with health and safety issues and the latter with a mainly education remit. This has been an issue for the whole early years workforce. However, for under threes, the workforce has been largely drawn from nursery nurses who have had a basic vocational training.

The Government, anxious to promote educational outcomes, has insisted that senior posts in the new government-funded Children's Centres will only go to those with qualified teacher status or with a postgraduate qualification. All regulatory and inspection functions (compulsory for all education and childcare premises in the United Kingdom) have been reallocated into a single inspection service within OfSTED, the education inspectorate agency. These changes in provision, promotion opportunities, training, regulation and inspection have left nursery nurses, who despite their basic training were likely to have more expertise with children under three, often feeling marginalized and devalued. Services for children under three run the risk of being conceptualized as merely an extension of nursery education for 3- and four-year-olds, while early years services in general are conceptualized as merely an extension of statutory schooling (see the Early Years Curriculum—United Kingdom entry).

A further major difficulty is that as the under threes sector has rapidly expanded, workforce development has struggled to keep up. Half the workforce is unqualified and the remainder often qualified to a relatively low level, certainly not graduate level. Mindful of this, the Government commissioned the development of materials (The Birth to Three Matters Framework) to support those working with under threes. However, given the highly diverse experience and training of the workforce, this Framework has had to be pitched at a basic level. Further, its implementation is very much at the discretion of individual nurseries and opportunities for working with it are highly varied.

Philosophical Divide

At a deeper level than these important organizational issues, the expansion of provision for babies and under threes has raised philosophical questions about the upbringing of the youngest children. Some of this has been due to a deep-rooted national suspicion of any nonmaternal care of babies and very young children.

Anxiety about the adequacy of any provision for babies that is nonmaternal is a continuing theme in media debate.

This anxiety has been underpinned by emerging evidence from two major studies showing that high levels of poor quality group care before the age of 3 may be associated with increased levels of antisocial behavior or lower levels of emotional regulation by the age of 3. The required ratios for group care of under threes in the United Kingdom are much more generous than in most countries but politicians have again questioned whether there is enough consistency of adult attention in most nurseries to enable infants to establish effective emotional regulation.

Developments in national standards and the training of the under threes workforce have reflected some of these concerns. A central principle of the Birth to Three Framework has been the importance of consistency and sensitivity of care in staff interactions with babies and under threes. This has been provided through the role of the "key person," a member of staff with responsibility for most of the day-to-day care of a small group of three or four children. Implementation of the key person role however is contentious and very variable. This is partly for organizational reasons—it very much reduces flexibility in the deployment of staff. However, it is also partly because the role places a particular emphasis on the importance of one to one relationships between infants and adults, to the detriment of other relationship opportunities in the nursery.

This issue is also evident in the National Standard, which has an additional Annex devoted to work with under twos. The tone of the standards is very much to emphasize the vulnerability of these youngest children and the importance of health and safety. Little is made of their resilience and the extended opportunities for interaction that care outside the home can provide.

Conclusion

At the close of the second Labour Government, provision in the United Kingdom for children under three has been the subject of major development. But it is development built on a number of major fault lines that continue to provoke contradictions and confusions.

The next phase of policy development will be shaped by a new Ten Year Child Care strategy. Almost certainly as a result of anxiety about the impact of nonparental care in the first 12 months, the strategy proposes an extension of parental leave to nine months (by April 2007) with the intention of a further extension to 12 months, to be shared by both parents, by 2010. However, it is doubtful if serious shifts in quality and accessibility can be achieved as long as philosophically there are basic, unresolved, conflicts of values.

Further Readings: Bruer, J. T. (1997). Education and the brain: A bridge too far. *Educational Researcher* 26(8), 4–16; Department for Education and Employment (1999). *National Child Care Strategy 1999*; Department for Education and Employment (2001). *National Standards of Day Care Provision*; Department for Education and Skills (2002). *Birth to three matters: A framework for supporting early years practitioners*. DfES Sure Start Unit; Gerhardt, S. (1994). *Why love matters: How affection shapes a baby's brain*. London: Routledge; HM Treasury (2005). *Choice for parents, the best start for children: A ten year strategy for childcare*. London. The Stationery Office. Available online at www.hm-treasury.gov.uk; House of Commons All Parliamentary Group for Children (2005). Minutes of the Joint Meeting of the All Party Parliamentary Groups for Childcare, children, maternity, parents and families. February 8, 2005; Land, D. (2004). Women, child poverty and child care. Day Care Trust Policy Paper; National Institute of Child Health and Human Development Early Child Care Research Network (1997). The Effect of Infant Child Care on Infant-Mother Attachment Security: Results of the NICHD Study of Early Child Care. *Child Development* 68(5), 860–879; Penn, H. (1997). *Comparing nursersies—staff and children in Italy, Spain and the UK*. London: Paul Chapman; Sylva, K., E. C. Melhuish, P. Sammons, I. Siraj-Blatchford, and B. Taggart (2004). The Effective Provision of Pre-School Education (EPPE) Project: Technical Paper 12 - The Final Report: Effective Pre-School Education. London: DfES / Institute of Education, University of London; Trevarthen, C. (2004). Making friends with infants. Paper Presented at Pen Green Conference, July 3, 2004. Edinburgh: Dept. of Psychology, The University of Edinburgh.

Peter Elfer

Inclusion

The Background to Current Legislation

The process toward a more inclusive education system for children with special educational needs began with Warnock's review of provision (1978). The major recommendation of the Warnock Report in the United Kingdom relates to the terminology used, and the underlying concepts implied by it. Using language such as "mentally handicapped" and "retarded" to classify children was identified as being within a medical deficit model framework. Thus, such language suggested that the "problem" was within the child rather than as a critique of the system or the type of provision on offer. This medical deficit terminology was therefore abandoned for the more generic term of "special educational need" (SEN).

However, even today, terminology still remains a contentious issue, with current critique concerning the concept of "special," "additional" and "need." Some conditions are themselves medically uncertain. For example, the diagnosis of "autistic spectrum disorder" is open to a wide variety of interpretations, and treatment might vary considerably. A further complication of terminology concerns the additional funding for provision or extra support often requested by parents or professionals working with children with special educational needs. The funding mechanism requires evidence of assessment that a special need exists and there is a perception that giving a child a specific label will ensure that funding follows. In addition, there are ambiguities within government legislation that aim to promote the notion of inclusion, while at the same time continuing to use terms rooted within the medical deficit model.

The Warnock Report was also significant because it recommended that professionals should work in partnership with parents; that there should be early identification of SEN; and that there should be an increase in working together in multidisciplinary teams. However, since the report was published the concept of partnership between parents and professionals and working together in multidisciplinary teams remains problematic, and its existence and its impact is difficult to measure. There is little direct evidence that the injunction to work in partnership has had an impact in terms of quality and effective delivery of provision to meet the individual needs of children with special educational needs.

Warnock (1978) promoted the concept that "all children should be the responsibility of all teachers." However, the recent appointment of Special Educational Needs Co-ordinators (SENCOs) to coordinate provision for children with special needs in schools suggests that responsibility for children with special educational needs is being viewed by other members of primary and secondary school staff as solely the responsibility of the SENCO.

Current UK Legislation

Current legislation in the United Kingdom regarding children with special educational needs (SEN) is arguably the most radical to date, and for the first time gives children with disabilities civil rights. The Special Educational Needs and Disability Act (SENDA) 2001, which came into effect in September 2002, embraces the full range of education provision, including early years settings, schools, and universities. This legislation begins with the premise that all children and young people will be placed in mainstream provision as opposed to a separate special school provision. Recent trends in England and Wales indicate a decrease in pupils being placed in special schools (Norwich, 2002). Over the past two decades, Local Education Authorities (LEAs) have had their powers reduced by a raft of legislation, but they still retain responsibility for ensuring that education provision is made for children with special educational needs. In the light of the demands of SENDA, many LEAs are reviewing their special school provision. As a result, the future for special schools is currently uncertain. A further issue is that the language contained within the Special Educational Needs and Disability Act (SENDA) 2001 is, despite efforts at clarification, still problematic and likely to require legal challenge to establish what inclusion actually means.

Early Education and Care

Early years provision, compared to other sectors of education provision, has been a leading force in developing inclusive policies and in identifying areas of positive practice for children with special educational needs.

Guidance from the government for all early years settings in receipt of any Department for Education and Skills (DfES) direct or indirect funding requires that they have "regard to the Code of Practice" (2001) in the early identification of a special educational need. All early years providers are expected to have a written SEN policy and to identify a staff member as the Special Educational Needs Coordinator (SENCO). Funding has been provided by the DfES for the professional development of SENCOs to ensure that national standards can be met. In the past, much of this funding has been targeted toward professional teachers working in primary and secondary schools. The training needs of those professionals have been largely determined on a local basis by the individual LEAs rather than as a systematic national program. This funding has now been extended to address the professional development of SENCOs in the early years sector through a program of nationally recognized training for all practitioners working in the early years (DfES, 2004) There are concerns about the assumption that training and expertise from one sector of education can be easily transported to, or is desirable in another, that is, from primary or secondary schooling to early years care.

To provide effective early intervention strategies for children with special educational needs, the UK government is also promoting an integrated approach to children's services. Crucial to this is the concept of the multidisciplinary team of health, education, and social services providing "joined up" assessment procedures and shared access to the records. To accommodate this shared access, a common database has been developed so that professionals working with a child can now easily share information. It is envisaged that one professional in the team will be responsible for coordinating the team in their work with individual families. Parents will certainly welcome the reduction of what often amounts to duplication of information (Mittler, 2000) by the introduction of the named professional acting as a conduit for the multidisciplinary team as a whole. However, this "named person" role is problematic because of the status of the named professional within the multidisciplinary team and because of the lack of training available for that person to manage a complex "team" with frequently competing professional agendas, funding mechanisms, and time constraints. There is also a continuing debate in the United Kingdom regarding the nature of the use of databases and implications for civil liberties. This debate has yet to be resolved.

The move toward inclusive provision has cost implications that cannot be underestimated, both in terms of training professionals working with children with special educational needs in inclusive settings, and raising the professional status of practitioners working in the early years.

Further Readings: DES (1978). Report of the Committee of Enquiry into the Education of Handicapped Children and Young People (The Warnock Report). London: HMSO; Department for Education and Skills (2001). The code of practice on the identification and assessment of special educational Needs. London: HMSO; Department for Education and Skills (2001). *Special educational needs and disability act.* London: HMSO; Department for Education and Skills (2003). *Every child matters.* London: HMSO; Department for Education and Skills (2004). *Removing barriers to achievement.* London: HMSO; Corbett, J. (1996). *Bad mouthing: The language of special needs.* London: Falmer Press; Mittler, P. (2000). *Working towards inclusive education: Social contexts.* London: David Fulton; Norwich, B. (2002). LEA Inclusion Trends in England 1997–2001: Statistics on Special Schools Placements and Pupils with Statements in Special Schools. Bristol: CSIE.

Helen Masterton

Children's Health and Well-Being

Children who are emotionally and physically healthy have the energy and motivation to play, explore, experiment, learn, and form relationships with others. A healthy childhood is not only important in its own right, it also lays the foundations for health in adult life. The focus of UK health policy has recently begun to reflect the need to ensure children's emotional and social well-being alongside their physical health.

Article 24 of the United Nations **Convention on the Rights of the Child** (UNCRC 1989) details the child's right to health, beginning with the basic necessities of clean drinking water and adequate nutritious foods. Article 24 refers to the differing global expectations for children's health, stating in section one that the child has the right to the "highest attainable standard of health." The need to ensure children's physical survival has to date focused attention on children's physical health with much less attention being given to social and emotional health.

National Health Service in the United Kingdom provides free health care and prescriptions for all children, and has traditionally reflected the emphasis on physical well-being. The development of comprehensive immunization programs, welfare foods, and child health clinics is supported by the inspection of water, sanitation, food, hygiene etc. by a variety of government agencies. However, in stating that a child has a right to the highest attainable standard of health, the UNCRC has set aspirational goals for children's social and emotional well-being alongside their physical health. In the United Kingdom there are major health concerns about the large number of young children living in relative poverty, experiencing behavior difficulties or mental health problems and those eating nutritionally poor diets and taking little exercise. In addition, a recent well-publicized case, the tragic death of Victoria Climbie at the hands of her foster parents, acted as a catalyst in highlighting the need for reform of children's services and for ensuring that children's voices should be heard in matters that concern them.

Families in the United Kingdom are experiencing many changes. As divorce and separation rates increase and support from traditional networks decrease, there is growing recognition that in the twenty-first century children's health, at least in developed countries where epidemics are relatively unknown, is determined more by social, environmental, and economic factors than by biological disorders.

Children Living in Relative Poverty

In 1979, when the Conservative government came into power, one in ten children were being raised in families living on 50 percent or less of the average income. When the Labour Government took office in 1997 the number of children being raised in poor households had risen to a staggering one in three. This fall into poverty that many families experienced has had dramatic effects on children's physical and emotional health. The Labour Government commissioned an independent inquiry into inequalities in health and the committee chaired by Sir Donald Acheson (1998) recommended that a high priority should be given to the health of families with young children and that further steps should be taken to improve the living standards of poor families. The government has subsequently pledged to tackle health inequalities and to end child poverty within a generation. It has raised the threshold for defining poverty from 50 percent to 60 percent of median income. The United Kingdom has developed a range of poverty indicators and recent research shows that an interim target of a 25 percent reduction in the number of children living in households with below 60 percent median income by 2005 is likely to be met, although long-term goals are more problematic (see the Poverty entry).

The impact of health inequalities on children's educational achievement has been recognized. The Department of Health and the Department for Education and Skills introduced the National Healthy Schools Standard where schools are encouraged to show a commitment to promoting emotional and physical health in order to reduce health inequalities, promote social exclusion and raise educational standards. Some schools in disadvantaged areas have also introduced school breakfast clubs to ensure a healthy start to the day. There has been increasing concern over the amounts of high fat, high sugar convenience foods that form part of many children's diets and the resulting levels of overweight and obesity amongst children. The national school fruit scheme was introduced in 2001, with the aim that every child between 4 and 6 years should be offered a piece of fresh fruit every day. Interestingly, celebrity chef Jamie Oliver has recently exposed the poor quality and lack of funding for school dinners in a popular television series. The result of this has been an announcement of tougher minimum standards for school dinners from 2006, and new minimum standards for processed foods to limit the amount of fat, salt, and sugar in products such as burgers, sausages, and cakes.

Supporting Families

Emotional and behavioral problems are now the foremost cause of functional disability in children, and concern has increasingly been expressed about the number of children in the United Kingdom who are exhibiting evidence of mental health problems. Bright Futures, the report from the Mental Health Foundation (1999), describes the incidence of mental health problems as follows:

> .... there are approximately 14.9 million children and young people under twenty living in the UK, representing 25% of the population. It is calculated that at any one time, 20% of children and adolescents experience psychological problems.

There has been increased recognition over the past two decades of the role of families and parenting in influencing children's social and emotional development. In 1999 the government produced a consultation paper "Supporting Families," to explore how families could be supported in their parenting role. It introduced the government's aspirations for family advice, work life balance, and tackling problems such as domestic violence. Subsequently, a National Family and Parenting Institute has been established to study and support family life. (Part of its funds have been devoted to Sure Start schemes to work innovatively in partnership with families with children under 4 years in disadvantaged areas—see introductory section, and sections on under twos and on poverty). Sure Start schemes have made a particular effort to incorporate health services. They have encouraged health, social services, education, and voluntary sector workers to work in partnership. But Sure Start projects are gradually being transformed into or merged with Children's Centres (see introductory section). These centers will now be funded (although not necessarily provided by) by local authorities and will focus on early education and encouraging parents to gain employment. Health workers will be separately funded, raising concerns about whether the innovative partnership services to support families and promote health and well-being can continue to be developed.

Protecting Children's Health and Well-Being

The death of Victoria Climbie, who was tortured by her foster parents, resulted in a public inquiry to investigate how such a tragedy could happen. The report highlighted many failings in the services to protect children. This led to a government consultation paper that outlined major changes to services. In particular the paper, Every Child Matters, emphasized five outcomes:

- Being healthy: enjoying good physical and mental health and living a healthy lifestyle
- Staying safe: being protected from harm and neglect
- Enjoying and achieving: getting the most out of life and developing the skills for adulthood
- Making a positive contribution: being involved with the community and society and not engaging in anti-social or offending behavior
- Economic well-being: not being prevented by economic disadvantage from achieving full potential in life

This paper laid the foundations for the new Children Act 2004, which also makes the provision for a new Children's Commissioner to act as an independent champion for children, particularly those suffering disadvantage.

Children in the United Kingdom had often been overlooked in a health service provision and services from one area to another were often fragmented. In 2004, a new National Service Framework (NSF) was introduced to set national health standards for children, young people and maternity services. This NSF focuses on early child-centered interventions with a new health promotion program to promote the health of children from conception to adulthood and a remit to tackle health inequalities.

There has been much recent progress in children's health policy but there is still much to be done. Many issues that impact on children's health (for instance domestic violence, or the responsibilities of being a "young carer") are only recently being highlighted. The focus is shifting from physical health to include mental health and well-being and toward listening to young children and their families, in an attempt to ensure that the highest attainable standards of health might be reached.

Further Readings: Acheson, Sir D. (1998). Independent inquiry into inequalities in health report. London: TSO; Bone, M., and H. Meltzer (1989). The prevalence of disability among children. OPCS Surveys of disability in Great Britain, Report 3. London: HMSO; DSS (Department of Social Security) (1999a). Households Below Average Income: A Statistical Analysis 1979-1995/96. London: HMSO; Department of Social Security (DSS) (1999b). *Opportunity for all: Tackling poverty and social exclusion, the first annual report.* London: HMSO; Hall, D., and Elliman, D. *Health for all children.* Oxford: Oxford University Press; The Mental Health Foundation (1999). *Bright futures.* London: The Mental Health Foundation; The United Nations Convention on the Rights of the Child (1989); United Nations Children's Fund (UNICEF) (2005). Child Poverty in Rich Countries. Innocenti Report Card

No. 6; United Nations Children's Fund (UNICEF) (2001). *The state of the world's children*. Oxford: Oxford University Press.

Angela Underdown

Teacher Preparation in the United Kingdom

Introduction

Training for work in early childhood services in the United Kingdom has historically been split between "care" and "education." Some kinds of provision have been seen as predominantly offering "care" and provided either because the child was seen to be at risk, or because the mother wanted or needed employment and was therefore unable to care for her child. Others have been seen as predominantly "education" and therefore directly beneficial for the child. Since a Labour Government was elected in 1997 government policies have produced continuous development in the early year's sector (see Early Childhood Education in the United Kingdom entry, above). Many policymakers and researchers hoped that these traditional understandings of care and education would be challenged in general, in the field of training in particular.

Recent Reforms

The Government paper, *Every Child Matters*, produced partly in response to a notorious child abuse case (see section on health), put forward major proposals for workforce reform in the *care* sector to ensure better protection for children. It aimed to improve the outcomes for children and produce a better integration of all services to children. The five outcomes envisioned were that children should be healthy, stay safe, enjoy and achieve, make a positive contribution, and achieve economic well-being. The implementation of these aims entailed major changes to a diverse range of regulations, including inspections, standards, and qualifications. The identification of a "common core of skills, knowledge, and competence for the widest possible range of workers in children's services" (DfES, 2004) was seen as a necessary step forward. Reviews of the National Standards have been conducted for both Under 8's Daycare and Childminding. Additional reviews have examined the National Occupational Standards (NOS) for Early Years Care and Education. Finally, revisions have been made to the qualifications framework for the children's workforce, including identifying a common core of skills and knowledge based on the five outcomes. A new Children's Workforce Development Council was also set up as part of the new Sector Skills Council for Social Care, Children and Young People.

During the time that these developments were undertaken by the Children's Workforce Unit of the Department for Education and Skills (DfES), another section (the Schools Workforce Unit) was also examining reform. However, these two different sections of the DfES, arriving separately at their conclusions, indicate the continuing divide in the way the children's workforce is conceptualized. Early year's teachers who have Qualified Teacher Status (QTS) are considered to be part of the schools' workforce, regulated by the Teacher Training Agency (TTA) and the General Teaching Council (GTC) while other child "care" workers are regulated by the Children's Workforce Development Council- a body in which, unlike the TTA, private employers are represented.

Early Childhood Education Staff Training Programs

The divisions outlined above are mirrored in the continuing divisions in content and levels of training. A qualified childcare worker at a supervisory level will have a level 3 National Qualifications Framework (NQF) qualification. This normally implies a two-year postsecondary education and training, which can be gained before the age of 18. A QTS teacher—as indicated below—is expected to demonstrate much higher levels of knowledge and competence.

Vocational qualifications. The level 3 NQF qualification can be gained by one of two main routes. One approach is to obtain a college diploma program that includes practicum placements. Alternately, students may obtain a vocational qualification (NVQ) via an employment-based route. The latter relies on outcome and competence assessed performance to achieve the qualification.

The content of these NVQs is being reviewed to match the revised National Occupational Standards (NOS). The standards were revised in 2004 in line with the five outcomes now given legal force in the Children Act 2004 (DfES 2004). They applied no longer only to the early years (0–8), but extended to age 16 and were renamed *National Occupational Standards in Children's Care, Learning and Development*.

Draft proposals for the revised level 3 NVQ suggest that it should be a nine-unit qualification, comprising five mandatory units. These include the following:
• develop and promote positive relationships;
• develop and maintain a healthy, safe, and secure environment for children;
• promote children's development;
• reflect on and develop practice; and
• protect and promote children's rights.
There are also four further units from a choice of thirty-six.

There is also a similar but lower NVQ qualification at level 2 (equivalent to a secondary school diploma) intended for other nonsupervisory workers in nurseries. At present, nearly half the child care workforce has either no qualification and training, or a level 2 qualification. There is high staff turnover and a shortage of skilled staff in the sector.

Teacher training programs. In contrast to the basic vocational level 2 and level 3 qualifications required for qualified child-care workers, qualified early year's teachers are normally required to complete four years of university level education, that is a basic three-year degree and a professional qualification: the postgraduate certificate of education (PGCE), which takes an additional year to complete. Once students have successfully completed their training and practice, they receive qualified teacher status (QTS). They are then qualified to teach children from age three onward in maintained sector nursery schools and classes. QTS teachers train to "teach across at least two consecutive key stages" (DfES/TTA, 2002). For those training as specialist early years teachers, this corresponds to the Foundation Stage of the National Curriculum (see section on curriculum) for children aged 3–5 and the Key Stage 1, for ages five to seven (See The Early Years Curriculum—United Kingdom entry, above).

Although students may obtain a variety of degrees leading up to the PGCE, the syllabus for the PGCE itself is tightly controlled by the Teacher Training Agency and enforced by frequent OfSTED inspections (Office for Standards in Education). Half of the 36-week course must be spent in mentored school practice. Knowledge of the National Curriculum for the appropriate age group is mandatory. There is relatively little opportunity to acquire any specialist knowledge of child development and early years.

Enhancing professionalism

Early Years QTS teachers have the same pay and conditions as those teaching primary and secondary-age school children. Teachers are therefore better paid and have better conditions of service than any other part of the "childcare/early years" workforce. On average they are likely to be paid almost twice as much as other members of the early years workforce. However, they are a very minor part of this workforce—less than 10 percent, and their training is heavily school based.

One attempt to improve the child care and teaching workforce, as well as to bolster recruitment, has been to introduce Foundation Degrees in Early Years. These are degree courses of two rather than three years, duration aimed at people already in relevant employment, such as nursery assistants working in primary schools. Doing a "Sure Start" Endorsed Foundation Degree would allow existing practitioners to improve their qualifications. Those who wish to continue may complete a further year to acquire an honors degree and/or become a qualified teacher. Unlike three-year honors degrees, in which individual universities decide on the content and delivery of the syllabus, the Sector Endorsed degree is strictly controlled. Those who gain the Foundation Degree can be given the title of "Senior Practitioner." However, this does not carry an increased salary. Nor is there any statutory requirement within the School Sector to appoint Senior Practitioners. There is some concern that this quick route to a teaching qualification may ultimately prove relatively worthless for those seeking to advance their careers within the sector.

The only current graduate education and training aimed specifically at crossing the care and education divide is the Early Childhood Studies (ECS) degree. The idea of an ECS degree was put forward during the 1980s and 1990s by various campaigners advocating for integrated early education and care provision, long before there was any government commitment to providing universal integrated children's centres. This integrated ECS degree is on offer to young students just beginning tertiary education, but is also intended to offer a route into training for staff with basic vocational qualifications working in the care sector who constitute the majority of the workforce. About forty higher education institutions now offer Early Childhood Studies degrees, often recruiting mature women from within the sector. These individuals help to professionalize work with children from birth to age eight. Their position differs from that of nursery teachers, who are not currently trained for work with children younger than three and focus mainly on curricular issues.

Future Goals

The government aspires to have a "better qualified workforce." Prompted by recent UK research which demonstrates that having qualified teachers in the early years improves young children's subsequent school performance (Sylva, Melhuish, Sammons et al., 2003), the government states two aims. The first is to improve "the qualifications and skills of early years workers, with more trained to degree level." The second is to ensure that all full day care settings are led by "fit-for-purpose" graduate qualified early year's professionals, such as pedagogues or "new teachers." (DfES, 2005, p. 25). So far, a new post-graduate professional qualification, the National Professional Qualification in Integrated Centre Leadership (NPQICL), is being piloted in order to meet the commitment to improve leadership. It has been recognized that workforce reform is necessary, and that a new core graduate professional may be needed. The choices put forward for consultation are between the Danish Social Pedagogue model and the "new" teacher model of Sweden or New Zealand (DfES, 2005). The barriers are a lack of commitment to changing statutory requirements for existing qualifications, especially teaching; and the failure to provide the finance necessary to achieve professional rates of pay and conditions of work throughout the sector.

Further Readings: Department for Education and Skills/Teacher Training Agency (2002). *Qualifying to teach.* Available online at www.dfes.gov.uk; HMSO (Her Majesty's Stationery Office). (2004). *Children's Act 2004.* London: HMSO; Department for Education and Skills (2004). *Every child matters: Change for children.* Nottingham. DfES Publications. Available online at www.everychildmatters.gov.uk; Department for Education and Skills (2005). *Common core of skills and knowledge for the children's workforce.* Available online at www.dfes.gov.uk; Department for Education and Skills (2005). *The children's workforce strategy.* Available online at www.dfes.gov.uk; Sylva, K., E. Melhuish, P. Sammons, L. Siraj-Blatchford, B. Taggart, and K. Eliot (2003). *The effective provision of pre-school education (EPPE) Project: Findings from the pre-school period. Summary of findings.* London: Institute of Education.

Pamela Calder

Financing Early Care and Education in the United Kingdom

Expenditure Levels

Expenditure on early education and care has been rising since 1997 when the Labour Government took office. The Government currently spends about £1500 per year per child on early years, compared with just over £3000 for a primary-school aged child and just under £4000 for a secondary-aged child.

The distribution of costs of early years education and care in England is illustrated in the chart below. Parents pay 45 percent of total costs of early education and care provision, or approximately 85 percent of the costs of child-care

Government expenditure on early years since 1997

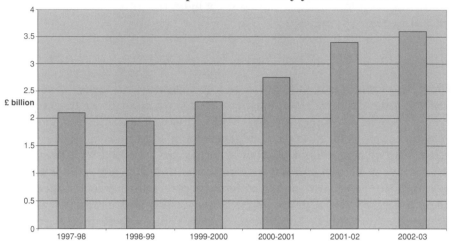

Source: National Audit Office, 2004

provision. The state contributes 38 percent for nursery education for 3- and 4-year-olds and a further 10 percent for Sure Start and other initiatives, and 5 percent in tax credits—a total of 53 percent of costs. Companies/employers pay approximately 2 percent of the costs.

How early years provision is paid for 2002-03

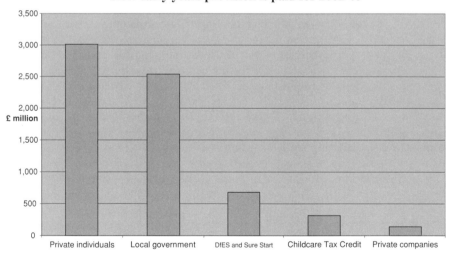

Source: National Audit Office, 2004

There are, or have been, a number of other short-term grants available for new initiatives. These include lottery money distributed through the New Opportunities Fund; training funds provided by the Learning and Skills Council (mainly for workplace-based basic vocational qualifications); special antipoverty initiative funds such as the Neighbourhood Renewal Fund, Single Regeneration Budget, and New Deal for Communities; and special European Social Fund collaborative

programmes. The plethora of these short-term funds, the complicated arrangements for applying for them, and the uncertainty about the future once the grant
expires, has deterred people from applying for them and take-up has been less
than predicted.

The Daycare Trust conducts an annual survey of childcare costs. The 2005
survey suggests that the costs parents pay to providers have been rising, with the
greatest increase in London where there has been an annual rise of 17 percent
over 2004/2005. For under-twos there has been a national 7.3 percent rise. Costs
generally are high. For a child aged 0–2 the average weekly cost is £138 and
for a child aged 3–4, £129. These averages mask considerable differences. The
highest reported costs are £350 per child per week in parts of London. There
is no evidence that cost is directly related to quality of provision, since all day
nurseries must meet minimum requirements for ratios, qualifications, and space
and are subject to regular inspection. The costs for childminding, or family day
care, are slightly lower. The average weekly cost for a child 0–2 is £129, and for
a child aged 3–4, £126. The survey data suggested that for 65 percent of parents
affordability was a problem.

Approximately 60–70 percent of costs are staff related, but property costs,
especially in London, are also high. Nursery staff, about half of whom have any
kind of qualification (usually the most basic), receive the minimum wage or just
above. The average gross salary of a child-care worker is £7,800 per annum
(compared to £22,662 for a graduate trained primary teacher). Staff turnover
is considered to be a problem by 84 percent of providers, suggesting that the
workforce is not stable enough to provide a high-quality service, despite the
regulations which are in place. Provider turnover is also high.

Key Questions

The affordability of care for parents, the costs of staffing, and capital costs,
particularly in urban areas, are unresolved issues in the Government's attempts
to expand and develop early education and care.

Early education is free for 3- and 4-year-old children, but of short daily duration.
Care is very expensive. The Government's preferred solution has been in the
form of tax credits, compensating parents for the costs that they pay toward
care. The childcare tax credit was introduced in 1999. However recent research
reported by Alakeson suggests that the childcare tax credit mainly benefits middle
class families. Unskilled women or lone parents are deterred from working, since
the low wages they are likely to earn will not compensate for the benefits they
lose by working. The child-care tax credit has almost no direct impact on child
poverty. As illustrated above, it only accounts for around 5 percent of the costs
of education and care. Any fiscal policy to support child care has to take a wider
view of the tax and benefit system.

The child-care sector is characterized by high staff turnover and low levels of
qualification. The Government has recognized that its current training requirements for nurseries have been set too low. The most recent Government consultation papers on workforce recruitment and training now suggest that levels
of training should be set higher with graduates in management posts (see UK

training section). However a better qualified workforce will require higher re-muneration, and since the costs parents pay are already high, it is unlikely that they will be able to meet increased costs. The Government has currently set aside £125 million for training, but this is a small proportion of the costs that will be incurred in achieving and maintaining a better-qualified workforce.

Much child-care provision, especially in urban areas, is in converted accom-modation, private houses, shop fronts, redundant churches, and so on. Although there are internal space requirements, the requirement for outside space for chil-dren can be waived in urban areas. The Government has allocated capital funds to support new buildings in urban areas of deprivation, where entrepreneurs are in any case unlikely to invest capital, but generally nursery stock is poor.

These problems of creating more nursery provision in poor districts, coupled with evidence from cost-benefit studies that suggest investment in early education and care brings significant returns in terms of education outcomes for children and for women's employment, have led some organizations to argue for a major shift from demand led child care to supply led child care, including a rethinking of the tax and benefit system. The consultants PriceWaterhouseCoopers were asked to cost various aspects of early years services, for example, parental leave, setting out costs as a percentage of GDP, and suggesting what level of parental contribution could reasonably be expected for each aspect. The likely increase in total costs were projected over a ten-year period. In a separate cost-benefit exercise, not listed here, PriceWaterhouseCooper also estimated the extra revenue that would accrue to the Exchequer as a result of greater workforce participation and in terms of improved circumstances for children who received early childhood services. They concluded that the increased costs could be gradually met, and would be significantly offset by increased revenue.

Estimated costs of vision for early years provision 2020

	Cost to government (%GDP)	Parental contribu-tion (% GDP)	Total cost (% GDP)	£billion at 2004/2005 GDP values
12 months parental leave	0.5	-	0.5	5.7
Home care allowance for 1-year-olds	0.1	-	0.1	1.6
Subsidized care alternative for 1-year-olds	0.3	0.1	0.4	4.8
20 hours pw free education for 2- to 4-year-olds	0.6	-	0.6	7.1
Wrap around care for 2- to 4-year-olds	0.4	0.2	0.6	7.1
Holiday/after-school care for 5- to 14-year-olds	0.3	0.1	0.4	4.1
Total costs	**2.2**	**0.4**	**2.6**	**30.4**

Source: PricewaterhouseCoopers report in Alakeson, The Social Market Foundation, 2005

Build-up of costs over time: SMF vision vs 10 year childcare strategy

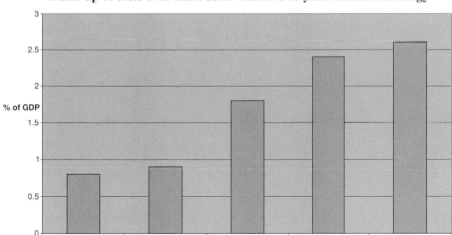

Source: PricewatherhouseCoopers report in Alakeson. The Social Market
Foundation, 2005

There is an additional argument about whether provision should be publicly provided or whether the private market is sufficiently flexible to provide accessible and affordable childcare for all. Early education is mainly provided in the public sector, child care in the private sector. The Government has acknowledged that in poorer districts of the United Kingdom, the local authority has at the very least to oversee, if not directly provide, the development of multipurpose children's centers which will cater for the poorest and most vulnerable children. An expansion program of 3,500 graduate led children's centers is currently being commissioned, although at the time of writing the revenue funds needed to run such centers have not yet been costed or allocated. It is unlikely that they will be long-term funding arrangements.

The Government has invested considerable new money in early education and care but it still spends less than most comparable European countries as a percentage of GDP. Unless both the levels and patterns of expenditure are revised, it is impossible for it to meet its ambitious targets.

Further Readings: Alakeson, V. (2005). *Too much, too late: Life chances and spending on education and training.* London: Social Market Foundation; Daycare Trust (2005). *Annual survey of childcare costs.* London: Daycare Trust; National Audit Office (2004). *Early years: Progress in developing high quality childcare and early education accessible to all.* London: The Stationery Office; PricewaterhouseCoopers (2004). *Universal early education and care in 2020: Costs, benefits and funding options.* London: Daycare Trust/Social Market Foundation; Toroyan, T., I. Roberts, A. Oakley, G. Laing, M. Mugford, and C. Frost (2003). Effectiveness of out-of-home day care for disadvantaged families: Randomized controlled trial. *British Medical Journal* 327, 906–909.

Helen Penn

Bibliography

Baratz, S. S., and J. C. Baratz (1970). Early childhood intervention: The social science base of institutional racism. *Harvard Educational Review* 40: 29–50.

Barnett, S., J. Hustedt, and K. Schulman (2005). *The state of preschool: 2005 state preschool yearbook.* New Brunswick, NJ: The National Institute for Early Education Research, Rutgers University.

Barnett, W. S. (1993). Benefit-cost analysis of preschool education: Findings from a 25-year follow-up. *American Journal of Orthopsychiatry* 63: 500–508.

Beatty, Barbara. (1995). *Preschool education in America: The culture of young children from the colonial era to the present.* New Haven, CT: Yale University Press.

Belsky, J., and L. D. Steinberg (1978). The effects of daycare: A critical review. *Child Development* 49: 929–949.

Berfenstam R., and I. William-Olsson (1973). Early child care in Sweden. *Early Child Development and Care* 2(2): 97–249.

Berk, L., and A. Winsler (1995). *Scaffolding children's learning: Vygotsky and early childhood education.* Washington, DC: NAEYC.

Bloch, M. N. (1987). Becoming scientific and professional: An historical perspective on the aims and effects of early education. In T. S. Popkewitz, ed., *The formation of school subjects.* Basingstoke, UK: Falmer, pp. 25–62.

Bloch, M. N. (1991). Critical science and the history of child development's influence on early education research. *Early Education and Development* 2(2): 95–108.

Cochran, M., ed. (1993). *The international handbook of child care policies and programs.* Westport, CT: Greenwood Press.

Cochran, M. (1997). Fitting early child care services to societal needs and characteristics. In Mary E. Young, ed. *Early child development: Investing in our children's future.* Amsterdam: Elsevier.

Cochran M. (2007). *Finding our way Amercan Eark care and education in global pres pectire.* Washington, DC: Zero to Three.

Cochran M. (2007). *Finding our way: American early care and education in global perspective.* Washington, DC: Zero to Three.

Committee on a Framework and Long-Term Research Agenda for International Comparative Education Studies (2003). *Understanding others, educating ourselves.* Edited by C. Chabbott and E. J. Elliott. Washington, DC: The National Academies Press.

Consortium for Longitudinal Studies (1983). *As the twig is bent: Lasting effects of preschool programs*. Hillsdale, NJ: Erlbaum.

David, M. and I. Lezine (1974). Early child care in France. *Early Child Development and Care* 4(1): 1–148.

Dickens, W., I. Sawhill, and J. Tebbs (2006). *The effects of investing in early education on economic growth*. Washington, DC: The Brookings Institution, Policy Brief #153.

Foucault, M. (1980). *Power/knowledge: Selected interviews and other writings, 1972–1977*. London: Harvester.

Frede, E. C. (1995). The role of program quality in producing early childhood program benefits. *The Future of Children* 5: 115–133.

Fuller, Bruce, Costanza Eggers-Pierola, Susan Holloway, Xiaoyan Liang, and Marylee F. Rambaud (1996). Rich culture, poor markets: Why do Latino parents forgo preschooling? *Teachers College Record* 97(3): 400–418.

Gandini, L., and C. P. Edwards, eds. (2001). *Bambini: The Italian approach to infant/toddler care*. New York: Teachers College Press.

Goffin, S., C. Wilson, J. Hill, and S. McAninch (1997). Policies of the early childhood field and its public: Seeking to support young children and their families. In J. Isenberg and M. R. Jalongo, eds. *Major trends and issues in early childhood education*. New York: Teachers College Press, pp. 13–28.

Goodnow, J. J., P. J. Miller, and F. Kessel, eds. (1995). *Cultural practices as contexts for development. New Directions for Child Development* (67). San Francisco: Jossey-Bass.

Hatch, A. (1995). *Qualitative research in early childhood settings*. Westport, CT: Praeger.

Hayes, C. (2002). *Thinking broadly: Financing strategies for comprehensive child and family initiatives*. Washington, DC: The Finance Project.

Hermann, A., and S. Komlos (1972). Early child care in Hungary. *Early Child Development and Care* 1(4): 337–459.

Hwang, C. P., M. E. Lamb, and I. E. Sigel, eds. (1996). *Images of childhood*. Mahwah, NJ: Erlbaum.

Kagan, S. L., and M. Neuman (2000). Early care and education: Current issues and future strategies. In S. Meisels and J. Shonkoff, eds. *Handbook of early childhood intervention*. 2nd ed. Cambridge: Cambridge University Press, pp. 339–360.

Kagan, S. L., and V. Steward (2005). A new world view: Education in a global era. *Phi Delta Kappan* 87(3): 184–187.

Kamerman, S. (2000). Early childhood education and care: An overview of developments in the OECD countries. *International Journal of Education Research* 33: 7–29.

Kamerman, S., and A. Kahn, eds. (1978). *Family policy: Government and families in 14 countries*. New York: Columbia University Press.

Kamerman, S., and A. Kahn (1981). *Child care, family benefits, and working parents: A study in comparative policy*. New York: Columbia University Press.

Kamerman, S., and A. Kahn, eds. (1991). *Child care, parental leave, and the under 3s: Policy innovation in Europe*. New York: Auburn House.

Kellmer-Pringle, M., and S. Naidoo (1974). Early child care in Britain. *Early Child Development and Care* 3(4): 299–473.

Khalakdina, Margaret. (1979). Early child care in India. *Early Child Development and Care* 5(3/4): 149–360.

Lamb, M., K. Sternberg, K-P. Hwang, and A. Broberg, eds. (1992). *Child care in context: Cross-cultural perspectives*. Hillsdale, NJ: Lawrence Erlbaum.

LeVine, R. A. (1980). Anthropology and child development. In C. Super and S. Harkness, eds., *Anthropological perspectives on child development: New directions for child development*. Vol. 8. San Francisco: Jossey-Bass, pp. 71–86.

LeVine, R. A., and Merry I. White (1986). *Human conditions: The cultural basis for educational developments*. New York: Routledge and Kegan Paul.

Lewis, C. (1995). *Educating hearts and minds: Reflections on Japanese preschools*. Cambridge: Cambridge University Press.

Lubeck, Sally. (2001). Early childhood education and care in cross-national perspective. *Phi Delta Kappan* 83(3): 213-215.

Luscher K., V. Ritter, and P. Gross (1973). Early child care in Switzerland. *Early Child Development and Care* 3(2): 89-210.

Mallory, B., and R. New, eds. (1994). *Diversity and developmentally appropriate practices: Challenges for early childhood education*. New York: Teachers College Press.

Meisels, S., and J. Shonkoff (2000). Early childhood intervention: A continuing evolution. In J. Shonkoff and S. Meisels, eds., *Handbook of early childhood intervention*. 2nd ed. Cambridge: Cambridge University Press, pp. 3-31.

Mitchell, A. (2005). *Stair steps to quality: A guide for states and communities developing quality rating systems for early care and education*. Alexandria, VA: United Way of America.

Myers, R. (1992). *The twelve who survive: Strengthening programmes of early childhood development in the third world*. London: Routledge.

New, R. (2003). Culture, child development, and early childhood education: Rethinking the relationship. In R. Lerner, F. Jacobs, and D. Wertlieb, eds., *Promoting positive child, adolescent, and family development: A handbook of program and policy innovations*. Thousand Oaks, CA: Sage Publications.

New, R. (2005). Learning about early childhood education from and with Western European nations. *Phi Delta Kappan* 87(3): 201-204.

New, R., and B. Mallory (1996). The paradox of diversity in early care and education. In E. J. Erwin, ed. *Putting children first: Visions for a brighter future for young children and their families*. Baltimore: Paul H. Brookes, pp. 143-67.

Nourot, P. M. (2000). Historical perspectives on early childhood education. In J. Roopnarine and J. Johnson, eds., *Approaches to early childhood education*. 3rd ed. Columbus, OH: Merrill.

OECD (2001). *Starting strong, early childhood education and care*. Paris: The Organization for Economic Cooperation and Development.

OECD (2006). *Starting strong II*. Paris: The Organization for Economic Cooperation and Development.

Olmstead, P., and D. Weikart, eds. (1989). *How nations serve young children: Profiles of child care and education in 14 countries*. Ypsilanti, MI: High/Scope Press.

Rapaport et al. (1976). Early child care in Israel. *Early Child Development and Care* 4(2/3): 149-345

Robinson, H., N. Robinson, M. Wolins, U. Bronfenbrenner, and J. Richmond (1973). Early child care in the United States of America. *Early Child Development and Care* 2(4): 359-582.

Sadovnik, Alan R., and Susan F. Semel (2002). *Founding mothers and others: Women educational leaders during the progressive era*. New York: Palgrave.

Saraceno, C. (1984). The social construction of childhood: Child care and education policies in Italy and the United States. *Social Problems* 31(3): 351-363.

U.S. Department of Health and Human Services. (1993). *Creating a 21st century head start: Final report of the advisory committee on head start quality and expansion*. Washington, DC: Author.

U.S. Department of Health and Human Services. (2002). *Making a difference in the lives of infants and toddlers and their families: The impacts of early head start*. Washington,

DC: The Commissioner's Office of Research and Evaluation and the Head Start Bureau, Administration on Children, Youth and Families.

Warner, M., S. Adriance, N. Baria, J. Hallas, B. Markeson, T. Morrissey, and W. Soref (2004). *Economic development strategies to promote quality child care.* Ithaca, NY: Cornell University, Department of City and Regional Planning. Available at http://www.earlychildhoodfinance.org/publicationspub.htm.

Woodill, G. A., J. Bernhard, and L. Prochner, eds. (1992). *International handbook of early childhood education.* New York: Garland.

Young, M., ed. *Early child development: Investing in our children's future.* Amsterdam: Elsevier.

Ziemska, Maria. (1978) Early child care in Poland. *Early Child Development and Care* 5(1/2): 1–148.

Zigler, E., and S. Muenchow. (1992). *Head Start: The inside story of America's most successful educational experiment.* New York: Basic, 1992.

Index

Boldface page numbers indicate main entries.

AAP. *See* American Academy of Pediatrics

AAPA. *See* American Adventure Playground Association

AAUW. *See* American Association of University Women

"Abbott District," 773

ABC. *See* Act for Better Child Care

ABC Bill, 544

Abecedarian Program, **1–2**, disabilities and, 293; SES and, 749

Ab/Mc. *See* Antibias/multicultural education

Aborigines: in Australia, 875; in Japan, 1163

About Behaviorism (Skinner), 733

ABS. *See* Australian Bureau of Statistics

The Absorbent Mind (Montessori), 524

Abstinence, 267

Abuse. *See* Child abuse; Parental substance abuse; Sexual abuse

Academic development: peers and friends and, 616

Academic expectations: learning disabilities and, 478

Academics, **3–5**; curriculum and, 177; definition of, 4; physical development and, 203–4

Academy for Early Childhood Program Accreditation, 542–43

ACC. *See* Augmentative and alternative communication

ACCES. *See* Cultural Association against Exclusion and Segregation

ACCESS. *See* American Associate Degree Early Childhood Educators

Accommodation, 11

Accreditation: curriculum and, 178; DAP and, 283; of early childhood programs, **5–9**; NAEYC and, 541; standards for, 27; structure of, 6–8. *See also* National Council for Accreditation of Teacher Education

Accuells parents-enfants, 1065, 1107

ACE. *See* Adverse Childhood Experiences Study

ACEI. *See* Association for Childhood Education International

ACEPP. *See* Association des Collectifs Enfants, Parents, Professionnels

Acheson, Donald, 1306

Achievement gap: parenting education and, 584

ACM. *See* Association of Children's Museums

ACT. *See* Association for Constructivist Teaching

Act and Observe, 208

Act for Better Child Care (ABC), **9–12**

Act for Early Childhood, Elementary, High School, Higher Vocational, and Other Education: in Czech Republic, 1045

Action Curriculum, 985

Action research, **12–13**, 333, 793

Activity-centered education. *See* Open education

Act of Content and Facilities of Kindergarten Education Guidelines: in Japan, 1168

Acts of Meaning (Bruner), 90

Actuarial Society of South Africa (ASSA), 1200

Adaptive development: developmental delay and, 273

ADD/ADHD. *See* Attention deficit disorder/Attention hyperactivity disorder

Addams, Jane, **13–14**; playgrounds and, 642

Addestramento, 1146

Addiction, 579–80

Adelaide Declaration on National Goals for Schooling, 902

ADHD. *See* Attention hyperactivity disorder

ADI. *See* Association of Direct Instruction

Adler, Alfred, 69, 501
Administration: of early care and education programs, 307–13
Administration for Children and Families, 808-9
Adolescence stage: in art, 104
Adoption, 14–18; children's development and, 15–16; parenting and, 16; preschool children and, 16; story of, 16
ADOS-G. See Autism Diagnostic Observation Schedule-Generic
Adventure playgrounds, 643
Adverse Childhood Experiences Study (ACE), 98, 579
Advisory Committee on Future Directions for Special Education in the 21st Century, 1187
Advocacy and leadership, 18–23, 22; administration, 311; data-based, 21; DEC and, 295; ECSE and, 326; individual vs. organizational, 21; internal vs. external, 21; through IRA, 458; McMillan, Margaret, and, 513; NARA and, 540; principles of, 20-22
Advocates for Children of New York, 21
AEI. See Aide Exceptionnelle à l'Investissement
Aesthetic perception, 199
Aesthetic principles, 948
AFDC. See Aid to Families with Dependent Children
AFEAMA. See Aide à la Famille pour l'Emploi d'une Assistante Maternelle
AFL-CIO, 123
African American Parents Project, 547
African Americans: Abecedarian Program and, 1; child abuse and, 98; culture and, 173; as gifted students, 389; rhythmic chants and, 199; SES and, 748; vernacular of, 476. See also Black caucus; National Black Child Development Institute
African National Congress (ANC), 1195

Afrikaans, 1225-26
AFT. See American Federation of Teachers
AFTEF. See American Federation of Teachers Educational Foundation
Agazzi, Rosa, 1126
Agazzi, Teresa, 1126
Age-appropriate strategies, 399
AGED. See Allocation de Garde d'Enfant à Domicile
Aggression: bullying and, 90; in Japan, 1160; peers and friends and, 615; social cognitive theory and, 60
Aide à la Famille pour l'Emploi d'une Assistante Maternelle (AFEAMA), 1103
Aide Exceptionnelle à l'Investissement (AEI), 1102
AIDS, 20, 1211; in China, 975; in South Africa, 1194, 1200, 1208; WHO and, 852
Aids: for communication, 53–54
Aid to Families with Dependent Children (AFDC), 113, 115, 809
Ainsworth, Mary, 45
Air pollutants, 344, 345
Akintetic seizures, 276
Alcohol: CP and, 276
Alcott, Bronson, 595
Alerting activities, 725
Alexander, F. Matthias, 557
Alfabetizzazione, 1130
Alfabetizzazione iniziale, 1130
Algebra, 507
Alger, Harriet, 549
Aliens, 491
Alive school, 1126
Alliance for Better Child Care, 9
Alliance for Curriculum Reform: ACEI and, 40
Allocation de Garde d'Enfant à Domicile (AGED), 1103
Allocation Parentale d'Éducation (APE), 1103
Allocation pour Jeune Enfant (APJE), 1103
A.L. Mailman Foundation, 620
Almy, Millie, 23–24
Alschuler, Rose, 551

Altruism, 265, 267; in Japan, 1162
Amazing Grace (Kozol), 20
Amber Was Brave, Essie Was Smart (Williams), 435
Ambientamento, 1139
Ambilinguism, 1050
Amblyopia, 275; screening for, 292
America 2000, 758
American Academy of Pediatrics (AAP), 147; television and, 801
American Adventure Playground Association (AAPA), 643
American Associate Degree Early Childhood Educators (ACCESS), 24–25, 545, 664
American Association for the Advancement of Science, 206
American Association of University Women (AAUW), 551
American Educational Research Association, 756
American Federation of Teachers (AFT), 94, 781
American Federation of Teachers Educational Foundation (AFTEF), 94
American Heart Association: physical development and, 202
American nursery school movement, 338
American Sign Language (ASL), 235, 238, 475
Americans with Disabilities Educational Act, 26; CP and, 96
AMI. See Association Montessori Internationale
Amygdala, 245
Anal stage, 727
ANC. See African National Congress
Andrews, J.D., 81–82
"Animal Intelligence: An Experimental Study of the Associative Processes in Animals" (Thorndike), 810-11
Animateurs, 1067, 1079
Anne E. Casey Foundation, 21

Annual New England Piaget Conference, 42

Anoxia: CP and, 276

Anthropology: Montessori and, 527; in social studies, 216

Antibias curriculum: culture and, 175; social studies and, 217

Antibias Curriculum: Tools for Empowering Young Children (NAEYC), 27

Antibias education, **25–32**

Antibias/multicultural education (Ab/Mc), 25

Anticonvulsants: for ADHD, 51

Antidepressants: for ADHD, 51

Antihypertensives: for ADHD, 51

Antipoff, Helen, 958

Antiretroviral Therapy, 1209

APAE. *See* Association of Parents and Friends of Exceptional Children

Apartheid, 1194, 1219

APE. *See* Allocation Parentale d'Éducation

APEEC. *See* Assessment of Practices in Early Elementary Classroom

Apgar score: disabilities and, 292

APJE. *See* Allocation pour Jeune Enfant

Apple, Michael, 694

Applied behavior analysts, 64

Applied kinesiology: for ADHD, 51

Apprentice children, 1129

Approval, 266

Apraxia: speech and, 52

April 19th Group, 544

Arab Americans, 26–27

ARACY. *See* Australian Research Alliance for Children and Youth

Art: in CK, 911; plastic, 1181–82; technology and, 230. *See also* Child art

Art as Experience (Dewey), 225

Articulation agreements, 661

The Art of Blockbuilding (Pratt), 654

ASCD. *See* Association for Supervision and Curriculum Development

ASD. *See* Autism spectrum disorders

Ashton-Warner, Sylvia, **32–33**

Asian/Pacific Americans, 26

Asili nido, 1111, 1137; caregivers for, 1146

Ask and Reflect, 208

ASL. *See* American Sign Language

Asperger Disorder, 56; SPD and, 723

Asphalt: on playgrounds, 642

ASSA. *See* Actuarial Society of South Africa

Assessment: administration of, 310; in Australia, 909–13; in China, 982–83; classroom discourse and, 139; *The Creative Curriculum for Preschool* and, 164; creativity and, 889–90; in Czech Republic, 1039–43; deaf children and, 237; developmental delay and, 273; developmental-interaction approach and, 281; documentation and, 296, 297, in early childhood, **34–38**; environmental, **340–44**; in France, 1005–00; Good Start, Grow Smart and, 392–393; of intelligence, 448; of IQ, 451; literacy curriculum and, 190; MI and, 536; multi-age grouping and, 520; readiness and, 691; school culture and, 712; standards for, 757; TPBA and, 237; in visual art, **38–40**. *See also* Standardized tests

Assessment of Practices in Early Elementary Classroom (APEEC), 343

Assessor: in play, 639

Assimilation, 41; in Australia, 877

Assistante maternelle, 1089, 1097

Associated disorders: with ADHD, 51

Associate degrees: ACCESS and, 24

Association des Collectifs Enfants, Parents,

Professionnels (ACEPP), 1070, 1075

Association for Childhood Education International (ACEI), **40–41**; Hymes, James, and, 426; IKU and, 458; Osborn and, 575; playgrounds and, 644; standardized tests and, 754; teacher certification and, 780; teacher education and, 789

Association for Constructivist Teaching (ACT), **41–42**

Association for Foreign Language Learning by the Immersion Method, 1051

Association for Supervision and Curriculum Development (ASCD): teacher certification and, 780–81

Association for the Study of Play, 644

Associationism, 154

Association Montessori Internationale (AMI), 524

Association of Children's Museums (ACM), 129

Association of Direct Instruction (ADI), 290

Association of parent cooperatives. *See* Association des Collectifs Enfants, Parents, Professionnels

Association of Parents and Friends of Exceptional Children (APAE), 959

Association of Teacher Educators (ATE), 780

Association of Waldorf Schools in North America (AWSNA), 835

Associative play, 593; peers and, 614

Asthma, 345, 346

Asylum for the Deaf and Dumb, 322

Ataxic CP, 96

ATE. *See* Association of Teacher Educators

Atelier, **42–44,** 698; in visual art curriculum, 230

Atheoid CP, 96

At Risk Child Care Program, 11, 115

Attachment, 16, **44–48**, 257; Bowlby and, 84; fathers and, 364; mothers and, 532; parental substance abuse and, 580–81; parents and, 589; peers and friends and, 613; play therapy and, 645; psychoanalysis and, 374; social competence and, 740; social development and, 269

Attachment (Bowlby), 85

Attachment disorders, 278

Attachment system, 246

Attachment theory, 1183

Attention deficit disorder/Attention hyperactivity disorder (ADD/ADHD), **48–52**, 277, 278, 292; behavior management and, 67; in boys, 385; in classroom, 49–50; at home, 50–51; in Japan, 1188; learning disabilities and, 483; SPD and, 723; temperament and, 806; treatment of, 51–52

Attention demand, 801

Attention hyperactivity disorder (ADHD), 48–52

Augmentative and Alternative Communication (AAC), **52–55**; literacy and, 490

Aurea magistrale, 1146

Australia, **867–913**; assessment in, 909–13; creativity in, 887–94; curriculum in, 894–97; exclusion in, 876; families in, 879–83; gender equity in, 906–8; Head Start in, 869; immigration in, 868, 876; infant mortality in, 868; language in, 868; multicultural education in, 874–76; numeracy in, 902–5; pedagogy in, 883–87; play in, 874; poverty in, 870; single-parent families in, 868

Australian Bureau of Statistics (ABS), 876

Australian Centre for Effective Partnerships, 887

Australian Council of Deans of Education, 895

Australian Research Alliance for Children and Youth (ARACY), 869

Authoritative parenting, 268

Authority: in social studies, 218

Autism, **55–59**, 277; in China, 1010; literacy and, 489; music and, 314; SPD and, 723; speech and, 52

Autism Diagnostic Observation Schedule—Generic (ADOS-G), 57

Autism spectrum disorders (ASD), 56, 291

Autistic Disorder, 56

Auto-education, 526

Autonomy: morality of, 625; parental substance abuse and, 580–81; psychosocial theory and, 675

Auxiliaires de puericulture, 1089, 1100

AWSNA. *See* Association of Waldorf Schools in North America

Baby hotels, 1184

Baby signs, 238

Bachelor's programs: for Chinese teachers, 1014; in Czech Republic, 1056

Back to basics, 910

"Back to Sleep" campaign, 100

Bad Boys: Public Schools in the Making of Black Masculinity, 385

Baer, Donald, 64

BAFA. *See* Brevet d'aptitude aux fonctions d'animateur

BAFD. *See* Brevet d'aptitude aux fonctions de directeur

Baker, Katherine Read. *See* Read, Katherine

Bake Sesame Seed Cakes, 991

Balancing traits, 338

Ballenger, Cynthia, 33

Bambini, 498, 1113, 1140

Bandura, Albert, **60–61,** 69; children's media and, 127; social cognitive theory and, 734

Banks, James, 25, 694

Bank Street, **61–62,** 279, 374, 517; documentation and, 296; pedagogy and, 603

Bank Street Readers, 62

Bantu education, 1225

Bao Yu Yuan, 986

Barker, Roger, 333

Bates, Elizabeth, 261

Bayley Scales of Infant Development, 454

Becker, Wesley, 290

Becoming a Kwoma (Whiting, John), 844

BEE. *See* Bureau of Educational Experiments

Beethoven Project, 620

Behavior: developmental delay and, 274; management of, 399; peers and friends and, 615

Behavioral play therapy, 647

Behavior and Misbehavior (Hymes, James), 425

Behavior disorders, 278

Behaviorism, **62–66,** 154; in Australia, 896; classroom environment and, 141; direct instruction model and, 290; Pavlov and, 594; Skinner and, 732–33; Watson and, 839

Behavior management and guidance, **66–72,** 67; obesity and, 568

The Behavior of Organisms (Skinner), 63, 733

Behavior Rating Scale, 454

Behavior Science and Child Rearing (Hunt), 424

Beijing Normal University, 1014

Being a Good Parent (Hymes, James), 425

Beliefs: culture and, 173

Beliefs *vs.* faith, 752–53

Bell, Alexander Graham, 524

Belongingness, 502

Benchmarking. *See* Standardized tests

Benchmarks for Scientific Inquiry, 207

Beneke, Sallee, 298

Benessere, 1139

Bentley, Alys, 557

Bereiter, Carl, 290

Better Baby Care, 544, 859

"Beyond the Best Interests of the Child" (Freud, Anna), 373

Biculturalism, 72–75

Biggers, John, 493

Bilingual education, 75–79, 475; biculturalism and, 73–74; culture and, 175; in Czech Republic, 1050-51; in Sweden, 1248. *See also* Second-language acquisition

Bilingual Education Act, 75

"A Bill of Rights for Children," 424

Bill of Rights for Children of Incarcerated Parents, 433

Binet, Alfred, **80–81,** 323, 446, 453; IQ and, 449

Biofeedback: for ADHD, 51

Biological factors: learning disabilities and, 478

Biology: Montessori and, 527

Biology and Knowledge (Piaget), 253

Bipolar disorder: SPD and, 723

The Birds Christmas Carol (Wiggin), 847

Birth Control Commission: in China, 1008

Birthrate: in Australia, 868; in Czech Republic, 1022, 1035; in Italy, 1139; in Japan, 1157, 1159; in Sweden, 1240. *See also* One-child policy

Birth to 3 Maters Framework: in United Kingdom, 1296-97

Birth trauma: developmental delay and, 274

Birth weight, 345; disabilities and, 292; Down Syndrome and, 303

Black caucus: of NAEYC, **81–82**

Blacks: in Brazil, 924-25

Blair, Tony, 1291

Blindness: in Brazil, 959; in China, 1009. *See also* Visual impairment

Bloch, Ernst, 558

The Block Book (Pratt), 654

Blocks, 1119, 1178; Pratt and, 654

Bloom, Benjamin, 323, 447

Blos, Peter, 348

Blow, Susan Elizabeth, **82–84,** 416; IKU and, 457

Bobo dolls, 60, 735

Body composition, 203

Bokasi, 1162

Bolsa Escola, 933

Bolsa Família, 933, 939

Books: for parenting guidance, 590

Boston Black, 131

Bouverat, Roberta Wong, 120

Bowen, Murray, 363

Bowlby, John, 44, **84–85,** 532, 1023

Bowman, Barbara, 82

Boys: ADD/ADHD and, 385; literacy in, 385

Boys' Clubs, 14

Braille language, 959

Brain development, **243–48,** 791; embodiment and, 728; IQ and, 451. *See also* Mental health

Brazelton, T. Berry, 807, 812, 858

Brazil, **914–70;** child care in, 938-43; CNE in, 916; creativity and imagination in, 952-57; culture in, 924-28; curriculum in, 947-52; ecology of childhood in, 919-24; ethnicity in, 924-28; FUNDEF in, 916; gender equity in, 966-70; inclusive education in, 961-65; National Educational Plan in, 916; play in, 957-61; poverty in, 928-34; race in, 924-28; teacher preparation in, 943-47; violence in, 934-38

Brazilian Institute of Geography and Statistics (IBGE), 930

Brazilian Legion of Assistance (LBA), 914

Brazilian Tribunal for Minors, 936

Brevet d'aptitude aux fonctions d'animateur (BAFA), 1108

Brevet d'aptitude aux fonctions de directeur (BAFD), 1108

Brevity of sequence, 801-2

Bridges, Ruby, 267

Briggs, Jean, 806

Bright Futures, 1307

Bright Horizons Family Solutions, 307

Brinquedotecas (toy-playing centers), 957

Brisset, Claire, 1099

British Infant Schools, 569

Bronfenbrenner, Urie, 67, **85–88,** 322; classroom environment and, 141; developmental systems theory and, 287; ecology of human development and, 333; environmental assessments and, 341; parent involvement and, 590; Touchpoints and, 813

Brownell, William, 194

Brown, Margaret Wise, 517

Bruner, Jerome, **88–90,** 195, 447, 959, 1116; constructivism and, 152; pedagogy and, 599; of play, 629; social studies curriculum and, 217

Bryan, Anna, 807

Building blocks: mathematics curriculum and, 194

Bullying, **90–93;** in Brazil, 935–36; gender differences in, 92

Bureau of Educational Experiments (BEE), 372, 517. *See also* Bank Street

Bureau of Women and Young Children: in China, 1007

Burlingame, Dorothy, 373

Burlingham, Dorothy, 348

Burrell, Rae, 549

Bush, George H.W., 10, 552

Bush, George W., 391, 560, 757; NCLB and, 669

CACFP. *See* Child and Adult Care Food Program

CAFs. *See* Caisses d'allocations familiales; Regional family allowance funds

CAH. *See* Department of Child and Adolescent Health and Development

CAI. *See* Computer-assisted instruction

Caisses d'allocations familiales
(CAFs), 1091, 1098
Caldwell, Grace, 550
California Cares, 95
California Early Childhood
Mentor Program, 95
Calming activities, 725
Camp Kilda (CK), 909
Canada: ERS and, 319
Canady, Helen, 545
Canter, Lee, 70
Capacity, 533
CAPTA. See Child Abuse
Prevention and Treatment Act
Cardiovascular disease, 563
Cardiovascular endurance,
202–3
Care: psychosocial theory and,
676
Career lattice, 661
Carini, Patricia, 795
Carlsson, Asplund, 1273
Carlsson-Paige, Nancy, 127
Carnegie Council on Children,
419
Carolina Abecedarian Project.
See Abecedarian Program
Caroline and Sigmund Schott
Foundation, 621
Carpenteria Preschool Program,
77
CARS. See Childhood Autism
Rating Scales
Casa dei Bambini, 523, 525, 528
Casa dei Bambini (Montessori),
323
Case studies, 680
Casey, Beth, 545
Cataracts, 275
Catlett, Elizabeth, 493
Cattell, James McKeen, 575, 810
Cattell, Raymond, 447
Cazden, Courtney, 135, 191
CBA. See Community Built
Association
CCB. See Child Care Benefit
CCDBG. See Child Care and
Development Block Grant
CCDF. See Child Care and
Development Fund
CCDLA. See Council for Child
Development Laboratory
Administrators

CCEP. See Child Care Employee
Project
CCR&R. See Child care resource
and referral
CCSA. See Child Care Services
Association
CCW. See Center for the Child
Care Workforce
CDA. See Child Development
Associate National
Credentialing Program
CDCs. See Child Development
Centers
CDF. See Children's Defense
Fund
CDGM. See Child Development
Group of Mississippi
CDLs. See Child development
laboratories
CEC. See Council for
Exceptional Children
CECF. See State Council on the
Conditions of Women
CEC Today, 163
CEI. See Classroom Ecological
Inventory
CEL. See Local educational
contracts
Center for Literacy and Disability
Studies, 491
Center for the Child Care
Workforce (CCW), 94–95;
Worth Wage Campaign and,
854
Center for the Study of Victims
of Violence: in Brazil, 935
Centers for Disease Control and
Prevention: autism and, 56;
disabilities and, 291; physical
development and, 202
Central Americans, 26
Centrality of meaning: in
qualitative research, 678
Centre for Research in Early
Childhood (CREC), 349
Centres of early excellence,
1282; in United Kingdom,
1300
Centro de Reabilitação de
Cegueira Dr. Newton Kara
José, 959
Centro Nazionale per la Scuola
Materna, 1111

CERC. See Council on
Employment, Incomes and
Social Cohesion
Cerebral cortex, 243;
development of, 245
Cerebral palsy (CP), 95–97, 276;
literacy and, 490; SPD and,
723; speech and, 52
Ceremonies: in Japan, 1165–66
CFGs. See Critical Friends'
Groups
Chafee, John, 10
Chaining, 63
Chandler, Beatrice, 387
Changing the World: A
Framework for the Study of
Creativity (Feldman,
Csikszentmihalyi, and
Gardner), 171
Channing, William Ellery, 595
Charcot, Jean-Martin, 80
Cheek, Carrie, 81
Chemistry: Montessori and, 527
Chen He-Qing, 985
Chicago Child-Parent Center
(CPC), 587
Child abuse, 97–100; attachment
and, 47; behavior disorders
and, 278; disabilities and, 292;
early intervention and, 330;
FAS and, 370; in Japan, 1160;
parenting education and, 584;
prevention of, 101–3; SES and,
749; in South Africa, 1205–6
Child Abuse Prevention and
Treatment Act (CAPTA), 97,
730
Child and Adult Care Food
Program (CACFP), 116;
after-school programs and,
709
Child and Dependent Care Tax
Credit, 118
Child and maternal health
centers (PMI), 1073, 1087,
1106, 1107
The Child and the Curriculum
(Dewey), 289
Child art, 103–7
Child-by-environment
perspective, 613
Child care, 107–11; behavior
and, 67; in Brazil, 938–43;

child's attachment with, 47; in China, 1005–9; in Czech Republic, 1058–62; licensing of, 12; preschool and, 655; quality of, 107–8. *See also* Day care

Child Care Act: in South Africa, 1196

Child Care and Development Fund (CCDF), 110, 111–12, 531; after-school programs and, 709; standards for, 757; TANF and, 809

Child Care and Early Education *Research Connections,* 112–13

Child Care Benefit (CCB), 870

Child Care Development Block Grant (CCDBG), 9, 11, 110, 113–14, 115, 419

Child Care Development Fund (CCDF): CCDBG and, 113

Child Care Employee Project (CCEP), 94

Childcare Information Exchange, 351. *See also* Exchange

Child Care Information Exchange Magazine: NARA and, 540

Child Care Partnership Initiative, 329

Child care resource and referral (CCR&R), 111, 543

Child Care Services Association (CCSA), 785

Child-care subsidies and tax provisions, 115–19; in France, 1103–4

Child-centered programs, 184. *See also* Open education

Child Development Associate (CDA) National Credentialing Program, 119–20, 242, 659, 711

The Child Development Associate National Program: The Early Years and Pioneers (Bouverat and Lichter), 120

Child Development Centers (CDCs), 242

Child Development Credential (CDA), 789

Child Development Group of Mississippi (CDGM), 120–25

Child development laboratories (CDLs), 471–72

A Child Development Point of View (Hymes, James), 425

Child Development System: of DoD, 240–43

Childhood and Society (Erikson), 348, 674, 727

Childhood Autism Rating Scales (CARS), 57

Childhood Disintegrative Disorder, 56

Childhood Education, 40, 457, 808

Childhouses, 1027

Child, Irvin, 844

Child labor, 871; in Brazil, 934

Childminders: in France, 1106; in Sweden, 1243, 1266

Child Nutrition Act, 849

Child Outcome Framework: social curriculum and, 215

Children: apprentice, 1129; constructive, 1127; domestic, 1129; expressive, 1127; manual and visual, 1127; as property, 972–73; searching, 129–1130; social, 1128

Children Act: in United Kingdom, 1282

Children and Families, 556

Children of the New Millennium, 898, 900

Children's Action Network: DEC and, 295

Children's Alliance of New Hampshire, 21

Children's Centres: in United Kingdom, 1300

Children's Defender, 1099

Children's Defense Budgets, 125

Children's Defense Fund (CDF), 12, 19–20, 125–26; ABC and, 10; advocacy by, 21; mental health and, 516; on race and ethnicity, 686

Children's Health Insurance, 651

Children's House, 14

Children's media, 126–29

Children's museums, 129–31

Children's Technology Review, 224

Children's Television Act, 804

Children's Television Workshop, 574

Children's Workforce Development Council: in United Kingdom, 1309

Children with Incarcerated Parents (CHIPS), 435

Child Sexual Abuse and Pornography Act, 730

The Child's Hour, 841

Child/staff ratio, 764–65; in China, 983

Child Study Association of America, 132; Hall and, 407; Owen, Grace, and, 575

Child study movement, 132–34, 374; creativity and, 167; kindergarten and, 467; Parten and, 592; progressive education and, 667

Child support, 365, 651

Child Support Grant: in South Africa, 1201

Child Training and Personality (Whiting, John; and Child), 844

Child Welfare Law: in Japan, 1157

Child Welfare League of America, 21; NARA and, 540

Child Welfare Services Demonstration, 329

Child Welfare Work Group, 859

China, 862, 971–1016; curriculum in, 984–89; families in, 976–79; literacy in, 1002–5; play in, 989–93; program quality in, 979–83; special education in, 1009–12; teacher education in, 1012–15

Chinese Children Development Guideline, 972

"Chinese Children Development Guidelines in the 1990's," 973

"Chinese Children Development Outline," 1008

CHIP. *See* State Children's Health Insurance Program

CHIPS. *See* Children with Incarcerated Parents

Chorionic villi sampling (CVS), 304

Christianity: corporal punishment and, 158–59; public schools and, 499

Christian, Linda, 363

Chromosomal disorders, 277; Down Syndrome and, 303

Ciari, Bruno, 1127; Malaguzzi and, 487

Citizen's Crusade Against Poverty, 123

Citizenship rationale: in advocacy, 19

Civic ideals: in social studies, 219

Civil Rights Movement, 19, 25, 422

CK. *See* Camp Kilda

Classes passerelles, 1086

Classroom discourse, **134–40**; Project Approach and, 672

Classroom Ecological Inventory (CEI), 343

Classroom environments, **140–45**; grouping and, 402; science curriculum and, 208

Classroom Practices Inventory (CPI), 343

Classrooms: assessment of, 340; environmental assessments and, 341; play within, 630–31

Client Centered Therapy: Its Current Practice, Implications, and Theory (Rogers), 703

Climbie, Victoria, 1306

Clinical Treatment of the Problem Child (Rogers), 703

Clinton, Bill, 552

CNAF. *See* National family allowance fund

CNDM. *See* National Council of Women's Rights

CNE. *See* National Council on Education

Coaching for Results, 513

Coalition building, 21–22

Cobb, Paul, 746

Cochlear implants, 235

Cochran, Moncrief, 88

Cockroaches, 344, 346

Codes of ethics, 663

Code switching, 716–17

Cognitive-behavioral play therapy, 647

Cognitive development, **248–55**, 1134; Abecedarian Program and, 1; creativity and, 168; curriculum and, 177; developmental delay and, 273; embodiment and, 728; fathers and, 365; gender stereotypes and, 382; Kohlberg and, 469; language and, 1049; literacy curriculum and, 187; MI and, 532; moral development and, 264; parenting education and, 584, 587; peers and friends and, 613, 616; play and, 627; role-playing and, 958–59; science curriculum and, 208; SES and, 749; technology and, 798; visual impairment and, 828

Cognitive development theory: of play, 627-28

Cognitive disorders, 277

Cognitively Guided Instruction, 153

Cognitive moral reasoning, 267

Cognitive play, 222

Cognitive psychology: Bruner and, 88

Cognitive theory: for artistic development, 226

Cohabitation: in Australia, 880

Cohen, Donald J., 856

Colburn, Warren, 194

Cole, Michael, 601

Coles, Robert, 267, 677

Collaborative Assessment Conference, 795

"Color Purple," 122

Comenius, John Amos, **145–46**, 1018, 1025-26, 1043, 1058; Froebel and, 376; Kurahashi and, 1169; playgrounds and, 641

Comitato di gestione, 1143

Commercialism: in Japan, 1159

Commission for Racial Equality: in United Kingdom, 1289

Committee of Nineteen of the International Kindergarten Union, 787

Committee on Children and Youth, 10

Committee on Nursing Schools, 457

Common Core standards, 782

Common School Movement, 595

Communication: administration and, 311; developmental delay in, 273; disorders in, 278; documentation for, 298; learning disabilities and, 481; visual impairment and, 828

Communicator: in play, 639

Community: theme of, 29

Community Action Programs, 412

Community Built Association (CBA), 645

Community Education Coordinating Committee: in China, 978

Community Opportunities Accountability, and Training and Educational Services Act, 358

Comparative theories: of play, 629

Competence: psychosocial theory and, 676

Complexity: in qualitative research, 678

Complexity of presentation, 802

Comprehensive Child Development Act, 110, 419; NBCDI and, 546

Comprehensive educational facility, 1158

Compulsory education: in Brazil, 914; in China, 1010; in Czech Republic, 1032, 1035; in Sweden, 1262

Computer and video game play, **146–49**; violence in, 821

Computer-assisted instruction (CAI), 799

Computer-assisted training: for ADHD, 51

Computer-based technologies, 222

Computer supported collaborative learning (CSCL), 149, 799

Concrete: on playgrounds, 642

Concrete operations, 266
Conditioned Reflexes (Pavlov), 594
A Conduct Curriculum for the Kindergarten and First Grade, 416
Conferring assurance, 7
Conformity, 266; in classroom, 270
Confucianism, 1164
Congenital disorders, 276-77
Congenital hyperthyroidism, 276
Consequences for Juvenile Offenders Act: NBCDI and, 546
Consolidation of the Labor Laws: in Brazil, 914
Consortium for Longitudinal Studies, 396
Constructionism, **149-52**
The Construction of Reality in the Child (Piaget), 625
Constructive children, 1127
Constructive play, 631-32
Constructivism, 28, 41-42, **152-55**; classroom environment and, 141; literacy curriculum and, 189; mathematical curriculum and, 195; Piaget and, 624-25
The Constructivist, 42
Consumer Product Safety Commission (CPSC), 643
Consumer surveys: in Sweden, 1259
Consumption: in social studies, 218
Contemporary Issues in Early Childhood, **155-56**
Content: of play, 630
Content standards, 757
Contingencies of reinforcement, 63
Continuing education: for Chinese teachers, 1015-16
Continuity. *See* Transitions/continuity
Contrat enfance, 1091, 1102
Controversy, 272
Conventional stage, 266
Convention on the Rights of the Child (CRC), 20, 75, **156-57**, 819, 871, 973, 1205, 1306; on

corporal punishment, 157, 161; United Kingdom and, 1285
Cooperative play, 593; peers and, 614
Cooper, Sarah, 846
Coordinatore pedagogico, 1138
Coordinatori, 1114
Copenhagen World Summit for Social Development, 1290
Copernicus turn, 1029
CORDE. *See National Coordination for the Integration of Disabled People*
Core competencies, 661
Corporal punishment, **157-62**; psychoanalysis and, 373
Correlational studies, 681
Corsaro, William, 128, 611
Corte Costituzionale, 1153
Cortisol, 246
Cost, Quality, and Child Outcomes Study, 317
Council for Child Development Laboratory Administrators (CCDLA), 473
Council for Exceptional Children (CEC), **162-63,** 798; curriculum and, 180; DEC of, 294; ECSE and, 325; inclusion and, 437; teacher certification and, 780
Council on Employment, Incomes and Social Cohesion (CERC), 1086
Count Me In, 903
CP. *See* Cerebral palsy
CPC. *See* Chicago Child-Parent Center
CPI. *See* Classroom Practices Inventory
CPSC. *See* Consumer Product Safety Commission
CRC. *See* Convention on the Rights of the Child
Creating Better Child Care Jobs, 95
Creative and Mental Growth (Lowenfeld), 104, 225, 493-94
Creative Curriculum: pedagogy and, 598

The Creative Curriculum for Preschool, **164-66**
Creative process: visual art curriculum and, 229
Creativity, **166-72**; in Australia, 887-94; in Brazil, 952-57; in China, 992-98; role-playing and, 958-59
CREC. *See* Centre for Research in Early Childhood
Crèches, 914, 1019, 1032, 1054, 1058-59; in Czech Republic, 1044; in France, 1064-65, 1083-84; reduction of, 1060-61; special education and, 1095
Cri du chat syndrome, 277
Criteria for Daycare Centers Child Caring that Respects Children's Fundamental Rights, 955-56
Critérios para um Atendimento em Creches que Respeite os Direitos Fundamentais das Crianças, 955-56
Critical Friends' Groups (CFGs), 795
Critical theories: in Australia, 886, 896
Cross-sectional field studies, 802
Cross, William, Jr., 88
CSCL. *See* Computer supported collaborative learning
Csikszentmihalyi, Mihaly, 171
Cultura generale, 1146
Cultural Association against Exclusion and Segregation (ACCES), 1070
Cultural diversity: in Australian families, 880-81
Culturally Responsive and Aware Dual Language Education Project, 329
Cultural pluralism, 26; in Australia, 877; conservatives and, 31; dichotomy of, 877-78
Cultural Revolution: in China, 986
Culture, **172-76**; in Brazil, 924-28; cognitive development and, 254; curriculum and, 177; in France, 1068-72; in Japan,

Culture, **172–76**; in Brazil, 1155, 1160–63; language development and, 260; learning disabilities and, 292, 478; moral development and, 268; music curriculum and, 199; pedagogy and, 604; peers and friends and, 616; in play, 1121; psychoanalysis and, 374; social competence and, 740; social studies and, 218; in Sweden, 1247-50; in United Kingdom, 1287-90

The Culture of Education (Bruner), 90

Cumulative recorder, 63

Curriculum, **176–81**; academics and, 3; accreditation and, 7; administration of, 310; in Australia, 883-84, 894-97; behavior management and, 69; in Brazil, 917-18, 947-52; in China, 984-89; classroom discourse and, 134; culture and, 175; in Czech Republic, 1043-48; DAP and, 283; emergent, **181–82**; emotional development, **183–86**; environmental assessments and, 341; in France, 1080-84; as fundamental architecture, 1125; grouping and, 402; in Italy, 1125-30; in Japan, 1172-76; for kindergarten, 467; literacy and, **186–92**, 490; mathematics, **192–98**; MI and, 535; multiculturalism and, 25; multidisciplinary approach to, 1147; music, **198–201**; negotiated, **182**; of open education, 572; open-ended, 227; pedagogy and, 596, 604; physical development, **201–5**; preschool/prekindergarten programs and, 655-56; process-based, 227; Reggio Emilia and, 699; science, **205–11**; social, **211–16**; social studies, **216–21**; in South Africa, 1219-24; standards for, 757; in Sweden, 1261-65; teacher-based, 227-28; technology, **221–25**; in

technology, 798; in United Kingdom, 1296-99; visual art, **225–31**; of Waldorf Schools, 775

Curriculum 2005: in South Africa, 1219

Curriculum Guidance for the Foundation Stage, 1297; in United Kingdom, 1288

Curriculum Is What Happens (Jones), 181

Curtis, Henry: playgrounds and, 642

Custodial rationale: in advocacy, 19

Customs: culture and, 173

CVS. *See* Chorionic villi sampling

Cycles of learning: in France, 1081

Cystic fibrosis, 276

Cytomegalovirus, 279

Czech Republic, **1017–62**; bilingual education in, 1050-51; child care in, 1058-62; curriculum in, 1043-48; families in, 1035-39; language in, 1048-53; pedagogy in, 1025-30; public policies in, 1031-34; quality of provision in, 1039-43; sociology of, 1021-25; teacher education in, 1053-58

Daily-life oriented education, 1170

Dalcroze Eurhythmics, 557

Dalton Plan: in Czech Republic, 1033

Damon, William, 265; moral development and, 264, 266

Daniel, Jack, 82

DAP. *See* Developmentally appropriate practice

Darwin, Charles, 170

Data analyses, 507

Data-based advocacy, 21

Dauntless Women in Early Childhood Education, 808

Davies, Bronwyn, 743

Davis, Michael, 545

Dawning realism stage, 104

Day care: in Brazil, 940; in Chinese businesses, 1005

Day Care Environmental Inventory and Observation Schedule for Physical Space, 342

Day nurseries, **232–34**

DCAP. *See* Dependent Care Assistance Plan

DCNEI. *See National Curricular Guidelines for Early Childhood Education*

Deaf children, **234–40**; language development and, 261

DEAFSA, 1230

DEC. *See* Division for Early Childhood

DECET. *See* Diversity in Early Childhood Education and Training

Declaration of Jomtien, 923

Declaration of Rights of Disabled People, 961

Declaration of the Rights of the Child, 818

DEC Recommended Practices: A Comprehensive Guide for Practical Application, 295

Decroly, O., 1078

Défenseur des enfants, 1099

Delegation for Gender Equality in Pre-school, 1257; in Sweden, 1255

Democracy: in Sweden, 1261-65

Democracy and Education (Dewey), 289, 668

Democratic parenting: styles of, 268

Demographics: SES and, 748

Department for Education and Employment (DfEE): in United Kingdom, 1282

Department for Education and Skills (DfES), 1304; in United Kingdom, 1283

Department of Child and Adolescent Health and Development (CAH), 852-53

Department of Child Study, 132

Department of Defense (DoD), **241–43**

Department of Defense Operation Child Care, 545

Department of Education: Office for Civil Rights of, 21

Department of Education, Science and Training (DEST), 869

Department of Family and Community Services (FaCS), 869

Department of Health: in South Africa, 1196

Department of Health and Human Services (HHS), 391

Department of Health, Education, and Welfare (HEW), 413

Dependent Care Assistance Plan (DCAP), 118

Depression: parental substance abuse and, 582

Descriptive Review of the Child, 795

Descriptive vocabulary, 261

Design technology, 221

Desirable Outcomes for Children's Learning, 1296

Despair: psychosocial theory and, 676

DEST. *See* Department of Education, Science and Training

Dethce, 1027

Developing Mathematical Ideas, 153

Developing Number Concepts, 153

Development: of brain, **243–48**; emotional, **256–59**; of language, **259–64**; moral, **264–68**; social, **269–73**; standards of, 251

Developmental Continuum, 164

The Developmental Continuum Assessment Toolkit for Ages 3-5, 166

Developmental delay, 273-75; IDEA and, 440; IQ and, 452; transitions and, 816; visual impairment and, 827

Developmental disorders of infancy and early childhood: taxonomy of, **275–79**

Developmental-interaction approach, 61, 279, **279–82**

Developmentally Appropriate Practice, 284

Developmentally appropriate practice (DAP), 167-68, **282–86,** 343, 909; in Australia, 884; curriculum and, 176; deaf children and, 236; ECSE and, 325; emotional development and, 184; families and, 353; history of, 283-84; literacy and, 485; MI and, 535; parents and, 589; pedagogy and, 597, 603, 604; reconceptualists and, 694; in science curriculum, 207

Developmentally Appropriate Practice in Early Childhood Settings, 67

Developmental psychology: Bronfenbrenner and, 85

Developmental quotient (DQ), 274

Developmental rationale: in advocacy, 19

Developmental screening, 691

Developmental systems theory, 252, **286–88,** 361

Developmental theory: for artistic development, 226

Developmental verbal apraxia: speech and, 52

Development as the Aim of Education (Kohlberg), 470

DeVries, Hugo, 526

Dewey, John, 132, 288-89, 958, 1013, 1169; Chen He-Qing and, 985; China and, 985; constructivism and, 152; developmental-interaction approach and, 279; feminism and, 367; Frank and, 371; Hall and, 408; Hill and, 416; Isaacs and, 459; laboratory schools and, 471; Malaguzzi and, 487; Mitchell, Lucy, and, 517; Naumburg and, 557; Parker and, 592; pedagogy and, 599, 602; playgrounds and, 641; progressive education and, 667; Reggio Emilia and, 697; social studies curriculum and, 217, 219-20; teacher research and, 794, 797; Temple and,

807; visual art curriculum and, 225; Xingzhi Dao and, 972

DfEE. *See* Department for Education and Employment

DfES. *See* Department for Education and Skills

DI. *See* Direct instruction

Diabetes, 563

The Diagnostic and Statistics Manual of Mental Disorders (DSM), 48, 56, 275

Diagnostic Classification of Mental Health and Development Disorders of Infancy and Early Childhood, 56, 275, 859

Dial, 596

Dialectical process, 744-45

Dialects, 476

Dick and Jane readers, 188

Didactic programs, 184; Montessori and, 526

Diet: for ADHD, 51

Dietary Guidelines for Americans, 564

Differential diagnosis: of ADHD, 51

Dimensions of Early Childhood, 751

Diplegia: CP and, 96

DIR. *See* Individual-Difference, Relationship-Based Model

Direct instruction (DI), 290; in kindergarten, 468

Direct instruction model, **289–91**

Direction Instructional System for Teaching and Remediation (DISTAR), 290

Directive play therapy, 646

Directorate of Research, Studies, Evaluation and Statistics (DRESS), 1086

Directors, 308; licensing of, 766

The Director's Link, 513

Directors' Technology Training, 513

Disabilities: in Australia, 875; CEC and, 163; in China, 1009; culture and, 172; developmental delay and, 274; Early Head Start and, 328; in France, 1093-94; with

Disabilities: in Australia, 875; language, 52; learning, 277; in South Africa, 1227; young children with, **291–94**. *See also* Handicapped Children's Early Education Program

Disabled Children's Action Group, 1230; in South Africa, 1227

Discipline, 66; in China, 973; Comenius and, 1026; group orientation and, 1161–62; MI and, 534; Montessori and, 526; parenting education and, 587; school culture and, 712

The Discovery of Grounded Theory (Glaser and Strauss), 680

Discrete trial training, 64

Discrimination, 25; biculturalism and, 73; obesity and, 567; in Sweden, 1247

Discursive subsystem: of language, 1049

Disorders. *See* Developmental disorders of infancy and early childhood

DISTAR. *See* Direction Instructional System for Teaching and Remediation

Distribution: in social studies, 218

Diversity, 27; in Australia, 878–79

Diversity in Early Childhood Education and Training (DECET), 1070, 1076

Division for Early Childhood (DEC), 163, **294–95**; curriculum and, 180; early intervention and, 331; ECSE and, 325; inclusion and, 437; teacher certification and, 780

Doctrine of integral protection, 936

Doctrine of irregular situation, 936

Documentation, **296–300**; of artwork, 38, 39; classroom discourse and, 139; families and, 353; for infant care, 443; Malaguzzi and, 487; MI and, 536; Project Approach and,

670; PZ and, 674; Reggio Emilia and, 699; science curriculum and, 208; teacher research and, 796

DoD. *See* Department of Defense

Dodd, Christopher, 10

Dogma, 753

Dole, Bob, 11

Doll, Edgar, 323

Dolls, 1119

Dolto, F., 1077, 1091

Domestic children, 1129

Domestic violence, **300–303**. *See also* Violence

Doubt: psychosocial theory and, 675

Down, John Langdon, 303

Down syndrome, 277, **303–6**; developmental delay and, 274; language development and, 261; SPD and, 723

Down Syndrome South Africa, 1230

DQ. *See* Developmental quotient

Dramatic play, 29–30, 213; Pratt and, 653

Drawing on the Right Side of the Brain (Edwards), 227

Dreikurs, Rudolf, 69–70

DRESS. *See* Directorate of Research, Studies, Evaluation and Statistics

Dr. Spock's Book of Baby and Child Care, 160

Drug abuse. *See* Parental substance abuse

DSM. *See The Diagnostic and Statistics Manual of Mental Disorders*

Du Bois, W.E.B., 25

Du Chenne's muscular dystrophy, 276

Duckworth, Eleanor, 409, 793

Dust mites, 344, 346

Dyson, Anne Haas, 128, 191, 612

Dyspraxia, 724

EA. *See* Emergency Assistance

Eager to Learn: Educating our preschoolers, 178

Early care and education programs: administration of, **307–13**

Early Child Development and Care, 314

Early Child Development: Investing in the Future, 863

Early Child Education Research Association: in China, 978

Early Childhood Care and Development Project (ECCD), 1008

Early Childhood Connections Journal of Music- and Movement-based Learning, 314

Early childhood education, care, and development (ECECD), 232

Early Childhood Education in Historical Perspective (Osborn), 575

Early Childhood Education Journal (ECEJ), **314–15**

Early Childhood Education: Living History Interviews (Hymes, James), 426

Early Childhood Education: Twenty years in Review (Hymes, James), 426

Early Childhood Environment Rating Scale—Revised (ECERS-R), 315, 342, 1293

Early Childhood Environment Rating Scales (ERS), **315–20**

Early Childhood Equity Alliance, 622

Early Childhood Funders Collaborative, 622

Early Childhood Investment Fund. *See* Fonds d'Investissement Petite Enfance

Early Childhood Music Education Commission (ECME), **320**

Early Childhood Physical Environment Observation Schedules and Rating Scales, 342

Early Childhood Program Accreditation: NAEYC and, 541

Early Childhood Programs: Human Relationships and Learning (Read; Gardner, Pat; and Mahler), 687

Early Childhood Research & Practice (ECRP), **320–21**

Early Childhood Research Quarterly (ECRQ), **321**; NAEYC and, 542

Early childhood special education (ECSE), 274, **321–27**, 322–23, 726; autism and, 58; in China, 1009–12; crèches and, 1095; early childhood, 274; in France, 1092–97; in Japan, 1187–90; learning disabilities and, 484; research in, 964–65; in Sweden, 1249; teacher certification and, 781; teachers education for, 1148; visual impairment and, 829

Early Childhood Studies (ECS), 1311

The Early Childhood Work Environment Survey (ECWES), 513

Early Education Center: in China, 1006

Early Head Start, **328–29**, 412; DEC of, 295; infant care and, 444; Osborn and, 574; parenting education and, 587, 590; PITC and, 666; SES and, 749; Zero to Three and, 858

Early infantile autism, 55

Early intervention (EI), **329–32**, 439; Abecedarian Program and, 2; Beethoven Project and, 620; in Brazil, 963; deaf children and, 235; DEC of, 295; disabilities and, 292; Down Syndrome and, 305; ecology of human development and, 336; FAS and, 370; in France, 1093; IDEA and, 440; intelligence and, 448; learning disabilities and, 481, 484; mental health and, 516; prekindergarten and, 771; in South Africa, 1227–30; technology

curriculum and, 223; visual impairment and, 827, 829

Early Language and Literacy Classroom Observation (ELLCO), 343

Early Learning Goals (ELGs), 1297

Early Learning Resource Unit (ELRU), 1216, 1223

Early literacy, 1130

Early reading, 239; grade retention and, 399

Early Reading First, 358; literacy curriculum and, 189

Early Symbolization and Transition to Literacy Project, 673

Early Years: An International Journal of Research and Development, **332**

Early Years Development and Care Partnerships (EYDCPs), 1283

Early Years Numeracy Project, 903

Early Years Trainers Anti-Racist Network (EYTARN), 1289

Earned Income Tax Credit (EITC), 10, 11, 651; CDF and, 126

Easter Seals: accreditation and, 8

ECA. *See* State of the Child and of the Adolescent

ECCD. *See* Early Childhood Care and Development Project

ECECD. *See* Early childhood education, care, and development

ECEJ. *See* Early Childhood Education Journal

ECERS-R. *See* Early Childhood Environment Rating Scale—Revised

ECME. *See* Early Childhood Music Education Commission

École maternelle, 1063, 1069

Ecological Congruence Assessment, 343

Ecological theory: of play, 628–29

Ecology: of childhood, 919; of human development, 85, **333–37**; in social studies, 214

The Ecology of Human Development: Experiments by Nature and Design (Bronfenbrenner), 86, 333

Economic Opportunity Act, 121

Economics: in social studies, 216

ECRP. *See* Early Childhood Research & Practice

ECRQ. *See* Early Childhood Research Quarterly

ECS. *See* Early Childhood Studies

ECSE. *See* Early childhood special education

Ecumenical Child Care, 623

ECWES. *See* The Early Childhood Work Environment Survey

Edelman, Marian Wright, 19

Edna McConnell Clark Foundation, 621

Edo period, 1164

Edo Shogunate, 1164

Educating Children with Autism, 56

Education Action Zones: in United Kingdom, 1291

Education Act of 1918, 575

Educational Act: in Czech Republic, 1018, 1044

Educational Equity Concepts, 385

Educational Guild, 575

Educational Handiwork Association, 575

Educational National Council Report of 1972: in Brazil, 944

Educational Psychology (Thorndike), 811

Education at a Glance, 573

Education by inducement, 1156

Education for All Handicapped Children Act, 20; deaf children and, 235; Down Syndrome and, 304; IEP and, 437

Éducation Nouvelle, 1077

Education of Man (Froebel), 376, 406

Education Policy Analysis, 573

Education Reform Act: in United Kingdom, 1288

Education 3-13, **338**

Education through environment theory, 1158

Education White Paper 1: in South Africa, 1196

Educatori, 1114

Educatrici, 1114, 1146

Edwards, Betty, 227

EECERA. *See* European Early Childhood Education Research Association

EECERJ. *See European Early Childhood Education Research Journal*

Effective Home-School Relations (Hymes, James), 425

The Effective Provision of Pre-School Education (EPPE), 1293

Effect of Reinforcement on Infant Performance Project, 395

Ego, 374

EI. *See* Early intervention

Einstein, Albert, 494

Elementarisation: of école maternelle, 1064

Elementary and Secondary Education Act (ESEA), 350, 757

Elementary Science Study (ESS), 409

The Elements of Psychology (Thorndike), 811

ELGs. *See* Early Learning Goals

Elias, Norbert, 161

Eliot, Abigail Adams, **338–40,** 515, 550; Owen, Grace, and, 575; Ruggles Street Nursery School Training School and, 705

Eliot-Pearson Children's School, 705

Elizabeth McCormick Memorial Fund: NAEYC and, 621

ELLCO. *See* Early Language and Literacy Classroom Observation

ELLs. *See* English-language learners

Ellsworth, Elizabeth, 694

ELRU. *See* Early Learning Resource Unit

Embodiment, 728

Emergency Assistance (EA), 809

Emergent curriculum, **181–82,** 909; progressive education and, 668; social constructivism and, 746

Emergent Curriculum (Jones), 181

Emergent literacy, 1130

Emerson, Ralph Waldo, 595

Emile (Rousseau), 704, 848

"Emmett Till," 121

Emotional attachments, 257

Emotional availability, 257

Emotional development, **256–59;** cerebral cortex and, 245; in China, 999–1001; Comenius and, 1026; developmental delay and, 273; gender stereotypes and, 382; parenting education and, 587; readiness and, 692; visual impairment and, 828. *See also* Curriculum; Development; Socioemotional development

Emotional disorders, 277–78

Emotional range, 802

Emotional restraint, 267

Emotion regulation, 257

Empathy, 265; fathers and, 364

Empire builder games, 147

Encouraging social relationships, 1170

Endorsed Foundation Degree, 1311

Engelmann Becker Corporation, 290

England. *See* United Kingdom

English as a Second Language (ESL), 76–77

English Immersion, 77

English-language learners (ELLs), 76, 713

Enhanced Home Visiting Demonstration, 329

Entering the College Zone, 547

Entrance ceremonies, 1165–66

Environmental assessments, **340–44**

Environmental contexts, 65

Environmental health, **344–47**

Environmental risk factors, 67; developmental delay and, 274

Environments: in social studies, 218; for visual art curriculum, 229

Epilepsy South Africa, 1230

EPPE. *See The Effective Provision of Pre-School Education*

Equilinguism, 1050

ERIC Clearinghouse on Elementary and Early Childhood Education, 320

Erikson, Erik, 322, **347–48;** creativity and, 167; developmental-interaction approach and, 280; gender formation and, 727; pedagogy and, 599; psychoanalysis and, 375; psychosocial development and, 674

Erikson Institute, 620

ERS. *See* Early Childhood Environment Rating Scales

Escola normal, 944

ESEA. *See* Elementary and Secondary Education Act

ESL. *See* English as a Second Language

ESS. *See* Elementary Science Study

The Essence of Kindergarten (Kurahashi), 1169, 1171

Essential learnings, 894

Ethical Behavior in Early Childhood (Katz and Ward), 663

Ethical principles, 948

Ethical rationale: in advocacy, 19

Ethic of care, 265

Ethics. *See* Professional ethics

Ethics in the Early Childhood Educator (Feeney and Freeman), 665

Ethnicity: in Brazil, 924–28; in Czech Republic, 1020; diversity in, 876; in France, 1068–72; in Japan, 1160; in United Kingdom, 1287–90. *See also* Race and ethnicity

Ethnographics, 679

Eugenics: in Brazil, 924–25

Eurhythmics, 557

European Commission Child Care Network, 1295
European Early Childhood Education Research Association (EECERA), 349
European Early Childhood Education Research Journal (EECERJ), **349–50**
European Social Fund, 1313
Evaluation. of parenting education, 587–88
Even Start, **350–51,** 358, 554–55
Every Child Matters, 1309
Evidence-based practices, 178
Evolutionary theory: of play, 629
"The Evolution of Human Intellect" (Thorndike), 811
Evolution, theory of, 170
Exceptional Children, 163
Exchange, **351**
Exclusion: in Australia, 876
Exercises of Practical Life, 527
Exosystems, 86, 334, 337
Expanded Programme of Immunisation, 1208
Experienced-based curriculum, 1172–73
Experimental analysis of behavior, 63
Experimental designs. *See* Quantitative Analyses/ experimental designs
Experimental Studies in Kindergarten Education, 416
Expressive children, 1127
Expressive language disorders, 278
Expressive play, 1178
Extended engagement: in qualitative research, 678
External advocacy, 21
Extracurricular activities: in China, 973
"Extreme aloneness," 55
EYDCPs. *See* Early Years Development and Care Partnerships
"The Eye of the Beholder" (Hawkins, Frances), 410
EYTARN. *See* Early Years Trainers Anti-Racist Network

FACES. *See Family and Child Experiences Study*
FaCS. *See* Department of Family and Community Services
Fading, 63
FAE. *See* Fetal alcohol effect
Failure to thrive, 279; developmental delay and, 274
Faith-based initiatives, 392, 393–94, 764
Faith *vs.* belief, 752–53
Families, **352–55**; accreditation and, 7–8; administration of, 310; in Brazil, 918; in China, 976–79; *The Creative Curriculum for Preschool* and, 164; culture and, 172; in Czech Republic, 1022, 1035–39; deaf children and, 236; in France, 1072–76; in Japan, 1164–68; peers and friends and, 616; psychoanalysis and, 374; in South Africa, 1211–15; theme of, 29
Families for Kids, 621
Family absence, 921
Family allowance funds. *See* Regional family allowance funds
Family and Child Experiences Study (FACES), 317
Family and Medical Leave Act, 531
Family child care (FCC), 242, **355–57**
Family Child Care Environment Rating Scale (FCCERS), 315
Family child care providers: child care and, 108
Family day care, 186; in Sweden, 1241
Family Day Care Rating Scale, 342
The Family Day Care Rating Scale (FDCRS), 356
Family differentiation, 16
Family home care, 963
Family literacy, **357–61**
Family Literacy Federal Work-Study Waiver, 358
Family Matters Project, 88
Family planning: in China, 973

Family resource centers: in Sweden, 1242
Family Resource Simulator, 548
Family systems theory (FST), 327, **361–64**
Family Therapy in Clinical Practice (Bowen), 363
FAPE. *See* Free appropriate public education
"Far-from-equilibrium" states, 41
FAS. *See* Fetal alcohol syndrome
Fatherhood Demonstration, 329
Fatherhood programs, 651
Fathers, **364–66**; in Japan, 1167; psychoanalysis and, 373; single, 531
FCC. *See* Family child care; Federal Communications Commission
FCCERS. *See* Family Child Care Environment Rating Scale
FDCRS. *See The Family Day Care Rating Scale*
Featherstone, Joseph, 569
Federal Communications Commission (FCC), 804
Federal Interagency Day Care Requirements (FIDCR), 769
Federation of Day Nurseries, 233
Feeney, Stephanie, 545, 665
Feldman, David Henry, 171, 673
Feminism, **366–68**; in Australia, 886; gender equality and, 906; Montessori and, 524; Wollstonecraft and, 847
Fertility. *See* Birthrate
Fetal alcohol effect (FAE), 368
Fetal alcohol syndrome (FAS), 68, **368–71**; SPD and, 723
FIDCR. *See* Federal Interagency Day Care Requirements
Filmore, Lily Wong, 78
Finances: in Brazil, 916–17, 927, 941; in China, 975–76; competition for, 313; in Czech Republic, 1019, 1032, 1061; in France, 1101–4; in South Africa, 1197–98, 1231–35; in Sweden, 1244; in United Kingdom, 1283–84, 1300–1301, 1312–15
Fine, Michelle, 694

FIPE. *See* Fonds d'Investissement Petite Enfance

First Discourse (Rousseau), 704

"First, do no harm," 761

The First Essay on the Principle of the Formation of Character (Owen, Robert), 577

First-person shooter (FPS) games, 147

First Steps to Numeracy, 903

Fisher Act, 513

Fisher, Ronald, 333

Fitness. *See* Physical development

Five Loves, 999

Five Million children—A Statistical Profile of Our Poorest Young Citizens, 548

Five-Year Plan for the Disabled, 1010

Flexibility, 203

Flexible design: in qualitative research, 679

Floor Time, 185

Florida Model, 395

FNS. *See* Food and Nutrition Service

Focus Newsletters, 40

Follow Through Program, 395

Fonds d'Investissement Petite Enfance (FIPE), 1098, 1102

Food and Nutrition Service (FNS), 849

Food Guide Pyramid for Young Children, 564

Food Stamps, 566

Ford Foundation, 620

Forebrain, 243

Foreign language. *See* Second-language acquisition

Formal education, 658

Formal operations, 266

Forman, George, 42

Formazione, 1145

Foster parents: parental substance abuse and, 582

Foucault, Michel, 693

Foundation for Child Development, 620

Foundation for Music-based Learning, 314

Foundation Phase, 1219

Foundation Stage Profile, 1298

4-2-1 Syndrome, 973

FPS. *See* First-person shooter games

Fragile-X disease, 277

Fraiberg, Selma, 516, 858

Frames of Mind (Gardner), 532, 536

France, 862, **1063–1109**; assessment in, 1085–88; culture, race, and ethnicity in, 1068–72; current trends in, 1097–1100; curriculum in, 1080–84; families in, 1072–76; finances in, 1101–4; inclusion in, 1092–97; infants in, 1088–96; pedagogy in, 1076–80; special education in, 1092–97; teacher education in, 1104–8

Frank, Lawrence, 133, 289, **371–72,** 422, 425

Frank Porter Graham Child Development Institute, 1

Free appropriate public education (FAPE), 437–38; IDEA and, 441

Freeman, Nancy K., 665

Free play, 467, 504, 958; in China, 991

"Free to Be You and Me," 384

Freinet, C., 1078, 1127

Freire, Paolo, 694

French language, 1082

Freud, Anna, **373–74**; developmental-interaction approach and, 280; Erikson and, 348; psychoanalysis and, 375; psychosocial development and, 674; Read and, 688; violence and, 823; war play and, 836

Freud, Sigmund, 322, **374–75,** 1023; creativity and, 167, 169; ecology of human development and, 333; Erikson and, 348; feminism and, 367; Hall and, 408; Isaacs and, 459; pedagogy and, 599; play and, 626; play therapy and, 645; sexuality and, 726

Friends, 614–15. *See also* Peers

Fröbelism, 1029

Froebel, Friedrich, 40, 69, 145, 322, **375–77,** 420, 523, 864, 958, 959, 1126; Blow and, 83; China and, 985; Czech Republic and, 1028; day nurseries and, 232; Dewey and, 289; embodiment and, 728; feminism and, 367; Hailmann, William, and, 405; Hall and, 407; IKU and, 457; Italy and, 1111; Japan and, 1168; kindergarten and, 466; Malaguzzi and, 487; Maslow and, 502; mathematics curriculum and, 193; Owen, Robert, and, 577; Peabody, Elizabeth, and, 596; pedagogy and, 598, 602; playgrounds and, 641; Pratt and, 653; progressive education and, 667; visual art curriculum and, 225; Wheelock and, 841; Wiggin and, 845

Froebel Institute, 405

Froebelseminariet, 1266

Froebel Society, 575

Fromberg, Doris, 545

Fromm, Erich, 501

Frontal cortex, 243

FST. *See* Family systems theory

Full coverage: in Sweden, 1242

Fuller, Margaret, 596

Fundação Dorina Nowill, 959

Fundação Laramara, 959

FUNDEB: in Brazil, 941

FUNDEF, 968; in Brazil, 916

Gabe method, 1168, 1169

Gage, Lucy, 289

Gakushyu-shido-yoryo, 1188

Galactosemia, 276

Gallas, Karen, 33

Galton, Francis, 446

Game play, 1177

Games with rules, 627

Gandhi's Truth (Erikson), 348

Gardner, Howard, 171, 673, 1116; child art and, 105; constructivism and, 152; MI and, 447, 532–37; visual art curriculum and, 226

Gardner, Pat, 687

Gastroesophageal reflux, 279

Gastrointestinal conditions, 279
Gates, Bill, 623
Gay, Geneva, 25, 694
Gay or Lesbian Parents, Children with, 378-82
Gays. *See* Homosexuals; Sexual orientation
GC. *See* General Curricula
GC ECE. *See* General Curriculum for Early Childhood Education
GEAR. *See* Growth, Employment and Redistribution
Gender, 382–87; formation of, 727-28; in play, 1121; play and, 628, 633-35; psychoanalysis and, 374; social studies and, 217; Whiting, John, and, 845. *See also* Feminism
Gender educators, 1257
Gender equity: in Australia, 906-8; in Brazil, 920, 966-70; in French parenthood, 1089; in Sweden, 1240, 1254-58
Gender in Early Childhood, 907
Gender play, 959
General Advice and Comments on Quality in Preschool in Sweden, 1246
General Curricula (GC), 1045
General curriculum, 179
General Curriculum for Early Childhood Education (GC ECE): in Czech Republic, 1045; in Czech Republic, 1020, 1033, 1036, 1039-43
General inspection of national education (IGEN), 1085
General Teaching Council (GTC), 1310
General teaching techniques: in Australia, 886
Generations of Hope, 17
Generative skill development, 199
Generativity: psychosocial theory and, 676
Genetic epistemology, 249
Genetics: disabilities and, 292
Genital stage, 727
Geography: in social studies, 214, 216
Geology: Montessori and, 527

Geometry, 196, 506; Montessori and, 527
Gergen, Kenneth, 742
German: as Czech foreign language, 1052
German measles, 279
Germany: Czec Republic and, 1028; ERS and, 319
Gesell, Arnold, 132, 322, 387–88, 454, 855; creativity and, 167; feminism and, 367; Hall and, 408; maturationism and, 509
Gestione sociale, 1112, 1134, 1141
Gestures, 53
Gibbons, Ira, 81
Gifted children, 388–91; CEC and, 163
Gilligan, Carol, 265; moral development and, 264, 266
Ginott, Haim, 69
Girardeau, Canary, 81
Giroux, Henry, 128, 694
Glaser, B.G., 680
Glasser, William, 70
Glossop, Robert, 334
Goals 2000, 759
Goal-setting: social cognitive theory and, 61
Golden Beads, 527
Goldenweiser, A.A., 558
Goldstein, Lisa, 266
Goodenough, Florence, 133, 226
Goodenough Harris Draw-A-Person Test, 226
Good Housekeeping, 585
Goodman, Nelson, 673
Goodman, Paul, 32
Good nature, 170
Goodness of fit, 258
Good practices, 1128-29
Goods and Services Tax (GST), 867
Good Start, Grow Smart, 391–95, 561; literacy curriculum and, 189; social curriculum and, 215; standards for, 757, 760
Gordon, Ira J., 395–96
Gordon, Thomas, 69
Governance: in social studies, 218

Grabbing: in domestic violence, 300
Grade retention, 396–400
Graduation ceremonies, 1165-66
Grand mal seizures, 276
Grandparents: in Australia, 881; in Czech Republic, 1022
Grant, Carl, 25
Graphic languages, 670
Grasping opportunities for intervention, 1170
Great Didactic (Comenius), 146
Greenberg, Mark, 186
Green, Judith, 712
Greenspan, Stanley, 858
Gross motor development: Abecedarian Program and, 1
Grounded theory studies, 680
Grouping, 212, 400–403; by age, 400-401; in China, 981; mixed-age, 401-2; size of, 764-65; in Sweden, 1245
Group orientation: in Japan, 1161
Group play therapy, 647
Groups: in social studies, 218
Growhouses, 1027
Growth, Employment and Redistribution (GEAR), 1201
Gruber, Howard, 170
Grumet, Madeline, 694
Gruppo Nazionale Nidi-Infanzia, 1113, 1140
GST. *See* Goods and Services Tax
GTC. *See* General Teaching Council
Guidance. *See* Behavior management and guidance
Guidelines for Developmentally Appropriate Practice, 694
Guidelines for the Curriculum Plan for Normal Schools for Preschool Teachers: in China, 1013
Guide to the Kindergarten and Moral Culture of Infancy (Peabody, Elizabeth), 595
Guilford, J.P., 169
Guilt: psychosocial theory and, 675
Gulick, Luther, Jr.: playgrounds and, 642
Gulou Kindergarten, 972

Habituation, 503
Hailmann, Eudora, **404–5**
Hailmann, William, 376, **405–7**
Haines, Henrietta, 83
Hale, Janice, 82
Hall, G. Stanley, 132, 374, **407–8**;
  Gesell and, 387; Hill and, 416;
  pedagogy and, 602
Haltes-garderies, 1065, 1093,
  1107
Hamer, Fannie Lou, 122
Handbook of Child Psychology,
  363
Handbook of Creativity
  (Sternberg), 169
*Handbooks for Public
  Playground Safety,* 644
Handicapped Children's Early
  Education Program (HCEEP),
  324, 648
Handicaps. *See* Disabilities
Handicrafts: in Japanese
  kindergarten, 1169
Hands-on experience: Almy and,
  23
Harlow, Harry, 501
Harper's, 289
Harré, Rom, 742, 743
Harris Foundation, 620
Hart, Betty, 688
Harvard Educational Review,
  20
Hatch, Orrin, 10
Hate crimes, 26
Hawk Catch Chickens, 991
Hawkins, David, **408–11**;
  constructivism and, 152
Hawkins, Frances P., 409–11,
  796–97
HCEEP. *See* Handicapped
  Children's Early Education
  Program
Head Start, 4, 20, 116, 307,
  411–14, 418, 656;
  Ashton-Warner and, 33;
  assessment and, 35; in
  Australia, 869;
  Bronfenbrenner and, 87;
  Bruner and, 89; CDF and, 125;
  CDGM and, 120; child care
  and, 107; day nurseries and,
  233; DEC of, 295; disabilities
  and, 293; early intervention

and, 330–31; ECSE and,
  323–24; Even Start and, 350;
  Good Start, Grow Smart and,
  391; Incredible Years and,
  185; infant care and, 444;
  intelligence and, 448; in Italy,
  1116; literacy curriculum and,
  189; Mitchell, Lucy, and, 517;
  NAEYC and, 541; NEGP and,
  552; nutrition and, 566;
  Osborn and, 574; parenting
  education and, 587, 590;
  PCER and, 654; pedagogy and,
  597; poverty and, 652; SES
  and, 749; social curriculum
  and, 215; standardized tests
  and, 755; standards and, 760;
  teacher certification and, 781.
  See also Early Head Start;
  National Head Start
  Association
Head Start Leadership Training
  Program, 512
Head Start National Reporting
  System (NRS), 755
Head Start-Planned Variations
  Program, 395
Head trauma: disabilities and,
  292
Health Action Zones: in United
  Kingdom, 1291
Health care: in Brazil, 939; SES
  and, 749; in South Africa,
  1207–11; in United Kingdom,
  1305–9; WHO and, 852
Healthy Child Care America, 544
Healthy Child Care America's
  Back to Sleep Campaign:
  NARA and, 540
Hearing: learning disabilities
  and, 482–83; loss in, 68;
  screening for, 34
Hearing impairment, 275; in
  China, 1010; literacy and, 489
Heath, Shirley Brice, 137, 712
Heavy metals: disabilities and,
  292
*Helping Children Cope with
  Crisis Guide,* 547
Hemiplegia: CP and, 96
Henry J. Kaiser Family
  Foundation, 801
Heqin Chen, 972, 1013

Here and Now Story Book
  (Mitchell, Lucy), 517
Herpes simplex, 279
HEW. *See* Department of Health,
  Education, and Welfare
Heynen, Jacques, 1051
HFCS. *See* High fructose corn
  syrup
HHS. *See* Department of Health
  and Human Services
Hierarchical theory of
  motivation, 501
Hierarchy of human needs, 501
Higashi, Motokichi, 169
High fructose corn syrup
  (HFCS), 565
High-need education areas
  (ZEP), 1064, 1074, 1080,
  1085, 1099
High/Scope Curriculum:
  pedagogy and, 598, 603
High/Scope Educational
  Research Foundation, 177,
  308, **414–15,** 427
High/Scope Perry Preschool
  Study, **415,** 1299; SES and, 749
Hildebrand, Verna, 545
Hilliard, Asa, 82
Hillis, Cora Bussey, 132
Hill, Patty Smith, **415–17,** 550;
  creativity and, 167; Dewey
  and, 289; feminism and, 367;
  Hall and, 408; IKU and, 457;
  McMillan, Margaret, and, 514;
  Pavlov and, 594; Pratt and,
  653; Wheelock and, 841;
  White and, 842
Hindbrain, 243
Hinde, Robert: Bowlby and, 84
HIPPY. *See* Home Instruction for
  Parents of Preschool
  Youngsters
Hiraganas, 1158
Hispanics: second-language
  acquisition by, 714; SES and,
  748
History: Montessori and, 527; in
  social studies, 214, 217
History of U.S. early childhood
  care and education, **417–23**
Hitting, 52–53; in domestic
  violence, 300
HIV. *See* AIDS

HLC. *See* Home Learning Center Approach to Early Stimulation

Hoiku, 1156

Hoikucn, 1189

Hoiku-en, 1184

Hoken Center, 1189

Holmes Partnership, 795

Home Instruction for Parents of Preschool Youngsters (HIPPY), 354

Home language use, 715

Home Learning Center Approach to Early Stimulation (HLC), 395

Homelessness: in Brazil, 934; parental substance abuse and, 582

Homeopathy: for ADHD, 51

Home-School Resource Teacher (HST), 2

Home visitation, 328–29

Homosexuals: as parents, **378–82**. *See also* Sexual orientation

Honesty, 267

Horizons of Early Childhood Professionals (Tsumori), 172

Horney, Karen, 501

Hospital class, 963

House Committee on Un-American Activities, 410

"How Gertrude Teaches Her Children" (Pestalozzi), 619

How to Help Your Child in School (Frank), 372

How to Tell Your Child About Sex (Hymes, James), 425

HPA. *See* Hypothalamic-pituitary-adrenal system

HST. *See* Home-School Resource Teacher

Hug-Hellmuth, H. von, 646

Hull-House, 13–14

Human capital rationale: in advocacy, 19

Human Development Index, 929

Humanistic education. *See* Open education

Human Nature Club (Thorndike), 811

Human rights: in South Africa, 1215–19

The Hundred Languages of Children, 562

Hunger: SPD and, 723

Hunt, J. McVicker, 323, **423–25,** 447

Hurd, Edith Thatcher, 517

Hygiene: in Brazil, 944; in China, 981; in Czech Republic, 1047

Hymes, Dell, 135

Hymes, James, L., Jr., **425–26**

Hyperactive/impulsive type, 48–52

Hyperactivity, 48–52. *See also* Attention deficit disorder/Attention hyperactivity disorder

Hyper-consumerism, 27

Hypersensitivity, 68

Hypnotherapy: for ADHD, 51

Hypothalamic-pituitary-adrenal (HPA) system, 244, 246

Hypothyroidism, 292

IA. *See* Increased activity

IASA. *See* Improving American School Act

IBGE. *See* Brazilian Institute of Geography and Statistics

ICCs. *See* Interagency Coordinating Councils

ICT. *See* Information and communications technologies

IDEA. *See* Individuals with Disabilities Education Act

IEA. *See* International Association for the Evaluation of Educational Achievement

IEA Preprimary Project, 4, **427–29**

IEP. *See* Individualized Education Plan

IERI. *See* Interagency Education Research Initiative

IFSP. *See* Individualized Family Service Plan; Infant Family Service Plan

IGEN. *See* General inspection of national education

IJEC. *See* International Journal of Early Childhood

IKU. *See* International Kindergarten Union

Imagination. *See* Creativity

Imaginative play, 213

IMCI. *See* Integrated Management of Childhood Illnesses

Imitation, 837

Immersion, 77; in bilingual education, 1051, 1225

Immigration, **429–32**; in Australia, 868, 876; biculturalism and, 73; in Brazil, 925; Chinese and, 78; conservatives and, 31; curriculum and, 179; in France, 1068; in Sweden, 1247–49; in United Kingdom, 1287

Imperial Education Act: in Czech Republic, 1028, 1053

Improving American School Act (IASA), 759

Improvisational play intervention, 607

Impulsiveness, 48–49

Inattentive type, 48

Incarcerated parents: children of, **432–35**

Incidental teaching, 64

Inclusion, 213, 343, **436–37**; in Brazil, 947, 961–65; early intervention and, 331; in France, 1064, 1092–97; in infant care, 445; in Japan, 1187–90; in South Africa, 1215–19; in United Kingdom, 1303; in visual art curriculum, 230

Increased activity (IA), 251

Incredible Years, 185

Independent normal schools: in China, 1013

Indicazioni, 1113

Indicazioni Nazionali per i Piani Personalizzati nella Scuola dell'Infanzia, 1128

Indigenous peoples: in Australia, 880; in Brazil, 927. *See also* Aborigines

INDIRE. *See Istituto Nazionale per la Documentazione e la Ricerca Educativa*

Individual advocacy, 21

Individual development: multi-age grouping and, 519–20; in social studies, 218

Individual-Difference, Relationship-Based Model (DIR), 185

Individual Family Service Plan, 58; ECSE and, 326; environmental assessment and, 343

Individualism: peers and friends and, 616; play and, 628

Individualized education plan (IEP), 343, **437–38**; in China, 1011; classroom environment and, 142; CP and, 97; early intervention and, 332; ECSE and, 326; environmental assessments and, 341; FAS and, 371; IDEA and, 440; inclusion and, 437; in Japan, 1189; transitions and, 815–16

Individualized Family Service Plan (IFSP), **438–40**; CP and, 96; deaf children and, 237; FAS and, 371

Individuals: in social studies, 218

Individuals with Disabilities Education Act (IDEA), 58, **440–42**; amendments to, 71; CDF and, 125; classroom environment and, 142; CP and, 96; curriculum and, 179; deaf children and, 235; developmental delay and, 274–75; disabilities and, 293; Down Syndrome and, 304; early intervention and, 331; ECSE and, 326; IEP and, 437; IFSP and, 438; inclusion and, 436; IQ and, 452; learning disabilities and, 481; teacher certification and, 781

Inducement in life, 1170–71

Industry: psychosocial theory and, 676

Inez, Maury, 435

Infance et Musique, 1070

Infant care, **442–46**; demand for, 1137–38; in Italy, 1137–41; in Japan, 1183–87

Infant Family Service Plan (IFSP), 815

Infant Health and Development Program, 293

Infant Mental Health Initiative, 859

Infant mortality: in Australia, 868; in Brazil, 931, 939; in China, 973; in Czech Republic, 1017; in France, 1073, 1077; in Japan, 1157; in South Africa, 1200, 1207

Infants: in CK, 910–11; in Czech Republic, 1055; in France, 1088–96

Infant School movement, 232; Owen, Robert, and, 577

Infant/toddler (IT), 343

Infant/Toddler Environment Rating Scale—Revised (ITERS-R), 315, 342

Infanzia, 1113, 1140

Infections, 279

Infectious diseases, 851

Information and communications technologies (ICT), 890, 898

Informatorium scholae maternae (Comenius), 1025, 1043, 1058

Informed Prace Collaboratives, 796

Initiation, response, evaluation (IRA), 135

Initiative: psychosocial theory and, 675

Innovations in Early Education: The International Reggio Exchange, 563

INP. *See* Integrated Nutrition Programme

Inquiry-based learning, 909

In Search of Understanding: The Case for Constructivist Classrooms, 152

Insegnanti, 1146

Inserimento, 1139, 1143–44

Institutional violence, 935

Institutions: in social studies, 218

Instituto Padre Chico, 959

Institut Universitaire de formation des maîtres (IUFM), 1105

Instructional Strategics in Infant Stimulation (ISIS), 395

Integral protection: doctrine of, 936

Integrated curriculum, 178

Integrated Management of Childhood Illnesses (IMCI), 1208

Integrated Nutrition Programme (INP), 1208

Integrated School Act: in Czech Republic, 1029

Integration: in adoptive families, 16

Integrity: psychosocial theory and, 676

Intellectual Growth of the Young Child (Isaacs), 460

Intelligence, **446–48**; creativity and, 169

Intelligence and Experience (Hunt), 424

Intelligence quotient (IQ), 81, 446, **449–53,** 453; creativity and, 169; DQ and, 274; gifted children and, 388; mental retardation and, 277; MI and, 532

Intelligence testing, 449, **453–55**

Intelligent tutoring systems (ITS), 799

Intent: bullying and, 90

Interacting with children with a warm heart, 1171

Interagency Coordinating Councils (ICCs), 331

Interagency Education Research Initiative (IERI), 197, **455,** 504; technology curriculum and, 223

Interdependence, 271; FST and, 361; play and, 628

Interdisciplinary Program for Leaders in Day Care, 23

Interethnic marriage, 686

Interference effects, 802

Internal advocacy, 21

International Association for the Evaluation of Educational Achievement (IEA), 427

International Children's Emergency Fund, 818

International Classification of Functioning, Disability, and Health, 965

International education exchanges, 1016

International Handbook of Child Care Policies and Programs, 863, 865

International Journal of Early Childhood (IJEC), **455–56,** 853

International Journal of Early Years Education, **456**

International Journal of Special Education, **456–57**

International Kindergarten Union (IKU), 416, 420, **457–58,** 807; Wheelock and, 841

International Perspectives, 314

International Play Association, 640

International Reading Association (IRA), 187, 284, **458,** 796

International Society for Music Education (ISME), 320

International Study Group for Early Child Care, 862

Interpersonal violence, 1204–5

Interracial marriage, 686

Interstate New Teacher Assessment and Support Consortium (INTASC), 789

Interview studies, 680

Intimacy, 271; psychosocial theory and, 676

Intra-family violence, 935

Intrapsychic conflicts, 626

An Introduction to the Theory of Mental and Social Measurements (Thorndike), 811

Introspection, 62

INVALSI. *See Istituto Nazionale per la Valutazionedel Sistema Scolastico Italiano;* National Institution for the Evaluation of the School System

I Passed This Way (Ashton-Warner), 33

IQ. *See* Intelligence quotient

IRA. *See* Initiation, response, evaluation; International Reading Association

Isaacs, Susan, **459–61;** developmental-interaction approach and, 279

ISIS. *See* Instructional Strategies in Infant Stimulation

ISME. *See* International Society for Music Education

Isolation, 278; psychosocial theory and, 676

Istituto Nazionale per la Documentazione e la Ricerca Educativa (INDIRE), 1149

Istituto Nazionale per la Valutazionedel Sistema Scolastico Italiano (INVALSI), 1149

Istituto Regionali per la Ricerca Educativa, 1149

IT. *See* Infant/toddler

Italy, 862, **1110–54;** curriculum in, 1125–30; education quality in, 1122–25; infant care in, 1137–41; literacy in, 1130–33; parents in, 1141–45; pedagogy in, 1115–18; play in, 1118–21; public policies in, 1150–54; socioemotional development in, 1133–36; teacher education in, 1145–50; toddlers in, 1137–41

Itard, Jean-Marc Gaspard, 523

ITERS-R. *See* Infant/Toddler Environment Rating Scale—Revised

ITS. *See* Intelligent tutoring systems

IUFM. *See* Institut Universitaire de formation des maîtres

JABA. *See Journal of Applied Behavior Analysis*

Jacklin, Carol, 384

Jackson, Phillip, 712

Jacques-Dalcroze method, 1181

Jaeger, Lloyd, 42

James, William, 810

Japan, **1155–93;** Chinese education and, 1013; culture in, 1160–63; curriculum in, 1172–76; families in, 1164–68;

group orientation in, 1161; inclusion in, 1187–90; infant care in, 1183–87; pedagogy in, 1168–72; play in, 1176–82; public policies in, 1191–93; special education in, 1187–90; special programs in, 1162–63; toddlers in, 1183–87

Jardinières d'enfants, 1107

JECTE. *See The Journal of Early Childhood Teacher Education*

Jefferson, Thomas, 499

JEI. *See Journal of Early Intervention*

Jenaplan Schools Association, 519

Jesuits: in Brazil, 936

Jidou-soudansho, 1189

Johnson, Harriet: developmental-interaction approach and, 279; Pratt and, 653

Johnson, Lyndon B., 121; Skinner and, 732; WIC and, 849

Johnson, Marietta: Naumburg and, 557

Jojo's Circus, 62

Jones, Elizabeth, 181

Jones, Fredric, 70

Jones, Kenneth, 369

Journal of Adolescent & Adult Literacy, 459

Journal of Applied Behavior Analysis (JABA), 64

Journal of Children and Media, 462

Journal of Early Childhood Research, **463**

The Journal of Early Childhood Teacher Education (JECTE), **463–64,** 546

Journal of Early Intervention (JEI), 65, 295, **464**

Journal of Experimental Psychology, 840

Journal of Research in Childhood Education, 40

The Journal of Special Education Leadership, 464

Journal of the Association, 349

Journal of the Experimental Analysis of Behavior, 63, 733

Journals, 40

Journey with Children (Hawkins, Frances), 410

Jumpstart, **464–65**

Jung, Carl: Hall and, 408

Junkai-Soudan, 1189

Junk food, 567

Kagan, Jerome, 806

Kahn, Alfred, 862

Kalff, Dora, 647

Kamehameha Early Education Program (KEEP), 74

Kamerman, Sheila, 862

Kamii, Constance: feminism and, 367

Kanji, 1158

Kanner, Leo, 55

Katakanas, 1158

Katz, Lilian G., 321, 663

Kazdin, Alan, 856

KEEP. *See* Kamehameha Early Education Program

Kellogg Foundation, 620

Kellogg, Rhoda: child art and, 105

Kenan Trust Family Literacy Project, 359

Kennedy, Edward, 550

Kennedy Krieger Institute, 95

Kergomard, Pauline, 1078, 1081

Key Learning Areas, 894

Keys to Quality, 555

KidPix, 230

Kids Count, 21

Kildee, Dale, 10

Kilpatrick, William, 524, 670

KinderCare, 307

Kindergarten, **466–69**; Blow and, 82; in Brazil, 958; child care and, 107; in China, 971; constructivism and, 154; in Czech Republic, 1028, 1043–44; DAP and, 283; day nurseries and, 232; Dewey and, 289; Froebel and, 69, 375; full day, 468–69; Hailmann, William, and, 406; Hall and, 407; Hill and, 415; IKU and, 457; in Japan, 1156, 1165–66; language

development and, 263; literacy and, 485; NAEYC and, 541; with overnight boarding, 975; PCER and, 654; Peabody, Elizabeth, and, 596; pedagogy and, 598, 602; peers and friends and, 616; progressive education and, 668; psychoanalysis and, 373; readiness and, 690; standardized tests and, 755; Temple and, 807; visual art curriculum and, 225; Waldorf, 834; Wiggin and, 845

The Kindergarten, 841

Kindergarten Culture in the Family and Kindergarten (Hailmann, William), 406

Kindergarten Department, 405

Kindergarten Education Guidelines: in China, 977, 986

The Kindergarten Messenger, 596, 846

Kindergarten Operation Regulations: in China, 977, 980

Kindergarten Provisional Guidelines: in China, 980

Kindergarten Provisional Operation Regulation, 971

Kindergarten Provisional Regulation: in China, 986

Kindergarten Provisional Teaching Outline: in China, 986

The Kindergarten Review, 416

King, Martin Luther, 123

Klein, Melanie, 84; psychoanalysis and, 375

Knowing and Education (Dewey), 289

Knowledge and Practices of Inclusion Early Childhood Education, 964

Knowledge-based learning, 912

Kohlberg, Lawrence, 265, **469–70**; moral development and, 264, 266; spiritual development and, 753

Kohn, Alfie, 69

Kokoro-mochi, 1170

Komenský, Jan Amos. *See* Comenius, John Amos

Koplow's therapeutic curriculum: pedagogy and, 598

Koryu-Kyoiku, 1188

Kozol, Jonathan, 20

Krauss, Ruth, 517

Ku Klux Klan, 121

Kung San, 589, 611

Kurahashi, Sozo, 1156, 1169–71

Kyoiku, 1156

Laboratory of Toys and Pedagogical Materials, 959

Laboratory schools, **471–73**; Parker and, 592

Laboratory studies, 802

LAD. *See* Language Acquisition Device

Ladies Home Journal, 585

Lady minder, 1053

Language: Abecedarian Program and, 1; in Australia, 868; in China, 987; classroom discourse and, 137–38; Comenius and, 1026; culture and, 173; in Czech Republic, 1048–53; deaf children and, 238–39; developmental delay and, 274; development of, **259–64**; DI and, 290; diversity in, 876; English, 1224; French, 1082; German, 1052; learning disabilities and, 481, 483; MI and, 535; parenting education and, 587; readiness and, 692; role-playing and, 958–59; science curriculum and, 208; screening for, 34; second, 175; social studies and, 217; in South Africa, 1231; subsystems of, 1049; symbolic, 230; television and, 803

Language Acquisition Device (LAD), 259

Language Acquisition Support System (LASS), 260

Language diversity, **473–77**

Language in Education Policy (LiEP), 1217, 1225

Language mixing, 716–17

Language of infancy, 256

Language of the turtle, 799

Lanham Act, 23
L'Année Psychologique, 80
LAP. *See* Lire à Paris
La Petite Academy, 307
LASS. *See* Language Acquisition Support System
Latinos: poverty and, 650
Laura Spelman Rockefeller Memorial (LSRM), 372, 422
Laurea, 1146
Law of Child Welfare: in Japan, 184
Law of Education: in France, 1064, 1074, 1085
Law of Guidelines and Bases of National Education (LDB), 944; in Brazil, 915, 939
Law of the Free Womb, 924
Law of the People's Republic of China on the Protection of Persons with Disabilities, 1010
Lazy eye, 275
LBA. *See* Brazilian Legion of Assistance
LD. *See* Learning disabilities
LDB. *See* Law of Guidelines and Bases of National Education
LEA. *See* Local education agency
Lead, 346, 383 and, 749
Leadership: advocacy and, 22. *See also* Advocacy and leadership
Leadership Connections, 513
Leadership Development Initiative, 859
Leadership Empowerment Action Project (LEAP), 95
League of Friends of the Blind, 1230
LEAP. *See* Leadership Empowerment Action Project
Learning: as teacher role, 600
Learning and Skills Council: in United Kingdom, 1313
Learning disabilities (LD), 277, 292, 479–84; incidence and characteristics of, 477–78; IQ and, 450; in Japan, 1188
Learning disorders, 277
Learning environment, 212
Learning to Read and Write: Developmentally Appropriate

Practices for Young Children, 187, 284
LEAs. *See* Local Education Authorities
Least restrictive environment (LRE), 437; IDEA and, 442
Leavitt, Robin, 367
Lectura y Vida, 459
Leeds, Jo Alice: child art and, 105
Lee, Joseph: playgrounds and, 642
Legend of three-year-old child, 1183
Leggi di iniziativa popolare, 1152
Leisure-time centers, 1241
Leiter International Performance Scale-Revised, 452
Lejeune, Jerome, 303
Lemish, Dafna, 462
Lemoine, Paul, 368
Leonard and Gertrude (Pestalozzi), 619
Leont'ev, A., 495, 959
Lesbians. *See* Homosexuals
Letters on Education (Macaulay), 848
Levin, Diane, 127
LeVine, Robert: culture and, 174
Levin, Kurt, 333
Levin, Tom, 121
Lewin, Kurt, 794; developmental-interaction approach and, 280
Lewis, Samela, 493
Lexical subsystem: of language, 1049
Lèzine, Iréne, 1077, 1113
Liberty, Equality, Fraternity, 1068
Libido, 727
Licensing: of child care, 12; in France, 1065, 1105; NARA and, 540. *See also* State licensing standards
Licensing Curriculum, 540
Licensors: case loads of, 768–69
Lichter, Harlene, 120
LiEP. *See* Language in Education Policy
Life Education, 972
Lifelong learning, 910
Lifeworld, 875

Lincoln, Abraham, 14
Linder, Eileen, 752
Lindfors, Judith, 600
Linguistically diverse students, 76
Linguistically isolated children: language development and, 261
Linguistic minority students, 76
Linkletter, Art, 248, 254
Lire à Paris (LAP), 1071
LISP, 150
Literacy, **485–88**; academics and, 3; in boys, 385; child care and, 107; in China, 1002–5; computer-enhanced curriculum and, 222; creative dimension of, 893; creativity and, 892–93; critical dimension of, 892; culture and, 172; curriculum and, 178, **186–92**; family, **357–61**; foundational dimension of, 892; Good Start, Grow Smart and, 392; human dimension of, 892; IRA and, 458; in Italy, 1130–33; kindergarten and, 468; language diversity and, 476; learning disabilities and, 483; Project Approach and, 672; Reggio Emilia and, 697; science curriculum and, 208; in Sweden, 1272–75; 3D view of, 898
Literacy and disabilities, **488–93**
Literacy Bill of Rights, 491–92
Literacy Involves Families Together Act, 350
Literature. Montessori and, 527
Little Red Riding Hood, 128
Lives on the Line: American Families and the Struggle to Make Ends Meet, 548
Local education agency (LEA), 438
Local educational contracts (CEL), 1080
Local Education Authorities (LEAs): in United Kingdom, 1304
Local Government Act: in Sweden, 1258
Locational expressions, 261

Locke, John: playgrounds and, 641

The Logic of Action (Hawkins, Frances), 410

Logo, 799

Longitudinal studies, 802; on temperament, 805

Longstaff, Ursula, 84

Looping, 213

Lorenz, Konrad: Bowlby and, 84

Loss (Bowlby), 85

Lourie, Reginald, 858

Lovaas, Ivar, 64

Love, 502; psychosocial theory and, 676; Rousseau and, 703

Love to Read Early Literacy Project, 547

Lowenfeld, Viktor, 104, **493–94**; visual art curriculum and, 225

Loyalty, 267, 271

LRE. *See* Least restrictive environment

LSRM. *See* Laura Spelman Rockefeller Memorial

Lubeck, Sally, 862

Luria, A.R., **494–96,** 959

Luther, Martin: playgrounds and, 641

Lyotard, Jacques, 693

MA. *See* Mental age

Macaulay, Catherine, 848

Maccoby, Eleanor, 383–84

Macrosystems, 86, 334

Magister, 1057

Mahler, Barbara Child, 687

Mainstreaming, 436

Make-believe play, 631

Making Learning Visible (MLV), 298, 674

Making the Most of Out-of-School Time (MOST), 708

Malaguzzi, Loris, 43, 410, **497–99,** 696, 700, 864, 1127, 1140; Australia and, 885; creativity and, 171; symbolic languages and, 777

Malaria: WHO and, 852

Managers, 308

Manifesto on Values, Education and Democracy, 1217

Mann, Horace, **499–501**

Mann, Marlis, 545

Mann, Mary Tyler Peabody, 595

Manual and visual children, 1127

Maori children, 32

Map and Track: State Initiatives for Young Children and Families, 548

Marbeau, F., 1076

Marenholz-Bulow, Bertha von, 377

Marketing: administration of, 310–11

Market-oriented strategy: in Czech Republic, 1059

Marshall Plan, 818

Marsuno, Clara, 1168

Marxism, 1030

Maslow, Abraham, **501–2,** 702

Massachusetts School for the Blind, 322

Massively multiplayer role playing games (MMRPG), 147

Materials: for visual art curriculum, 229

Maternal leave: in France, 1090

Maternal mental health: disabilities and, 292

Maternity school: in Czech Republic, 1028

Materská škola, 1018

Mathematica Policy Research (MPR), 655

Mathematics, **502–9**; academics and, 3; cognitive development and, 251; constructivism and, 153; curriculum for, **192–98**; DAP and, 285; DI and, 290; learning disabilities and, 483; MI and, 535; Montessori and, 527; social constructivism and, 746; standardized tests and, 755; technology and, 798. *See also* Numeracy

Mathematics curriculum. *See* Curriculum

A Matter of Consequences (Skinner), 733

Maturationism, **509–12**

MC. *See* Middle childhood

MCAA. *See* Military Child Care Act

McCarthy, Cameron, 694

McCormick Tribune Center for Early Childhood Leadership, **512–13**

McCormick Tribune Foundation, 622

McFee, June, 227

M-CHAT. *See* Modified Checklist for Autism in Toddlers

McLaren, Peter, 694

McLaughlin, Barry, 715

McMillan, Margaret, 339, **513–14**; creativity and, 167; White and, 842

McMillan, Rachel, **514–15**; creativity and, 167; White and, 842

MDG. *See* Millennium Development Goals

MDS. *See* Ministry of Social Development

Mead, George Herbert, 333

Mead, Margaret: culture and, 174

Meaning systems, 173

Measles, 279

Measurement, 507

Measurement and patterning, 196

MEC. *See* Ministry of Education

Media: for parenting guidance, 589; play and, 630; in symbolic languages, 778; war play and, 838–39. *See also* Children's media; *Journal of Children and Media*

Mediator: in play, 639

Medicaid, 651

Meeting the Highly Qualified Teachers Challenge, 561

"Meeting the Needs of Young Children," 621

Meiji Restoration, 1164

Melting pot, 26

MENC. *See* Music Educators National Conference

Mental Affections of Childhood and Youth (Down), 303

Mental age (MA), 453

Mental health, **515–16**

Mental retardation, 277; CEC and, 163; in China, 1010; literacy and, 489

Mentoring, 399

Merriam, Eve, 517

Merrill-Palmer Motherhood and HomeTraining School, 515
Mesosystems, 86, 334, 337
"Messing About in Science" (Hawkins, David), 410
Meta-analysis, 802, 803
The Method of Kindergarten Education (Higashi), 169
Mexican Americans, 26
MEXT. *See* Ministry of Education, Culture, Sports, Science and Technology
MI. *See* Multiple intelligences
Michiko (Empress), 1162
Microsystems, 86, 334
Microworlds, 230
Midbrain, 243
Middle childhood (MC), 343
Migratory labor systems, 861
Military Child Care Act (MCAA), 241
Millennium Development Goals (MDG), 819; WHO and, 852
Miller, George, 10
Miller, Janet, 694
Mind/body techniques: for ADHD, 51
The Mind of Bringing up Children (Kurahashi), 1169
Mindstorms. Children, computers and powerful ideas (Papert), 150
Minimum highest entry, 784
Ministries of Health, Social Affairs, Youth and Sport: in France, 1063, 1067
Ministry of Education: in China, 974; in France, 1097
Ministry of Education (MEC): in Brazil, 914
Ministry of Education and Science: in Sweden, 1243, 1266
Ministry of Education, Culture, Sports, Science and Technology (MEXT), 1165, 1187, 1191; in Japan, 1157
Ministry of Education, Youth and Sport: in Czech Republic, 1018
Ministry of Health: in China, 974
Ministry of Health and Welfare: in Sweden, 1243, 1266

Ministry of Health, Labor and Welfare: in Japan, 1165
Ministry of Social Affairs: in France, 1086, 1097
Ministry of Social Development (MDS): in Brazil, 916–17, 939
Ministry of Social Welfare: in Japan, 1184
Ministry of Welfare and Labor: in Japan, 1157
Minor Legal Code: in Brazil, 936
Minuchin, Patricia, 363
Minuchin, Salvador, 363
"Mississippi Burning," 122
Mississippi Child Development Program, 33
Mitchell, George, 11
Mitchell, Lucy Sprague, 61, 279, 372, **517–18**; documentation and, 296; Pratt and, 653
Mitchell, Wesley Clair, 372
MIT Logo Group, 150
Mixed-age grouping, 212, **518–23**
MLV. *See* Making Learning Visible
MMRPG. *See* Massively multiplayer role playing games
Modeling, 734–36
Models: of parenting education, 586–87
Modesty, 267
Modified Checklist for Autism in Toddlers (M-CHAT), 57
Modulation for effect: parental substance abuse and, 580–81
Mold, 346
Mondale, Walter, 88
Mong Yang Yuan, 984
Montessori education, 308, **525–29,** 1111; accreditation for, 6; in Czech Republic, 1033; day nurseries and, 232; Erikson and, 348; play in, 1135; Ruggles Street Nursery School Training School and, 705; social curriculum and, 215
Montessori, Maria, 323, **523–25,** 864, 958, 1113, 1127; Australia and, 884; China and, 985; feminism and, 367; France and, 1078; Freud,

Anna, and, 373; Kurahashi and, 1169; mixed-age grouping and, 518; Naumburg and, 557; pedagogy and, 598; Pratt and, 654
Moore, Evelyn, 82
Moral absolutism, 264
Moral development, **264–68**; Kohlberg and, 469; stages of, 266
Moral education: public schools and, 499
Morality: culture and, 173; ethics and, 662–63; in Sweden, 1276–79
Moral reasoning, 267
Moral relativism, 264, 266
Moral socialization, 267
Moravcik, Eva, 665
Morphographs, 290
Morphology, 138
Morpho-syntactic subsystem: of language, 1049
Morrison, Phillip, 409
MOST. *See* Making the Most of Out-of-School Time
Mother Care: day nurseries and, 233
Mother-, Play- and Nursery Songs (Froebel), 376
Mothers, **529–32**
Motivation: creativity and, 888; Maslow and, 501; self-esteem and, 720
Motivation and Experience (Hunt), 424
Motor development, 1134; Abecedarian Program and, 1; learning disabilities and, 482; readiness and, 692; screening for, 34; visual impairment and, 828
Mott Foundation, 620
Mountain View Center for Environmental Education, 409
Mouse Paint, 210
Movies: violence in, 821
MPR. *See* Mathematica Policy Research
Multi-accueils, 1091, 1102
Multi-Age Association, 519
Multi-age grouping: in Australia, 895

Multicare services, 1066
Multicultural education: in Australia, 874–76; in Brazil, 927, 947; in Italy, 1114–15; superficial, 877; in United Kingdom, 1287. *See also* Antibias/multicultural education
Multiculturalism: culture and, 175. *See also* Biculturalism
Multidimensional tasks, 904
Multiliteracies: in Australia, 897–901; map of, 899
Multimedia, 897
Multiple intelligences (MI), 39, 171, 447, **532–37**; PZ and, 673
Multisystem Developmental Disorder, 56
Mumford, Lewis, 558
Muscular dystrophy, 276
Muscular strength, 203
Museums. *See* Children's museums
Music and movement, 29, 557; in China, 992–98; Comenius and, 1026; in Japanese kindergarten, 1168, 1180
Music curriculum, **198–201**
Music Educators National Conference (MENC), 320
Music for children (Orff), 1181
Muslims, 26–27; in France, 1069
Muth, Guts, 641
Myelination, 244, 246
Myers, Hector, 82
Myers, Robert, 863
My Mother and I Are Getting Stronger (Inez), 435
Myoclonic seizures, 276
Myrdal, Alva, 853
Myths: culture and, 173

NAACP. *See* National Association for Advancement of Colored People
NACCRRA. *See* National Association of Child Care Resource and Referral Agencies
NAECSSDE. *See* National Association of Early Childhood Specialists in State Departments of Education

NAECS/SDE. *See* National Association of Early Childhood Specialists in State Departments
NAECTE. *See* National Association of Early Childhood Teacher Educators
NAECTEF. *See* NAECTE Foundation
NAECTE Foundation (NAECTEF), 546
NAEYC. *See* National Association for the Education of Young Children
NAFCC. *See* National Association of Child Care
Nakamura, Masanao, 1168
NALS. *See* National Association of Laboratory Schools
NAMBLA. *See* North American Man-Boy Love Association
Name calling, 91–92
NANE. *See* National Association for Nursery Education
Nanjing Normal University, 1014
NARA. *See* National Association for Regulatory Administration
NARA Licensing Magazine, 541
Narrative, 90, **538–40**
Narrative frameworks for thinking, 631
Narrative studies, 680
Narrative text environment, 1274
NASBE. *See* National Association of State Boards of Education
NASPE. *See* National Association for Sport and Physical Education
The Nation, 289
National Academy of Sciences, 206
National Adoption Information Clearinghouse, 15, 17
National Adult Literacy Survey, 492
The National Affiliate Network, 547
National After-School Association, 708
National Agency for Education: in Sweden, 1245

National Agency for Higher Education: in Sweden, 1268
National Agency for School Improvement: in Sweden, 1245
National Agenda for Early Childhood, 869
National Association for Advancement of Colored People (NAACP): NBCDI and, 547
National Association for Nursery Education (NANE), 340, 842
National Association for Regulatory Administration (NARA), **540–41**
National Association for Sport and Physical Education (NASPE), 202
National Association for the Education of Young Children (NAEYC), 3, 21, 377, 421, **541–42**; accreditation by, 5–6, 242; antibias curriculum and, 27; assessment and, 34; black caucus of, 81–82; child abuse and, 101–3; CHIPS and, 435; classroom discourse and, 138; corporal punishment and, 162; curriculum and, 176, 180; DAP and, 282; early intervention and, 331; ECRQ by, 321; ECSE and, 325; Eliot and, 340; Elizabeth McCormick Memorial Fund and, 621; emotional development and, 184; environmental assessment and, 341; ethics and, 662; Hill and, 289; IKU and, 457; inclusion and, 437; literacy curriculum and, 187; mental health and, 516; NANE and, 842; NARA and, 540; playgrounds and, 644; Read and, 688; sexuality and, 729; standardized tests and, 756; teacher certification and, 780; teacher education and, 788; *Young Children* and, 856
National Association for the Education of Young Children Academy of Early Childhood

Program Accreditation, 542–43

National Association of Child Advocates, 21

National Association of Child Care (NAFCC), 356

National Association of Child Care Resource and Referral Agencies (NACCRRA), 543–45

National Association of Early Childhood Specialists in State Departments (NAECS/SDE), 35; curriculum and, 180; DAP and, 284

National Association of Early Childhood Specialists in State Departments of Education (NAECSSDE), 756

National Association of Early Childhood Teacher Educators (NAECTE), 463, 545–46, 664

National Association of Laboratory Schools (NALS), 473

National Association of State Boards of Education (NASBE), 781

National Black Child Development Institute (NBCDI), 546–47

National Care and Education Guideline for Children under Three: in China, 980

National Center for Children in Poverty (NCCP), 112, 547–49; mental health and, 516; SES and, 748

National Center for Educational Statistics, 21

National Center for Family Literacy (NCFL), 359

National Center for Infants Toddlers and Families, 56

National Center for Maternal Schools, 1111

National Center for Measurement in Education (NCME), 756

National Child Care Accreditation Council, 870

National Childcare Accreditation Council (NCAC), 869

National Child Care Association: NARA and, 540

National Child Care Information Center (NCCIC), 762

The National Child Care Staffing Study, 95, 317

National Childcare Strategy: in United Kingdom, 1283, 1291

National Coalition for Campus Children's Centers (NCCCC), 473, 549–50

National Commission for the Rights of Children: ACEI and, 40

National Commission on Children, 621

National Commission on Excellence in Education (NCEE), 758

National Commission on Special Needs in Education and Training: in South Africa, 1228

National Commission on Teaching and America's Future, 62, 787, 791

National Committee on Education Support Services: in South Africa, 1228

National Committee on Nursery Schools, 550–51

National Congress of Mothers, 585

National Coordination for the Integration of Disabled People (CORDE), 965

National Council for Accreditation of Teacher Education (NCATE), 41, 551–52, 782, 788

National Council of Churches, 123

National Council of Primary Education, 458, 808

National Council of Teachers of English (NCTE), 795

National Council of Teachers of Mathematics, 195

National Council of Women's Rights (CNDM), 967

National Council on Education (CNE): in Brazil, 916

National Curricular Guidelines for Early Childhood Education (DCNEI), 948, 955; in Brazil, 917, 940

National Curricular References for ECE (RCNEI), 949, 969

National Curriculum (NC), 1045

National Curriculum Guideline: in China, 980

National Curriculum Standards for Kindergartens, 1173–74, 1180; in Japan, 1171

National Doll Campaign, 544

National Down Syndrome Society, 304

National ECD Audit: in South Africa, 1235–36

National Educational Plan: in Brazil, 916

National Education Association (NEA), 132; Kindergarten Committee of, 596; Kindergarten Department of, 405

National Education Goals, 20

National Education Goals Panel (NEGP), 36, 552–54; readiness and, 691–92; social curriculum and, 215; standards and, 758

National Electronic Injury Surveillance System, 644

National Even Start Association (NESA), 554–55

National family allowance fund (CNAF), 1065, 1086, 1101

National Family and Parenting Institute: in United Kingdom, 1307

National Family Education Association: in China, 978

National Food Consumption Survey: in South Africa, 1208

National Governor's Association (NGA), 758

National Guidelines for Special Education in Basic Education, 962

National Head Start Association (NHSA), 555–56

National Health Service: in United Kingdom, 1306

National Healthy Schools Standard: in United Kingdom, 1307

National Household Education Survey (NHES), 656; school-age care and, 707

National Infant and Toddler Child Care Initiative, 859

National Institute for Early Childhood Professional Development, **556–57**

National Institute for Early Education Research (NIEER): curriculum and, 180; prekindergarten and, 773

National Institute of Direct Instruction (NIFDI), 290

National Institute of Mental Health, 363

National Institute of Special Education (NISE), 1190

National Institutes of Health (NIH): NBCDI and, 547; physical development and, 202

National Institution for the Evaluation of the School System (INVALSI), 1122

National Investment for the Early Years (NIFTeY), 869

National Kindergarten Association, 289

National Mental Health Association, 516

National Movement in Defense of Disabled People's Rights, 961

National Network of Continuing Education of Teachers in Basic Education: in Brazil, 946

National Occupational Standards (NOS), 1309

National Occupational Standards in Children's Care, Learning and Development, 1310

National Professional Qualification in Integrated Centre Leadership (NPQICL), 1312

National Qualifications Framework (NQF), 1197, 1235, 1310

National Recreation and Park Association (NRPA), 642

National Regulations for the Qualification of Program Directors: in China, 981

National Reporting System, 755

National Report on the State of Early Childhood Upbringing, Education and Care of Pre-school Age in the Czech Republic, 1037

National Research Council: assessment and, 37; literacy curriculum and, 190; quantitative analyses and, 681

National Resource Center for the Health and Safety of Children in Child Care (NRC), 762

National School Reform Faculty (NSRF), 795

National Science Foundation, 210

National Service Framework (NSF), 1308

National Strategy for Screening, Identification, Assessment and Support: in South Africa, 1228

National Teacher Recruitment Campaign, 561

National testing. *See* Standardized tests

National vocational qualification (NVQ), 1310

National Women's Federation: in China, 974

National Writing Project, 795

A Nation at Risk, 572, 758

Native Americans: child abuse and, 98; Erikson and, 348; Even Start and, 350

Natural communities of reinforcement, 64

Natural settings: in qualitative research, 678

Naumburg, Margaret, **557–58**

NBCDI. *See* National Black Child Development Institute

NC. *See* National Curriculum

NCAC. *See* National Childcare Accreditation Council

NCATE. *See* National Council for Accreditation of Teacher Education

NCCCC. *See* National Coalition of Campus Children's Centers

NCCIC. *See* National Child Care Information Center

NCCP. *See* National Center for Children in Poverty

NCEE. *See* National Commission on Excellence in Education

NCFL. *See* National Center for Family Literacy

NCLB. *See* No Child Left Behind Act

NCME. *See* National Center for Measurement in Education

NCTE. *See* National Council of Teachers of English

NEA. *See* National Education Association

Neglect, **97–100,** 272; attachment and, 47; behavior disorders and, 278; disabilities and, 292; early intervention and, 330; FAS and, 370; parenting education and, 584; prevention of, **101–3;** SES and, 749

Negotiated curriculum, **182**

Neighbourhood nurseries, 1282

Neighbourhood Renewal Fund, 1313

Nelson, Waldemar, 620

Neoliberal reforms: in Brazil, 967–68

Neonatal intensive care unit (NICU), 815

NESA. *See* National Even Start Association

NESB. *See* Non-English speaking background

Neubauer, Peter, 858

Neuromotor disorders, 276

Neurons, 244

New Beginnings, 62

New Deal for Communities, 1313; in United Kingdom, 1291

New Education, 404–5, 406

New Institution for the Formation of Character, 578

New Opportunities Fund, 1313

News: violence on, 821

New schools movement, 557

Newsletters, 40

A New View of Society (Owen, Robert), 577

New York State School Age Care Credential (NYS SACC), 710

Next Step Advanced Leadership Training, 513

NGA. *See* National Governor's Association

NGOs. *See* Nongovernmental organizations

NHES. *See* National Household Education Survey

NHSA. *See* National Head Start Association

NHSA Dialog, **559–60**

NICU. *See* Neonatal intensive care unit

Nidi, 1111, 1112, 1133–34

Nidi d'infanzia, 1137

NIEER. *See* National Institute for Early Education Research

Nicnhius, Albert, 527

NIFDI. *See* National Institute of Direct Instruction

NIFTeY. *See* National Investment for the Early Years

NIH. *See* National Institutes of Health

1968 generation, 1065

NISE. *See* National Institute of Special Education

Nixon, Richard: veto by, 9, 110, 417

Nobel Prize: by Addams, 14; Montessori and, 525; by Pavlov, 594

Noble savage, 704

No Child Left Behind Act (NCLB), 421, **560–62**; assessment and, 35; bilingual education and, 76; Bruner and, 90; CDF and, 125; classroom discourse and, 139; corporal punishment and, 158; embodiment and, 728; family literacy and, 358; Good Start, Grow Smart and, 391; IEP and, 438; laboratory schools and, 473; language diversity and, 476; literacy curriculum and, 189; PCER and, 654; play and, 632; progressive education and, 667; reconceptualists and, 695; standardized tests and,

755; standards and, 759; teacher certification and, 781; teacher education and, 791

Noddings, Nel, 265–66

Noncompliance: with Good Start, Grow Smart, 393

Nondirective play therapy, 646

Non-English speaking background (NESB), 876

Nongovernmental organizations (NGOs): in Brazil, 938; in Czech Republic, 1020; in South Africa, 1195, 1216, 1223, 1230; in United Kingdom, 1285

Nonverbal communication: in music curriculum, 200

Nonverbal period, 715

Nonviolence: in Brazil, 938; Comenius and, 1026

Normalcy, 962

Normalization, principle of, 66

Normal Superior, 945

Normative age/stage theory: creativity and, 167

North American Man-Boy Love Association (NAMBLA), 730

North American Reggio Emilia Alliance (NAREA), **562–63**

Northern Ireland. *See* United Kingdom

NOS. *See* National Occupational Standards

Nover, Robert, 858

NPQICL. *See* National Professional Qualification in Integrated Centre Leadership

NQF. *See* National Qualifications Framework

NRC. *See* National Resource Center for the Health and Safety of Children in Child Care

NRPA. *See* National Recreation and Park Association

NRS. *See* Head Start National Reporting System

NSF. *See* National Service Framework

NSRF. *See* National School Reform Faculty

Nuclear families, 861; in Japan, 1159

Numbers, 503

Numeracy: in Australia, 902–5; in Japan, 1171

Numeracy for All Report, 903

Numeration Activities, 527

Nuovi Orientamenti, 1113

Nuovi Orientamenti per la Scuola Materna, 1128

Nursery Logic (Wiggin), 847

Nursery or primordial, practical, self-explanatory, versatile teaching to the little ones for real perfection of reason and cultivation of the heart point to reading, arithmetics and technical drawing for teachers, fosterers and parents (Svoboda), 1027

The Nursery School (McMillan, Margaret), 339, 514

The Nursery School: A Human Relationships Laboratory (Read), 687

Nursery School Association, 575

Nursery School Education (Owen, Grace), 575, 727

Nursery schools: in Czech Republic, 1018, 1019–20, 1032, 1044; in Italy, 1126; in United Kingdom, 1282. *See also* Owen, Grace

Nurses, 1107; teachers as, 1055

Nutrition, **563–66**; in Brazil, 931–32, 944; in Czech Republic, 1047; developmental delay and, 274; parental substance abuse and, 580; SES and, 749; in South Africa, 1207

NVQ. *See* National vocational qualification

NYS SACC. *See* New York State School Age Care Credential

OBE. *See* Outcomes based education

Obedience, 267

Obesity, 563, **567–69**; SES and, 749; television and, 803

Observation: as assessment, 36

Observational learning, 735

Observing: as teacher role, 600

Occupational therapists, 54
OECD. *See* Organisation for Economic Co-Operation and Development; Organisation for Economic Co-operation and Development
Oedipal stage, 727
OEEC. *See* Organisation for European Economic Cooperation
OEO. *See* Office of Economic Opportunity
Office for Civil Rights, 21
Office of Economic Opportunity (OEO), 121; Head Start and, 412
OMEP. *See* World Organisation for Early Childhood Education
Omoiyari, 1162
Onchocerciasis, 827
One-child policy, 1005; in China, 973
O'Neill, Barbara, 607
Onlooker, 593
ONMI. *See* Opera Nazionale Maternità e Infanzia; Opera Nazionale Maternità e Infanzia
Open education, **569–72**; general features of, 570–71
Open-ended curriculum, 227
Open preschools, 1242
Open University BA in Childhood: in United Kingdom, 1286
Opera Nazionale Maternità e Infanzia (ONMI), 1111, 1151
Operants, 63
Operating Parenting Edge, 329
Opportunity for All, 1291
Oral stage, 727
Orbis Pictus (Comenius), 145
Order of School Education: in Japan, 1168
Ordinal Scales of Psychological Development, 424
Ordinance on Quality Reports in the Education System: in Sweden, 1245
Orff, K., 1181
Organic Law of Social Assistance: in Brazil, 939
Organisation for Economic Co-operation and

Development (OECD), 572–74, **863**; in Czech Republic, 1033
Organisation for European Economic Cooperation (OEEC), 572
Organizational advocacy, 21
Organized child care facilities: child care and, 108
Organizing activities, 725
Orientamenti, 1113, 1120
Orientamenti per la Scuola Materna, 1128
Original Stories from Real Life (Wollstonecraft), 848
Osborn, D. Keith, **574–75**
Otitis media, 275
OT/SI. *See* Sensory integration-based occupational therapy
Our Gracie Aunt (Woodson), 435
Outcomes based education (OBE), 1198
Outlook, 409
Overprotection, 1159
Owen, Grace, 513, **575–77**, 727
Owen, Robert, **577–78**
Ozone, 345

PAA. *See* Playground Association of America
PACE. *See* Parent and Child Education Program
Packard Foundation, 22, 622
PAJE. *See* Prestation d'Accueil du Jeune Enfant
Paley, Vivian Gussin, 33, 128, 272, 539, 612, 638; pedagogy and, 599–600
Palimpsest, 910
Pan-African Reading for All, 458
Papert, Seymour, 150, 799
Paradigmatic framework for thinking, 631
Parallel play, 593, 614
Pardos, 925
Parens patriae, 585
Parental drug abuse: prenatal exposure to, 581–82
Parental substance abuse, **579–84**; interventions and, 582–83

Parent and Child Education Program (PACE), 359
Parent Central, 545
Parent Child Centers, 396
Parent Committee: in China, 978
Parent Education Program (PEP), 395
The Parent Empowerment Program, 547
Parenting: child's self-esteem and, 719; education for, 531; peers and friends and, 616; social competence and, 739–40; styles of, 268
Parenting education, **584–89**
Parent ratings: as assessment, 36
Parents: child's attachment with, 47; in Italy, 1141–45; in Sweden, 1250–54
Parents and parent involvement, **589–91**
Parent Teacher Association (PTA), 585
Parker, Francis, 416, **592**; progressive education and, 667
Parker, Samuel, 807
Park, Rose, 42
Partecipazione, 1112, 1141–42
Parten, Mildred, 271, **592–93**; constructive play and, 632; peers and, 614
Participant observation studies, 679
Participants' perspective: in qualitative research, 678
Partidos dos Trabalhadores, 929
PAS. *See* Program Administration Scale
Passive text environment, 1274
Pastoral da Criança, 939
Paternal leave: in France, 1090
PATHS. *See* Providing alternative thinking strategies
Patriarchy: in Brazil, 936; in Japan, 1155
Patronages, 1066
Pavlov, Ivan Petrovich, **594–95**; Watson and, 839
PBS. *See* Public Broadcasting System
PDD. *See* Pervasive development delay

PDD-NOS. *See* Pervasive developmental disorder-not otherwise specified

PDS. *See* Professional Development Schools

Peabody, Elizabeth Palmer, **595–96**; day nurseries and, 232; feminism and, 367; Wheelock and, 841; Wiggin and, 845

Peabody, Mary Tyler. *See* Mann, Mary Tyler Peabody

Peace culture: in Brazil, 938

Pearson, Henry Greenleaf, 339, 705

La pedagogia culturale, 1117–18

La pedagogia dela documentazione, 1117

La pedagogia del benessere, 1117

La pedagogia del gusto, 1117

La pedagogia della continuità, 1117

La pedagogia della partecipazione, 1117

Pedagogical project, 947

Pedagogical proposal, 947

Pedagogista, 698, 1114, 1138

Pedagogy, **596–98**; academic achievement, 610; active/participatory, 610; activity-based/experimental, **598–601**; in Australia, 883–87; in Brazil, 945, 954; caring/loving/passionate, 610; child-centered, **601–4**; critical/reflexive, 608; culturally relevant and responsive, 609; curriculum and, 177, 187; in Czech Republic, 1025–30; democratic, 610; developmental-interaction approach and, 279; documentation and, 297–98; emergent curriculum and, 181; of foreign language teaching, 1051–52; in France, 1076–80; in Italy, 1115–18; in Japan, 1168–72; MI and, 536; multicultural and antioppressive, 609–10; play and, 960; play-based, **604–8**;

school culture and, 712–13; social justice/equity, **608–10**

Pedagogy for Nursery Schools: in Czech Republic, 1056

Pederasty, 936

Pediatricians: in crèches, 1065; for parenting guidance, 590

Peers, 128, **611–13, 613–18**; group relations with, 615; infants as, 1139; in Japan, 1159–60, 1162; language development and, 262; literacy and, 1131; mixed age grouping and, 522; poverty and, 269; social competence and, 739; social contracts with, 1135; technology and, 800; writing and, 191

Peller, Lili: psychoanalysis and, 375

Pell Grants, 651

Pennsylvania Training School for Feeble Minded Children, 387

People: in social studies, 218

PEP. *See* Parent Education Program

Perceptual theory: for artistic development, 227

Percutaneous umbilical blood sampling (PUBS), 304–5

Performance standards, 757

Performative skill development, 199

Perkins, David, 673

Perkins Institute, 322

Personality Developing Model, 1030

Personal Responsibility and Work Opportunity Reconciliation Act (PRWORA), 110, 113, 809; NBCDI and, 546

Pervasive developmental disorder-not otherwise specified (PDD-NOS), 56, 277

Pervasive development delay (PDD), 723

Pestalozzi, Johann, 145, 322, 523, **618–19**; Froebel and, 376; Hailmann, William, and, 405; Italy and, 1111; Kurahashi and, 1169; Owen, Robert, and, 577; pedagogy

and, 602; playgrounds and, 641; progressive education and, 667

Pestalozzi, Joseph, 194

Pesticides, 344, 346

Pestovat, 1027

Petit mal seizures, 276

Pew Charitable Trusts, 622

P&G. *See* Proctor and Gamble

PGCE. *See* Postgraduate certificate of education

Pharmacotherapy: for ADHD, 51–52

Phelps, Winthrop, 95

Phenylketonuria (PKU), 292

Philanthropy and young children, **619–24**; limits of, 622–23

Philosophical rationalism, 504

A Philosophy of Freedom (Steiner), 774

Phonemes: in Japanese, 1158

Phonetics: in China, 1003

Phonological disorders, 278

Phonological subsystem: of language, 1049

Phonology, 138

Phylketonuria, 276

Physical attractiveness, 719

Physical bravery, 267

Physical development: Comenius and, 1026; curriculum in, **201–5**; developmental delay and, 273; gender stereotypes and, 382; screening for, 34

Physical education. *See* Curriculum, physical development

Physical therapists, 34

Piaget, Jean, 41, 253, 322, 447, **624–26**, 864, 873, 953, 959, 1118; Almy and, 23; Binet and, 80; Bruner and, 89; cognitive development and, 249; constructionism and, 150–51; constructivism and, 152, 153–54; creativity and, 166; culture and, 174; curriculum and, 177; developmental-interaction approach and, 280; ecology of human development and, 333;

Piaget, Jean, 41, 253, 322, 447, embodiment and, 728; feminism and, 367; Hunt and, 424; imitation and, 837; Italy and, 1113; mathematics curriculum and, 194, 503; MI and, 532; moral development and, 264, 266; pedagogy and, 599, 604; peers and friends and, 613; play and, 627; Reggio Emilia and, 697; science curriculum and, 206; sensory motor play and, 1177; social studies curriculum and, 219; spiritual development and, 753; Vygotsky and, 831
Piaget on Piaget (Piaget), 624
Piazza, Giovanni, 777
Pinching, 52–53
Pinyin, 1002
PISA. *See* Programme for International Student Assessment
PITC. *See* Program for Infant-Toddler Caregivers
PKU. *See* Phenylketonuria
PL. *See* previous level
Places: in social studies, 218
Plan and Predict, 208
Planner: in play, 639
Plastic, 243
Plastic arts, 1181–82
Plato, 704; creativity and, 169; playgrounds and, 641
Play, **626–45**; Almy and, 23; in Australia, 874; in Brazil, 957-61; in China, 989-93; CK and, 909; cognitive, 222; *The Creative Curriculum for Preschool* and, 164; creativity and, 167; DAP and, 283; deaf children and, 236; development of, 630; emergent curriculum and, 181; fathers and, 364; free, 958; gender, 959; grouping and, 400; in Italy, 1118–21; in Japan, 1158, 1176–82; in Japanese kindergarten, 1168; language development and, 263, 474–75; mathematical curriculum and, 194; in Montessori education, 1135;

obesity and, 568; Parten and, 592-93; pedagogy and, 599; peers and, 614; Piaget and, 168; preferred, 958; progressive education and, 668; psychoanalysis and, 374; respect for, 1170; Ruggles Street Nursery School Training School and, 705; in Sweden, 1244, 1269-72; turbulent, 959; in Waldorf Education, 834. *See also* War play
Play and gender, **633–35**
Play and teacher's role, **637–641**
Play as storytelling, 627, **635–37**
Play-based learning, 912
Play-based pedagogies, 885
The Playground, 642
Playground and Recreation Association of America (PRAA), 642
Playground Association of America (PAA), 642
Playgrounds, 204, **641–45**; assessment of, 340; embodiment and, 728; obesity and, 567
Playground standards movement, 643
Play rhetorics, 629
Play therapy, 627, **645–48**
Play with rules: in China, 991
Playworlds, 606
Plot of silence, 935
Plowden Report, 570
PMI. *See* Child and maternal health centers
PMTCT. *See* Prevention of Mother-to-Child Transmission
Policy Briefs on Early Childhood, 820
Policy of the Preparation of the Early Childhood Education Professional: in Brazil, 945
Political principles, 948
Political science: pedagogy and, 597; in social studies, 217
Political violence, 1203-4
Pollen, 346
Ponty, Merleau: child art and, 105
Popularity, 272
Pornography, 730

The Portage Guide to Early Education, 649
Portage Project, **648–49**
Portfolios: in art education, 39
Postcolonialism: in Australia, 886
Postconventional stage, 266
Postgraduate certificate of education (PGCE), 1310
Postgraduate programs: for Chinese teachers, 1014; in Czech Republic, 1057
Postmodernism: in Australia, 886, 896
Poststructuralism: in Australia, 896; gender equality and, 906
Posttraumatic stress disorder (PTSD), 301, 823
Postural disorder, 724
A Pound of Prevention (Hymes, James), 425
Pouponnières, 1107
Poverty, 25; in Australia, 870, 875; biculturalism and, 73; in Brazil, 926, 928-34; culture of, 174; definition of, 649-50; disabilities and, 293; early intervention and, 330; environmental health and, 345; fathers and, 366; Head Start and, 411; mothers and, 531; nutrition and, 563; parental substance abuse and, 582; parenting education and, 585; race and ethnicity and, 686; SES and, 748; social development and, 269; in South Africa, 1199-1203; in United Kingdom, 1290-93, 1306-7; WHO and, 852
Poverty and Social Exclusion Survey, 1291
Poverty, family, and child, **649–52**
Powell, Gregg, 559
Power: bullying and, 90; in social studies, 218
The Power of Documentation: Children's Learning Revealed, 298
PRAA. *See* Playground and Recreation Association of America
Practice-close research, 1275

Prader-Willi syndrome, 277
Pragmatic subsystem: of language, 1049
Pragmatism: Dewey and, 288
Pratt, Caroline, 194, 517, **653–54**; developmental-interaction approach and, 279
Preconventional stage, 266
Preferred play, 958
Prefrontal cortex, 243
Pregnancy: developmental delay and, 274; prevention of, 651; TANF and, 529
Pregnancy Discrimination Act, 531
Prejudice: social studies and, 217
Prekindergarten. *See* State prekindergarten programs
Pre-Kindergarten Study, 317
Prematurity: developmental delay and, 274
Prenatal asphyxia: disabilities and, 292
Preparation for Art (McFee), 227
Prepared environment, 526
Preparing a good environment, 1170
Preschematic stage, 104
Preschool Curriculum Evaluation Research Program (PCER), **654–55**
The Preschool Education (Kurahashi), 1169
Preschool Environmental Rating Scale, 342
Preschoolers: in CK, 911–12; creative curriculum for, 164–66; electronic play for, 148
Preschool/prekindergarten programs, **655–58**; enrollment at, 657
Preschools: in Brazil, 940; Malguzzi and, 497–99; open, 1242
Presidential Task Force on Child Development, 424
President's Council for Early Childhood Education, 574
President's Council on Television, 574

Prestation d'Accueil du Jeune Enfant (PAJE), 1097, 1104
Pretend play, 1118–19
Preventing Reading Difficulties in Young Children, 188
Prevention of Mother-to-Child Transmission (PMTCT), 1209
previous level (PL), 251
Primary emotions, 256
Primary Methods and Kindergarten Instruction (Hailmann, William), 406
Primary/Native Language Programs, 77
Primary School Nutrition Programme (PSNP), 1208
Principals, 308
Principles of Teaching (Thorndike), 811
Private Baby-Sitting Station, 1006
Privatization: in Japan, 1186
Process-based curriculum, 227
Proctor and Gamble (P&G), 547
Production: in social studies, 218
Productive language, 716
Productive Pedagogies, 884
Profeseur des écoles, 1064
Professional development, 312, **658–62**; ECSE and, 325; through IRA, 458; NAEYC and, 542; Reggio Emilia and, 699
Professional Development Schools (PDS), 795
Professional ethics, 662–65; codes of, 663; Comenius and, 1026; in Sweden, 1276–79
Professional learning communities, 299–300
Proficiency standards, 757
Progettazione, 182, 628, 670, Reggio Emilia and, 698
Program Administration Scale (PAS), 513
Program Architectural Design Regulation: in China, 981
Program for Infant-Toddler Caregivers: infant care and, 444
Program for Infant-Toddler Caregivers (PITC), **665–67**
Programme for International Student Assessment (PISA), 573

Program of Educational Work in Crèches and Nursery Schools, 1044
Program of Initial In-Service Training of Teachers in Early Childhood Education, 946; in Brazil, 917
Program of Upbringing for Nursery Schools, 1044
Progressive Education, **667–69,** 794, 1169; Dewey and, 288. *See also* Open education
Progressive Education, 425, 668
ProInfantil. *See* Program of Initial In-Service Training of Teachers in Early Childhood Education
Project Approach, 182, 508, **670–73**; mixed-age grouping and, 518; pedagogy and, 603
Project Care, 293
Project Spectrum, 181, 673
Project to Reinvent NAEYC Accreditation, 6
Project Zero (PZ), 226, 298, **673–74,** 795
Projcto Fome Zero, 929
Promise-keeping, 267
Promotion: multi-age grouping and, 520
Proprioceptive sense, 722
Protection of Children Against Sexual Exploitation Act, 730
Provence, Sally, 858
Providing: as teacher role, 600
Providing alternative thinking strategies (PATHS), 186
Pruning, 244
PRWORA. *See* Personal Responsibility and Work Opportunity Reconciliation Act
Pseudonaturalistic stage, 104
PSNP. *See* Primary School Nutrition Programme
Psychoanalysis, 516; in France, 1077; in Italy, 1113. *See also* Freud, Anna; Freud, Sigmund
Psychoanalytic theory: for artistic development, 226; Freud, Anna, and, 373; of play, 626–27
Psychological Review, 840

Psychological violence, 935–36

Psychology: behaviorism and, 62

"Psychology as the Behaviorist Views It" (Watson), 840

The Psychology of Sex Differences (Maccoby and Jacklin), 383–84

Psychosexual theory, 169

Psychosocial theory, **674–77**

PTA. *See* Parent Teacher Association

PTSD. *See* Posttraumatic stress disorder

Public Broadcasting System (PBS), 802

Public Playground Safety Checklist, 342

Public policies: in Czech Republic, 1031–34; in Italy, 1150–54; in Japan, 1191–93

Public relations: administration of, 310–11

Public schools: Mann and, 499

Public systems: of education, 862

Public Television, 802

PUBS. *See* Percutaneous umbilical blood sampling

Puericultrici, 1146

Puericultura programs, 943, 1100

Puériculture, 1077

Punishment, 70; corporal, 157–62

Purpose: psychosocial theory and, 676

Push-down curriculum, 177

Pushing: in domestic violence, 300

Puzzles, 147

PZ. *See* Project Zero

Qing Dynasty, 984

QTS. *See* Qualified Teacher Status

Quadriplegia: CP and, 96

Qualified Teacher Status (QTS), 1309, 1310

Qualitative research, **678–81**

Quality Assurance, 544

Quantitative analyses/ experimental designs, **681–84**

The Quest for Certainty (Dewey), 289

Quest program, 329

Quincy system, 592

QWERTY keyboard, 55

Race: in Brazil, 924–28; in France, 1068–72; in United Kingdom, 1287–90

Race and ethnicity, **685–87**

Race Relations Amendment Act: in United Kingdom, 1288

Rachel McMillan Nursery School and Training Centre, 705

Racial democracy, 925

Racism, 25; biculturalism and, 73; in Brazil, 925; social studies and, 217; in South Africa, 1194

Radical behaviorism, 63

Raising Cain: Protecting the Emotional Life of Boys, 385

RAM. *See* Relais Assistantes Maternelles

Rambush, Nancy, 525, 527

Ramsey, Marjorie, 545

Randomized controlled trial designs, 683

Rank, Otto, 333, 647

Rationalism, 504

RCNEI. *See* National Curricular References for ECE

Read-alouds and vocabulary development, **688–90**

Readiness, 4, **690–92**; Gesell and, 387; Good Start, Grow Smart and, 392; maturationism and, 510; NEGP and, 553–54; parenting education and, 584; prekindergarten and, 771; school culture and, 712

Reading: MI and, 535

Reading Excellence Act, 358

Reading First, 358

Reading in Paris. *See* Lire à Paris

Reading Online, 459

Reading Research Quarterly, 459

The Reading Teacher, 459

Reading wars, 188

Read, Katherine, **687–88**

Read Schools Resource Group, 554

Ready-to-Read, 62

Real Boys: Rescuing Our Sons from the Myths of Masculinity, 385

Realism, 264

Real time strategy (RTS) games, 147

Rearview Mirror: Reflections of a Preschool Car Project (Beneke), 298

Rebecca of Sunnybrook Farm (Wiggin), 845

Reception Year: in South Africa, 1196

Receptive aphasias, 278

Receptive language disorders, 278

Reciprocal causation, 734

Reciprocal determinism, 734

Reciprocity, 335

Recognition of prior learning (RPL), 1237

Reconceptualists, **693–96**

Reconceptualizing Early Childhood Research, Theory and Practice Conference, 695

Record of a School (Peabody, Elizabeth), 595

Redshirting, 468, 691

Reflexivity: in qualitative research, 679

Reformism: in Czech Republic, 1029–30

Reggio Emilia, 33, 38, 39, 308, 410, 508, 674, 1110, 1113, 1116, 1127, 1136, 1143, 1260; approach to early childhood education, **696–700**; atelier and, 43; Australia and, 884, 885; Bruner and, 90; child art and, 106; classroom discourse and, 138–39; classroom environment and, 143; creativity and, 171; curriculum and, 177; documentation and, 296; emergent curriculum and, 182; families and, 353; laboratory schools and, 473; Malaguzzi and, 497; open education and, 572; pedagogy and, 598; play and, 628; Pratt and, 653; Project Approach and, 670; science curriculum and, 207; symbolic languages and, 776; visual art curriculum and, 225, 230. *See also* North American Reggio Emilia Alliance

Reggio-inspired teacher education (RITE), **700–702,** 796

Regional family allowance funds (CAFs), 1065, 1066, 1070, 1091, 1101

Registration and referral (R&R), 242

Regular Education Initiative, 436

Regulated market, 763

Reinforcement: in behaviorism, 63–64; positive, 70; social cognitive theory and, 735

Reis, Meirelles, 958

Rejection, 272

Relais Assistantes Maternelles (RAM), 1091, 1106-7

Relationship play therapy, 647

Relationships: creativity and, 893; developmental systems theory and, 286; Rousseau and, 703

Relatives: child care and, 108

Release play therapy, 646–47

Reliability: in assessment, 36

Report and Reflect, 208

Republic (Plato), 704

Republicans: in France, 1072

Research: in Brazil, 941–42, 964-65; in Czech Republic, 1037, 1061-62; on play, 1121

Research Connections, **112–13**

Researcher as instrument: in qualitative research, 678

Research Institute: autism and, 56

Research Notes, 513

Research Triangle Institute (RTI): PCER and, 654

Resilience, 67

Respect for play, 1170

Respiratory infections, 346

Responding: as teacher role, 600

Response facilitation, 735

Retention: kindergarten, 691; multi-age grouping and, 520

Retrolental fibroplasia, 275

Retts Disorder, 56

Revised National Curriculum Statement (RNCS), 1218, 1219; details of, 1220; in South Africa, 1198

RH blood incompatibility: CP and, 276

Rhetoric of progress, 629

Rhythm, 834

Rhythmic patterning, 198

Rights Council: in Brazil, 937

"The Rights of Children," 20

The Rights of Children (Wiggin), 847

Right to share worlds, 1277

Riley, Richard, 552

Risk factors: for child abuse, 98; disabilities and, 292; early intervention and, 329-32; environmental, 344

Risley, Todd, 64, 65, 688

RITE. *See* Reggio-inspired teacher education

Rituals: culture and, 173

River blindness, 827

RNCS. *See* Revised National Curriculum Statement

Robert F. Kennedy Council for Campus Child Care, 549

Robertson, James, 84

Robert Taylor Homes, 620

Rodney, Clare, 545

Rogers, Carl, 69, 647, **702–3;** Maslow and, 501

Rogers, Katherine, 559

Rogoff, Barbara, 601; Australia and, 885

Role confusion: psychosocial theory and, 676

Role-playing, 29, 958

Role playing games (RPG), 147

Roles: of art teacher, 228; culture and, 173

Romany, 1020; in Czech Republic, 1035

Ross, Gail, 89

Rothenberg, Dianne, 321

Rousseau, Jean-Jacques, 322, 703–4, 848; Kurahashi and, 1169; Maslow and, 502; Montessori and, 525; pedagogy and, 602; Pestalozzi and, 618; playgrounds and,

641; progressive education and, 667

RPG. *See* Role playing games

RPL. *See* Recognition of prior learning

R&R. *See* Registration and referral

RTI. *See* Research Triangle Institute

RTS. *See* Real time strategy games

Rubella, 279; CP and, 96

Ruggles Street Nursery Training School, 338-39, 471, 515, **705-6**

Runnymede Trust, 1287

Saberes e Práticas da Inclusão—Educação Infantil, 964

SAC. *See* School-age care

SACC. *See* School Age Care Credential

SACERS. *See* School-Age Care Environment Rating Scale

Sacrifice, 267

Safety, 502

Salaries: for Brazilian teachers, 946; in Czech Republic, 1057; in Sweden, 1243

Salles d'asile, 1078, 1080

Sameroff, Arnold, 363

SAMSHA. *See* Substance Abuse and Mental Health Services Administration

Samuelsson, Pramling, 1273

Sandpaper Letters, 527

Sand tray play therapy, 647

Sapon-Shevin, Mara, 390

SAQA. *See* South African Qualifications Authority

SATs. *See* Standard Attainment Tests

Savage Inequalities (Kozol), 20

Save the Children, 1285

SBA. *See* Standards-based accountability

SC. *See* School curricula

Scandinavia, 862

Schedules of reinforcement, 63

Schematic stage, 104

Schickedanz, Judith, 545

Schlick, Calvert, 42

Schoggen, Phillip, 333
School-age care (SAC), 242, 707–11
School Age Care Credential (SACC), 710
School-Age Care Environment Rating Scale (SACERS), 315, 343
School and Society (Dewey), 289
The School and Society (Dewey), 668
School Construction Act: NBCDI and, 546
School culture, 174–75, 711–13
School curricula (SC), 1045
Schooling: stages of, 894–95
School of Infancy (Comenius), 145
School professors: in France, 1074
School readiness: early intervention and, 330; social curriculum and, 215
Schools Where Children Learn (Featherstone), 569
School System Reform Plan: in China, 985
School violence, 935
Schulthess, Anna, 618
Science: curriculum in, **205–11**; in social studies, 219
Science Research Associates (SRA), 290
ScienceStart!, 208, 210
Science, technology, engineering, mathematics (STEM), 221
Scienze della Formazione Primaria, 1146
Scotland. *See* United Kingdom
Screaming, 52–53
Screening, 34; for amblyopia, 292; developmental, 691; WIC and, 849
Scribbling, 104
Scribe: in play, 639
Scripted curriculum, 179; in science, 206
Scuole dell'infanzia, 1110, 1111; teachers for, 1146
Scuole materne, 1110, 1111
Scuole paritarie, 1148

Searching children, 1129–30
SECA. *See* Southern Early Childhood Association
SECA Reporter, 751
Secondary emotions, 256
Second-language acquisition, 475, **713–17**; in Czech Republic, 1048–53; sensibility in, 1050; in South Africa, 1224–26; in Sweden, 1248, 1261
Sector Skills Council for Social Care, Children and Young People: in United Kingdom, 1309
Segregation: in Brazil, 925–26
Seguin, Edouard, 527
Seidel, Steve, 673
SEIT. *See* Special Education Itinerant Teacher
Seizure disorders, 276
Selah, 33
Selective mutism, 278
Self-actualization, 501; Rogers and, 702
Self concept, 702, **718–21**
Self-confidence: in China, 999–1000
Self-conscious emotions, 256
Self-correcting, 526
Self-disclosure, 271
Self-efficacy, 734, 736–37; technology and, 800
Self-esteem, **718–21**; in China, 999–1000; creativity and, 888; obesity and, 568; parental substance abuse and, 580–81; Rogers and, 702
Self-evaluation, 1041
Self-help: Abecedarian Program and, 1; visual impairment and, 828
Self-judgment, 737; social cognitive theory and, 61
Self-observation, 737; social cognitive theory and, 61
Self-reaction: social cognitive theory and, 61
Self-regulation, 734, 737; amygdala and, 245; prefrontal cortex and, 245; social cognitive theory and, 61
Self-report: as assessment, 36

Semilinguism, 1050
Semiotic theory, 897
SEN. *See* Special education need
SENCOs. *See* Special Educational Needs Co-ordinators
SENDA. *See* Special Educational Needs and Disability Act
Senn, Milton, 855
Sensibility: in second language acquisition, 1050
Sensitive periods, 244, 526
Sensorial Activities, 527
Sensorimotor integration disorders, 276
Sensorineural hearing loss, 275
Sensory defensive, 723
Sensory discrimination dysfunction, 724
Sensory disorders, 275–76
Sensory integration. *See* Sensory processing disorder
Sensory integration-based occupational therapy (OT/SI), 725
Sensory integration training: for ADHD, 51
Sensory modulation dysfunction (SMD), 723
Sensory motor play, 1177
Sensory processing disorder (SPD), **721–26**
Separation (Bowlby), 85
Services of public interest, 1151
Services on individual demand, 1151
Servizio Nazionale per la Scuola Materna, 1149
SES. *See* Socioeconomic status
Sesame Street, 802
Setting events, 66
Sex and sexuality in young children, **726–30**
Sexual abuse, 98, 579, 728–29, **730–32**; in Brazil, 935; psychoanalysis and, 374; in South Africa, 1194
Sexual orientation, 26, 28; conservatives and, 31
Shabazz, Betty, 82
Shame: psychosocial theory and, 675
Shanghai School for the Blind and Low Vision, 1009

Shaping, 63
Shelters: in Brazil, 934
Shinsho-Gakkyu, 1188
Shiritori, 1178
Shougai-Fukushi Center, 1189
Shoving: in domestic violence, 300
Shriver, R. Sargent, 121
Shulman, Lee, 1221
Sign language, 53, 235
Simon, Théodore, 80-81, 449
Simon, Theophile, 446, 453
Simulation games, 147
Single Health System: in Brazil, 939
Single-parent families: in Australia, 868, 880; in Sweden, 1240
Single Regeneration Budget, 1313
Skinner box, 63
Skinner, Burrhus Frederic, 63, 595, 732–34; Pavlov and, 594; Watson and, 839
Slapping: in domestic violence, 300
Slavery: in Brazil, 924
Sleeter, Christine, 694
SMD. See Sensory modulation dysfunction
Smith, David, 369
Smith, Linda K., 544
Smith, Marilyn, 82
Smith, Nora Archibald, 847
Smith, Robert, 545
Smith, Wilfred Cantwell, 752
SNCC. See Student Nonviolent Coordinating Committee
Snowe, Olympia, 10, 550
Social and psychological adjustment: peers and friends and, 616
Social capital: of children, 872-73
Social children, 1128
Social cognitive theory, 60, 70, 734–38
Social competence, 270, 738–41; The Creative Curriculum for Preschool and, 164; fathers and, 364
Social constructionism, 741–44

Social constructivism, 138, 744–47; classroom environment and, 141; emergent curriculum and, 181; family literacy and, 358; Reggio Emilia and, 43; Vygotsky and, 832
Social contracts: with peers, 1135
Social conventions, 265
Social-cultural theory, 744
Social curriculum, 271
Social development, 211–16, 269–73; Abecedarian Program and, 1; in China, 999-1001; developmental delay and, 273; gender stereotypes and, 382; parenting education and, 587; readiness and, 692; visual impairment and, 828. See also Socioemotional development
Social Development of the Young Child (Isaacs), 460
Social disorders, 277-78
Social emotions, 256
Social expressions, 261
Socialization: in France, 1081
Social justice: in South Africa, 1215-19
Socially constructed child, 871
Social phobias, 278
Social play. See Play
Social position: bullying and, 90
Social referencing, 258
Social Security Act, 769
Social Security Law for Disabled Persons: in China, 1011
Social Services Block Grant (SSBG), 115, 809
Social studies curriculum, 216–21
Social violence, 935
Social withdrawal, 278
Society for Research in Child Development, 183
Sociocultural theory: in Australia, 896; of play, 628-29; Reggio Emilia and, 43; Vygotsky and, 832
Socioeconomic status (SES), 747–50; in Australia, 880; in Brazil, 918; disabilities and,

292; in France, 1093; in South Africa, 1194
Socioemotional development: in Italy, 1133–41
Sociohistorical school, 494
Sociology: of Czech childhood, 1021-25; in social studies, 214, 217; of United Kingdom childhood, 1284
Socrates: constructivism and, 152
Solemn silence, 527
Solitary play, 593
Solnit, Albert J., 855, 858
"Some Current Dimensions of Applied Behavior Analysis" (Baer, Wolf, and Risley), 64
Songs, Games, and Rhymes (Hailmann, Eudora), 405
Sorensen, C.Th., 643
Sounds, 1180-81
South Africa, 862, 1194–1239; curriculum in, 1219-24; early intervention in, 1227-30; families in, 1211-15; finances in, 1231-35; health care in, 1207-11; human rights in, 1215-19; inclusion in, 1215-19; poverty in, 1199-1203; second language acquisition in, 1224-26; social justice in, 1215-19; stereotypes in, 1221; teacher education in, 1235-39; violence in, 1203-7
South African Broadcasting Corporation Educational TV, 1213
South African Qualifications Authority (SAQA), 1197
South African Schools Act, 1196
Southern Early Childhood Association (SECA), 426, 751
Spanking. See Corporal punishment
SPARK. See Supporting Partnerships to Assure Ready Kids
Sparks, Louise Derman, 1216
Spatial reasoning, 506
SPD. See Sensory processing disorder

Special education. *See* Early childhood special education

Special Educational Needs and Disability Act (SENDA): in United Kingdom, 1304

Special Educational Needs Co-ordinators (SENCOs), 1304

Special Education Itinerant Teacher (SEIT), 607

Special education need (SEN), 1303

Special teaching techniques: in Australia, 886

Speech: in Japanese kindergarten, 1169; learning disabilities and, 481

Speech disorders, 278, 1049

Speech pathologists, 54

Spina bifida, 276, 291; SPD and, 723

Spiritual development, **751–54**

Spodek, Bernard, 545

Sports games, 147

Spring, Joel, 694

Sputnik, 597

Squatters, 491

SRA. *See* Science Research Associates

SSBG. *See* Social Services Block Grant

Staff: environmental assessments and, 341; shortage of, 313

Stage and Sequence: The Cognitive Developmental Approach to Socialization (Kohlberg), 470

Stage manager: in play, 639

Stage theories, 753

Stagnation: psychosocial theory and, 676

Standard Attainment Tests (SATs), 1296

Standardized teaching: in Brazil, 955–56

Standardized tests, **754–57**; in art, 38; in Australia, 895, 912; language diversity and, 476; MI and, 534; NCLB and, 669

Standards, **757–61**. *See also* State licensing standards

Standards-based accountability (SBA), 757

Standards for Early Professional Preparation, 788

Standards for Educational and Psychological Testing, 754

Standards for Public Playground Equipment, 644

Stanford-Binet Intelligence Scale, 446, 453

Starting Strong: Early Childhood Education and Care, 573

Star Wars, 128

State Children's Health Insurance Program (CHIP), 126

State Council on the Conditions of Women (CECF), 967

State Farm Insurance Companies, 547

State licensing standards, **761–71**

State of America's Children, 21, 125, 686

State of nature, 704

State of the Child and of the Adolescent (ECA): in Brazil, 936

State prekindergarten programs, **771–74**

Statute of Mong Yang Yuan and Family Education, 984

Statute of the Child and Adolescent: in Brazil, 939

Steiner, Rudolf, **774–76**; Australia and, 884; Waldorf Education and, 833

STEM. *See* Science, technology, engineering, mathematics

Step by Step Program: in Czech Republic, 1033

Stereotypes, 27; gender, 382–87; obesity and, 567; play and, 628; social studies and, 217; in South Africa, 1221

Sternberg, Robert, 169, 447

Stern, William, 453

Stimulants: for ADHD, 51

Stimuli, 63

Stimulus-response theory, 194

Stolz, Lois Meek, 425, 551

Story building: in CK, 911

The Story of Patsy (Wiggin), 847

StoryQUEST: Celebrating Beginning Language and Literacy, 329

Storytelling, 475, 627; pedagogy and, 599

Strabismus, 275

"The Strange Situation," 45

Strategies: for communication, 54–55; for diversity, 878; for opportunity, 878

Strauss, A.L., 680

Stress, 346

Stress system development, 246

Structural violence, 1203

Structure: of play, 630

Student Nonviolent Coordinating Committee (SNCC), 123

The Study of Children in Family Child Care and Relative Care, 317

Subjectivity: in qualitative research, 678

Subsidies. *See* Child care subsidies and tax provisions

Substance Abuse and Mental Health Services Administration (SAMSHA), 292

Summer Institute, 854

Sunshine Center, 1230

Suole dell'infanzia, 1133–34

Superego, 374

Superheroes in the Doll Corner (Paley), 612

Supervisors, 308

"Supporting Families," 1307

Supporting Partnerships to Assure Ready Kids (SPARK), 547

Supporting the motivation for achievement and self-satisfaction, 1170

Sure Start, 1283, 1307, 1311; in United Kingdom, 1291–92

Survey research, 802

Sutton-Smith, Brian, 629

Svoboda, Jan Vladimír, 1027

Sweden, **1240–80**; corporal punishment and, 157–62; culture in, 1247–50; curriculum in, 1261–65; democracy in, 1261–65; ECERS and, 319; education

quality in, 1258-61; ethics in, 1276-79; gender equity in, 1254-58; literacy in, 1272-75; morality in, 1276-79; parents in, 1250-54; play in, 1269-72; teacher education in, 1265-69
Swedish Early Childhood Education and Care System, 1262, 1276
Sword, Jean, 545
Symbolic languages, 230, 776–79; Malaguzzi and, 487; Reggio Emilia and, 697
Symbolic play, 627, 1121, 1177
Symbol machines, 897
Symbols, 53; in music curriculum, 199
Synaptogenesis, 244
Syntax, 138

Tactile defensiveness, 276
Tactile sense, 722
TACTYC. See Training, Advancement and Co-operation in Teaching Young Children
Taking Charge of Change, 512-13
Taking on Turnover, 95
Talented children. See Gifted children
TANF. See Temporary Assistance for Needy Families
Task Force on Culture and Development, 859
Tax credits, 118-19; in United Kingdom, 1313
Tax provisions. See Child care subsidies and tax provisions
Tay-Sachs disease, 276
Teachable moments, 30
TEACH Early Childhood Project Technical Assistance and Quality Assurance Center, 785-86
Teacher (Ashton-Warner), 32
Teacher certification/licensure, 660, 780–85
Teacher Corp., 396
Teacher-directed curriculum, 227-28
Teacher education, 786–93; at Bank Street, 281; in China,

1008, 1012-15; in Czech Republic, 1021, 1033-34, 1053-58; in France, 1096, 1104-8; in Italy, 1145-50; NAECTE and, 545; in South Africa, 1235-39; for special education, 1148; in Sweden, 1265-69; in United Kingdom, 1309-12
Teacher Education and Compensation Helps (TEACH), 785–86
Teacher Education Commission: in Sweden, 1266
Teacher Listen, the Children Speak (Hymes, James), 425
Teacher preparation: in Brazil, 940-41, 943-47
Teacher ratings: as assessment, 36
Teacher research, 793–98
Teachers: as nurses, 1055
Teachers Network Leadership Institute (TNLI), 796
Teacher Training Agency (TTA), 1311; in United Kingdom, 1310
Teaching: styles of, 268
TEACHING Exceptional Children, 163
Teaching Exceptional Children (TEC), 798
Teaching the NAEYC Code of Ethical Conduct (Feeney, Freeman, and Moravcik), 665
Teasing, 91
TEC. See Teaching Exceptional Children
Technology, 798–801; administration and, 311; art and, 230; curriculum in, 221–25; electronic, 223; in social studies, 219
TECSE. See Topics in Early Childhood Special Education
Telecommunications Act, 804
Telegraphic and formulaic speech, 715-16
Television, 147, 574, 801–5; in Japan, 1166; obesity and, 567; violence on, 821

Temperament, 46, 67, 805–7; emotion regulation and, 258; peers and friends and, 615
Temple, Alice, 289, 807–8; creativity and, 167
Temple School, 595
Tempo per le Famiglie, 1138
Temporary Assistance for Needy Families (TANF), 113, 115, 651, 808–10; Head Start and, 413; mothers and, 529; TEACH and, 785
Ten Year Strategy for Childcare, 1291, 1293, 1302
Terakoya, 1164
Terman, Lewis, 388, 446, 453
Terrible twos, 511
Testing: as assessment, 36; standardized, 38
Te Whariki, 74, 178
TFR. See Total fertility rate
Thematic Review of Early Childhood Education and Care Policy: in Czech Republic, 1037
Then and Now: Changes in Child Care Staffing, 1994-2000, 95
Theory into Practice, 796
Theory of evolution, 170
Thinking Classroom, 459
Thomas, Dorothy, 333
Thomas, William, 333
Thorndike Arithmetics (Thorndike), 811
Thorndike, Edward Lee, 501, 810–11; mathematics curriculum and, 193; Pavlov and, 594; pedagogy and, 602
Thoughts on the Initiation of Daughters (Wollstonecraft), 848
3D view of literacy, 898
Three Period Lesson, 526, 527
Three strikes laws, 432
Threshold values, 1124
Throw Handkerchief, 991
Thurstone, Louis, 447
Tiered strategies: in standards, 768
Timbral, 198
Time: in social studies, 218
Time for Families, 1138

Timothy's Quest (Wiggin), 847

Tirocinio, 1147–48

TNLI. *See* Teachers Network Leadership Institute

Tobacco: WHO and, 852

Tobacco smoke, 344, 345–46

Tobin, Joseph, 128

Toddlers: in CK, 910–11; in Czech Republic, 1055; in Italy, 1137–41; in Japan, 1183–87

Tokubetu-Shien-Kyoiku, 188

Tokushu-Gakkyu, 1188

Tokushu-kyoiku, 188

Tokyo Women's Teachers College, 1156, 1168

Tolman, Edward, 333

Topics in Early Childhood Special Education (TECSE), 65, **811–12**

Torrance Tests of Creative Thinking, 170

Torres Strait. *See* Aborigines

Total fertility rate (TFR): in Australia, 868

Touchpoints, 807, **812–14**

Toward a Psychology of Being (Maslow), 501

Toward a Theory of Instruction (Bruner), 89

Toxins: disabilities and, 292

Toynbee Hall, 13

Toy-playing centers, 957

TPBA. *See* Transdisciplinary, play-based assessment model

Training, Advancement and Co-operation in Teaching Young Children (TACTYC), 332

Training and Resources in Early Education (TREE), 1210

Traits: peers and friends and, 615

Transcendence, 502

Transdisciplinary, play-based assessment model (TPBA), 237

Transitional Child Care, 113, 115

Transitional programs, 691

Transitions/continuity, **814–17**

Transvaal Memorial Institute, 1230

Trauma: of domestic violence, 301

Traumatic brain injury: speech and, 52

TREE. *See* Training and Resources in Early Education

Tribunal de Menores, 936

Trisomy 21. *See* Down Syndrome

Trotter, Yorke, 557

Trust: parental substance abuse and, 580–81; psychosocial theory and, 675

Trusting threes, 511

Tsumori, Makoto, 1172

TTA. *See* Teacher Training Agency

Tuberculosis: WHO and, 852

Tufts Educational Day Care Center, 705

Tukyu, 1188

Turbulent play, 958

Tur Er Suo, 975

Turiel, Elliot, 265; moral development and, 264

Tutoring, 399

The Twelve Who Survive (Myers), 863

21st Century Community Learning Centers, 358, 710

Twenty Years at Hull-House (Addams), 14

Two Worlds of Childhood: U.S. and U.S.S.R. (Bronfenbrenner), 86

Understanding Others, Educating Ourselves, 864

Understanding Your Child (Hymes, James), 425

UNESCO. *See* United Nations Educational, Scientific, and Cultural Organization

UNICEF. *See* United Nations Children's Fund

Unified Kindergarten and First Grade Teaching (Temple and Parker), 807

United Kingdom, **1281–1317**; culture in, 1287–90; curriculum in, 1296–99; educational services in, 1299–1303; education quality in, 1293–96; ethnicity in, 1287–90; finances in, 1312–15; health care in,

1305–9; inclusion in, 1303; poverty in, 1290–93; race in, 1287–90; teacher education in, 1309–12

United Nations: ACEI and, 40; Convention on the Rights of the Child and, 20, 75; CRC and, 156

United Nations Children's Fund (UNICEF), **818–19**; in Brazil, 914, 923; China and, 1008

United Nations Educational, Scientific, and Cultural Organization (UNESCO), 320, 524, **819–20**, 962; in Brazil, 914, 923; OMEP and, 853

United Parcel Service (UPS), 547

United Way: accreditation and, 8

Universal Declaration of Human Rights, 961

University Institutes for Teacher Training. *See* Institut Universitaire de formation des maîtres

UN Millennium Development Goals. *See* Millennium Development Goals

Unoccupied behavior, 593

UN Relief and Rehabilitation Administration, 818

UPS. *See* United Parcel Service

Urban Kindergarten Provisional Regulation: in China, 980

U.S. Army School Age Credential, 710

Utopian community: Owen, Robert, and, 578

Uzgiris, Ina C., 424

Vaccinations: in Brazil, 939; in South Africa, 1208

Vaccines for Children Program, 125

Validity: in assessment, 37

Vanderwalker, Nina: day nurseries and, 232

V-chips, 127, 804

Velvet Revolution, 1035

Ventre Livre, 924

Verbal Behavior (Skinner), 733

Verbs, 261

Vestibular sense, 722

Victorian Schools Innovation Commission (VSIC), 887
Video games. *See* Computer and video game play
A Vindication of the Rights of Woman (Wollstonecraft), 848
Violence, **821–26**; domestic, 67; early intervention and, 330; institutional, 935; intra-family, 935; parental substance abuse and, 582; prevention of, 825; social, 935; social cognitive theory and, 60; in South Africa, 1194, 1203-7; structural, 934; in television, 802; Wollstonecraft and, 847
Vision: learning disabilities and, 482-83; screening for, 34
Visual art: assessment in, 38-40; in China, 992-98; curriculum in, **225–31**
Visual impairment, 275, **826–29**; in China, 1010; literacy and, 489
Visual orientation, 802
Vocabulary development. *See* Read-alouds and vocabulary development
Vocational high schools: for Chinese teachers, 1011
Voices for Katrina's Children, 22
Voices of Practitioners: Teacher Research in Early Childhood Education, 796
The Voyage of Mimi, 62
VSIC. *See* Victorian Schools Innovation Commission
Vygotsky, Lev, 41, 267, 322, **829–33**, 873, 953, 959, 1119, 1273; Australia and, 885; Bruner and, 88; child art and, 105; constructivism and, 152; creativity and, 166; culture and, 174; developmental-interaction approach and, 280; ecology of human development and, 333; feminism and, 367; Italy and, 1113; Luria and, 494; make-believe play and, 631; multi-age grouping and, 520; pedagogy and, 597, 599, 604-5; peers and friends and,

613; play and, 168, 627; play as storytelling and, 637; Reggio Emilia and, 697; social studies curriculum and, 219; visual art curriculum and, 229; Whiting, John, and, 845

Wada, Minoru, 1169
Wadsworth, Barry, 42
Walden School, 557
Walden Two (Skinner), 733
Wald, Lillian, 557
Waldorf Early Childhood Association of North America (WECAN), 835
Waldorf Education, 774-76, **833–35**; in Czech Republic, 1033; pedagogy and, 598
Wales. *See* United Kingdom
Wallon, Henri, 1113
Wann, Kenneth, 447
Ward Council: in Brazil, 937
Ward, Evangeline, 81, 82, 663
Warnock Report, 1303-4
War on Poverty, 25; NHSA and, 555; Osborn and, 574; parenting education and, 585; WIC and, 849
War play, **836–39**
Watson, John B., 62, 132, **839–40**; Pavlov and, 594
WECAN. *See* Waldorf Early Childhood Association of North America
Wechsler-Bellevue Scale, 449
Wechsler, David, 449, 453
Wechsler Preschool and Primary Scale of Intelligence (WPPSI), 453
Week-of-the-Young-Child, 21
Weikart, David P., 414
Welfare to Work, 1291
Well-being. *See* Health care
Werner, Heinz, 280
Wertheimer, Max, 501
Wesley, Susanna, 158
WestEd, 665-66
What Do We Learn in the École Maternelle?, 1082
What Matters Most: Teaching and America's Future, 788
Wheelock, Lucy, 339, **840–41**; IKU and, 457

Whispering, 527
White Book, 1045
White, Edna Noble, 340, 515, 550, **841–42**
White Paper 6 on Inclusive Education: in South Africa, 1217
White Paper for Social Welfare: in South Africa, 1196
Whiting, Beatrice, **842–44**; culture and, 174
Whiting, John W.M., 843, **844–46**; culture and, 174
WHO. *See* World Health Organization
Whole child, 535; progressive education and, 667
Wholeness Pedagogy, 985
WIC. *See* Women, Infants and Children
Wiggin, Kate Douglas, **846–47**
The Wild Boy of Aveyron (Itard), 322
William F. Goodling Even Start Family Literacy Program, 358
Williams, Vera B., 435
Wilson, Woodrow, 524
Winnicott, David: Read and, 688
Winnicott, Donald: psychoanalysis and, 375
Wisdom: psychosocial theory and, 676
Wishon, Phil, 545
Wolf, Montrose, 64
Wollstonecraft, Mary, **847–49**
Women: in Australian workforce, 879, 880-81; in Brazil, 920; as Chinese teachers, 1012; in Czech Republic, 1017-18; in Czech workforce, 1023-24; in French workforce, 1100
Women, Infants and Children (WIC), 531, 566, **849–50**
Women's Education Association, 339
Women's Federation: in China, 1008
Women's International League for Peace and Freedom, 14
Women's Normal School Regulation: in China, 1013
Wood, David, 89

Woodsen, Carter, 25
Woodson, Jacqueline, 435
Wooley, Helen Thompson, 550
Work: theme of, 29
Workforce Investment Act, 358
Work Sampling System, 36
World Association for Infant
 Mental Health, 516
World Bank, 862; in Brazil, 923
World Forum Foundation, 850
The World Forum on Early Care
 and Education, **850**
World Health Organisation
 (WHO), 44, **851–53**; Bowlby
 and, 84; obesity and, 567
World Literacy Day, 104
World Organisation for Early
 Childhood Education (OMEP),
 853–54
World Summit for Children, 819
World Trade Center, 27
World War II: day nurseries and,
 232
Worldwide Declaration of
 Education for All, 962
Worthy Wage Campaign, 95, **854**
Worthy Wage day, 854
WPPSI. *See* Wechsler Preschool
 and Primary Scale of
 Intelligence
Wright, Frank Lloyd, 377

Wright, Herbert, 333
Wright, Marian, 123
Writer's Laboratory, 517

Xingzhi Dao, 972
Xuemen Zhang, 972

Yale University Child Study
 Center, **855–56**
Yanshi Women's School,
 1013
Yarrow, Leon, 858
YMCA, 708
Yochien, 1189
Yoji-kyoiku, 1156
York, Mary Elizabeth,
 545
You Can't Say You Can't Play
 (Paley), 272
You Er Yuan, 974, 984
Yougo-Gakkou, 188
Young Children, 9, 363, 796,
 856–57; code of ethics in,
 664; NAEYC and, 542
Young Citizen Protection Law:
 in China, 973
Young Exceptional Children,
 295
Young Man Luther (Erikson),
 348
Young Scientist series, 210

Your Child and his Art
 (Lowenfeld), 494
You Zhi Yuan, 984
Yu Yin Yuan, 1008

Zacharias, Jerrold, 409
Zachry, Caroline, 425
Základní škola, 1018
Zao Jiao Zhong Xin, 975
ZEP. *See* High-need education
 areas; Zone d'éducation
 prioritaire
Zero exclusion policy, 52
Zero Hunger Project, 929
Zerosix, 498
ZERO TO THREE, 56, **858–59**;
 Early Head Start and, 329;
 mental health and, 516
Zhang Zhi-Dong, 984
Zhang Zue Men, 985
Zhou dynasty, 994
Zigler, Edward, 413
Zone d'éducation prioritaire
 (ZEP), 1069, 1101
Zone of proximal development
 (ZPD), 168, 229, 267, 627,
 1119; pedagogy and, 605;
 Vygotsky and, 832
Zoology: Montessori and, 527
ZPD. *See* Zone of proximal
 development

List of Editors and Contributors

VOLUME EDITORS

Rebecca S. New
Tufts University
Medford, Massachusetts

Moncrieff Cochran
Cornell University
Ithaca, New York

EDITORIAL ASSISTANT

Joanna K. Nelson
Tufts University
Medford, Massachusetts

**CONTRIBUTORS—VOLUMES
1–3**

Mona M. Abo-Zena
Tufts University
Medford, Massachusetts

Leah Adams
Eastern Michigan University
Ypsilanti, Michigan

Susan Matoba Adler
University of Illinois
Urbana-Champaign, Illinois

Betty N. Allen
Tufts University
Medford, Massachusetts

Jason Almerigi
Tufts University
Medford, Massachusetts

Rika Alper
Montclair State University
Montclair, New Jersey

Charlotte Anderson
*Texas State University-San
Marcos*
San Marcos, Texas

Carol Aubrey
University of Warwick
Coventry, United Kingdom

Megina Baker
Tufts University
Medford, Massachusetts

Nancy Baptiste
New Mexico State University
Las Cruces, New Mexico

Margaret S. Barrett
University of Tasmania
*Launceston, Tasmania,
Australia*

Lindsay Barton
Tufts University
Medford, Massachusetts

Angie Baum
University of South Carolina
Columbia, South Carolina

Glenda Bean
*Southern Early Childhood
Association*
Little Rock, Arkansas

Neda Bebiroglu
Tufts University
Medford, Massachusetts

Sherry Mee Bell
University of Tennessee
Knoxville, Tennessee

Maria Benejan
Bank Street College
New York, New York

Maggie Beneke
Tufts University
Medford, Massachusetts

Ann C. Benjamin
*University of
Massachusetts–Lowell*
Lowell, Massachusetts

Susan Benner
University of Tennessee
Knoxville, Tennessee

John Bennet
*Education Directorate,
OECD*
Paris, France

Marina Umaschi Bers
Tufts University
Medford, Massachusetts

Srilata Bhattacharyya
New York Institute of
Technology
New York, New York

Camille L.Z. Blachowicz
National-Louis University
Evanston, Illinois

Helen Blank
National Women's Law
Center
Washington, D.C.

Marianne Bloch
University of Wisconsin
Madison, Wisconsin

Paula Jorde Bloom
National-Louis University
Wheeling Campus
Wheeling, Illinois

Barbara Bodner-Johnson
Gallaudet University
Washington, DC

Elena Bodrova
Mid-continent Research for
Education and Learning
Aurora, Colorado

Mary Boscardin
University of Massachusetts
Amherst, Massachusetts

Barbara Bowman
Erikson Institute
Chicago, Illinois

Sue Bredekamp
Council for Professional
Recognition
Washington, D.C.

Susan Jane Britsch
Purdue University
West Lafayette, Indiana

Christopher Brown
University of Texas
Austin, Texas

Mark Brundrett
University of Manchester
Manchester, United
Kingdom

Eric S. Buhs
University of
Nebraska–Lincoln
Lincoln, Nebraska

Maria Pelzer Bundy
University of North
Carolina
Chapel Hill, North Carolina

Barbara M. Burns
University of Louisville
Louisville, Kentucky

Meena Cabral de Mello
Department of Child and
Adolescent Health and
Development
World Health Organization
Geneva, Switzerland

Beth Cady
International Reading
Association
Newark, Delaware

Stephen N. Calculator
University of New
Hampshire
Durham, New Hampshire

Gaile S. Cannella
Arizona State University
Tempe, Arizona

Nancy Carlsson-Paige
Lesley University
Cambridge, Massachusetts

Margaret Caspe
New York University
New York, New York

Kathryn Castle
Oklahoma State University
Stillwater, Oklahoma

Corinne G. Catalano
Montclair State University
Montclair, New Jersey

Susan Catapano
University of Missouri–St.
Louis
St. Louis, Missouri

Stephen Ceci
Cornell University
Ithaca, New York

Sylvia Chard
University of Alberta
Edmonton, Alberta, Canada

Clement Chau
Tufts University
Medford, Massachusetts

Yi Che
Arizona State University
Tempe, Arizona

Jie-Qi Chen
Erikson Institute
Chicago, Illinois

Soo-Hyang Choi
UNESCO
Paris, France

Shunah Chung
Sookmyung Women's
University
Seoul, South Korea

Ann-Marie Clark
Appalachian State
University
Boone, North Carolina

Douglas Clark
National-Louis University
Wheeling Campus
Wheeling, Illinois

Sydney Gurewitz Clemens
New College of California
San Francisco, California

Douglas H. Clements
University at Buffalo
State University of New
York
Buffalo, New York

Moncrieff Cochran
Cornell University
Ithaca, New York

Judith A. Colbert
Early Care and Education
Consultant
London, Ontario, Canada

Kathy Conezio
The Warner School
University of Rochester
Rochester, New York

Abby Copeman
Tufts University
Medford, Massachusetts

Marg Csapo
University of British
Columbia
Vancouver, British
Columbia, Canada

Stacey D. Cunningham
National Black Child
Development Institute
Washington, D.C.

Lori Custodero
Columbia University
New York, New York

Yasmine Daniel
Children's Defense Fund
Washington, D.C.

Kim Davenport
Child Care Network at
Beansprout Networks
Chelmsford, Massachusetts

Cynthia R. Davis
Tufts University
Medford, Massachusetts

Carol Brunson Day
Council for Professional
Recognition
Washington, D.C.

Louise Derman-Sparks
Pacific Oaks College
Pasadena, California

Karen Diamond
Purdue University
West Lafayette, Indiana

Nancy DiMarco
Texas Woman's University
Denton, Texas

Adrienne Dixon
Ohio State University
Columbus, Ohio

Diane Trister Dodge
Teaching Strategies Inc.
Washington, D.C.

Joan Riley Driscoll
Tufts University
Medford, Massachusetts

M. Ann Easterbrooks
Tufts University
Medford, Massachusetts

Caroline Ebanks
National Center for
Education Research
U.S. Department of
Education
Washington, D.C.

Carolyn Pope Edwards
University of
Nebraska-Lincoln
Lincoln, Nebraska

Mary Eisenberg
Tufts University
Medford, Massachusetts

Linda M. Espinosa
University of
Missouri-Columbia
Columbia, Missouri

Eve Essery
Texas Woman's University
Denton, Texas

Demetra Evangelou
Purdue University
West Lafayette, Indiana

Roy Evans
Brunel University
Uxbridge, United Kingdom

Stephanie Feeney
University of Hawaii
Honolulu, Hawaii

David Henry Feldman
Tufts University
Medford, Massachusetts

Sue Fernandez
Montclair, New Jersey

David Fernie
Wheelock College
Boston, Massachusetts

Peter J. Fisher
National-Louis University
Evanston, Illinois

Catherine Twomey Fosnot
The City University of New
York (CUNY)
New York, New York

Susan Douglas Franzosa
University of
Washington-Bothell
Bothell, Washington

Nancy K. Freeman
University of South Carolina
Columbia, South Carolina

Lucia French
University of Rochester
Rochester, New York

Doris Pronin Fromberg
Hofstra University
Hempstead, New York

Joe L. Frost
University of Texas
Asutin, Texas

Jeanne Galbraith
Ohio State University
Columbus, Ohio

Kathleen Cranley Gallagher
University of North
Carolina
Chapel Hill, North Carolina

Alice Galper
University of Maryland
College Park, Maryland

Lella Gandini
University of Massachusetts
Amherst, Massachusetts

Lori Geismar-Ryan
Clayton Schools Family
Center
Clayton, Missouri

Celia Genishi
Columbia University
New York, New York

Steinunn Gestsdottir
Tufts University
Medford, Massachusetts

Calvin Gidney
Tufts University
Medford, Massachusetts

Eric Gidseg
Arlington Center School
District
Poughkeepsie, New York

Mark R. Ginsberg
National Association for the
Education of Young
Children (NAEYC)
Washington, D.C.

Stacie G. Goffin
Education Consultant
Washington, D.C.

Dale Goldhaber
University of Vermont
Burlington, Vermont

Jeanne Goldhaber
University of Vermont
Burlington, Vermont

Elizabeth Graue
University of Wisconsin
Madison, Wisconsin

Kelly Graydon
University of
California-Santa Barbara
Santa Barbara,
California

Polly Greenberg
National Association
for the Education
of Young
Children (NAEYC)
Washington, D.C.

Susan Grieshaber
Queensland University of
Technology
Brisbane,
Queensland,
Australia

James A. Griffin
National Center for
Education Research
U.S. Department of
Education
Washington, D.C.

Lori Grine
Heidelberg College
Tiffin, Ohio

Amita Gupta
The City University of New
York (CUNY)
New York,
New York

Michael J. Guralnick
University of Washington
Seattle, Washington

Maria Rosario T. de Guzman
University of
Nebraska–Lincoln
Lincoln, Nebraska

Ellen Hall
Boulder Journey School
Boulder, Colorado

Susan Hall
University of the Incarnate
Word
San Antonio, Texas

Rena Hallam
University of Tennessee
Knoxville, Tennessee

Patrice Hallock
Utica College
Utica, New York

Sia Haralampus
Tufts University
Medford, Massachusetts

Thelma Harms
University of North
Carolina
Chapel Hill, North Carolina

J. Amos Hatch
University of Tennessee
Knoxville, Tennessee

Robert Leibson Hawkins
New York University
New York, New York

Kisha M. Haye
University of
Nebraska–Lincoln
Lincoln, Nebraska

Judy Harris Helm
Best Practices Inc.
Brimfield, Illinois

Sue Henry
*National Even Start
Association
San Diego, California*

Dorothy W. Hewes
*San Diego State University
San Diego, California*

William Bryan Higgins
*University of Tennessee
Knoxville, Tennessee*

Toni L. Hill-Menson
*University of
Nebraska—Lincoln
Lincoln, Nebraska*

Blythe Hinitz
*The College of New Jersey
Ewing, New Jersey*

Hollie Hix-Small
*University of Oregon
Eugene, Oregon*

Jim Hoot
*University at Buffalo
State University of New
York
Buffalo, New York*

Amy Hornbeck
*Rutgers, The State University
of New Jersey
New Brunswick, New Jersey*

Sherri L. Horner
*Bowling Green State
University
Bowling Green, Ohio*

John Hornstein
*University of New
Hampshire
Durham, New Hampshire*

Carol S. Huntsinger
*College of Lake County
Grayslake, Illinois*

Terry Husband
*Ohio State University
Columbus, Ohio*

Marilou Hyson
*National Association for the
Education of Young
Children (NAEYC)
Washington, D.C.*

Eunsook Hyun
*Kent State University
Kent, Ohio*

Hatice Zeynep Inan
*Ohio State University
Columbus, Ohio*

Joan Isenberg
*George Mason University
Fairfax, Virginia*

Sonia Susan Issac
*Tufts University
Medford, Massachusetts*

Mary Jalongo
*Editor, Early Childhood
Education Journal
Indiana, Pennsylvania*

Shane R. Jimerson
*University of
California–Santa Barbara
Santa Barbara, California*

Elizabeth Jones
*Pacific Oaks College
Pasadena, California*

Jacqueline Jones
*Educational Testing Service
Princeton, New Jersey*

Sharon Judge
*University of Tennessee
Knoxville, Tennessee*

Lucy Kachmarik
Williamsburg, Virginia

Sharon Lynn Kagan
*Columbia University
New York, New York*

Barbara Kaiser
*Education Consultant
Grand Pre, Nova Scotia,
Canada*

Michael Kalinowski
*University of New
Hampshire
Durham, New Hampshire*

Constance Kamii
*University of
Alabama–Birmingham
Birmingham, Alabama*

Elizabeth Kane
*National Head Start
Organization
Alexandria, Virginia*

Rebecca Kantor
*Ohio State University
Columbus, Ohio*

Margot Kaplan-Sanoff
*Boston University School of
Medicine
Boston, Massachusetts*

Yasuhiko Kato
*Sophia University
Tokyo, Japan*

Laurie Katz
*Ohio State University
Columbus, Ohio*

Lilian G. Katz
*University of Illinois
Urbana-Champaign, Illinois*

Kristie Kauerz
*Columbia University
New York, New York*

Ko Eun Kim
*University of Wisconsin
Madison, Wisconsin*

Anna Kirova
*University of Alberta
Edmonton, Alberta, Canada*

Jane Knitzer
*National Center for
Children in Poverty
New York, New York*

Heather Koball
National Center for
Children in Poverty
New York, New York

Pauline Koch
National Association for
Regulatory Administration
(NARA)
Newark, Delaware

Derry Koralek
National Association for the
Education of Young
Children (NAEYC)
Washington, D.C.

Carol Kranowitz
Editor-in-chief
SI Focus Magazine
Bethesda, Maryland

Lee Kreader
National Center for
Children in Poverty
New York, New York

Mara Krechevsky
Project Zero
Harvard Graduate School of
Education
Cambridge, Massachusetts

Maria K. E. Lahman
University of Northern
Colorado
Greeley, Colorado

Susan Laird
University of Oklahoma
Norman, Oklahoma

J. Ronald Lally
WestEd Center for Child and
Family Studies
Sausalito, California

Faith Lamb-Parker
Columbia University
New York, New York

Martha Latorre
Southern Illinois University
Edwardsville
Edwardsville, Illinois

Stephanie F. Leeds
Cazenovia College
Cazenovia, New York

Dafna Lemish
Tel Aviv University
Tel Aviv, Israel

Deborah Leong
Metropolitan State College
of Denver
Golden, Colorado

Richard M. Lerner
Tufts University
Medford, Massachusetts

Sarah A. Leveque
Tufts University
Medford, Massachusetts

Diane E. Levin
Wheelock College
Boston, Massachusetts

Robert A. LeVine
Harvard University
Cambridge, Massachusetts

Cathy Grist Litty
Western Carolina University
Cullowhee, North Carolina

Carrie Lobman
Rutgers, The State University
of New Jersey
New Brunswick, New Jersey

Mary Ellin Logue
University of Maine
Orono, Maine

M. Elena Lopez
Senior Consultant
Harvard Family Research
Project
Mountain View, California

John M. Love
Mathematica Policy
Research Inc.
Princeton, New Jersey

Kelly Brcy Love
University of
Nebraska–Lincoln
Lincoln, Nebraska

Amy E. Lowenstein
Columbia University
New York, New York

Alison Lutton
Northampton Community
College
Bethlehem, Pennsylvania

Samara Madrid
Ohio State University
Columbus, Ohio

Bruce L. Mallory
University of New
Hampshire
Durham, New Hampshire

John P. Manning
University of Central
Florida
Orlando, Florida

Ben Mardell
Tufts University
Medford, Massachusetts

Hermine Marshall
San Francisco State
University
San Francisco, California

Kamilah Martin
National Association for the
Education of Young
Children (NAEYC)
Washington, D.C.

Linda C. Mayes
Yale Child Study Center
New Haven, Connecticut

Lisa McCabe
Cornell University
Ithaca, New York

Sarah-Kathryn McDonald
Data Research and
Development Center
Chicago, Illinois

Gillian D. McNamee
Erikson Institute
Chicago, Illinois

Anissa Meacham
University of Tennessee
Knoxville, Tennessee

Kim Means
NAEYC Academy for Early
Childhood Accreditation
Washington, D.C.

Daniel Meier
San Francisco State
University
San Francisco, California

Claudia Miranda
Tufts University
Medford, Massachusetts

Jayanthi Mistry
Tufts University
Medford, Massachusetts

Mary Ruth Moore
University of the Incarnate
Word
San Antonio, Texas

Mary Jane Moran
University of Tennessee
Knoxville, Tennessee

Gwen Morgan
Wheelock College
Boston, Massachusetts

Dori Mornan
Center for the Child Care
Work Force
Washington, D.C.

Taryn W. Morrissey
Cornell University
Ithaca, New York

Sarah A. Mulligan
NAEYC Academy for Early
Childhood Accreditation
Washington, D.C.

Nancy Nager
Bank Street College of
Education
New York, New York

Joanna K. Nelson
Tufts University
Medford, Massachusetts

Bonnie Neugebauer
Co-Editor, Child Care
Information Exchange
Redmond, Washington

Roger Neugebauer
Co-Editor, Child Care
Information Exchange
Redmond, Washington

Staccy Ncuharth-Pritchett
University of Georgia
Athens, Georgia

Michelle J. Neuman
Columbia University
New York, New York

Rebecca S. New
Tufts University
Medford, Massachusetts

John Nimmo
University of New
Hampshire
Durham, New Hampshire

Jan Nisbet
University of New
Hampshire
Durham, New Hampshire

Vey M. Nordquist
University of Tennessee
Knoxville, Tennessee

Maryann O'Brien
Tufts University
Medford, Massachusetts

Samuel Odom
Indiana University
Bloomington, Indiana

Pam Oken-Wright
St. Catherine's School
Richmond, Virginia

Maril Olson
National Association for the
Education of Young
Children (NAEYC)
Washington, D.C.

Carole J. Oshinsky
Columbia University
New York, New York

Veronica Pacini-Ketchabaw
University of Victoria
Victoria, British Columbia,
Canada

Vivian Paley
Sturgeon Bay, Wisconsin

Boyoung Park
University of Georgia
Athens, Georgia

Rod Parker-Rees
University of Plymouth
Plymouth, United Kingdom

Christine Pascal
University College Worcester
Worcester, United Kingdom

Alan Pence
University of Victoria
Victoria, British Columbia,
Canada

Ellen C. Perrin
Tufts New England Medical
Center
Boston, Massachusetts

Gail Perry
National Association for the
Education of Young
Children (NAEYC)
Washington, D.C.

Nancy L. Peterson
University of Kansas
Lawrence, Kansas

Rae Pica
*Moving and Learning
Center Barnstead, New
Hampshire*

Ellen E. Pinderhughes
*Tufts University
Medford, Massachusetts*

Alison Pitzer
*Jumpstart
Boston, Massachusetts*

Sarah Pletcher
*University of
California–Santa Barbara
Santa Barbara, California*

Toni Porter
*Bank Street College of
Education
New York, New York*

Martha Pott
*Tufts University
Medford, Massachusetts*

Douglas R. Powell
*Purdue University
West Lafayette, Indiana*

Laurel Preece
*University of Illinois
Urbana-Champaign, Illinois*

Larry Prochner
*University of Alberta
Edmonton, Alberta, Canada*

Elizabeth S. Pufall
*Tufts University
Medford, Massachusetts*

Peter B. Pufall
*Smith College
Northampton,
Massachusetts*

Helen Raikes
*University of
Nebraska–Lincoln
Lincoln, Nebraska*

Patricia G. Ramsey
*Mount Holyoke College
South Hadley, Massachusetts*

Edna Ranck
*Westover Consultants Inc.
Washington, D.C.*

Judy Sklar Rasminsky
*Westmount, Quebec,
Canada*

Aisha Ray
*Erikson Institute
Chicago, Illinois*

Stuart Reifel
*University of Texas
Austin, Texas*

Gretchen Reynolds
*Algonquin College
Ottawa, Canada*

Shannon S. Rich
*Texas Woman's University
Denton, Texas*

Elizabeth Rigby
*Columbia University
New York, New York*

Christine Rioux
*Tufts University
Medford, Massachusetts*

Jeri Robinson
*Boston Children's Museum
Boston, Massachusetts*

Alison Rogers
*Early Childhood Mental
Health Consultant
Ashfield, Massachusetts*

Diane Rothenberg
*University of Illinois
Urbana-Champaign, Illinois*

Melanie S. Rudy
*University of
Nebraska–Lincoln
Lincoln, Nebraska*

Frances Rust
*New York University
New York, New York*

Sharon Ryan
*Rutgers, The State University
of New Jersey
New Brunswick, New Jersey*

Tom Salyers
*Zero to Three
Washington, D.C.*

Ingrid Pramling Samuelson
*Göteborg University
Göteborg, Sweden*

Charlotte Sanborn
*Texas Woman's University
Denton, Texas*

Cornelia Santschi
*Saint Barnabas Institute of
Neurology and
Neurosurgery
West Orange,
New Jersey*

Wendy Sapp
*Visual Impairment
Education Services
Cohutta, Georgia*

Julie Sarama
*University at Buffalo
State University of New
York
Buffalo, New York*

W. George Scarlett
*Tufts University
Medford, Massachusetts*

Melissa Schultz
*University of Cincinnati
Cincinnati, Ohio*

Charles Schwall
*St. Michael School
St. Louis, Missouri*

Lawrence J. Schweinhart
*High/Scope Educational
Research
Ypsilanti, Michigan*

Dorothy G. Singer
*Yale University Family
Television Research and
Consultation Center
Yale University
New Haven, Connecticut*

Jerome L. Singer
*Yale University Family
Television Research and
Consultation Center
Yale University
New Haven, Connecticut*

Iram Siraj-Blatchford
*University of London
London, United Kingdom*

Barbara J. Smith
*University of
Colorado—Denver
Denver, Colorado*

Patricia Snyder
*Vanderbilt University
Medical Center
Nashville, Tennessee*

Antoinette Spiotta
*Montclair State University
Montclair, New Jersey*

Barbara Sprung
*Academy for Education
Development
Washington, D.C.*

Vickie D. Stayton
*Western Kentucky
University
Bowling Green, Kentucky*

Kate Stimmel
*University of New
Hampshire
Durham, New Hampshire*

Murray A. Straus
*University of New
Hampshire
Durham, New Hampshire*

Beth Blue Swadener
*Arizona State University
Tempe, Arizona*

Mallory I. Swartz
*Tufts University
Medford, Massachusetts*

Susan M. Swearer
*University of
Nebraska-Lincoln
Lincoln, Nebraska*

Louisa Banks Tarullo
*Mathematica Policy
Research Inc.
Washington, D.C.*

Jane Thomas
*Harper College
Palatine, Illinois*

Christine Marmé Thompson
*Pennsylvania State
University
University Park,
Pennsylvania*

Candra Thornton
*Auburn University
Auburn, Alabama*

Joseph Tobin
*Arizona State University
Tempe, Arizona*

Sandra Twardosz
*University of Tennessee
Knoxville, Tennessee*

Lynda Van Kuren
*Council for Exceptional
Children
Arlington, Virginia*

Cheri A. Vogel
*Mathematica Policy
Research Inc.
Princeton, New Jersey*

Marissa McClure Vollrath
*Penn State University
University Park,
Pennsylvania*

Alice Wakefield
*Old Dominion University
Norfolk, Virginia*

Charlotte Wallinga
*University of Georgia
Athens, Georgia*

Michelle Banyai Walsh
*Child Development
Specialist
Santa Barbara, California*

Cixin Wang
*University of
Nebraska-Lincoln
Lincoln, Nebraska*

Dorothy E. Warner
*Harvard Medical School
Waltham, Massachusetts*

Valora Washington
*Unitarian Universalist
Service Committee
Cambridge, Massachusetts*

Tara N. Weatherholt
*University of Louisville
Louisville, Kentucky*

Graham F. Welch
*University of London
London, United Kingdom*

Edyth J. Wheeler
*Towson State University
Towson, Maryland*

Marcy Whitebook
*University of California
Berkeley, California*

Marian Whitehead
*Educational Consultant
Norwich, United Kingdom*

Gay Wilgus
*City College of New York
(CCNY)
New York, New York*

Meredith Willa
*National Center for
Children in Poverty (NCCP)
New York, New York*

Arthur E. Wise
*National Council for
Accreditation of Teacher
Education
Washington, D.C.*

Janice Witte
*Office of the Secretary of
Defense
Washington, D.C.*

Nicola Yelland
*Victoria University
Melbourne, Australia*

Marci Young
*Center for the Child Care
Workforce
Washington, D.C.*

Francie Zimmerman
*Education Consultant
Philadelphia, Pennsylvania*

Contributors—Volume 4

Australia

Mindy Blaise
Monash University
*Peninsula Campus
Frankston, Victoria,
Australia*

Jennifer Bowes
*Associate Professor
Head, Institute of Early
Childhood
Macquarie University
Sydney, Australia*

Bill Cope
*RMIT University
Melbourne, Australia*

Susan Grieshaber
*Queensland University of
Technology
Brisbane, Australia*

Alan Hayes
*Director, Australian
Institute of Family Studies
Melbourne, Australia*

Susan Hill
*University of South
Australia
Magill Campus
Magill, South Australia,
Australia*

Mary Kalantzis
*RMIT University
Melbourne, Australia*

Anna Kilderry
*Queensland University of
Technology
Brisbane, Australia*

Libby Lee
*Murdoch University
Perth, Australia*

Felicity McArdle
*Queensland University of
Technology
Brisbane, Australia*

Maureen O'Rourke
*Victoria University
Melbourne, Australia*

Nicola Yelland
*Victoria University
Melbourne, Australia*

Brazil

Angela Rabelo Barreto
*Interforums Movement for
Early Childhood Education
Brasília, Brazil*

Maria Malta Campos
*Senior Researcher-Carlos
Chagas Foundation
Catholic University of São
Paulo*

Marina Célia Moraes Dias
*Faculty of Education
University of São Paulo
São Paulo, Brazil*

Adriana Friedmann
*Research Director and
Teacher at NEPSID
Center of Studies and
Research in Symbolism,
Childhood and Development
São Paulo, Brazil*

Lenira Haddad
*Federal University of
Alagoas
Maceió, Al, Brazil
EDUCERE-Training Center
for Early Childhood
Education
São Paulo, SP, Brazil*

Tizuko Morchida Kishimoto
*Faculty of Education
University of São Paulo
São Paulo, SP, Brazil*

Marieta Lúcia Nicolau
Machado
*Faculty of Education
University of São Paulo
São Paulo, SP, Brazil*

Maria Letícia Nascimento
*Mackenzie Presbyterian
University
São Paulo, SP, Brazil*

Mônica Appezzato Pinazza
*Faculty of Education
University of São Paulo
São Paulo, SP, Brazil*

Zilma Ramos de Oliveira
*Faculty of Education
University of São Paulo
São Paulo, SP, Brazil*

Fúlvia Rosemberg
*Senior Researcher-Carlos
Chagas Foundation
Professor of Social
Psychology*

Catholic University of São
Paulo
São Paulo, SP, Brazil

Marie Claire Sekkel
Institute of Psychology
University of São Paulo
São Paulo, SP, Brazil

Ana Paula Soares da Silva
Faculty of Philosophy,
Science and Letters of
Ribeirão Preto
University of São Paulo
Ribeirão Preto, SP, Brazil

Sandra Unbehaum
Researcher, Carlos Chagas
Foundation
São Paulo, SP, Brazil

Sonia Larrubia Valverde
Municipal Secretariat of
Education-Prefecture of São
Paulo
São Paulo, SP, Brazil

Cláudia Vianna
Faculty of Education
University of São Paulo
São Paulo, SP, Brazil

Telma Vitória
General Coordenadora for
Early Childhood Education
Centers
Santo Agostinho Association
São Paulo, SP, Brazil

CHINA

Bisheng Lou
Associate Professor
Department of Early
Childhood Education
Nanjing Normal University,
Nanjing, China

Jingbo Liu
Associate Professor
Department of Early
Childhood Education
Nanjing Normal University,
Nanjing, China

Lan Gao
Professor
Department of Early
Childhood Education
South China Normal
University, Guang Zhou,
China

Meiru Tu
Professor
Department of Early
Childhood Education
Nanjing Normal University,
Nanjing, China

Wei Li-Chen
Researcher
Yew Chung Education
Foundation, Hong Kong

Wen Qian
Associate Professor
Department of Early
Childhood Education
East China Normal
University, Shanghai, China

Xin Zhou
Professor
Department of Early
Childhood Education
East China Normal
University, Shanghai, China

Xueqin Qiu
Associate Professor
Department of Early
Childhood Education
Nanjing Normal
University,Nanjing, China

Yunfei Ji
Doctoral student
Department of Early
Childhood Education
Nanjing Normal University,
Nanjing, China

THE CZECH REPUBLIC

Lucie Kozáková
Doctoral student
Department of Educational
Sciences

Faculty of Arts,
Masaryk University in Brno

Eva Opravilová
Associate Professor
Faculty of Education
Charles University in
Prague

Milada Rabušicová
Associate Professor
Department of Educational
Sciences
Faculty of Arts
Masaryk University in Brno

Klára Šeďová
Assistant Professor
Department of Educational
Sciences
Faculty of Arts
Masaryk University in Brno

Kateřina Smolíková
Senior Researcher
Research Institute of
Education, Prague

Jana Uhlířová
Associate Professor
Faculty of Education
Charles University in
Prague

FRANCE

Brigitte Belmont
Ingénieurs de recherche
(CERLIS, University Paris 5)

Catherine Bouve
Trainer (ITSRS, Montrouge)
and associate researcher
(CERLIS, University Paris
5-REEFI, University
Paris X)

Véronique Francis
Maître de conférences
(IUFM Orléans-Tours)

Pierre Moisset
(CERLIS, University Paris 5)

Alexandra Moreau
Ph.D. student
(GREC-University Paris 13)

Sylvie Rayna
Maître de conférences
(INRP-University Paris 13)

Aliette Vérillon
Ingénieurs de recherche
(CERLIS-University Paris 5)

Marie-Laure Vitali
Ingénieur d'études
(CRF-CNAM), Ph.D. student
(CNAM-University Paris 13)

ITALY

Anna Bondioli
Professor of Pedagogy
University of Pavia

Battista Quinto Borghi
Director, Early Childhood
Education Services
City of Torino

Chiara Bove
Researcher in Education
University of Milan-Bicocca

Aldo Fortunati
Research Director
Istituto degli Innocenti
Firenze

Susanna Mantovani
Professor of Pedagogy
University of Milan-Bicocca

Tullia Musatti
Senior Researcher
Institute of Cognitive
Sciences and Technologies
National Research Council,
Rome

Elisabetta Nigris
Associate Professor in
Teaching Methodologies
University of Milan-Bicocca

Lilia Teruggi
Researcher in Didactics
University of Milan-Bicocca

JAPAN

Junko Enami
Professor, Department of
Early Child Education and
Care
Tokiwa Junior College,
Ibaraki

Keiko Gondo
Professor, Department of
Early Childhood Education
St. Margaret's Junior
College, Tokyo

Tomohisa Hirata
Professor, Department of
Early Childhood Education
Jumonji University, Saitama

Miwako Hoshi-Watanabe
Professor, Department of
Developmental Psychology
Jumonji University, Saitama

Kyoko Imagawa
Associate Professor,
Department of Early
Childhood Education
St. Margaret's Junior
College, Tokyo

Reiko Irie
Professor, Department of
Child Science
Kyoritsu Women's
University, Tokyo

Nobuko Kamigaichi
Professor, Department of
Early Childhood Education
Jumonji University, Saitama

Takako Kawabe
Associate Professor,
Department of Education
University of the Sacred
Heart, Tokyo

Kazuko Matsumura
Professor, Department of
Human Studies
Director, University
Kindergarten
Bunkyo Gakuin University,
Saitama

Takako Noguchi
Assistant Professor,
Department of Early
Childhood Education
Jumonji University, Saitama

SOUTH AFRICA

Eric Atmore
Director, Center for Early
Childhood Development

Linda Biersteker
Head of Research, Early
Learning Resource Unit

Carole Bloch
Co-ordinator of Early
Literacy Unit, Project for the
Study of Alternative
Education in South Africa
(PRAESA)
University of Cape Town

Laetitia Brümmer
Training
Coordinator–Inclusive
Education Western Cape

Andrew Dawes
Research Director, Child
Youth and Family
Development
Human Sciences Research
Council of South Africa

Beryl Hermanus
Antibias and Human Rights
Project Manager
Early Learning Resource
Unit

Annie Leatt
Child Poverty Programme
Manager

Children's Institute,
University of Cape Town

Ian Moll
Education Specialist,
Teacher Education and
Early Childhood
Development
South African Institute for
Distance Education

Mary Newman
Educational Associate, Early
Learning Resource Unit

Patsy Pillay
Chairperson, South African
Training Institute for Early
Childhood Development

Ann Short
Early Childhood
Development Consultant

Victoria Sikhakhana
Training and Resources in
Early Education (TREE)

SWEDEN

Maj Asplund Carlsson
Department of Education
Göteborg University

Björn Flising
Department of Education
Göteborg University

Lisbeth Flising
Department of Education
Göteborg University

Lars Gunnarsson
Department of Education
Göteborg University

Karin Gustafsson
Department of Education
Göteborg University

Eva Johansson
Department of Education
Göteborg University

Maelis Karlsson Lohmander
Department of Education
Göteborg University

Johannes Lunneblad
Department of Education
Göteborg University

Elisabeth Mellgren
Department of Education
Göteborg University

Ingrid Pramling Samuelsson
Department of Education
Göteborg University

UNITED KINGDOM

Lynn Ang
Senior Lecturer
University of East London

Pamela Calder
Visiting Fellow
University of the South
Bank

Peter Elfer
Principal Lecturer
Roehampton University

Eva Lloyd
Senior Lecturer
University of Bristol

Helen Masterton
Principal Lecturer
University of East London

Berry Mayall
Institute of Education
University of London

Peter Moss
Institute of Education
University of London

Helen Penn
University of East London

Raymonde Sneddon
Visiting Fellow
University of East London

Angela Underdown
Senior Lecturer
Warwick University